Lecture Notes in Computer Science   12131

More information about this series at http://www.springer.com/series/7412

Aurélio Campilho · Fakhri Karray ·
Zhou Wang (Eds.)

Image Analysis and Recognition

17th International Conference, ICIAR 2020
Póvoa de Varzim, Portugal, June 24–26, 2020
Proceedings, Part I

 Springer

Editors
Aurélio Campilho 🄾
University of Porto
Porto, Portugal

Fakhri Karray 🄾
University of Waterloo
Waterloo, ON, Canada

Zhou Wang 🄾
University of Waterloo
Waterloo, ON, Canada

ISSN 0302-9743   ISSN 1611-3349 (electronic)
Lecture Notes in Computer Science
ISBN 978-3-030-50346-8   ISBN 978-3-030-50347-5 (eBook)
https://doi.org/10.1007/978-3-030-50347-5

LNCS Sublibrary: SL6 – Image Processing, Computer Vision, Pattern Recognition, and Graphics

This Springer imprint is published by the registered company Springer Nature Switzerland AG
The registered company address is: Gewerbestrasse 11, 6330 Cham, Switzerland

Preface

ICIAR 2020 was the 17th edition of the series of annual conferences on Image Analysis and Recognition, organized, this year, as a virtual conference due to the pandemic outbreak of Covid-19 affecting all the world, with an intensity never felt by the humanity in the last hundred years. These are difficult and challenging times, nevertheless the situation provides new opportunities for disseminating science and technology to an even wider audience, through powerful online mediums. Although organized as a virtual conference, ICIAR 2020 kept a forum for the participants to interact and present their latest research contributions in theory, methodology, and applications of image analysis and recognition. ICIAR 2020, the International Conference on Image Analysis and Recognition took place during June 24–26, 2020. ICIAR is organized by the Association for Image and Machine Intelligence (AIMI), a not-for-profit organization registered in Ontario, Canada.

We received a total of 123 papers from 31 countries. The review process was carried out by members of the Program Committee and other external reviewers. Each paper was reviewed by at least two reviewers, and checked by the conference co-chairs. A total of 73 papers were accepted and appear in these proceedings. We would like to sincerely thank the authors for their excellent research work and for responding to our call, and to thank the reviewers for dedicating time to the review process and for the careful evaluation and the feedback provided to the authors. It is this collective effort that resulted in a strong conference program and a high-quality proceedings.

We were very pleased to include three outstanding keynote talks: "Deep Learning and The Future of Radiology" by Daniel Rueckert (Imperial College London, UK); "Towards Human-Friendly Explainable Artificial Intelligence" by Hani Hagras (University of Essex, UK); and "Embedded Computer Vision and Machine Learning for Drone Imaging" by Ioannis Pitas (Aristotle University of Thessaloniki, Greece). We would like to express our gratitude to the keynote speakers for accepting our invitation to share their vision and recent advances made in their areas of expertise.

This virtual conference was organized in two parallel tracks, corresponding to nine sessions, each one corresponding to the following chapters in this proceedings with two volumes:

1. Image Processing and Analysis
2. Video Analysis
3. Computer Vision
4. 3D Computer Vision
5. Machine Learning
6. Medical Image Analysis
7. Analysis of Histopathology Images
8. Diagnosis and Screening of Ophthalmic Diseases
9. Grand Challenge on Automatic Lung Cancer Patient Management

Chapter 8 and 9 correspond to two successful parallel events: Special Session on "Novel Imaging Methods for Diagnosis and Screening of Ophthalmic Diseases" co-chaired by Ana Mendonça (University of Porto, Portugal) and Koen Vermeer (Roterdam Eye Hospital, The Netherlands); and "Grand Challenge on Automatic Lung Cancer Patient Management" organized by João Pedrosa, Carlos Ferreira, and Guilherme Aresta from Institute for Systems and Computer Engineering, Technology and Science (INESC TEC), Portugal.

We would like to thank the program area chairs: Armando Pinho (University of Aveiro, Portugal) and Ed Vrscay (University of Waterloo, Canada), chairs for the area on Image Processing and Analysis; José Santos Victor (Instituto Superior Técnico, University of Lisbon, Portugal) and Petia Radeva (University of Barcelona, Spain), chairs for the area on Computer Vision; Jaime Cardoso (University of Porto, Portugal) and J. Salvador Sanchez Garreta (University of Jaume I, Spain), chairs for the area on Machine Learning; and Ana Mendonça (University of Porto, Portugal) and Roberto Hornero (University of Valladolid, Spain), chairs for the area on Medical Image Analysis; who have secured a high-quality program. We also would like to thank the members of the Organizing Committee from INESC TEC, for helping with the local logistics, and the publications and web chairs, Carlos Ferreira and Khaled Hammouda, for maintaining the website, interacting with the authors, and preparing the proceedings. We are also grateful to Springer's editorial staff, for supporting this publication in the LNCS series. As well, we would like to thank the precious sponsorship and support of the INESC TEC, the Faculty of Engineering at the University of Porto, Portugal, the Waterloo Artificial Intelligence Institute, the Faculty of Engineering of the University of Waterloo, and the Center for Pattern Analysis and Machine Intelligence at the University of Waterloo. We also appreciate the valuable co-sponsorship of the IEEE EMB Portugal Chapter, the IEEE Computational Intelligence Society, Kitchener-Waterloo Chapter, and the Portuguese Association for Pattern Recognition. We also would like to acknowledge Lurdes Catalino from Abreu Events for managing the registrations.

We were very pleased to welcome all the participants to ICIAR 2020, a virtual conference edition. For those who were not able to attend, we hope this publication provides a good overview into the research presented at the conference.

June 2020   Aurélio Campilho
                                                               Fakhri Karray
                                                               Zhou Wang

Organization

General Chairs

Aurélio Campilho   University of Porto, Portugal
Fakhri Karray   University of Waterloo, Canada
Zhou Wang   University of Waterloo, Canada

Local Organizing Committee

Catarina Carvalho   INESC TEC, Portugal
João Pedrosa   INESC TEC, Portugal
Luís Teixeira   University of Porto, Portugal

Program Chairs

Image Processing and Analysis

Armando Pinho   University of Aveiro, Portugal
Ed Vrscay   University of Waterloo, Canada

Computer Vision

J. Santos Victor   Instituto Superior Técnico, Portugal
Petia Radeva   University of Barcelona, Spain

Machine Learning

Jaime Cardoso   University of Porto, Portugal
J. Salvador Garreta   University of Jaume I, Spain

Medical Image Analysis

Ana Mendonça   University of Porto, Portugal
Roberto Hornero   University of Valladolid, Spain

Grand Challenge on Automatic Lung Cancer Patient Management

João Pedrosa   INESC TEC, Portugal
Carlos Ferreira   INESC TEC, Portugal
Guilherme Aresta   INESC TEC, Portugal

Novel Imaging Methods for Diagnosis and Screening of Ophthalmic Diseases

Ana Mendonça   University of Porto, Portugal
Koen Vermeer   Rotterdam Eye Hospital, The Netherlands

Publication and Web Chairs

Carlos Ferreira   INESC TEC, Portugal
Khaled Hammouda   Shopify, Canada

Supported and Co-sponsored by

AIMI – Association for Image and Machine Intelligence

Center for Biomedical Engineering Research
INESC TEC – Institute for Systems and Computer Engineering,
Technology and Science
Portugal

Department of Electrical and Computer Engineering
Faculty of Engineering
University of Porto
Portugal

Faculty of Engineering
University of Waterloo
Canada

CPAMI – Centre for Pattern Analysis and Machine Intelligence
University of Waterloo
Canada

Waterloo AI Institute
Canada

IEEE Engineering in Medicine and Biology Society
Portugal

IEEE Computational Intelligence Society
Kitchener-Waterloo Chapter

APRP - Portuguese Association for Pattern Recognition
Portugal

Program Committee

Alaa El Khatib	University of Waterloo, Canada
Alberto Taboada-Crispi	Universidad Central Marta Abreu de Las Villas, Cuba
Alexander Wong	University of Waterloo, Canada
Ambra Demontis	Università di Cagliari, Italy
Ana Filipa Sequeira	INESC TEC, Portugal
Ana Maria Mendonça	University of Porto, Portugal
Andreas Uhl	University of Salzburg, Austria
Angel Sappa	ESPOL Polytechnic University, Ecuador, and Computer Vision Center, Spain
António Cunha	University of Trás-os-Montes and Alto Douro, Portugal
Arjan Kujiper	TU Darmstadt, Fraunhofer IGD, Germany
Armando Pinho	University of Aveiro, Portugal
Aurélio Campilho	University of Porto, Portugal
Beatriz Remeseiro	Universidad de Oviedo, Spain
Bob Zhang	University of Macau, Macau
Carlos Thomaz	FEI, Brazil
Catarina Carvalho	INESC TEC, Portugal
Chaojie Ou	University of Waterloo, Canada
Dariusz Frejlichowski	West Pomeranian University of Technology, Poland
Dipti Sarmah	Sarmah's Algorithmic Intelligence Research Lab, The Netherlands
Dominique Brunet	Environment and Climate Change Canada (Toronto Area), Canada
Edward Vrscay	University of Waterloo, Canada
Fabian Falck	Imperial College London, UK
Fakhri Karray	University of Waterloo, Canada
Farzad Khalvati	University of Toronto, Canada
Francesco Camastra	University of Naples Parthenope, Italy
Francesco Renna	University of Porto, Portugal
Francesco Tortorella	Universita' degli Studi di Salerno, Italy
Gerald Schaefer	Loughborough University, UK
Giang Tran	University of Waterloo, Canada
Gilson Giraldi	LNCC, Brazil
Giuliano Grossi	University of Milan, Italy
Guillaume Noyel	International Prevention Research Institute, France
Hasan Ogul	Baskent University, Turkey
Hassan Rivaz	Concordia University, Canada
Hélder Oliveira	INESC TEC, Portugal
Hicham Sekkati	National Research Council of Canada, Canada
Howard Li	University of New Brunswick, Canada
Huiyu Zhou	Queen's University Belfast, UK
Jaime Cardoso	University of Porto, Portugal
Jinghao Xue	University College London, UK
João Pedrosa	INESC TEC, Portugal

João Rodrigues	University of the Algarve, Portugal
Johan Debayle	École nationale supérieure des Mines de Saint-Étienne, France
Jonathan Boisvert	CNRC, Canada
Jorge Batista	University of Coimbra, Portugal
Jorge Marques	University of Lisbon, Portugal
Jorge Silva	University of Porto, Portugal
José Alba Castro	University of Vigo, Spain
José Garreta	University of Jaume I, Spain
José Rouco	University of Coruña, Spain
José Santos-Victor	University of Lisbon, Portugal
Jose-Jesus Fernandez	CNB-CSIC, Spain
Juan José Rodríguez	Universidad de Burgos, Spain
Juan Lorenzo Ginori	Universidad Central Marta Abreu de Las Villas, Cuba
Kaushik Roy	North Carolina A&T State University, USA
Kelwin Fernandes	NILG.AI, Portugal
Koen Vermeer	Rotterdam Eye Hospital, The Netherlands
Linlin Xu	University of Waterloo, Canada
Luc Duong	École de technologie supérieure, Canada
Luís Alexandre	University of Beira Interior, Portugal
Luís Teixeira	University of Porto, Portugal
Mahmoud El-Sakka	University of Western Ontario, Canada
Mahmoud Hassaballah	South Valley University, Egypt
Mahmoud Melkemi	Univeristé de Haute-Alsace, France
Manuel Penedo	University of Coruña, Spain
María García	University of Valladolid, Spain
Marie Muller	North Carolina State University, USA
Mariella Dimiccoli	Institut de Robòtica i Informàtica Industrial, Spain
Mario Vento	Università di Salerno, Italy
Markus Koskela	CSC - IT Center for Science, Finland
Mehran Ebrahimi	University of Ontario, Canada
Mohammad Shafiee	University of Waterloo, Canada
Nicola Strisciuglio	University of Groningen, The Netherlands
Oliver Montesdeoca	Universitat de Barcelona, Spain
Parthipan Siva	Sportlogiq, Canada
Pascal Fallavollita	University of Ottawa, Canada
Pavel Zemčík	Brno University of Technology, Czech Republic
Pedro Carvalho	INESC TEC, Portugal
Pedro Pina	University of Lisbon, Portugal
Petia Radeva	University of Barcelona, Spain
Philip Morrow	Ulster University, UK
Radim Kolář	Brno University of Technology, Czech Republic
Reyer Zwiggelaar	Aberystwyth University, UK
Robert Fisher	University of Edinburgh, UK
Robert Sablatnig	TU Wien, Austria
Roberto Hornero	University of Valladolid, Spain

Rosa María Valdovinos   Universidad Autónoma del Estado de México, Mexico
Rui Bernardes   University of Coimbra, Portugal
Sajad Saeedi   Imperial College London, UK
Sébai Dorsaf   National School of Computer Science, Tunisia
Shamik Sural   Indian Institute of Technology, India
Vicente García-Jiménez   Universidad Autónoma de Ciudad Juérez, Mexico
Víctor González-Castro   Universidad de Leon, Spain
Xosé Pardo   CiTIUS, Universidade de Santiago de Compostela, Spain
Yasuyo Kita   National Institute AIST, Japan
Yun-Qian Miao   General Motors, Canada
Zhou Wang   University of Waterloo, Canada

Additional Reviewers

Américo Pereira   INESC TEC, Portugal
Audrey Chung   University of Waterloo, Canada
Devinder Kumar   Stanford University, USA
Dongdong Ma   Tsinghua University, China
Guilherme Aresta   INESC TEC, Portugal
Honglei Su   Qingdao University, China
Isabel Rio-Torto   University of Porto, Portugal
Juncheng Zhang   Tsinghua University, China
Khashayar Namdar   University of Toronto, Canada
Lu Zhang   INSA Rennes, France
Mafalda Falcão   INESC TEC, Portugal
Pedro Costa   INESC TEC, Portugal
Saman Motamed   University of Toronto, Canada
Tânia Pereira   INESC TEC, Portugal
Tom Vicar   Brno University of Technology, Czech Republic
Youcheng Zhang   Tsinghua University, China

Contents – Part I

Image Processing and Analysis

3D Computer Vision

Contents – Part II

Medical Image Analysis

Analysis of Histopathology Images

Diagnosis and Screening of Ophthalmic Diseases

Grand Challenge on Automatic Lung Cancer Patient Management

Image Processing and Analysis

Exploring Workout Repetition Counting and Validation Through Deep Learning

Bruno Ferreira[1](✉), Pedro M. Ferreira[2], Gil Pinheiro[2], Nelson Figueiredo[3], Filipe Carvalho[3], Paulo Menezes[1], and Jorge Batista[1]

[1] Institute of Systems and Robotics, Department of Electrical and Computer Engineering, University of Coimbra, Coimbra, Portugal
{bruno.ferreira,PauloMenezes,batista}@isr.uc.pt
[2] Nixfuste Nova, Porto, Portugal
{pedro.ferreira,gil.pinheiro}@nixfuste-nova.pt
[3] Prozis.Tech, Maia, Portugal
{nelson.figueiredo,filipe.scarvalho}@prozis.com

Abstract. Studying human motion from images and videos has turned into an interesting topic of research given the recent advances in computer vision and deep learning algorithms. When focusing on the automatic procedure of tracking physical exercises, cameras can be used for full human pose estimation in relation to worn sensors. In this work, we propose a method for workout repetition counting and validation based on a set of skeleton-based and deep semantic features that are obtained from a 2D human pose estimation network. Given that some of the individuals' body parts might be occluded throughout physical exercises, we also perform a multi-view analysis on supporting cameras to improve our recognition rates. Nevertheless, the obtained results for a single-view approach show that we are able to count valid repetitions with over 90% precision scores for 4 out of 5 considered exercises, while recognizing more than 50% of the invalid ones.

Keywords: Workout repetition counting · Human physical activity analysis · 2D human pose estimation · Deep learning

1 Introduction

Performing exercise on a regular basis is crucial to a healthy lifestyle, being motivated and recommended at all ages. When carried out properly, it promotes the strengthening of our immune and cardiovascular system while balancing the stress and anxiety we are exposed on a daily basis [7]. However, individuals are frequently demotivated to perform it alone and therefore end up searching for

---

B. Ferreira and P. M. Ferreira—Both authors contributed equally to this work.

© Springer Nature Switzerland AG 2020
A. Campilho et al. (Eds.): ICIAR 2020, LNCS 12131, pp. 3–15, 2020.
https://doi.org/10.1007/978-3-030-50347-5_1

new ways to stay committed. Nowadays, there are several gadgets and commercial applications that try to make users engaged with physical activities by establishing daily/weekly/monthly milestones [10]. For instance, counting the number of daily steps and the corresponding energy expenditure by using the information gathered from IMUs (Inertial Measurement Unit) present in smartphones, smartwatches or even cheap smartbands. Also, more complete systems that make use of wearable inertial sensors can be used to precisely predict and study how the user is moving. In Skawinski et al. [8], 3D acceleration sensors were used alongside a standard Convolutional Neural Network (CNN) for exercise recognition and peak detection with an adaptive threshold for workout repetition counting. Another example considering the same type of approach for workout repetition counting is presented in [9] by Soro et al. It adopts an end-to-end deep learning approach, trained on data collected using two smartwatches, one worn on the wrist and another on the ankle. The raw sensor data is fed to a CNN with a sliding window for exercise recognition and to another CNN that outputs the beginning of a repetition for counting. Yet, these methods are usually impractical and not suitable for every type of exercise, or even commonly require distinct setups for different actions.

Relying on the success of computer vision applications, researchers and developers are turning to these techniques to assess and create new challenges to motivate physical exercise. The prime example of this type of approach is the GymCam, developed by Khurana et al. [6]. It detects, recognizes and tracks multiple motion trajectories in unconstrained scenes to infer the type and count repetitions of the existing exercises. However, a major weakness across all these methodologies is that repetition counting is typically performed independently from the exercise validation, that is, the repetitions are counted even if their execution are incorrect.

In this work, we present the creation of a system that counts and validates repetitions for five different physical exercises commonly used in CrossFit workout routines[1]. Different from the methodologies mentioned above, our model predicts at the frame level the current moment of the exercise execution. Accordingly, the proposed system is capable of providing feedback to the individual with much more detail while recognizing invalid repetitions promptly. More specifically, our main contributions can be summarized as follows:

- The acquisition and annotation of a novel dataset of video recordings of five CrossFit-specific exercises that comprises both valid and invalid repetitions.
- The proposal of a repetition counting and validation system that is composed by a *2D Pose Estimation Network* along with a *Moment-classifier* that infers the current moment of the exercise execution. Specifically, the moment-classifier is trained with a highly discriminative feature representation that comprises: (i) skeleton-based features, computed from the keypoints coordinates, and (ii) deep semantic features, learned from the probabilistic inferences (heatmaps) of the body joints. Later, repetition counting and validation can be performed when there is a transition from the last to the first

---

[1] Demo: https://youtu.be/zu5p0eZUEsQ.

moment of the exercise, while all the moments within the current repetition must appear in the right order.
- A comparison between different features and machine learning algorithms for the moment-classification task.

The rest of the article is organized as follows. Section 2 presents our created dataset for the considered exercises, while Sect. 3 explains the proposed methodology to achieve our goals. Section 4 explores the best combination between several extracted features and machine learning models. It also provides a multiview analysis on how different cameras may support each other to improve occlusions robustness. Section 5 reports the experimental results for repetition counting and validation. Finally, conclusions and some topics for future work are presented in Sect. 6.

2 Dataset

To the best of our knowledge, there are no publicly available datasets of video recordings of physical exercises, comprising both valid and invalid repetitions. In this regard, we have collected a video-based dataset of five of the most common CrossFit-specific exercises from a total of 22 subjects: Squats, Burpees, Push-Ups, Sit-Ups, and Jumping Jacks.

The acquisition setup contains a total of 4 Intel RealSense Depth Cameras D435 with the following arrangement: two central cameras D0 and D1, placed at ≈47.5 cm and ≈187 cm from the floor, respectively; and two lateral cameras D2 and D3, both placed at the same height centred at D1, but with a horizontal displacement of approx. ≈80 cm from each other. All the exercises were naturally executed by the subjects under a non-controlled scenario, regarding both the subjects' clothing and the acquisition conditions (e.g., lighting, background, clutter, etc.). Moreover, all the samples were recorded using an image resolution of 720×1280 at ≈30 frames-per-second.

For evaluation and training purposes, all the videos were manually annotated by an expert physiologist concerning both temporal and categorical annotations of the repetitions. The temporal annotation process includes two types of labels for each video frame: *key poses* and *phases*. *Key poses* represent the most important human poses that should be accomplished during a given exercise, while a given *phase* is the period between two *key poses*. Therefore, all the frames within the period of a *phase* have the same label. In addition, repetitions are also categorically labeled either as valid or invalid at the *phase* level in terms of their execution, and the set of associated categorical errors is also available. For instance, when performing Burpee exercise, individuals should reach a specific key pose where they stand and jump with their hands above the head. Figure 1 illustrates all the key poses and phases associated to this exercise, whereas Table 1 gives a complete overview of the considered phases and identified key poses on our dataset.

Throughout the rest of the paper, let $\mathbb{X}^{(z)} = \{X_t, m_t, y_t\}_{t=1}^{N}$ denote a labeled sequence of N frames of an exercise $z, z = 1, ..., 5$, where X_t denotes the input colour image at frame t, and m_t represents the current moment of the exercise execution. Moments of a given exercise comprise the key poses as well as the phases of the exercise, whereas $y_t \in \{0, 1\}$ belongs to one of two classes, denoting whether the t-th frame belongs either to a valid or invalid repetition.

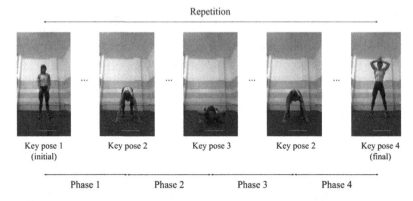

Fig. 1. Visual description for the difference between key poses and phases that were manually annotated in our dataset.

Table 1. General overview of our dataset with the number of the existing phases and description of the identified key poses for each exercise, as well as the number of valid/not valid repetitions.

Exercise	# Reps	# Phases	List of Key Poses
Squats	318/389	2	1: Standing upright position*
			2: Bent knees (hips aligned/lower than knees)
Burpees	109/70	4	1: *; 2: Squat with hands on the floor
			3: Push-up position: down
			4: Stand and jump with hands above the head
Push-Ups	178/251	2	1: Plank position (full elbow extension)
			2: Down position (bent elbows)
Sit-Ups	137/98	2	1: Sitting position (feet soles together)
			2: Lay down, hands touch the floor above head
Jumping Jacks	469/474	2	1:* (feet together, hands down)
			2: Feet apart (shoulder width), hands touch above head

3   Methodology

To better understand the following, the proposed work focuses on counting valid repetitions for the previously five mentioned exercises, while still providing feedback regarding their execution in an online-fashion. To accomplish this purpose, our system combines a *2D Pose Estimation Network* along with a *Moment-classifier* that infers the current moment of the exercise execution at frame level. The underlying idea of inferring the moment of the exercise is two-fold: (i) to provide information about the exercise execution with a fine-level of detail, and (ii) the ability to detect invalid repetitions promptly.

As illustrated in Fig. 2, the proposed system comprises four main modules: (i) a *2D human pose network*, (ii) a *representation module*, (iii) a *moment-classifier*, and (iv) a *repetition counting* and *validation module*. Specifically, the 2D human pose network aims at mapping from an input image X_t to a confidence heatmap H_t and a set of J keypoints image coordinates K_t. The set $K_t = (k_1, ..., k_J)$ comprises the keypoints coordinates pairs (x, y), where $k_j \in \mathbb{R}^2, j \in \{1, ..., J\}$ and J represents the number of considered human joints.

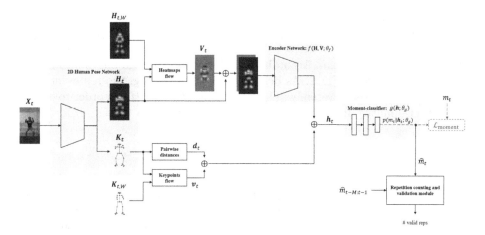

Fig. 2. Global overview of our method for counting and validation of workout repetitions.

The representation block operates on top of both outputs of the 2D human pose network, H_t and K_t, in order to produce a highly discriminative feature representation h for the moment classification task. In this regard, the representation h comprises a set of hand-crafted skeleton-based features computed from K_t as well as a set of features learned from the heatmaps H_t. The moment-classifier is then trained on these highly discriminative representations. Formally, a moment-specific function can be denoted as $g(h; \theta_g)$, which is parameterized by θ_g and maps from h to the predicted probabilities $p(m|h; \theta_g)$ of each moment class.

Finally, repetition counting and validation module receives the predicted moment $\hat{m} = \arg \max p(m|h; \theta_g)$ and outputs the current number of valid repetitions that the individual has been performing based on an internal state machine.

3.1   2D Human Pose Network

Within a sequence of frames, there are numerous poses that a human can perform and each of them are associated with a certain type of activity. The ability to understand human motion that was captured on still images comes along with the necessity of estimating the configuration of the human skeleton. Therefore, we have considered one popular and state-of-the-art approach for real-time human pose estimation developed by researchers at the *Carnegie Mellon University*, the *OpenPose* [2]. This framework consists on a bottom-up approach that is capable of jointly detecting human body, hand, facial and foot *keypoints* from multiple individuals in the same image. Its architecture is based on a two branch multi-stage CNN that has been trained on a large dataset concerning heterogeneous conditions.

From here, we make use of the OpenPose network in order to extract, from a given input image X_t, a set of J keypoints coordinates of the human joints K_t and a set of 2D confidence maps (or *heatmaps*). We then compute an overall heatmap H_t from the set of extracted heatmaps, which is given by the maximum value per pixel among them. Accordingly, H_t encodes the local information of all keypoints, as shown in Fig. 2. As described in the following, the representation module of the proposed system will be fed by both K_t and H_t, in order to create highly discriminative features for the moment classification task.

3.2   Representation Module

Given the previously data provided by the 2D Human Pose Network, K_t and H_t, there are different features that can be arranged and later fed to the desired moment-classifier. Specifically, the set of keypoints coordinates K_t are used to compute a set of skeleton-based features that encode the configuration of the human skeleton (i.e., the pose) as well as how the skeleton pose changes over time (i.e., the notion of movement). As a complement to these skeleton-based features, we also extract a set of features from the overall heatmap H_t. Our proposed advantage of using heatmap-based features is to gain robustness to partially occluded and/or miss-detected body joints.

Skeleton-Based Features. Based on the direct usage of the image coordinates of *keypoints*, one can calculate pairwise l^2 distances between them or even their flow among some desired frames. The pairwise distances among the set of extracted keypoints coordinates K_t are used to give the model an idea of the current configuration of the human skeleton. Accordingly, the i-th element of such pairwise distance vector $\mathbf{d}$ at frame t contains the Euclidean distance between two different keypoints i and j, such that:

$$d_{t,i} = ||\boldsymbol{k}_{t,i} - \boldsymbol{k}_{t,j}||_2, \forall i, i = 1, ..., J : i \neq j, \tag{1}$$

where $|| \cdot ||_2$ is the l^2-norm.

On the other side, the difference between all the current *keypoints* and the previous ones allows us to have a notion regarding the direction of the movement that the individual is performing. For instance, when performing a Squat exercise, the flow should point down during the descending phase, and vice-versa. Therefore, the flow or rate of change $\mathbf{v}$ at frame t is computed as the 1st order derivative of the keypoints coordinates:

$$v_{t,W} = \left[\mathbf{K}_t - \mathbf{K}_{(t-1)}; \ \mathbf{K}_t - \mathbf{K}_{(t-2)}; \ \ldots; \ \mathbf{K}_t - \mathbf{K}_{(t-W-1)} \right], \tag{2}$$

where W is the window size for calculating the flow. For instance, having $W = 2$ means that we are only considering the current t and the previous $(t-1)$ frames to compute the pose flow. When $W > 2$, one can encode different velocities of movement that may naturally arise among different individuals' executions.

Heatmaps-Based Features. As explained before, the 2D Human Pose Network is also used to extract an overall confidence map or heatmap $\mathbf{H}$ of all considered human joints. The overall extracted 2D heatmap $\mathbf{H}$ encodes information concerning the full estimated human pose. Therefore, it can be used as a complement to the distance feature vector $\mathbf{d}$, since there are still values for the occluded body parts. Moreover, similarly to the *keypoints*, we also compute their semantic flow as follows:

$$V_{t,W} = \left[\mathbf{H}_t - \mathbf{H}_{(t-1)}; \ \mathbf{H}_t - \mathbf{H}_{(t-2)}; \ \ldots \ \mathbf{H}_t - \mathbf{H}_{(t-W-1)} \right] \tag{3}$$

As depicted in Fig. 2, the heatmap flow $\mathbf{V}$ at frame t captures the spatial changes on the activations of the heatmaps from the previous to the current frames. At this stage, the skeleton-based and the heatmaps-based features are at a completely different semantic level. Besides, heatmaps-based features are still images (i.e., a 2D representation) that still encode the local spatial information of the body parts. Therefore, the representation module comprises an encoder network, which aims at learning an encoding function $f(\mathbf{H}, \mathbf{V}; \theta_f)$, parameterized by θ_f, that maps from both heatmaps-based representations, $\mathbf{H}$ and $\mathbf{V}$, to a high-level feature representation. Specifically, the encoder network consists of a sequence of L_e 3×3 convolutional layers with Rectified Linear Units (ReLUs) as nonlinearities. The output activation map is then flattened to be concatenated with the skeleton-based feature vectors.

Summing up, the representation module produces a feature representation h that comprises a set of hand-crafted skeleton-based features computed from the keypoints coordinates as well as a set of features learned from the heatmaps.

3.3 Moment-Classifier

The moment-classifier $g(\cdot, \theta_g)$ receives as input the feature representation h, produced by the representation module, and aims to predict the moment of the exercise execution m. Specifically, the moment-classifier is composed by a sequence of L_m fully connected layers, with ReLUs as the nonlinear functions, for predicting the moment class $\hat{m} = \arg\max p(\mathrm{m}|\boldsymbol{h};\theta_g)$. Accordingly, the last fully connected layer has a softmax activation function which outputs the probabilities for each moment class.

The learning process of the proposed system is then performed by jointly training the encoder network and the moment-classifier. That is, the parameters of the encoder θ_f and the moment-classifier θ_g are jointly optimized by minimizing the negative log-likelihood of the correct moment predictions:

$$\min_{\theta_f,\theta_g} \mathcal{L}_{\mathrm{moment}}(\theta_f,\theta_g) = -\frac{1}{N}\sum_{t=1}^{N}\log p(m_t|\boldsymbol{d}_t, \boldsymbol{v}_t, f(\boldsymbol{H}_t, \boldsymbol{V}_{t,W};\theta_f);\theta_g). \qquad (4)$$

3.4   Key Poses Augmentation

Labeling the exercises for each key moment provides a naturally imbalanced dataset. As the exercises are typically performed in a repetitive and cyclic fashion, the large majority of the frames will tend to belong to their inherent phases rather to their key poses. Taking the Squat exercise as an example, most of the frames will belong either to the descending or ascending phase of the exercise and, hence, just a few of them will be related to the key poses (e.g., Standing upright position). When a model is trained in such an unbalanced dataset, it will just predict the most representative classes, which in our case corresponds to the considered phases to achieve those key poses.

As illustrated in Fig. 3, we have addressed this issue by artificially generating new samples for the key poses with the aim of balancing the dataset regarding all the moments of the exercise. The augmentation process is performed at the feature level around every annotated key pose label. That is, for each extracted feature, R random samples are created based on the magnitude that each feature takes around every key pose label with some random noise, as depicted in Fig. 3 by the Euclidean distance between the right hip and the right ankle, and the y flow of the right hip. Note that the shadow areas represent the artificially augmented poses and the y flow becomes close to zero when the individual reaches a given key pose.

3.5   Repetition Counting and Validation Module

Building on top of the moment predictions, the *Repetition Counting and Validation module* updates the current number of valid repetitions at each frame t. Specifically, this module receives the moment prediction of the current frame $\hat{m}_t$ as well as the M past moment predictions $\hat{m}_{t-M:t-1}$, which are used for smoothing the current prediction of the moment-classifier. Afterwards, the current number of valid repetitions is incremented if there is a transition from the last moment to the first moment of the exercise and if all the moments of the exercise appear in the right order within the current repetition.

4 Exploring the Best Combination of Features and Cameras

Considering all the extracted features as explained in Sect. 3.2, one can arrange them in different manners to assess which is the most suitable data vector to train a given model. To this end, we have carried out tests with four combinations of these features for each physical exercise by employing different state-of-the-art machine learning models to the presented problem. In addition, our evaluation protocol throughout the rest of the article relies on the division of the presented dataset into the following sets: 18 participants for training and validation (80% and 20%, respectively) and the remaining 4 participants for testing. Every model presented below was equally optimized through a cross-validation and exhaustive grid search over specified parameter values.

The results for a *per-frame* phase classification regarding only the information acquired from one camera can be seen in Table 2. Note that tests $1 - 4$ refer to the exploitation of the following combinations of features: 1) $\mathbf{d}_{t,i}$; 2) $\mathbf{d}_{t,i} + \mathbf{v}_{t,2}$; 3) $\mathbf{d}_{t,i} + \mathbf{v}_{t,2} + \mathbf{H}_t$; 4) $\mathbf{d}_{t,i} + \mathbf{v}_{t,2} + \mathbf{H}_t + \mathbf{V}_{t,2}$. A first round of the results was performed for the K-Nearest Neighbors (KNN) [1], Support-Vector Machine (SVM) [3] and Random Forest (RF) [4] classifiers. We noticed that the combination used for Test #4 shows to be the most suitable for the intended purpose in a global fashion. Therefore, providing not only the direct skeleton-based features, but also the ones that can be extrapolated from a more semantic level, can indeed increase the overall performance of an exercise's phase classifier.

Given our previously described approach, we have trained a Multilayer Perceptron (MLP) both with and without the Encoder Network using this

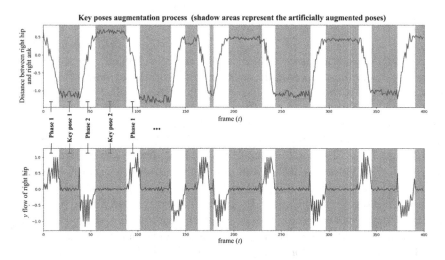

Fig. 3. Illustration of the key poses augmentation process.

Table 2. Accuracy comparison between different kinds of classifiers and our approach to workout phase recognition *per-frame*.

Exercise	Test #	Accuracy (%)				
		KNN	SVM	RF	MLP	MLP + Encoder
Squats	1	58.26	62.12	68.33	–	–
	2	87.80	90.89	92.18	–	–
	3	88.19	91.49	92.65	–	–
	4	88.38	93.01	95.28	94.90	**95.53**
Burpees	1	49.59	54.77	60.86	–	–
	2	59.79	56.22	73.73	–	–
	3	63.74	56.52	78.52	–	–
	4	63.68	56.22	77.02	89.46	**91.74**
Push-Ups	1	54.95	54.39	54.53	–	–
	2	80.85	80.51	84.35	–	–
	3	80.71	81.96	83.77	–	–
	4	81.84	82.02	87.37	83.43	**91.71**
Sit-Ups	1	66.59	70.30	70.34	–	–
	2	75.90	76.98	79.89	–	–
	3	76.43	76.95	80.03	–	–
	4	77.21	77.03	82.60	84.32	**84.64**
Jumping Jacks	1	65.50	77.94	74.66	–	–
	2	89.39	89.97	93.43	–	–
	3	90.64	91.87	93.48	–	–
	4	92.29	91.82	95.68	**97.52**	97.01

best combination of features. As it can be seen in Table 2, the MLP + an Encoder Network has successfully overcome the previous models in 4 out of the 5 considered Cross-Fit exercises while having a similar performance on the last one.

On the other side, during the execution of exercises that have one or more phases with key poses where the human body is parallel to the floor, there are higher changes of having occluded limbs. However, given that our dataset was created with videos recorded from distinct point-of-views over the "workout area", one can explore how different cameras might support each other during this *per-frame* phase classification. Hence, we have combined information of two concurrent cameras concerning the best combination of the single-view analysis to perform a multi-view study that would improve our results, as shown in Table 3. It suggests that complementing the frontal view with a lateral camera enhances the previously obtained results, specifically for the exercises with

Table 3. Multi-view analysis for the best combination of features.

Exercise	D0	D0 & D1	D2 & D3	D0 & D2
Squats	95.53	95.12	95.52	**96.75**
Burpees	91.74	92.04	77.34	**95.95**
Push-Ups	91.71	89.38	80.20	**92.75**
Sit-Ups	84.64	84.00	**88.97**	87.58
Jumping Jacks	**97.52**	95.57	93.83	97.41

floor-parallel phases (e.g, Push-Ups and Burpees), as it lowers the chances of having occluded upper body parts. In addition, there is a significant gain in accuracy ($\approx$4%) for the Burpees exercise, but a single-view approach appears to be sufficient for the Jumping Jacks. This may be due to the fact that unlike Squats, Jumping Jacks doesn't have straightforward variants (e.g, people don't performing the ascending phase with arm trajectories). The Sit-Ups exercise shows to benefit from the upper camera (D1) and one lateral camera, which can be explained by the fact that upper body is also commonly occluded to the lower one (D0). Lastly, experiments with the combination of three or more cameras were not conducted, since it would highly increase the execution time of our system and lead us to offline solutions for the presented problem.

5   Experimental Results on Workout Repetition Counting and Validation

As explained before, we have artificially augmented the labelled data to comprise every moment for the exercises and trained a new model for the MLP + Encoder Net. It is noteworthy to mention that we were able to promptly identify repetitions that were performed incorrectly by this procedure, but it shouldn't be seen as a correct practice, since the live data will not comprehend a balanced dataset. Nevertheless, the new results can be seen in Table 4, which clearly shows that the overall scores decreased with the increase of the classes number.

Table 4. *Per-frame* recognition for the exercises augmented moments.

Exercise	# Phases/Classes	Accuracy (%)	# Moments/Classes	Accuracy (%)
Squats	2	95.53	4	95.48
Burpees	4	91.74	8	70.62
Push-Ups	2	91.71	4	93.24
Sit-Ups	2	84.64	4	80.87
Jumping Jacks	2	97.52	4	98.50

Table 5. Counting valid repetitions.

Exercise	Precision (%)	Recall (%)
Squats	90.50	95.00
Burpees	91.30	84.00
Push-Ups	92.31	100.00
Sit-Ups	71.01	87.72
Jumping Jacks	96.08	92.45

Table 6. Recognition rate for invalid repetitions.

Exercise	Recognition rate (%)
Squats	64.71
Burpees	51.51
Push-Ups	68.97
Sit-Ups	83.33
Jumping Jacks	78.05

Under the scope of our approach, a repetition is considered valid and properly executed if the individual has passed through every phase, reaching each subsequent key pose, and if all the moments of the exercise appear in the right order. Moreover, we consider that our method counts those repetitions correctly if within the right moment or at least in a given time window (3 past frames, current frame and 3 future frames), e.g when the individual move from the final key pose to the initial one. Therefore, we present our system's precision and recall[2] for the single-view repetition counting process in Table 5. In this sense, a true positive is considered when the repetition is adequately counted within the mentioned time window. A false negative consists on a repetition that is counted outside this time frame. Finally, a false positive is when the system counts a non-existing valid repetition. But, since individuals might try to trick our system on the execution of the exercises, we have tested our models with only invalid reps to understand how robust it would be. As shown in Table 6, our system can automatically identify more than 50% of the provided badly executed repetitions for all the exercises. When carefully observing this table, it can recognize 83.33% of the invalid repetitions for the Sit-Ups exercise. This suggests that our system tends to be robust during the execution of invalid repetitions despite the fact that we have trained our moment-classifier with only valid repetitions.

---

[2] From [5] – Precision is the fraction of relevant instances among the retrieved instances: $Precision = \frac{tp}{tp+fp}$. Recall measures the proportion of actual positives that are correctly identified: $Recall = \frac{tp}{tp+fn}$.

6 Conclusion

In this work we have proposed a new method for counting valid repetitions among 5 different CrossFit physical exercises. We have evaluated the performance of different state-of-the-art machine learning algorithms on four possible combinations for distinct features. Given the best combination, we have successfully trained a MLP classifier along with an Encoder Network that is able of identifying in which moment the individual is for a given exercise. Despite our promising results, we consider that recurrent networks with more sophisticated architectures can be the next step to help us identify errors that individuals are performing throughout the exercises. For instance, while performing Squats there are some errors that people tend to execute over time, such as excessive feet rotation or knees abduction. Moreover, improving the presented system could also aid preventing sport-related injuries or even teach fit enthusiasts beginners on how to correctly perform those exercises through machine supervision.

References

1. Altman, N.S.: An introduction to kernel and nearest-neighbor nonparametric regression. Am. Stat. **46**(3), 175–185 (1992)
2. Cao, Z., Hidalgo, G., Simon, T., Wei, S.E., Sheikh, Y.: OpenPose: real-time multi-person 2D pose estimation using part affinity fields. arXiv preprint arXiv:1812.08008 (2018)
3. Cortes, C., Vapnik, V.: Support-vector networks. Mach. Learn. **20**(3), 273–297 (1995). https://doi.org/10.1007/BF00994018
4. Ho, T.K.: Random decision forests. In: Proceedings of 3rd International Conference on Document Analysis and Recognition, vol. 1, pp. 278–282. IEEE (1995)
5. Kent, A., Berry, M.M., Luehrs Jr., F.U., Perry, J.W.: Machine literature searching viii. Operational criteria for designing information retrieval systems. Am. Doc. **6**(2), 93–101 (1955)
6. Khurana, R., Ahuja, K., Yu, Z., Mankoff, J., Harrison, C., Goel, M.: Gymcam: detecting, recognizing and tracking simultaneous exercises in unconstrained scenes. In: Proceedings of the ACM on Interactive, Mobile, Wearable and Ubiquitous Technologies, vol. 2, no. 4, pp. 1–17 (2018)
7. Rêgo, M.L., Cabral, D.A., Costa, E.C., Fontes, E.B.: Physical exercise for individuals with hypertension: it is time to emphasize its benefits on the brain and cognition. Clin. Med. Insights: Cardiol. **13**, 1179546819839411 (2019)
8. Skawinski, K., Montraveta Roca, F., Findling, R.D., Sigg, S.: Workout type recognition and repetition counting with CNNs from 3D acceleration sensed on the chest. In: Rojas, I., Joya, G., Catala, A. (eds.) IWANN 2019. LNCS, vol. 11506, pp. 347–359. Springer, Cham (2019). https://doi.org/10.1007/978-3-030-20521-8_29
9. Soro, A., Brunner, G., Tanner, S., Wattenhofer, R.: Recognition and repetition counting for complex physical exercises with deep learning. Sensors **19**(3), 714 (2019)
10. Åkerberg, A., Soderlund, A., Lindén, M.: Technologies for physical activity self-monitoring: a study of differences between users and non-users. Open Access J. Sports Med. **8**, 17–26 (2017). https://doi.org/10.2147/OAJSM.S124542

FlowChroma - A Deep Recurrent Neural Network for Video Colorization

Thejan Wijesinghe, Chamath Abeysinghe, Chanuka Wijayakoon$^{(\boxtimes)}$,
Lahiru Jayathilake, and Uthayasanker Thayasivam

University of Moratuwa, Moratuwa, Sri Lanka
{thejanwijesinghe.14,chamath.14,chanuka.14,lahiruj.14,
rtuthaya}@cse.mrt.ac.lk

Abstract. We develop an automated video colorization framework that minimizes the flickering of colors across frames. If we apply image colorization techniques to successive frames of a video, they treat each frame as a separate colorization task. Thus, they do not necessarily maintain the colors of a scene consistently across subsequent frames. The proposed solution includes a novel deep recurrent encoder-decoder architecture which is capable of maintaining temporal and contextual coherence between consecutive frames of a video. We use a high-level semantic feature extractor to automatically identify the context of a scenario including objects, with a custom fusion layer that combines the spatial and temporal features of a frame sequence. We demonstrate experimental results, qualitatively showing that recurrent neural networks can be successfully used to improve color consistency in video colorization.

Keywords: Video colorization · Image colorization · Recurrent neural networks

1 Introduction

Colorizing a grayscale image to achieve a natural look has been a much-explored research problem in the recent years, especially with the rise of deep learning-based approaches for image processing. A primary goal has been to produce diverse colorizations, while also providing plausible colorizations that apply correct colors to identified objects. Desaturating an image is a surjective operation, but it is not injective. Hence, there are multiple possible colors to choose from when considering a pixel in a grayscale image - it is a one-to-many mapping.

Compared to the image colorization problem, colorizing black and white videos has largely been left behind. This problem has abundant training data, as one could easily convert a video to grayscale and test the colorization against the original video. Video colorization could be used as a video preprocessing technique, such as to enhance CCTV footage, and to restore old movies and

Supported by Amazon Cloud Credits for Research.

A. Campilho et al. (Eds.): ICIAR 2020, LNCS 12131, pp. 16–29, 2020.
https://doi.org/10.1007/978-3-030-50347-5_2

documentaries. One could argue that video colorization could be taken as a direct extension of image colorization, where successive application of frame colorization would produce a colorized video. But obviously, there is no guarantee that the selected image colorization technique would color successive frames consistently, known as temporal coherence, since it would consider each frame as a separate task, ignoring the contextual connections between frames. This would result in flickering colors, reducing the usefulness of such results.

The other prime obstacle has been the high computational costs in colorizing videos [14, 26] - it adds another dimension across time on top of the already computationally intensive image colorization.

Furthermore, we observed that the most realistic image colorization results from current techniques are produced when some sort of human intervention is made, such as user scribbles that guide the colorization process [6,14]. While this is feasible for a few images, it certainly does not scale up for videos with thousands of consecutive frames, as commercial videos run at 24 or more frames per second. Thus, efficiently colorizing a video with resource constraints and minimal supervision poses an interesting research problem.

There's a plethora of early video content shot in black and white that was enjoyed by older generations and remembered fondly. Such classical content is mostly forgotten and the later generations prefer colored content. Colorizing existing content is much cheaper than reproducing them entirely in color today.

Our research contributions are as follows;

1. We propose a new fully automated video colorization framework focusing on improved temporal and contextual coherence between frames and scene changes.
2. We use a Recurrent Neural Network (RNN) based architecture to maintain contextual information across frames for consistent coloring.
3. We study the effects of using RNNs on the colorization of videos.

2   Related Work

Most of the previous work in the colorization domain has been done for image colorization, and video colorization is now gaining momentum with their success. The current image colorization algorithms can broadly be put into two major categories: parametric methods [1–7] and non-parametric methods [9–20]. Parametric methods learn predictive functions from large datasets of color images; once the predictive function's parameters are learned with an appropriate optimization objective, it is ready to predict colors in a fully automatic manner. Alternatively, non-parametric methods require some level of human intervention.

There are mainly two non-parametric methods explored in the literature: scribble-based and transfer-based. Scribble-based colorization schemas [12,14, 17,18,20] require manually chosen color scribbles on the target grayscale image. In few instances, scribble-based colorization methods are extended to video colorization as well [14,17]. Transfer-based colorization schemas [9–11,13,15,16,19] require the user to select semantically similar colorful reference images to match similar segments of the target grayscale image.

Applying non-parametric methods on both image and video colorization has a number of drawbacks, the most prominent among which is the inability to fully automate the colorization process. In color transferring approaches, there is a manual intervention in searching for colorful reference images. Scribble-based colorization may require tens of well-placed scribbles plus a carefully chosen, rich pallet of colors in order to achieve convincing, natural results for a complex image.

Both scribble-based and transfer-based video colorization schemas can only be automated within a frame sequence without a scene change; i.e. at each scene change, if the process is scribble-based, the user will have to introduce a new set of scribbles. If it is transfer-based, a new selection of swatches with or without a new reference image will be required.

Comparatively, parametric colorization schemas can fully automate the colorization process. Deshpande et al. [3] proposed a parametric image colorization schema which formulates the colorization problem as a quadratic objective function and trained it using the LEARCH framework [24]. With the unparalleled success of deep neural networks, solutions that utilize DNNs have been proposed as parametric image colorization schemas. Cheng et al. [2] proposed an image colorization schema which leverages a three-layer fully connected neural network that was trained by the inputs of a set of image descriptors: luminance, DAISY features [28] and semantic features. More recently, many authors have employed convolutional neural networks (CNN) and generative adversarial networks (GAN) in their colorization schemas rather than conventional deep neural networks (DNN). Zhang et al. [5] proposed a CNN-based colorization schema which predicts a probability distribution of possible colors for each pixel in order to address the typical ambiguous and multimodal nature of image colorization [9].

They also introduced a CNN based color recommender system [6] that propagates user-provided scribbles while satisfying high level color preferences of the user. Larsson et al. [7] trained an end-to-end network to predict colors of an image with the hypercolumns [8] for each pixel generated from a pre-trained VGG-16 network without a classification layer. Iizuka et al. [4] proposed a colorization method that utilizes a CNN based architecture, combining a high-level semantic feature extractor, a mid-level feature network and a colorization network. More recently, inspired by the colorization model of Iizuka et al. [4], Baldassarre et al. [1] replaced the high-level semantic feature extractor in the colorization model of Iizuka et al. [4] with a pre-trained CNN image classifier: Inception-ResNet-v2 [27]. This transfer learning approach significantly reduces the computational time as well as the need for extreme amounts of data and hardware resources to train the colorization network to yield a quality colorization result.

Most of the fully-automatic, parametric image colorization solutions can be extended to video colorization domain by treating a video merely as a sequence of independent frames. But considering video frames independently causes colors to shift erratically, failing to maintain temporal coherence throughout the frame sequence, causing visual fatigue for viewers. For an example, a wall in one frame may be colored in one shade of yellow and the same wall should maintain that color in subsequent frames, rather than changing to a shade of white. Failing to capture these details drastically reduces the quality of colored videos, because the user can notice color mismatches and flickering between video frames. In this research, we explore the effectiveness of employing RNNs to preserve the temporal coherence in video colorization while mitigating the challenges of computational time and need for large amounts of data, with the help of a transfer learning application.

3   Proposed Approach

When modeling the video colorization problem as a learnable function, we have chosen the CIE La*b* color space to represent video frames. According to Ruderman et al. [25], La*b* color space was developed to minimize correlation between the three coordinate axes of the color space. La*b* color space provides three decorrelated, principal channels corresponding to an achromatic luminance channel L and two chromatic channels as a* and b*. If we have a grayscale frame, that means we already have the luminance layer of that particular frame, the next step is finding a plausible a*, b* combination and fusing them together to come up with a final colored frame, given that there is temporal coherence when predicting a* and b* combinations. Therefore, the main assumption here is that for every luminance component of video frames

$$X_t{}^L \in R^{H \times W \times 1} \tag{1}$$

there exists a function F such that

$$F : \{X_t{}^L, X_{t-1}{}^L, ..., X_{t-(T-1)}{}^L\} \rightarrow (X_t{}^{a^*}, X_t{}^{b^*}) \tag{2}$$

Here, $X_t{}^k$ represents the a or b color layer in t^{th} time frame, while H, W and T represent frame height, width and total number of previous frames used for prediction, respectively.

The chromatic channels a* and b* define an Euclidean space where the distance to the origin determines the chroma. Change of values in one channel imposes minimal effect on values of the other two. This decorrelation of the three channels allows us to combine the luminance with the predicted chromatic channels, ensuring an image construction with high level of detail but with almost non-existent cross-channel artifacts.

3.1   Proposed Architecture

FlowChroma architecture can be divided into five main components, as shown in Fig. 1: the CNN encoder, global feature extractor, stacked LSTM, fusion layer and the CNN decoder. We include Inception-ResNet-v2 network as a global feature extractor; this is a transfer learning technique, drawing inspiration from

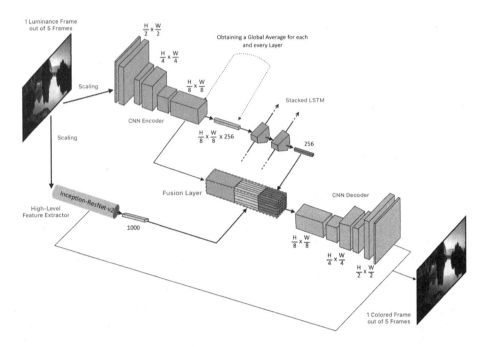

Fig. 1. FlowChroma architecture diagram

the works of Iizuka et al. [4] and Baldassarre et al. [1] This significantly reduces the computational complexity in training the model.

Although the use of Long Short-Term Memory (LSTM) units [29] to support video colorization has been proposed before, this is one of the first architectures to produce experimental results showing the effectiveness of it specifically towards video colorization. An LSTM is a special form of recurrent neural networks (RNNs). All RNNs have loops within their architecture, acting as a memory cell allowing information to persist for a certain period. They are able to connect previously learned information to the present task. LSTMs specifically outperform regular RNNs in many scenarios, as they have a superior ability to learn longer-term dependencies against vanilla RNNs. When considering an arbitrary frame sequence, it can include scene changes as well. Therefore, our model also needs to learn how much it should remember or forget while generating a frame sequence - this criteria makes LSTMs an ideal candidate for our use case over vanilla RNNs.

As shown in Fig. 1, the CNN encoder extracts local features such as texture and shapes while the Inception-ResNet-v2 extracts high level semantic information such as objects and environments from an individual frame. A stacked LSTM is being employed to grasp temporal features of a sequence of frames. The outputs from the CNN encoder, Inception network and the LSTM are then fused together in the fusion layer to provide inputs to the colorization network or the CNN decoder. The CNN decoder is used to predict a* and b* layers related to the input luminance frame at the current time step in a spatio-temporal manner.

Encoder			Stacked LSTM		Decoder		
Layer	Kernels	Stride	Layer	Hidden Cells	Layer	Kernels	Stride
Conv	64 x (3 x 3)	2 x 2	LSTM	256	Conv	256 x (1 x 1)	1 x 1
Conv	128 x (3 x 3)	1 x 1	LSTM	256	Conv	128 x (3 x 3)	1 x 1
Conv	128 x (3 x 3)	2 x 2	Dense	-	Upsampling	-	-
Conv	256 x (3 x 3)	1 x 1			Conv	64 x (3 x 3)	1 x 1
Conv	256 x (3 x 3)	2 x 2			Conv	64 x (3 x 3)	1 x 1
Conv	512 x (3 x 3)	1 x 1			Upsampling	-	-
Conv	512 x (3 x 3)	1 x 1			Conv	32 x (3 x 3)	1 x 1
Conv	256 x (3 x 3)	1 x 1			Conv	2 x (3 x 3)	1 x 1
					Upsampling	-	-

Fig. 2. FlowChroma architecture: The CNN encoder extracts local features while the Inception network extracts high level semantic information from a frame. The stacked LSTM grasps temporal features from a sequence of frames. The outputs from the CNN encoder, Inception network and the LSTM are then fused together in the fusion layer to provide inputs to the colorization network or the CNN decoder. Note that the CNN encoder, decoder, fusion layer and Inception network are all applied to every temporal slice of the input.

3.2 Grasping Local and Global Features of Each Individual Frame

In order to grasp local features such as shapes in frame at each time step, we apply a CNN encoder to every temporal slice of the input. It processes a $t \times H \times W$ grayscale frame sequence and outputs a sequence of $t \times H/8 \times W/8 \times 256$ feature encodings.

Global features such as objects and environments are helpful for the CNN decoder to provide an appropriate colorization. The high-level feature extractor is a pre-trained Inception-Resnet-v2 model without the last SoftMax layer. When training FlowChroma, we keep Inception's weights static. At each time step, we scale the input luminance frame to 299×299, and then stack itself to obtain a three channel frame in order to satisfy Inception's input dimensionality requirements. Then we feed the resultant frame to Inception and obtain its logits output (the output before the softmax layer). When the results at each time step are combined, we get a final embedding of $t \times 1000$ for the entire sequence.

3.3 Capturing Temporal Features

In order to grasp temporal variations of the frame sequence, we use a 2-layer stacked LSTM model. The CNN encoder provides a local feature encoding of $t \times H/8 \times W/8 \times 256$. By employing global average pooling operation on that encoding at each time step, we obtain an embedding of $t \times 256$, which can be used as inputs to the stacked LSTM. Stacked LSTM has two LSTM layers, each having 256 hidden states, thus giving us an output with the dimensions of $t \times 256$. This output improves temporal coherence of the video colorization predictions.

3.4 Fusing Local and Global Spatial Features with Temporal Features

Fusing local and global level spatial features with temporal features will be done by a specially crafted fusion layer, first introduced by Iizuka et al. [4] Similar to CNN encoder, we apply the fusion layer to every temporal slice of the input. The fusion layer takes the output embeddings from Inception and stacked LSTM to replicate it $H/8 \times W/8$ times and then concatenates them with the output provided by the CNN encoder. The fusion mechanism is more comprehensively illustrated in Fig. 3.

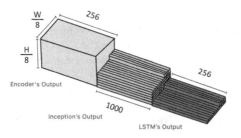

Fig. 3. Fusion Layer - the outputs of the Inception network and the LSTM are replicated and stacked with the CNN encoder's output.

3.5 Colorization Decoder Network

Once the local and global spatial features are fused with temporal features, they are processed by a set of convolutions and up-sampling layers in the CNN decoder. Similar to the CNN encoder and Fusion layer, we apply the CNN decoder to every temporal slice of the input. The decoder takes a $t \times H/8 \times W/8 \times 1512$ input and results in a final output with dimension of $t \times H \times W \times 2$. The resultant sequence can be considered as the sequence of a* and b* layers for the input sequence of luminance frames, once this result is appropriately merged with the input sequence, we can obtain the final colorized frame sequence.

3.6 Optimization and Learning

Optimal model parameters were found by minimizing an objective function defined over predicted outputs and actual results. To quantify the loss, mean squared error between each pixel in a*, b* layers of predicted and actual results were used. If we consider a video V, the MSE loss is estimated by,

$$C(X, \Theta) = \frac{1}{2nHW} \sum_{t=0}^{n} \sum_{k \in a, b} \sum_{i=1}^{H} \sum_{j=1}^{W} (X^k{}_{t_{i,j}} - \hat{X}^k{}_{t_{i,j}})^2 \qquad (3)$$

Here θ represents all model parameters and $X^k{}_{t_{i,j}}$ represents the (i,j) pixel in t^{th} time frame's k layer. This objective function can be extended to batch level by taking the average.

$$C(X,\beta) = \frac{1}{|\beta|} \sum_{X \in \beta} C(X,\Theta) \tag{4}$$

To optimize the above objective function, we used Adam optimizer [23].

3.7   Training

FlowChroma was trained for roughly 50 h on 50,000 short, preprocessed video clips, taken from the FCVID [22] video dataset. Videos were randomly selected from the dataset, converted to LAB color space and resized to match the input shape of the network. We used a batch size of 20 and a validation split of 10%. Training was done on an AWS EC2 instance that had 32 virtual CPUs and four NVIDIA Tesla P100 GPUs, with a total video memory of 64 GB.

4   Experiments

We compare FlowChroma's video colorization performance by taking the Deep Koalarization framework proposed by Baldassarre et al. [1] as our baseline model. There are mainly two reasons for this choice, rather than another image colorization framework or a state-of-the-art technique.

1. Both FlowChroma and Deep Koalarization use the same transfer learning application of obtaining global features of an image or a video frame from a pre-trained object classifier and fusing them in the fusion layer, similar to Iizuka et al. [4]
2. The main purpose of our research is emphasizing the use of sequence models in preserving temporal coherence between frames and scene changes rather than extremely realistic colorizations; to achieve that, comparison of our framework with a good enough image colorization framework is sufficient.

To evaluate the performance of FlowChroma against our baseline model, we randomly selected 1,000 videos from the FCVID dataset, belonging to various categories depicting a wide range of scenarios, derived their grayscale variants and colorized them with the two models.

In order to provide a fair comparison of the two model's colorization performance, we used Inception-ResNet-v2, pre-trained object classifier as the global feature extractor for both FlowChroma and the baseline model. We also trained both models on the same dataset and hardware environment upto a close validation loss. Subsequently, a qualitative assessment of the colorizations was performed.

Our model only takes a sequence of 5 frames as an input at once, but when running inference we need to colorize videos with hundreds of frames. Thus, we use a sliding window approach during inference. In contrast to that, our baseline model only takes a single frame as input at a time, thereby coloring each frame in a video independently.

We first confirm that our model performs well in colorization, and verify that although we use a recurrent architecture, it still converges. Next, we show that we can achieve temporal and contextual coherence through video frames with LSTMs. Finally, we discuss the weaknesses of the proposed architecture and discuss possible solutions.

5   Results and Discussion

In general, we observed that our model produces appropriate colorization results, assigning realistic colors to objects within each scenario. Furthermore, the system successfully maintains color information between frames, keeping a natural flow and a high spatio-temporal coherence at both global and local levels for videos with common objects and environments in the training dataset. We also observed that for sudden or quick object movements, our model added blobs of flickering that followed the movement of the object (Fig. 5).

Fig. 4. FlowChroma generalizes commonly encountered scenes and objects and assigns them appropriate colors during inference. It also generates an acceptable variation of colors in each scene throughout the colorization results, as demonstrated in 4a, 4b and 4c. In 4a, note how the parachute and the flag are colored in red hues while the sky is in blue. In 4c, the eye color and skin tones over different regions in the face make the frame appear more realistic. (Color figure online)

In terms of raw colorization, our model generalizes commonly encountered scenes and objects and assigns them appropriate colors during inference. Figure 4b depicts a scene with a large field in the foreground and the sky in the background. This type of colorizations are observed throughout the results, and stand to reason that the system generalizes the scenes in the training dataset.

We observe LSTM's sequence learning capabilities on colorization at two scales; locally and globally. At a global scale, FlowChroma maintains the overall color composition of a scene throughout the video better than the baseline image colorization model. At a local level, the baseline model sometimes mistakenly colorizes small regions of a frame with inappropriate colors, but FlowChroma avoids such mistakes.

An example of this is shown in Fig. 6a, which depicts a herd of elephants strolling about. FlowChroma maintains the dry tone of the environment across the video while the baseline model shows colors changing between green and off-brown even for slight movements of elephants and their tails. Similarly, in Fig. 6b, FlowChroma again maintains the grass field in green while the baseline flickers from brown to green for the slight movements of the shooter and his gun. In Fig. 6c, note how the baseline system bleeds color from the smartphone's clock into the background while our model does a better job of keeping the background uniform.

At a local scale, the LSTM affects how FlowChroma decides colors should be assigned even when it cannot fully identify the progression of a previously detected region. In Fig. 6a, the background contains a wall that is uniformly colored throughout the frames by FlowChroma, while having blue patches in the baseline model's output. This is an example of the downsides of considering each frame as a separate colorization task, as done by image colorization models. Figure 6b contains an off-white board that is consistently colored by FlowChroma, whereas the baseline model again adds blue color patches. Blue color patches have appeared probably due to erroneously identifying those regions as sky or water in some frames.

Based on our observations, we can divide the factors affecting the consistency of colorization as temporal and non temporal. Non-temporal factors include

1. extreme pixel values of input grayscale image e.g. extreme dark color of asphalt roads or extreme bright color of snow,
2. the prevalence of a context in the training dataset. These factors affect both image colorization extensions to video colorization as well as FlowChroma. If the pixel values are extreme, such as in the case of snow or asphalt roads, both the baseline model and FlowChroma tend to leave them as extremes without assigning new colors.

Furthermore, when colorizing commonly encountered contexts, both the baseline and our model provided consistent appropriate colors because of the high level feature extractor; Inception-ResNet-v2 that is pre-trained on the ImageNet dataset, which contains images of commonly encountered context.

Temporal factors mainly relate to the movement of objects in a scenario, where the action frequency confuses the system's perception of the trajectory of the scene. This is applicable only to FlowChroma. When the movements in a video are smooth, our system identifies the objects and applies appropriate, temporally coherent coloring. When the movement in the scenario speeds up, the perceived flow of movement breaks and thus the colorization quality degrades fast, especially in terms of segmentation and appropriate coloring.

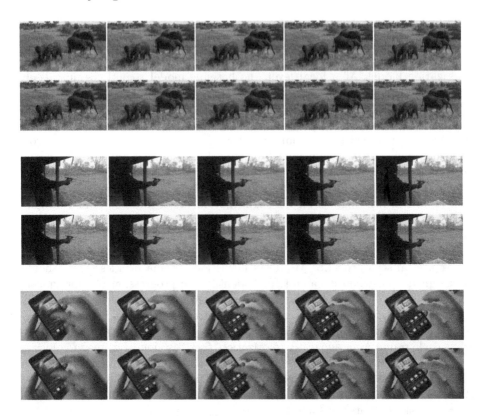

Fig. 5. In each sub-figure, the top and bottom rows show the video frame sequences colored by FlowChroma and the baseline model respectively. These show the superior global color palette maintenance throughout the scene by our model. (Color figure online)

Lastly, we observe when the colorization of FlowChroma becomes inconsistent and also propose possible solutions for them.

1. The introduction of new objects into a scene changes its context, introducing momentary flickering before stabilizing again. Training the model further may alleviate this problem.
2. When there is a high object frequency in a scene, the aptness of the colorization gets reduced. An example would be a surface with a complex pattern. A potential solution would be to train the system on more videos with high object frequency.
3. The action frequency also adversely affects the system's performance. Normalizing the action speed is one possible solution. This could be done by increasing the number of frames containing the movement by predicting intermediate frames, as recently demonstrated by Nvidia [21], and then slowing down the video to achieve the desired speed. Another potential solution is to train the system with more time steps.

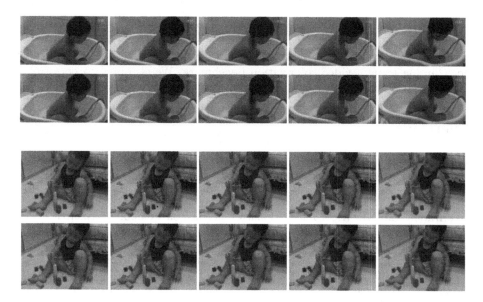

Fig. 6. In each sub-figure, the top and bottom row are from FlowChroma and the baseline model, respectively, showing how the local color uniformity is better maintained by FlowChroma. Note how the baseline model flickers with blue color patches as the camera angle changes in a and as the boy moves his hands in b. (Color figure online)

6 Conclusions

Contemporary image colorization techniques are not directly applicable to video colorization as they treat each video frame as a separate colorization task, without maintaining temporal coherence between frames. We propose FlowChroma, a novel colorization framework with a recurrent neural network - LSTM - added to maintain temporal and contextual information between frames.

Inherent capability of LSTMs to learn how much each hidden cell should remember or forget while reading or generating a sequence stands as a justification for using LSTMs in FlowChroma rather than vanilla RNNs - this is the basis for their usage in video colorizations with scene changes.

We show that the LSTM maintains the image colorization quality of current methods intact while also successfully minimizing flickering between frames. It maintains the overall color palette of a scenario across subsequent frames at a global level, while coloring identified objects within a scene consistently at a local level.

We observed some limitations in the use of recurrent architectures for video colorization, which may be common to other techniques as well. FlowChroma specifically generates inconsistent colorizations in the following scenarios;

1. Sudden introduction of new objects into the scene
2. High object frequency or having high number of objects in a scene
3. High action frequency or fast movements in a scene.

Finally, from these preliminary results, we have a promising research direction in maintaining temporal and contextual coherence in video colorization with LSTMs. As future work, we hope to quantitatively assess the performance of FlowChroma using a video colorization benchmark. We also plan to perform a visual Turing test of colorized videos from various frameworks.

References

1. Baldassarre, F., Morín, D.G., Rodés-Guirao, L.: Deep koalarization: image colorization using CNNS and inception-ResNet-v2. CoRR, abs/1712.03400 (2017)
2. Cheng, Z., Yang, Q., Sheng, B.: Deep colorization. CoRR, abs/1605.00075 (2016)
3. Deshpande, A., Rock, J., Forsyth, D.: Learning large-scale automatic image colorization. In: 2015 IEEE International Conference on Computer Vision (ICCV), pp. 567–575, December 2015
4. Iizuka, S., Simo-Serra, E., Ishikawa, H.: Let there be color!: joint end-to-end learning of global and local image priors for automatic image colorization with simultaneous classification. ACM Trans. Graph. 35(4), 110:1–110:11 (2016)
5. Zhang, R., Isola, P., Efros, A.A.: Colorful image colorization. CoRR, abs/1603.08511 (2016)
6. Zhang, R., et al.: Real-time user-guided image colorization with learned deep priors. CoRR, abs/1705.02999 (2017)
7. Larsson, G., Maire, M., Shakhnarovich, G.: Learning representations for automatic colorization. CoRR, abs/1603.06668 (2016)
8. Hariharan, B., Arbeláez, P.A., Girshick, R.B., Malik, J.: Hypercolumns for object segmentation and fine-grained localization. CoRR, abs/1411.5752 (2014)
9. Charpiat, G., Hofmann, M., Schölkopf, B.: Automatic image colorization via multimodal predictions. In: Forsyth, D., Torr, P., Zisserman, A. (eds.) ECCV 2008. LNCS, vol. 5304, pp. 126–139. Springer, Heidelberg (2008). https://doi.org/10.1007/978-3-540-88690-7_10
10. Chia, A.Y.-S., et al.: Semantic colorization with internet images. ACM Trans. Graph. 30(6), 156:1–156:8 (2011)
11. Gupta, R.K., Chia, A.Y.-S., Rajan, D., Ng, E.S., Zhiyong, H.: Image colorization using similar images. In: Proceedings of the 20th ACM International Conference on Multimedia, MM 2012, pp. 369–378. ACM, New York (2012)
12. Huang, Y.-C., Tung, Y.-S., Chen, J.-C., Wang, S.-W., Wu, J.-L.: An adaptive edge detection based colorization algorithm and its applications. In: Proceedings of the 13th Annual ACM International Conference on Multimedia, MULTIMEDIA 2005, pp. 351–354. ACM, New York (2005)
13. Irony, R., Cohen-Or, D., Lischinski, D.: Colorization by example. In: Proceedings of the Sixteenth Eurographics Conference on Rendering Techniques, EGSR 2005, pp. 201–210. Eurographics Association, Aire-la-Ville (2005)
14. Levin, A., Lischinski, D., Weiss, Y.: Colorization using optimization. ACM Trans. Graph. 23(3), 689–694 (2004)
15. Tai, Y.-W., Jia, J., Tang, C.-K.: Local color transfer via probabilistic segmentation by expectation-maximization. In: 2005 IEEE Computer Society Conference on Computer Vision and Pattern Recognition (CVPR 2005), vol. 1, pp. 747–754, June 2005
16. Welsh, T., Ashikhmin, M., Mueller, K.: Transferring color to greyscale images. ACM Trans. Graph. 21(3), 277–280 (2002)

17. Yatziv, L., Sapiro, G.: Fast image and video colorization using chrominance blending. IEEE Trans. Image Process. **15**(5), 1120–1129 (2006)
18. Luan, Q., Wen, F., Cohen-Or, D., Liang, L., Xu, Y.-Q., Shum, H.-Y.: Natural image colorization. In: Proceedings of the 18th Eurographics Conference on Rendering Techniques, EGSR 2007, pp. 309–320. Eurographics Association, Aire-la-Ville (2007)
19. Morimoto, Y., Taguchi, Y., Naemura, T.: Automatic colorization of grayscale images using multiple images on the web. In: SIGGRAPH 2009: Posters, SIGGRAPH 2009, pp. 32:1–32:1. ACM, New York (2009)
20. Qu, Y., Wong, T.-T., Heng, P.-A.: Manga colorization. ACM Trans. Graph. (SIGGRAPH 2006 issue) **25**(3), 1214–1220 (2006)
21. Jiang, H., Sun, D., Jampani, V., Yang, M., Learned-Miller, E.G., Kautz, J.: Super slomo: high quality estimation of multiple intermediate frames for video interpolation. CoRR, abs/1712.00080 (2017)
22. Jiang, Y.-G., Wu, Z., Wang, J., Xue, X., Chang, S.-F.: Exploiting feature and class relationships in video categorization with regularized deep neural networks. IEEE Trans. Pattern Anal. Mach. Intell. **40**(2), 352–364 (2018)
23. Kingma, D.P., Ba, J.: Adam: a method for stochastic optimization. CoRR, abs/1412.6980 (2014)
24. Ratliff, N.D., Silver, D., Bagnell, J.A.: Learning to search: functional gradient techniques for imitation learning. Auton. Robots **27**(1), 25–53 (2009). https://doi.org/10.1007/s10514-009-9121-3
25. Ruderman, D.L., Cronin, T.W., Chiao, C.-C.: Statistics of cone responses to natural images: implications for visual coding. J. Opt. Soc. Am. A **15**, 2036–2045 (1998)
26. Sheng, B., Sun, H., Magnor, M., Li, P.: Video colorization using parallel optimization in feature space. IEEE Trans. Circuits Syst. Video Technol. **24**(3), 407–417 (2014)
27. Szegedy, C., Vanhoucke, V., Ioffe, S., Shlens, J., Wojna, Z.: Rethinking the inception architecture for computer vision. CoRR, abs/1512.00567 (2015)
28. Tola, E., Lepetit, V., Fua, P.: A fast local descriptor for dense matching. In: 2008 IEEE Conference on Computer Vision and Pattern Recognition, pp. 1–8, June 2008
29. Hochreiter, S., Schmidhuber, J.: Long short-term memory. Neural Comput. **9**(8), 1735–1780 (1997)

Benchmark for Generic Product Detection: A Low Data Baseline for Dense Object Detection

Srikrishna Varadarajan[(✉)], Sonaal Kant, and Muktabh Mayank Srivastava

ParallelDots, Inc., Gurugram, India
{srikrishna,sonaal,muktabh}@paralleldots.com

Abstract. Object detection in densely packed scenes is a new area where standard object detectors fail to train well [6]. Dense object detectors like RetinaNet [7] trained on large and dense datasets show great performance. We train a standard object detector on a small, normally packed dataset with data augmentation techniques. This dataset is 265 times smaller than the standard dataset, in terms of number of annotations. This low data baseline achieves satisfactory results (mAP = 0.56) at standard IoU of 0.5. We also create a varied benchmark for generic SKU product detection by providing full annotations for multiple public datasets. It can be accessed at this URL. We hope that this benchmark helps in building robust detectors that perform reliably across different settings in the wild.

Keywords: Dense object detection · Grocery products · Retail products · Benchmark · Generic SKU detection

1 Introduction

The real-world applications of computer vision span multiple industries like banking, agriculture, governance, healthcare, automotive, retail, and manufacturing. A few prominent ones include self-driving cars, automated retail stores like Amazon Go, and automated surveillance. The use of object detectors is absolutely a critical part of such real-world products. The area of research in object detectors has been quite vibrant, with a considerable number of datasets spanning various domains. However, the sub-topic of object detection in dense scenes is rarely explored. Dense object detection is quite relevant to multiple applications, for example, in surveillance and retail industries. Some of these applications are crowd counting, monitoring and auditing of retail shelves, insights into brand presence for sales, marketing teams, and so on.

Exemplar based object detection refers to the detection and classification of objects from scene images with the supervision of an exemplar image of the object. Most object detection datasets are quite large, with enough number of instances of every object category. Most of the object detection methods [10]

© Springer Nature Switzerland AG 2020
A. Campilho et al. (Eds.): ICIAR 2020, LNCS 12131, pp. 30–41, 2020.
https://doi.org/10.1007/978-3-030-50347-5_3

depend on balanced and large object detection datasets to perform well in every category. These guarantees cannot be made for real-world applications where the object categories vary widely both in variety and in availability. For example, in the retail domain, the gathering of data to train an end to end object detection model is highly time-consuming as well as costly. This is because gathering enough data which covers all the variants of objects and has equal representation of each object is going to be much harder. For example, making sure that our dataset contains a specific rare Mercedes logo design requires us to search across multiple showrooms or market places. We cannot collect a balanced dataset for object detection due to the availability of various logos. A similar case can be made when we need to monitor retail shelves, which has thousands of SKUs (Stock Keeping Units) having different availability and frequency.

Moreover, in a dynamic world, where new products, new marketing materials, new logos keep getting introduced, the importance of incorporating incremental learning in real-world applications becomes greatly necessary. Unfortunately, the methods of incremental learning for object detection lead to a vast and unacceptable drop in performance [11]. A lot of these applications also involve distinguishing between extremely fine-grained classes. E.g., retail shelf monitoring, logo monitoring, face recognition. Building an end-to-end detector that would do both the dense object detection and fine-grained recognition is a very challenging task whose real-world performance is quite bad. Hence, to tackle this problem, we introduce to decouple detection and classification. We propose to use a general object detector that predicts bounding boxes of objects that is of interest. The detected objects can then be classified by a suitable fine-grained classifier.

Contributions. This brings us to the current work of generic object detection in densely packed scenes. Previous works [6] have shown that training dense object detectors like RetinaNet [7] on large dense object detection datasets works well. In this work, we explore the effectiveness of standard object detectors, trained on very low data. Our training data is 265 times smaller than the other methods, in terms of number of annotations. We provide a low data baseline for dense object detection task. We train a standard detector, namely Faster-RCNN [10], on a small dataset of normal scenes. This achieves a satisfactory performance (mean Average Precision, mAP) at the standard IoU (Intersection over Union) of 0.5.

We also create a varied benchmark for generic SKU product detection by annotating every SKU in multiple datasets. The motivation behind this is to create detectors that are robust across different settings. It is quite common for deep learning based detectors to transfer poorly to other datasets. In the industry, there is a high need for robust detectors that perform reliably in the wild. This benchmark consists of 6 datasets (Table 1) used solely as test sets. Models trained on any dataset can be tested on this benchmark to measure the progress of robust generic SKU detection. The benchmark datasets, evaluation code, and the leaderboard are available at this URL[1]

---

[1] https://github.com/ParallelDots/generic-sku-detection-benchmark.

2   Related Work

Focal loss for dense object detection was introduced by [7]. A method to localize objects more precisely in dense scenes was proposed by [6]. This achieves significant increase in performance (mAP) at higher IoUs. Identifying real-world products (in situ) by training on exemplar template product images (in vitro) was initially proposed by [9]. They released a database of 120 SKUs for product classification. Six in vitro images were collected from the web for each product and used for training. The in situ images were provided from frames of videos captured in a grocery store. There have been a few retail product checkout datasets by [15] and [2]. Both of them are densely packed product datasets arranged in the fashion of a checkout counter, with many overlapping regions between objects as well.

3   Benchmark Datasets

[6] recently released a huge benchmark dataset for product detection in densely packed scenes. To increase diversity to the task of generic product detection, we release a benchmark of datasets. Details of the datasets are shown in Table 1. Please note that all of these datasets are used as a test set on which we benchmark our models. We welcome the community to participate in this benchmark by submitting their results.

Table 1. Details of the datasets in the benchmark. # represents the count. Object sizes (Mean and Standard Deviation) are relative to the image size. Average Image size is shown in Megapixels

Dataset	#Images	#Objects	#Obj/Img	Object Size (Mean)	(Std)	Avg Img Size
SKU110K-Test	2941	432,312	146	0.27%	0.21%	7.96
WebMarket	3153	118,388	37	1.20%	1.09%	4.40
TobaccoShelves	354	13,184	37	1.1%	0.65%	6.08
Holoselecta	295	10,036	34	0.99%	0.80%	15.62
GP	680	9184	13	3.66%	2.59%	7.99
CAPG-GP	234	4756	20	3.09%	3.04%	12.19

3.1   WebMarket

[16] released a database of 3153 supermarket images. They also provided information regarding what product is present in each image. We annotate every object in the entire dataset to provide ground truth for the evaluation of general object detection. The average number of objects per image in this dataset is 37, while the average object area is roughly 0.052 megapixels.

3.2   Grocery Products (GP)

A multi-label classification approach was proposed by [5] accompanied by 680 annotated shop images from their GP dataset. The annotation provided by them covered a group of same products in a bounding box rather than bounding boxes for individual boxes. A subset of 70 images was chosen by [13] and annotated with the desired object-level annotations. We provide individual bounding box annotation for every product for all 680 images in this dataset. The average number of objects per image in this dataset is 13, while the average object size is roughly 0.293 megapixels.

3.3   CAPG-GP

A fine-grained grocery product dataset was released by [4]. It consists of 234 test images taken from 2 stores. The authors annotated only the products belonging to certain categories. To create ground truth for generic object detection, we decided to annotate every product in the entire dataset. The average number of objects per image in this dataset is 20, while the average object area is roughly 0.377 megapixels.

3.4   Existing General Product Datasets

Holoselecta. Most recently, [3] released a dataset of 300 real-world images of Selecta vending machines containing 10,000 objects belonging to 90 categories of packaged products. The images in this dataset were quite varied in their sizes, as shown in Table 2.

Table 2. Details of Holoselecta dataset. # represents the count. Average size of the entire image is shown in megapixels

Type of Images	Avg Img Size	#Images
Type 1 (HoloLens)	1.11	30
Type 2	8.13	8
Type 3 (OnePlus-6T)	16.03	208
Type 4	24	49
Total	15.62	295

TobaccoShelves. A retail product dataset was released by [14] containing 345 images of tobacco shelves collected 40 stores with four cameras. The annotations of every product were also released by the authors. The average number of objects per image in this dataset is 37, while the average object area is roughly 1.1% of the entire image. The images in this dataset were also quite varied in size, ranging from 1.4 megapixels to 10.5 megapixels.

SKU110K. Recently, [6] released a huge dataset for precise object detection in densely packed scenes. This dataset contains 11,762 images that were split into train, validation, and test sets. The test set consists of 2941 images with the average number of objects per image being 146. The average object area is roughly 0.27%, making it the lowest among all the datasets in this benchmark.

3.5   Denseness of the Datasets

The denseness of the datasets depends on two factors. The average number of objects and the relative sizes of the objects. SKU110K [6] is by far one of the most dense datasets for object detection. An analysis of the denseness of other datasets in the current benchmark is shown in Table 3.

Table 3. Analysis on the denseness of the generic product datasets. # represents the count.

Dataset	#Images	#Images with SKU count greater than						
		100	80	60	40	20	10	5
SKU110K-Test	2941	2822	2902	2926	2934	2939	2941	2941
WebMarket	3153	57	121	349	1119	2526	3048	3139
TobaccoShelves	354	2	3	18	130	308	349	354
Holoselecta	295	0	0	0	113	249	293	293
GP	680	0	0	1	9	101	407	604
CAPG-GP	234	0	0	4	33	82	160	209

4   Low Data Baseline Approach

We collected close to 300 images encompassing various shapes in which retail products occur by querying images from the public domain (e.g., GoogleImages, OpenImages). The total number of annotations in our dataset is 4556. This is in contrast with SKU110K-Train, the data on which [6] was trained, where the total number of annotations is 1.2 million, as shown in Table 4. This makes our training dataset 265 times smaller than the SKU110K-Train.

Table 4. Statistics of trainset. # represents the count. Number of Annotations is denoted by #Anns

Dataset	#Images	#Obj/Img	#Anns
Our trainset	312	14.6	4556
SKU110K-train	8233	147.4	1,210,431

We apply standard object detection augmentations from [1]. Our product detector is based on the Faster-RCNN [10] model, trained on our dataset described above as a low data baseline for this benchmark. We call this model *LDB300* (Low Data Baseline). We measure the performance across different datasets, to test the robustness of the model in the wild and its effectiveness in generic product detection.

5   Implementation and Results

We use standard post-processing of non-max suppression (NMS) after our detections. We use multi-scale testing (2 scales) since lot of the datasets have high variance in object sizes. For the SKU110K dataset, only one scale is used. The inference settings of the compared *Full Approach* can be obtained from the code base released by the authors at URL. Multi-scale testing can be employed on the *Full Approach* as well, but this might be highly time consuming. For example, it is 10 times slower (FPS) than Faster-RCNN, as shown in [6].

Table 5. Performance of *LDB*300 across different general product datasets. Performance numbers of Faster-RCNN, RetinaNet and Full Approach, trained on entire SKU110K-train set, are obtained from [6]. * denotes results obtained using the trained model provided by the authors at URL as is.

Dataset	Method	AP	$AP^{.50}$	$AP^{.75}$	AR_{300}	$AR_{300}^{.50}$
SKU110K-Test	RetinaNet	0.455	–	0.389	0.530	–
	Full Approach	0.492	–	0.556	0.554	–
	Full Approach*	0.514	0.853	0.569	0.571	0.872
	Faster-RCNN	0.045	–	0.010	0.066	–
	LDB300	0.186	**0.560**	0.052	0.264	0.647
WebMarket	Full Approach*	0.383	0.773	0.332	0.491	0.855
	LDB300	**0.322**	0.621	0.248	0.455	0.684
TobaccoShelves	Full Approach*	0.534	0.948	0.560	0.615	0.970
	LDB300	0.108	0.442	0.009	0.159	0.491
Holoselecta	Full Approach*	0.454	0.835	0.447	0.581	0.955
	LDB300	0.239	0.707	0.072	0.347	0.816
GP	Full Approach*	0.259	0.520	0.241	0.403	0.716
	LDB300	**0.234**	**0.596**	0.125	0.334	0.713
CAPG-GP	Full Approach*	0.431	0.684	0.519	0.481	0.721
	LDB300	0.312	**0.745**	0.169	0.434	0.895

We use the same evaluation metric as the recent work [6]. This is the standard evaluation metric used by COCO [8]. Average precision (AP) and Average Recall (AR_{300}) are reported at IoU = .50:.05:.95 (averaged by varying IoU between 0.5 and 0.95 with 0.05 intervals). 300 here represents the maximum number of objects in an image. AP and AR at specific IoUs (0.50 and 0.75) are also reported.

We report the accuracies of *Full Approach* and *LDB300* on various datasets in the benchmark[2]. Our baseline results on the SKU110K dataset (Table 5) shows satisfactory performance of mAP = 0.560 at 0.5 IoU, even while trained on very low data (265 times smaller in terms of number of annotations). For some of the datasets like GP, CAPG-GP, our baseline results are quite close to the state-of-the-art. This could be because of the huge variation in object sizes as well the non-dense nature of the scenes in these datasets, which can be seen from Table 1 and Table 3. This method serves as a simple baseline while methods exploiting the shape of the objects and structure of densely packed scenes look promising.

6   Discussion

The varying results from Table 5 shows that evaluating on a benchmark of datasets is necessary to have a detector perform reliably in the wild. For example, the *Full Approach* [6] trained on the huge SKU110K dataset does not perform well on the GP [5] dataset as is.

A qualitative output of our method on different datasets are shown in Fig. 2, 1, 3, 5, 4. The performance on TobaccoShelves was a bit low (Table 5), which is seen qualitatively in Fig. 4. One can see that, our method performs well when homogeneous objects are present throughout the image. It also detects objects of different aspect ratios comfortably. Current limitations of this baseline model include precise detection of the objects, detecting objects with occlusion from shelves, as well as handling multi-scale objects ranging from 0.1% to 20% of the scene. Precise detection can be helped by EM-Merger module from [6]. Better scale-invariant object detectors [12] can be tried as future work.

---

[2] Note that *Full Approach* is trained on SKU110K-Train while *LDB300* is trained on our low shot dataset.

7 Qualitative Outputs

Fig. 1. Ouputs of our method spanning different type of objects on SKU110K [6] dataset. Blue boxes denote groundtruth objects, while Red boxes denotes predictions. (Color figure online)

Fig. 2. Sample predictions of our method on GP [5] dataset. Blue boxes denote groundtruth objects, while Red denotes predictions. (Color figure online)

Fig. 3. Ouputs of our method on WebMarket [16] dataset. Red boxes denotes predictions. (Color figure online)

Fig. 4. Ouputs of our method on TobaccoShelves [14] dataset. Blue boxes denote groundtruth objects, while Red boxes denotes predictions. (Color figure online)

Fig. 5. Ouputs of our method on Holoselecta [3] dataset. Blue boxes denote groundtruth objects, while Red boxes denotes predictions. (Color figure online)

References

1. Buslaev, A.V., Parinov, A., Khvedchenya, E., Iglovikov, V.I., Kalinin, A.A.: Albumentations: fast and flexible image augmentations. CoRR abs/1809.06839 (2018). http://arxiv.org/abs/1809.06839
2. Follmann, P., Böttger, T., Härtinger, P., König, R., Ulrich, M.: Mvtec D2S: densely segmented supermarket dataset. CoRR abs/1804.08292 (2018). http://arxiv.org/abs/1804.08292
3. Fuchs, K., Grundmann, T., Fleisch, E.: Towards identification of packaged products via computer vision: convolutional neural networks for object detection and image classification in retail environments. In: Proceedings of the 9th International Conference on the Internet of Things, IoT 2019, pp. 26:1–26:8. ACM, New York (2019). https://doi.org/10.1145/3365871.3365899
4. Geng, W., et al.: Fine-grained grocery product recognition by one-shot learning. In: Proceedings of the 26th ACM International Conference on Multimedia, MM 2018, pp. 1706–1714. ACM, New York (2018). https://doi.org/10.1145/3240508.3240522
5. George, M., Floerkemeier, C.: Recognizing products: a per-exemplar multi-label image classification approach. In: Fleet, D., Pajdla, T., Schiele, B., Tuytelaars, T. (eds.) ECCV 2014. LNCS, vol. 8690, pp. 440–455. Springer, Cham (2014). https://doi.org/10.1007/978-3-319-10605-2_29
6. Goldman, E., et al.: Precise detection in densely packed scenes. CoRR abs/1904.00853 (2019). http://arxiv.org/abs/1904.00853
7. Lin, T.Y., Goyal, P., Girshick, R., He, K., Dollar, P.: Focal loss for dense object detection. In: 2017 IEEE International Conference on Computer Vision (ICCV), October 2017. https://doi.org/10.1109/iccv.2017.324
8. Lin, T., et al.: Microsoft COCO: common objects in context. CoRR abs/1405.0312 (2014). http://arxiv.org/abs/1405.0312
9. Merler, M., Galleguillos, C., Belongie, S.: Recognizing groceries in situ using in vitro training data. In: 2007 IEEE Conference on Computer Vision and Pattern Recognition, pp. 1–8, June 2007. https://doi.org/10.1109/CVPR.2007.383486

10. Ren, S., He, K., Girshick, R.B., Sun, J.: Faster R-CNN: towards real-time object detection with region proposal networks. CoRR abs/1506.01497 (2015). http://arxiv.org/abs/1506.01497

11. Shmelkov, K., Schmid, C., Alahari, K.: Incremental learning of object detectors without catastrophic forgetting. CoRR abs/1708.06977 (2017). http://arxiv.org/abs/1708.06977

12. Singh, B., Davis, L.S.: An analysis of scale invariance in object detection - SNIP. CoRR abs/1711.08189 (2017). http://arxiv.org/abs/1711.08189

13. Tonioni, A., di Stefano, L.: Product recognition in store shelves as a sub-graph isomorphism problem. CoRR abs/1707.08378 (2017). http://arxiv.org/abs/1707.08378

14. Varol, G., Salih, R.: Toward retail product recognition on grocery shelves, p. 944309 (2015). https://doi.org/10.1117/12.2179127

15. Wei, X., Cui, Q., Yang, L., Wang, P., Liu, L.: RPC: a large-scale retail product checkout dataset. CoRR abs/1901.07249 (2019). http://arxiv.org/abs/1901.07249

16. Zhang, Y., Wang, L., Hartley, R., Li, H.: Where's the weet-bix? In: Yagi, Y., Kang, S.B., Kweon, I.S., Zha, H. (eds.) ACCV 2007. LNCS, vol. 4843, pp. 800–810. Springer, Heidelberg (2007). https://doi.org/10.1007/978-3-540-76386-4_76

Supervised and Unsupervised Detections for Multiple Object Tracking in Traffic Scenes: A Comparative Study

Hui-Lee Ooi[1]([✉]), Guillaume-Alexandre Bilodeau[1], and Nicolas Saunier[2]

[1] LITIV, Department of Computer and Software Engineering,
Polytechnique Montréal, Montréal, Canada
`hui-lee.ooi@polymtl.ca`
[2] Department of Civil, Geological and Mining Engineering,
Polytechnique Montréal, Montréal, Canada

Abstract. In this paper, we propose a multiple object tracker, called MF-Tracker, that integrates multiple classical features (spatial distances and colours) and modern features (detection labels and re-identification features) in its tracking framework. Since our tracker can work with detections coming either from unsupervised and supervised object detectors, we also investigated the impact of supervised and unsupervised detection inputs in our method and for tracking road users in general. We also compared our results with existing methods that were applied on the UA-Detrac and the UrbanTracker datasets. Results show that our proposed method is performing very well in both datasets with different inputs (MOTA ranging from 0.3491 to 0.5805 for unsupervised inputs on the UrbanTracker dataset and an average MOTA of 0.7638 for supervised inputs on the UA Detrac dataset) under different circumstances. A well-trained supervised object detector can give better results in challenging scenarios. However, in simpler scenarios, if good training data is not available, unsupervised method can perform well and can be a good alternative.

Keywords: Multiple object tracking · Urban traffic scene · Supervised detection · Unsupervised detection

1 Introduction

Multiple object tracking (MOT) in the context of traffic scenes essentially means following the target objects (road users) in the scene to obtain an accurate representation of their trajectories across frames, usually as feedback information to eventually improve traffic management systems or to better plan the layout of the roads. To follow an object, we must see it first; to track a road user in a scene, the importance of getting correct detection inputs for the tracking paradigm must not be overlooked. Compared to single object tracking, MOT has to keep track of the presence of more than one target object while dealing with

© Springer Nature Switzerland AG 2020
A. Campilho et al. (Eds.): ICIAR 2020, LNCS 12131, pp. 42–55, 2020.
https://doi.org/10.1007/978-3-030-50347-5_4

Fig. 1. Examples of selected frames from videos in the UA-Detrac dataset [16] used for evaluation in the experiments.

the possible occlusions and mismatches of objects as a result of interactions of the moving objects with the background and other objects, making it a challenging problem that is still actively researched. In the case of traffic scenes, the MOT method must also deal with various lighting and weather conditions (See Fig. 1). There are also multiple classes of objects.

Generally, there are two types of object detection methods to be used for tracking: supervised and unsupervised. The former is the more modern approach using labeled data to train models that can detect the target objects in a particular domain [9,14]. This approach usually delineates an object with a bounding box, and also attributes a class label to each detected object. The latter typically corresponds to the classical approach of foreground extraction and outputs objects that are not part of the background in the frame [1,13]. This method does not need supervised training as it segments the scene in two classes based on a model of the background. It is designed for cameras that are not moving and provides an object segmentation mask, but no labels.

In this paper, we address the MOT problem for traffic scenes by proposing a new tracker that integrates classical features (spatial distances and colours) and modern features (detection labels and re-identification features), as well as object prediction in its tracking framework. Our tracker can be applied to either supervised and unsupervised object detections. Therefore, while designing our method we raised the question: *which type of detection should be used?* To answer this question, we investigated formally the impact of the choice of the type of detections in the design of the tracker.

The contributions of this paper are: 1) a new MOT tracker that combines various features and that can capitalize on both unsupervised and supervised object detections and 2) a formal analysis of the performance of unsupervised and supervised object detectors in road tracking scenarios and their impact on MOT.

2   Related Works

The study of MOT on traffic scenes has undergone many changes and evolution over the years. Conventionally, before the advent of deep learning in computer vision, the extraction of target objects in the application of MOT were generic and unsupervised, as in [5,8,17]. In Yang et al. [17], background subtraction detections were combined with kernelized correlation filters (KCF) for solving the MOT problem in urban traffic scenes. KCF is used as an appearance model as well as for predicting the object position in the next frame. Similarly, Jodoin et al. [8] used background subtraction to extract potential unknown road users for their proposed finite state machine to handle the different target objects. Keypoints are used as an appearance model. Other works, like the one of Saunier et al. [12], instead used optical flow information to detect and track road users.

Recently, most works on MOT use detections from supervised learning methods that output bounding boxes around learned object classes. The use of a deep learning-based detector as the only source of input for multiple object tracking involving several different types of road users was presented in [11], but with disappointing results. Ooi et al. [10] then further improved the method on the same dataset (UrbanTracker [8]) by applying classical unsupervised object detection outputs coupled with modern supervised learning-based detector outputs, achieving some progress with the use of detector labels as part of the feature description as well.

Meanwhile, the reported results on the UA-Detrac dataset [16] on its official website are based on supervised object detectors. UA-Detrac does not consider bikes, motorcycles and pedestrians. At the time of conducting our experiments, the reported top trackers on the dataset are Evolving Boxes (EB)+Kalman+IOUT (extension of [4]), EB+IOUT [4] and RCNN+IOUT [4]. These three methods are rather similar, essentially working by the overlap of the intersection over union (IOU) of the bounding boxes that represent the objects in each frame, with the assumptions that the high frame rate of the videos does not leave "gaps" between the detections [4]. The Kalman filter used in the EB+Kalman+IOUT approach is meant to allow skipping frames via predictions to improve processing speed.

Hence, in this study, we are interested in evaluating and understanding the effects of unsupervised and supervised detections for MOT in varying traffic scenarios under different environmental conditions as provided by these two datasets, UA-Detrac and UrbanTracker. We therefore devised a novel tracker that can work with both kinds of inputs.

3   Method

We proposed a novel tracker (MF-Tracker) that combines classical features as well as deep learning features for the matching of objects across frames. We are also interested in investigating the effects of supervised and unsupervised detections on MOT performance. Our tracker was thus designed to work with both types of detections.

Our multiple object tracker consists of several components: (i) Object detection, (ii) Feature generation from objects and (iii) Data association to produce the final tracking outputs that describe the trajectory of each target object across frames, as shown in Fig. 2.

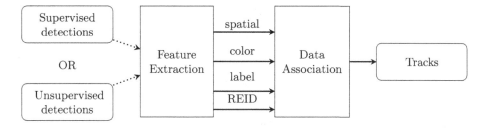

Fig. 2. Overview of our proposed tracker (MF-Tracker). Detections from supervised or unsupervised approaches are fed into the Feature Extraction module for further processing in Data Association to produce the final trajectory outputs.

3.1 Inputs for the Tracker

Since we intend to compare the performances of different input objects for tracking, we used a state-of-the-art background subtraction method (IMOT [2] with PAWCS (Pixel-based Adaptive Word Consensus Segmenter) [13]) as unsupervised input source and the deep learning-based detector (RetinaNet [9]) as supervised input source. Both approaches give bounding boxes of target objects for each frame.

The next step for MF-Tracker is to extract the information contained within the bounding boxes for the subsequent tracking module.

3.2 Classical Features and Modern Features

The proposed method integrates both classical features and modern features to generate overall similarity scores to compare the objects across frames.

The similarity costs from classical features are:

– the spatial cost C_d: based on the spatial distances of the four coordinates of the bounding boxes, it is defined as:

$$C_d = 1 - max(0, \frac{T_d - \overline{SD}}{T_d})$$ (1)

$$\overline{SD} = \frac{1}{4}(|x_{D,min} - x_{T,min}| + |y_{D,min} - y_{T,min}| +$$
$$|x_{D,max} - x_{T,max}| + |y_{D,max} - y_{T,max}|),$$ (2)

where $\overline{SD}$ is the mean bounding box spatial distance and x_{min}, y_{min}, x_{max} and y_{max} denote the minimum and maximum coordinates of an object bounding box. T represents an object that is currently tracked while D represents a detected object in a frame. $\overline{SD}$ denotes the mean spatial distance of the x coordinates and y coordinates of all the four corners of the bounding boxes of the compared objects. A fixed parameter T_d is used to normalize C_d and to bound the maximal distance between bounding boxes.

- the color cost C_c: it is the Bhattacharyya distances of the color histograms of the bounding boxes. It is defined as:

$$C_c = \sqrt{1 - \frac{1}{\sqrt{\overline{H_i^D} \overline{H_j^T} N^2}} \sum_N \sqrt{H_i^D H_j^T}},$$ (3)

where H_i^D denotes the color histogram of a detection i, H_j^T denotes the color histogram of a currently tracked object j and N is the total number of histogram bins (256 is used in this work). $\overline{H_m^D}$ and $\overline{H_m^T}$ are the histogram bin means of the detected object and currently tracked object, given by Eq. 4 and Eq. 5 respectively.

$$\overline{H_m^D} = \frac{1}{N} \sum H_m^D$$ (4)

$$\overline{H_m^T} = \frac{1}{N} \sum H_m^T$$ (5)

Meanwhile, the similarity costs from modern features are:

- the label cost C_l: the label information from the detector inputs are used as a similarity cost. It is defined as:

$$C_l = \begin{cases} 1 - \frac{W_i + W_j}{2} & \text{if } L_i = L_j \\ 1 & \text{if } L_i \neq L_j, \end{cases}$$ (6)

where L_i denotes the class label of object i and W_i its confidence value (between 0 and 1). Using the confidence value from the object class label, and not just the class label for the cost is a beneficial strategy because confidence values tend to be similar in consecutive frames for a given object.
- the re-identification (REID) cost C_r: the deep-learned REID features of OSNet [18] are also used for object description, where the REID cost is computed with the Euclidean distance as

$$C_r = 1 - \sqrt{\sum_n (r_n^i - r_n^j)^2}$$ (7)

where r_n^i and r_n^j denote respectively the n_{th} REID feature value of object i and j, and n is the number of REID features. We used OSNet pre-trained on Multi-Scene Multi-Time person ReID dataset (MSMT17) [15]. The features were not specifically tuned for our application.

All these features are applied and combined to give a final similarity score given by

$$C_{final} = \alpha C_d + \beta C_c + \gamma C_l + \lambda C_r,$$ (8)

that ranges from 0 to 1, and where $\alpha, \beta, \gamma, \lambda$ denotes the weights for the corresponding cost.

This procedure is performed in the extracted bounding boxes of detections from both supervised and unsupervised sources. In the experiment, for the case of unsupervised detections, due to lack of label information from the unsupervised method itself, detections from the supervised detector are matched with the ones from the unsupervised approach, thus assigning the label accordingly to the bounding boxes given by the unsupervised detector. Alternatively, an object classifier could be applied. Input detection boxes from the unsupervised approach are given null labels if there is no overlapping boxes from the supervised approach.

3.3 Data Association

Based on the similarity score computed from the features, the Hungarian algorithm is used for matching the detected objects (detection list) from the supervised or unsupervised approaches in each frame to the tracked objects (tracked list) accumulated from the previous frames.

Corresponding objects from the two lists (detection list and tracked list) are marked as matched detection and the information for the objects is updated accordingly. Objects from the detection list that are not successfully matched with any object in the tracked list are initialized as new objects and taken in as part of the tracked list for the subsequent frame. Unmatched objects from the tracked list could either be objects that are occluded or objects that already left the scenes, or invalid objects that are incorrectly detected. A Kalman filter is used to make prediction in the subsequent frames, accounting for occlusion cases, so that occluded objects in the tracked list proceed with possible trajectories when they were momentarily not detected at certain frames.

For each object trajectory, there is also an analysis on the position histories so as to remove invalid objects that are not relevant or to terminate the trajectory when the objects were confirmed to have left the scene.

4   Experiments

The UA-Detrac [16] and UrbanTracker [8] datasets were used for the evaluation in this study because they include four challenging real-world traffic videos with 4 to 20 targets in the same frame simultaneously under different environmental conditions with varying types of annotated road users. The videos contain 600 to 1000 frames respectively. Evaluation of performances for the two datasets is performed using the standardized CLEAR MOT metrics [3]. Because unsupervised detections are less precise in their localization and extent (see Fig. 3), an intersection over union of 0.3 is used for computing the evaluation metrics as in previous work [2].

Fig. 3. Examples of extracted bounding boxes from supervised and unsupervised detections of road users in evaluated sequence.

4.1 Experimental Setup for the UA-Detrac Dataset

Comparing supervised and unsupervised detections is not trivial because datasets are designed with one or the other in mind. UA-Detrac does not include annotations for pedestrians, bikes and motorcycles. Due to the nature of unsupervised methods in producing the input objects for the tracker, it is observed that the presence of these unannotated road users in the frames will severely affect the quality of inputs for tracking and perhaps good trajectories without corresponding annotations will be produced, but penalized in the MOTA. Hence, in order to allow for fair comparisons of performance for the two sources of inputs in the tracking phase, we have chosen 22 videos from the training set for this evaluation where there are no (or very few) pedestrians, bikes and motorcycles. The videos are recorded at 25 fps (frame per seconds) with resolution of 960x540 pixels. The chosen videos include different angles of observations with varying illumination and weather conditions. Comparison of existing methods on the dataset is done by running the trackers on these videos individually to obtain their MOTA and MOTP results.

For an unsupervised method, to get the detections, the background subtraction method typically observes the video for some time to learn the background. In UA-Detrac, objects have to be detected and tracked from the first frame of the video. Therefore, to simulate the normal condition in which an unsupervised method would be applied, for each selected video, k frames are selected randomly over the whole video for learning the background. That way, foreground objects can then be detected from frame 1 in the tracking evaluation. Hence practically, for the unsupervised approach to work on this dataset, it has to "see" certain portion of the frames of the video before doing the actual foreground detection. Hence to allow fair comparison with the supervised methods, we are conducting experiment on videos of the training set, where the detector has "seen" the data as well.

In practical applications where the evaluation is performed on new unseen data, it is expected that the tracking performance will be lower for both type of detectors because of some deterioration in quality of the detections obtained.

For the supervised detections as used in our method, RetinaNet with VGG-16 as backbone is trained on the training set of UA-Detrac. The detected objects with confidence lower than 0.4 are filtered out before tracking. As for unsupervised detections, only bounding boxes with areas that are greater than 2000 pixels are allowed as input to the tracker. These steps are to ensure that only input objects that are valid in terms of size and confidence will be used for our MOT evaluation. Indeed, presence of spurious noise and incorrect detections can have a detrimental effect on the overall tracking performances. The supervised and unsupervised detections used in our experiments with UA-Detrac can be downloaded at this link (https://github.com/HuiLee-Ooi/MF-Tracker).

Besides comparing results of our proposed tracker with the different detection sources, tracking performances of existing trackers, under similar experimental settings with supervised and unsupervised detections, are presented as well in Table 3.

At the time of writing, the current reported three best trackers in the dataset official website are based on [4] with detection results from [14] and [7]. However, since we are not able to run the tracker version with the Kalman filter on the individual videos presented in this study (the public code does not work), only results of EB+IOU and RCNN+IOU are reported (as IoU + EB and IoU + RCNN in the table).

4.2 Experimental Setup for the UrbanTracker Dataset

In this experiment, all four videos in the UrbanTracker dataset are used to evaluate and compare with existing methods.

The optimal filter for the size of detections varies depending on video due to the inherently different scenarios. For a fair comparison, we are using the same parameter settings as presented by [8]. Meanwhile, due to the limited amount of data in the dataset, supervised detection inputs are results of RetinaNet detection with VGG-16 backbone trained on the UA-Detrac training set. The confidence threshold for filtering out the input bounding boxes from supervised sources is set at 0.4 for all videos. For unsupervised detections, extra frames are available before the annotated video segments. They are thus used to learn the background model.

The MOT performances for our proposed MF-Tracker (with supervised and unsupervised detections) compared to existing methods are presented in Table 1.

5   Results

For the UA-Detrac dataset, generally, the trackers with supervised detections give better tracking performances than the ones with unsupervised detections, as shown in Table 3. MF-Tracker outperformed all the compared methods when coupled with supervised detections.

Table 1. Comparison of MOTA and MOTP performances of trackers on the UrbanTracker dataset. For tracker names, the part following "+" indicates the method used to obtain the detections. **Boldface** indicates the best result, <u>Underline</u> indicates the second best result and *Italicized green* indicates the third best result. * indicates that the reported results are taken from original published works without re-running the methods. RL indicates Rene-Levesque and Sher. indicates Sherbrooke

Video Seq.	Unsupervised detections								Supervised detections			
	MF-Tracker + IMOT-PAWCS		UrbanTracker + IMOT * [2]		MKCF + ViBe * [17]		MF-Tracker + RetinaNet		Ooi et al. [11] + RFCN [6]	
	MOTA	MOTP	MOTA	MOTP	MOTA	MOTP	MOTA	MOTP	MOTA	MOTP
Rouen	<u>0.5805</u>	*0.6035*	**0.670**	<u>0.620</u>	*0.501*	0.582	0.133	0.885	−0.188	**0.687**
Sher.	<u>0.609</u>	0.5771	**0.690**	*0.590*	0.317	0.553	*0.3771*	**0.915**	0.027	<u>0.7490</u>
St-Marc	<u>0.643</u>	*0.6849*	**0.653**	0.682	*0.463*	0.652	0.1124	**0.951**	−0.366	<u>0.723</u>
RL	<u>0.3491</u>	<u>0.712</u>	**0.613**	*0.705*	*0.334*	0.531	0.273	**0.901**	NA	NA

Supervised detections on the UA-Detrac dataset work very well, where MF-Tracker + RetinaNet achieved a mean MOTA of 0.7638 and a mean MOTP of 0.8884, whereas unsupervised detections are not as good with MF-Tracker + IMOT-PAWCS only achieving mean MOTA of 0.2673 and mean MOTP of 0.6527, despite the use of a state-of-the-art background subtraction method.

Despite the trend of supervised detectors overwhelmingly giving better performances than unsupervised detectors, it is interesting to note that for some videos (MVI_40241, MVI_40243 and MVI_40244), our tracker with unsupervised detections ranked in third place, being quite competitive with the second ranked method (IoU + RCNN) that is based on supervised detections. These three videos are observed to have fast vehicles moving, causing motion blur. It is also observed that the use of state-of-the-art background subtraction (PAWCS [13]) with MKCF (Multiple Kernelized Correlation Filters) improves the performance of the original MKCF that uses ViBe background subtraction. Similarly, the use of PAWCS [13] with IMOT with our tracker has improved the tracking performance compared to the original implementation of the IMOT approach based on ViBe [1]. IMOT post-process results from background subtraction by using optical flow and edges to solve object merging.

On the contrary, the results on the UrbanTracker dataset are showing a different trend. Table 1 shows that trackers with unsupervised detections give better performances in terms of multiple object tracking accuracy (MOTA), especially UrbanTracker + IMOT [2]. Our proposed tracker with unsupervised detections (IMOT boxes from PAWCS background subtraction) ranked second in the comparison. However, it must be noted that the results reported in both [2] and [17] are using parameters that are specifically tuned to each video in the dataset. In contrast, aside from the filter for input size in the tracker that varies according to video (which is a useful step given the disparity of target input size among the videos and because those filter sizes were used by the competing methods), the proposed MF-Tracker is applied with identical parameter settings for all the evaluated videos in the dataset. Still, MF-Tracker with unsupervised detections obtains competitive results with respect to [2,17] for Rouen, Sherbrooke and St-Marc, although tracking performance on Rene-Levesque is significantly worse.

Table 2. Comparison of tracking results on videos from UrbanTracker dataset based on the different individual features

Features	Correct Tracks	Misses	FP	Mismatches	MOTP	MOTA
Distance	19358	5491	5182	89	0.677	0.567
Color	19292	5557	5371	141	0.677	0.555
Label	18968	5881	5193	271	0.679	0.543
REID	19090	5759	6761	654	0.678	0.470

Effects of the four different feature cost on our proposed tracker were studied individually on the UrbanTraccker dataset with supervised inputs in Table 2, where number of correct tracks, misses, false positives (FP) and mismatches of the four videos are accumulated. It is observed that the compared features gives fairly similar MOTP (0.68) and MOTA ranges from 0.47 to 0.57. Spatial distance appears to be the best performing feature whereas REID is the worst performing feature. Therefore we used the following weights $\alpha = 0.7, \beta = 0.1, \gamma = 0.1$ and $\lambda = 0.1$ in the experiments.

6   Discussion

The quick impression from the presented results is that supervised methods give better detections for the UA-Detrac dataset and conversely, unsupervised detections work better on the UrbanTracker dataset.

For UA-Detrac, while the use of state-of-the-art background subtraction might help improving the tracking results (comparing original MKCF with ViBe and MKCF with PAWCS), it is obvious that the methods with supervised detections are the clear winners. While one could argue that good results are expected since the videos are part of the training set, similar conditions can be said on the unsupervised methods as well since each video are "seen" to build the background model before producing foreground outputs (detections) for tracking purposes. However, despite a similar amount of learning on the data itself, methods with unsupervised detections with fixed parameter settings still yield poor results overall.

Unsupervised object detection methods struggle with high density traffic were all objects become merged together. Supervised object detection methods handle these cases better because each road user is individually detected. Also, for unsupervised detection methods, in night conditions, car headlights generate foreground regions that are then tracked as ghost objects. They are ignored by supervised detection methods.

In any case, our proposed tracker with unsupervised detections (MF-Tracker + IMOT-PAWCS) is the best performing method among the methods with such detections, and it managed to rank third on three of the videos in terms of MOTA, effectively outperforming a method with supervised detections (IoU + EB). These videos are revealed to be containing high speed vehicles that appear slightly blurry in the frame, possibly causing the supervised detector to produce less accurate detections for the tracking framework. On the other hand, the camera that is statically positioned ensure that the backgrounds of the videos are properly learned without a lot of noise by the unsupervised detector, thereby producing detections of satisfactory quality to proceed with tracking. It must be noted that while the videos in the UA-Detrac dataset are taken from fixed camera setups, some inevitable environmental conditions such as windy weather can affect the quality of foreground given by unsupervised detectors as the camera is slightly moving and vibrating. In these cases, results show that newer methods (e.g. PAWCS) can better handle this issue than older methods (e.g. ViBe), where street markings and highways dividers are detected as objects.

As we delve deeper in interpreting the results, it is observed that the supervised detectors do not perform as well on the UrbanTracker dataset as on the UA-Detrac dataset because the datasets contain inherently very different scenarios. The UA-Detrac dataset contains a large number of videos in similar locations and angles with subtle differences, such as illumination at different time of day. In contrast, the four videos in the UrbanTracker dataset are captured at entirely different locations and the different heights of installation of the cameras cause the captured objects in the frames to be highly varied in sizes and scales. UrbanTracker also contains a larger variety of viewpoints. The work of [11] on UrbanTracker dataset has previously shown that a supervised detector performed poorly on the dataset, due to detector that produces too many false positive objects for tracking. Both MF-Tracker + RetinaNet and the tracker presented in [11] are not trained on UrbanTracker itself due to the lack of available training videos. It is plausible that better results could be achieved by supervised detectors with more relevant training data, which is unfortunately lacking for proper training.

The best performances on the UrbanTracker dataset are from UrbanTracker + IMOT [2], while our proposed tracker with unsupervised detections ranked second in terms of MOTA for all the videos. However, aside from the size filter for the unsupervised detections to be fed into the tracker, our proposed tracker retained all the same parameters and settings for all the videos. This is not the case for the tracker parameters in the works of [2] and [17] that have been tuned to each of the specific videos in the dataset to achieve competitive final results. It is important to note that this could be the main reason why UrbanTracker + IMOT generally fare better on the UrbanTracker dataset. In practical real applications, however, it is desirable to have generic settings that is not overly tuned (overfit) to individual video sequence.

Table 3. Comparison of MOTA and MOTP performances of trackers with supervised and unsupervised detections on selected videos of UA-Detrac. For tracker names, the part following "+" indicates the method used to obtain detections. **Boldface** indicates best result, Underline indicates second best result and *Italicized green* indicates third best result.

Video Seq.	Unsupervised detections								Supervised detections					
	MKCF + ViBe		IMOT + ViBe		MKCF + PAWCS		MF-Tracker + IMOT-PAWCS		IoU + EB		IoU + RCNN		MF-Tracker + RetinaNet	
	MOTA	MOTP	MOTA	MOTP	MOTA	MOTP	MOTA	MOTP	MOTA	MOTP	MOTA	MOTP	MOTA	MOTP
MVI_39801	−1.1280	0.5624	−1.1493	0.5301	0.1309	0.5399	0.1970	0.5859	*0.6085*	0.8146	0.6773	*0.7485*	**0.8351**	**0.8536**
MVI_39861	−2.3416	0.5928	−2.0680	0.5319	−0.7905	0.5392	−0.0244	0.6201	0.7529	0.8423	*0.5502*	*0.7312*	**0.7824**	**0.8546**
MVI_40191	−1.1280	0.5624	−0.6120	0.6227	0.1679	0.6001	0.3050	0.7227	0.7201	0.8979	*0.5156*	*0.8397*	**0.8549**	**0.9123**
MVI_40192	−1.6718	0.5357	−1.0181	0.5948	0.3896	0.6055	0.3615	0.6915	0.5273	0.8807	*0.4574*	*0.8145*	**0.7999**	**0.8918**
MVI_40201	−2.4787	0.5489	−0.7528	0.5861	0.4245	0.6182	0.3321	0.6687	0.4643	**0.8897**	0.6324	*0.8168*	**0.8009**	0.8873
MVI_40204	−0.9831	0.5456	−0.7504	0.5700	0.2506	0.6050	0.2368	0.6651	**0.7799**	0.8645	0.6676	*0.7647*	0.5312	**0.8715**
MVI_40211	−5.1159	0.6144	−3.0001	0.5892	0.1305	0.6642	0.3414	0.6514	**0.8491**	0.9011	0.6354	*0.7703*	0.7019	**0.9017**
MVI_40212	−3.3782	0.6059	−1.9731	0.5858	0.0832	0.6576	0.2650	0.6438	**0.8446**	0.8952	0.6485	*0.7731*	0.7452	0.8841
MVI_40213	−3.1261	0.5969	−1.7845	0.5928	0.2929	0.6594	0.3957	0.6430	**0.8458**	0.9023	0.5389	*0.7699*	0.7028	**0.8920**
MVI_40241	−0.5776	0.5802	−0.3539	0.6214	0.3978	0.6246	*0.4493*	0.6880	0.3936	0.8998	0.6279	*0.7821*	**0.7535**	**0.9116**
MVI_40243	−0.0120	0.5995	−0.0934	0.6424	0.3950	0.6177	*0.4828*	0.6862	0.2845	0.9009	0.5216	*0.7860*	**0.7695**	**0.9116**
MVI_40244	0.1491	0.5771	0.0872	0.6458	0.4985	0.6091	*0.5448*	0.6770	0.1784	0.9044	0.5818	*0.7843*	**0.7316**	**0.9139**
MVI_40752	−0.5572	0.5888	−0.3374	0.6301	−0.0946	0.5952	0.2330	0.6586	0.6464	**0.8799**	*0.5782*	*0.7521*	**0.7607**	0.8788
MVI_40871	−0.4175	0.4671	−0.5729	0.4176	−0.1294	0.5151	0.0418	0.5522	*0.1642*	0.8861	0.4538	*0.8061*	**0.8208**	**0.9208**
MVI_40962	−0.4033	0.5940	0.0078	0.6796	−0.2181	0.5943	0.3114	0.7298	*0.6969*	0.9140	0.8478	*0.8488*	**0.8696**	**0.9240**
MVI_40963	−0.3398	0.5442	−0.0243	0.6428	−0.1518	0.5237	0.2407	0.6730	**0.7308**	0.8637	0.7056	*0.7699*	*0.5945*	0.8441
MVI_40981	−0.6972	0.5346	−0.4488	0.5951	−2.0140	0.4758	0.0065	0.6000	*0.7529*	0.8915	0.8122	*0.7932*	**0.8964**	**0.9168**
MVI_41063	0.1081	0.6198	0.1116	0.6271	0.4788	0.6399	0.3598	0.6507	0.7666	0.8738	*0.7283*	*0.7868*	**0.7939**	**0.8870**
MVI_41073	−1.1475	0.6197	−0.6290	0.6440	−0.4349	0.6355	0.2526	0.6520	**0.8098**	0.8889	0.7954	*0.7699*	*0.7320*	0.8732
MVI_63552	−3.2291	0.5804	−2.2304	0.5329	−0.1617	0.6421	0.1696	0.6249	0.6236	0.8334	*0.5364*	*0.7487*	0.7518	**0.8549**
MVI_63553	−3.0276	0.5699	−1.5817	0.5530	−0.1176	0.6256	0.1720	0.6161	0.7878	0.8455	0.5474	*0.7433*	**0.8032**	**0.8499**
MVI_63554	−3.0283	0.5657	−1.9908	0.5631	0.0836	0.6122	0.2065	0.6278	0.7213	0.8739	0.5668	*0.7698*	**0.7707**	0.8660
Average	−1.5696	0.5730	−0.9620	0.5908	−0.0177	0.6000	0.2673	0.6527	0.6341	0.8793	*0.6194*	*0.7802*	**0.7638**	**0.8864**

7 Conclusion

We presented a novel multi-feature tracker (MF-Tracker) that comprises classical and modern features for the matching of objects across frames. In addition, we evaluated our tracker with either unsupervised or supervised object detection approaches to investigate their differences in MOT performance. Compared to the existing trackers evaluated on the datasets, our proposed tracker achieved the best performances on the UA-Detrac dataset and is highly competitive on the UrbanTracker dataset with fixed parameters for all videos during tracking. Supervised inputs, when sufficiently trained with available data, produce good inputs that lead to more accurate tracking of objects. Nevertheless, in simpler scenarios, if good training data is not available, unsupervised method can perform well and can be a good alternative that should not be neglected.

Acknowledgments. This research is funded by FRQ-NT (Grant: 2016-PR- 189250) and Polytechnique Montréal PhD Fellowship. The Titan X used for this research was donated by the NVIDIA Corporation. We acknowledge the contribution of Hughes Perreault for providing the RetinaNet detections.

References

1. Barnich, O., Van Droogenbroeck, M.: Vibe: a universal background subtraction algorithm for video sequences. IEEE Trans. Image Process. **20**(6), 1709–1724 (2010)
2. Beaupré, D.A., Bilodeau, G.A., Saunier, N.: Improving multiple object tracking with optical flow and edge preprocessing. arXiv preprint arXiv:1801.09646 (2018)
3. Bernardin, K., Stiefelhagen, R.: Evaluating multiple object tracking performance: the clear mot metrics. J. Image Video Process. **2008**, 1 (2008). https://doi.org/10.1155/2008/246309
4. Bochinski, E., Eiselein, V., Sikora, T.: High-speed tracking-by-detection without using image information. In: 2017 14th IEEE International Conference on Advanced Video and Signal Based Surveillance (AVSS), pp. 1–6. IEEE (2017)
5. Breitenstein, M.D., Reichlin, F., Leibe, B., Koller-Meier, E., Van Gool, L.: Online multiperson tracking-by-detection from a single, uncalibrated camera. IEEE Trans. Pattern Anal. Mach. Intell. **33**(9), 1820–1833 (2010)
6. Dai, J., Li, Y., He, K., Sun, J.: R-FCN: Object detection via region-based fully convolutional networks. In: Advances in Neural Information Processing Systems, pp. 379–387 (2016)
7. Girshick, R., Donahue, J., Darrell, T., Malik, J.: Rich feature hierarchies for accurate object detection and semantic segmentation. In: Proceedings of the IEEE Conference on Computer Vision and Pattern Recognition, pp. 580–587 (2014)
8. Jodoin, J.P., Bilodeau, G.A., Saunier, N.: Tracking all road users at multimodal urban traffic intersections. IEEE Trans. Intell. Transp. Syst. **17**(11), 3241–3251 (2016)
9. Lin, T.Y., Goyal, P., Girshick, R., He, K., Dollár, P.: Focal loss for dense object detection. In: Proceedings of the IEEE International Conference on Computer Vision, pp. 2980–2988 (2017)

10. Ooi, H.-L., Bilodeau, G.-A., Saunier, N.: Tracking in urban traffic scenes from background subtraction and object detection. In: Karray, F., Campilho, A., Yu, A. (eds.) ICIAR 2019. LNCS, vol. 11662, pp. 195–206. Springer, Cham (2019). https://doi.org/10.1007/978-3-030-27202-9_17

11. Ooi, H.-L., Bilodeau, G.-A., Saunier, N., Beaupré, D.-A.: Multiple object tracking in urban traffic scenes with a multiclass object detector. In: Bebis, G., et al. (eds.) ISVC 2018. LNCS, vol. 11241, pp. 727–736. Springer, Cham (2018). https://doi.org/10.1007/978-3-030-03801-4_63

12. Saunier, N., Sayed, T.: A feature-based tracking algorithm for vehicles in intersections. In: The 3rd Canadian Conference on Computer and Robot Vision (CRV 2006), pp. 59–59. IEEE (2006)

13. St-Charles, P.L., Bilodeau, G.A., Bergevin, R.: Universal background subtraction using word consensus models. IEEE Trans. Image Process. $25(10)$, 4768–4781 (2016)

14. Wang, L., Lu, Y., Wang, H., Zheng, Y., Ye, H., Xue, X.: Evolving boxes for fast vehicle detection. In: IEEE International Conference on Multimedia and Expo (ICME), pp. 1135–1140 (2017)

15. Wei, L., Zhang, S., Gao, W., Tian, Q.: Person transfer GAN to bridge domain gap for person re-identification. In: Proceedings of the IEEE Conference on Computer Vision and Pattern Recognition, pp. 79–88 (2018)

16. Wen, L., et al.: UA-DETRAC: a new benchmark and protocol for multi-object detection and tracking. arXiv preprint arXiv:1511.04136 (2015)

17. Yang, Y., Bilodeau, G.A.: Multiple object tracking with kernelized correlation filters in urban mixed traffic. In: 2017 14th Conference on Computer and Robot Vision (CRV), pp. 209–216. IEEE (2017)

18. Zhou, K., Yang, Y., Cavallaro, A., Xiang, T.: Omni-scale feature learning for person re-identification. arXiv preprint arXiv:1905.00953 (2019)

Variation of Perceived Colour Difference Under Different Surround Luminance

Thilan Costa[1]($\boxtimes$), Vincent Gaudet[1], Edward R. Vrscay[2], and Zhou Wang[1]

[1] Department of Electrical and Computer Engineering, Faculty of Engineering,
University of Waterloo, Waterloo, ON N2L 3G1, Canada
{tcosta,vcgaudet,zhou.wang}@uwaterloo.ca
[2] Department of Applied Mathematics, Faculty of Mathematics,
University of Waterloo, Waterloo, ON N2L 3G1, Canada
ervrscay@uwaterloo.ca

Abstract. With the wider availability of High Dynamic Range (HDR) Wide Colour Gamut (WCG) content, both consumers and content producers have become more concerned about the preservation of creative intent. While the accurate representation of colour plays a vital role in preserving creative intent, there are relatively fewer objective image and video quality assessment methods that are available which consider the colour quality. This paper will study the effect of surrounding luminance on perception of a colour stimulus, specifically, whether the perceptual uniformity is preserved in colour spaces and colour differencing methods as the surrounding luminance changes. The work presented in this paper provides important information and insight required for the future development of a successful colour quality assessment model.

Keywords: Perceptual uniformity · Delta E 2000 · ICtCp · CIECAM02 · HDR · WCG · Colour quality assessment · Surrounding luminance

1 Introduction

With the popularity of High Dynamic Range (HDR) Wide Colour Gamut (WCG) displays that boast the ability to reproduce content as graded in expensive grading studios, the ability to measure colour fidelity becomes an important topic of interest in the field of image and video quality assessment.

In order to measure fidelity, one requires the means to measure differences in colour in a way that correlates with the perceived difference by the human visual system (HVS). Ideally, a colour difference measure should provide a similar difference value for all colour pairs that are only different by the smallest noticeable perceptual difference for those particular colours (referred to as the *Just Noticeable Difference* (JND)) [10]. A colour space that satisfies this property for all colours represented within the space is called a perceptually uniform colour space [10]. A perceptually uniform colour space is highly desirable for colour

© Springer Nature Switzerland AG 2020
A. Campilho et al. (Eds.): ICIAR 2020, LNCS 12131, pp. 56–60, 2020.
https://doi.org/10.1007/978-3-030-50347-5_5

difference applications in image and video production and distribution since it supplies the foundation to formulate objective quality assessment methods and standards for evaluating degradation of colour.

Additionally, various factors affecting the viewing conditions such as the surround luminance, surrounding colours and ambient luminance, can also affect how a patch of colour would be perceived by the HVS. While the colour difference value may change for different background luminance values, ideally we would prefer the colour space to still be perceptually uniform i.e. for the JND of each colour observed under the same background luminance to remain similar.

Various colour differencing models and methods have been proposed over the years based on approximately perceptually uniform colour spaces. $\Delta E2000$ based on the L*a*b* is such a method that comes recommended by the International Commission on Illumination (CIE) for evaluating colour difference [5]. Then there are are other newer proposed methods based on the IC_tC_p [6] and CIECAM02 colour spaces [7]. CIECAM02 is claimed to also be more perceptually uniform than $\Delta E2000$ [8], while IC_tC_p claims to be more perceptually uniform than them both [9,11].

In this paper, we discuss work performed to evaluate the perceptual uniformity of commonly used colour spaces and colour difference methods under different background luminance levels. This is especially relevant since a particular colour is not usually observed by itself when viewing images and video. In images and video, the colour is surrounded by other colours that could have a lower or higher luminance in comparison to the observed colour. Thus, it becomes important to evaluate the effect of background luminance on the perceptual uniformity of the colour space. We first describe the experimental design, and present the results obtained from the experimental data. Since it is infeasible to consider different surrounding colours with different luminances, our experiment is limited to an achromatic stimulus as the surrounding luminance. The data and insight obtained from this experiment will be used to formulate an objective colour quality assessment method for HDR WCG image and video content.

2   Experiment Design

For this experiment, we sampled colour points from the colours contained within BT 2020 primaries [1,3]. 12 reference colour samples were randomly chosen per luminance level, for a total of 72 reference colours at 6 luminance levels of 0.05, 0.5, 5, 50, 150, and 300 nits. While HDR WCG content supports up to 10,000 nits, the current HDR WCG displays are limited to the 1000 nits range, and the higher luminances are usually used for highlights in an image/frame of video. Thus, a maximum luminance of 300 nits is a realistic choice since a large colour patch would be less likely to be graded to be displayed at higher luminance levels.

The sampling of the colours were performed in the xyY colour space. For each reference colour, 1500 test colour points were sampled at fixed distances from the reference colour (by manually verifying the intra-distance between the points to be far smaller than the perceptual difference, but also such that the furthest point to clearly be perceptually different from the reference colour) along a randomly chosen direction on the xy plane of the xyY colour space, holding the luminance level constant. The colour for the surrounding luminance was chosen to be achromatic, and luminance levels of 0, 0.01, 1, 10, and 100 were chosen for the background.

The test was carried out on a Canon DP-2420 Reference monitor in a dark room with a backlight of approximately 5 nits to reduce eye fatigue. The test procedure is described in the following steps.

– Each reference colour and the furthest sampled test point from the 1500 sampled test points corresponding to the reference colour would be shown on two squares as shown in Fig. 1. The region in which the surrounding luminance will be changed is shown in white in the same Figure. Note that the entire monitor screen was not used to show the same surrounding luminance for this experiment since the peak luminance capability/stability of a display decreases as the pixel arrays on the entire screen is activated. Keeping the activated surround region smaller enables the display luminance to be reliably maintained at the desired value.
– The Canon Reference monitor used in this experiment is not an OLED display that can support black levels at 0 nits. Therefore, the display was covered using non-reflective blackout materials, exposing only the two squares to simulate the 0 nits surround luminance. When the other surround luminance values were displayed, the region outside of the chosen surround luminance region was covered using the blackout materials to keep the surrounding luminance at 0 nits.
– The left or right square will be randomly chosen at the start of each test pair to contain the reference colour, while the other contains the test colour. The test subject would be able to adjust the colour in the test square by navigating through the 1500 samples test points using a slider. When the slider is at the leftmost position, the two squares would look the most different in appearance while the two squares would contain the identical colour at the rightmost position. Subjects are instructed to choose the leftmost position at which the two squares look the same.
– Once the leftmost position is found, the subject would press a button and the next test case would be displayed.
– The test consists of 72 test pairs per set, which takes about 15 minutes to complete. The surround luminance was fixed for the entire set at one of the chosen six luminance levels. Once the set is complete, the test subject would have a five minute break, and the next set is started which would contain the same 72 pairs of colours, but a different surround luminance. Each subject required approximately 2 hours to complete the test with the breaks.

3   Results

There were 30 test subjects in total, and outlier detection was performed to filter the data as defined in BT.500 [4].

Fig. 1. Test setup for testing the impact of surround luminance on the perception of colour difference.

We then first computed the JND for each test case for each test subject. Then we computed the final JND value for the test case as the average of the JND values for each subject. If the colour space or colour difference method is perceptually uniform, then the variation of the final JND value for each test case should be minimal. Therefore, we evaluate the perceptual uniformity of each colour space using the coefficient of variation (CV) given as follows [2],

$$CV = \frac{The\ standard\ deviation\ of\ the\ final\ JND\ values}{The\ mean\ of\ the\ final\ JND\ values}. \tag{1}$$

The CV was computed for each background luminance level, and is reported in Table 1.

Table 1. Coefficient of Variation (CV) measuring perceptual uniformity of the space (lower the CV, better the perceptual uniformity of the space).

Method	0 nits	0.01 nits	1 nits	10 nits	100 nits
ΔRGB	1.083	1.0917	1.0243	0.9969	0.8265
ΔICtCp	0.6057	0.6328	0.5840	0.5438	0.4884
ΔYCbCr	1.0215	1.0269	0.9649	09288	0.7827
ΔE2000	0.7956	0.8444	0.7739	0.7726	0.7555
CIECAM02-UCS	0.7191	0.7864	0.7249	0.6752	0.6768

It appears from the results that the perceptual uniformity of all the colour spaces improve with increasing surrounding luminance. We also see confirmation of previous results [8,9,11] that indicated better performance by IC_tC_p over existing colour spaces, and also the better performance of CIECAM02-UCS over $\Delta E2000$.

4 Conclusions

In this paper, we present an experiment performed to study the perceptual uniformity of prominent colour spaces as the perceived colour stimulus by the HVS is affected by a fixed surround luminance. The results show that the perceptual uniformity of the colour spaces that were tested increases as the surround luminance increases, which is an unintuitive result.

References

1. BT.2100: Image parameter values for high dynamic range television for use in production and international programme exchange. Standard, Radiocommunication Sector of International Telecommunication Union (2017)
2. Abdi, H.: Coefficient of variation. Encycl. Res. Des. **1**, 169–171 (2010)
3. BT.2020-2, I.R.R.: Parameter values for ultra-high definition television systems for production and international programme exchange, October 2015
4. BT.500-13, I.R.R.: Methodology for the subjective assessment of the quality of television pictures, January 2012
5. Goldstein, P.: Non-macadam color discrimination ellipses. In: Novel Optical Systems Design and Optimization XV, vol. 8487, p. 84870A. International Society for Optics and Photonics (2012)
6. Dolby Laboratories: ICtCp white paper Version 7.2
7. Moroney, N., Fairchild, M.D., Hunt, R.W.G., Li, C., Luo, M.R., Newman, T.: The CIECAM02 color appearance model. In: Color and Imaging Conference, vol. 2002, pp. 23–27. Society for Imaging Science and Technology (2002)
8. Moroney, N., Huan, Z.: Field trials of the CIECAM02 color appearance. CIE 25th Quadrennium (2003)
9. Pieri, E., Pytlarz, J.: Hitting the mark-a new color difference metric for HDR and WCG imagery. SMPTE Mot. Imaging J. **127**(3), 18–25 (2018)
10. Poynton, C.: Digital Video and HD: Algorithms and Interfaces. Elsevier, Amsterdam (2012)
11. Pytlarz, J., Pieri, E., Atkins, R.: Objectively evaluating high dynamic range and wide color gamut color accuracy. SMPTE Moti. Imaging J. **126**(2), 27–32 (2017)

4K or Not? - Automatic Image Resolution Assessment

Vyas Anirudh Akundy[(⊠)] and Zhou Wang

Department of Electrical and Computer Engineering,
University of Waterloo, 200 University Avenue W,
Waterloo, ON N2L 3G1, Canada
{vaakundy,zhou.wang}@uwaterloo.ca

Abstract. Recent years have witnessed a growing popularity of 4K or
ultra high definition (UHD) content. However, the acquisition, production, post-production, and distribution pipelines of such content often go
through stages where the actual video resolution goes below 4K/UHD
level and is then upscaled to 4K/UHD resolution at later stages. As
a result, the claimed 4K content in the real world often drops below
the intended 4K quality, while final consumers are not well informed
about such quality degradation. Here, we present our recent research
progress on automatic image resolution assessment methods that determine whether a given image has true 4K resolution or not. Specifically,
we developed a largest of its kind database of more than 10,000 true and
fake 4K/UHD images with ground-truth labels. We have also made some
initial attempts on constructing edge feature, Fourier transform feature,
and deep learning based methods for the classification task. We believe
that the built database and the attempted methods will help accelerate
the research progress on automatic image resolution assessment.

Keywords: Image quality assessment · 4K · Ultra high definition
(UHD) · Video resolution · Perceptual image quality

1 Introduction

There has been a significant trend in recent years in the media and entertainment
industry of producing and delivering 4K or ultra high definition (UHD) content
to consumers. Strictly speaking, 4K and UHD represent two different spatial
resolutions of 4096×2160 and 3840×2160, respectively, but the UHD resolution
is most commonly used in consumer electronics, and thus 4K and UHD are often
used interchangeably in practice for 3840×2160 resolution. 4K/UHD videos
offer the potential to present significantly increased sharpness and fine details
for better quality-of-experience (QoE) of end viewers. However, the acquisition,
production, post-production, and distribution pipelines often go through stages
where the actual video resolution goes below 4K/UHD level and is then upscaled
to 4K/UHD resolution at later stages. Consequently, the claimed 4K content

© Springer Nature Switzerland AG 2020
A. Campilho et al. (Eds.): ICIAR 2020, LNCS 12131, pp. 61–65, 2020.
https://doi.org/10.1007/978-3-030-50347-5_6

in the real world often drops below the intended 4K quality in terms of their sharpness and fine details, but consumers are often not well informed about such quality degradation. The objective of this research is to develop image resolution assessment methods without access to the pristine-quality reference image that can automatically determine whether a given image has true 4K resolution or not.

Traditional full-reference (FR) image quality assessment (IQA) algorithms such as PSNR and SSIM [1] do not apply because they require access to the reference image. No-reference (NR) methods are desirable but not much NR-IQA work has been dedicated to detecting images whose resolutions have been increased by upscaling from lower resolutions. In [2], a Discrete Fourier Transform (DFT) based technique is proposed with focuses on observing the difference in Fourier power spectra between natural and upscaled images. Natural scene statistics (NSS) based approaches [3,4] have been developed based on examining the statistical dependencies in natural against artificially generated images. Deep learning approaches have also been explored [5,6] by detecting manipulation in images during forgeries. Nevertheless, there are still significant gaps in achieving reliable image resolution assessment. In particular, large-scale high-quality databases that cover a wide variety of image content are missing, making it difficult to perform sufficient and convincing validation of objective models. Furthermore, the lack of big data also impedes the development of machine-learning, specifically deep learning, based approaches because of the risk of overfitting. Therefore, our first focus of this work is on database construction, which is followed by a few first attempts on objective NR resolution assessment algorithms developed upon the database.

2   Database Construction

We develop a large-scale database containing images of real and fake 4K/UHD resolutions together with ground-truth labels. To the best of our knowledge, it is the first and largest database of its kind. The database consists of two classes of images: "True 4K" and "Fake 4K" images. A visual example of a pair of true and fake 4K images are shown in Fig. 1. Both images are cropped and enlarged for visualization purpose. In this particular example, it is apparent that the true 4K image presents more crisp texture details and sharper edges than the fake 4K image. Depending on the native resolution, the up-scaling factor, the up-scaling method, and the image content, the fake 4K images may exhibit reduced perceptual sharpness at different levels.

In constructing the database, the "True 4K" images are acquired by taking videos recorded in 4K and extracting the frames from the videos. The "Fake 4K" images includes two sub-datasets created from two sources. The first dataset is constructed by extracting frames from 1080p resolution (1920×1080) videos, and up-scaling to 4K/UHD resolution. The second set of images is obtained from [9], which is a dataset consisting of 102 classes of flowers with a wide variety of resolutions. This complements the first dataset in that the variation in source

Fig. 1. Sample "true" and "fake" 4K images in the built database. Images are cropped and enlarged for visualization purpose.

image resolution reduces the bias towards the 1080p resolution which has a fixed up-scaling factor of 2 to 4K/UHD images. In both datasets, three up-scaling filters, bicubic, fast-bilinear and lanczos, have been used to up-scale the images. All operations are performed using the open-source FFMPEG tools.

The full database is divided into two parts with 8,437 and 2,393 images, respectively. The two parts have no overlap in terms of image content, and each contains both "True 4K" images and "Fake 4K" images upscaled from 1080p as well as other arbitrary resolutions (e.g., 667×500, 754×500, 674×500, and 500×533) that help improve the robustness of the models being trained and tested with the database. The division is intended for machine learning methods that require independence between a training and a testing sets. The division is flexible in practical use of the database, and does not necessarily follow the suggested division here.

3   "True" and "Fake" 4K Image Classification

Starting from the built database, we make a few first attempts training objective models that classify "True" and "Fake" 4K images. These models are geared towards exploiting potential feature extraction and classification methodologies and are at a premature stage. Diagrams of these methods are illustrated in Fig. 2.

The first method is based on edge features. Specifically, four edge detection filters, Laplacian, Sobel, Prewitt and Scharr, are applied to a test image, and various statistic features are extracted (including variance, mean, median, maximum, among others) from the filtered images. Such features have been successfully used previously in other classification tasks such as shark fish classification [7]. The second method works in the discrete Fourier transform (DFT) domain where a similar statistical feature extraction process is applied. In both cases, support vector machine (SVM) models, namely Model-1 and Model-2 in Fig. 2, are trained to predict the classification labels based on the extracted features. The third method is based on deep convolutional neural networks (CNN), where features learned from other classification tasks (specifically the Inception V3 network [8] features learned for ImageNet large scale visual recognition challenge) are transferred to the current task and the fully-connected layers after the CNN layers are trained for classification.

Input Image

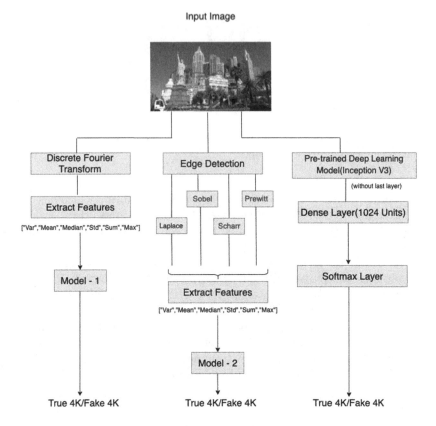

Fig. 2. Diagram of objective image resolution assessment models

Using the database division described earlier, we train the three models using the training set (within which 33% of images are used for validation), and test the models using the testing set, which is completely independent from the training set. The overall classification accuracy on the testing set is 79.70%, 79.07% and 72.8%, respectively, of the three models. In terms of speed, to test a 4K image, the time required to run the three models are 4.17 s (feature extraction 2.51 s and classification 1.66 s), 3.96 s (feature extraction 2.19 s and classification 1.77 s), and 1.66 s, respectively, on a machine with a 1.8 GHz Dual-Core Intel Core i5 Processor, a 8 GB 1600 MHz DDR3, and an Intel HD Graphics 6000 1536 MB. These results are promising as initial attempts, but also leave significant space for improvement, especially the CNN based approach, for which end-to-end training and other network architectures may be investigated. Methods that incorporate both knowledge-driven approaches (such as feature extractions in Model-1 and Model-2) and data-driven approaches (such as the CNN model) may also be combined to improve the classification performance.

4 Conclusion

We present our recent research progress on image resolution assessment, specifically targeting at automated classification of "true" and "fake" 4K image content. We build a first of its kind database that contains over 10,000 "true" and "fake" 4K images with ground truth labels. The database will be made publicly available and is expected to greatly help accelerate the research progress on the topic. We also make several initial attempts in developing image classification methods based on edge features, DFT features and deep CNN predictions. These methods demonstrate promising results but also leave significant space for improvement. Future work includes thorough comparisons with other NR-IQA methods especially those focusing on perceptual sharpness and blur assessment, and further development of advanced methods based on machine learning and perceptual modeling approaches.

References

1. Wang, Z., Bovik, A.C., Sheikh, H.R., Simoncelli, E.P.: Image quality assessment: from error visibility to structural similarity. IEEE Trans. Image Process. **13**(4), 600–612 (2004)
2. Mavridaki, E., Mezaris, V.: No-reference blur assessment in natural images using Fourier transform and spatial pyramids. In: 2014 IEEE International Conference on Image Processing (ICIP), pp. 566–570 (2014)
3. Moorthy, A.K., Bovik, A.C.: Blind image quality assessment: from natural scene statistics to perceptual quality. IEEE Trans. Image Process. **20**(12), 3350–3364 (2011)
4. Sheikh, H.R., Bovik, A.C., Cormack, L.: No-reference quality assessment using natural scene statistics: JPEG2000. IEEE Trans. Image Process. **14**(11), 1918–1927 (2005)
5. Bayar, B., Stamm, M.C.: On the robustness of constrained convolutional neural networks to JPEG post-compression for image resampling detection. In: 2017 IEEE International Conference on Acoustics, Speech and Signal Processing (ICASSP), pp. 2152–2156 (2017)
6. Bayar, B., Stamm, M.C.: A deep learning approach to universal image manipulation detection using a new convolutional layer. In: Proceedings of the 4th ACM Workshop on Information Hiding and Multimedia Security, pp. 5–10 (2016)
7. Shrivakshan, G.T., Chandrasekar, C.: A comparison of various edge detection techniques used in image processing. Int. J. Comput. Sci. Issues (IJCSI) **9**(5), 269–276 (2012)
8. Szegedy, C., Vanhoucke, V., Ioffe, S., Shlens, J., Wojna, Z.: Rethinking the inception architecture for computer vision. CoRR abs/1512.00567 (2015)
9. Nilsback, M.-E., Zisserman, A.: Automated flower classification over a large number of classes. In: Proceedings of the Indian Conference on Computer Vision, Graphics and Image Processing (2008)

Detecting Macroblocking in Images Caused by Transmission Error

Ganesh Rajasekar[✉] and Zhou Wang[✉]

Department of Electrical and Computer Engineering,
University of Waterloo, 200 University Ave W, Waterloo, ON N2L 3G1, Canada
{g3rajase,zhou.wang}@uwaterloo.ca

Abstract. Macroblocking is a type of widely observed video artifact where severe block-shaped artifacts appear in video frames. Macroblocking may be produced by heavy lossy compression but is visually most annoying when transmission error such as packet loss occurs during network video transmission. Since receivers do not have access to the pristine-quality original videos, macroblocking detection needs to be performed using no-reference (NR) approaches. This paper presents our recent research progress on detecting macroblocking caused by packet loss. We build the first of its kind macroblocking database that contains approximately 150,000 video frames with labels. Using the database, We make initial attempts of using transfer learning based deep learning techniques to tackle this challenging problem with and without using the Apache Spark big data processing framework. Our results show that it is beneficiary to use Spark. We believe that the current work will help the future development of macroblocking detection methods.

Keywords: Macroblocking · Packet loss · Transmission artifacts · No-reference image quality assessment · Deep learning · Apache Spark

1 Introduction

Macroblocking is a video artifact in which objects or areas appear to be made up of blocks rather than proper details in the original content. The blocks may appear throughout the image, or just in certain regions. Macroblocking may occur due to heavy video compression, especially in video frames of fast motion or abrupt scene changes, but the most annoying types of macroblocking in practical visual communication systems are often caused by transmission errors such as packet loss. The latter is the main focus of the current research.

Early work in detecting macroblocking caused by packet loss [1] used subjective test to identify circumstances of packet loss, and constructed a classifier that uses objective factors to predict macroblocking. A strong correlation is observed in the variability of mean opinion scores against packet loss levels [2]. The impact of packet loss on QoE in video streaming services is reviewed in [3]. In [4,5], various pixel level statistical features are extracted to detect macroblocking. However, packet loss based assessment is not applicable in the scenarios

© Springer Nature Switzerland AG 2020
A. Campilho et al. (Eds.): ICIAR 2020, LNCS 12131, pp. 66–70, 2020.
https://doi.org/10.1007/978-3-030-50347-5_7

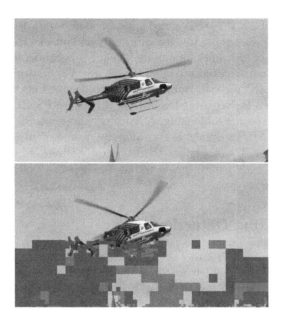

Fig. 1. Sample images without (top) and with (bottom) macroblocking

that the packet information is not available, for example, when the video frames are decoded. In addition, they are not capable of localizing the macroblocking artifacts in the exact video frames and spatial locations. In [6], a neural image assessment model based on transfer learning is proposed that is claimed to produce quality scores well correlated with distributions of subjective scores in a limited test. Nevertheless, the performance of existing methods has not been fully validated largely due to the lack of large-scale high-quality databases that cover a wide range of image content and packet loss levels. Furthermore, the potentials of transfer learning [7] has not been thoroughly investigated.

2   Macroblocking Database Construction

We create the largest of its kind database of video frames of macroblocking caused by packet loss. The database construction is divided into three steps: video clip/frame extraction, macroblocking simulation, and image labeling.

A set of original videos (around 25) of 10-second in length, 1080p resolution (1920 × 1080), and 24 or 30 frames per second (fps), are collected and all individual frames are extracted. Each video is encoded using 3 types of video codecs of MPEG2, H.264 and H.265, respectively. Macroblocking is simulated by randomly dropping packets from different frames of the video using OpenCV library at 7 drop rate percentages of 1, 5, 10, 20, 50 and 100%, respectively. The 100% drop rate was used to augment the macroblocked class to reduce class imbalance.

Therefore, a total of 25*3*7 = 525 video clips are generated with around 150,000 frames. Figure 1 shows sample images with and without macroblocking.

Given the number of frames, manually labeling all of them is infeasible. Thus we use a semi-automatic method to label the images. We first compute the PSNR values of all images and pre-determine two threshold values on the scale of PSNR. Any frame that has a PSNR value larger than the higher PSNR threshold is considered a frame free of macroblocking. Any frame that has a PSNR value smaller than the lower PSNR threshold is considered a frame of macroblocking. Any frame that has a PSNR value larger than the lower threshold and smaller than the higher threshold is visually inspected and assigned a label (macroblocking or not) by a human subject.

3   Macroblocking Detection

The built database allows us to explore machine learning approaches for macroblocking detection, for which we present the results of our initial attempts here. Motivated by the success of transfer learning based approaches designed for other image classification problems [8], we opt to use the framework and pipelines shown in Fig. 2.

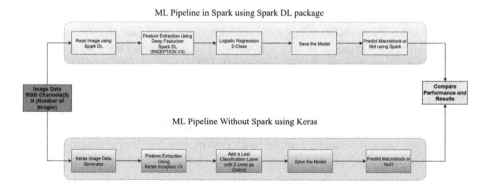

Fig. 2. Methodology comparison of Spark and non-Spark way to classify images

For data loading, in terms of pipeline 2, in the non-Spark way we use keras image data generator that reads images in batches from file directory and converts them into tensors on the go. In pipeline 1, the spark way we use the efficient readImages library from SparkDL package. This reads a directory of images into a spark dataframe. The dataframe encodes the images as an ImageSchema which contains all the pixel level data and other metadata of the image. This efficient read is a parallel read and on the go, stores all the image data in a spark dataframe. For feature extraction, we use a state-of-the-art pre-trained machine learning model (Inception V3) and remove the last classification layer. We feed the Inception V3 feature vector to our own classification model trained

Table 1. Classification accuracy and speed (second/test image) comparison.

Method	Train (70%)	Validation (15%)	Test (15%)	Speed
Transfer learning (Keras)	87.6%	82.1%	78.7%	2.10 s
Transfer learning (Spark)	88.3%	83.4%	80.1%	0.38 s

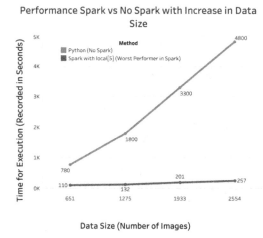

Fig. 3. Running time for Spark vs No-Spark methods as functions of data size

to classify the images. In the non-Spark way we directly use the Keras Inception V3 model and extract the features sequentially. In the spark pipeline we use SparkDL DeepImageFeaturizer library which performs the same task but extracts the Image features in parallel from the Image loader step. This way it extracts features much faster. In model training we use logistic regression on top of the Inception V3 features. We create the Spark ML pipeline using the "pyspark.ml.Pipeline" package and add DeepImageFeaturizer and LogisticRegression as the stages and run for 20 epochs with regularization parameter of 0.05. In the non-Spark pipeline we use a fully-connected last layer with output units as 2. For the pipeline we use a keras pipeline with the keras image data generator, Inceptionv3 feature extraction and the fully connected last layer as stages and we finally fit the model on the training data. The model once trained is saved and used to predict on the testing data. In spark pipeline we do this parallelly using the transform method from sparkdl and in the keras pipeline we have to do this sequentially.

We use accuracy (percentage of correct classification) to evaluate the prediction results on the test set, and compute the training time for the 20 epochs to compare the run time of both the models. Accuracy here refers to the ratio between correct classification and total number of samples. We use a 10×10 fold validation approach. We ensure each fold represents the original data distribution as close as possible. The results are tabulated in Table 1. The same model was tested on two different frameworks while varying the size of the data (number of images) and the running time was compared and plotted in Fig. 3. It can be observed that the non-Spark method does not scale well with the data size whereas using Spark achieves the same accuracy at roughly $\frac{1}{10^{th}}$ of the time.

4   Conclusion and Future Work

In this paper we present our recent research progress on automatic detection of macroblocking caused by transmission errors such as packet loss. We construct the largest database of its kind that is composed of around 150,000 images with or without macroblocking artifacts. Using the database, we investigated two transfer learning approaches with and without using the Apache Spark big data processing framework. The results clearly show that the model performs well on the database with close to 80% accuracy with minimal fine tuning, and it is beneficiary to use Spark. The major bottleneck in terms of training with large number images is that a sequential disk read training is much slower when compared to a distributed training on spark cluster. We believe that the built database and the attempted methods will help the future development of macroblocking detection methods. In the future, the built database may be used for other machine learning based approaches. Pixel based approaches may also be incorporated as an additional feature layer on top of the transfer learning approach to further improve the accuracy of macroblocking detection.

References

1. Reibman, A.R., Kanumuri, S., Vaishampayan, V., Cosman, P.C.: Visibility of individual packet losses in MPEG-2 video. In: 2004 International Conference on Image Processing, Singapore, vol. 1, pp. 171–174 (2004)
2. Nightingale, J., Wang, Q., Grecos, C., Goma, S.: Subjective evaluation of the effects of packet loss on HEVC encoded video streams. In: 2013 IEEE Third International Conference on Consumer Electronics Berlin (ICCE-Berlin), Berlin, pp. 358–359 (2013)
3. Greengrass, J., Evans, J., Begen, A.C.: Not all packets are equal, part 2: the impact of network packet loss on video quality. IEEE Internet Comput. **13**(2), 74–82 (2009)
4. Glavota, I., Vranješ, M., Herceg, M., Grbić, R.: Pixel-based statistical analysis of packet loss artifact features. In: 2016 Zooming Innovation in Consumer Electronics International Conference (ZINC), Novi Sad, pp. 16–19 (2016)
5. Vranjes, M., Herceg, M., Vranjes, D., Vajak, D.: Video transmission artifacts detection using no-reference approach. In: 2018 Zooming Innovation in Consumer Technologies Conference (ZINC), Novi Sad, pp. 72–77 (2018)
6. Talebi, H., Milanfar, P.: NIMA: neural image assessment. IEEE Trans. Image Process. **27**(8), 3998–4011 (2018)
7. Brownlee, J.: Transfer Learning in Keras with Computer Vision Models, September 2019
8. Sellami, Z.: Making Image Classification Simple With Spark Deep Learning. https://medium.com/linagora-engineering/making-image-classification-simple-with-spark-deep-learning-f654a8b876b8

Bag of Tricks for Retail Product Image Classification

Muktabh Mayank Srivastava[(✉)]

ParallelDots, Inc., Gurugram, India
muktabh@paralleldots.com
https://www.paralleldots.com/

Abstract. Retail Product Image Classification is an important Computer Vision and Machine Learning problem for building real world systems like self-checkout stores and automated retail execution evaluation. In this work, we present various tricks to increase accuracy of Deep Learning models on different types of retail product image classification datasets. These tricks enable us to increase the accuracy of fine tuned convnets for retail product image classification by a large margin. As the most prominent trick, we introduce a new neural network layer called Local-Concepts-Accumulation (LCA) layer which gives consistent gains across multiple datasets. Two other tricks we find to increase accuracy on retail product identification are using an instagram-pretrained Convnet and using Maximum Entropy as an auxiliary loss for classification.

Keywords: Convolutional Neural Networks · Retail image recognition · Grocery image recognition · Image classification

1 Introduction

Retail product image classification is the problem of deciphering a retail product from its image. This recognition of products from images is needed in a lot of Computer Vision applications in the real world like self-checkout shops, retail execution measurement and shopper behavior observation. Convnets (Convolutional Neural Networks) have been shown to give the best performance for many image classification datasets. Transfer Learning is a method to train a Deep Learning model on a small dataset by finetuning a model pretrained on a larger dataset. This practice is especially more prevalent with convnets which respond very well to this method. This work aims to figure out the best method to finetune deep convnets for different types of retail product classification datasets.

Classifying and identifying retail product images is a very important component of systems where one needs to automate or analyze retail practices. It can help in making a self-checkout store by providing an interface to recognize products for automatic billing, help make retail supply chain more efficient by automating product logging, can help automatically evaluate retail-execution

© Springer Nature Switzerland AG 2020
A. Campilho et al. (Eds.): ICIAR 2020, LNCS 12131, pp. 71–82, 2020.
https://doi.org/10.1007/978-3-030-50347-5_8

evaluation when combined with a retail product object detector or help analyze consumer behavior in retail stores in combination with a video analysis system.

Deep Learning algorithms have gathered interest recently due to their performance and applicability in the real world [12]. Convolutional Neural Networks (convnets), a subset of Deep Learning algorithms, have beaten the state of the art results for various Computer Vision tasks like image classification [24], object detection [9] and image matching [3]. In scenarios like identifying retail products, where often only a relatively small number of training images per class are available (sometimes just a few product packshots [23]), finetuning [25] of pretrained weights is generally the preferred mode to train the convnet in use. Few shot classification techniques [4] are often used in combination with finetuning when only a few images per class are present. Our aim in this work is to come up with a set of tricks which give high accuracy across different retail product classification datasets when finetuning convnets.

Our contributions in this work are: 1. We introduce Local-Concepts-Accumulation layer, which gets consistent accuracy gains across datasets, 2. We show that Maximum-Entropy loss [4] can be used as an auxiliary loss in combination with Local-Concepts-Accumulation to increase the classification accuracy even more, 3. We show that a model of the exact same size pretrained on Instagram and then imagenet [15] gives better accuracy than a model pretrained just on Imagenet.

2   Related Work

Deep Learning [12] systems have been making inroads into many cognitive automation tasks. In case of retail, there is a lot of scope to make existing workflows efficient using Deep Learning. Localizing and classifying retail objects on retail shelves has been studied in the past. Traditional Image Processing features SIFT [14] and Harris corners [10] have been used for detecting and identifying retail products. [2] proposes using SIFT features [14] with a hybrid approach combining SVM with HMM/CRF for context aware product detection and identification. [16] introduces Grozi-120 dataset and uses SIFT [14] for product identification as baseline. [7] introduces CAPG-GP dataset and uses a combination of Deep Learning [25] and SIFT [14]/BRISK [13] for product recognition. [6] compares visual bag of words and deep learning on grozi dataset for both detection on shelves and classification. [8] tries out dense pixel based matching, bag of words and genetic algorithms for exemplar based product matching. [11] uses Object Detection algorithms for one-shot product detection and identification. [21] uses BRISK features [13] and graphs to verify planograms. [20] uses GAN based training of convnet embeddings for fine-grained product image classification.

With the recent introduction of generic retail object detectors from retail shelves like [9] and [22], the problem of retail object detection from shelves and retail object identification can be separately solved. In this work, we show methods to improve finetuning [25] of convnets for image classification of retail objects.

Convnets have been shown to work very well for image classification problems [19]. It has also been shown that models pretrained on imagenet dataset can be finetuned on other smaller datasets [25] for classification to achieve better accuracy. ResNext architecture [24] is one of the best-performing deep learning architectures for image classification. ResNext architecture has residual connections with bottleneck dimensions between layers and also has multiple paths within each layer. Resnext architecture when trained on a larger instagram dataset and finetuned on imagenet, gives state of the art accuracy on imagenet [15]. It is shown, such a network trained on instagram [5], also called ResNext-WSL is very robust to image noise and perturbations [17].

While traditional image classification methods not using Deep Neural Networks are effective for some datasets, a lot of careful feature engineering is needed to make them work. Manually configured features might be very useful for differentiating some products, but might not work for others. Deep Learning based algorithms do not require feature engineering and an off-the-shelf pretrained convnet can be finetuned to get close to best accuracies without any fuss. We worked under the hypothesis that adding some custom layers to deep networks for recognizing retail products and adding a few tricks addressing unique characteristics of retail product images, we should be able to improve accuracy of convnets.

In the past, image matching techniques using descriptors like BRISK [13] and SIFT [14] have also been used to identify retail products. Superpoint [3] is a convnet based keypoint detection and keypoint matching algorithms that has recently shown better results than SIFT. Superpoint is trained on a synthetic dataset and then finetuned on image augmentations to become invariant to various distortions. We use Superpoint as a baseline in all benchmark tasks.

Fine-grained classification is a classification task where classes of images are visually similar to each other. Maximum Entropy Loss [4] has been used to make classification in such scenario more effective. We use Maximum Entropy loss as we find the 'lack of diversity of features' hypothesis true in all retail product image classification, just like it is true in fine-grained classification.

3 Methodology

We present three tricks which make convnets more effective at recognizing retail product images. We try these techniques on three different datasets which represent different scenarios which arise while working with retail images in real world and observe gain in accuracy across all three. First trick we present is that a convnet [15] pretrained on instagram [5] images and then finetuned later on imagenet works better for retail product classification than a convnet pretrained on imagenet [19] alone. The second trick is the new type of neural network layer called Local-Concepts-Accumulation we introduce, which can be used while finetuning convnets for retail product image classification. Local-Concepts-Accumulation layer is a simple layer which can be added while finetuning any off-the-shelf

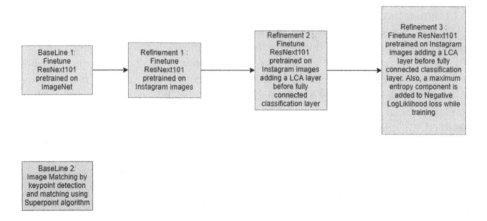

Fig. 1. The three tricks we propose to increase the accuracy of convnets on retail product classification datasets applied one on the top of other.

convnet. The third trick is to train a multitask learning based classifier using Maximum Entropy loss as an auxiliary loss. We show that these tricks incrementally give good gains for retail product image classification. The tricks are implemented one on the top of other as depicted in Fig. 1.

3.1   Finetuning an Instagram Pretrained Model

ResNext [24] architecture has shown state of the art classification accuracy on classification tasks in the past. We thus chose it as our baseline architecture to finetune for retail product image classification. It has been shown that a ResNext model, pretrained on instagram [5] images using hashtags as training labels, before finetuning it on imagenet [19], gives state of the art results on imagenet classification [15]. This convnet, also known as ResNext-WSL model, has been shown to have more robustness on common image corruptions and perturbations [17]. We show that using a pretrained ResNext-WSL with the same number of parameters gives better accuracy than a pretrained ResNext on imagenet (we refer this ResNext model pretrained just on imagenet as ResNext-INet henceforth to contrast it with ResNext-WSL). We use the "resnext-101_32X8" pretrained models (both ResNext-INet and ResNext-WSL) available from pytorch [18] repositories for finetuning. Both the networks require exactly the same resources for finetuning as they have the same number of parameters and we finetune them with exactly the same hyperparameters. We find that finetuning ResNext-WSL gets gains in accuracy for all datasets we work on. It seems that ResNext-WSL gets better gain in accuracy on datasets where test images have more noise and distortions.

3.2   Local-Concepts-Accumulation Layer

We introduce a new layer called Local-Concepts-Accumulation (LCA layer) which can be added to any convnet architecture as its penultimate layer while training or finetuning. We show that adding LCA layer while finetuning convnets for retail product image classification gives sizable gains in accuracy across all datasets we present our results on. The hypothesis to use this layer is that there are multiple large or small 'local concepts' in retail product images which when individually recognized and then aggregated can be used to recognize the product better (Fig. 2).

Fig. 2. Figure showing hypothesized local concepts on a retail product. The top left image is of the retail object itself. The top right image is of various possible local concepts marked on image. The bottom row has possible local concepts shown individually.

The hypothesis further is that when a convnet is trained to classify globally pooled features from the last layer, it focuses more on the global look and feel of the retail product rather than on the local features. When we use different local concepts as embeddings and aggregate their contribution with equal importance, the classifier focuses on both individual local concepts and global look and feel. It is proposed that focusing on local concepts would give a boost in classification accuracy.

Implementation-wise, in a LCA layer, we build embeddings for all possible local concepts in an image and aggregate them by averaging. These aggregated embeddings are then fed to the classifier layer. This LCA layer can be used during finetuning any pretrained convnet when placed between pretrained layers and classification layer. The implementation of LCA layer can be visualized in Fig. 3.

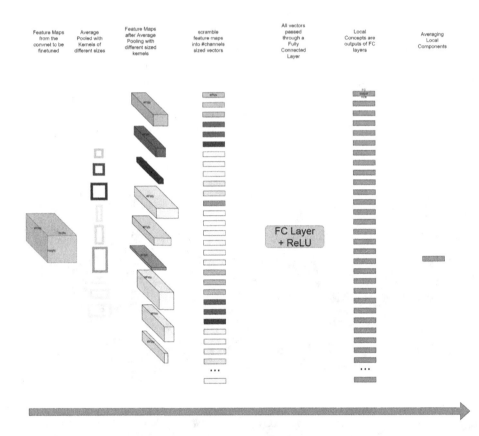

Fig. 3. This figure explains the implementation of Local Context Aggregation Layer (LCA Layer). The feature maps of pretrained convnet (size #FMs X Height X Width) are averaged pooled by different kernels of all possible sizes (larger than 1X1 and smaller than or equal to Height X Width) and the pooled feature maps are then flattened across width and height to get a list of vectors of #FMs size each. These vectors are then passed through a Fully Connected layer to give rise to different "Local Concepts" embeddings. The Local Concepts Embeddings are then aggregated by averaging into the final representation for the image.

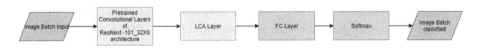

Fig. 4. This figure shows the final Neural Network being finetuned for the retail product image classification problem statement. The LCA layer is placed between the final classification layer and pretrained convolutional layers of ResNext.

For a resnext-101_32X8 architecture, LCAlayer is placed between the pre-trained convolutional layers of the ResNext architecture and the last FC classification layer. All possible rectangle and square kernels larger than 1X1 are used to average pool the feature map from pretrained network and get corresponding pooled feature maps. The number of feature maps remains the same before and after each individual average pool operation. Now all the pooled feature maps are flattened across height and width into a list of vectors, each of dimension of number of feature maps in ResNext pretrained output. Each of these vectors is passed through a common fully connected layer followed by Relu nonlinearity to get embedding for the local concept. The local concept embeddings are averaged to get the representation for the image. Figure 4 shows arrangement of layers when finetuning the ResNext architecture along with LSA layer. The Neural Network is trained with Stochastic Gradient Descent with Momentum.

3.3 Maximum Entropy Loss as an Auxiliary Loss

Maximum Entropy loss has been previously used for fine grained visual classification [4]. We show that using Maximum Entropy loss as an auxiliary loss in retail product image classification loss betters the accuracy of the convnet. This might be due to the fact that the diversity of features across classes in retail dataset is not as high as real world objects and diversity of features within classes is not that high too. Authors of [4] propose that Maximum Entropy loss can be useful in such circumstances. The structure of the loss function is

$$\theta^* = argmin_\theta \mathbb{E}_{x \varepsilon D}[\mathbb{D}_{KL}\bar{y}(x)||p(y|x;\theta)) - \gamma H[p(y|x;\theta)]]$$

where x represents images belonging to the dataset D, $\bar{y}(x)$ is the actual output and $p(y|x;\Theta)$ is the predicted class probabilities. Here the regular classification loss $\theta^* = argmin_\theta \mathbb{E}_{x \varepsilon D}[\mathbb{D}_{KL}\bar{y}(x)||p(y|x;\theta))]$ is combined with a entropy component H, γ being a weightage hyperparameter.

The description of Entropy (quantity H in equation of Maximum Entropy Loss) over a conditional distribution is

$$H[p(.|x;\theta))] = -\sum_{i=1}^{m} p(y_i|x;\theta)log(p(y_i|x;\theta))$$

where m is the number of classes in dataset D.

The expected value (and the multitask learning loss function) comes out to be weighted average between Negative Likelihood loss and Maximum Entropy loss. This is used as the final loss term for finetuning the neural networks. The weightage γ is a hyperparameter.

4   Datasets

In this section, we describe the various datasets used for experiments. We also explain how these datasets are analogues to real-world problem statements.

4.1   Baselines

We choose two baselines to show the effectiveness of our method. The first baseline is a simple finetuning [25] of a ResNext [24] model pretrained on imagenet only (referred to as ResNext-INet). These baselines give an idea about how much the tricks we implement one on the top of other, aid classification accuracy. The other baseline is keypoint detection and matching using convnet based Superpoint algorithm [3]. This is because keypoint matching based identification is common in many retail product image classification systems. Also, Superpoint is one of the leading methods for keypoint detection and feature matching. Superpoint algorithm can thus be treated as a good representative of what retail product identification systems using image matching could achieve.

4.2   Grozi-120 Dataset

Grozi-120 dataset [16] (URL) is a dataset having images of 120 retail products. Some products in the dataset are for example: Cheerios, Cheez-it, Snickers etc. We take in-vitro images of retail products as training data and in-situ images were taken as testing data. Typically, the number of in-vitro images is 4–6 per class. These in-vitro training images are packshots [23] taken from the internet and thus many augmentation techniques were applied on the images before finetuning the convnet for classification. Figure 5 shows a few pairs of in-vitro/in-situ images. In real world use cases, such type of classification problem often comes up where one gets only pack shots for training and the classifier trained has to work on images from shops/retail outlets.

Fig. 5. Sample train and test pairs of images from Grozi-120 dataset.

4.3   CAPG-GP Dataset

CAPG-GP [7] (URL) dataset has 102 retail products for fine grained one-shot classification. All products have just one training image. However, the training images are not pack shots but a small number of good quality images of actual products. In real world, an analogous classification problem often comes up where a few high quality images are available to train the classifier and the classifier trained is supposed to work on product images from shops/retail outlets. Image augmentations to incorporate different types of distortions into train set are introduced while the convnet is finetuned. Figure 6 shows a few pairs of train and test set images.

4.4   DM4VM Dataset

DM4VM dataset [1] (URL) is a dataset of 10 retail products with 60–70 images in training set per product and approximately 30 images per product in the test set. Both the training and test images appear to be real world images taken from shelves. Figure 7 shows pairs of train and test set images. A real world usecase analogous to this dataset is when data is collected from real world shelves and is annotated in a considerable number to train a classifier which again has to work in similar domain as training data.

5   Results

We now present the results of our experiments on various datasets to show the accuracy gains the proposed tricks achieve. As mentioned earlier, our baselines are classification by image matching (keypoint detection + keypoint matching) using Superpoint [3] and finetuning Resnext [24] pretrained on Imagenet (ResNext-INet) using Negative Log-Likelihood loss. We then show accuracy of suggested tricks applied one after the other. We show results when finetuning ResNext-WSL [15] using Negative Log-Likelihood loss on the retail product classification datasets. When ResNext-WSL is trained with LCA layer using Negative Log-Likelihood loss, the model thus obtained is referred to as ResNext-WSL-LCAlayer. When Resnext-WSL with LCA layer is finetuned with a mutlitask learning loss combining Negative Log-Likelihood loss and Maximum-Entropy loss, the model is called ResNext-WSL-LCAlayer-ME. The performance numbers shown in Table 1 are test set classification accuracy in Percentage.

When we analyze the results, we can come to a set of conclusions. ResNext-WSL gets better accuracy than ResNext-INet for all datasets, but its gets a relatively higher accuracy boost in Grozi-120, where the test images have a lot of distortions and noise. We can attribute this to the robustness pretraining on instagram gives to the model. Adding an LCAlayer gives a sizable accuracy boost in all the datasets showing it is a good methodology for any type of retail product image classification problem. Max-Entropy loss gives an accuracy boost across all datasets too, reinforcing that the hypothesis of the inventors that it is a good add-on loss wherever low-diversity of features is seen in the training data.

Fig. 6. Sample train and test pairs of images from CAPG-GP dataset.

Fig. 7. Sample train and test pairs of images from DM4VM dataset.

Table 1. Accuracy of various baselines and proposed methods

Method/dataset	Grozi-120	CAPG-GP	DM4VM
Image matching with superpoint	44.8%	84.7%	96.16%
ResNext-INet	58.66%	83.9%	99.3%
ResNext-WSL	60.4%	84.1%	100%
ResNext-WSL-LCAlayer	70.8%	90.4%	100%
ResNext-WSL-LCAlayer-ME	72.3%	92.2%	100%

6   Conclusions

We propose multiple tricks that better the accuracy of retail product image classification in multiple datasets. The technique of using a instagram and later imagenet pretrained convnet instead of imagenet pretrained convnet only is very simple to apply and gives performance boost without adding any parameters. A new layer for neural networks is proposed called LCA layer which, when added during finetuning, gives consistent accuracy gain across all datasets. We also show that using maximum-entropy loss as an auxiliary loss makes the classifier work better. Future scope of the work is adapting the techniques to hierarchical retail product datasets where one has to classify products at different levels of hierarchy. Local Concepts can also be studied to see if they are useful on other few shot fine grained classification problems.

References

1. Akgul, C.B.: Color histogram descriptors, data mining for visual media 2015, Assignment 04 (2015). http://www.cba-research.com/pdfs/DM4VM_A04_ColorDescriptors.pdf
2. Baz, I., Yoruk, E., Cetin, M.: Context-aware hybrid classification system for fine-grained retail product recognition. In: 2016 IEEE 12th Image, Video, and Multi-dimensional Signal Processing Workshop (IVMSP), pp. 1–5. IEEE (2016)
3. DeTone, D., Malisiewicz, T., Rabinovich, A.: SuperPoint: self-supervised interest point detection and description. In: Proceedings of the IEEE Conference on Computer Vision and Pattern Recognition Workshops, pp. 224–236 (2018)
4. Dubey, A., Gupta, O., Raskar, R., Naik, N.: Maximum-entropy fine grained classification. In: Advances in Neural Information Processing Systems, pp. 637–647 (2018)
5. Facebook Inc: Instagram (2020). https://www.instagram.com/
6. Franco, A., Maltoni, D., Papi, S.: Grocery product detection and recognition. Expert Syst. Appl. **81**, 163–176 (2017)
7. Geng, W., et al.: Fine-grained grocery product recognition by one-shot learning. In: 2018 ACM Multimedia Conference on Multimedia Conference, pp. 1706–1714. ACM (2018)
8. George, M., Floerkemeier, C.: Recognizing products: a per-exemplar multi-label image classification approach. In: Fleet, D., Pajdla, T., Schiele, B., Tuytelaars, T. (eds.) ECCV 2014. LNCS, vol. 8690, pp. 440–455. Springer, Cham (2014). https://doi.org/10.1007/978-3-319-10605-2_29
9. Goldman, E., Herzig, R., Eisenschtat, A., Goldberger, J., Hassner, T.: Precise detection in densely packed scenes. In: Proceedings of the IEEE Conference on Computer Vision and Pattern Recognition, pp. 5227–5236 (2019)
10. Harris, C.G., Stephens, M., et al.: A combined corner and edge detector. In: Alvey Vision Conference, vol. 15. Citeseer (1988). 10-5244
11. Karlinsky, L., Shtok, J., Tzur, Y., Tzadok, A.: Fine-grained recognition of thousands of object categories with single-example training. In: Proceedings of the IEEE Conference on Computer Vision and Pattern Recognition, pp. 4113–4122 (2017)
12. LeCun, Y., Bengio, Y., Hinton, G.: Deep learning. Nature **521**(7553), 436 (2015)

13. Leutenegger, S., Chli, M., Siegwart, R.: BRISK: binary robust invariant scalable keypoints. In: 2011 IEEE International Conference on Computer Vision (ICCV), pp. 2548–2555. IEEE (2011)
14. Lowe, D.G.: Distinctive image features from scale-invariant keypoints. Int. J. Comput. Vis. **60**(2), 91–110 (2004). https://doi.org/10.1023/B:VISI.0000029664.99615.94
15. Mahajan, D., et al.: Exploring the limits of weakly supervised pretraining. In: Ferrari, V., Hebert, M., Sminchisescu, C., Weiss, Y. (eds.) ECCV 2018. LNCS, vol. 11206, pp. 185–201. Springer, Cham (2018). https://doi.org/10.1007/978-3-030-01216-8_12
16. Merler, M., Galleguillos, C., Belongie, S.: Recognizing groceries in situ using in vitro training data. In: 2007 IEEE Conference on Computer Vision and Pattern Recognition, pp. 1–8. IEEE (2007)
17. Orhan, A.E.: Robustness properties of Facebook's ResNeXt WSL models. arXiv preprint arXiv:1907.07640 (2019)
18. Paszke, A., et al.: PyTorch: an imperative style, high-performance deep learning library. In: Advances in Neural Information Processing Systems, pp. 8024–8035 (2019)
19. Russakovsky, O., et al.: ImageNet large scale visual recognition challenge. Int. J. Comput. Vis. **115**(3), 211–252 (2015). https://doi.org/10.1007/s11263-015-0816-y
20. Tonioni, A., Di Stefano, L.: Domain invariant hierarchical embedding for grocery products recognition. Comput. Vis. Image Underst. **182**, 81–92 (2019)
21. Tonioni, A., Di Stefano, L.: Product recognition in store shelves as a sub-graph isomorphism problem. In: Battiato, S., Gallo, G., Schettini, R., Stanco, F. (eds.) ICIAP 2017. LNCS, vol. 10484, pp. 682–693. Springer, Cham (2017). https://doi.org/10.1007/978-3-319-68560-1_61
22. Varadarajan, S., Kant, S., Srivastava, M.M.: Benchmark for generic product detection: a low data baseline for dense object detection (2019)
23. Wikipedia Contributors: Packshot – Wikipedia, the free encyclopedia (2019). https://en.wikipedia.org/w/index.php?title=Packshot&oldid=904468054. Accessed 2 Apr 2020
24. Xie, S., Girshick, R., Dollár, P., Tu, Z., He, K.: Aggregated residual transformations for deep neural networks. In: Proceedings of the IEEE Conference on Computer Vision and Pattern Recognition, pp. 1492–1500 (2017)
25. Yosinski, J., Clune, J., Bengio, Y., Lipson, H.: How transferable are features in deep neural networks? In: Advances in Neural Information Processing Systems, pp. 3320–3328 (2014)

Detection and Recognition of Food in Photo Galleries for Analysis of User Preferences

Evgeniy Miasnikov[1(✉)] and Andrey Savchenko[1,2]

[1] St. Petersburg Department of Steklov Institute of Mathematics,
St. Petersburg, Russia
[2] Laboratory of Algorithms and Technologies for Network Analysis,
National Research University Higher School of Economics,
Nizhny Novgorod, Russia
deeprehension@gmail.com

Abstract. Food analysis is one of the most important parts of user preference prediction engines for recommendation systems in the travel domain. In this paper, we describe and study the neural network method that allows you to recognize food in a gallery of photos taken with mobile devices. The described method consists of three main stages, including the classification of scenes, food detection, and subsequent classification. An essential feature of the developed method is the use of lightweight neural network models, which allows its usage on mobile devices. The development of the method was carried out using both known open data and a proprietary data set.

Keywords: Scene recognition · Food detection · Food recognition · Convolutional neural networks (CNN)

1 Introduction

The continuous increase in the number of smartphones and the improvement of their characteristics has led to the accumulation of a huge amount of photos, both posted on social networks and stored in user galleries. Such photos can be used not only for entertainment purposes but also to extract information useful to the user.

Food can play an essential role in such photographs. Custom photographs containing food images can be used to solve a number of practical problems, such as calorie management, dietary assessment, search for recipes, building recommendation systems, etc. In all such cases, it is necessary to solve many computer vision tasks, such as scene analysis, food detection, recognition, volume estimation, extraction of ingredients, and so on.

In this paper, the solution to the problem of food analysis is considered mainly from the viewpoint of constructing recommendation systems. Depending on the user's profile, it is possible to recommend suitable products, shops,

© Springer Nature Switzerland AG 2020
A. Campilho et al. (Eds.): ICIAR 2020, LNCS 12131, pp. 83–94, 2020.
https://doi.org/10.1007/978-3-030-50347-5_9

and content [1]. In particular, food preferences can be used in restaurant recommendation engines. The cold-start problem could be alleviated if the companies can get access to reliable preference information without the need for rating elicitation of monitoring users closely over time.

Using a smartphone imposes quite strict restrictions on the food analysis methods used. In particular, heavy convolutional neural networks (CNN) and ensembles of neural networks are unsuitable, despite the fact that they give the best quality characteristics when solving such problems. For this reason, lightweight mobile neural networks are used in this paper.

The paper has the following structure. Section 2 gives a brief review of relevant literature. Section 3 introduces the proposed food analysis pipeline and practical examples of its usage. Section 4 describes experimental results, provides details on the tuning of all the necessary components. The paper ends up with a conclusion.

2   Literature Survey

The topic of food image analysis seems to be well-studied in literature. Hence, we present in this section only a relatively small number of relevant sources that correspond to the tasks being solved.

In the food detection problem, both traditional computer vision and neural network approaches are applied. In [2], several types of detectors are used, including the deformable part model (DPM), a circle detector, the JSEG region segmentation. The Difference of Gaussian (DoG), grid-based, and circle-based descriptors based on color and gradient information are applied in [3]. In [4], the following descriptors are studied: Bag of SIFT, PRICoLBP, and Bag of Textons. In [5], SVM (Support Vector Machine) and SoftMax–based classifiers are trained on top of the AlexNet, VGG, and Network in Network models. The GoogLeNet CNN model to detect food images is utilized in [6]. In [7], the authors use ResNet50-based features to detect food items. In the paper [8], authors propose their own CNN and calibrate kernels and the number of layers. In [9], the authors utilize GoogLeNet. In [10], the authors build a state-of-the-art model with GoogLeNet, principal component analysis, and support vector machine.

The analysis of food recognition techniques shows that the list of the most commonly used classic techniques includes both color and texture features [11,12], as well as SIFT [13,14] and HoG [11,12] descriptors. The list of neural network models used to classify food images include GoogLeNet [15,16], AlexNet [8,17], ResNet [18–20], VGG [21], Inception [20,22] and some others. It is worth noting that the state-of-the-art results are achieved with deep neural networks, their ensembles, and combinations with classical techniques.

3   Materials and Methods

3.1   Datasets

Despite conventional Flickr and MS COCO, the following datasets are used in this work to train and evaluate neural networks. The UNICT-FD889 dataset [23] is composed of 3583 large-scale images related to 889 distinct dishes of food of different nationalities and aimed to study the representation of food images.

The FoodX-251 dataset [24] consists of 158k images of 251 categories. It is designed for the food classification task. The images in the dataset are split into a training set of 118k images and human-verified labels for both the validation set of 12k images and the test set of 28k images. Unfortunately, the groundtruth data contains only fine-grained (prepared) food categories without super-categories (classes).

The Food-101 dataset [24] consists of 101,000 images of 101 categories, and it is aimed at the food classification task. The photos are downloaded from a photo-sharing website (hrefhttp://foodspotting.comfoodspotting.com). The test data was manually cleaned by the authors, whereas the training data consists of cross-category noise, i.e., images with multiple food items labeled with a single class.

Unfortunately, we could not indicate any special dataset devoted to the localization of food in a user photo. For this reason, we prepared the dataset for food detection ourselves.

To do this, we prepared food-related image queries, containing various keywords related to mealtimes (breakfast, dinner, supper), national cuisines (Italian, Chinese, Indian, Mexican, Russian, etc.), places (restaurants, cafes), actors (family, friends, pairs), etc. After downloading images and removing duplicates and non-relevant images, we selected slightly more than 1 thousand images. Then we tagged food items located in plates, pans, cutting boards, or just placed on tables, etc. The distribution of the number of food items tagged in images is shown in the Fig. 1 (top). Figure 1 (bottom) shows the distribution of tagged item sizes. Totally, more than 5 thousand items were tagged. This is actually ongoing work, and we show here our first results.

3.2   Proposed Approach

In this section, we describe our approach to analyzing food in user images. We considered two main types of food images. The first type contains large-scale images of food. In this case, the food can be placed in a plate, pan, cutting board, table, or another context, but this context is not important for us. The second type of images corresponds to scenes containing one or more containers with food. As it is relatively easy to detect containers of standard forms such as plates, cutting boards, or pans, we mainly rely on the features of the containers to detect food.

Hence, the main idea behind our approach consists in splitting the analysis task into three tasks, namely, "food/non-food" classification, food detection (localization), and food recognition. The proposed processing pipeline is shown in Fig. 2.

Here we independently process each photo from the gallery of a mobile device. At first, the "food/non-food" classification block analyses an input image to make the binary decision if the photo contains the large-scale image of food or not. In the last case, the depicted food is classified into one of the food classes.

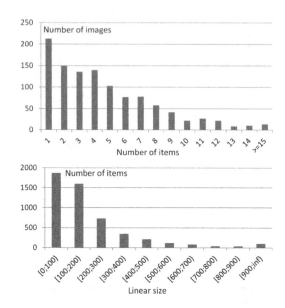

Fig. 1. Dataset characteristics: the number of food items per image (top), the number of food items with the given linear pixel size (bottom).

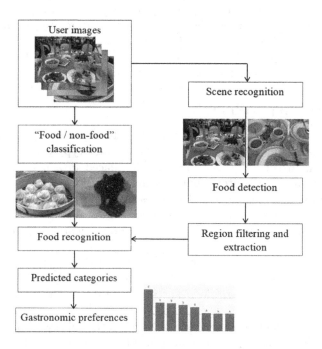

Fig. 2. The proposed approach to food analysis.

Otherwise, the "scene analysis" block makes a decision if the image depicts a scene related to a restaurant, cafe, or home dinner/breakfast. We are using the scene classification MobileNet v2 model from [1] that allows classifying image scenes from Places2 dataset with 51.3% top 1 and 80.7% top 5 accuracy. The main purpose of the considered block in the pipeline is to avoid further analysis of irrelevant images.

If the scene is classified as a relevant one, the "food detection" block will look for objects containing food items in the image. We trained several versions of the YOLO v3 network on our specially gathered dataset (Subsect. 3.1). Taking into account that mobile platforms are of particular interest, we used the Mobilenet backbone and tiny versions of the YOLO detector. Next, we filter these objects to create the list of regions, which have high enough size and resolution to be reliably classified. Then the food recognition task is solved to predict the category of the food depicted in an image. It is supposed that the image contains the food, which can be attributed to exactly one of the categories. The "Food recognition" module in our pipeline performs per-region classification of food and produces the list of predicted food categories.

Finally, the recognition results for all photos from the gallery are aggregated into a single histogram (profile of interests), and the top frequent objects may be used in a recommendation engine.

3.3   Practical Example

Some results of food predictions using our YOLO-based object detector are shown in Fig. 3. Several examples with generated solutions for food detection and recognition are shown in Fig. 4.

Fig. 3. Samples of food detection using YOLO v3 with the MobileNet backbone.

Finally, we gathered publicly available photos of famous chef Gordon Ramsay from his Instagram accounts. The results for our pipeline are shown in Fig. 5. Here one could notice that most frequently occurred scenes are related to food. The resulted profile (Fig. 5b) demonstrates that our model successfully detects many relevant food items.

Fig. 4. Sample results of food recognition with the proposed approach

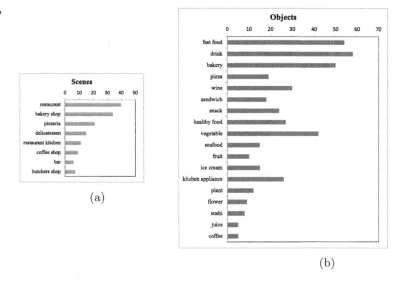

(a)

(b)

Fig. 5. Processing of Instagram photos of Gordon Ramsay (chef): (a) scene recognition, (b) Profile based on object detection.

4   Experimental Results

4.1   "Food/Non-food" Classification

As our target is a mobile platform, we tried to build our solution on the base of mobile networks. We started with training the MobileNet v2 classifier using an existing combination of food and non-food datasets. In particular, we used the UNICT-FD889+Flickr dataset described in the paper [5]. It consists of 3583 food images from the UNICT-FD889, 4805 food images from Flickr-Food, and 8005 non-food images from Flickr-NonFood. According to the above-mentioned paper, we used all the UNICT-FD889 dataset + 3583 images from Flickr-NonFood as a training set. The validation set was composed of the entire Flickr-Food dataset and the rest 4422 images from the Flickr-NonFood dataset.

We trained the MobileNet v2 network for 70 epochs from scratch with SGD to perform two-class ("food/non-food") classification and achieved 84.3% accuracy on the validation set. In order to improve this result, we trained SVM on top of the MobileNet-based embeddings. The latter allowed us to improve our results to 87.5% and 90.0% for linear and RBF kernels, respectively. We compared our results to the paper [5] in Table 1.

As can be seen in the table, our MobileNet is about 5% worse than the best approach from the considered paper. On the other hand, our results are obtained using the mobile network, and these results are comparable to other described results. In addition, we trained the Inception v3 network for 70 epochs and achieved 93.3% accuracy. It is only 1.6% lower than the best one and outperforms

Table 1. Food/non-food classification accuracy (%) for UNICT-FD889+Flickr dataset

Method	Pre-trained model	Fine-tuned model
AlexNet + SoftMax [5]	–	86.41%
AlexNet + SVM [5]	84.95%	**94.86%**
VGG + SoftMax [5]	–	91.84%
VGG + SVM [5]	92.47%	91.46%
NetworkInNetwork + SoftMax [5]	–	84.77%
NetworkInNetwork + SVM [5]	90.82%	84.85%
MobileNet v2	–	84.3%
MobileNet v2 + SVM(linear)	–	87.5%
MobileNet v2 + SVM(RBF)	–	90.0%
Inception 3	–	93.3%

any other result in the considered table. However, the use of SVM did not allow us to improve it.

To further improve our results, we created two more datasets, namely, FoodX-251+COCO and Food-101+COCO. The FoodX-251+COCO dataset is based on the FoodX-251 dataset [18] and the COCO dataset. The images from FoodX-251 serve as positive examples for the image classification, and images from the COCO serve as negative ones. To ensure that COCO does not contain food-related images, we excluded all the images belonging to 'kitchen' and 'food' super-categories from COCO. Thus, the COCO nonfood split contains 63223 images in the training part and 31096 images in the test part. To create a balanced set, after random shuffling, we took 63223 images from foodX-251 for training, and 31096 for validation. As a result, we ended up with 126446 images for training and 62192 for validation.

Analogously, the Food-101+COCO dataset was based on Food-101 [24] and COCO. We used a similar procedure to create a balanced set of the same size as above. It is worth noting that some images from both COCO and food datasets were unused due to the procedure. After the training of the MobileNet v2, we performed the cross estimation of the detection accuracy for both created datasets and the UNICT-FD889+Flickr dataset, which was used earlier. The results of the estimation are shown in Table 2.

Table 2. Cross-estimation of food/non-food classification accuracy (%)

Training set	Evaluation dataset		
	UNICT+ Flickr	FoodX-251+ COCO	Food-101+ COCO
UNICT + Flickr	84.3%	87.9%	87.7%
FoodX-251 + COCO	83.7%	**98.9%**	80.8%
Food-101 + COCO	**95.5%**	95.8%	**98.4%**

Here we achieved 80% or higher accuracy in all the considered cases. The MobileNet v2 trained on Food-101+COCO is the best one, resulting in 95.5–98.4% accuracy. It is worth noting that this our result for the UNICT-FD889+Flickr dataset (95.5%) outperforms the best result (94.86%) reported in Table 1, while our solution is based on lightweight MobileNet v2 network.

4.2   Food Detection and Localization

To tackle the problem of food detection and localization, we trained several versions of the YOLO network on our constructed dataset. For each YOLO-based detector, at first, we took the pre-trained versions of backbone CNNs and tuned YOLO weights for 150 epochs. In particular, we used the Darknet weights from YOLO v3-416 and YOLO v3-tiny pre-trained on the COCO Dataset as the backbone for YOLO 3 and its Tiny version. In addition, we used the Mobilenet model pre-trained on the ImageNet-1000 for the MobileNet versions of YOLO v3.

After tuning the YOLO weights, we unfroze the backbone CNN of networks and fine-tuned them for 100 epochs. In each case, we used the Adam optimizer, reduced the learning rate on a plateau, and stopped training after 10 epoch of patience. Depending on the particular version of the network, we used batch size equal to 4 or 8. Almost in all the considered cases, the training was early stopped before the maximum number of iterations reached.

The results of the evaluation are shown in Table 3. Here the best accuracy is achieved by conventional Darknet YOLO v3.

Table 3. Validation results for food detection

Model	Average precision (AP), %	Model file size, Mb
YOLO v3 (Darknet backend)	71.35	235
YOLO v3 (MobileNet backend)	60.15	92.5
Tiny YOLO v3 (Darknet backend)	47.54	33.1
Tiny YOLO v3 (MobileNet backend)	42.77	33.1

4.3   Food Recognition

We started the food recognition part by training the MobileNet v2 network on the FoodX-251 dataset [18]. We took the network pre-trained on ImageNet-1000 and trained all the layers. The data augmentation assumed random horizontal flips, scaling up to 20%, and random horizontal and vertical shifts. We used the stochastic gradient descent with 1e−4 starting value with a momentum equal to 0.9 and reduced the learning rate on a plateau with 5 epochs patience. This led us to 58.2% top-1 accuracy and 76.8% top-3 accuracy after 20 epochs of training. This result is 6.2 pt lower than the baseline result reported in [18], but our MobileNet-based solution has an order of magnitude lower memory consumption than the ResNet-based solution [18].

To find a better solution, we varied training parameters and fine-tuned the previous solution with augmentation extended by up to 30 degrees random rotations and up to 5% brightness distortions. This allowed us to get approximately 1% better top 3 accuracy (77.6%).

After that, we studied several training techniques, which could improve our current results. In particular, we found that the mixup training strategy [25] combined with our previous augmentation procedure gave some improvement in both top1 and top3 accuracy. In particular, the fine-tuning of our previous model with this technique gave us 60.7% top-1 accuracy and 79.5% top-3 on MobileNet v2. Thus, we improved our previous MobileNet v2 result by 2.5% and 1.9% correspondingly.

For comparison purposes, we extended the list of models with Squeeze and Excitation (SE-) [26] SE-Inception network. The training with the described above augmentation without mixup gave us 62.0% top-1 accuracy and 80.5% top-3 accuracy.

Table 4 contains a summary of all the described results. Although the food recognition solution is not more accurate than the published result [18], it shows comparable accuracy, and have an order of magnitude lower memory consumption and running time.

Table 4. Food recognition accuracy (%)

Model	Top 1 accuracy	Top 3 accuracy	Size, mb
MobileNet v2	58.1	76.8	14
MobileNet v2 (extended augmentation)	58.1	77.6	14
MobileNet v2 (mixup)	60.3	79.1	14
SE-Inception	62.0	80.5	102
ResNet-101 [18]	–	83	171

5   Conclusions

In this paper, we proposed the pipeline (Fig. 2) to the food analysis problem in the gallery of a mobile device based on the lightweight CNNs. Though we considered the solution to the problem of food analysis mainly from the viewpoint of constructing recommendation systems, the stages of the analysis are universal and can be used to solve other mentioned problems. In particular, we prepared our dataset for food detection and used the combination of the public and proprietary datasets to train food detection and classification neural networks. It was demonstrated that the proposed solution provides excellent state-of-the-art accuracy to the "food/non-food" classification problem and acceptable quality to the food detection problem. We suppose that under the considered restrictions to the class of mobile neural networks, the food classification problem can be solved with acceptable quality for generalized food categories.

Acknowledgements. This research is based on the work supported by Samsung Research, Samsung Electronics.

References

1. Savchenko, A.V., Demochkin, K.V., Grechikhin, I.S.: User preference prediction in visual data on mobile devices. arXiv preprint 1907.04519 (2019)
2. Matsuda, Y., Yanai, K.: Multiple-food recognition considering co-occurrence employing manifold ranking. In: Proceedings of the 21st International Conference on Pattern Recognition, ICPR 2012, pp. 2017–2020, November 2012
3. Kitamura, K., Yamasaki, T., Aizawa, K.: FoodLog: capture, analysis and retrieval of personal food images via web. In: Proceedings of the ACM Multimedia 2009 Workshop on Multimedia for Cooking and Eating Activities, CEA 2009, pp. 23–30. Association for Computing Machinery, New York (2009)
4. Farinella, G.M., Allegra, D., Stanco, F., Battiato, S.: On the exploitation of one class classification to distinguish food vs non-food images. In: Murino, V., Puppo, E., Sona, D., Cristani, M., Sansone, C. (eds.) ICIAP 2015. LNCS, vol. 9281, pp. 375–383. Springer, Cham (2015). https://doi.org/10.1007/978-3-319-23222-5_46
5. Ragusa, F., Tomaselli, V., Furnari, A., Battiato, S., Farinella, G.M.: Food vs non-food classification. In: Proceedings of the International Workshop on Multimedia Assisted Dietary Management (MADiMa), pp. 77–81. ACM (2016)
6. Myers, A., et al.: Im2Calories: towards an automated mobile vision food diary. In: 2015 IEEE International Conference on Computer Vision (ICCV), pp. 1233–1241, December 2015
7. Anzawa, M., Amano, S., Yamakata, Y., Motonaga, K., Kamei, A., Aizawa, K.: Recognition of multiple food items in a single photo for use in a buffet-style restaurant. IEICE Trans. Inf. Syst. **E102.D**(2), 410–414 (2019)
8. Kagaya, H., Aizawa, K., Ogawa, M.: Food detection and recognition using convolutional neural network. In: Proceedings of the 22nd ACM International Conference on Multimedia, MM 2014, pp. 1085–1088. Association for Computing Machinery, New York (2014)
9. Singla, A., Yuan, L., Ebrahimi, T.: Food/non-food image classification and food categorization using pre-trained GoogLeNet model. In: Proceedings of the 2nd International Workshop on Multimedia Assisted Dietary Management. MADiMa 2016. Association for Computing Machinery, New York (2016)
10. Aguilar, E., Bolaños, M., Radeva, P.: Exploring food detection using CNNs. In: Moreno-Díaz, R., Pichler, F., Quesada-Arencibia, A. (eds.) EUROCAST 2017. LNCS, vol. 10672, pp. 339–347. Springer, Cham (2018). https://doi.org/10.1007/978-3-319-74727-9_40
11. Oliveira, L., Costa, V., Neves, G., Oliveira, T., Jorge, E., Lizarraga, M.: A mobile, lightweight, poll-based food identification system. Pattern Recogn. **47**(5), 1941–1952 (2014)
12. Martinel, N., Piciarelli, C., Micheloni, C., Foresti, G.L.: A structured committee for food recognition. In: 2015 IEEE International Conference on Computer Vision Workshop (ICCVW), pp. 484–492 (2015)

13. Zheng, J., Wang, Z., Zhu, C.: Food image recognition via superpixel based low-level and mid-level distance coding for smart home applications. Sustainability **9**(5), 856 (2017)

14. Bettadapura, V., Thomaz, E., Parnami, A., Abowd, G.D., Essa, I.: Leveraging context to support automated food recognition in restaurants. In: Proceedings of the Winter Conference on Applications of Computer Vision (WACV), pp. 580–587. IEEE (2015)

15. Bolanos, M., P., R.: Simultaneous food localization and recognition. In: International Conference on Pattern Recognition, pp. 3140–3145 (2017)

16. Wu, H., Merler, M., Uceda-Sosa, R., Smith, J.R.: Learning to make better mistakes: semantics-aware visual food recognition. In: Proceedings of the 24th International Conference on Multimedia (MM), pp. 172–176. ACM (2016)

17. Ciocca, G., Napoletano, P., Schettini, R.: Food recognition: a new dataset, experiments, and results. IEEE J. Biomed. Health Inform. **21**(3), 588–598 (2016)

18. Kaur, P., Sikka, K., Wang, W., Belongie, S., Divakaran, A.: FoodX-251: a dataset for fine-grained food classification. arXiv preprint 1907.06167 (2019)

19. Ming, Z.-Y., Chen, J., Cao, Y., Forde, C., Ngo, C.-W., Chua, T.S.: Food photo recognition for dietary tracking: system and experiment. In: Schoeffmann, K., et al. (eds.) MMM 2018. LNCS, vol. 10705, pp. 129–141. Springer, Cham (2018). https://doi.org/10.1007/978-3-319-73600-6_12

20. Aguilar, E., Bolaños, M., Radeva, P.: Food recognition using fusion of classifiers based on CNNs. In: Battiato, S., Gallo, G., Schettini, R., Stanco, F. (eds.) ICIAP 2017. LNCS, vol. 10485, pp. 213–224. Springer, Cham (2017). https://doi.org/10.1007/978-3-319-68548-9_20

21. Xin Wang, Kumar, D., Thome, N., Cord, M., Precioso, F.: Recipe recognition with large multimodal food dataset. In: Proceedings of the International Conference on Multimedia Expo Workshops (ICMEW), pp. 1–6. IEEE (2015)

22. Liu, C., Cao, Y., Luo, Y., Chen, G., Vokkarane, V., Ma, Y.: DeepFood: deep learning-based food image recognition for computer-aided dietary assessment. In: Chang, C.K., Chiari, L., Cao, Y., Jin, H., Mokhtari, M., Aloulou, H. (eds.) ICOST 2016. LNCS, vol. 9677, pp. 37–48. Springer, Cham (2016). https://doi.org/10.1007/978-3-319-39601-9_4

23. Farinella, G.M., Allegra, D., Stanco, F.: A benchmark dataset to study the representation of food images. In: Agapito, L., Bronstein, M.M., Rother, C. (eds.) ECCV 2014. LNCS, vol. 8927, pp. 584–599. Springer, Cham (2015). https://doi.org/10.1007/978-3-319-16199-0_41

24. Bossard, L., Guillaumin, M., Van Gool, L.: Food-101 – mining discriminative components with random forests. In: Fleet, D., Pajdla, T., Schiele, B., Tuytelaars, T. (eds.) ECCV 2014. LNCS, vol. 8694, pp. 446–461. Springer, Cham (2014). https://doi.org/10.1007/978-3-319-10599-4_29

25. Zhang, H., Cissé, M., Dauphin, Y.N., Lopez-Paz, D.: Mixup: beyond empirical risk minimization. CoRR abs/1710.09412 (2017)

26. Hu, J., Shen, L., Sun, G.: Squeeze-and-excitation networks. CoRR abs/1709.01507 (2017)

Real Time Automatic Urban Traffic Management Framework Based on Convolutional Neural Network Under Limited Resources Constraint

Antoine Meicler[1(✉)] , Assan Sanogo[1], Nadiya Shvai[1] , Arcadi Llanza[1] ,
Abul Hasnat[1] , Marouan Khata[1] , Ed-Doughmi Younes[1], Alami Khalil[1],
Yazid Lachachi[1] , and Amir Nakib[1,2]

[1] CYCLOPE.AI, Paris, France
{antoine.meicler,assan.sanogo,nadiya.shvai,
arcadi.llanza,hasnat.abul,marouan.taha,
younes.eddoughmi,khalil.alami,yazid.lachachi}@cyclope.ai
[2] Laboratoire LISSI, University Paris Est CRETIL, 94400 Vitry sur Seine, France

Abstract. Automatic traffic flow monitoring and control systems have become one of the most in-demand tasks due to the massive growth of the urban population, particularly in large cities. While numerous methods are available to address this issue with an unconstrained use of computational resources, a resource-constrained solution is yet to become publicly available. This paper aims to propose a real-time system framework to control the traffic flow and signals dealing with resource limitation constraints. Experimental results showed a high accuracy performance on the desired task and the scalability of the proposed framework.

Keywords: Multi-target detection and tracking · GPU-based embedded system

1 Introduction

Automatic traffic management (ATM) has become one of the most important concerns of today's urban/city life [3,4,10,11,13,14]. The impact is particularly significant in big cities, where hundreds of thousands of peoples can either benefit or suffer from good or bad traffic management policies. Indeed, today an obvious way to significantly improve the city traffic management is to develop an automatic system that exploits the video streams provided by the surveillance cameras located all around the cities. This paper proposes such an automatic system that combines powerful computer vision techniques, such as the deep convolutional neural network (CNN) [5], as well as low-cost devices powered by the Graphics Processing Units (GPU) [1,9]. More specifically, the framework aims at facilitating non-motorized transportation (pedestrians, bikes, and kick scooters) as opposed to motorized ones (light vehicles, trucks, and motorbikes).

© Springer Nature Switzerland AG 2020
A. Campilho et al. (Eds.): ICIAR 2020, LNCS 12131, pp. 95–106, 2020.
https://doi.org/10.1007/978-3-030-50347-5_10

A variety of different ATM methods have been recently proposed in the literature from different perspectives [3, 4, 10, 11, 13, 14], see Sect. 2 for a detailed study and comparison. However, the main differences with the existing methods are as follows: (a) problem domain: we consider the problem through a fine-grained (e.g., vehicle classes, human, etc.) analysis, while others consider it from coarser level (vehicle only) [4, 10, 11, 13, 14] (b) computational resource constraint: while we consider low-cost near sensor solution, many others consider it as an offline service [10] or a transfer of data to powerful devices via web services [4, 11, 13, 14]; and (c) application domain: we take into account multiple tasks, such as detailed traffic flow estimation, counting and controlling, existing methods [4, 11, 13, 14] focus only a subset of them. These differences do not only point out the additional challenges addressed herein, but also highlight the necessity to develop a more complete and independent framework.

This paper proposes a real-time ATM (monitoring and controlling) system, which consists of: (1) pre-processing the 360° view images obtained from the fish-eye camera; (2) light-weight multiple-classes vehicle and pedestrian detector; (3) fast and low-cost object tracker and (4) an estimator module for the flow and count measurements. The proposed system is deployed within an embedded device, called Jetson AGX Xavier (from Nvidia) [12] to independently control the traffic signals based on traffic flow observed through the camera lenses located in the city crossroads. Results show that while it is able to successfully perform real-time ATM, it provides interesting perspectives and challenges for the larger-scale deployments.

Our key contributions in this paper are: (a) present ATM problem with its real-world constraints; (b) propose a full framework to deal with this problem; (c) achieved high accuracy in real-time and (d) provides an in-depth analysis and discussion to discover the further development.

The rest of the paper is organized as follows: related work is in Sect. 2, problem formulation and dataset in Sect. 3 and 4, respectively. The proposed method is presented in Sect. 5, while, experimental results is in Sect. 6 and the conclusion is in Sect. 7.

2   Related Work

ATM problems have been addressed from different perspectives, and hence the proposed solutions differ based on the tasks [3, 4, 10, 11, 13, 14]. Naphade et al. [10] reported a set of traffic analysis approaches, which were presented at the NVIDIA AI city challenge. Thirteen papers have been proposed for the traffic flow analysis where the detection ground truths were already available. Moreover, they do not impose any constraint on computational resources or real-time related issues. Therefore, they are not quite comparable to our proposed method.

Several recent works [3, 4, 11, 13, 14] considered the problem without any given detection information and aimed to perform real-time traffic flow processing. However, an important distinction among these methods relies on the use of on-device (embedded) vs. off-device (web-service oriented) solutions. While our method considers providing a resource-constrained solution, the off-device solutions, e.g., [4,11,13,14], can be considered as the unbounded resource methods. Besides, this research considers the input images captured from a relatively different imaging device - the fish-eye camera, which clearly distinguishes itself from the related methods listed above.

Recently, Chauhan et al. [3] presented an ATM problem that is very close to this research concerning image capturing contexts, resource constraints and the different types of objects needed to be treated by the system. However, their target application was rather unspecific compared to this research.

Several differences remain concerning the individual elements of the proposed pipeline, which primarily used the object detection and tracking modules. Three detectors have been mostly experimented: [3] used YOLO, [11,14] used SSD and [4,11] used Faster R-CNN. In our approach, we use a lightweight version of YOLO, which is quite different from the other detectors used in other works. To track objects, [4] used the SORT [16] tracker and [14] used a custom tracker based on different types of image features, weighted similarity measure, and bipartite graph-based association approach. Although our tracker is similar to SORT [16], it is suited to perform on a lower frame rate.

3   Problem Formulation

To integrate the data on active transportation (such as pedestrians, bikes, kick scooters) in the traffic light control, it was required to build a visual-based traffic monitoring system that would be able to detect, track and count following classes of traffic subjects: *light vehicle, truck, bus, motorcycle, bicycle, kick scooter, pedestrian*. Such a pipeline should be able to provide the following output:

– **low-level counting:** number of pedestrians, kick scooters and bikes waiting at the junction in order to cross the street. This type of response should be given at the rate of 3 responses per second:

$$res_{micro}^t = n_{non\text{-}motorized}^t = \sum_{e:e\in A^t} \mathbb{1}\{e \in W^t\},$$

where e denotes a tracked entity, A^t - set of non-motorized entities (pedestrian, kick scooters, and bikes) at the moment t, and W^t - set of entities that are located in a pre-assigned waiting areas in the moment t.
– **high-level counting:** number of motorized object (light vehicles, trucks and buses) that went through the junction in the specified direction, and the number of non motorized objects (pedestrians, kick scooters and bikes) that crossed the street in the given timeframe of 3 min. This type of response should be sent every 3 min:

$$res_{macro}^{t,M,P} = \sum_e \mathbb{1}\{\exists t_0 : e \in M^{t_0} \cap P^{t_0}, t - t_0 < 180\},$$

$$res_{macro}^{t,A,(P_1,P_2)} = \sum_e \mathbb{1}\{\exists t_1 < t_2 : t - t_1 < 180,$$

$$e \in P_1^{t_1} \cap A^{t_1}, e \in P_2^{t_2} \cap A^{t_2}\},$$

where e denotes a tracked entity, A^t and M^t - sets of non-motorized and motorized entities at the moment t respectively, P^t - set of entities that are located in a pre-assigned crossroad area in the moment t.

4   Dataset

The data has been collected with a fish-eye camera installed on one of the crossroads in Paris, France.

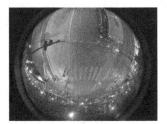

(a) Daytime view   (b) Nighttime view

Fig. 1. Examples of the fish-eye images from the collected dataset (10,017 images) obtained at different times of the day. Pictures illustrate the setup of the camera, the variability in objects (vehicle vs. truck) dimensions, and the environment illumination (shadows, saturation, brightness, etc.).

As shown in Fig. 1, images from this camera are wide-angle and must be unwrapped and registered to train our detection model (with bounding boxes surrounding recognizable shapes). Original wide-angle images have a resolution of 2592×1944 pixels.

Overall the dataset consists of 10,000 images. These images were collected in a two-fold procedure:

- First, around 8,000 images were collected from videos distributed uniformly through different times of the day,
- The trained detection model was used, then, to collect around 2,000 images containing low represented classes: *bus* and *kick scooter*.

The images from the dataset were (according to a fixed region of interest in the crossroad) registered to decrease the radial distortion, and annotated with bounding boxes. An example of a resulting image is given in Fig. 4.

In summary, 10,017 annotated images contained 57,323 instances of objects of interest. The overall statistics of the number of instance per class is given in Table 1. These images were collected in various hours of the day with an emphasis over morning and evening rush hours. The distribution of images over the day is illustrated on the frequency histogram in Fig. 2.

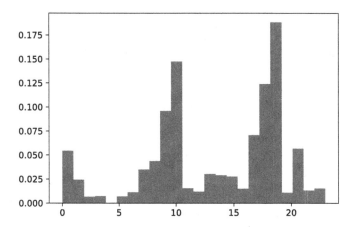

Fig. 2. Distribution of collected images over the hours of the day. The maximum number of images have been collected from 10 to 11 pm. (1,503 images) and from 6 to 7 pm. (1,853 images). These time-frames coincide with rush-hours, periods particularly crucial to the use-case.

5   Proposed Method

Figure 3 is a block diagram illustrating the proposed approach. It considers the continuous video stream as input and provides the micro and macro responses as the output. It consists of three main components: image pre-processing, object detector and multi-object tracker. The following subsections provide a brief discussion of each component.

5.1   Image Pre-processing

The fish-eye camera placed above the crossroad produces strongly distorted images; Fig. 1 provides an example. Indeed, directly using the object detector on this type of high-resolution images is challenging due to: (a) longer image pre-processing time; (b) objects (pedestrians) size become very small and (c) distorted object shapes. In order to avoid these, we apply image pre-processing. Interestingly, only part of the image contains relevant information to monitor the traffic. Therefore, the image pre-processor initially focuses and extracts only the *image Region of Interest (ROI)*.

Table 1. Number of class instances among the collected dataset, and the splitted training and test set. In parenthesis are displayed the distribution of the instances based on the total amount of objects available. Furthermore, it is presented the split of images in the set of data.

Class name	Training set	Test set	Total
light vehicle	20929	1260	22189 (0.387)
truck	1579	171	1750 (0.031)
bus	1483	578	2061 (0.036)
motorcycle	2272	164	2436 (0.042)
bicycle	3842	933	4775 (0.083)
kick scooter	668	82	750 (0.013)
pedestrian	21056	2306	23362 (0.408)
Total	**51829**	**5494**	**57323**
Number of images	**8994**	**1023**	**10017**

A common way to proceed with fish-eye camera images is to undistort images using either known camera parameters or estimating parameters using checkerboard calibration. However, none of these options were available to us due to computational constraints. Thus as an alternative, we opt to do simple *rotation and cropping* of the image, equivalent to tensor slicing and multiplication. The crop is used to select only the mask regions of interest, and rotation optimizes the crop size (i.e. fits the region of interest to the rectangular as close as possible) and facilitates the labeling (due to more "upright" positioning of pedestrians, kick scooters, bikes).

5.2   Detection

The model has been trained for 130,000 steps with a batch size equal to 64 and a fixed learning rate equal to 0.001. The input image size for the model is 832 × 832. This is four times larger than the default size for this model (416 × 416). We increased the input size to ease the detection of small-scale objects such as pedestrians, kick scooters, and bikes. Out of 10,000 images available in the data set we used 9,000 images for training and 1,000 images for validation.

The foundation of our detection module is a widely adopted YOLOv3-tiny [6] detector. This choice was made for multiple reasons. First, YOLOv3 family of architectures are current state-of-the-art in many detection benchmarks [7] and provide a solid starting point in any detection task. Secondly, our use case imposed real-time application and YOLOv3-tiny represents one of the fastest detection models (7.57 fps on an NVIDIA Jetson AGX Xavier).

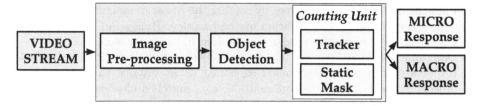

Fig. 3. A representation of the technical pipeline of the complete system. The data flow comes from a fish-eye camera in a video stream format. Afterwards, the pre-processing module is applied based on an image rotation and extraction of the Region of Interest (ROI). Then, Object Detection model is used to detect all the classes of interest and the tracking module is used to follow the instances in a temporal sequence. Finally, a MICRO (every 0.33 s) and MACRO (every 3 min) responses are delivered.

Fig. 4. Example of an image after rotation, extraction of the region of interest, and detection using the YOLOv3-tiny object detector. Green, yellow, and violet boxes stand for the "motorcycle", "pedestrian", and "light vehicle" objects respectively. (Color figure online)

5.3   Objects Tracking

The main objective of the tracker is to follow the different object entities (multiple types of vehicles, pedestrians, bikes, and kick scooters) across multiple frames. We adopt the tracking-by-detection [2] based multi-object tracking approach. The basic assumption of this tracker is that the detected objects in the consecutive frames should have sufficient overlap, which can be quantified by the intersection-over-union (IoU) among the object bounding boxes in the consecutive frames. Our core tracking pipeline follows the steps below:

a. Compute the IOU scores among the object bounding boxes detected in two consecutive frames t and $t-1$.

b. Find the object correspondences by solving the linear re-assignment problem with a combinatorial optimization method named: Hungarian algorithm [8], where the IOU scores are used as the desired distance measures.

c. Determine the matched and unmatched objects by verifying the associated IoU scores w.r.t. a predetermined threshold value. Finally, characterize the objects using the associated information, *e.g.*, matched identifier.

This pipeline tends to lose objects due to occlusions. To tackle this, we incorporate an additional predictor based on the Kalman filter [15], which predicts the object location in the next frame given its current location as input. Therefore, at every frame, the decisions from the core tracker and the prediction from Kalman filter are fused based on the object appearance state. Particularly, for an object, we exploit the Kalman filter prediction as its current location in case of occlusion or lost position by the core tracker.

5.4   Counting

Counting the entities depending on their zone location (or sometimes direction) implies that each zone is fully identified. We manually drew masks on a standard image transmitted to the detection model. That way each pixel belongs to a zone of the crossroad. Every time an object is detected, its centroid position is assigned to the corresponding zone.

We identify five different zones: P4, P4bis, P4-P4bis, E8, and S8 corresponding respectively to the right and the left pedestrian waiting zones, the pedestrian crossing path section, the vehicle entrance road and the vehicle exit road.

Combining the zone identification of the object and the tracking over time, our system counts the objects either crossing the street or passing through either the road entrance or exit.

Fig. 5. Visualization of manual masks displaying the different traffic zones. Where P4 and P4bis correspond to the sidewalks (green), P4-P4bis corresponds to the pedestrian crossing path section (grey), E8 corresponds to the motorized entrance road (yellow), and S8 corresponds to the motorized exit road (dark green). (Color figure online)

6   Experiments and Results

Implementation. The presented pipeline was implemented on an Nvidia Jetson AGX Xavier. This device was installed on the crossroad, near the camera. This "enclosed" solution allowed us to avoid any data transfer out of premises, and thus ensuring data privacy protection.

Detection. We adopt the common object detection metric, *mean average precision* (mAP). We also provide average precision (AP) for each of the classes separately at IoU threshold = 50%. The evaluation was performed on 1 k images previously unseen by the model. Table 2 reports evaluation results. We can see that class *kick scooter* has AP significantly lower than the other classes. This is explained by the small size of instances of kick scooter class comparing to the image size, the sparsity of this class and the fact that this class can easily be confused with *pedestrian* class.

Table 2. Average precision per class and mean average precision for trained model. It can be observed a low AP in kick scooter and in pedestrian because the objects in the image appear to be quite small, and quite often they appear in groups making it more challenging for the non maximum suppression from the object detector.

Class name	AP	Number of instances in test set
light vehicle	85.10%	1260
truck	84.43%	171
bus	90.44%	578
motorcycle	83.12%	164
bicycle	89.44%	933
kick scooter	34.00%	82
pedestrian	67.93%	2306
Overall mean	**76.35%**	**5494**

Counting and Tracking. For the macro-response, the evaluation relied on nine intervals of 3 min, computing each time the error rate when counting motorized vehicles entering (E8) and exiting the zone (S8), and the non-motorized entities traversing the crossroad. We finally compute the average error rate and the median error rate (results in Table 3). Computing the median error rate is justified as, in particular for non-motorized vehicles, the small number of observations lead to a high error rate (1 non-motorized entity crossing missed out of 1 lead to 100% error rate). The median error rate shows that despite some extreme values, the error rate remains in the majority at 0%. For the micro response, the results correspond to detection evaluation for classes *pedestrian, bike and kick scooter*.

Finally, we examine the real-time performance of our solution: on average the proposed method takes 230 milliseconds to process 1 frame, which means it processes 4.19 frames per second. An in-depth analysis reveals that it takes 41.18 milliseconds for image pre-processing, 132.01 milliseconds for object detection and 56.82 milliseconds for tracking, counting and flow estimation.

Table 3. Average and median error of instances counting. Four zones are taken into consideration (E8, S8, P4 to P4bis and P4bis to P4). Important to highlight that it is taken into account the direction of the object in the pedestrian crossing path section. That is why the average error seems to increase.

	Motorized		Non-motorized	
	E8	S8	P4-P4bis	P4bis-P4
Average error	2,66%	3,94%	31,48%	14,81%
Median error	0%	3,33%	0%	0%

Discussion. Here we tackle multiple challenges encountered in this research paper by discussing what could be improved and propose unexplored enhancement approaches.

- **Challenging detection of minority classes.** Visually similar classes of *pedestrian, kick scooter* and, in some conditions, *bicycle* pose a challenge for object detector. Additionally, the size of these classes instances is small compared to the whole image size. As follows from Table 2, the most difficult detection task is associated with *kick scooter* class, which is also most underrepresented. Similarly, we observed that many strollers are misdetected and decrease average precision on the *pedestrian* class. By including strollers as an extra class, we hope to improve the detection accuracy on *pedestrians* and the overall model precision. Overall, those particular issues could be tackled by increasing the number of underrepresented classes instances either by further data collection or oversampling with advanced data augmentation techniques.
- **Image quality.** One of the particular challenges constituted the light reflections and multiple shadows observed during dawn and dusk hours. In that regard, we would propose for the next experiments the usage of appropriate image augmentation techniques.
- **Variety of points of view.** To have a wider field of view, we believe that adding two or more cameras at the intersection with overlapping views can improve detection. Indeed, the fish-eye view shows poor detection accuracy on the edges of the camera due to high distortion. However, by adding more cameras, we increase the processing time on the AGX Jetson Xavier. Thus a balance should be found between the number of frames per second and time processing.

– **Tracking by interlaced video-sequence.** Recently, *Mhalla et al.* have proposed an improvement to tracking-by-detection by exploiting detection on interlaced video-sequences. This method could be explored to improve tracking on *pedestrians*. As the current tracking approach is highly dependent on detection precision of the detection, using an *temporal interlaced object tracker* seems to be a promising way to improve the detection performance. However, while very accurate, this method requires heavy annotations on multiple video-sequences.

7   Conclusion

This work presents a lightweight detection-and-tracking pipeline able to operate on a GPU-based embedded device without the need for an additional ground station, and, as a consequence, data transfer. We show that it is possible to train an object detector without full image unwarping (for fish-eye camera images), simply using instead image rotation and cropping. In the experimental phase, the implemented solution was successfully incorporated within the traffic control system to analyze the traffic and enable better integration of active transportation in the city.

References

1. Almeida, M., Laskaridis, S., Leontiadis, I., Venieris, S.I., Lane, N.D.: EmBench: quantifying performance variations of deep neural networks across modern commodity devices. CoRR abs/1905.07346 (2019)
2. Bochinski, E., Eiselein, V., Sikora, T.: High-speed tracking-by-detection without using image information. In: International Conference on Advanced Video and Signal Based Surveillance, pp. 1–6 (2017)
3. Chauhan, M.S., Singh, A., Khemka, M., Prateek, A., Sen, R.: Embedded CNN based vehicle classification and counting in non-laned road traffic. In: Proceedings of the International Conference on Information and Communication Technologies and Development, p. 5. ACM (2019)
4. Fedorov, A., Nikolskaia, K., Ivanov, S., Shepelev, V., Minbaleev, A.: Traffic flow estimation with data from a video surveillance camera. J. Big Data **6**(1), 73 (2019). https://doi.org/10.1186/s40537-019-0234-z
5. Gu, J., et al.: Recent advances in convolutional neural networks. Pattern Recogn. **77**, 354–377 (2017)
6. Huang, R., Pedoeem, J., Chen, C.: YOLO-LITE: a real-time object detection algorithm optimized for non-GPU computers. In: 2018 IEEE International Conference on Big Data (Big Data), pp. 2503–2510. IEEE (2018)
7. Jiao, L., et al.: A survey of deep learning-based object detection. IEEE Access **7**, 128837–128868 (2019)
8. Kuhn, H.W.: The Hungarian method for the assignment problem. Naval Res. Logist. Q. **2**(1–2), 83–97 (1955)
9. Mittal, S.: A survey on optimized implementation of deep learning models on the NVIDIA Jetson platform. J. Syst. Archit. **97**, 428–442 (2019)

10. Naphade, M., et al.: The 2018 NVIDIA AI city challenge. In: Proceedings of the IEEE CVPR Workshops, pp. 53–60 (2018)

11. Peppa, M., Bell, D., Komar, T., Xiao, W.: Urban traffic flow analysis based on deep learning car detection from CCTV image series. Int. Arch. Photogram. Remote Sens. Spat. Inf. Sci. **42**(4), 499–506 (2018)

12. Pujol, R., Tabani, H., Kosmidis, L., Mezzetti, E., Abella, J., Cazorla, F.J.: Generating and exploiting deep learning variants to increase heterogeneous resource utilization in the NVIDIA Xavier. In: Euromicro Conference on Real-Time Systems (2019)

13. Rathore, M.M., Son, H., Ahmad, A., Paul, A.: Real-time video processing for traffic control in smart city using Hadoop ecosystem with GPUs. Soft Comput. **22**(5), 1533–1544 (2018). https://doi.org/10.1007/s00500-017-2942-7

14. Wei, P., Shi, H., Yang, J., Qian, J., Ji, Y., Jiang, X.: City-scale vehicle tracking and traffic flow estimation using low frame-rate traffic cameras. In: Proceedings of the ACM International Joint Conference on Pervasive and Ubiquitous Computing and Proceedings of the 2019 ACM International Symposium on Wearable Computers, pp. 602–610 (2019)

15. Welch, G., Bishop, G., et al.: An introduction to the Kalman filter (1995)

16. Wojke, N., Bewley, A., Paulus, D.: Simple online and realtime tracking with a deep association metric. In: IEEE International Conference on Image Processing, pp. 3645–3649 (2017)

Slicing and Dicing Soccer: Automatic Detection of Complex Events from Spatio-Temporal Data

Lia Morra$^{(\boxtimes)}$, Francesco Manigrasso, Giuseppe Canto, Claudio Gianfrate, Enrico Guarino, and Fabrizio Lamberti

Department of Control and Computer Engineering,
Politecnico di Torino, 10129 Turin, Italy
`lia.morra@polito.it`

Abstract. The automatic detection of events in sport videos has important applications for data analytics, as well as for broadcasting and media companies. This paper presents a comprehensive approach for detecting a wide range of complex events in soccer videos starting from positional data. The event detector is designed as a two-tier system that detects *atomic* and *complex events*. Atomic events are detected based on temporal and logical combinations of the detected objects, their relative distances, as well as spatio-temporal features such as velocity and acceleration. Complex events are defined as temporal and logical combinations of atomic and complex events, and are expressed by means of a declarative Interval Temporal Logic (ITL). The effectiveness of the proposed approach is demonstrated over 16 different events, including complex situations such as tackles and filtering passes. By formalizing events based on a principled ITL, it is possible to easily perform reasoning tasks, such as understanding which passes or crosses result in a goal being scored. To counterbalance the lack of suitable, annotated public datasets, we built on an open source soccer simulation engine to release the synthetic SoccER (Soccer Event Recognition) dataset, which includes complete positional data and annotations for more than 1.6 million atomic events and 9,000 complex events. The dataset and code are available at https:// gitlab.com/grains2/slicing-and-dicing-soccer.

Keywords: Sport analysis · Event detection · Interval temporal logic · Computer graphics

1 Introduction

Data-driven sport video analytics attracts considerable attention from academia and industry. This interest stems from the massive commercial appeal of sports programs, along with the increasing role played by data-driven decisions in soccer and many other sports [17]. We focus here on the challenging problem of temporal event recognition and localization in soccer, which requires considering the positions and actions of several players at once.

© Springer Nature Switzerland AG 2020
A. Campilho et al. (Eds.): ICIAR 2020, LNCS 12131, pp. 107–121, 2020.
https://doi.org/10.1007/978-3-030-50347-5_11

Sports analytics systems relies on a variety of data sources for event detection, including broadcast videos [7,13,17], multi-view camera setup [12,17] and wearable trackers and sensors [3,14]. Large outdoor soccer stadiums are usually equipped with multiple wide-angle, fixed position, synchronized cameras. This setup is particularly apt at event recognition as the spatio-temporal location of all players can be inferred in an unobtrusive and accurate fashion, without resorting to ad-hoc sensors, as will be detailed in Sect. 3.3.

Previous attempts at sports event recognition fall in two main categories: machine learning techniques applied to spatio-temporal positional data [3,14,15] or knowledge-based systems based, e.g., on finite state machines, fuzzy logic or first-order logic [7,17]. The latter approach has several advantages in this context: it does not require large training set, takes full advantage of readily available domain knowledge, and can be easily extended with reasoning engines.

We propose here a comprehensive event detection system based on Interval Temporal Logics (ITL). Khan et al. applied a similar approach to identify events of interest in broadcast videos [7]: the distance-based event detection system takes as input bounding boxes associated with a confidence score for each object category, and applies first-order logic to identify simple and complex events. Complex events combine two or more simple events using logical (AND, OR) or temporal (THEN) operators.

Our work extends previous attempts in literature [7] in several ways. First, we work on spatio-temporal data instead of broadcast videos: we are thus able to detect events that require the position of multiple players at once (e.g. filtering pass), or their location within the field (e.g., cross). We thus cover a much wider range of events, determining which can be accurately detected from positional data, and which would need integration with other visual inputs (e.g., pose estimation). Lastly, we extend existing rule-based systems by using more expressive ITLs, which associate to each event a time interval and are capable of both qualitative and quantitative ordering.

A severe limitation for developing sports analytics systems is the paucity of available datasets, which are usually small and lack fine-grained event annotations. This is especially true for multi-view, fixed setups comparable to those available in modern outdoor soccer stadiums [12]. A large scale dataset was recently published based on broadcast videos [6], but annotations include only a limited set of events (Goal, Yellow/Red Card, and Substitution).

With the aim of fostering research in this field, we have generated and released the synthetic Soccer Event Recognition (SoccER) dataset, based on the open source Gameplay Football engine. The Gameplay Football engine was recently proposed as a training gym for reinforcement learning algorithms [9]. We believe that event recognition can similarly benefit from this approach, especially to explore aspects such as the role of reasoning and the efficient modeling of spatial and temporal relationships. We used the dataset to demonstrate the feasibility of our approach, achieving precision and recall higher than 80% on most events.

The rest of the paper is organized as follows. Section 2 introduces the SoccER dataset. In Sect. 3, the event detector is described. Experimental results are presented in Sect. 4 and discussed in Sect. 5.

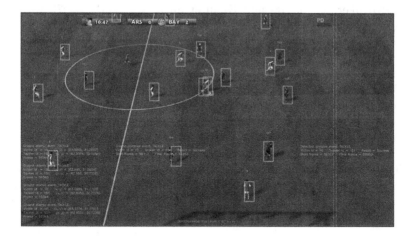

Fig. 1. Example of scene generated by the Gameplay Football engine, with superimposed ground truth bounding boxes and IDs of each player and the ball. The ground truth and detected events are also overlaid on the bottom of the scene: in this frame, a tackle attempt is correctly detected.

2 The SoccER Dataset

2.1 Modified Gameplay Football Engine

We designed a solution to generate synthetic datasets starting from the open source Gameplay Football game [16], which simulates a complete soccer game, including all the most common events such as goals, fouls, corners, penalty kicks, etc. [9]. While the graphics is not as photorealistic as that of commercial products, the game physics is reasonably accurate and, being the engine open source, it can be inspected, improved and modified as needed for research purposes. The opponent team is controlled by means of a rule-based bot, provided in the original Gameplay Football simulator [9].

For each time frame, we extract the positions and bounding boxes of all distinct 22 players and the ball, the ground truth event annotation and the corresponding video screenshots. We adopt the same field coordinate system used in the Alfheim dataset, which includes the position of players obtained from wearable trackers [12]. All the generated videos have a resolution of 1920 × 1080 pixels (Full HD) and frame rate of 30 fps. An example of generated frame is reported in Fig. 1. We envision that event detectors can be trained and tested directly on the generated positional data, focusing on the high-level relational reasoning aspects of the soccer game, independently of the performance of the player detection and tracking stages [7,13].

2.2   Events and Generated Datasets

Events are automatically logged by the game engine in order to generate the ground truth annotation. We define the notion of event based on previous work by Tovinkere et al. [18] and Khan et al. [7]. Similarly to [7], we distinguish between *atomic* and *complex* events, with a slightly different approach (as discussed in the next sub-section). Atomic events are those that are spatio-temporally localized, whereas complex (compound) events are those that occur across an extended portion of the field, involve several players or can be constructed by a combination of other events. Stemming from this difference, an atomic event is associated to a given time frame, whereas a complex event is associated to a time interval, i.e., to a starting and ending frame. Atomic events include ball possession, kicking the ball, ball deflection, tackle, ball out, goal, foul and penalty. Complex events include ball possession, tackle, pass and its special cases (filtering pass, cross), shot and saved shot. A complex ball possession, or tackle, event corresponds to a sequence of consecutive atomic events that involve the same players. The ground truth also includes examples of chains of events, such as a pass, filtering pass or cross that led to a goal.

Table 1. Distribution of atomic and complex events (training and test set).

Atomic event	Train Set	Test set
KickingTheBall	3,786	3,295
BallPossession	812,086	797,224
Tackle	34,929	26,286
BallDeflection	172	78
BallOut	182	168
Goal	45	36
Foul	3	10
Penalty	3	1

Complex event	Train Set	Test set
Pass	2,670	2,389
PassThenGoal	33	31
FilteringPass	37	27
FilterPassThenGoal	4	4
Cross	197	165
CrossThenGoal	9	9
Tackle	1,413	1,130
Shot	282	224
ShotThenGoal	41	36
SavedShot	104	64

The annotations are generated leveraging information from the game engine bot, independently from the detection system: different finite state machines detect the occurrence of several types of events based on the decisions of the bot or the player, their outcomes and the positions of all the players. The definition of each event was double-checked against the official rules of the Union of European Football Association (UEFA), and the annotations were visually verified.

For the present work, eight matches were synthesized through various modalities (player vs. player, player vs. AI, AI vs. AI), for a total of 500 min of play with 1,678,304 atomic events and 9,130 complex events, divided in a training and testing set as reported in Table 1. The game engine and dataset are available at https://gitlab.com/grains2/slicing-and-dicing-soccer.

3   Soccer Event Detection: A Temporal Logic Approach

The designed event detection system comprises two modules: an *atomic event detector* and a *complex event detector*. The first module takes as input the x and y coordinates of the players and the ball, and recognizes atomic (low-level) events through feature extraction and the application of predefined rules. The atomic events are stored in memory, and a temporal logic is then used to model and recognize low- and high-level complex events [2,4].

The proposed system is capable of detecting overall five atomic events and 10 complex events, including all events defined in the ground truth except for fouls, penalties and goals, which would require additional information (such as the referee position and the z coordinate of the ball).

We adopt a methodology and notation similar to that used in [7], grounded on declarative logic, for the rule-based system. Briefly, an atomic event is defined as follows:

$$SE = \langle ID, seType, t, \langle role_1, p_1 \rangle, ..., \langle role_i, p_i \rangle \rangle$$

where ID is an event identifier, *seType* is the type of the event, and t is the time at which the event occurred; the event is associated to one or more objects, each identified as p_i and associated to a specific $role_i$, which identifies the function played by the player in the event and is assigned automatically when the rule is verified. The event can be associated to conditions to be satisfied, e.g., based on the distance between the player and the ball.

Complex events are built by aggregating other simple or complex events using temporal (temporal complex events) or logical operators (logical complex events):

$$LCE = \langle ID, ceType, (t_s, t_e), L = \langle e_1 ope_2 op...ope_n \rangle \rangle$$
$$TCE = \langle ID, ceType, (t_s, t_e), L = \langle e_1 THEN e_2 THEN...THEN e_n \rangle \rangle$$

In all cases, *ID* corresponds to the event identifier, *ceType* to the event type, (t_s, t_e) is the time interval in which the event occurred, and e_i is used to identify the sub-events. In the following, we do not differentiate between logical or temporal complex events. The main difference between our approach and that proposed in [7] is that we model time using intervals, rather than instants. Rule parameters were optimized using a genetic algorithm (see Sect. 4.2).

3.1   Atomic Event Detector

Feature Extraction. Starting from the player and ball x and y positions, the following features were calculated: *velocity, acceleration, direction* with respect to the field, *distance from the ball*, which players move, *distance from the target line* of both teams, *expected cross position on target line* and angle covered by the *change of direction*. For a more detailed definition of the individual features, the reader is referred to the paper by Richly et al. [14].

Rules. Atomic events are detected by applying a set of rules. Even if they are associated to a single time instant t_i, in order to reduce the computational time and calculate stable values for the features, a sliding window approach was implemented: given a time instant t_i, the event E_i is recognized if the corresponding rule is satisfied by the values in the interval (t_i, t_{i+k}), where k is equal to the window size. Feature extraction and rule checking were implemented in Python. Specifically, atomic events are defined as follows:

1. **KickingTheBall** consists in a simple kick aimed at executing a cross, pass or shot. Starting from a position close to the player, the ball should move away from the player over the course of the window k, with a sudden acceleration and a final increased speed.

$$\langle ID, KickingTheBall, t, L = \langle\langle KickingPlayer, p_i\rangle, \langle KickedObject, b\rangle\rangle\rangle$$
$$player(p_i), ball(b), Distance(p_i, b, t) < T_{id_1}$$
$$\forall k = 1 \ldots n, D(p_i, b, t+k) < D(p_i, b, t+k+1),$$
$$speed(b, t+n) < T_{s_1} \exists k | acceleration(b, t+k) < T_{a_1}$$

2. **BallPossession** is defined taking into account not only the player who has the control of the ball (i.e., the closest player), but also the player status (i.e., whether it is moving or not). Secondly, since the z coordinate of the ball is not available, we used the ball speed to avoid accidentally triggering ball possession during cross events.

$$\langle ID, BallPossession, t, L = \langle\langle PossessingPlayer, p_i\rangle, \langle PossessedObject, b\rangle\rangle\rangle$$
$$player(p_i), ball(b), Distance(p_i, b, t) < T_{id_2}$$
$$\forall j \neq i, player(p_j), D(p_j, b, t) > D(pi, b, t)$$
$$\forall k = 1 \ldots n, D(p_i, b, t+k) < T_{id_2}$$
$$\forall k = 0 \ldots n, \forall j \neq i, team(p_j) \neq team(p_i), D(p_i, p_j, t+k) < T_{od_2},$$
$$speed(b, t+k) < T_{s_2}$$

3. **Tackle** occurs when a player (TacklingPlayer) tries to gain control of the ball against a player of the opposite team (PossessingPlayer). As a direct consequence, the presence of a member of the opposite team nearby is a condition to trigger the event.

$$\langle ID, Tackle, t, L = \langle\langle PossessingPlayer, p_i\rangle, \langle TacklingPlayer, p_j\rangle,$$
$$\langle PossessedObject, b\rangle\rangle,$$
$$player(p_i), player(p_j), ball(b),$$
$$Distance(p_i, b, t) < T_{id_3}$$
$$\forall u \ldots i, player(p_u), D(p_u, b, t) > D(p_i, b, t)$$
$$\forall k = 1 \ldots n, D(p_i, b, t+k) < T_{id_3}$$
$$\forall k = 0 \ldots n, \exists player(p_i) | D(p_i, p_j, t+k) < T_{od_3}, team(p_i) \neq team(p_j),$$
$$speed(b, t+k) < T_{s_3}$$

4. **BallDeflection** occurs when the ball has a sudden change in direction, usually due to a player or the goalkeeper deflecting it. The ball in this event undergoes an intense deceleration reaching an area far from the deflecting player.

$$\langle ID, BallDeflection, t, L = \langle\langle DeflectingPlayer, p_i\rangle\rangle DeflectedObject, b\rangle\rangle\rangle$$
$$player(p_i), ball(b), Distance(p_i, b, t) < T_{id_4}$$
$$\forall k = 1\ldots n, D(p_i, b, t+k) < D(p_i, b, t+k+1),$$
$$speed(b, t+n) > T_{s_4}$$
$$\exists k | acceleration(b, t+k) < -T_{a_4}$$

5. **BallOut** is triggered when the ball goes off the pitch.
6. **Goal** occurs when a player scores a goal.

3.2   Complex Event Detector

This module was implemented based on a temporal logic; specifically the Temporal Interval Logic with Compositional Operators (TILCO) [8] was used. TILCO belongs to the class of ITLs, where each event is associated to a time interval. TILCO was selected among several available options because it implements both qualitative and quantitative ordering, and defines a metric over time: thus, we were able to impose constraints on the duration of the events, as well as to gather statistics on their duration. The ETALIS (Event TrAnsaction Logic Inference System) open source library, based on Prolog, was used for implementation [4]. The complex event detector is characterized by few parameters, which were manually optimized on the training set.

For the complex events, the rules were formalized as reported in the following.

1. **Pass** and **Cross** events occur when the ball is passed between two players of the same team, and hence can be expressed as a sequence of two atomic events, KickingTheBall and BallPossession, where the passing and receiving players belong to the same team. A cross is a special case in which the ball is passed from the sideline area of the field to the goal area. An additional clause is added to the pass detection (not reported for brevity) to evaluate the position of the players, straightforward in our case as the coordinate system coincides with the field.

$$\langle ID, Pass, (t, t+k), t, L = \langle ID, KickingTheBall,$$
$$\langle KickingPlayer, p_i, t\rangle, \langle KickedObject, b, t\rangle\rangle$$
$$THEN \langle ID, BallPossession, \langle PossessingPlayer, p_j, t+k\rangle,$$
$$\langle PossessedObject, b, t\rangle\rangle\rangle$$
$$player(p_i), player(p_j), ball(b), team(p_i) = team(p_j), k < Th3$$

2. **FilteringPass** allows to create goal opportunities when the opposite team have an organized defence. According to the UEFA definition, it consists of a

pass over the defence line of the opposite team. In our definition, the player that receives the ball has to be, at the time the pass starts, nearer to the goal post than all the players from the opposite team.

$$\langle ID, FilteringPass, t, t + k, t, L = \langle ID, Pass, \langle PossessingPlayer, p_i, t \rangle,$$
$$\langle ReceivingPlayer, p_j, t + k \rangle, \langle PossessedObject, b, t \rangle \rangle \rangle$$
$$player(p_i), player(p_j), ball(b), team(p_i) = team(p_j),$$
$$\forall k, player(p_k), team(p_k) \neq team(p_j), goal(g, p_k),$$
$$D(p_j, g, t + k) < D(p_k, g, t + k)$$

3. **PassThenGoal, CrossThenGoal** and **FilteringPassThenGoal** are defined by the concatenation of two temporal sub-sequences: an alternation of Pass/FilteringPass/Cross followed by a Goal, where the receiver of the pass is the same player who scores.
4. **Tackle,** as a complex event, is a sequence of one or more atomic tackles, followed by a ball possession (which indicates the end of the action). A **Won-Tackle** terminates with the successful attempt to gain the ball by the opponent team. A **LostTackle** is obtained by the complementary rule.
5. **ShotOut, ShotThenGoal** and **SavedShot** represent possible outcomes of an attempt to score. The SavedShot event, where the goalkeeper successfully intercepts the ball, is formalized as KickingTheBall followed by a BallDeflection or BallPossession, where the deflecting player is the goal keeper.

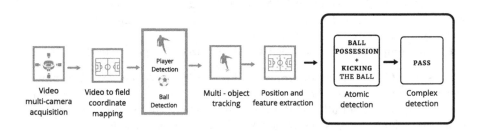

Fig. 2. Deployment of the proposed system in a real-life scenario.

3.3   Event Recognition from a Multi-view Camera Setup

In a real setting, spatio-temporal data would need to be extracted from a multi-view video stream using a multi-object detection and tracking system (see Fig. 2). A multi-camera setup is required in order to solve occlusions and cover the entire playing field. For instance, Pettersen et al. used three wide-angle cameras to cover the Alfheim stadium [12]; modern acquisition setup like Intel True View© include up to 38 5K cameras. The players and the ball can be detected using e.g., Single Shot Detector or another real-time object detector [7,13]. Pixel coordinates are then mapped to the field coordinate systems using a properly calibrated setup; alternatively, field lines can be used to estimate the calibration parameters [13]. For accurate event detection the system should be able to distinguish and track different players, assign them to the correct team, and minimize identity switches during tracking. For instance, certain events can only occur between players of the same team, other between players of competing teams. Developing the detection and tracking system is beyond the scope of this paper. Instead, we exploit the game engine to log the position of the players and the ball at each frame, and focus on the final event detection step, which is further divided into atomic and complex event detection.

4   Experimental Results

In this section, the evaluation protocol and the experimental results of the proposed detector on the SoccER dataset are reported. We focus first on the detection of atomic events, for which optimal parameters were found by means of a multi-objective genetic algorithm. Starting from the optimal solution of the atomic event detector, the performance of the complex event detector is analyzed and compared with the state of the art.

4.1   Evaluation Protocol

A ground truth atomic event is detected if an event of the same type is found within a temporal window of three frames. For complex events, we use the common OV20 criterion for temporal action recognition: a temporal window matches a ground truth action if they overlap, according to the Intersection over Union, by 20% or more [5]. For each event, we calculate the recall, precision and F-score.

4.2   Parameter Optimization: An Evolutionary Strategy

Genetic or evolutionary algorithms are effective techniques for parameter optimization, as they only require the ability to evaluate the fitness function and are applicable when an analytic formulation of the loss is not available [11]. In our case, the fitness value is based on the weighted average of the recall and precision metrics over all the event types. Since precision and recall are competing requirements, we opted for a multi-objective implementation, the Strength Pareto Evolutionary Algorithm or SPEA2 [19]. SPEA2 is a Pareto-based optimization technique which seeks to approximate the Pareto-optimal set, i.e., the set of individuals that are not dominated by any others, while maximizing the diversity of the generated solutions.

Each individual's genome encodes the set of 16 parameters associated to all rules. The parameters of each rule are defined in Sect. 3.1 (i.e., Inner Distance (T_{id_N}), Outer Distance (T_{od_N}), speed (T_{s_N}) and acceleration (T_{a_N}), where N ranges from 1 to 4). In addition, the window for each rule is separately optimized. Finally, since the rules are not mutually exclusive, the order in which they are evaluated is also encoded using the Lehmer notation. A range and discretization step is defined for each real-valued parameter to limit the search space. All window sizes are limited in the range 3–30 frames (with unitary step), all thresholds on speed were limited in the range 1–15 with step 1.0, and all thresholds on distance were limited in the range 0.1–2.0 m with step 0.1. The genetic algorithm was run for 50 generations starting from a population of 200 individuals; genetic operators were the BLX-0.5 crossover [1], with probability 90%, and random mutation with probability 20%. An archive of 100 individuals was used to store the Pareto front. The optimal parameters were determined on the training set and evaluated on the testing set. The experiment was repeated twice to ensure, qualitatively, the reproducibility of the results. Genetic algorithms are sensitive to random initialization and more runs would be needed to estimate the variability in the results.

The final set of solutions, which approximate the Pareto front, is shown in Fig. 3a. The four solutions which maximize F-score for each event are compared in Fig. 3. The BallOut event (not reported) reaches perfect scores for all parameter choices. The easiest events to detect are KickingTheBall, with an average F-score of 0.94, and BallPossession, with an average F-score of 0.93. For Tackle, the average precision is high (0.94), but the recall is much lower (0.61). The worst result is obtained for BallDeflection, with values of F-score consistently lower than 0.4. Some events are more difficult to detect based on positional data alone, i.e., without considering the position of the joints or the action performed by the players [10]. The best performing solution for the Tackle event (0.65 vs. 0.42 recall) corresponds to a lower recall for BallPossession (0.91 vs. 0.87), largely due to the similarity between the two classes; the difference in absolute values is easily explained by the higher frequency of BallPossession events.

4.3 Parameters Evolution

The distribution of the parameter values at different iterations provides additional insight on the role of each parameter and the effectiveness of each rule. Two competing factors are responsible for the convergence towards specific parameter values: lack of diversity in the population, leading to premature convergence, and the existence of a narrow range of optimal values for a given parameter. We ruled out the first factor by repeating the experiment: we assume that parameters that converge to a stable value across multiple runs are more critical to the overall performance, especially if they are associated to high detection performance.

Let us consider for instance the parameters for the KickingTheBall rule, represented in Fig. 4. The window size and distance threshold both converge to a very narrow range, suggesting that a strong local minimum was found. On the other hand, the threshold on the ball speed appears less critical.

Other parameters tend to behave in a similar way, although there are exceptions. Generally speaking, the system is very sensitive to the distance thresholds, and in fact they converge to very narrow ranges for all events except BallDeflection (results are not reported for brevity). For most events, the window size

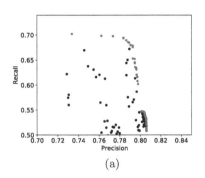

	Metrics	KtB	BallP	Tackle	BallD	Avg
KtB	Precision	0,96	0,96	0,96	0,97	0,96
	Recall	0,92	0,87	0,91	0,86	0,93
	Fscore	0,94	0,91	0,93	0,91	0,94
BallP	Precision	0,99	0,99	0,99	0,99	0,99
	Recall	0,88	0,91	0,87	0,86	0,88
	Fscore	0,93	0,95	0,93	0,92	0,93
Tackle	Precision	0,95	0,97	0,87	0,96	0,94
	Recall	0,6	0,42	0,65	0,47	0,61
	Fscore	0,73	0,59	0,74	0,63	0,74
BallD	Precision	0,28	0,28	0,26	0,26	0,27
	Recall	0,37	0,36	0,39	0,39	0,35
	Fscore	0,32	0,31	0,31	0,31	0,31

(a)   (b)

Fig. 3. Visualization of the Pareto front after 50 generations (a) and performance of the four best solutions generated (b). In (a) each dot represents a possible solution, and those belonging to the Pareto front are highlighted in red. In (b), each column represents the solution which maximize the F-score with respect to a specific event: KickingTheBall (KtB), BallPossession (BallP), Tackle and BallDeflection (BallD). For each event (row), the average performance is reported in the last column. (Color figure online)

has a larger variance then KickingTheBall and, in general, the rules seem quite robust with respect to the choice of this parameter.

The existence of an optimal parameter value is not necessarily associated to a high detection performance: for instance, the distribution of the acceleration threshold for the BallDeflection has a very low standard deviation and very high mean (not shown), as the change of direction usually causes an abrupt acceleration. At the same time, acceleration alone is probably not sufficient to recognize the event. Finally, the order in which the rules are processed does not seem to play a fundamental role.

4.4   Overall Performance

The performance for complex events (precision and recall) is reported in Fig. 5. In eight out of 11 cases, the system was able to reach an F-score between 0.8 and 1. Sequences of events, such as passes that result in a goal, can be detected effectively. However, performance suffers when the detection of the atomic events is not accurate, e.g., for Tackle and SavedShot, which depend on the atomic events Tackle and BallDeflection, respectively.

Comparison with previous literature is difficult due to differences in the datasets, experimental settings, and types of events. Few previous works were based on positional data, extracted either from wearable trackers or using cameras covering the entire field [10,14,15]. In the latter case, the accuracy of the positional data may further vary, depending on whether the ball and players are manually identified [14] or detected by a multi-object detector and tracker [10].

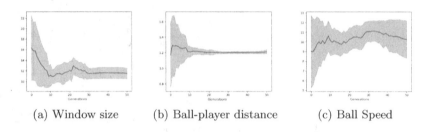

(a) Window size   (b) Ball-player distance   (c) Ball Speed

Fig. 4. Distribution (mean and standard deviation) of each parameter of the rule KickingTheBall calculated over the entire population at each iteration.

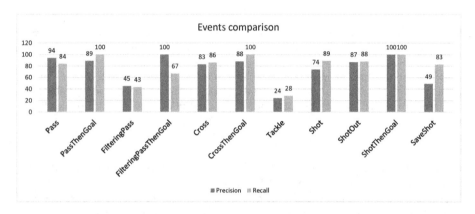

Fig. 5. Precision and Recall for each complex event

Despite these limitations, in Table 2 we attempt a comparison for two events: pass (complex event) and kicking the ball (atomic event). For both events, our results are comparable or better than previous literature, confirming that the proposed events can be successfully detected using (i) positional data (as in [14,15]) and (ii) temporal logic (as in [7]). It should be noticed that the SoccER dataset is much larger than those used in competing approaches, including 1,203 passes and 1,728 kicking the ball events: datasets included in Table 2 range between 14 and 134 events).

5   Discussion and Conclusions

Event recognition in soccer is a challenging task due to the complexity of the game, the number of players and the subtle differences among different actions. In this work, we introduce the SoccER dataset, which is generated by an automatic system built upon the open source Gameplay Football engine. With this contribution, we strive to alleviate the lack of large scale datasets for training and validating event recognition systems. We modified the Gameplay Football engine to log positional data, as could be generated by a fixed multi-camera

Table 2. Comparison between state of the art and proposed approach.

Solution	Input	Method	Precision	Recall	F-score
Kicking the ball					
Richly (2017) [14]	Positional data	Feature extraction + neural networks	95%	92%	93%
Khan (2018) [7]	Broadcast video	Object detection + temporal logic	–	92%	89%
Ours	Positional data	Temporal logic	96%	93%	94%
Pass					
Khan (2018) [7]	Broadcast video	Object detection + temporal logic	94%	84%	89%
Richly (2016) [14]	Positional data	Feature extraction + SVM	42.6%	64.7%	51%
Lee (2017) [10]	Fixed camera, Entire pitch	Action recognition + finite state machine	–	60%	–
Ours	Positional data	Temporal logic	96%	93%	94%

setup covering the whole field. Compared to the use of broadcast footage, we are thus able to consider the position of all players at once and model sequences of complex and related events that occur across the entire field. In the future, the game engine could be further extended to generate data on-the-fly, e.g., for the training of deep neural networks.

A second contribution is the design and validation of ITLs for soccer event recognition. ITLs provide a compact and flexible representation for events, exploiting readily available domain knowledge, given that sports are governed by a well-defined set of rules. The capability of reasoning about events is key to detect with high accuracy complex chains of events, such as "passes that resulted in a scored goal", bypassing the need for extensive training and data collection. Relationships between events are also easy encoded.

Spatio-temporal positional data in the SoccER dataset may be more accurate than those extracted from real video streams, as explained in Sect. 3.3. Previous works reported a tracking accuracy of about 90% for the players and 70% for the ball in a multi-camera setup [10]. It is possible to accurately and fairly compare different event detection techniques using synthetic data. Nonetheless, investigating the performance on real video streams, in the presence of noise, will require further investigation.

In conclusion, we have shown that ITLs are capable of accurately detecting most events from positional data extracted from untrimmed soccer video streams. Future work will exploit the SoccER dataset for comparing other event detection techniques, for instance based on machine learning [6].

References

1. Alcalá, R., Gacto, M.J., Herrera, F., Alcalá-Fdez, J.: A multi-objective genetic algorithm for tuning and rule selection to obtain accurate and compact linguistic fuzzy rule-based systems. Int. J. Uncertain. Fuzziness Knowl.-Based Syst. **15**(05), 539–557 (2007)
2. Anicic, D., Fodor, P., Stuhmer, R., Stojanovic, N.: Event-driven approach for logic-based complex event processing. In: 2009 International Conference on Computational Science and Engineering, vol. 1, pp. 56–63. IEEE (2009)
3. Cannavó, A., Calandra, D., Basilicó, G., Lamberti, F.: Automatic recognition of sport events from spatio-temporal data: an application for virtual reality-based training in basketball. In: 14th International Conference on Computer Graphics Theory and Applications, GRAPP 2019, pp. 310–316. SCITEPRESS (2019)
4. D. Anicic, P. Fodor, R.S.: Etalis Home. http://code.google.com/p/etalis
5. Gaidon, A., Harchaoui, Z., Schmid, C.: Actom sequence models for efficient action detection. In: Proceedings of the IEEE Conference on Computer Vision and Pattern Recognition, pp. 3201–3208. IEEE (2011)
6. Giancola, S., Amine, M., Dghaily, T., Ghanem, B.: SoccerNet: a scalable dataset for action spotting in soccer videos. In: Proceedings of the IEEE Conference on Computer Vision and Pattern Recognition Workshops, pp. 1711–1721 (2018)
7. Khan, A., Lazzerini, B., Calabrese, G., Serafini, L.: Soccer event detection. In: 4th International Conference on Image Processing and Pattern Recognition, IPPR 2018, pp. 119–129. AIRCC Publishing Corporation (2018)
8. Konur, S.: Real-time and probabilistic temporal logics: an overview. Computing Research Repository - CoRR, May 2010
9. Kurach, K., et al.: Google research football: a novel reinforcement learning environment. CoRR (2019)
10. Lee, J., Nam, D., Moon, S., Lee, J., Yoo, W.: Soccer event recognition technique based on pattern matching. In: 2017 Federated Conference on Computer Science and Information Systems (FedCSIS), pp. 643–646, September 2017
11. Morra, L., Coccia, N., Cerquitelli, T.: Optimization of computer aided detection systems: an evolutionary approach. Expert Syst. Appl. **100**, 145–156 (2018)
12. Pettersen, S.A., et al.: Soccer video and player position dataset. In: Proceedings of the 5th ACM Multimedia Systems Conference, MMSys 2014, pp. 18–23. Association for Computing Machinery, New York (2014)
13. Rematas, K., Kemelmacher-Shlizerman, I., Curless, B., Seitz, S.: Soccer on your tabletop. In: Proceedings of the IEEE Conference on Computer Vision and Pattern Recognition, pp. 4738–4747 (2018)
14. Richly, K., Bothe, M., Rohloff, T., Schwarz, C.: Recognizing compound events in spatio-temporal football data. In: International Conference on Internet of Things and Big Data, vol. 2, pp. 27–35. SCITEPRESS (2016)
15. Richly, K., Moritz, F., Schwarz, C.: Utilizing artificial neural networks to detect compound events in spatio-temporal soccer data, August 2017
16. Schuiling, B.K.: Gameplay Football. https://github.com/BazkieBumpercar/GameplayFootball
17. Shih, H.C.: A survey of content-aware video analysis for sports. IEEE Trans. Circuits Syst. Video Technol. **28**(5), 1212–1231 (2017)

18. Tovinkere, V., Qian, R.J.: Detecting semantic events in soccer games: towards a complete solution. In: IEEE International Conference on Multimedia and Expo, ICME 2001, pp. 833–836, August 2001
19. Zitzler, E., Laumanns, M., Thiele, L.: SPEA2: improving the strength Pareto evolutionary algorithm for multiobjective optimization. In: Proceedings of the EURO-GEN 2001 Conference, Athens, Greece (2001)

Video Analysis

RN-VID: A Feature Fusion Architecture for Video Object Detection

Hughes Perreault[1]($\boxtimes$), Maguelonne Heritier[2], Pierre Gravel[2],
Guillaume-Alexandre Bilodeau[1], and Nicolas Saunier[1]

[1] Polytechnique Montreal, Montreal, Canada
{hughes.perreault,gabilodeau,nicolas.saunier}@polymtl.ca
[2] Genetec, Montreal, Canada
{mheritier,pgravel}@genetec.ca

Abstract. Consecutive frames in a video are highly redundant. Therefore, to perform the task of video object detection, executing single frame
detectors on every frame without reusing any information is quite waste-
ful. It is with this idea in mind that we propose RN-VID (standing for
RetinaNet-VIDeo), a novel approach to video object detection. Our contributions are twofold. First, we propose a new architecture that allows
the usage of information from nearby frames to enhance feature maps.
Second, we propose a novel module to merge feature maps of same
dimensions using re-ordering of channels and 1×1 convolutions. We
then demonstrate that RN-VID achieves better mean average precision
(mAP) than corresponding single frame detectors with little additional
cost during inference.

Keywords: Video object detection · Feature fusion · Road users ·
Traffic scenes

1 Introduction

Convolutional neural network (CNN) approaches have been dominant in the last
few years for solving the task of object detection, and there has been plenty of
research in that field. On the other hand, research on video object detection
has received a lot less attention. To detect objects in videos, some approaches
try to speed up inference by interpolating feature maps [17], while others try to
combine feature maps using optical flow warping [31]. In this work, we present
an end-to-end architecture that learns to combine consecutive frames without
prior knowledge of motion or temporal relations.

Even though research on video object detection has been less popular
than its single frame counterpart, the applications are not lacking. To name
a few: autonomous driving, intelligent traffic systems (ITS), video surveillance,
robotics, aeronautics, etc. In today's world, there is a pressing need to build reliable and fast video object detection systems. The number of possible applications
will only grow over time.

© Springer Nature Switzerland AG 2020
A. Campilho et al. (Eds.): ICIAR 2020, LNCS 12131, pp. 125–138, 2020.
https://doi.org/10.1007/978-3-030-50347-5_12

Using multiple frames to detect the objects on a frame presents clear advantages, if used correctly. It can help solve problems like occlusion, motion blur, compression artifacts and small objects (see in Fig. 1). When occluded, an object might be difficult or nearly impossible to detect and classify. When moving, or when the camera is moving, motion blur can occur in the image making it more challenging to locate and recognize objects because it changes their appearance. In digital videos, compression artifacts can alter the image quality and make some parts of the frame more difficult to analyze. Small objects can be difficult to locate and recognize, and having multiple frames allows us to use motion information (implicitly or explicitly) as a way to help us find them. Implicitly by letting the network learn how to do it, explicitly by feeding the network optical flow or frame differences.

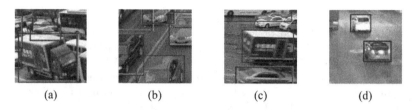

(a)   (b)   (c)   (d)

Fig. 1. Qualitative examples where our model (blue) performs better than the RetinaNet baseline (red). (a) the two cars in the back are heavily occluded by the green truck, (b) the car in the bottom center is being occluded by the frame boundary, (c) the green truck is blurry due to motion blur, (d) as cars become smaller, they become harder to detect, like the white one at the top. (Color figure online)

Our model relies on the assumption that a neural network can learn to make use of the information in successive frames to address these challenges, and this paper demonstrates the advantages of such a model. Frame after frame, the object instances are repeated several times under slightly different angles, occlusion levels and illuminations, in a way that could be thought as similar to data augmentation techniques. We seek to make the network learn what is the best fusion operation for each feature map channel originating from several frames. Our proposed method contains two main contributions: an object detection architecture based on RetinaNet [16] that merges feature maps of consecutive frames, and a fusion module that merges feature maps without any prior knowledge or handcrafted features. Combined together, these two contributions form an end-to-end trainable framework for video object detection and classification.

Since this domain contains a lot of interesting challenges and applications, our evaluation is concentrated on traffic surveillance scenes. The effectiveness of our method is evaluated on two popular object detection datasets composed of video sequences, namely UA-DETRAC [29] and UAVDT [8]. We compare both with the RetinaNet baseline from which we build upon, and state-of-the-art methods from the public benchmarks of those datasets. Results show that our method outperforms both the baseline and the state-of-the art methods.

2   Related Work

2.1   Object Detection

Over the last few years, the research focus for object detection has been on single frame detectors. Deep learning-based methods have been dominant on all benchmarks. The two main categories are two-stage detectors, which use a region proposal network, and single-stage detectors, which do not. R-CNN [10], a two-stage detector, was the first dominant object detector to use a CNN. It used an external handcrafted object proposal method called selective search [26] to produce bounding boxes. It would then extract features for each bounding box using a CNN and would classify those features using SVM. Fast R-CNN [9] builds upon this idea by addressing the bottleneck (passing each bounding box in a CNN). The way it solves this problem is by computing deep features for the whole image only once and cropping these corresponding features for each bounding box proposals. Faster R-CNN [24] improves furthermore by making the architecture completely trainable end-to-end by using a CNN to produce bounding box proposals, and by performing a classification and regression to refine the proposals. R-FCN [5] improves Faster R-CNN by introducing position sensitivity of objects, and by doing so can localize them more precisely. It divides each proposal into a regular grid and classifies each cell separately. In Evolving Boxes [27], the authors build an architecture specialized for fast vehicle detection that is composed of a proposal and an early discard sub-network to generate candidates under different feature representation, as well as a fine-tuning sub-network to refine those boxes.

Single-stage object detectors aim to speed up the inference by removing the object proposal phase. That makes them particularly well suited for real-time applications. The first notable single-stage network to appear was YOLO [21], which divides the image into a regular grid and makes each grid cell predict two bounding boxes. The main weakness of YOLO is thus large numbers of small objects, due to the fact that each grid cell can only predict two objects. A high density of small objects is often found in the traffic surveillance context. Two improved versions of YOLO later came out, YOLOv2 [21] and YOLOv3 [23]. SSD [19] tackles the problem of multi-scale detection by combining feature maps at multiple levels and applying a sliding window with anchor boxes at multiple aspect ratio and scale. RetinaNet [16] works similarly to SSD, and introduces a new loss function, called focal loss that addresses the imbalance between foreground and background examples during training. RetinaNet also uses the state-of-the-art way of tackling multi-scale detection, Feature Pyramid Network (FPN) [15]. FPN builds a feature pyramid at multiple levels with the help of lateral and top-down connections and performs classification and regression on each of these levels.

2.2   Video Object Detection

Here we present an overview of some of the most notable work on video object detection. In Flow Guided Feature Aggregation (FGFA) [31], the authors use optical flow warping in order to integrate feature maps from temporally close frames, which allows them to increase detection accuracy. In MANet [28], the authors use a flow estimation and train two networks to perform pixel-level and instance-level calibration. Some works incorporate the temporal aspect explicitly, for example, STMM [30] uses a recurrent neural network to model the motion and the appearance change of an object of interest over time. Other works focus on increasing processing speed by interpolating feature maps of intermediate frames, for instance in [17] where convolutional Long Short-Term Memories (LSTMs) are used. These previous works use some kind of handcrafted features (temporal or motion), while our work aims to train a fusion module completely end-to-end. Kim *et al.* [2] trained a model by using deformable convolutions that could compute an offset between frames. Doing so allowed them to sample features from close frames to better detect objects in a current frame. This helps them in cases of occlusion or blurriness. In 3D-DETNet [14], to combine several frames, the authors focus on using 3D convolutions on concatenated features maps, generated from consecutive frames, to improve them. MF-SSD [3], standing for Recurrent Multi-frame Single Shot Detector, extends the SSD [19] architecture to merge features of multiple sequential frames with a recurrent convolutional module. Perreault *et al.* [20] trained a network on concatenated image pairs for object detection but could not benefit from pre-trained weights and therefore had to train the network from scratch to outperform the detection on a single frame.

2.3   Optical Flow by CNNs

Works on optical flow by CNNs showed that we can train a network to learn motion from a pair of images. Therefore, similar to our goal, these works put together information from consecutive frames. FlowNet [7] is the most notorious work in this field, being the first to present an end-to-end trainable network for estimating optical flow. In the paper, two models are presented, FlowNetSimple and FlowNetCorr. Both models are trained on an artificial dataset of 3D models of chairs. FlowNetSimple consists of a network that takes as input a pair of concatenated images, while FlowNetCorr used a correlation map between higher level representation of each image of the pair. The authors later released an improved version named FlowNet 2.0 [11] that works by stacking several slightly different versions of FlowNet on top of each other to gradually refine the flow.

3   Proposed Method

Formally, the problem we want to solve is as follows: given a target image, a window of n preceding and n future frames and predetermined types of objects, place a bounding box around and classify every object of the predetermined types in the target image.

To address this problem, we propose two main contributions, a novel architecture for object detection and a fusion module to merge feature maps of the same dimensions. We crafted this architecture to allow the usage of pre-trained weights from ImageNet [6] in order to build over methods from the state-of-the-art.

3.1   Baseline: RetinaNet

We chose to use the RetinaNet [16] as a baseline upon which to build our model, due to its high speed and good performance. To perform detection at various scales, RetinaNet uses an FPN, which is a pyramid of feature maps at multiple scales (see Fig. 2). The pyramid is created with top-down and side connections from the deepest layers in the network, and going back towards the input, thus growing in spatial dimension. A sliding window with boxes created with multiple scales and aspect ratios is then applied at each pyramid level. Afterwards, every box is passed through a classification and a regression sub-network. Finally, non maximal suppression is performed to remove duplicates. The detections with the highest confidence scores are the ones that are kept. As a backbone extractor, we used VGG-16 [18] for the good trade-off between speed and size that it offers. RetinaNet uses the focal loss for classification:

$$FL(p') = -\alpha_t(1 - p')^\gamma log(p') \tag{1}$$

where γ is a factor that diminish the loss contributed by easy examples. α_t is the inverse class frequency, and its purpose is to give more representation to underrepresented classes during training. p' is the probability that the predicted label corresponds to the ground-truth label.

So, if the network predicts with a high probability and is correct, or a low probability and is incorrect, the loss will be marginally affected due to those examples being easy. For the cases where the network is confident (high probability) and incorrect at the same time, the examples will be considered hard and the loss will be affected more.

3.2   Model Architecture

The main idea of the proposed architecture is to be able to compute features for every frame of a sequence only once, and to be able to use these pre-computed features to enhance the features for a target frame t. The fusion module thus comes somewhat late in the network.

Our network uses multiple input streams that eventually merge into a single output stream, as shown in Fig. 2. For computing the feature pyramid for a frame at time t, we will use n preceding frames and n future frames. All the $2n+1$ frames are passed through the VGG-16 network, and we keep the outputs of blocks B3, B4 and B5 for each frame. In RetinaNet, these outputs are used

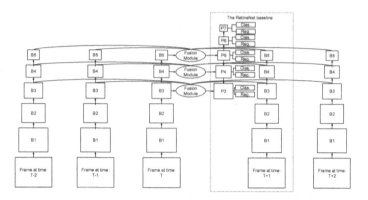

Fig. 2. A representation of our architecture with $n = 2$. Each frame is passed through a pre-trained VGG-16, and the outputs of block 3, block 4 and block 5 are collected for fusion. B1 to B5 are the standard VGG-16 [18] blocks, and P3 to P7 are the feature pyramid levels. In the dotted frame is an overview of our baseline, a RetinaNet [16] with VGG-16 as a backbone.

to create the feature pyramid. We then use our fusion module to merge the corresponding feature maps of each frame (block B3 outputs together, block B4 outputs together, etc.) in order to enhance them, before building the feature pyramid. This allows us to have higher quality features and to better localize objects. We then use the enhanced maps as in the original RetinaNet to build the feature pyramid.

During the training process, we have to use multiple frames for one ground-truth example, thus slowing down the training process. However, for inference on video, the features computed for each frame are used multiple times making the processing time almost identical to the single frame baseline.

3.3   Fusion Module

In order to combine equivalent feature maps of consecutive frames, we designed a lightweight and trainable feature fusion module (see Fig. 3). The inspiration for this module is the various possible way a human would do the task. Let us say you wanted to combine feature map channels of multiple consecutive frames. Maybe you would look for the strongest responses and only keep those, making the merge operation an element-wise maximum. Maybe you would want to average the responses over all the frames. This 'merge operation' might not be the same for all channels. The idea is to have a network learn the best way to merge feature maps for each channel separately, with 1×1 convolutions over the channels.

In our fusion module, we use 1×1 convolutions in order to reduce the dimension of tensors. In the Inception module [25] of the GoogLeNet, the 1×1 convolution is actually used as a way to reduce the dimensions which inspired our work. The inception module allowed them to build a deeper and wider network while staying computationally efficient. In contrast, in our work, we use 1×1 convolutions for learning to merge feature maps.

The module takes as input $2n + 1$ feature maps of dimension $w * h * c$ (for width, height and channels respectively), and outputs a single enhanced feature maps of dimension $w * h * c$. The feature maps that we are combining come from corresponding pre-trained VGG-16 layers, so it is reasonable to think that corresponding channels are responses from corresponding 'filters'. The idea is to take all the corresponding channels from the consecutive frames, and combine them to end up with only one channel, and thus re-build the wanted feature map, as shown in Fig. 3.

Formally, for $2n + 1$ feature maps of dimension $w * h * c$, we extract each c channels one by one and concatenate them, ending up with c tensors of dimension $w * h * (2n+1)$. We then perform a 2D convolution with a 1×1 convolution kernel $(1 * 1 * (2n+1))$ on the c tensors, getting c times $w * h * 1$ as an output. The final step is to concatenate the tensors channel-wise to finally get the $w * h * c$ tensor that we need. The module is entirely learned, so we can interpret this module as the network learning the operation that best combines feature maps, for each channel specifically, without any prior knowledge or handcrafted features.

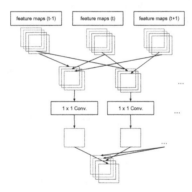

Fig. 3. Our fusion module consists of channel re-ordering, concatenation, 1×1 convolution, and a final concatenation (better seen in color).

4   Experiments

4.1   Datasets

The training process of our method requires consecutive images from videos. We chose two datasets containing sequences of moving road users: UA-DETRAC [29] (fixed camera, 960×540, 70000 images, 4 possible labels, see Fig. 4a) and the Unmanned Aerial Vehicle Benchmark (UAVDT) [8] (mobile camera, 3 possible labels, 80000 images, high density of small objects, see Fig. 4b).

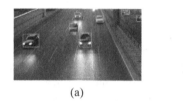 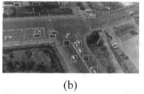

(a)   (b)

Fig. 4. (a) An example frame of UA-DETRAC and its ground-truth annotations. (b) An example frame of UAVDT and its ground-truth annotations.

4.2   Implementations Details

We implemented the proposed model in Keras [4] using TensorFlow [1] as the backend. We used a standard RetinaNet as our baseline, without any bells and whistles or post-processing. We want to keep the models simple in order to properly show the contributions of our architecture and fusion module.

We built a feature pyramid with five different levels, called P3, P4, P5, P6, P7, with the outputs of block 3, 4, 5 of VGG-16. P3 to P5 are the pyramid levels corresponding to block 3 to 5. P6 and P7 are obtained via convolution and down-sampling of P5, and their size is reduced in half at each level: P6 is the half the size of P5, and P7 is the half the size of P6. This is standard for RetinaNet.

For UAVDT and UA-DETRAC, we adapted the scales used for the anchor boxes by reducing them, due to the high number of small objects in the tested datasets. Instead of using the classic $2^0, 2^{(1.0/3.0)}, 2^{(2.0/3.0)}$ scale ratios, we used $2^0, 1/(2^{(1.0/3.0)}), 1/(2^{(2.0/3.0)})$. This modification did not affect the results on UA-DETRAC, but improved them on UAVDT, causing a bigger gap with the reported state-of-the-art results in the paper. Since we use the same scales for our baseline, this has no effect on our conclusions. The focal loss parameter γ is 2 and we used an initial learning rate of 1e−5.

To train both the model and the baseline, we used the adam optimizer [12]. In order to fit the model into memory, we had to freeze the first four convolutional blocks of the VGG-16 model during training, and only retrained the other weights, with a batch size of one. For a fair comparison, we used the same training setting for our baseline. Despite this limitation, we still achieve state-of-the-art results when compared to single frame object detectors. Even though the first four convolutional blocks are frozen, they are still initialized with fine-tuned weights for each dataset. Note that the weights used to initialize the backbone are the same for the baseline and the model.

To select the hyperparameter n of our method (the number of frames used before and after), we used a validation set and tried a few values. $n = 2$ was the value that worked best for us, so that is the value we use for the final results. We show the results of different values of n in an ablation study in Table 3.

4.3 Performance Evaluation

For the two datasets, the test set is predetermined and cannot be used for training or to fix hyperparameters. We split the training data into training and validation by choosing a few whole sequences for validation, and the others for training. We did this to prevent overfitting on the validation data that would likely happen if we would split randomly between all frames. We trained the models until the validation loss started to increase, meaning the model was overfitting.

The performance measure used for evaluation is the mAP, meaning Mean Average Precision. The mAP is the mean AP for every class. The AP is the average precision considering the recall and precision curves; thus, it is the area under the precision-recall curve. The minimum intersection over union (IOU) between the ground-truth and the prediction bounding box, to consider a detection valid, is 0.7 for UA-DETRAC and UAVDT, as defined by the dataset's protocols. The IOU, or the Jaccard index, is the intersection area between two rectangles divided by the union area between them.

4.4 Results

Results on UA-DETRAC. Results on the UA-DETRAC dataset are reported in Table 1. We drew the ROC curves for our model, the baseline and few other state-of-the-art models in Fig. 5a. Our detector outperforms all classic state-of-the-art models evaluated on UA-DETRAC as well as the baseline by a significant margin.

Something interesting to notice is that our model outperforms R-FCN for the categories labeled "hard" and "cloudy", confirming our hypothesis that the features are indeed enhanced for hard cases like occlusion and blur (from motion or from clouds). As a result, it raised the mAP for "overall" above R-FCN's "overall". We have to keep in mind that most VGG-16 layers are frozen during training, and that the final score would probably be much higher if this was not case. Nonetheless, our model convincingly surpasses the baseline in all categories, showing that features are enhanced not only for hard cases, but at all times. We outperform other video object detection for which we found results on UA-DETRAC, that is, 3D-DETNet [14] and RN-D-from-scratch [20]. The other video object detectors mentioned in the related works section did not produce results on this dataset.

Results on UAVDT. The results on UAVDT dataset are reported in Table 2. We drew the ROC curves for our model, the baseline and few other state-of-the-art models in Fig. 5b. Our detector outperforms all classic state-of-the-art models evaluated on UAVDT as well as the baseline by a significant margin. The mAP scores on this dataset are quite low compared to UA-DETRAC due to its very challenging lighting conditions, weather conditions and smaller vehicles. We show that by adapting the scales used for the anchor boxes on each dataset, we can greatly improve results. Also, our model shows results on UAVDT that are

Table 1. mAP reported on the UA-DETRAC test set compared to our baseline as well as classic state-of-the-art detectors. Results for "Ours" and "RN-VGG16" are generated using the evaluation server on the UA-DETRAC website, 3D-DETNet [14] is reported as in their paper, and others are as reported in the results section of the UA-DETRAC website. **Boldface:** best result, *Italic:* baseline.

Model	Overall	Easy	Medium	Hard	Cloudy	Night	Rainy	Sunny
RN-VID (Ours)	**70.57%**	87.50%	75.53%	**58.04%**	**80.69%**	69.56%	56.15%	83.60%
R-FCN [5]	69.87%	**93.32%**	**75.67%**	54.31%	74.38%	**75.09%**	**56.21%**	**84.08%**
RN-VGG16	69.14%	86.82%	73.70%	56.74%	79.88%	66.57%	55.21%	82.09%
EB [27]	67.96%	89.65%	73.12%	53.64%	72.42%	73.93%	53.40%	83.73%
Faster R-CNN [24]	58.45%	82.75%	63.05%	44.25%	66.29%	69.85%	45.16%	62.34%
YOLOv2 [22]	57.72%	83.28%	62.25%	42.44%	57.97%	64.53%	47.84%	69.75%
RN-D [20]	54.69%	80.98%	59.13%	39.23%	59.88%	54.62%	41.11%	77.53%
3D-DETnet [14]	53.30%	66.66%	59.26%	43.22%	63.30%	52.90%	44.27%	71.26%

consistent with UA-DETRAC's results, having an improvement of ~1.2 mAP points against the ~1.4 on UA-DETRAC.

Table 2. mAP reported on the UAVDT test set compared to our baseline as well as classic state-of-the-art detectors. Results for "Ours" and "RN-VGG16" are generated using the official Matlab toolbox provided by the authors, others are reported as in their paper. **Boldface:** best result, *Italic:* baseline.

Model	Overall
RN-VID (Ours)	**39.43%**
RN-VGG16	38.26%
R-FCN [5]	34.35%
SSD [19]	33.62%
Faster-RCNN [24]	22.32%
RON [13]	21.59%

5   Discussion

To explain the gains we get from our model, we now discuss a few reasons why aggregating features from adjacent frames is beneficial.

5.1   Analysis

Small Objects: The smaller the object, the harder it will be to detect and classify, as a general rule. There is a large number of small objects in the evaluated datasets, as there is in traffic surveillance scenes in general. Having multiple

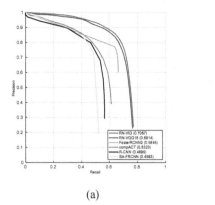 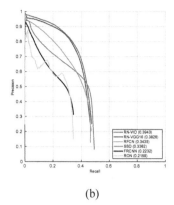

(a)   (b)

Fig. 5. Precision-Recall curves on UA-DETRAC [29] (a) and UAVDT [8] (b) for RN-VID (Ours), RN-VGG16 (Baseline) and a few other state-of-the-art methods.

frames allows RN-VID to see the object from slightly different angles and lighting conditions, and a trained network can combine these frames to obtain richer features.

Blur: Blur is omnipresent in traffic surveillance datasets due to road users' constant motion (motion blur), and weather/lighting conditions. A blurred object can be harder to classify and detect. Since its appearance is changed, the network could recognize it as none of the predetermined labels, and not considering it as a relevant object. Having multiple slightly different instances of theses objects allows the network to refine the features and output finer features to the classification sub-network, finer than each single frame separately. It could also simply choose the best frame is that seems useful. A convincing example of our model performing better in blurry conditions is the "Cloudy" category in which it got the best result.

Occlusion: Occlusion from other road users or from various road structures is very frequent in traffic surveillance scenes. Having access to adjacent frames gives our model a strong advantage against temporary occlusions, allowing it to select features from less occluded previous or future frames, making the detections more temporally stable. Figure 1 shows a qualitative example of our model performing better than the baseline in a case of occlusion.

5.2   Ablation Study

To properly assess the contribution of each part of our model, we performed an ablation study. We tried to isolate, as best as we could, our two contributions and looked at the impact of each of them. We justify the choice of using five consecutive frames with an experiment in which we varied this parameter on the UAVDT dataset. We tried several combinations and reported results in Table 3. We can see than using five frames is better than using three, and that using

three is better than using only one. We did not test with seven frames due to
GPU memory issues.

To remove the contribution of the fusion module, we trained a model where
instead of merging the feature maps, we would simply concatenate them and
continue to build the feature pyramid as usual, by adjusting the kernel size of
the convolutions to adapt to the new input size. Doing this actually degrades
the performance a lot as shown by the RN-VID-NO-FUSION model in Table 3.
This is easily understandable by the fact that combining feature maps like this
is noisy, and we might need much more data and parameters in order to make
this work. We can conclude from this that the fusion module is an essential part
of our model.

Table 3. mAP reported on the UAVDT test set for different variations of our model
to conduct an ablation study. Results are generated using the official Matlab toolbox
provided by the authors. Number of frames is the number of frames used for each
detection.

Model	Num. frames	Overall
RN-VID (Ours)	5	**39.43%**
RN-VID	3	39.05%
RN-VGG16 (Baseline)	1	38.26%
RN-VID-NO-FUSION	5	26.95%

5.3   Limitations of Our Model

A limitation of our model is for border situations, the first and last frames of
a sequence where we cannot use our architecture to its full potential. However,
this is not a problem since we can do a padding by repeating the first and last
frame the number of times needed to without a real loss of performance. Also, it
takes more memory to train the model then its single frame counterpart, due to
the fact that we need multiple frames to train one single ground-truth example.

6   Conclusion

A novel approach for video object detection named RN-VID was introduced,
composed of an object detection architecture and a fusion module for merging
feature maps. This model was trained and evaluated on two different traffic
surveillance datasets, and compared with a baseline RetinaNet model and several
classic state-of-the-art object detectors. We show that by using adjacent frames,
we can increase mAP by a significant margin by addressing challenges in the
traffic surveillance domain like occlusion, motion and general blur, small objects
and difficult weather conditions.

Acknowledgments. We acknowledge the support of the Natural Sciences and Engineering Research Council of Canada (NSERC), [RDCPJ 508883 - 17], and the support of Genetec. The authors would like to thank Paule Brodeur for insightful discussions.

References

1. Abadi, M., et al.: TensorFlow: large-scale machine learning on heterogeneous systems (2015). http://tensorflow.org/
2. Bertasius, G., Torresani, L., Shi, J.: Object detection in video with spatiotemporal sampling networks. In: Ferrari, V., Hebert, M., Sminchisescu, C., Weiss, Y. (eds.) ECCV 2018. LNCS, vol. 11216, pp. 342–357. Springer, Cham (2018). https://doi.org/10.1007/978-3-030-01258-8_21
3. Broad, A., Jones, M., Lee, T.Y.: Recurrent multi-frame single shot detector for video object detection. In: BMVC, p. 94 (2018)
4. Chollet, F., et al.: Keras (2015). https://keras.io
5. Dai, J., Li, Y., He, K., Sun, J.: R-FCN: object detection via region-based fully convolutional networks. In: Advances in Neural Information Processing Systems 29, pp. 379–387. Curran Associates, Inc. (2016)
6. Deng, J., Dong, W., Socher, R., Li, L.J., Li, K., Fei-Fei, L.: ImageNet: a large-scale hierarchical image database. In: CVPR 2009 (2009)
7. Dosovitskiy, A., et al.: FlowNet: learning optical flow with convolutional networks. In: The IEEE International Conference on Computer Vision (ICCV) (2015)
8. Du, D., et al.: The unmanned aerial vehicle benchmark: object detection and tracking. In: Ferrari, V., Hebert, M., Sminchisescu, C., Weiss, Y. (eds.) ECCV 2018. LNCS, vol. 11214, pp. 375–391. Springer, Cham (2018). https://doi.org/10.1007/978-3-030-01249-6_23
9. Girshick, R.: Fast R-CNN. In: The IEEE International Conference on Computer Vision (ICCV) (2015)
10. Girshick, R., Donahue, J., Darrell, T., Malik, J.: Rich feature hierarchies for accurate object detection and semantic segmentation. In: The IEEE Conference on Computer Vision and Pattern Recognition (CVPR) (2014)
11. Ilg, E., Mayer, N., Saikia, T., Keuper, M., Dosovitskiy, A., Brox, T.: FlowNet 2.0: evolution of optical flow estimation with deep networks. In: The IEEE Conference on Computer Vision and Pattern Recognition (CVPR) (2017)
12. Kingma, D.P., Ba, J.: Adam: a method for stochastic optimization. arXiv preprint arXiv:1412.6980 (2014)
13. Kong, T., Sun, F., Yao, A., Liu, H., Lu, M., Chen, Y.: RON: reverse connection with objectness prior networks for object detection. In: IEEE Conference on Computer Vision and Pattern Recognition, vol. 1, p. 2 (2017)
14. Li, S., Chen, F.: 3D-DETNet: a single stage video-based vehicle detector. In: Third International Workshop on Pattern Recognition, vol. 10828, p. 108280A. International Society for Optics and Photonics (2018)
15. Lin, T.Y., Dollar, P., Girshick, R., He, K., Hariharan, B., Belongie, S.: Feature pyramid networks for object detection. In: The IEEE Conference on Computer Vision and Pattern Recognition (CVPR) (2017)
16. Lin, T.Y., Goyal, P., Girshick, R., He, K., Dollár, P.: Focal loss for dense object detection. IEEE Trans. Pattern Anal. Mach. Intell. (2018)
17. Liu, M., Zhu, M.: Mobile video object detection with temporally-aware feature maps. In: The IEEE Conference on Computer Vision and Pattern Recognition (CVPR) (2018)

18. Liu, S., Deng, W.: Very deep convolutional neural network based image classification using small training sample size. In: 2015 3rd IAPR Asian Conference on Pattern Recognition (ACPR), pp. 730–734 (2015). https://doi.org/10.1109/ACPR.2015.7486599

19. Liu, W., et al.: SSD: single shot multibox detector. In: Leibe, B., Matas, J., Sebe, N., Welling, M. (eds.) ECCV 2016. LNCS, vol. 9905, pp. 21–37. Springer, Cham (2016). https://doi.org/10.1007/978-3-319-46448-0_2

20. Perreault, H., Bilodeau, G.A., Saunier, N., Gravel, P.: Road user detection in videos. arXiv preprint arXiv:1903.12049 (2019)

21. Redmon, J., Divvala, S., Girshick, R., Farhadi, A.: You only look once: unified, real-time object detection. In: Proceedings of the IEEE Conference on Computer Vision and Pattern Recognition, pp. 779–788 (2016)

22. Redmon, J., Farhadi, A.: YOLO9000: better, faster, stronger. In: The IEEE Conference on Computer Vision and Pattern Recognition (CVPR) (2017)

23. Redmon, J., Farhadi, A.: YOLOv3: an incremental improvement. arXiv preprint arXiv:1804.02767 (2018)

24. Ren, S., He, K., Girshick, R., Sun, J.: Faster R-CNN: towards real-time object detection with region proposal networks. In: Advances in Neural Information Processing Systems, pp. 91–99 (2015)

25. Szegedy, C., et al.: Going deeper with convolutions. In: Proceedings of the IEEE Conference on Computer Vision and Pattern Recognition, pp. 1–9 (2015)

26. Uijlings, J.R., Van De Sande, K.E., Gevers, T., Smeulders, A.W.: Selective search for object recognition. Int. J. Comput. Vis. **104**(2), 154–171 (2013). https://doi.org/10.1007/s11263-013-0620-5

27. Wang, L., Lu, Y., Wang, H., Zheng, Y., Ye, H., Xue, X.: Evolving boxes for fast vehicle detection. In: 2017 IEEE International Conference on Multimedia and Expo (ICME), pp. 1135–1140. IEEE (2017)

28. Wang, S., Zhou, Y., Yan, J., Deng, Z.: Fully motion-aware network for video object detection. In: Ferrari, V., Hebert, M., Sminchisescu, C., Weiss, Y. (eds.) ECCV 2018. LNCS, vol. 11217, pp. 557–573. Springer, Cham (2018). https://doi.org/10.1007/978-3-030-01261-8_33

29. Wen, L., et al.: UA-DETRAC: a new benchmark and protocol for multi-object detection and tracking. arXiv CoRR abs/1511.04136 (2015)

30. Xiao, F., Lee, Y.J.: Video object detection with an aligned spatial-temporal memory. In: Ferrari, V., Hebert, M., Sminchisescu, C., Weiss, Y. (eds.) ECCV 2018. LNCS, vol. 11212, pp. 494–510. Springer, Cham (2018). https://doi.org/10.1007/978-3-030-01237-3_30

31. Zhu, X., Wang, Y., Dai, J., Yuan, L., Wei, Y.: Flow-guided feature aggregation for video object detection. In: Proceedings of the IEEE International Conference on Computer Vision, pp. 408–417 (2017)

Color Inference from Semantic Labeling
for Person Search in Videos

Jules Simon[1(✉)], Guillaume-Alexandre Bilodeau[1(✉)], David Steele[2],
and Harshad Mahadik[2]

[1] LITIV Lab., Polytechnique Montréal, Montréal, QC H3T 1J4, Canada
{jules.simon,gabilodeau}@polymtl.ca
[2] Arcturus Networks, Etobicoke, ON M9C 1A3, Canada
{dsteele,harshad}@arcturusnetworks.ca

Abstract. We propose an explainable model for classifying the color
of pixels in images. We propose a method based on binary search trees
and a large peer-labeled color name dataset, allowing us to synthesize
the average human perception of colors. We test our method on the
application of Person Search. In this context, persons are described from
their semantic parts, such as *hat, shirt, ...* and person search consists
in looking for people based on these descriptions. We label segments
of pedestrians with their associated colors and evaluate our solution on
datasets such as PCN and Colorful-Fashion. We show a precision as high
as 83% as well as the model ability to generalize to multiple domains
with no retraining.

Keywords: Color classification · Person search · Semantic color
labeling

1 Introduction

Security matters are prevalent today, and so does the use of video surveillance.
Therefore, efforts are being made to develop automatic methods for labeling
videos and searching inside them for people or events. Given bounding boxes of
people in images, we aim to generate labels that can be used for person search
in videos using colors and semantic parts. Our goal is to answer queries such as:
Find in these videos a person with a red shirt and blue pants. The answer to such
query can then be used to obtain or filter candidates for person re-identification.

Within our context of person search, colors are an efficient way of describing
people. As the images produced by cameras used in surveillance often suffer from
defects such as low resolution, dirty lenses, haze and video compression artifacts,
we can use colors as a discriminative feature to easily filter out true negatives
from a query.

Thus, we are interested in classifying colors accurately in images. This task
is not often the main focus of computer vision works and for instance, most
datasets, such as Colorful-Fashion Parsing [14], DukeMTMC-attribute [26] and

© Springer Nature Switzerland AG 2020
A. Campilho et al. (Eds.): ICIAR 2020, LNCS 12131, pp. 139–151, 2020.
https://doi.org/10.1007/978-3-030-50347-5_13

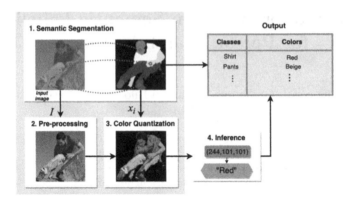

Fig. 1. Overview of the main steps of our method: Segmentation, color pre-processing, quantization and classification.

Market-1501-attribute [25] only provide 8 to 13 discrete color attributes in their labels. A richer color model would enable the generation of more organic and convincing textual descriptions of images, and fit these descriptions closer to human perception, making natural language queries more streamlined for person search.

Since color labels are meant to be used by humans, we ask ourselves the following question: *How can we generate meaningful, non-ambiguous semantic color labels for describing persons?* Trying to answer this question calls for the following requirements: 1) we need a model that reflects the human visual system, 2) we need an appropriate way of sampling colors in images in order to associate them to semantic classes, and 3) we have to make sure that good classification results translate well into the real-world application of person search.

We aim to satisfy these requirements with the following contribution: we introduce a new method for generating semantic labels of persons in videos using colors. It uses semantic segmentation [17] in order to associate semantic meaning to pixels in the images. Images are pre-processed and the colors of each semantic part are quantized in order to extract their dominant color. Finally, color classification is performed on these dominant colors. Figure 1 gives an overview of our method.

2   Background and Related Work

2.1   Color Perception

To work on color label inference, we first try to understand how the brain perceives colors and how to emulate this perception with a computer. According to [23] our visual system's perception of colors is intrinsically non-uniform and thus calls for more flexible models. In addition to this property of our vision, as highlighted by [7], the perceived color of an object varies with the properties of its materials and its environment. To describe formally this phenomenon, a given pixel in an image can be described as the product of its illuminance (the quantity of light hitting a surface) and its reflectance (the quantity of light reflected of a surface). By separating the illuminance and reflectance information, our visual system perceives colors consistently regardless of the illumination through a mechanism called "color constancy".

In order to process an image such that its colors are represented as our visual system would see them, and bridge the gap between the colors we see and the ones we experience, the popular algorithm Retinex [12] can be used. A lightness-color constancy algorithm such as Retinex must achieve three tasks [10]: 1) compress the dynamic range of the scene, 2) make colors independent of the illumination of the scene and 3) keep the color and lightness rendition. Improvements over the original Retinex algorithm allow for more general use cases, for example, the Automated Multiscale Retinex with Color Restoration [21] is an image independent Retinex algorithm that solves the issue of graying out (images becoming desaturated after Retinex).

Color constancy is still an ongoing problem to solve, and there are some more recent works on the subject [3,6] using advances in machine learning. However only [3] is trained to handle lightness constancy, and [6] achieves only color constancy, i.e. the second requirement of lightness-color constancy.

2.2 Color Inference

There are already existing methods for color inference, working mostly on a one-to-one association of color to label. There are a number of color names lookup tables built by committees available for use such as the ISCC–NBS System of Color Designation [11] or the X11 color names [1]. These tables however feature a low number of unique names, for instance the X11 color table is 783 lines long, and moreover while some of these tables are bigger (the ISCC-NBS table features 42,000 points) they do not contain descriptive names. In addition, color lookup tables only feature one RGB triplet per color name and therefore require interpolation to cover the whole spectrum. Considering that the human perception of color is not linear, this interpolation is non-trivial to define. Finally, color tables do not capture the notion of clusters and ambiguity in perception: color names do not have variances, cluster shapes, cluster sizes and cannot overlap.

This observation comes from Mojsilovic [18] when proposing a computational model for color naming. Starting from the ISCC-NBS [11] dictionary, this model uses three color naming experiments in order to define a more accurate color vocabulary. The model proposed in [18] works with 267 named color points spread around the color spectrum and allows the generation of color names for any input color. However, these names follow a strict pattern and are only abstract names with modifiers such as *light, vivid, etc.* Thus, while this work is related to our problem, it does not handle semantics and ambiguity in color names (i.e. when several names could be applied to an input color).

PCN-CNN [9] is a more recent and comprehensive method for pedestrian color naming, based on the VGG convolutional neural network, and it is able to achieve state of the art performance for pixel-level color naming. However, like many CNN, it has to be trained on domain-specific datasets and therefore is not a general solution for color naming.

3   Problem Statement

Person search requires a textual description of a person. Therefore, for a given image of a person I, we want to generate k color name labels l_i for each of the k semantic classes present in the image. These classes can be for instance *shirt, shoes, scarf, etc*, and the color labels should be meaningful and reflect the many different possibilities for naming colors based on perception.

4   Method

We focus our work on a data-driven model for color naming. Our algorithm has four main steps as highlighted in Fig. 1, and we detail them in the following sections. In a first step, we perform semantic segmentation on a pedestrian image to extract binary masks corresponding to different body parts. In a second step, we process the image to enhance its colors, then we quantize them within each semantic mask. Finally, we perform color classification using the semantic binary masks computed in the first step and the image computed in the third step. As an output, we generate for a given image of a pedestrian a table associating semantic classes and colors.

4.1   Semantic Segmentation

Let I be an input image consisting of a crop of a person. As a first step, we compute the semantic segmentation of I for k classes: $M = \phi(I)$, where M is a tensor of k two-dimensional binary masks. They correspond to the semantic parts of the person such as *torso, legs, feet, etc.* from which we can sample colors.

The semantic segmentation and labelling is achieved with a GAN, the MMAN architecture [17], that we selected for its good ability to generalize. We train it on the PPSS dataset [16] as it features images of people in low contrast situations that correspond to a worst case scenario for city video surveillance footage.

As we show in our experiments in Sect. 6.3, the quality of the semantic segmentation part is not critical to our method, and our goal at this step is to obtain a rough localisation of body parts.

4.2   Image Pre-processing

In this second step, we process the input images to prepare them for color classification. This is required as the images captured from city cameras often suffer from haze (pollution) and low contrast, as well as low saturation. As the scene illumination is simple for street scenes in daylight (there is only one illuminant), we do not find the need for complex methods such as neural networks.

Therefore, we kept two approaches for pre-processing:

- A domain specific approach, in which we search for the optimal contrast, brightness and saturation enhancements to apply to the input images using the validation set.
- A general approach, using the Multi-Scale Retinex with Chromacity Preservations (MSRCP) algorithm. We use the automatic method MSRCP [21] as it performs better than MSRCR [20] under even and white illumination [21], which is often the case in outdoor scenes.

4.3   Color Quantization

We erode each of the binary semantic masks in order to avoid border effects as the segmentation is less precise around the borders, and can introduce noise from the background or other body parts. Then, for each mask, we quantize the colors of the underlying pixels of the pre-processed image using K-means clustering in RGB space with a small K, fixed to 5 in this paper. We then keep the biggest cluster and use its centre as the RGB color triplet to classify.

4.4   Color Classification

To classify the colors, we use the results of the XKCD Color Survey that was opened in 2010 by the cartoonist Randall Munroe [19]. In this survey, volunteer Internet users were shown patches of plain colors on their web browser, and for each color they were tasked with filling a free-form text box with the name they would choose for the color. In total 3,083,876 unique RGB tuples were assigned 183,401 unique textual color names, with a total of 3.4 million entries, that are available online.

The data extracted from this survey addresses some of the shortcomings of the aforementioned color lookup tables. For instance, it contains both abstract and descriptive labels : the abstract names allow us to capture the common perception of the survey participants while the descriptive ones allow us to capture intrinsic semantic knowledge of the objects used for naming. For instance, labels *apple, peach, sky, etc.* each have distinct color shades associated to them. Thus, this dataset should be able to capture the variability of naming colors. Moreover, due to its crowd-sourced nature, this dataset uses a varied vocabulary and allows to generate more realistic labels. For the same reason, this survey was filled using different screen technologies and thus is closer to the variance in color perception that would happen in real-world scenarios. However, there is a noteworthy problem introduced by the free-form text boxes used for the survey, which is the introduction of noise in the labels as participants can input any answers, including irrelevant ones. Thus we need to remove these outliers.

Using the results of the survey, we classify the RGB triplets using a binary decision tree. Our choice of a decision tree is motivated by the fact that it does not use distances but instead binary comparisons, making it efficient regardless of the color spaces. Moreover, decision trees can be used for multi-label classification and thus allow us to deal better with ambiguity by outputing several possible color names for a given pixel value. Finally, a tree model has the advantage of being explainable and easy to visualize, even more so with color values as decision variables, and is fast at inference time.

Decision Tree Training. During the first filtering step in line 1 of Algorithm 1, we sort the color names dataset by label occurrences and only keep the most common color names, such that only a given portion τ of the dataset is represented. This ratio τ allows us to filter out names that are too unique to be representative. We find that in our situation, because the labels were generated using a free-form survey, $\tau = 0.65$ is a good choice as this corresponds to labels having more than 2000 occurrences and therefore representative of a consensus. This gives a dataset of 140 unique labels and 2,263,631 samples. This data is available to download[1].

Algorithm 1. Building the decision tree

Require: D color names dataset
Require: L the set of colors labels on which to train

Sort D by occurences
1: $D' \leftarrow$ MostFrequentLabels(D, τ)
2: $D'' \leftarrow$ RemoveOutliers(D')
3: $D''' \leftarrow$ Resample(D'')
4: $D^* \leftarrow \{d \| d_{label} \in L \ \forall \ d \in D'''\}$
5: $T \leftarrow$ DecisionTree(D^*)

Following this step (at line 2), we perform class-wise outliers removal using K-Nearest Neighbors [22]. This step allows us to remove any data point that has less than K neighbors and is used to make the convex hull of each color cluster smoother, which is useful for the following re-sampling step as well as to reduce ambiguity between small clusters of colors.

In the next step (line 3), re-sampling is done using Synthetic Minority Oversampling Technique (SMOTE [8]). This oversampling algorithm works by generating new samples within the convex hull of the minority classes. This allows us to balance the dataset as some colors are underreesented.

In the end we obtain D^* (line 4), the final dataset from which we can train the tree T (at line 5) with the subset of labels L. We train it on a subset of prototype color names, such as the 11 colors *(black, white, red, green, yellow, blue, brown, pink, orange, purple, and gray)* as defined by Berlin and Kay [5]. This choice can also be made according to the domain of the application at hand.

---

[1] The data is available at https://github.com/Smoltbob/XKCDColors-Dataset.

Pooling Images in Videos. We can make use of the additional information offered in a video by sampling using several frames. For a given pedestrian, sampling on several frames allows us to reduce the uncertainty and be more robust to noisy events that alter color rendition such as walking in the shade.

If several images are available for a given person, we can use them for the classification using one of three following pooling methods: 1) randomly using one image per person, 2) averaging the colors per mask for all of the images of each person or 3) sorting the colors by saturation and classifying on the most saturated images.

5   Experiments

In order to evaluate performance for person search, we use the Region Annotation Score (RAS) [9]. This score is a region-wise metric, computed over the dataset using region labels. It is equivalent to the Precision for regions. We compute it using

$$RAS = \frac{TP}{TP + FP}$$

where TP, FP are the number True and False positives and FN are the number of False negatives. A true positive corresponds in practice to a successful retrieval of an attribute for a given query. We use this metric as it allows us to compare our methods to the benchmark of [16]. However, we also include a study of the recall in Sect. 6.3. We performed our experiments using MSRCP pre-processing on the images. For training, we used SMOTE resampling and outlier removal. Finally, we used average pooling when computing the final classification result.

5.1   Datasets

The first dataset used is the Pedestrian Color Naming (PCN) Dataset [9]. It is a color-balanced split of the Market-1501 dataset [25]. Market-1501 is made for person re-identification and features 1501 identities captured in 32,668 bounding boxes. The images in this dataset are similar to a real world situation, with low quality street scenes.

PCN is augmented by pixel-level color annotation maps, rather than image-level as in Market-1501-Attribute. We used it to compare our method with the other methods that were tested in [9] on this dataset. We followed the same procedure as described in the original paper: we use the dataset ground truth, and we measure the RAS for color prediction.

We also used the Colorful-Fashion dataset [14], that focuses on women fashion and provides clothes description for each of its 2682 images, semantic segmentation masks and a color for each class. The dataset is generated automatically with SLIC superpixel segmentation [2]. With this dataset, we used the provided masks instead of computing new ones, as they have more granular classes. As this dataset is vivid and well lit, we did not apply any pre-processing on it and used the images as is.

Table 1. Classifier RAS study. Boldface indicates best results, *italic* second best.

Method	PCN	Colorful-Fashion
PLSA [24]	68.4	71.4
PFS [4]	68.5	60.5
SVM [14]	62.2	45.4
DCLP [15]	62.0	54.8
PCN-CNN [9]	**80.8**	*81.9*
Ours	75.0	76.1
Ours, retrained	*80.4*	**83.0**

5.2   Results and Discussion

Results are reported in Table 1. For our method, we used two training settings: in a first setting, we used the model trained on XKCD as described in the method section, and in a second setting, we retrained the model on the pixel distributions of the datasets. This is done in order to compare our method with methods such as PCN-CNN [9] or SVM [14], that are trained on specific datasets as well.

We show that with retraining, our model achieves its best performance on both dataset and gives results close to the state of the art, and that without retraining it remains close to the state of the art, losing about 6 to 9 points in precision.

6   Study of the Model

In this part, we look into the limits of our model as well as into ways of optimizing it.

We used the Market-1501-Attributes dataset [13], that is built from the Market-1501 dataset [25]. Market-1501 Attributes [13] is an augmentation of this dataset with 28 hand annotated attributes, such as gender, age, sleeve length, flags for items carried, as well as upper clothes colors and lower clothes colors. Here we used the upper clothes or lower clothes labels, that we matched with the classes of the same name from the PPSS dataset. We selected this dataset in order to test the whole person search pipeline as described in our methodology going from the segmentation to the classification of colors.

Results in this section correspond to the average for 10,000 picture queries over 500 identities from the Market-1501 Attributes dataset [13].

6.1   Evaluation of Pre-processing Approaches

To facilitate the distinction between colors and improve the person search results, we can pre-process the input images, as described in 4.2. In this experiment we compared the two approaches (using learned hyper parameters or using MSRCP) to a baseline.

We also compared the three pooling methods of images mentioned in Sect. 4.4: random sampling, average pooling and saturation sort (Sat Sort), applied on the dataset. We measured the RAS for the upper clothes and the lower clothes. Results are reported in Table 2.

Table 2. RAS for Market-1501 under different pre-processing configurations. Boldface indicates best results, *italic* second best.

	None	Learned	MSRCP
Random	69.6	68.6	65.2
Average	69.1	74.4	72.3
Sat Sort	69.7	*73.1*	71.2

For the average pooling of images, we notice that using the parameters learned from the data improves the RAS by 5 points compared to the baseline. However this pre-processing method is costly and domain dependant and we see that using a method independent of the domain such as MSRCP can also improve results, by a significant margin (3 points).

As shown in Fig. 2, with no pre-processing, most of the failure cases concern shades of white and the pre-processing step helps alleviate this issue.

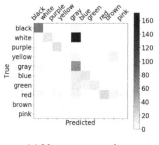
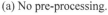
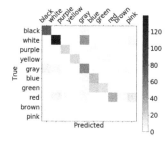

(a) No pre-processing.   (b) MSRCP pre-processing.

Fig. 2. Confusion matrices for predictions in Market-1501, with and without pre-processing the images.

Compared to the saturation sort, the simple method of average pooling gives a better overall result and has a lower processing time We hypothesize that while saturation sort increases the performance on vivid colors, it does so at the cost of reduced performance on neutral colors and makes them more sensitive to color noise and compression artifacts. Random pooling, which uses a single image, by far gives the worst results. This shows that in situations where several images of the same object are available, such as in videos, we can noticeably improve the performance by adding a pooling step.

6.2 Training Strategy

Using average pooling and MSCRP pre-processing, we compare our different training data processing steps using the XKCD dataset as synthetic data as well as the Market-1501 dataset. These steps can consist of removing outlier points (Clean) or applying SMOTE resampling to balance the dataset. Results are given in Table 3.

Table 3. Model performance study. **Boldface** indicates best results, *italic* second best. Synthetic is the XKCD test set.

SMOTE	Clean	Synthetic	Market
		87.6	72.3
	✓	*97.5*	74.9
✓		89.2	72.3
✓	✓	**97.7**	*73.7*

In Market-1501, results do not vary much regardless of the training parameters, while there is up to a 10-point difference between combinations when classifying the synthetic data. We explain this difference by the non-uniform distribution of colors: in Market-1501, the most common colors are *green, blue, purple* and the least common are *white, black, gray*. These last colors are the hardest to classify because of the color constancy problem, which does not occur with synthetic data.

6.3 Robustness of the Method to Segmentation Maps

In this experiment, we show that our method is robust to the quality the segmentation maps it is provided with, and that it can achieve good results even when the segments are altered. To do so, we introduce an operation that we named "Semantic Smoothing". For a given semantic map M made of k labels, we computed its smoothed version M' with the Eq. 1.

$$M'(x, y) = \arg\max_k [\sum_{s=-h}^{h} \sum_{t=-h}^{h} w(s, t, \sigma) * M_k(x - s, y - t)] \tag{1}$$

where $w(x, y, \sigma)$ is a Gaussian kernel of size h and M_k the semantic map of label k.

This operation is parameterized by σ, the standard deviation of the Gaussian function. We defined this operation as it is fast, reproducible and simulates an inaccurate semantic map as if it was outputted by a generative neural network in a failure case. The main characteristics of these maps are ill-defined borders, in particular for small segments. We show, in Fig. 3, examples of alterations of a semantic map for different values of σ.

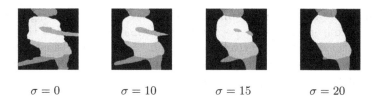

$\sigma = 0$ $\sigma = 10$ $\sigma = 15$ $\sigma = 20$

Fig. 3. Smoothing of a semantic map for different values of σ. Small details are lost while the structure remains.

For this experiment we use the optimal parameters as described in Sects. 6.1 and 6.2. For different values of σ, we alter the semantic maps and perform person search, for the whole test set. We plotted the resulting measures for each sigma in Fig. 4.

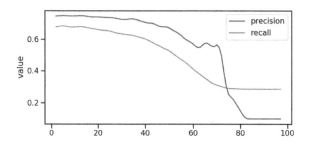

Fig. 4. Evolution of the precision (RAS) and recall in function of σ on the PCN dataset. Performance stays stable even for high σ.

We notice a sharp decline where σ reaches 60, which is the moment at which some of the bigger parts of the segments disappear. Therefore, we conclude that full, accurate pixel-wise segmentation is not required for accurate color estimation.

7   Conclusions

We propose a method for generating color semantic labels from still images or videos following four main steps of 1) semantic segmentation, 2) image pre-processing, 3) color quantization, 4) color classification. We found that in a urban context, pre-processing the images is useful to achieve a better classification. This can be done automatically with a lightness-color constancy algorithm such as MSRCP. We also noticed that using a crowd-sourced dataset to represent the complexity of human color vision produces results close to those of models trained using state of the art datasets such as Market-1501 or Colorful-Fashion.

We tested our method through experiments reflecting real-world situations using datasets such as PCN and Colorful-Fashion. We achieve better results than color naming methods when retraining is not allowed. When allowing retraining, we show that our method achieves similar performance to state of the art deep learning solutions with respectively 80.4% and 83.0% of precision. This shows that we retain the same classification capabilities as state of the art trained methods while being more general domain-wise.

Acknowlegments. We acknowledge the support of the Natural Sciences and Engineering Research Council of Canada (NSERC), [CRDPJ 528786 - 18], and the support of Arcturus network.

References

1. X11 Color Names. GitLab
2. Achanta, R., Shaji, A., Smith, K., Lucchi, A., Fua, P., Süsstrunk, S.: Slic superpixels. Technical report (2010)
3. Baslamisli, A.S., Le, H.A., Gevers, T.: CNN based learning using reflection and Retinex models for intrinsic image decomposition. In: The IEEE Conference on Computer Vision and Pattern Recognition (CVPR), June 2018
4. Benavente, R., Vanrell, M., Baldrich, R.: Parametric fuzzy sets for automatic color naming. J. Opt. Soc. Am. A: **25**(10), 2582 (2008)
5. Berlin, B., Kay, P.: Basic Color Terms: Their Universality and Evolution. Center for the Study of Language and Information (1999)
6. Bianco, S., Cusano, C.: Quasi-unsupervised color constancy. In: The IEEE Conference on Computer Vision and Pattern Recognition (CVPR), June 2019
7. Billmeyer Jr., F.W.: Color Science: Concepts and Methods, Quantitative Data and Formulae, 2nd edn. Color Research & Application (1983)
8. Chawla, N.V., Bowyer, K.W., Hall, L.O., Kegelmeyer, W.P.: SMOTE: synthetic minority over-sampling technique. J. Artif. Intell. Res. **16**, 321–357 (2002)
9. Cheng, Z., Li, X., Loy, C.C.: Pedestrian color naming via convolutional neural network. In: Lai, S.-H., Lepetit, V., Nishino, K., Sato, Y. (eds.) ACCV 2016. LNCS, vol. 10112, pp. 35–51. Springer, Cham (2017). https://doi.org/10.1007/978-3-319-54184-6_3
10. Jobson, D.J., Rahman, Z., Woodell, G.A.: Properties and performance of a center/surround retinex. IEEE Trans. Image Process. **6**(3), 451–462 (1997)
11. Kelly, K.L., Judd, D.B.: Inter-Society Color Council.: The ISCC-NBS Method of Designating Colors and a Dictionary of Color Names. National Bureau of Standards Circular, United States (1955)
12. Land, E.H., McCann, J.J.: Lightness and retinex theory. Josa **61**(1), 1–11 (1971)
13. Lin, Y., et al.: Improving person re-identification by attribute and identity learning. Pattern Recogn. **95**, 151–161 (2019)
14. Liu, S., et al.: Fashion parsing with weak color-category labels. IEEE Trans. Multimedia **16**(1), 253–265 (2014)
15. Liu, Y., Yuan, Z., Chen, B., Xue, J., Zheng, N.: Illumination robust color naming via label propagation. In: 2015 IEEE International Conference on Computer Vision (ICCV), pp. 621–629. IEEE, Santiago, December 2015
16. Luo, P., Wang, X., Tang, X.: Pedestrian parsing via deep decompositional network. In: Proceedings of the IEEE International Conference on Computer Vision, pp. 2648–2655 (2013)

17. Luo, Y., Zheng, Z., Zheng, L., Guan, T., Yu, J., Yang, Y.: Macro-micro adversarial network for human parsing, July 2018
18. Mojsilovic, A.: A computational model for color naming and describing color composition of images. IEEE Trans. Image Process. **14**(5), 690–699 (2005)
19. Munroe, R.: Color Survey Results. xkcd, May 2010. https://blog.xkcd.com/2010/05/03/color-survey-results/
20. Parthasarathy, S., Sankaran, P.: An automated multi Scale Retinex with Color Restoration for image enhancement. In: 2012 National Conference on Communications (NCC), pp. 1–5 (2012)
21. Petro, A.B., Sbert, C., Morel, J.M.: Multiscale Retinex. Image Processing On Line, pp. 71–88 (2014)
22. Ramaswamy, S., Rastogi, R., Shim, K.: Efficient algorithms for mining outliers from large data sets, p. 12, May 2000. https://doi.org/10.1145/335191.335437
23. Szeliski, R.: Computer Vision: Algorithms and Applications, p. 979, September 2010. http://szeliski.org/Book/
24. van de Weijer, J., Schmid, C., Verbeek, J., Larlus, D.: Learning color names for real-world applications. IEEE Trans. Image Process. **18**(7), 1512–1523 (2009)
25. Zheng, L., Shen, L., Tian, L., Wang, S., Wang, J., Tian, Q.: Scalable person re-identification: a benchmark. In: Proceedings of the IEEE International Conference on Computer Vision (2015)
26. Zheng, Z., Zheng, L., Yang, Y.: Unlabeled samples generated by GAN improve the person re-identification baseline in vitro. arXiv preprint arXiv:1701.07717 (2017)

2D Bidirectional Gated Recurrent Unit Convolutional Neural Networks for End-to-End Violence Detection in Videos

Abdarahmane Traoré🔟 and Moulay A. Akhloufi$^{(\boxtimes)}$🔟

Perception, Robotics, and Intelligent Machines Research Group (PRIME),
Department of Computer Science, Université de Moncton,
Moncton, NB E1A 3E1, Canada
{eat4651,moulay.akhloufi}@umoncton.ca

Abstract. Abnormal behavior detection, action recognition, fight and violence detection in videos is an area that has attracted a lot of interest in recent years. In this work, we propose an architecture that combines a Bidirectional Gated Recurrent Unit (BiGRU) and a 2D Convolutional Neural Network (CNN) to detect violence in video sequences. A CNN is used to extract spatial characteristics from each frame, while the BiGRU extracts temporal and local motion characteristics using CNN extracted features from multiple frames. The proposed end-to-end deep learning network is tested in three public datasets with varying scene complexities. The proposed network achieves accuracies up to 98%. The obtained results are promising and show the performance of the proposed end-to-end approach.

Keywords: CNN · GRU · Abnormal behavior detection · Violence detection · Video classification

1 Introduction

Nowadays we face growing violence and criminality due to the increase in population especially in large cities [11]. The surveillance systems as we know them are not reliable nor efficient because it takes a person behind the monitors to detect abnormal behavior. In the case of a grocery store we have 2 or 3 screens, but in the case of an airport, with hundreds of monitors, it is almost impossible for a human to be efficient in this security task. Over time we have seen several approaches proposed to solve this problem using computer vision. But these methods were limited by the need of a manual extraction of the characteristics and then their classification using a classifier such as SVM. With the progress in terms of hardware and software and with the rise of deep learning, new end-to-end image processing techniques have emerged. Indeed, deep architectures such

Thanks to the Natural Sciences and Engineering Research Council of Canada (NSERC), [funding reference number RGPIN-2018-06233].

© Springer Nature Switzerland AG 2020
A. Campilho et al. (Eds.): ICIAR 2020, LNCS 12131, pp. 152–160, 2020.
https://doi.org/10.1007/978-3-030-50347-5_14

as EfficientNet achieved a 97.1% accuracy in the challenge of classifying images among 1000 categories [19]. For videos, we are interested in action recognition. This last term defines several other sub-domains including the one studied in this article, namely violence detection. The main challenge of action recognition in this context is to recognize acts of violence from video images. We need to take into account two important factors: the image itself and the correlation that exists between the images over time. Many deep learning and vision-based techniques were proposed for violence detection. In general, they can be categorized into five type of approaches as described in the following.

The first category of algorithms use 3D CNN. These algorithms are computationally expensive. However, they have proven to be efficient [3,8,16,21]. For example, Song et al. [16] propose the use of 3D CNN to enable the extraction of both spatial and temporal characteristics. The CNN is mainly composed of eight 3D convolutional layers and five 3D max pooling. In [21], the authors propose a three stage deep learning approach for violence detection. They first detect persons in surveillance videos using CNN. Then, they feed a 3D CNN with a sequence of 16 frames with the detected persons. The extracted spatiotemporal features are sent to a Softmax classifier for violence detection.

Other algorithms use 2D CNN in a time series approach and then refine the characteristics with a Long short-term memory (LSTM). This end-to-end method is very efficient in term of computation and gives very interesting results as reported in [1].

Algorithms that use feature extraction followed by an LSTM are the most popular. They use several types of feature extraction, ranging from classical methods based on a simple CNN as in [18] to more sophisticated approaches as in [4]. In [4], Ditsanthia et al. use a method called multiscale convolutional features extraction to handle variations in the video data, and feeds the LSTMs with these multiscale extracted characteristics.

Other techniques, use both optical flow and frames as input in a fusion scheme and then classify the data to detect specific actions [14,22].

The final category uses ConvLSTMs which are LSTMs whose matrix operations have been replaced by convolutions [10,17]. Sudhakaran et al. [17] use this special convolutions to classify actions from the extracted 3D data.

In this work, we propose an end-to-end 2D deep learning approach to automate violence detection from video sequences. The proposed architecture outperforms many available techniques. The effectiveness of our approach is validated on three public datasets.

2   Proposed Method

In this work we develop an end-to-end deep learning network which is easy to train and capable of reaching the same level of performance as existing state-of-the-art methods. Our network is able to classify a video sequence as violent or not. We use a 2D CNN distributed in time to capture the temporary spatial characteristics. We combine it with a bidirectional GRU (BiGRU) to refine our detections.

2.1   Convolutional Neural Network

Our CNN network is based on a VGG16 adapted to our purpose and distributed over time to handle a sequence of images. We pre-trained VGG on the INRA person dataset introduce by [2] which contains images of people as positives and random images as negatives. The objective is to identify persons in an image and ignore the background. After training on INRA, we remove the fully connected layers and use a flatten layer to forward the features to the BiGRU network.

2.2   Gated Recurrent Unit

To better consider all the spatial-temporal relationship between frames we use a GRU (See Fig. 1) to refine our characteristics. The choice of the GRU is made to avoid the gradient vanishing problem of the LSTMs. GRU is more robust to noise [20] and outperforms the LSTM in several tasks [6]. Moreover, the GRUs are less computationally expensive as they have two gates unlike the LSTM which has four. In addition, we use our GRU in a bidirectional position to consider not only the previous sequences but also the following sequences. This means that forward propagation is done twice, in one direction and its opposite. Both outputs are used for gates operations. This allowed the increase in classification accuracy.

Equation 1 gives the GRU functions used in this work, the update gate z_t decides what information to keep or to drop, the reset gate r_t decides how much past information to forget, h_t is the output gate and h_{t-1} is the hidden state of previous cell (output of the previous cell). W, U are weights matrices that will be learnt and b is the biais, σ_g is a sigmoid activation function and σ_h is a hyperbolic tangent function. Finally x_t is the input vector.

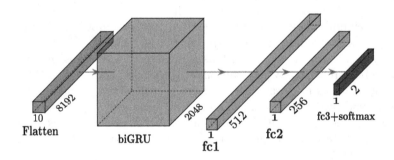

Fig. 1. BiGRU used to capture temporal features

$$z_t = \sigma_g(W_z x_t + U_z h_{t-1} + b_z)$$
$$r_t = \sigma_g(W_r x_t + U_r h_{t-1} + b_r)$$
$$h_t = z_t \circ h_{t-1} + (1 - z_t) \circ \sigma_h(W_h x_t +$$
$$U_h(r_t \circ h_{t-1}) + b_h)$$

(1)

The full network resulting from merging both our VGG-based CNN and BiGRU is illustrated by Fig. 2. We used 10 frames of each video as input to our network.

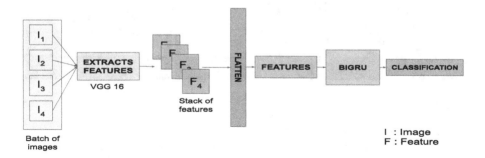

Fig. 2. 2D BiGRU-CNN architecture

3   Experiments and Results

To evaluate our network, we used three datasets: Hockey dataset [12], Violent Flow dataset [5] and Real Life Violence Situations dataset [9]. We used the accuracy metric to assess the performance of our network.

3.1   Datasets

We divided each dataset randomly into 2 parts, training (80%) and validation/testing (20%). Even if Violentflow doesn't have as much data as the other datasets, this will allow us to demonstrate the network generalization capacity on a small dataset.

Hockey Dataset. Hockey fight dataset [12], is a dataset that contains 1000 videos of fights between hockey players and 1000 other videos of non-violent game times (see Fig. 3). In this dataset, the classes are balanced. Each clip lasts approximately 2 s and consists of about 41 frames with a resolution of 360×288. The details captured by the sequences are quite similar, especially the background. We resized the images to 128×176.

Violent Flow Dataset. Violent Flow Dataset [5] is a dataset of real-world video footage of crowd violence (see Fig. 4). The dataset contains 246 videos. The shortest clip duration is 1.04 s, the longest clip is 6.52 s, and the average length of a video clip is 3.60 s. We also resized the images to 128×128.

Fig. 3. Frames from the Hockey dataset

Fig. 4. Frames from the ViolentFlow dataset

Real Life Violence Situations Dataset. Real-Life Violence Situations Dataset [9] is a dataset of real-life violence videos (see Fig. 5). It contains 1000 fight and 1000 no fight videos captured in various situations (classes are balanced). We resized the images to 128×128 pixels.

3.2   Parameters and Sampling

For the implementation of our network, we used Keras with the TensorFlow backend. Since we do not have the same video lengths and the videos are at average 30 fps, we have chosen a different number of frames for each dataset and we used a uniform sampling method. With this sampling, not only the number of parameters to compute decreases, but we avoid unnecessary calculations of redundant frames. Before starting the training on the datasets, we pretrained the VGG-based CNN on INRA for 100 epochs using SGD, a learning rate of 0.001 and a batch size of 8. Then, we combined our 2D CNN with BiGRU followed by 3 fully connected layers.

Fig. 5. Frames from real life violence situations dataset

The proposed 2D BiGRU-CNN was trained on all the datasets using SGD as optimizer with a batch size of 10. The learning rate was set to 0.0008 for the Hockey and Real Life Violence datasets. The best learning rate for Violent Flow was 0.0006. The network was trained for 250 epochs. It takes as input a sequence of 10 frames for each dataset.

3.3   Results and Discussions

In Table 1 and 2 we present an accuracy, input and sampling comparison for the two datasets Hockey and Violent Flow with previously published techniques. On the Hockey dataset we obtained an accuracy of 98%, and on Violent Flow we obtained an accuracy of 95.5%. We can see from Tables 1 and 2 that our approach outperforms most of the previously published techniques. It is only surpassed by the use of 3D CNNs in [16] for Hockey and [21] for Violent Flow. Still we obtain better results in Hockey compared to the work in [21] and in Violent Flow compared to the model proposed in [16]. These last techniques use computationally intensive 3D convolutions [7], whereas we only use 2D CNN.

Finally, Real-Life Violence Situations is the dataset that allows us to confirm that the proposed network is robust, because this last dataset contains various situations (We find Hockey scenes, outdoor scenes, etc.). With the obtained accuracy of 90.25%, we can say that our network has a good generalization. This recent dataset was only used in another previous work [15]. The authors used VGG16 with LSTM and achieved an accuracy of 88.2% which is lower than our result.

In term of computation complexity, our approach depends more on CNN than on GRU. Indeed, in our case we use VGG16 having 138 million parameters. We use it with smaller image sizes, which reduces the number of parameters. Moreover the use of GRU helps reduce the overall complexity of the architecture when compared with other solutions such as those based on LSTM [1].

Table 1. Hockey Dataset violence detection, comparison with other methods (W represent words, H represent histogram bins, F are frames, C is a CXC window, "?" means not specified and "-" means not used)

Method	Inputs	Sampling	Accuracy (%)
HOF + BoW	1000 (W)	-	88.6 [16]
HOG + BoW	1000 (W)	-	91.7 [16]
MoSIFT + BoW	1000 (W)	-	90.9 [16]
MoWLD + BoW	900 (W)	-	91.9 [16]
MoWLD + Sparse Coding	1000 (W)	-	93.7 [16]
MoSIFT + KDE + Sparce Coding	500 (W)	-	94.3 [16]
MoWLD + KDE + Sparce Coding	500 (W)	-	94.9 [16]
MoIWLD + KDE +SRC	1800 (W)	-	96.8 [16]
3D-CNN	16 (F)	Uniform	91 [16]
3D ConvNet	16 (F)	Intervall of 8	96 [21]
FightNet	25 (F)	Random	97 [23]
VGG19+LSTM	40 (F)	?	97 [1]
ConvLSTM	20 (F)	Custom	97.1 [17]
Our approach	10 (F)	Uniform	**98**
3D ConvNet	16 (F)	Uniform	98.96 [16]
3D ConvNet	32 (F)	Uniform	99.62 [16]

Table 2. ViolentFlow Dataset violence detection, comparison with other methods (W, H, F, C, "?" and "-" are the same as in Table 1)

Method	Inputs	Sampling	Accuracy (%)
LTP	20 (H)	-	71.53 [16]
ViF	20 (H)	-	81.3 [16]
MoWLD + BoW	500 (W)	-	82.56 [16]
RVD	4 × 4 (C) /5 frames	-	82.79 [16]
MoWLD + Sparse Coding	500 (W)	-	86.39 [16]
VGG19+LSTM	40 (F)	?	85.71 [1]
MoSIFT + KDE + Sparce Coding	500 (W)	-	89.05 [16]
MoWLD + KDE + Sparce Coding	500 (W)	-	89.78 [16]
MoWLD + KDE +SRC	1800 (W)	-	93.19 [16]
3D ConvNet	?	Uniform	93.5 [16]
ConvLSTM	20 (F)	?	94.57 [17]
Our approach	10 (F)	Uniform	**95.5**

4   Conclusion and Future Work

In this work we proposed a simple end-to-end deep learning approach to detect violence in video sequences. The new architecture combines 2D CNN and bidirectional GRU. The CNN uses a modified VGG16 pretrained on a person dataset to learn how to extract persons from video images. The CNN features from multiple images are sent to the bidirectional GRU which takes into account temporal and local motion characteristics. Tests were performed on 3 public datasets. The obtained results show that the proposed approach outperforms many previous approaches. It is only slightly surpassed by 3D CNN models. However, since we used 2D CNN our approach is less computationally intensive. Future work includes the use of different sampling approaches that have been shown to increase the performance in video classification [16]. In addition, we will explore the fusion of frames with optical flow [22] in order to improve accuracy. Finally, as our approach is modular, we can get closer to real-time performance using light CNNs such as MobileNets [13].

References

1. Abdali, A.M.R., Al-Tuma, R.F.: Robust real-time violence detection in video using CNN And LSTM. In: 2019 2nd Scientific Conference of Computer Sciences (SCCS), pp. 104–108, March 2019
2. Dalal, N., Triggs, B.: Histograms of oriented gradients for human detection. In: 2005 IEEE Computer Society Conference on Computer Vision and Pattern Recognition (CVPR 2005), vol. 1, pp. 886–893, June 2005
3. Ding, C., Fan, S., Zhu, M., Feng, W., Jia, B.: Violence detection in video by using 3D convolutional neural networks. In: Bebis, G., et al. (eds.) ISVC 2014. LNCS, vol. 8888, pp. 551–558. Springer, Cham (2014). https://doi.org/10.1007/978-3-319-14364-4_53
4. Ditsanthia, E., Pipanmaekaporn, L., Kamonsantiroj, S.: Video representation learning for CCTV-based violence detection. In: 2018 3rd Technology Innovation Management and Engineering Science International Conference (TIMES-iCON), pp. 1–5, December 2018
5. Hassner, T., Itcher, Y., Kliper-Gross, O.: Violent flows: real-time detection of violent crowd behavior. In: 2012 IEEE Computer Society Conference on Computer Vision and Pattern Recognition Workshops, pp. 1–6, June 2012
6. Kanai, S., Fujiwara, Y., Iwamura, S.: Preventing gradient explosions in gated recurrent units. In: Proceedings of the 31st International Conference on Neural Information Processing Systems. NIPS 2017, pp. 435–444. Curran Associates Inc., Red Hook (2017)
7. Kanojia, G., Kumawat, S., Raman, S.: Exploring temporal differences in 3D convolutional neural networks (2019)
8. Li, C., Zhu, L., Zhu, D., Chen, J., Pan, Z., Li, X., Wang, B.: End-to-end multiplayer violence detection based on deep 3D CNN. In: Proceedings of the 2018 VII International Conference on Network, Communication and Computing, ICNCC 2018, Taipei City, Taiwan, pp. 227–230. ACM, New York (2018)
9. Mohamed, E., Mohamad, H., Massih, M.A.E.: Real life violence situations dataset. https://kaggle.com/mohamedmustafa/real-life-violence-situations-dataset. Accessed January 2020

10. Morales, G., Salazar-Reque, I., Telles, J., Díaz, D.: Detecting violent robberies in CCTV videos using deep learning. In: MacIntyre, J., Maglogiannis, I., Iliadis, L., Pimenidis, E. (eds.) AIAI 2019. IAICT, vol. 559, pp. 282–291. Springer, Cham (2019). https://doi.org/10.1007/978-3-030-19823-7_23

11. Mt, S.: Increasing crimes vs. population density in megacities. Sociol. Criminol.-Open Access **4**(1), 1–2 (2016)

12. Bermejo Nievas, E., Deniz Suarez, O., Bueno García, G., Sukthankar, R.: Violence detection in video using computer vision techniques. In: Real, P., Diaz-Pernil, D., Molina-Abril, H., Berciano, A., Kropatsch, W. (eds.) CAIP 2011. LNCS, vol. 6855, pp. 332–339. Springer, Heidelberg (2011). https://doi.org/10.1007/978-3-642-23678-5_39

13. Sandler, M., Howard, A., Zhu, M., Zhmoginov, A., Chen, L.C.: Mobilenetv 2: inverted residuals and linear bottlenecks. In: The IEEE Conference on Computer Vision and Pattern Recognition (CVPR), June 2018

14. Simonyan, K., Zisserman, A.: Two-stream convolutional networks for action recognition in videos. In: Ghahramani, Z., Welling, M., Cortes, C., Lawrence, N.D., Weinberger, K.Q. (eds.) Advances in Neural Information Processing Systems, vol. 27, pp. 568–576. Curran Associates, Inc. (2014)

15. Soliman, M.M., Kamal, M.H., El-Massih Nashed, M.A., Mostafa, Y.M., Chawky, B.S., Khattab, D.: Violence recognition from videos using deep learning techniques. In: 2019 Ninth International Conference on Intelligent Computing and Information Systems (ICICIS), pp. 80–85, December 2019. https://doi.org/10.1109/ICICIS46948.2019.9014714

16. Song, W., Zhang, D., Zhao, X., Yu, J., Zheng, R., Wang, A.: A novel violent video detection scheme based on modified 3D convolutional neural networks. IEEE Access **7**, 39172–39179 (2019)

17. Sudhakaran, S., Lanz, O.: Learning to detect violent videos using convolutional long short-term memory. In: 2017 14th IEEE International Conference on Advanced Video and Signal Based Surveillance (AVSS), pp. 1–6, August 2017

18. Sumon, S.A., Shahria, M.D.T., Goni, M.D.R., Hasan, N., Almarufuzzaman, A.M., Rahman, R.M.: Violent crowd flow detection using deep learning. In: Nguyen, N.T., Gaol, F.L., Hong, T.-P., Trawiński, B. (eds.) ACIIDS 2019. LNCS (LNAI), vol. 11431, pp. 613–625. Springer, Cham (2019). https://doi.org/10.1007/978-3-030-14799-0_53

19. Tan, M., Le, Q.V.: EfficientNet: rethinking model scaling for convolutional neural networks. arXiv:1905.11946 [cs, stat], May 2019. arXiv: 1905.11946

20. Tang, Z., Shi, Y., Wang, D., Feng, Y., Zhang, S.: Memory visualization for gated recurrent neural networks in speech recognition. In: 2017 IEEE International Conference on Acoustics, Speech and Signal Processing (ICASSP), pp. 2736–2740, March 2017. https://doi.org/10.1109/ICASSP.2017.7952654

21. Ullah, F.U.M., Ullah, A., Muhammad, K., Haq, I.U., Baik, S.W.: Violence detection using spatiotemporal features with 3D convolutional neural network. Sensors (Basel, Switz.) **19**(11), 2472 (2019)

22. Xu, X., Wu, X., Wang, G., Wang, H.: Violent video classification based on spatial-temporal cues using deep learning. In: 2018 11th International Symposium on Computational Intelligence and Design (ISCID), vol. 01, pp. 319–322, December 2018

23. Zhou, P., Ding, Q., Luo, H., Hou, X.: Violent interaction detection in video based on deep learning. J. Phys: Conf. Ser. **844**, 012044 (2017)

Video Based Live Tracking of Fishes in Tanks

José Castelo(✉), H. Sofia Pinto, Alexandre Bernardino, and Núria Baylina

Instituto Superior Técnico, Lisbon (INESC-ID & ISR),
Oceanário de Lisboa, Lisbon, Portugal
jbcastelo@hotmail.com

Abstract. We explore video tracking and classification in the context of real time marine wildlife observation. Among other applications it can help biologists by automating the process of gathering data, which is often done manually. In this paper we present a system to tackle the challenge of tracking and classifying fish in real time. We apply Background Subtraction techniques to detect the fish, followed by Feature Matching methods to track their movements over time. To deal with the shortcomings of tracking by detection we use a Kalman Filter to predict fish positions and a local search recovery method to re-identify fish tracks that are temporarily lost due to occlusions or lack of contrast. The species of tracked fish is recognized through Image Classification methods, using environment dependent features. We developed and tested our system using a custom built dataset, with several labeled image sequences of the fish tanks in the *Oceanário de Lisboa*. The impact of the proposed tracking methods are quantified and discussed. The proposed system is able to track and classify fish in real time in two scenarios, main tank and coral reef, reflecting different challenges.

Keywords: Object detection · Video tracking · Image classification · Real time · Fish

1 Introduction

Almost everything we know about animals comes from observing and analyzing their behaviours. In the past, biologists spent most of their time observing their subjects. Advances in technology allowed for better ways to make these observations. Film cameras proved to be a powerful tool when collecting data, as they convey more information than still pictures. Analog films allowed biologists to study behaviour or trait in more detail, as they can be played back multiple times. Furthermore, rare phenomenons, which could take a lifetime to encounter and understand, become objectively shareable among the community. Finally, the appearance of the digital video camera unlocked the potential to automatically process videos.

Video observations of animals, as everything, come with a set of advantages: a non intrusive way of observing animals, unaffected by the human presence;

© Springer Nature Switzerland AG 2020
A. Campilho et al. (Eds.): ICIAR 2020, LNCS 12131, pp. 161–173, 2020.
https://doi.org/10.1007/978-3-030-50347-5_15

Fig. 1. Two of the tanks at the *Oceanário de Lisboa*.

continuous observation, potentially revealing previously unseen behaviours that take place under very specific scenarios; an objective portrait of animals and their traits/behaviours, not limited by the observation of the biologists in the field; relatively low cost, as cameras and computing power become more economically viable; the possibility of remote observation or analysis. However, they have also drawbacks: produce a significant amount of data, requiring considerable amounts of data storage capacity; their output needs to be processed, as only small portions of the observations convey useful information; a limited viewport, in the sense that only what is in front of a camera is captured, potentially leaving out relevant information.

The *Oceanário de Lisboa* hosts a range of exhibition tanks that simulate environments from marine biomes all around the globe, two of which can be seen in Fig. 1. Part of its work, whether for maintenance, monitoring or research purposes, involves close observation of fish. We captured image sequences from some of its main tanks to create a dataset that captures significant diversity of scenarios and allow us to develop and test a system to automatically track and identify several classes of fish.

The *Oceanário de Lisboa* is interested in detecting many events that require a timely and long term observation of the fish, for example, when a given species is displaying a behaviour that is rarely seen. This motivated us to enable our system to constantly monitor the observed tanks and relay information regarding fish species and trajectories in real-time. Different environments and tanks, as illustrated in Fig. 1, have distinct properties and challenges: (1) the depth of each tank influences the perceived colors typically resulting in a blue tint; (2) the size of the fish greatly impacts their behaviour, with smaller fish displaying faster and more unpredictable movements; (3) the uniformity of certain groups of fish species makes their distinction in videos an extremely difficult task; (4) the size of certain tanks limit the visibility of fishes that are swimming at considerable distances from the camera; (5) the presence of marine flora hinders detecting fish, due to their movement and provided camouflage (6) variations in lighting present a constantly changing environment; (7) tank features, such as rocks, conceal the fish swimming behind them.

The Fish4Knowledge project [1,5,6,8] aimed at surveying fish populations with a remote network of underwater cameras. They successfully applied computer vision techniques to the captured footage in order to track and classify the fish. Our scenarios pose different challenges to the ones seen in Fish4Knowledge, in particular the much shorter ranges and lower resolution footage.

2   Problem Statement and Objectives

The problem of tracking and classifying fish in real-time can be broken into three major sub-problems as follows:

1. Detect the set of fish present in each video frame t, $D^{(t)} = \{d_{n_t}^{(t)}\}, n_t = 1..N_t$, where N_t is the number of fish at frame t and $d = (x, y, w, h, m, t)$ where x, y are the horizontal and vertical bounding box position coordinates, w, h its width and height, respectively, m a mask of the pixels within the bounding box and t the frame timestamp.
2. Associate each detected fish, $d_{n_t}^{(t)}$ with the appropriate track $T_k = \{d_{i_k(t)}\}, t = t_{0k} : t_{fk}$, where $i_k(t)$ is the index of the detected blob at timestamp t which corresponds to track T_k.
3. Identify the species, c_i, out of the species set $C = c_0 : c_N$, corresponding to each track T_k.

A few restrictions and assumptions have to be taken into consideration, based on our environment: (1) the scene is captured by a statically positioned camera, from outside of the tanks to minimize the intrusiveness of the system; (2) the resolution of the video output by the camera must be at least 720×480 pixels. A lower resolution means there is not enough detail to analyse the scene; (3) there is a limited number of fish in each species which limits the size of the dataset used to train the fish classifiers; (4) a closed environment is assumed, meaning that the possible species of the observed fish will not change from those originally in the system.

We aim at developing a practical and low cost fish observation system through the use of videos, whether for research, monitoring or entertainment purposes. By providing video tracking and species classification of fish in real-time, we seek to provide the framework for applications that require a real-time information feed containing the position and species of each fish.

Our primary objective is to provide a live feed of location and species for each fish in a video stream of a tank. An example frame of a tank video stream can be seen in Fig. 2(a), where the desired output is the location of each fish (highlighted with a bounding box) and species (bounding box color), exemplified in Fig. 2(b).

Our system should be able to support different environment conditions that fish can be observed in, as well as the ability to adapt to new environments with little setup and parameterization. It is our goal to have the system running in real-time on ordinary computers. This makes our system economically viable for most people, with no need for extra investment in specialized hardware.

(a) Example frame   (b) Desired output

Fig. 2. Goal: live feed of locations and species for each fish in a tank.

3 Detection

The detection module is responsible for localizing the set of fish, $D^{(t)}$, present in video frame t. To do this, it must first be able to recognize the parts of a fish. We used the Adaptive Gaussian Mixture Model (AGMM [4]) implemented in *opencv* that follows the specification in [9] and is composed of three stages: Background modelling, Background subtraction and Connected Components. In the following paragraphs, we succinctly describe each of the steps.

Background Modelling - In the AGMM algorithm, each pixel in the background is modeled as a Gaussian Mixture. During the background modelling stage the Gaussian mixtures for each pixel are updated. The Gaussians in the mixture are given a weight, based on their relevance to the model. This allows the model to contain information regarding more infrequent samples, while not overestimating their importance. At each update, every Gaussian has its weight, mean, and variance updated according to the newly observed data. The modelling process is detailed next.

Consider the sample history of the last T timesteps, with the rgb color values for each pixel, $\boldsymbol{x}^{(t)}$, at timestep t: $X_T = \boldsymbol{x}^{(t)}, ..., \boldsymbol{x}^{(t-T)}$. At each time step t, an estimated probability density $\hat{p}$ function models the observed values, which might contain both foreground (FG) and background (BG) related values:

$$\hat{p}(\boldsymbol{x}|X_T, BG + FG) = \sum_{m=1}^{M} \hat{\pi}_m \mathcal{N}(\hat{\boldsymbol{\mu}}_m, \hat{\sigma}_m^2 I) \tag{1}$$

In this equation $\hat{\boldsymbol{\mu}}_m$, $\hat{\sigma}_m^2$ and $\hat{\pi}_m$ are respectively mean, variances and weight estimates for each Gaussian component m. When a new value $\boldsymbol{x}^{(t)}$ is observed, each component is updated recursively as follows:

$$\hat{\pi}_m \longleftarrow \hat{\pi}_m + \alpha(o_m^{(t)} - \hat{\pi}_m) \tag{2}$$

$$\hat{\mu}_m \longleftarrow \hat{\mu}_m + o_m^{(t)}(\alpha/\hat{\pi}_m)\boldsymbol{\delta}_m \tag{3}$$

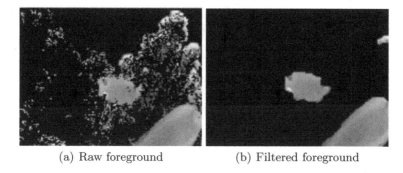

(a) Raw foreground   (b) Filtered foreground

Fig. 3. Applying morphological filters (opening and closing) to the pixels flagged as foreground.

$$\hat{\sigma}_m^2 \longleftarrow \hat{\sigma}_m^2 + o_m^{(t)}(\alpha/\hat{\pi}_m)(\boldsymbol{\delta}_m^T\boldsymbol{\delta}_m - \hat{\sigma}_m^2) \tag{4}$$

where $\boldsymbol{\delta}_m = \boldsymbol{x}^{(t)} - \hat{\boldsymbol{\mu}}_m$ and α is the learning rate parameter. $o_m^{(t)}$ is a binary selector, whose value is 1 when a component is the most relevant (largest weight π_m) within the components close to the observed value, according to the Mahalanobis Distance [3], and 0 otherwise. In the case where there are no close components, a new one is generated. If the amount of components exceeds the limit, the least important (lowest weight π_m) component is discarded.

Background Subtraction - During this stage a background subtraction algorithm identifies which pixels belong to the foreground. This is done by first considering the N most important Gaussian components for each pixel. N is determined as:

$$N = argmin_n(\frac{\sum_{i=0}^n \hat{\pi}_i}{\sum_{i=0}^{N_m} \hat{\pi}_i} >= 0.75) \tag{5}$$

which translates into the N most important components that exceed a total summed relative weight of 75%. These components model the colors that most likely belong to the background. Then we check if the Mahalanobis Distance between the observed value $x^{(t)}$ and any of these N components is bellow a threshold (80 in our case, determined empirically). As the used implementation considers that the color channels are independent, their covariance matrix is the Identity matrix. In this case, the Mahalanobis Distance [3] between a Gaussian component m with mean value $\boldsymbol{\mu}$ and an observed value $\boldsymbol{x}$ is:

$$D_M(\boldsymbol{\mu}, \boldsymbol{x}) = \sqrt{(\boldsymbol{x} - \boldsymbol{\mu})(\boldsymbol{x} - \boldsymbol{\mu})^T} \tag{6}$$

Once all the pixels are processed we now have a frame labeled into background and foreground pixels. An example of a set of pixels that have been labeled as foreground can be seen in Fig. 3(a).

Morphological Operations and Connected Components - The foreground (Fig. 3(a)) is then manipulated with morphological filters. These help remove noise, such as isolated pixels identified as foreground, and close small holes within big regions of foreground pixels. The impact of these operations can be seen in Fig. 3(b). Each separate foreground region is then uniquely identified by a two-pass connected component algorithm. This process identifies pixels identified as foreground that form connected regions, uniquely identifying each separate region.

4 Tracking

The first important aspect is to discuss the features to take into account when comparing a blob to a track, and how this comparison is made.

Position Similarity - The position of a fish does not usually change significantly between consecutive frames. Moreover, this movement is relatively predictable given the short time elapsed between frames. As such, the position of the detected blobs are compared to the predicted position of each track. This prediction is computed through a Kalman Filter, which takes into account the position history of each track. A Kalman Filter also takes into account noise in position measurements, which could occur, for example, due to faulty detection. For a given detected blob d_j and track T_k, the position similarity function is computed as follows:

$$S_p(d_j, T_k) = 1 - \frac{\|P_K(T_k) - P(d_j)\|}{M_d} \tag{7}$$

where M_d is the maximum Euclidean Distance in the frame, which can be computed based on the video resolution. $P(d_j)$ is the position of blob d_j and $P_K(T_k)$ is the position predicted by a Kalman Filter for the track T_k.

Color Similarity - The second feature is based on the appearance of a fish. It consists of a color description of a blob, computed in the form of a relative frequency color histogram. This normalized histogram contains a set of bins for each color channel (red, green and blue). Each bin describes the relative frequency in which that color intensity interval appears within a blob. When comparing two normalized histograms, the Bhattacharyya coefficient, B_c, computes a similarity value between them. This coefficient is simply the ratio of overlap between two histograms. It can be computed as follows, for two histograms H_1 and H_2 with n bins:

$$B_c(H_1, H_2) = \sum_{i=0}^{n} \sqrt{H_1^i H_2^i} \tag{8}$$

where H^i is the value of the ith bin in the histogram. For a detected blob d_j and track T_k the color similarity function, S_c, is:

$$S_c(d_j, T_k) = B_c(H(D_j), H(T_k)) \tag{9}$$

where $H(d_j)$ is the histogram computed at the pixels of the blob mask and $H(T_k)$ is the histogram of the last blob associated with the considered track.

Data Association - We then attempt to associate each existing track with a detected blob. Consider the set of active tracks at time-step $t-1$, $T^{(t-1)}$, as well as the set of detected blobs $D^{(t)}$. A track T_k will be associated with the blob D_j when:

$$S_p(d_j, T_k) \geq \theta_p - \gamma_{p,T_k} \tag{10}$$

$$S_c(d_j, T_k) \geq \theta_c - \gamma_{c,T_k} \tag{11}$$

$$k = \mathrm{argmax}_i(S_c(d_j, T_i)) \tag{12}$$

where θ_p and θ_c are minimum thresholds for each similarity function. To improve the behaviour of the associations, we add a decay, γ_{p,T_k} and γ_{c,T_k}, to the minimum similarity thresholds required. This decay is based on how long an existing track has not been matched with a blob. This helps when a tracked fish significantly changes in appearance, or moves in an unexpected way such that the predicted position is not accurate.

Local Search Recovery Method - After every detected blob has been considered for association with a given track there is still a chance that it has not been matched with a detected blob. This, however, does not guarantee that the tracked fish isn't present in the scene and can occur when the detection module fails to identify the presence of a fish. So when a track is not associated with any detected blob a recovery tracking method is applied. This method consists in building an appearance heat-map around the predicted position of the tracked fish. For each pixel in the area surrounding the predicted position the estimated probability of the color fitting the tracked fish color histogram is computed. This is done with the color histogram of past blobs for that track. Then each pixel is flagged as either positive (meaning it probably is part of the fish) or negative, using a threshold parameter. A two-pass connected component algorithm then removes isolated false-positives and identifies the biggest connected region of positive pixels. If the area of this region is larger than $\frac{3}{4}$ of the area of the last blob then it is associated to the track as the blob for that frame. A given track, however, cannot repeatedly use this recovery method alone. This would cause a drift of the color histogram for that track, possibly resulting in the repeated tracking of a background region.

Track Lifespan - Detected blobs that were not matched to an existing track, through the method described in Sect. 4, get assigned to a new track. Finally, tracks that have not been associated with a blob (detected or recovered) for longer than 2 seconds (or equivalent number of frames when running the system in frame-by-frame mode) are deleted. This happens when a fish leaves the scene or is occluded behind an object.

5   Classification

For fish classification is required a collection of sample photos for each species of interest. For each species were collected about 20 examples, with the background removed.

Coral Reef Scenario. One of the environments is a coral reef. In this environment, the colors are well defined, the water is clear and the depth is not a factor impairing visibility. These conditions allow us to classify the fish through color similarity metric, the Bhattacharyya coefficient.

Features - Consider two relative frequency color histograms, H_1 and H_2, computed from the colors of the pixels in two distinct blobs. If the overlap of these histograms is significant, the two blobs probably belong to two fishes of the same species. This assumption has drawbacks which are discussed later. The function that describes this overlap is the Bhattacharyya coefficient, B_c.

Classification - In order to classify a track we consider the average Bhattacharrya coefficients, B_c, of the last $k \leq 5$ blobs of that track and each of the species images within our dataset. The species set with the highest average coefficient becomes our classification for that track. This simple classification method proves reliable when the colors of the species are well defined and there is not much overlap among the appearance of the present species. However, it does suffer in performance when lighting is not stable enough or the colors are washed out.

Main Tank Scenario. The second environment of our test scenarios displays conditions that make it hard to distinguish fish species by relying on their color. First, due to depth, it wears out colors, leaving everything with a blue tint. Secondly, the dimensions of the tank allow fish to wander further from the camera and thus appear smaller and with less contrast. To overcome these two problems, a solution that does not rely on color cues or the scale of the fish is required. An histogram of oriented gradients (HOG) [2] fits these requirements, when treating images scaled to the same dimensions.

Features - An HOG describes directional changes in color, capturing features such as edges, that would otherwise not be considered. The magnitude and direction of the gradients are computed based on the vertical and horizontal per-pixel gradients. Then, the image is divided into blocks. The gradients within each block are normalized, which makes the features more robust to variations in brightness. The histograms of gradients are then computed on a per-block basis.

Classification - In order to compute the similarity between two images we use linear regression to reconstruct the HOG features of a detected fish based on the HOG features of each species dataset. The species dataset that best reconstructs the HOG features of the detected blob becomes the class associated with that blob. By down-scaling the sample images and blobs we are able to keep this method running in real time. This linear regression approach is based on the work in [7].

Let μ be the vector of HOG features of a given image. A set of n images belonging to a class dataset (indexed j), can then be concatenated into a matrix ζ_j, where the columns are: $\mu_1, ..., \mu_n$. Given a new image, i, whose class we want to identify we need to first compute its vector of HOG features, γ_i. Assuming that μ_i can be written following the linear hypothesis:

$$\gamma_i = \zeta_j \theta_j \tag{13}$$

where θ_j are the linear regression coefficients, we project the HOG features onto the class j feature subspace, as follows:

$$\theta_j = (\zeta_j^T \zeta_j)^{-1} \zeta_j^T \gamma_i \tag{14}$$

$$\hat{\gamma}_j = \zeta_j \theta_j \tag{15}$$

The difference between the values of γ_i and $\hat{\gamma}_i$ form the residuals, R_i^j for that image:

$$R_i^j = ||\gamma_i - \hat{\gamma}_i|| \tag{16}$$

A smaller residual value means the regressed feature vector is closer to the original than otherwise. To arrive at a final classification we cast an exponentially weighted vote based on the residuals R^j for each species image set j. Each residual, for image i, R_i^j, casts an exponentially weighted vote support class j:

$$\omega_i^j = e^{-\beta R_i^j} \tag{17}$$

Then, we select the class j, with the maximum summed vote weight:

$$c = argmax_j \left(\sum_i \omega_i^j \right) \tag{18}$$

Temporal Consistency - Regardless of which of the two methods used, to further improve the stability of our classification module we take the most frequent classification of blobs in a track for the previous $n = 20$ time steps. We allow our blob classifiers a significant error margin while keeping the overall track classification accurate.

6   Evaluation

Detection and Tracking - We tested our system with and without Kalman Filter based prediction & Local Search Recovery on both scenarios, Fig. 4.

On the main tank environment, as expected, our system performs better with both methods enabled. Looking at them individually we see that the Kalman Filter position prediction does not have a considerable impact on its own. Similarly, the Local Search Recovery Method only seems to improve the global accuracy by 0,6%. When used together, these methods show a slight (1,4%) improvement on the global accuracy.

On the coral reef scenario we see that, while the recovery method improves the global accuracy, the Kalman filter position prediction method seems to affect performance negatively with and without the recovery method enabled. This can be attributed to the more random nature of movement presented by the smaller

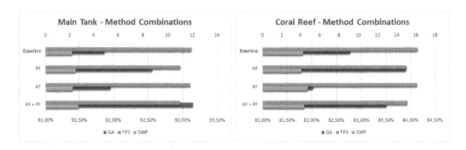

Fig. 4. Impacts of the proposed methods in each environment. GA - Global accuracy; FPS - Processed frames per second; SWP - Number of identity swaps.

fish in this environment. The metrics of the tests in the coral reef are overall worse than on the main tank for two reasons: the fish remain on scene longer, meaning that target losses are expected to be higher, as there are more opportunities for missing detections and other issues such as crossing fish; the *yellowtailed* fish are so small that they sometimes remain undetected for long periods of time, explaining the few mostly lost tracks and the overall lower global accuracy.

Classification - In the case of the main tank, in Fig. 5, the F1-score of the ray species is significantly lower than the rest. Rays have a unique way of moving. They have "wings" which flap in order to swim through the water. This way of swimming results in considerable deformation of their bodies as they present a wide range of shapes, as seen in Fig. 6. This explains why a classifier based on shape features would present a lower precision value for the ray species.

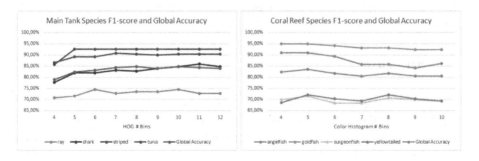

Fig. 5. Global Accuracy and F1-Score for the species in the Main tank (left) and Coral Reef (right) scenarios.

On the coral reef scenario, in Fig. 5, we observe two values that stand out. The *yellowtailed* recall (56,5%) and the *surgeonfish* precision (56,9%). When considering blobs of these two species, the few background pixels around the smaller fish make up for a bigger portion of the blob than in the case of the *surgeonfish*, throwing off the expected color histogram. Although it might be

Fig. 6. Part of the ray classification dataset.

easy for us to distinguish between these two, specially due to their size, they are quite similar in color under certain lighting. Figure 7 illustrates how similar the histograms of the two species can be.

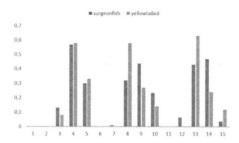

Fig. 7. Color histogram comparison between the blobs of a "yellowtailed" and a surgeonfish. (Color figure online)

7   Conclusions and Future Work

We first discussed the motivation and benefits of tracking and classifying fish in real-time. Video tracking is a hot topic in the domain of computer vision, but that has not been discussed much in the realm of marine wildlife observation. Marine environments, and thus fish, are facing ever growing sustainability problems due to human interference. A proper application of video tracking and image classification could aid biologists in gaining a better understanding of marine wildlife and how they are impacted.

We proposed and implemented an approach to track and classify fish in real-time on a unique dataset built in the *Oceanário de Lisboa*. We implemented methods supporting the usual approaches that we deemed appropriate for our problem. These were able to deal with some of the shortcomings that are associated with tracking based on detection. We also implemented classification methods able to deal with the unique challenges presented by the different environments in our dataset.

The presented system is just one of the possible approaches to our problem. The biggest hurdle is dealing with the restraints associated with enabling our system to run in real-time. This heavily limited the feasibility of most methods. We also had to deal with the problem of having a limited dataset to work with, as most classification algorithms require large training data-sets for adequate results.

Some of the challenges presented remain unaddressed by our proposed solution. The main problem that affects our system is the overlap of fish. Solving it requires proper segmentation on a per-object basis which we were unable to achieve. Our approach to tracking, based in tracking by detection, is prone to unrelated moving objects. While we were somewhat successful in addressing the issue of repetitive background movement, which mostly appears due to coral and algae, our system is still vulnerable to unrelated moving entities that could appear in other environments. While we successfully implemented classification methods for our defined problem, it was significantly simplified by grouping species with similar appearance. We would like to see a more complete discretization of fish species and a solution that is able to deal with that, significantly harder, problem.

Acknowledgments. This work was supported by Fundação para a Ciência e a Tecnologia, under project UIDB/50021/2020, Project E-ARK3 and partially supported by FCT with the LARSyS - FCT Plurianual funding 2020–2023.

References

1. Beauxis-Aussalet, E., Palazzo, S., Nadarajan, G., Arslanova, E., Spampinato, C., Hardman, L.: A video processing and data retrieval framework for fish population monitoring. In: Proceedings of the 2nd ACM International Workshop on Multimedia Analysis for Ecological Data (MAED), pp. 15–20 (2013)
2. Dalal, N., Triggs, B.: Histograms of oriented gradients for human detection. In: Proceeding of the IEEE Computer Society Conference on Computer Vision and Pattern Recognition (CVPR), vol. 1, pp. 886–893 (2005)
3. De Maesschalck, R., Jouan-Rimbaud, D., Massart, D.L.: The mahalanobis distance. Chemometr. Intell. Lab. Syst. **50**(1), 1–18 (2000)
4. Friedman, N., Russell, S.: Image segmentation in video sequences: a probabilistic approach. In: Proceedings of the 13th Conference on Uncertainty in Artificial Intelligence (UAI), pp. 175–181 (1997)
5. Kavasidis, I., Palazzo, S.: Quantitative performance analysis of object detection algorithms on underwater video footage. In: Proceedings of the 1st ACM International Workshop on Multimedia Analysis for Ecological Data (MAED), pp. 57–60 (2012)
6. Kavasidis, I., Spampinato, C., Giordano, D.: Generation of ground truth for object detection while playing an online game: productive gaming or recreational working? In: Proceedings of the IEEE Conference on Computer Vision and Pattern Recognition (CVPR) Workshops, pp. 694–699 (2013)
7. Nadeem, U., Shah, S.A.A., Bennamoun, M., Togneri, R., Sohel, F.: Real time surveillance for low resolution and limited-data scenarios: an image set classification approach. arXiv:1803.09470 (2018)

8. Spampinato, C., Chen-Burger, Y.-H., Nadarajan, G., Fisher, R.B.: Detecting, tracking and counting fish in low quality unconstrained underwater videos. In: Proceedings of the 3rd International Conference on Computer Vision Theory and Applications (VISAPP), vol. 2, pp. 514–519 (2008)
9. Zivkovic, Z.: Improved adaptive gaussian mixture model for background subtraction. In Proceedings of the 17th International Conference on Pattern Recognition (ICPR), vol. 2, pp. 28–31 (2004)

Using External Knowledge to Improve Zero-Shot Action Recognition in Egocentric Videos

Adrián Núñez-Marcos[1]([✉])(ID), Gorka Azkune[2](ID), Eneko Agirre[2](ID),
Diego López-de-Ipiña[1](ID), and Ignacio Arganda-Carreras[3,4,5](ID)

[1] Deustotech Institute, University of Deusto,
Avenida de las Universidades, No. 24, 48007 Bilbao, Spain
{adrian.nunez,dipina}@deusto.es

[2] IXA NLP Group, Faculty of Computer Science, University of the Basque Country,
P. Manuel Lardizabal 1, 20018 San Sebastian, Spain
{gorka.azcune,e.agirre}@ehu.es

[3] Department of Computer Science and Artificial Intelligence,
University of the Basque Country, P. Manuel Lardizabal 1,
20018 San Sebastian, Spain
ignacio.arganda@ehu.eus

[4] Ikerbasque, Basque Foundation for Science, Maria Diaz de Haro 3,
48013 Bilbao, Spain

[5] Donostia International Physics Center (DIPC),
Manuel Lardizabal 4, 20018 San Sebastian, Spain

Abstract. Zero-shot learning is a very promising research topic. For a vision-based action recognition system, for instance, zero-shot learning allows to recognise actions never seen during the training phase. Previous works in zero-shot action recognition have exploited in several ways the visual appearance of input videos to infer actions. Here, we propose to add external knowledge to improve the performance of purely vision-based systems. Specifically, we have explored three different sources of knowledge in the form of text corpora. Our resulting system follows the literature and disentangles actions into verbs and objects. In particular, we independently train two vision-based detectors: (i) a verb detector and (ii) an active object detector. During inference, we combine the probability distributions generated from those detectors to obtain a probability distribution of actions. Finally, the vision-based estimation is further combined with an action prior extracted from text corpora (external knowledge). We evaluate our approach on the EGTEA Gaze+ dataset, an Egocentric Action Recognition dataset, demonstrating that the use of external knowledge improves the recognition of actions never seen by the detectors.

Keywords: Egocentric Action Recognition · Zero-Shot Learning · External knowledge

© Springer Nature Switzerland AG 2020
A. Campilho et al. (Eds.): ICIAR 2020, LNCS 12131, pp. 174–185, 2020.
https://doi.org/10.1007/978-3-030-50347-5_16

1   Introduction

Vision-based action recognition is a major emerging field, mainly due to the broad range of applications in domains such as health [9] or surveillance [3,4,11]. The majority of the research has focused on exocentric videos, where the action is being observed from a third-person's perspective. Nonetheless, in the last decade, thanks to the growth in the amount of wearable camera devices, the Egocentric Action Recognition (EAR) field has attracted the interest of the computer vision community. EAR is specially well suited to recognise actions performed by a person, since the visual information of the working space is usually perfectly visible. From the application point of view, such potential makes EAR interesting for Ambient Assisted Living, where the visual information captured by egocentric devices can be used to assist users.

Egocentric action videos are usually labelled with a verb and a set of objects, creating an action when combined, e.g., "open fridge" or "cut cucumber". However, datasets are quite limited in the number of combinations of verbs and objects, thus constraining the scalability of the developed systems. In fact, for an action recognition system to be useful in real world settings, being able to generalise to any action is crucial. This problem is known as Zero-Shot Learning (ZSL). In the zero-shot action recognition literature it is common to find solutions that disentangle the action classification into the verb (the movement) and the active object (the visually manipulated object) classification [13,18]. Following such approach, both the verb and the active object would be separately inferred. Therefore, should the system receive a never seen action, it would be able to make a prediction by combining the knowledge acquired from those two separated branches, as long as the verb and the object have been previously seen. More formally, assuming $|V|$ and $|O|$ are the number of verbs and objects in the training set respectively, the system would be able to recognise $|V| \times |O|$ actions only requiring $|V| + |O|$ labels.

Nonetheless, naively combining verbs and objects may wind up with action predictions that do not exist, such as "cut fridge", following the previous examples, or action predictions that are rare, instead of those that are performed more frequently. Thus, we propose to add external knowledge to the system to address those problems. As the action prediction can be represented as a string of text, external text corpora containing pairs of verbs and objects (actions) can be efficiently used to create an action prior. The latter provides a probability distribution over the set of possible actions created from the Cartesian product between a set of verbs and objects (those learnt from the two separate verb and object detectors).

In that sense, it is important to find a suitable source of external knowledge, since different action priors from different knowledge domains may have different results and effects. For example, using a cooking book corpus will benefit actions often appearing in recipes, whilst a corpus created from several books may provide more general knowledge. We raised this question and proposed several experiments to test a number of corpora in order to provide insights on the matter.

Therefore, this paper presents the following two main contributions:

1. A novel method which uses external knowledge in form of text corpora to improve the performance of vision-based action recognition systems for ZSL in egocentric videos.
2. A thorough analysis to measure the effects of applying action priors extracted from different sources.

2   Related Work

Even though the EAR field has gained popularity in the last decade [2,10,16], the Zero-Shot EAR subfield is still developing, and, to the best of our knowledge, the number of works is quite limited.

The idea of fusing verbs and objects to infer new combinations is already introduced by Zhang et al. [18]. They used the Fisher Vector encoding of features such as Improved Dense Trajectories or Histogram of oriented Gradients and visual CNN features, respectively. In fact, the idea of dividing the verb and the object influenced other researchers, as well as this work. In addition, they analysed various fusion methods among *early*, *late*, and *early+late* stage fusion. In a similar fashion, Al-Naser et al. [1] used a Myo armband sensor and a Multi-layer Perceptron to classify verbs and a gaze-point-based cropping of video frames as input to a GoogleNet [15] to predict objects. Any new action composed from the combination of the learnt verbs and objects can be inferred from their system.

Guadarrama et al. [5] aimed at inferring descriptions of the actions in videos. When unseen actions appeared, they used a semantic hierarchy built from free annotations to provide a less specific and more general answer. In their case, they used triplets of subject, verb and object in their hierarchy. In our case, we only include verb and object, as the subject in first-person videos is always the one recording the video, and we use text corpora to build a probability distribution to help us decide which prediction of the system is more suitable, rather than to be able to provide a more generic answer.

Although there are other approaches in the exocentric vision domain using zero-shot learning [7], we would like to highlight the work performed by Shen et al. [13]. In particular, they aim to recognise Human-Object Interactions in images using a system based on a Faster Region-Based CNN [12] that branches, on top of it, into two streams: the verb and the object detection networks. The output of the system provides two probability distributions: one for verbs and the other one for objects. By multiplying these, a matrix is obtained where the probability at a position (i, j) refers to the probability of the action created by fusing the ith verb with the jth object.

In general, our work follows those where the verb and the active object are separately modelled. However, instead of focusing on improving those detectors by means of new computer vision and/or machine learning techniques, we provide a novel way to leverage external knowledge on top of those vision-based detectors and improve the overall action recognition performance. Hence, in principle, our proposal could be used to improve any approach which relies on separated verb and object detectors.

3   Methodology

In the context of EAR, a ZSL approach aims to create a model which is capable of recognising actions that have never been seen during the training phase. Inspired by the literature, we separate an action into a verb and an active object. In consequence, recognising the verb and the active object in a given video, we can infer the performed action. Following that idea, we built two identical neural networks to detect the verb and the active object. We pose the problem as a classification problem, where given a video, i.e., a sequence of frames, the detectors have to estimate the probability distribution over the set of verbs and active objects. Then, we combine both probability distributions to infer the action such that $a = max_i\{p^v(a_i)\}$, where a is the action label and $p^v(a_i)$ denotes the probability for the ith action estimated by the vision-based system. This probability is calculated as $p^v(a_i) = p(v_{a_i}) \times p(o_{a_i})$, where $p(v_{a_i})$ and $p(o_{a_i})$ denote the probability of the verb and object disentangled from a_i. Those probabilities are estimated by the neural networks D_V and D_O.

Moreover, we use external knowledge in form of text corpora to compute a probability distribution of all the combinations of verbs and objects. Specifically, we look for co-occurrences of those verbs and objects within N-grams extracted from text corpora to create the probability distribution which we call the action prior. This prior is combined with the probabilities of the actions obtained from the combination of the verb and object detectors. The final action prediction is the one with the highest probability. More formally, given $p^v(a_i)$ and $p^t(a_i)$ (the action prior for the ith action), the inferred action a is calculated as $a = max_i\{p^v(a_i) \times p^t(a_i)\}$. An overview of the system is shown in Fig. 1.

3.1   System Architecture

Both D_V and D_O, the verb and object detectors, take as input a video $X = \{F_1, F_2, ..., F_n\}$, an ordered list of frames of the video, where $F_i \in \mathbb{R}^{224x224x3}$. As the videos have a varying length, we uniformly sample 25 frames from each one. The network architecture is based on the work of Sudhakaran et al. [14], being composed of a Convolutional Neural Network (CNN) with a Recurrent Neural Network (RNN) on top, as the feature extraction part, and a single Fully-Connected (FC) layer as the classifier. Specifically, in this work we use a ResNet50 [6] architecture as the CNN (with a 1×1 convolution of 256 filters on top to reduce the dimensionality) and a Convolutional Long Short-Term Memory (ConvLSTM) [17] as the RNN. The detector outputs a probability distribution $p = \{p_1, p_2, ..., p_n\}$, where $p_i \in [0, 1]$ is the probability of the class i for a given video such that $\sum_{i=1}^{n} p_i = 1$. Depending on the task of the network, i.e., predicting verbs or active objects, p is defined as $p(v)$ (output of D_V) or $p(o)$ (output of D_O), respectively, and p_i as $p(v_i)$ and $p(o_i)$.

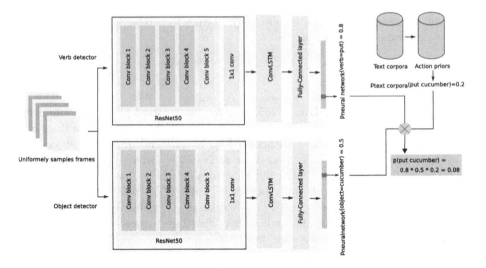

Fig. 1. Architecture overview: two neural networks composed of a ResNet50 and a ConvLSTM take as input a video (uniformly sampled frames) and output two probability distributions (verbs and objects). The resulting probability distributions are combined with an action prior sampled from text corpora to infer the most probable action. The layers or blocks of layers in orange are frozen while the yellow ones are trained. (Color figure online)

3.2   Action Priors

The action prior $p^t(a)$ is the probability distribution over the set of actions coming from the Cartesian product of the set of verbs and objects from a given dataset, i.e., $\{(v_j, o_k) : \forall j, \forall k | v_j \in V \text{ and } o_k \in O\}$ and $a_i = (v_j, o_k)$. The objective of the action prior is to estimate the likelihood of a given combination of verb and object, i.e., $p^t(a_i)$, based on external knowledge completely independent from the action recognition videos. We propose to estimate those priors using different textual corpora.

In our work, the following external knowledge sources are used to estimate action priors:

- Cookbook wiki: using the Cookbook wiki page[1], we extract a corpus containing recipes and, thus, actions related to cooking recipes. We selected this knowledge source to further narrow the domain of the egocentric videos and see how specialised knowledge can help for ZSL.
- Google searcher API[2]: we use the API to search for actions and get the number of results as the number of occurrences. This knowledge source was chosen to have a more general prior estimation which is not focused on a specific domain, in contrast to Cookbook wiki.

---

[1] https://en.wikibooks.org/wiki/Cookbook:Recipes.
[2] https://developers.google.com/custom-search/v1/overview.

– *Phrasefinder* searcher API[3]: similar to the Google API, the *Phrasefinder* source has no specific domain, as it searches through Google Books' N-grams. We chose this as a more controlled alternative to the Google API prior, whose results come from a wilder environment (any site indexed in Google).

In order to create the prior, for the Cookbook source, we scrapped the Wikicook to obtain a corpus and cleaned it. With the raw corpus, we removed non-ascii characters, lowercased the text, eliminated stop words and applied the WordNet lemmatiser[4]. Finally, we experimentally decided to extract N-grams of size 4. To determine that an action appears in an N-gram, both the verb and the object of the action are taken separately and both must appear within the N-gram, not necessarily in adjacent positions. In fact, instead of just taking the verb and the object as they are, we manually defined a list of synonyms for each one and, for each possible combination of synonyms of a verb and an object, their appearance in the N-gram is checked. If at least a synonym of the verb and a synonym of the object are contained in the N-gram, it is considered that the action is contained in it. The number of N-grams where the action is found divided by the total number of N-grams is the final prior of the action.

In the case of the Google and *Phrasefinder* sources, for a given action, the API returns the number of results given by the query. This query is created with the expression "verb * object" with the Google API and "verb ? object" with the *Phrasefinder* API. The symbol "*" and "?" are wildcards, placeholders for strings such as "a", "the", and so on; the use of wildcards allows for searches that are more natural than just searching for "verb object". The query returns the number of results, which is used as the frequency of the action. Again, we use synonyms for verbs and objects, using the mean of all the non-zero results as the final frequency of the action. The latter is normalised by the sum of all actions' frequencies to obtain the action prior.

Finally, in order to estimate an upper bound of our proposed system, we created the so called *perfect prior* using the test set distribution of classes. We computed the frequency of each action and normalised them by the total number of videos of the test set. Although very informative, this upper bound is, in fact, empirically unreachable by other means, as the perfect prior is unique to the test set.

4   Experimental Setup

4.1   Dataset and Evaluation Metrics

We chose the EGTEA Gaze+[5] dataset for our experiments. Launched in 2017, this dataset contains 28 h of egocentric videos with 32 subjects performing

---

[3] https://phrasefinder.io/api.

[4] http://www.nltk.org/_modules/nltk/stem/wordnet.html#WordNetLemmatizer.

[5] Georgia Tech: Extended GTEA Gaze+. http://webshare.ipat.gatech.edu/coc-rim-wall-lab/web/yli440/egteagp.

cooking related actions. It is composed of 10,325 action segments, with 19 verbs, 53 nouns and 106 actions.

To evaluate the performance of the tested systems, apart from reporting the accuracy over the predicted actions, we also chose to present the F1 score in its macro variant, due to the unbalanced nature of the EGTEA Gaze+ dataset: classes with few samples that may not be learnt have low impact in the accuracy, in contrast, they have a significant impact on the F1 score. In addition, in the F1 computation, we include an artificial class in which all predictions out of the set of test actions are included. This class is taken into account to compute the F1 score.

4.2   Zero-Shot Splits

EGTEA Gaze+ consists of three official training and test splits that provide a common ground to evaluate action recognition systems. However, those official splits are not suitable for ZSL, since the actions in the test set are also represented in the train set. Therefore, in our experiments, we employ new splits. Using all the data in EGTEA, we followed the guidelines given by Shen et al. [13] for a similar problem. First, we removed action videos containing verbs and objects that only appear once, as they are not appropriate for the zero-shot task, as formulated in this paper. This left us with 9 verbs and 29 objects. Second, to generate the test set, we randomly took 20% of the action classes under the condition that any verb and object contained in that test set must appear in the training set (in any action). That is, all the verbs and objects must appear in the training set. The validation set is created taking a stratified subset from the resulting training set, using the 10% of the videos in train. Note that the validation set is important not for the ZSL task itself, but to train and tune the detectors.

Since we aim at measuring the effects of specialised and generic knowledge in the system, we propose two types of splits: the first one, denoted as the Recipe split (R split), is built explicitly discarding some verbs, objects and actions which have nothing to do with recipes. Specifically, we banned the verb *Inspect/Read*, the objects *cabinet, sponge, grocery bag, eating utensil, drawer*, and *fridge drawer* and the action *wash pan*. The split created with this rules has 6121 training videos and 1464 test videos. The second one, called the No Recipe split (NR split), avoids any bias. To create the test set we do not impose any other condition apart from the ones given by Shen et al. [13]. We assume that the Cookbook prior will not be as effective in this type of split as in the R split, as such prior produces a specific type of probability distribution focused on actions related to recipes. In this case, the split has 6277 training videos and 1308 test videos.

4.3   Experiments

We performed several experiments to validate the hypothesis posed in this paper, i.e., that we can improve zero-shot EAR using external knowledge. We compare our proposed system with a baseline system which only relies on D_V and D_O. For this baseline, we infer the action of a given video computing $a = max_i\{p^v(a_i)\}$. Moreover, we test our system with the proposed three action priors (provided by Cookbook, Google and *Phrasefinder*) on both ZSL splits (R and NR).

For each split, both D_V and D_O, as in Sect. 3.1, are trained for 100 epochs with early stopping with a patience of 10 epochs (the macro-F1 metric in the validation set is used to stop). The CNN weights are initialised with an Imagenet pre-training and are frozen up to the 4th convolutional block, being the 5th fine-tuned (see Fig. 1). We use Adam [8] optimiser with a batch size of 16, initial learning rate of $1e^{-4}$ and 25 timesteps per video. To avoid over-fitting as much as possible we use class weights in training (for the loss function, they penalise errors in classes with fewer samples) and data augmentation: (i) standard random horizontal flipping and (ii) multi-scale random corner cropping, i.e., one of the four corners or the centre position are randomly selected as a possible crop, the initial crop size is set to 224×224, but is scaled with a factor randomly chosen among $1, 0.875, 0.75, 0.65625$ and then re-scaled again to 224×224.

The code of our proposed approach is publicly available[6].

5   Results

The results for verb and object classification per split, using D_V and D_O independently, are shown in Tables 1 and 2, respectively. As it can be observed, the performance in the test set with respect to the validation set suffers a significant drop, specially for the case of D_O. We believe a possible explanation why D_V does not deteriorate as much is the number of classes that must be learnt (9 for verbs and 29 for objects). Besides, we hypothesise that this drop may be a consequence of the different shapes and poses that objects have in the test set compared to the training or the validation set. For instance, a tomato observed during the action "take" may look different from a tomato which is being "cut", especially since the tomato may be partially occluded or even sliced during the latter. This observation suggests that the active object detection is highly correlated with the verb and thus, active object detectors specially suffer in ZSL conditions.

Table 1. Verb classification results with verb detector. The results are given as the mean of 3 runs, with the standard deviation.

	Split	Train		Validation		Test	
		Accuracy	Macro-F1	Accuracy	Macro-F1	Accuracy	Macro-F1
Verb detector	R	99.37%	99.22	75.69%	67.93	60.31%	31.08
		(± 0.10)	(± 0.19)	(± 0.35)	(± 0.58)	(± 1.10)	(± 0.06)
	NR	98.44%	97.64	76.65%	66.42	53.49%	42.90
		(± 0.61)	(± 0.80)	(± 0.42)	(± 3.11)	(± 1.44)	(± 1.46)

---

[6] https://github.com/AdrianNunez/zeroshot-action-recognition-action-priors.

Table 2. Active object classification results with object detector. The results are given as the mean of 3 runs, with the standard deviation.

	Split	Train		Validation		Test	
		Accuracy	Macro-F1	Accuracy	Macro-F1	Accuracy	Macro-F1
Object detector	R	99.37%	99.22	75.69%	67.93	27.14%	13.48
		(±0.10)	(±0.19)	(±0.35)	(±0.58)	(±0.74)	(±0.73)
	NR	98.70%	98.35	76.43%	68.64	31.75%	15.34
		(±0.56)	(±0.76)	(±0.34)	(±0.39)	(±0.81)	(±0.51)

Using the presented D_V and D_O, we carried out all the experiments of Sect. 4.3 and show the results in Table 3. To analyse the results, paying attention to the type of split is pivotal.

On the one hand, we have the R split, with a test set created specifically with actions related to recipes. The baseline result for this split in Table 3 is higher than for the NR split. Apart from that, the R split benefits the most from the prior built from a corpus of recipes (Cookbook), having an improvement of 5.47 points in accuracy compared to the baseline. However, it is also important to point out that the Google prior grants a slight improvement of 1.73 points, even though it is not as appropriate as the Cookbook prior for this type of split. The reason may well be that the Google prior helps discarding non-existing actions and promoting actions that are more common.

Results per class of the test set of the R split are shown in Table 4. It can be seen that the Cookbook experiments are the ones that show the largest improvement on the majority of the classes, although the Google and the *Phrasefinder* priors have also some classes where they can surpass the Cookbook priors. In fact, this is the expected behaviour given the prior of each class. Classes where the Google or the *Phrasefinder* prior is the highest among these three are also the ones where they have the best accuracy.

On the other hand, the NR split shows an accuracy improvement on every experiment, having a higher accuracy with the Cookbook prior but higher F1 with the Google and the *Phrasefinder* priors. Observing Table 5, it is clear that the Cookbook prior has the potential to improve a few classes to a high accuracy, but this effect is localised in some classes and zeroes out others. Meanwhile, the Google prior has a higher F1 due to the balanced effect it has, i.e., it only zeroes out a class with a baseline low accuracy (divide/pull apart lettuce) while it obtains the best accuracy in 5 classes. In fact, this is the expected behaviour, as the Cookbook prior has a few non-zero action probabilities due to the constrained domain used and the Google prior has broader knowledge, thus including more actions and a more balanced distribution.

Moreover, half of the classes do not have any performance gain in any experiment (those in which the baseline is highlighted in bold). There may be some reasons why this can happen in any split: (i) the presence of meta-objects (such as *eating* or *cooking utensil*), as discussed by [14], can affect the performance, as a single label (hyperonym) covers various objects (hyponyms) and learning them is more difficult; and (ii) difficult to learn verbs and objects whose performance affect the learning of the action, a problem caused by the detectors, because of the few samples in training or their intrinsic variance.

We can conclude that specific domain knowledge applied in the same domain can be beneficial, as in the case of the Wikicook prior in the R split. In fact, not only is it helpful to be in the same domain, approximating the prior to the distribution of actions is very promising too, as seen with the perfect prior. In the case of this dataset, the actor had controlled actions but, different people usually have different routines and, thus, a different action distribution. Adjusting the prior to each one could potentially be a huge improvement. In the opposite side, we have the Google prior, whose generic knowledge seems to be more balanced and helpful in almost all the classes but not as beneficial as a prior specific to a domain of actions.

Table 3. Table of zero-shot action classification results: comparison between the baseline and the experiments using the Cookbook, the Google, the *Phrasefinder* and the perfect priors. Results in bold highlight the best result.

Split	Baseline		Cookbook prior		Google prior		*Phrasefinder* prior		Perfect prior	
	Acc.	F1	Acc.	F1	Acc.	F1	Acc.	F1	Acc.	F1
R	12.61%	16.52	**18.08%**	**22.65**	14.89%	18.89	14.34%	18.29	51.46%	44.14
	(±0.56)	(±0.23)	(±0.99)	(±0.80)	(±0.93)	(±0.64)	(±0.90)	(±1.05)	(±1.45)	(±0.97)
NR	8.03%	11.46	**11.47%**	9.73	9.17%	**12.58**	10.37%	11.48	54.31%	45.51
	(±0.54)	(±1.21)	(±1.41)	(±1.25)	(±0.91)	(±1.46)	(±1.01)	(±1.16)	(±0.42)	(±1.68)

Table 4. Table of zero-shot action classification results by class in the R split using the accuracy: comparison between the baseline and the experiments using the Cookbook, the Google, the *Phrasefinder* and the perfect priors. Results in bold highlight the best result (not taking into account the perfect prior experiments).

Class (R split)	Baseline	Cookbook prior	Google Prior	*Phrasefinder* prior	Perfect prior
Cut bell pepper	14.22% (±6.04)	**23.28% (±6.64)**	14.46% (±6.36)	6.86% (±1.93)	63.97% (±9.92)
Cut onion	0.57% (±0.00)	**8.05% (±0.47)**	1.92% (±0.27)	2.87% (±0.47)	57.47% (±2.15)
Put bread	18.09% (±4.51)	25.89% (±7.39)	25.53% (±4.84)	**29.79% (±6.26)**	64.18% (±8.74)
Put cup	7.92% (±3.58)	14.17% (±5.62)	14.58% (±5.62)	**15.42% (±4.60)**	41.67% (±10.27)
Put lettuce	21.36% (±3.46)	**41.75% (±3.46)**	25.57% (±2.29)	37.86% (±1.59)	77.67% (±1.37)
Put onion	2.56% (±3.63)	**10.26% (±5.54)**	2.56% (±2.09)	5.98% (±3.20)	5.13% (±2.09)
Put plate	21.32% (±5.73)	29.41% (±4.33)	25.25% (±5.58)	**29.66% (±5.71)**	61.52% (±10.54)
Put pot	14.52% (±3.99)	**28.05% (±1.23)**	16.50% (±2.60)	25.08% (±1.23)	50.17% (±1.23)
Put tomato	4.37% (±1.48)	3.17% (±1.48)	**5.95% (±0.97)**	1.59% (±1.12)	13.49% (±0.56)
Take bowl	30.00% (±7.08)	18.00% (±5.19)	**32.22% (±7.31)**	18.44% (±6.02)	75.11% (±6.19)
Take egg	0.00% (±0.00)	0.98% (±1.39)	**2.94% (±4.16)**	0.98% (±1.39)	6.86% (±3.67)
Take onion	6.11% (±1.57)	**17.22% (±1.57)**	8.33% (±2.72)	7.78% (±2.08)	39.44% (±2.08)
Take pan	17.11% (±1.07)	**17.98% (±3.28)**	17.54% (±3.10)	8.33% (±4.34)	73.25% (±4.07)
Take pot	2.99% (±1.60)	**7.26% (±1.60)**	2.99% (±2.63)	2.99% (±1.60)	16.24% (±1.21)
Take tomato	2.63% (±2.15)	**3.07% (±1.24)**	2.63% (±1.07)	0.88% (±1.24)	17.54% (±1.64)
Wash pot	10.85% (±1.10)	**13.95% (±3.29)**	9.30% (±1.90)	11.63% (±1.90)	57.36% (±3.95)

Table 5. Table of zero-shot action classification results by class in the NR split using the accuracy: comparison between the baseline and the experiments using the Cookbook, the Google, the *Phrasefinder* and the perfect priors. Results in bold highlight the best result (not taking into account the perfect prior experiments).

Class (NR split)	Baseline	Cookbook prior	Google prior	*Phrasefinder* prior	Perfect prior
Close drawer	7.41% (±5.24)	0.00% (±0.00)	**15.56% (±6.54)**	8.89% (±5.44)	53.33% (±10.10)
Cut cucumber	6.41% (±2.27)	0.96% (±0.00)	**8.65% (±3.07)**	3.21% (±0.60)	84.78% (±9.50)
Cut lettuce	**5.80% (±3.69)**	1.45% (±1.02)	3.62% (±1.02)	1.45% (±2.05)	38.41% (±9.11)
Divide/pull apart lettuce	**0.42% (±0.59)**	0.00% (±0.00)	0.00% (±0.00)	0.42% (±0.59)	16.25% (±3.06)
Divide/pull apart onion	**0.00% (±0.00)**	0.00% (±0.00)	0.00% (±0.00)	0.00% (±0.00)	22.44% (±7.08)
Open fridge drawer	**0.00% (±0.00)**	0.00% (±0.00)	0.00% (±0.00)	0.00% (±0.00)	42.32% (±7.42)
Put bell pepper	5.67% (±5.31)	0.00% (±0.00)	**17.02% (±6.95)**	0.71% (±1.00)	24.82% (±14.15)
Put bowl	16.55% (±3.65)	**48.55% (±4.66)**	22.82% (±3.05)	31.77% (±3.12)	77.85% (±3.05)
Put cheese container	0.00% (±0.00)	0.00% (±0.00)	0.00% (±0.00)	0.00% (±0.00)	9.40% (±7.93)
Put cup	5.83% (±1.56)	8.33% (±0.59)	**10.42% (±0.59)**	10.42% (±0.59)	30.42% (±4.71)
Put cutting board	28.67% (±3.40)	29.33% (±12.26)	**34.00% (±5.89)**	25.33% (±12.26)	63.33% (±8.22)
Put plate	14.95% (±0.92)	**37.50% (±6.24)**	22.30% (±2.27)	26.47% (±2.40)	70.83% (±3.81)
Take bell pepper	**11.95% (±3.21)**	0.00% (±0.00)	6.92% (±4.71)	0.00% (±0.00)	70.83% (±6.23)
Take cheese container	**2.38% (±2.23)**	0.00% (±0.00)	0.60% (±0.84)	0.00% (±0.00)	48.81% (±3.04)
Take sponge	**8.33% (±3.90)**	0.00% (±0.00)	4.17% (±1.95)	4.69% (±1.28)	56.25% (±9.20)
Wash eating utensil	**4.97% (±1.09)**	2.34% (±0.41)	2.92% (±1.09)	1.75% (±0.72)	49.42% (±11.42)

6   Conclusions

Throughout this manuscript, we have presented our system of Zero-Shot Egocentric Action Recognition, a branched approach composed of a verb detector and an object detector whose results are fused to infer an action. This is further improved by the main contribution of the work: the addition of action priors. We have presented several priors from different sources and made experiments with each of them, highlighting their pros and cons. As future work, we aim to improve the base verb and object detectors and how the action priors are fused with them, as this research path has not been extensively exploited.

Acknowledgments. We gratefully acknowledge the support of the Basque Government's Department of Education for the predoctoral funding of the first author. This work has been supported by the Spanish Government under the FuturAAL-Ego project (RTI2018-101045-A-C22) and the FuturAAL-Context project (RTI2018-101045-B-C21) and by the Basque Government under the Deustek project (IT-1078-16-D).

References

1. Al-Naser, M., et al.: Hierarchical model for zero-shot activity recognition using wearable sensors. In: ICAART, vol. 2, pp. 478–485 (2018)
2. Bambach, S.: A survey on recent advances of computer vision algorithms for egocentric video. arXiv preprint arXiv:1501.02825 (2015)
3. Brezovan, M., Badica, C.: A review on vision surveillance techniques in smart home environments. In: 2013 19th International Conference on Control Systems and Computer Science, pp. 471–478. IEEE (2013)
4. deCampos, T.: A survey on computer vision tools for action recognition, crowd surveillance and suspect retrieval. In: XXXIV Congresso da Sociedade Brasileira de Computacao (CSBC), pp. 1123–1132. Citeseer (2014)
5. Guadarrama, S., et al.: Youtube2text: recognizing and describing arbitrary activities using semantic hierarchies and zero-shot recognition. In: Proceedings of the IEEE International Conference on Computer Vision, pp. 2712–2719 (2013)
6. He, K., Zhang, X., Ren, S., Sun, J.: Deep residual learning for image recognition. In: Proceedings of the IEEE Conference on Computer Vision and Pattern Recognition, pp. 770–778 (2016)
7. Junior, V.L.E., Pedrini, H., Menotti, D.: Zero-shot action recognition in videos: a survey. arXiv preprint arXiv:1909.06423 (2019)
8. Kingma, D.P., Ba, J.: Adam: a method for stochastic optimization. arXiv preprint arXiv:1412.6980 (2014)
9. Luo, Z., et al.: Computer vision-based descriptive analytics of seniors' daily activities for long-term health monitoring. In: Machine Learning for Healthcare (MLHC) (2018)
10. Nguyen, T.H.C., Nebel, J.C., Florez-Revuelta, F., et al.: Recognition of activities of daily living with egocentric vision: a review. Sensors 16(1), 72 (2016)
11. Rege, A., Mehra, S., Vann, A., Luo, Z.: Vision-based approach to senior healthcare: Depth-based activity recognition with convolutional neural networks, Semantic Scholar (2017)
12. Ren, S., He, K., Girshick, R., Sun, J.: Faster R-CNN: towards real-time object detection with region proposal networks. In: Advances in Neural Information Processing Systems, pp. 91–99 (2015)
13. Shen, L., Yeung, S., Hoffman, J., Mori, G., Fei-Fei, L.: Scaling human-object interaction recognition through zero-shot learning. In: 2018 IEEE Winter Conference on Applications of Computer Vision (WACV), pp. 1568–1576. IEEE (2018)
14. Sudhakaran, S., Lanz, O.: Attention is all we need: nailing down object-centric attention for egocentric activity recognition. arXiv preprint arXiv:1807.11794 (2018)
15. Szegedy, C., et al.: Going deeper with convolutions. In: Proceedings of the IEEE Conference on Computer Vision and Pattern Recognition, pp. 1–9 (2015)
16. Tadesse, G.A., Cavallaro, A.: Visual features for ego-centric activity recognition: a survey. In: Proceedings of the 4th ACM Workshop on Wearable Systems and Applications, pp. 48–53. ACM (2018)
17. Xingjian, S., Chen, Z., Wang, H., Yeung, D.Y., Wong, W.K., Woo, W.C.: Convolutional LSTM network: a machine learning approach for precipitation nowcasting. In: Advances in Neural Information Processing Systems, pp. 802–810 (2015)
18. Zhang, Y.C., Li, Y., Rehg, J.M.: First-person action decomposition and zero-shot learning. In: 2017 IEEE Winter Conference on Applications of Computer Vision (WACV), pp. 121–129. IEEE (2017)

A Semantics-Guided Warping for Semi-supervised Video Object Instance Segmentation

Qiong Wang[1,2](✉), Lu Zhang[2], and Kidiyo Kpalma[2]

[1] College of Computer Science and Technology,
Zhejiang University of Technology, Hangzhou 310023, China
wangqiong819@gmail.com
[2] Univ Rennes, INSA Rennes, CNRS, IETR (Institut d'Electronique et de
Télécommunication de Rennes) - UMR 6164, 35000 Rennes, France

Abstract. In the semi-supervised video object instance segmentation domain, the mask warping technique, which warps the mask of the target object to flow vectors frame by frame, is widely used to extract target object. The big issue with this approach is that the generated warped map is not always of high accuracy, where the background or other objects may be wrongly detected as the target object. To cope with this problem, we propose to use the semantics of the target object as a guidance during the warping process. The warping confidence computation firstly judges the confidence of the generated warped map. Then a semantic selection is introduced to optimize the warped map with low confidence, where the target object is re-identified using the semantics-labels of the target object. The proposed method is assessed on the recently published large-scale Youtube-VOS dataset and compared to some state-of-the-art methods. The experimental results show that the proposed approach has a promising performance.

Keywords: Warping flow · Semantics · Semi-supervised video object instance segmentation

1 Introduction

Video object segmentation aims to segment objects from backgrounds. It assigns object IDs to the pixels belonging to objects, and assigns 0 values to other pixels. It has numerous applications in autonomous driving, video surveillance, object recognition, etc.

According to the object to be segmented, video object segmentation can be roughly classified into three categories: video foreground segmentation, video semantic object segmentation and video object instance segmentation. Video foreground segmentation aims at segmenting all probable objects. For real-world scenes, the detected region may contain multiple objects. Decomposing the detected region into different objects is more meaningful and is better for

© Springer Nature Switzerland AG 2020
A. Campilho et al. (Eds.): ICIAR 2020, LNCS 12131, pp. 186–195, 2020.
https://doi.org/10.1007/978-3-030-50347-5_17

video understanding. Video semantic object segmentation segments the region based on the semantic label. The objects belonging to the same semantic label are grouped together. In the output map of video object instance segmentation, the pixels are grouped into multiple sets and assigned to consistent object IDs. Pixels within the same set belong to the same object.

Video object instance segmentation attracts more interests and has not been fully investigated. One popular way for video object instance segmentation is called as Semi-supervised video object segmentation. Human-guidance is adopted to define the objects that people want to segment. It is usually delineated in the frame that the object appears in the first time. By propagating the manual labels to the rest of the video sequence, the object instance is segmented in the whole video sequences. Semi-supervised video object segmentation can be regarded as a tracking problem but with the mask output. This paper focuses on semi-supervised video object instance segmentation.

For semi-supervised video object segmentation based on the human-guidance, one challenge is how to segment a pre-defined object in a video based on its provided mask of the frame in which the object appears at the first time. An initial way for semi-supervised video object segmentation is to firstly train the parent network which detects all foreground objects (also called as offline learning), secondly fine-tune the parent network for the particular object using the manual label (also called as online learning), as in state-of-the-art method Segflow [2]. However, it is very time-consuming. Segmenting the target object just from each static frame is not sufficient.

Most works adopt "Mask warping", which combines the necessary appearance information and the temporal context together, to generate the warped map. "Mask warping" is faster than online learning, which benefits the video object segmentation. However, the warped map generated in this way is vulnerable to lighting changes, deformations, etc. The wrongly detected regions in one frame can be propagated to the following ones, thus more background is warped.

The semantics label of the object instance in the first frame is another useful cue for semi-supervised video object segmentation. In the method [11], a semantics instance segmentation algorithm is leveraged to obtain the semantics label of the target object in the first frame, and then the semantics label is propagated to the following frames. In the method [6], objects are divided into human and non-human object instances which are propagated using different networks.

Mask warping and semantics label guidance are not mutually exclusive, and could be taken simultaneously. Few studies combine the advantages of two aforementioned cues. In order to take merits of mask warping and semantics label guidance, a novel semi-supervised video object instance segmentation is proposed with following contributions:

- we propose a new method, named Warping Confidence Computation (WCC), to differentiate the warped maps by classifying them into low-confidence or high-confidence.
- Semantics selection is introduced when a low-confidence warped map is detected. With the semantics label, the optimized warped map is generated

through re-identifying the target object. Different from [11], the temporal information (optical flow) is also used for the optimization of the mask hboxwarping.

The remaining of this paper is organized as follows. Section 2 introduces an overview of state-of-the-art methods. Section 3 presents the proposed method in detail. In Sect. 4, we show and discuss the performance of the proposed method. Section 5 concludes the paper.

2   An Overview of State-of-the-Art Methods

Recent works are introduced based on the way to use the human-guidance.

2.1   Online-Offline Learning

The methods [1,12] employ the combination of offline and online learning strategies. Caelles *et al.* [1] design a network to learn the foreground object, which consists of a foreground branch and a contour branch. Compared with OSVOS [1], OnAVOS [16] updates the result based on online selected training example. It aims at adapting the changes in appearance. Cheng *et al.* [2] propose a network which has two branches: the segmentation branch and the flow branch to predict the foreground objects. MaskTrack [12] predicts the segmentation mask with a rough estimated map of the previous frame.

2.2   Mask Warping

The initial way of mask warping is to directly warp the mask of the target object to the optical flow vectors to generate warped map frame by frame [7,8,15,17,19]. Leibe *et al.* [9] propose to optimize the generated warped map in each step with an objectness score; Khoreva *et al.* [5] propose to optimize the generated warped map by removing the possibly spurious blobs.

3   Proposed Method

The proposed algorithm (semantic-guided warping for semi-supervised video object segmentation (SWVOS)) consists of three main steps: (1) according to the provided pixel-wise mask of the first frame, target object is firstly segmented using mask warping technique, where warped maps are generated; (2) the warping confidence is computed for each warped map, which is then divided into high-confidence map and low-confidence map; (3) the warped map with high-confidence is directly used as the final segmentation map, while the low-confidence warped map is optimized using a semantics selection. The block-diagram of the proposed algorithm is shown in Fig. 1.

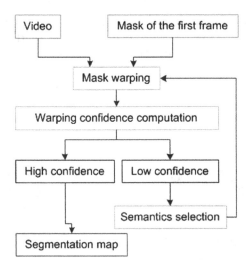

Fig. 1. The proposed block-diagram SWVOS.

3.1 Mask Warping

The optical flow vectors between pairs of successive frames are generated using the Flownet [4]. Then the warped map of each frame is obtained by warping the proposal of the previous frame to the optical flow vector. The warping function is defined as:

$$f_j = \omega(f_i, V_{i \to i+1}) \tag{1}$$

where f_j denotes the warped map of the frame j, ω is the bilinear warping function, f_i denotes the warped map of the previous frame i (for the first frame, the proposal is the provided mask), $V_{i \to j}$ is the optical flow vectors between pairs of successive frames i and j.

3.2 Warping Confidence Computation

For the generated warped map, overlap ratio and contiguous groups number are used for warping confidence computation (WCC). Overlap ratio (OR) is the ratio of the object that belongs to the warped map (WM) and the foreground map (FM), the larger is better.

$$OR = \frac{|WM \cap FM|}{|FM|} \tag{2}$$

Contiguous groups number (CGN) is the number of contiguous regions in the warped map, the smaller is better. The warped map with a low OR value or a high CGN is regarded as low-confidence in the WCC.

The foreground map (FM) is obtained with a fully covolutional network (FCN), which is a modified NLDF (Non-Local Deep Features) network [10]. Our

FCN differs from the NLDF [10] in that (1) the NLDF resizes the input image to a fixed size while our FCN uses it with its original size; (2) the NLDF adopts the VGG [14] as the baseline and uses the output of the 5-th block in the VGG as the global feature, while our FCN removes this global feature which may bring noises for complex scenes; (3) the NLDF uses the cross entropy loss and the boundary IOU loss for training while our FCN only uses the cross entropy loss since our pre-experiment showed that the boundary IOU loss does not influence a lot our method's performances.

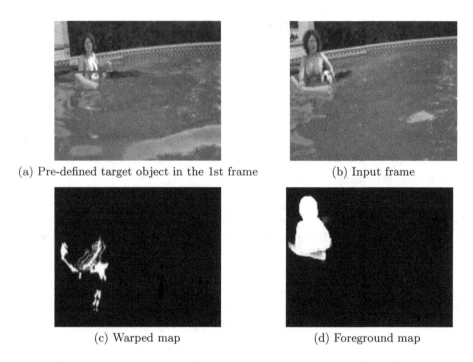

(a) Pre-defined target object in the 1st frame   (b) Input frame

(c) Warped map   (d) Foreground map

Fig. 2. One example of the warping confidence computation. The target object is denoted in red box in (a). (Color figure online)

One example of the WCC is given in Fig. 2. In this example, we can see that the warped map not only contains many contiguous groups, but also has low overlap region with the foreground map. Thus, it is judged to be a warped map with low-confidence. In this paper, the threshold for the OR is just set to be a small number 0.001. The threshold for the CGN is set to be 10, i.e. about five times of the average number of objects in each frame in the video sequence.

3.3 Semantics Selection

The warped map with low-confidence is optimized using semantic selection (SS) as following. Firstly, the semantic label of the target object in the first frame is detected using the MASK R-CNN [3]. Secondly, for the frame with low-confidence warped map, semantics of all objects are detected using the MASK R-CNN. Thirdly, the object in the frame that satisfies two conditions is segmented to generate the optimized warped map: (1) the object has the same semantic label as the target object, (2) the object is the closest one to the center of gravity of the low-confidence warped map. Here the MASK R-CNN is fine-tuned with the YouTube-VOS-train dataset [18] in order to recognize categories in this dataset. An example is given in Fig. 3.

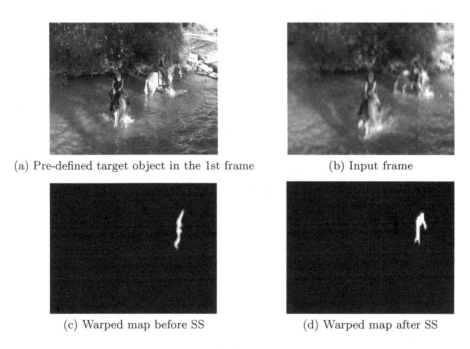

(a) Pre-defined target object in the 1st frame   (b) Input frame

(c) Warped map before SS   (d) Warped map after SS

Fig. 3. Example of semantics selection (SS). The target object is denoted in red box in (a). (Color figure online)

For a video sequence with multiple pre-defined objects, target objects are detected separately, and then merged together to generate the final segmentation map. If the pixel is detected belonging to multiple target objects, it is set to the one that has the smallest size in the provided manual labels in the first frame.

4   Experiments and Analysis

This section firstly introduces the used dataset and metrics, and then shows the performance of our approach.

4.1 Datasets

The YouTube-VOS dataset [18] is a recently published and the largest dataset with high resolution for semi-supervised video object segmentation. It is the most challenging dataset, and it contains three sets: Train, Validation and Test. It has the total number 197,272 of object annotations. For the Test set, it contains 508 video sequences with the first-frame ground truth provided. 65 categories of objects in the Test set appear in Train set, which are called as "seen objects"; and 29 categories of objects in the Test set do not appear in Train set, which are called as "unseen objects".

4.2 Evaluation Metrics

For semi-supervised video object segmentation, Region Similarity J and Contour Accuracy F [13] are used to measure the similarity between the generated segmentation map (M) and the ground truth (GT). Region Similarity J is defined as the intersection-over-union of M and GT. Contour Accuracy F is computed by the contour-based precision Pc and recall Rc.

$$J = \frac{|M \bigcap GT|}{|M \bigcup GT|} \quad F = \frac{2P_c R_c}{P_c + R_c} \tag{3}$$

A larger J value and a larger F value mean a better performance. For the overall evaluation, the final measure is the average of four scores: J for seen categories, J for unseen categories, F for seen categories and F for unseen categories.

4.3 Results and Discussions

Table 1 compares our proposed method with the state-of-the-art methods. We can see that the proposed method achieves better overall performance than Segflow [2] on the YouTube-VOS-test dataset. We must note that the compared methods OSVOS, OnAVOS and MaskTrack perform better than our proposed method. However they all use the time-consuming online learning step, which is not suitable for real-world applications. Our proposed method has not this limitation.

Table 1. Performance comparison between the proposed method (SWVOS) and existing models over the YouTube-VOS-test dataset. The best score is in **bold**.

Methods	J_seen↑	J_unseen↑	F_seen↑	F_unseen↑	Overall↑
OnAVOS	0.557	0.568	0.613	0.623	0.590
MaskTrack	0.569	**0.607**	0.593	0.637	0.602
OSVOS	**0.591**	0.588	**0.637**	**0.639**	**0.614**
SWVOS	0.513	0.367	0.494	0.419	0.448
Segflow	0.404	0.385	0.350	0.327	0.367

The first frame and its manual labels

Input frames

Segmentation results

Fig. 4. Some examples of segmentation maps generated by proposed SWVOS.

Figure 4 shows some segmentation maps generated by the proposed approach.
For the semi-supervised video object segmentation task, the YouTube-VOS
Challenge on video object segmentation 2018 uses YouTube-VOS-test dataset for
competition. Our method achieves the 8th result in YouTube-VOS Challenge on
video object segmentation 2018. In Table 2, we show the performance of our
proposed models (named "SnowFlower") in the benchmarking table. Note that
only 8 models are selected and listed.

Table 2. Performance benchmarking in the YouTube-VOS Challenge.

Team Name	Overall	J_seen	J_unseen	F_seen	F_unseen	Rank
Jono	0.722(1)	0.737(1)	0.648(2)	0.778(1)	0.725(2)	1st
speeding_zZ	0.720(2)	0.725(3)	0.663(1)	0.752(3)	0.741(1)	2nd
mikirui	0.699(3)	0.736(2)	0.621(4)	0.755(2)	0.684(4)	3rd
hi.nine	0.684(4)	0.706(5)	0.623(3)	0.728(5)	0.677(5)	4th
sunpeng	0.672(5)	0.707(4)	0.598(6)	0.736(4)	0.648(6)	5th
random_name	0.672(6)	0.672(6)	0.609(5)	0.709(6)	0.697(3)	6th
kduarte	0.539(7)	0.594(7)	0.483(7)	0.578(7)	0.502(7)	7th
SnowFlower	0.448(8)	0.513(8)	0.367(8)	0.494(8)	0.419(8)	8th

5   Conlusion

In this study, we have proposed a novel semi-supervised video object instance segmentation method that extracts each target object from each frame. This goal is achieved by using the mask warping technique. By employing the warping confidence computation, the method can firstly detect the warped map in low-level confidence. Then the optimized warped flow map is achieved through re-identifying the target object with semantics selection. The target object is extracted with better performance.

For the evaluation of video object segmentation, one recently published large-scale dataset: Youtube-VOS is used. Experimental results demonstrate that the proposed method achieves high J value and F value. Our method has not the time-consuming limitation caused by online learning step. Since, the proposed method is a combination of traditional method and deep-learning method, we will further investigate to improve its performance by training a network in an end-to-end way.

Acknowledgment. This work was supported in part by the China Scholarship Council (CSC) under Grants 201504490048, in part by National Key Research and Development Program of China (No. 2018YFE0126100).

References

1. Caelles, S., Maninis, K., Pont-Tuset, J., Leal-Taixé, L., Cremers, D., Gool, L.V.: One-shot video object segmentation. In: 2017 IEEE Conference on Computer Vision and Pattern Recognition, CVPR 2017, Honolulu, HI, USA, 21–26 July 2017, pp. 5320–5329 (2017)
2. Cheng, J., Tsai, Y., Wang, S., Yang, M.: SegFlow: joint learning for video object segmentation and optical flow. In: IEEE International Conference on Computer Vision, ICCV 2017, Venice, Italy, 22–29 October 2017, pp. 686–695 (2017)
3. He, K., Gkioxari, G., Dollár, P., Girshick, R.B.: Mask R-CNN. IEEE Trans. Pattern Anal. Mach. Intell. **42**(2), 386–397 (2020)
4. Ilg, E., Mayer, N., Saikia, T., Keuper, M., Dosovitskiy, A., Brox, T.: FlowNet 2.0: evolution of optical flow estimation with deep networks. In: 2017 IEEE Conference on Computer Vision and Pattern Recognition, CVPR 2017, Honolulu, HI, USA, 21–26 July 2017, pp. 1647–1655 (2017)
5. Khoreva, A., Benenson, R., Ilg, E., Brox, T., Schiele, B.: Lucid data dreaming for video object segmentation. Int. J. Comput. Vis. **127**(9), 1175–1197 (2019)
6. Le, T.N., et al.: Instance re-identification flow for video object segmentation. In: The 2017 DAVIS Challenge on Video Object Segmentation-CVPR Workshops (2017)
7. Li, X., Loy, C.C.: Video object segmentation with joint re-identification and attention-aware mask propagation. In: Ferrari, V., Hebert, M., Sminchisescu, C., Weiss, Y. (eds.) ECCV 2018. LNCS, vol. 11207, pp. 93–110. Springer, Cham (2018). https://doi.org/10.1007/978-3-030-01219-9_6
8. Li, X., et al.: Video object segmentation with re-identification. In: The 2017 DAVIS Challenge on Video Object Segmentation-CVPR Workshops (2017)

9. Luiten, J., Voigtlaender, P., Leibe, B.: PReMVOS: proposal-generation, refinement and merging for video object segmentation. In: Jawahar, C.V., Li, H., Mori, G., Schindler, K. (eds.) ACCV 2018. LNCS, vol. 11364, pp. 565–580. Springer, Cham (2019). https://doi.org/10.1007/978-3-030-20870-7_35

10. Luo, Z., Mishra, A.K., Achkar, A., Eichel, J.A., Li, S., Jodoin, P.: Non-local deep features for salient object detection. In: 2017 IEEE Conference on Computer Vision and Pattern Recognition, CVPR 2017, Honolulu, HI, USA, 21–26 July 2017, pp. 6593–6601 (2017)

11. Maninis, K., et al.: Video object segmentation without temporal information. IEEE Trans. Pattern Anal. Mach. Intell. **41**(6), 1515–1530 (2019). https://doi.org/10.1109/TPAMI.2018.2838670

12. Perazzi, F., Khoreva, A., Benenson, R., Schiele, B., Sorkine-Hornung, A.: Learning video object segmentation from static images. In: 2017 IEEE Conference on Computer Vision and Pattern Recognition, CVPR 2017, Honolulu, HI, USA, 21–26 July 2017, pp. 3491–3500 (2017)

13. Perazzi, F., Pont-Tuset, J., McWilliams, B., Gool, L.V., Gross, M.H., Sorkine-Hornung, A.: A benchmark dataset and evaluation methodology for video object segmentation. In: 2016 IEEE Conference on Computer Vision and Pattern Recognition, CVPR 2016, Las Vegas, NV, USA, 27–30 June 2016, pp. 724–732 (2016)

14. Simonyan, K., Zisserman, A.: Very deep convolutional networks for large-scale image recognition. arXiv preprint arXiv:1409.1556 (2014)

15. Sun, J., Yu, D., Li, Y., Wang, C.: Mask propagation network for video object segmentation. In: The 2018 DAVIS Challenge on Video Object Segmentation-CVPR Workshops (2018)

16. Voigtlaender, P., Leibe, B.: Online adaptation of convolutional neural networks for video object segmentation. In: British Machine Vision Conference 2017, BMVC 2017, London, UK, 4–7 September 2017 (2017)

17. Xiao, H., Feng, J., Lin, G., Liu, Y., Zhang, M.: MoNet: deep motion exploitation for video object segmentation. In: 2018 IEEE Conference on Computer Vision and Pattern Recognition, CVPR 2018, Salt Lake City, UT, USA, 18–22 June 2018, pp. 1140–1148 (2018)

18. Xu, N., et al.: YouTube-VOS: a large-scale video object segmentation benchmark. CoRR abs/1809.03327 (2018)

19. Xu, S., Bao, L., Zhou, P.: Class-agnostic video object segmentation without semantic re-identification. In: The 2018 DAVIS Challenge on Video Object Segmentation-CVPR Workshops (2018)

Two-Stream Framework for Activity Recognition with 2D Human Pose Estimation

Wei Chang, Chunyang Ye$^{(\boxtimes)}$, and Hui Zhou

School of Computer Science and Cyberspace Security,
Hainan University, Haikou, China
cyye@hainanu.edu.cn

Abstract. Two-Stream framework with spatial information and optical flow information have reached the great performance for action recognition task in video. The optical flow information captures the low-level motion characteristics via a fixed quantity of consecutive video frames, which however contains noise information and is incompetent to characterize different actions with varying posture and duration. Usually ten frames before and after a frame are used as optical flow information, which may be too long or too short to capture the useful motion features for different actions. Moreover, the cost of calculating optical flow information from several consecutive video frames is high. To solve these issues, we propose a novel framework to recognize actions by capturing a high-level motion feature, human pose estimation, instead of the optical flow. Our framework uses 2D human pose estimation as the motion feature, and fuses it with the spatial information using attention mechanisms. We handle extensive experiments on two excellent and challenging datasets of realistic human action, HMDB-51 and UCF-101. The experimental results illustrate that our two-stream framework outperforms state-of-the-art approaches in terms of accuracy.

Keywords: Two-Stream Framework · 2D pose estimation · Action recognition

1 Introduction

The task of human action recognition in video is a highly active research area of computer vision. With the deepening and intricacy of the convolutional neural network, the accuracy of action recognition is getting better and better. However, it is still far from human performance.

The accuracy of action recognition in video is affected by multiple factors such as lighting conditions, various perspectives, composite backgrounds, and huge intra-class changes. It is generally believed that optical flow information represents the motion information of video without background information. Therefore, it can complement the image information, improving the effect of

© Springer Nature Switzerland AG 2020
A. Campilho et al. (Eds.): ICIAR 2020, LNCS 12131, pp. 196–208, 2020.
https://doi.org/10.1007/978-3-030-50347-5_18

the two-stream model. Sevilla-Lara et al. [19] explored the role of optical flow in action recognition and have the following observations: (1) optical flow is almost invariant to appearance as the target object, so it is useful for action recognition and (2) the popular method for optimizing optical flow information is to minimize end-point-error (EPE), while it is not well correlated with the performance of action recognition network.

In the traditional two-stream framework, the cost of calculating optical flow information is high. Usually ten frames before and after a frame are used as optical flow information, which may be too long or too short to capture the useful motion features for different actions. Moreover, the motion features extracted by the optical flow information is at a low level with noise, and it is not clear what useful functions optical streaming provides for action recognition.

To solve these issues, we propose a novel two-stream framework to recognize actions by capturing a high-level motion feature, pose estimation, in place of the optical flow. We observe that many actions have specific characters of pose. Therefore, our two-stream framework uses the 2D human pose estimation as the motion feature to remove the redundant background information and highlight the description of the human motion. By getting only human pose estimation corresponding to the image frames, our approach can effectively reduce the amount of calculation. Moreover, to effectively fuse the features from the two-stream framework, we add the attention mechanism in the fusion layer, which not only highlights the local features, but also allows the network to give distinct attention between original image frames and pose estimation. In addition, we use DenseNet-121 [10] as the convolutional neural network, because DenseNet-121 achieves a better performance on multiple image recognition datasets including CIFARA-100, SVHN and ImageNet with fewer parameters. We conduct extensive experiments on two excellent and challenging datasets of realistic human action: HMDB-51 and UCF-101. The experimental results illustrate that our two-stream framework outperforms the state-of-the-art methods in terms of accuracy. That is, our two-stream framework has a significant improvement (up to 83.6%, 98.4%, respectively), especially in the sports scenes that can clearly distinguish the human pose estimation.

The rest of this paper is arranged as follows: Sect. 2 reviews state-of-the-art research efforts in action recognition of computer vision. Section 3 describes our current methodology. Section 4 evaluates our proposal with extensive experiments. Section 5 summarizes our work and highlights some future directions.

2   Related Work

2.1   Action Recognition

In recent years, two methods, namely Deep Convolutional Neural Network (DCNN) and Recurrent Neural Network (RNN) are frequently used for human action recognition of computer vision. DCNN is further divided into 3D Convolution Network and Two-Stream Framework.

Two-Stream framework was first proposed by Simonyan and Zisserman [23]. They found that video can spontaneously be disintegrated into two parts: spatial and temporal components. Therefore, they proposed a network architecture with two-stream. The spatial stream learns the features of action recognition from several consecutive video frames, whilst the temporal stream is trained to recognize action from motion in the form of dense optical flow. Each stream captures the features using a DCNN, and two stream information are integrated by SVM. Feichtenhofer et al. [7] also studied how to fuse each stream.

Shuiwang et al. [21] first proposed a 3D convolution model for action recognition in video with only a few layers of convolution and full connected layer. As the neural network gets deeper and deeper, Tran et al. [28] proposed to learn spatial and temporal components in video clips with 3D convolutional networks. Compared with 2D ConvNet, 3D ConvNet has better ability to model temporal and spatial information simultaneously, due to the addition of 3D convolution and 3D pooling operations. In 3D ConvNets, convolution and pooling operations can learn spatio-temporal information, whereas in 2D ConvNets they are done only spatially. However 3D ConvNet cannot capture long-term sequence features.

Long short-term memory networks (LSTM) is characterized by the advantage to learn long-term dependency information in variable-length videos. Wu et al. [35] applied LSTM to explore long-term temporal information for action recognition of human. They use the wealth of information (time information, spatial information, audio information) in the video to construct a Multi-Stream Fusion Framework. Later, Ma et al. [18] proposed an approach to integrate Two-Stream Networks with LSTM, but the training efficiency of action recognition methods based on LSTM has not been fully studied.

2.2 Attention Mechanisms

Attention mechanism originates from the study of human vision, by selectively focusing on different information in scene. It can also find parts of the scene that provide the most pertinent information. When neural networks recognize images or languages, they focus on more important features each time. Attention models were first proposed for object recognition task with RNN, drawing on the experience of Reinforce Algorithm [34]. In particular, Ba et al. [1] proposed to apply attention mechanisms adaptively selecting a sequence of regions to extract information from an image and sequentially considering the selected regions at a higher resolution. Xu et al. [36] proposed two Attention methods to the image application: Soft Attention and Hard Attention. Soft Attention method calculates the weights of each feature first, and then sums the weights of the features. The larger the weights, the greater the contribution of the features to the current recognition. In the Hard Attention, the role of weight is the probability that the features will be selected at a certain time, and only one feature will be selected.

Subsequently, this soft attention model was used in video classification tasks. Sharma et al. [20] proposed a novel approach to combine soft attention mecha-

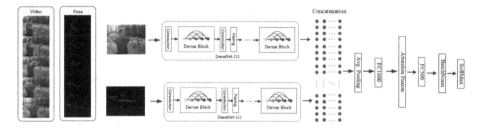

Fig. 1. An illustration of our model. One stream uses image sequence as input and the other one uses 2D pose estimation as input. The feature map obtained after DenseNet-121 and attention fusion is performed. Finally, calculate the score of action.

nisms with LSTM. This framework based on multi-layered lstm units to selectively concentrate on different information of the image sequence and classify videos after taking a few glimpses. Li et al. [16] proposed an end-to-end sequence learning network model which hardwires convolutions in the Soft-Attention LSTM, called VideoLSTM. Since the attention model was introduced to the deep learning, it has been widely used in various models, and diverse deformations have emerged in an endless stream, but attention modeling adds a significant burden to the computation.

3   Approach

Our method is based on the traditional Two-Stream network framework, but we propose to use a high-level motion feature, the 2D human pose estimation, instead of the low-level motion feature (traditional optical flow information), as shown in Fig. 1. The image frame and the 2D pose estimation image are trained as two separate networks, respectively. In our approach, the two-stream network acts as an extractor for high-dimensional features. Vast literatures show that using deeper convolutional neural networks can boost the overall performance of the Two-Stream Network. Distinctly, experiments on Googlenet [26], BN Inception [11] and ResNet [9] have proved this point. DenseNet-121 has a good performance on CIFARA-100 [12], ImageNet and other image classification datasets, which proves that it has good static image feature extraction ability. It has more information flow between each layer, and the parameters are much less than the traditional networks. So we choose the DenseNet-121 to investigate fusion methods at different stages of the Two-Stream Network. The results show that late fusion can obtain better fusion performance. Therefore, we use the last layer from a two-stream network to explore the attention fusion mechanism.

3.1   Original Image Frame

Consider the sequence of image frames as X_l that is passed through a convolutional network. It consists of L layers in total, each layer implements a non-linear transformation $H_l(\Delta)$, where l represents one of the layers. $H_l(\Delta)$ can be an operation of composite function such as convolution (Conv), sigmoid function, rectified linear units (ReLU) [8], batch normalization (BN), or pooling [15]. We denote the output of the lth layer as X_l.

DenseNet connects all layers directly on the premise of guaranteeing the largest information transmission between each layer in the network. The traditional convolutional networks connect the output of the lth layer as the input to the $(l+1)^{th}$ layer, which caused the following transition between each of two layers:

$$X_l = H_l(X_{l-1}) \tag{1}$$

Based on traditional network, ResNet adds skip connection blocks that bypasses the non-linear transformations with an identity function:

$$X_l = H_l(X_{l-1}) + X_{l-1} \tag{2}$$

In order to greatly improve the interaction of information flow between each layer, DenseNet directly connects the previous layer to all subsequent layers. As shown in Fig. 2, the lth layer takes the all feature-maps of previous layers, X_l is represented by the following:

$$X_l = H_l([X_0, X_1, ..., X_{l-1}]) \tag{3}$$

Where $X_0, X_1, ..., X_{l-1}$ refers to the concatenation of the feature-maps generated in layers $0, ..., l-1$. The DenseNet-121 is fine-tuned on the fully connected and output layers to fit two datasets.

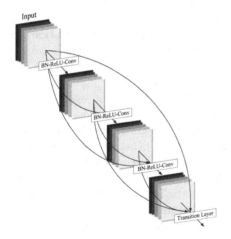

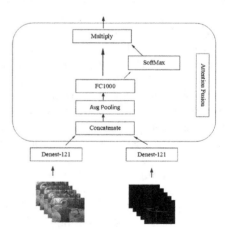

Fig. 2. A 4-layer denes block. Each layer receives all previous feature-maps of layers as input.

Fig. 3. Attention Fusion. We removed the structure after fully connected layer on top of the DenseNet121 and connected two sensors directly.

3.2   2D Human Pose Estimation

The key element in enabling machines to have an comprehending of human behavior in images and even videos is real-time 2D pose estimation method. We use the open source project OpenPose [2,3,22] from CMU to generate 2D pose estimates. OpenPose is released as the earliest open-source real-time multi-person system used in the field of 2D pose detection, including hand, facial, foot and body key points. We use the pose estimation of human body only. We take the divided images frame as input, as shown in Fig. 4, to get the corresponding 2D pose estimation. We can observe from Fig. 4 that 2D pose estimation can highlight the description of human motion while removing complex background, and can be used as supplementary information of image frames.

Fig. 4. 2D human pose estimation corresponding to picture frames.

3.3   Attention Mechanisms in Our Model

In previous section, we have described a video classification model that can extract features from single input. To fully exploit the multiple modalities, we consider two different multi-model fusion methods.

Feature Fusion: This fusion method is widely used by researchers. It is the most intuitive and easiest fusion method, connecting different modalities within the same time period, directly. Hence, we can fuse image frames feature sequences $\{a_1, a_2, ..., a_n\}$ and pose estimation feature sequences $\{b_1, b_2, ..., b_n\}$ into a single feature sequence $c = [a_i, b_i]$.

Attention Fusion: Unlike Feature Fusion, this method does not have to directly link the features of multiple modalities within each local time interval. It can pay attention to the information in diverging time periods for different modalities and in that the network still has the ability to extract interactions between multiple modalities. Suppose sequence c is obtained by feature fusion, the output vector f is calculated from the expected value using the attention fusion mechanism:

$$f = \sum_{i=1}^{N} \lambda_i c_i \tag{4}$$

The weight of each c_i is computed by:

$$e_i = \omega^T c_i \tag{5}$$

$$\lambda_i = \frac{exp(e_i)}{\sum_{j=1}^{N} exp(e_j)} \tag{6}$$

Where the ω is a learnable parameter. For intuitiveness, we represent the attention fusion model's output as $f = Attention(\{a_i\})$.

This attention vector needs to be computed at each time step in the two-stream network. The operation to compute the attention weights of tensors after feature fusion in this attention fusion framework is essentially realized by a Softmax layer. Long et al. [17] evaluated various other methods to compute the attention weights, but found that the performance of model was not significantly improved for more complex architectures. Hence, we design a simple and intuitive model structure, as shown in Fig. 3.

3.4 Loss Function

In the training stage, we represent the real classes for i^{th} video clips as a one-hot vector y_i and the amount of all videos contained in the dataset is denoted as N. We calculate the categorical cross-entropy as loss function:

$$Loss = -\sum_{i=1}^{N} y_i \log(\hat{y}_i) \tag{7}$$

Where $\hat{y}_i$ is the predictions class. This loss function is usually used for multi-class classification tasks or softmax output units.

4   Evaluation

This section evaluates our proposal using two experimental datasets. We first illustrate the experiments on the two datasets (HMDB-51 and UCF-101) with our proposed methods and use a part of dataset (UCF-101) to study which datasets has better performance on our approach. Then, we compare our framework with some of state-of-the-art approaches.

4.1   Datasets

We evaluate our approach on two excellent and challenging datasets of realistic human action. For HMDB-51 and UCF-101, each dataset is divided into three standard training and testing splits for model evaluation, respectively. In order to facilitate comparison with other methods, the mean average accuracy over the three testing splits is computed.

HMDB-51 [13] is a widely used action recognition data set, mainly collected from open-source movies, and a small part is from public video sites on the web,

Table 1. Experiment on single input with different models (split 1), accuracy (%).

Methods	HMDB-51	UCF-101
	RGB/Pose	*RGB/Pose*
InceptionV3	63.8/62.4	85.0/83.4
ResNet101	62.9/61.0	81.2/79.8
DenseNet121	64.7/62.8	86.9/84.1

Table 2. The performance on three testing splits of UCF-101, accuracy (%).

Methods	UCF-101		
	Split 1	*Split 2*	*Split 3*
RGB	86.9	88.3	86.1
Feature fusion	93.0	94.2	93.5
Attention fusion	98.1	98.7	98.4

such as the YouTube, Prelinger archive and Google videos. This dataset contains 6849 video clips in fifty-one human action types, which is divided into 5 groups, each type including at least 101 video clips.

UCF-101 [24] is an extensive video classification data set of realistic human action, all collected from YouTube, having 101 human action types. UCF101 provides the greatest variety in terms of actions and with large diversity in camera motion, object scale, illumination conditions, viewpoint, cluttered background, object appearance and pose, etc. The dataset contains 101 human action categories, which is divided into twenty five groups, and each group consists of about six video clips of a human action.

4.2   Experimental Setup

Our network structure, parameter settings and input data format are the same on the two datasets. The image frames with data augmentation (horizontal flip) and the corresponding pose estimation are resized to 224×224 for standard DenseNet-121 model to extract feature maps respectively. DesNet-121 has four dense blocks that each has an identical amount of layers. We just fine-tuned it, removing the structure after fully connected layer at the top of the network. At the end of the last dense block, a global average pooling is performed on two sensors as inputs of the attention Fusion. For the attention fusion, we directly concatenate the two sets of learned sensors and multiply the attention weights. Then, we normalize the output and use the softmax to classify the actions.

Here, we compare the three different Convolution Networks architectures on both datasets. Specifically, we compare ResNet-121, Inception-V3 [27] and DenseNet-121. Experiments on the three networks are shown in Table 1. The DenseNet-121 has excellent performance in both image frames and human pose estimation. At the same time, DenseNet-121 has fewer parameters. Therefore, we choose DenseNet-121 as a default architecture for two-stream.

Table 3. The performance on three testing splits of HMDB-51, accuracy (%).

Methods	HMDB-51		
	Split 1	Split 2	Split 3
RGB	64.7	63.4	62.0
Feature Fusion	80.1	79.8	81.8
Attention Fusion	84.2	82.7	83.9

Table 4. Experiment on different types of data, accuracy (%).

Methods	Datasets	
	Sports	Human-object interaction
RGB	62.6	58.8
Pose estimation	68.7	52.3
Two-stream	81.2	74.0

4.3 Results of Multimodal Fusion

In this section, we analyze the performances of previous experimental on all the three testing splits of two datasets using our proposed methods. We also analyze the two different proposed multimodal fusion methods.

The performances of our method on HMDB-51 and UCF-101 are reported in Table 2 and 3, respectively. As can be seen from Table 2, the two-stream late fusion structure could vastly improve the accuracy over than single stream framework. We also empirically expose that our method with an attention fusion for the two stream network ensures the highest accuracy.

Partly, the performances of our method on HMDB-51 shown in Table 3 is less satisfied than that on UCF-101. One potential reason is that actions in the videos of HMDB-51 are more difficult to identify than that of UCF-101. Similarly, a later attention fusion for the two stream has a best performances on HMDB-51.

4.4 Which Datasets Are More Suitable for Our Model

In order to study which datasets has better performance on our model, we take ten types of UCF-101 datasets split 1: sports (golf, diving, archery, etc.) and human-object interactions (makeup, brushing teeth, cooking, etc.), respectively, as test data to explore the role of human pose estimation in action recognition. As show in Fig. 5 below, pose estimation of human can clearly describe golf, but the effect is not good enough for makeup.

The experimental results can be seen from Table 4. We can easily observe that in the sports category, the effect of 2D pose estimation is better, even exceeding that of the image frames. The addition of pose estimation in both types of data can enhance the performance, especially for the sports category. This show our network is more effective for simple and can estimate the complete pose.

Fig. 5. Contrast of human pose estimation and image frame (Golf and Makeup).

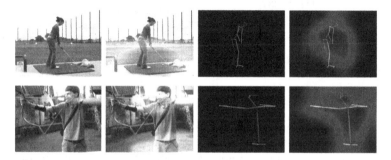

Fig. 6. Heatmaps of Golf and Archery.

4.5 Comparison with the State-of-the-Art

Finally, we compare our approach against some of the state-of-the-art methods in action recognition area. The mean average accuracy on the three testing splits of HMDB-51 and UCF-101 is reported. We compare it with some of the existing published traditional methods [14,30,32] as well as deep learning approaches [4–7,23,25,29,31,33,37]. Our approach achieves a highest level of accuracy both on HMDN-51 and UCF-101, 83.6% and 98.4% respectively, as shown in Table 5. In order to visually find out which part of an image plays a key role in human action recognition, we output the feature map through the top of the convolution layer of DenseNet and get the corresponding heatmaps, as shown in Fig. 6. We can observe that neural networks pay attention to those characteristic regions.

Table 5. Comparison with the State-of-the-Art, accuracy (%).

Methods	Datasets	
	HMDB-51	UCF-101
IDT [30]	57.2	85.9
MoFAP [32]	61.7	88.3
MIFS [14]	65.1	89.1
Two-Stream [23]	59.4	88.0
TDD [33]	63.2	90.3
FstCN [25]	59.1	88.1
LTC [29]	64.8	91.7
TSN [31]	70.7	94.9
3DConv+3DPool [7]	69.2	93.5
ST-ResNet [6]	66.4	93.4
TLE [5]	71.1	95.6
DTPP [37]	74.8	95.8
I3D+PoTion [4]	80.9	98.2
Ours	83.6	98.4

5   Conclusion

Two-Stream Networks have been extensively used in video analysis, especially action recognition of human. In many previous studies, various methods have been explored to combine image frames with optical flow to identify action, using temporal and spatial stream. However, human pose estimation is rarely used in two stream architecture. We design a novel two-steam framework using the 2D human pose estimation instead of the optical flow information as supplementary information of the original image frames, which can remove the interference of complex background information and multi-angle illumination. We also compared the performance of two fusion methods (feature fusion and attention fusion) at the fusion layer and explore which datasets are more suitable for our model. The experimental results show that our model has excellent performance in action recognition tasks.

In the future, we plan to fuse the 2D human pose estimation with optical flow information adaptively for action recognition.

Acknowledgment. This work was supported in part by the National Key Research and Development Program of China under Grant No. 2018YFB2100805, National Natural Science Foundation of China under the grant No. 61562019, 61379047, 60903092, and grants from State Key Laboratory of Marine Resource Utilization in South China Sea and Key Laboratory of Big Data and Smart Services of Hainan Province.

References

1. Ba, J., Mnih, V., Kavukcuoglu, K.: Multiple object recognition with visual attention. arXiv preprint arXiv:1412.7755 (2014)
2. Cao, Z., Hidalgo, G., Simon, T., Wei, S.E., Sheikh, Y.: OpenPose: real-time multi-person 2D pose estimation using part affinity fields. arXiv preprint arXiv:1812.08008 (2018)
3. Cao, Z., Simon, T., Wei, S.E., Sheikh, Y.: Realtime multi-person 2D pose estimation using part affinity fields. In: CVPR, pp. 7291–7299 (2017)
4. Choutas, V., Weinzaepfel, P., Revaud, J., Schmid, C.: Potion: pose motion representation for action recognition. In: CVPR, pp. 7024–7033 (2018)
5. Diba, A., Sharma, V., Van Gool, L.: Deep temporal linear encoding networks. In: CVPR, pp. 2329–2338 (2017)
6. Feichtenhofer, C., Pinz, A., Wildes, R.: Spatiotemporal residual networks for video action recognition. In: NIPS, pp. 3468–3476 (2016)
7. Feichtenhofer, C., Pinz, A., Zisserman, A.: Convolutional two-stream network fusion for video action recognition. In: CVPR, pp. 1933–1941 (2016)
8. Glorot, X., Bordes, A., Bengio, Y.: Deep sparse rectifier neural networks. In: AISTATS, pp. 315–323 (2011)
9. He, K., Zhang, X., Ren, S., Sun, J.: Deep residual learning for image recognition. In: CVPR, pp. 770–778 (2016)
10. Huang, G., Liu, Z., Van, L., Weinberger, K.Q.: Densely connected convolutional networks. In: CVPR, pp. 4700–4708 (2017)
11. Ioffe, S., Szegedy, C.: Batch normalization: accelerating deep network training by reducing internal covariate shift. arXiv preprint arXiv:1502.03167 (2015)
12. Krizhevsky, A., Hinton, G.: Learning multiple layers of features from tiny images, Technical report, Citeseer (2009)
13. Kuehne, H., Jhuang, H., Garrote, E., Poggio, T., Serre, T.: HMDB: a large video database for human motion recognition. In: ICCV, pp. 2556–2563. IEEE (2011)
14. Lan, Z., Ming, L., Li, X., Hauptmann, A.G., Raj, B.: Beyond gaussian pyramid: multi-skip feature stacking for action recognition. In: CVPR, pp. 204–212 (2015)
15. LeCun, Y., Bottou, L., Bengio, Y., Haffner, P., et al.: Gradient-based learning applied to document recognition. Proc. IEEE 86(11), 2278–2324 (1998)
16. Li, Z., Gavrilyuk, K., Gavves, E., Jain, M., Snoek, C.G.: VideoLSTM convolves, attends and flows for action recognition. CVIU 166, 41–50 (2018)
17. Long, X., et al.: Multimodal keyless attention fusion for video classification. In: AAAI, pp. 1–8 (2018)
18. Ma, C.Y., Chen, M.H., Kira, Z., AlRegib, G.: TS-LSTM and temporal-inception: exploiting spatiotemporal dynamics for activity recognition. SPIC 71, 76–87 (2019)
19. Sevilla-Lara, L., Liao, Y., Güney, F., Jampani, V., Geiger, A., Black, M.J.: On the integration of optical flow and action recognition. In: Brox, T., Bruhn, A., Fritz, M. (eds.) GCPR 2018. LNCS, vol. 11269, pp. 281–297. Springer, Cham (2019). https://doi.org/10.1007/978-3-030-12939-2_20
20. Sharma, S., Kiros, R., Salakhutdinov, R.: Action recognition using visual attention. arXiv preprint arXiv:1511.04119 (2015)
21. Shuiwang, J., Ming, Y., Kai, Y.: 3D convolutional neural networks for human action recognition. TPAMI 35(1), 221–231 (2013)
22. Simon, T., Joo, H., Matthews, I., Sheikh, Y.: Hand keypoint detection in single images using multiview bootstrapping. In: CVPR, pp. 1145–1153 (2017)

23. Simonyan, K., Zisserman, A.: Two-stream convolutional networks for action recognition in videos. In: NIPS, pp. 568–576 (2014)
24. Soomro, K., Zamir, A.R., Shah, M.: UCF101: a dataset of 101 human actions classes from videos in the wild. arXiv preprint arXiv:1212.0402 (2012)
25. Sun, L., Jia, K., Yeung, D.Y., Shi, B.E.: Human action recognition using factorized spatio-temporal convolutional networks. In: ICCV, pp. 4597–4605 (2015)
26. Szegedy, C., et al.: Going deeper with convolutions. In: CVPR, pp. 1–9 (2015)
27. Szegedy, C., Vanhoucke, V., Ioffe, S., Shlens, J., Wojna, Z.: Rethinking the inception architecture for computer vision. In: CVPR, pp. 2818–2826 (2016)
28. Tran, D., Bourdev, L., Fergus, R., Torresani, L., Paluri, M.: Learning spatiotemporal features with 3D convolutional networks. In: ICCV, pp. 4489–4497 (2015)
29. Varol, G., Laptev, I., Schmid, C.: Long-term temporal convolutions for action recognition. TPAMI 40(6), 1510–1517 (2017)
30. Wang, H., Schmid, C.: Action recognition with improved trajectories. In: ICCV, pp. 3551–3558 (2013)
31. Wang, L., et al.: Temporal segment networks: towards good practices for deep action recognition. In: Leibe, B., Matas, J., Sebe, N., Welling, M. (eds.) ECCV 2016. LNCS, vol. 9912, pp. 20–36. Springer, Cham (2016). https://doi.org/10.1007/978-3-319-46484-8_2
32. Wang, L., Yu, Q., Tang, X.: MoFAP: a multi-level representation for action recognition. IJCV 119(3), 254–271 (2016)
33. Wang L, Qiao Y, Tang, X.: Action recognition with trajectory-pooled deep-convolutional descriptors. In: CVPR, pp. 4305–4314 (2015)
34. Williams, R.J.: Simple statistical gradient-following algorithms for connectionist reinforcement learning. Mach. Learn. 8(3–4), 229–256 (1992). https://doi.org/10.1007/BF00992696
35. Wu, Z., Jiang, Y.G., Wang, X., Ye, H., Xue, X.: Multi-stream multi-class fusion of deep networks for video classification. In: ACMMULTIMEDIA, pp. 791–800. ACM (2016)
36. Xu, K., Ba, J., Kiros, R., Cho, K., Bengio, Y.: Show, attend and tell: neural image caption generation with visual attention. Computer Science, pp. 2048–2057 (2015)
37. Zhu, J., Zhu, Z., Zou, W.: End-to-end video-level representation learning for action recognition. In: ICPR, pp. 645–650. IEEE (2018)

Video Object Segmentation Using Convex Optimization of Foreground and Background Distributions

Jia-Wei Chen and Jin-Jang Leou[(✉)]

Department of Computer Science and Information Engineering,
National Chung Cheng University, Chiayi 62102, Taiwan, ROC
{chwei106m,jjleou}@cs.ccu.edu.tw

Abstract. In this study, a video object segmentation approach using convex optimization of foreground and background distributions is proposed. The proposed approach consists of four stages. First, optical flow computation and superpixel segmentation are performed on video frames. Second, convex optimization with a mixed energy function is employed to estimate the initial foreground and background distributions of video frames. Third, binary label maps for video frames are generated by maximum a posteriori (MAP) estimation. Fourth, the binary label maps are refined to obtain the final video object segmentation maps. Based on the experimental results obtained in this study, the performance of the proposed approach is better than those of three comparison approaches.

Keywords: Video object segmentation · Convex optimization · Superpixel segmentation · Gaussian mixture model (GMM) · Markov random field (MRF)

1 Introduction

Video object segmentation is to partition foreground objects (regions) from the background in all video frames in a video sequence. Video object segmentation is an active research area in computer vision applications, such as video content analysis and summarization, content-based video retrieval, human action recognition, etc.

Video object segmentation approaches can be classified into three categories: supervised [1–4], semi-supervised [5–8], and unsupervised [9–14]. Supervised object segmentation approaches [1–4] usually cope with the object segmentation problem by employing user annotations on a few selected frames. Bai et al. [1] proposed a video object segment approach, in witch adaptive local classifiers are used to cutout dynamic video objects. Tsai et al. [2] proposed a video object segmentation and tracking approach, in which video information is described by a multi-label Markov random field. Wen et al. [3] proposed a joint online tracking and segmentation approach, in which multi-part tracking and segmentation are integrated into a unified energy optimization framework. Tsai et al. [4] proposed a video object segmentation approach using modified optical flow computations.

© Springer Nature Switzerland AG 2020
A. Campilho et al. (Eds.): ICIAR 2020, LNCS 12131, pp. 209–219, 2020.
https://doi.org/10.1007/978-3-030-50347-5_19

Semi-supervised video segmentation approaches [5–8] usually propagate the pattern of one or more noted frames to the entire video sequence. Grundmann et al. [5] proposed a video object segmentation approach using a layered hierarchical graph-based algorithm. Perazzi et al. [6] proposed a video object segmentation approach to segment objects in unconstrained video sequences using multiple object proposals. Jang et al. [7] developed an online video object segmentation approach using the convolutional trident network (CTN). Calles et al. [8] proposed a one-shot video object segmentation (OSVOS) approach using the fully convolutional networks architecture.

For unsupervised video object segmentation, Zhang et al. [9] proposed a layered directed acyclic graph (DAG) framework for detecting and segmenting prominent objects in a video sequence. Taylor et al. [10] proposed a video object segmentation approach using the convex optimization framework, which deals with the object occlusion problem. Luo et al. [11] proposed a video object segmentation approach using video complexity awareness and segmentation parameters. Jang et al. [12] proposed a video object segmentation approach, in which an alternating convex optimization (ACO) scheme converting the mixed energy function into two quadratic programs is employed. Wang et al. [13] proposed a video object segmentation approach using the superpixel and geodesic distances. Wang et al. [14] proposed a deep learning approach for video saliency detection by using convolutional neural networks (CNN). In this study, an unsupervised video object segmentation approach using convex optimization is proposed.

The paper is organized as follows. In Sect. 2, the proposed video object segmentation approach is addressed. In Sect. 3, experimental results are presented, followed by concluding remarks.

2 Proposed Approach

2.1 System Architecture

In this study, as shown in Fig. 1, a video object segmentation using convex optimization of foreground and background distributions is proposed. The proposed approach consists of four stages. First, optical flow computation and superpixel segmentation are performed on video frames. Second, convex optimization with a mixed energy function is employed to estimate the initial foreground and background distributions of video frames. Third, binary label maps for video frames are generated by maximum a posteriori (MAP) estimation. Fourth, the binary label maps are refined to obtain the final video object segmentation maps.

2.2 Pre-processing

In this study, the input is a video sequence containing n video frames, $\tau_t, t = 1, 2, \ldots, n$, and an optical flow algorithm [15] is used to determine the correspondences between two consecutive video frames.

Based on the characteristics of the human visual system (HVS), human eyes usually focused on prominent object regions (superpixels), instead of pixels. A superpixel refers to a group of perceptual pixels formed by adjacent pixels with similar texture and structural features. In this study, video frames are converted from RGB color space into CIELAB color space and the simple linear iterative clustering (SLIC) method [16] is employed to perform superpixel segmentation on video frames. Video frame τ_t is split into a superpixel set $sp_t^i, t = 1, 2, \ldots, n, i = 1, 2, \ldots, N$, where N denotes the number of superpixels in video frame τ_t.

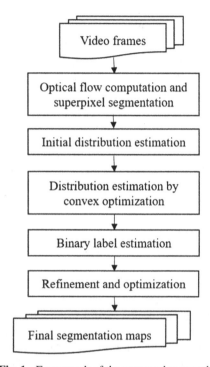

Fig. 1. Framework of the proposed approach.

2.3 Convex Optimization

The proposed approach using convex optimization contains three estimations: initial distribution, energy function, and foreground and background distribution estimations.

2.3.1 Initial Distribution Estimation

In this study, the manifold ranking algorithm [17] is employed to compute boundary prior. First, a k-ring graph $G = (V, E)$ for video frame τ_t is generated, where a set of superpixels are represented as the set of nodes $V = \{v_1, \ldots, v_N\}$ and $E = \{e_{ij}\}$ denotes the set of edges between node pairs. For video frame τ_t, the affinity matrix $W_t = [w_{t,i,j}], 1 \leq i, j \leq N$ is calculated from the edge linking nodes v_i and v_j and defined as:

$$w_{t,i,j} = \begin{cases} exp(-\mu^2(v_i, v_j)/\sigma^2), & \text{if } e_{ij} \in E, \\ 0, & \text{otherwise}, \end{cases} \quad (1)$$

where $\mu(v_i, v_j)$ denotes the feature-based distance between nodes v_i and v_j and σ^2 denotes a scale parameter. The affinity matrix W_t is normalized symmetrically by normalized affinity matrix $SM_t = [sm_{t,i,j}]$, $1 \leq i, j \leq N$, i.e.,

$$SM_t = D^{-1/2} W_t D^{-1/2}, \tag{2}$$

where D denotes an $N \times N$ diagonal matrix and the sum of the i-th row of W_t will determine the elements of D. Different ranking scores can be proportionally assigned to the respective confidences if the confidences of queries are known. Hence, a background query column vector $y_{b,t} = [y_{b,t,1}, \ldots, y_{b,t,N}]^T$ is defined, in which $y_{b,t,i} = 1$ if node v_i is a query and $y_{b,t,i} = 0$, otherwise. The initial background ranking column vector $r_{b,t} = [r_{b,t,1}, \ldots, r_{b,t,N}]^T$ is defined as

$$r_{b,t} = (I - \alpha \cdot SM_t)^{-1} \cdot y_{b,t}, \tag{3}$$

where $\alpha \in [0, 1)$ denotes the relative dedication to the ranking score from the adjacent region and the initial ranking score and I is an $N \times N$ identity matrix. In this study, different LAB colors are calculated [10], and to use the average of LAB color differences, the average of optical flow differences between two nodes is used to calculate each element of the affinity matrix W_t.

Let $sm_{t,i,j}$ be the element of the normalized affinity matrix. A relatively large amount of query will be assigned to a highly scalable node, which can be connected to many similar nodes. Therefore, a query amount $y_{b,t,i}$ at node v_i is proportional to $1/max_i\{sm_{t,i,j}\}$ when v_i is on the frame boundary, and 0, otherwise. Based on the background query vector $r_{b,t}$ in Eq. (3), we will obtain the background ranking column vector which is used as the column vector of the initial background distribution $r_{b,t} = [r_{b,t,1}, \ldots, r_{b,t,N}]^T$. Similarly for foreground indexing, the background distribution is converted into a foreground query vector through an inverse proportional relationship between the foreground query vector at the node and the background distribution to obtain the column vector of the initial foreground distribution $r_{f,t} = [r_{f,t,1}, \ldots, r_{f,t,N}]^T$ (via Eq. (3)).

2.3.2 Energy Function Estimation

In this study, prominent object segmentation is mainly divided into two stages. In the first (forward) stage, the prominent object in each video frame is sequentially depicted from the first video frame to the last video frame. The segmentation results (the label maps) of the previous two video frames will be used to generate the segmentation results of the current video frame. In the second (backward) stage, the above process is similarly performed backward from the last video frame to the first video frame. The corresponding probabilities $r_{b,t}$ and $r_{f,t}$, $t = 1, 2, \ldots, n$ for n video frames are combined to determine the priority distribution of each video frame, and then the region with the highest priority distribution is determined as the prominent object.

For video frame τ_t, let $d_{f,t} = [d_{f,t,1}, \ldots, d_{f,t,N}]^T$ and $d_{b,t} = [d_{b,t,1}, \ldots, d_{b,t,N}]^T$ be the column vectors of the foreground and background distributions, respectively. To segment prominent objects, the mixed energy function consists of Markov, spatiotemporal, and mutually exclusive energy functions.

2.3.2.1 Markov Energy Function

In this study, the segmentation results of video frame τ_t are obtained by the segmentation results of the previous two video frames and the background and foreground distributions $d_{b,t}$ and $d_{f,t}$ of the current video frame τ_t. In a k-ring graph, when k is a large value, a k-ring graph node will be connected to a great number of nodes. The transition matrix $A_t = [a_{t,i,j}], t = 1, \ldots, n, 1 \leq i, j \leq N$ can be defined as

$$a_{t,i,j} = w_{t,i,j} / \sum_{k=1}^{N} w_{t,k,j}. \tag{4}$$

The squared distance between the transition matrix and the stationary distribution can be defined as

$$\left\| A_t d^{(t)} - d^{(t)} \right\|^2, \tag{5}$$

where d denotes the distribution defined as

$$d^{(t+1)} = A_t d^{(t)}, \tag{6}$$

where t denotes the temporal variable.

The distribution of pixels in each video frame can be treated as a Markov random field, and image segmentation can be treated as image clustering. First, regions with dense distribution have high probabilities and regions with dispersed distribution have low probabilities. Second, adjacent pixels having similar probabilities will be assigned to the same cluster. Based on the above two clustering characteristics, the Markov energy function can be defined as

$$\varepsilon_M \left(d_{f,t} \right) = \left\| A_t d_{f,t} - d_{f,t} \right\|^2, \tag{7}$$

where A_t is the transition matrix of video frame τ_t.

2.3.2.2 Spatiotemporal Energy Function

To accurately segment prominent objects in a video sequence, both spatial and temporal information should be employed together. Here, initial foreground and background distributions are combined with the segmentation results of the previous two video frames.

For video frame τ_t, the column vector of the initial foreground distribution $r_{f,t} = [r_{f,t,1}, \ldots, r_{f,t,N}]^T$ is initially estimated [10] and then the column vector of the foreground temporal information $\varphi_{f,t} = [\varphi_{f,t,1}, \ldots, \varphi_{f,t,N}]^T$ is calculated. First, the propagation matrix $C_{(t,\tilde{t})}$ with size $N \times N$ is defined, which transfers the binary labels of video frame $\tilde{t}$ to video frame t. Based on optical flow computations, if at least one pixel in node v_i of video frame t and the pixels in node v_j of video frame $\tilde{t}$ are matching, the element $c_{(t,\tilde{t}),i,j}$ of $C_{(t,\tilde{t})}$ is 1, and otherwise 0. Afterwards, the segmentation results of two previous video frames, $t-1$ and $t-2$, are transferred into video frame t to produce temporal information, which can be defined as

$$\varphi_{f,t} = C_{(t,t-1)} L_{t-1} + C_{(t,t-2)} L_{t-2}, \tag{8}$$

where L_{t-1} and L_{t-2} are column vectors of binary label at video frames $t-1$ and $t-2$, respectively. Combining spatial and temporal information, the foreground spatiotemporal distribution $s_{f,t} = \left[s_{f,t,1}, \ldots, s_{f,t,N} \right]^T$ (a column vector) is defined as

$$s_{f,t} = \beta \times \left(\varphi_{f,t} \otimes r_{f,t} \right), \tag{9}$$

where $\otimes$ denotes element-by-element multiplication and β denotes a normalized constant. Finally, the spatiotemporal energy function can be defined as

$$\varepsilon_S \left(d_{f,t} \right) = \left\| d_{f,t} - s_{f,t} \right\|^2. \tag{10}$$

2.3.2.3 Mutually Exclusive Energy Function

The object segmentation results are more obvious when the foreground probability is very high. However, if both the foreground and background distributions have high probabilities in the same region, the segmentation results will be poor. Based on the fact, the mutually exclusive energy function is defined as

$$\varepsilon_{ME} \left(d_{f,t}, d_{b,t} \right) = \sum_{i=1}^{N} \sum_{j \in M_i} w_{t,i,j} \cdot d_{f,t,i} \cdot d_{b,t,j}, \tag{11}$$

where M_i represents the set of related nodes for node v_i and $w_{t,i,j}$ represents the affinity matrix between the node pair v_i and v_j of video frame τ_t.

2.3.3 Foreground and Background Distribution Estimation

In this study, the mixed energy function combing the above three energy functions is defined as

$$\varepsilon \left(d_{f,t}, d_{b,t} \right) = \varepsilon_M \left(d_{f,t} \right) + \varepsilon_M \left(d_{b,t} \right) + \theta \cdot \varepsilon_S \left(d_{f,t} \right)$$
$$+ \ \theta \cdot \varepsilon_S \left(d_{b,t} \right) + \delta \cdot \varepsilon_{ME} \left(d_{f,t}, d_{b,t} \right), \tag{12}$$

where θ is a nonnegative parameter and δ is a balance parameter. If $d = \left[d_{f,t}^T, d_{b,t}^T \right]^T$ denotes the total distribution column vector, the mixed energy function can be redefined as

$$\varepsilon(d) = d^T B d - 2\theta \left[s_{f,t}^T, s_{b,t}^T \right] d + \theta s_{f,t}^T s_{f,t} + \theta s_{b,t}^T s_{b,t}, \tag{13}$$

where B is an $N \times N$ control matrix defined as

$$B = \begin{bmatrix} (A_t - I)^T (A_t - I) + \theta I & \frac{\delta}{2} W_t \\ \frac{\delta}{2} W_t & (A_t - I)^T (A_t - I) + \theta I \end{bmatrix}. \tag{14}$$

Note that there are some constraints on the mixed energy function so that minimizing the mixed energy function can be changed into a quadratic program [12]. Here, two constraints are given as

$$\sum_{i=1}^{N} d_{f,t,i} = 1, \ 0 \le d_{f,t,i} \le 1, \tag{15}$$

$$\sum_{i=1}^{N} d_{b,t,i} = 1, \ 0 \le d_{b,t,i} \le 1. \tag{16}$$

In Boyd et al. [18], the minimization problem is solved via two quadratic programs, which was employed in this study. To minimize the foreground distribution, the initial background distribution is used, whereas to minimize the background distribution, the resulting foreground distribution is employed. For video frame τ_t, based on the constraints of Eqs. (15)–(16), the foreground and background distributions can be computed iteratively as

$$\min_{d_{f,t}}\{d_f^T\left((A_t - 1)^T(A_t - 1) + \theta I\right)d_{f,t} - \left(2\theta s_{f,t}^T - \delta d_{f,t}W\right)d_{f,t}\}, \tag{17}$$

$$\min_{d_{b,t}}\{d_b^T\left((A_t - 1)^T(A_t - 1) + \theta I\right)d_{b,t} - \left(2\theta s_{b,t}^T - \delta d_{b,t}W\right)d_{b,t}\}. \tag{18}$$

For each iteration of the quadratic program, the foreground and background distributions may reduce the mixed energy function value gradually. When the mixed energy function value will not be decreased, the foreground and background distributions are obtained.

2.4 Foreground and Background Label Estimation

For video frame τ_t, after obtaining the foreground and background distributions via convex optimization, the maximum a posteriori (MAP) estimation [19] is used to determine the binary partition label of each superpixel. In this study, the foreground probability of node v_i in video frame τ_t is determined by the likelihood function $p(v_i|d_{f,t})$ of the foreground and the priori probability $p(d_{f,t})$ of the foreground in τ_t. Similarly, the background probability of node v_i in video frame τ_t is determined by the likelihood function $p(v_i|d_{b,t})$ of the background and the priori probability $p(d_{b,t})$ of the background in τ_t. The foreground posterior probability probability of node v_i in video frame τ_t can be defined as

$$p(d_{f,t}|v_i) = \frac{p(v_i|d_{f,t})p(d_{f,t})}{p(v_i|d_{f,t})p(d_{f,t}) + p(v_i|d_{b,t})p(d_{b,t})}. \tag{19}$$

In this study, the prior probabilities of foreground and background in video frame τ_t are estimated by using the distribution of the previous video frame. Because each distribution contains the number of nodes with the reciprocal of its uniform probability, the prior probabilities of foreground and background in video frame τ_t can be defined as

$$p(d_{f,t}) = \frac{1}{\max_i\left(d_{f,t-1,i}\right)}, \tag{20}$$

$$p(d_{b,t}) = \frac{1}{\max_i\left(d_{b,t-1,i}\right)}. \tag{21}$$

Based on the prior probabilities of foreground and background, the segmentation label of node v_i in video frame τ_t is defined as

$$l_{t,i} = \begin{cases} 1, & if \ p(d_{f,t}|v_i) > p(d_{b,t}|v_i), \\ 0, & otherwise. \end{cases} \tag{22}$$

2.5   Refinement and Optimization

In the refinement stage, both Gaussian mixture model (GMM) for obtaining the position information of the prominent object and the pixel-wise optical flow $op_e(x, y)$ between video frame pairs are used to refine the obtained results, followed by Markov random field (MRF) optimization [20]. GMM considers mainly the pixels, which is improved by MRF introducing neighboring relationships between pixels. After obtaining the prominent object in a video frame, the object suggestion information is embedded in MRF model to accurately segment the object. The nodes and edges in the graph are defined in Zang et al.'s [9]. Here, the priori information h and label superpixels $g = [g_1, g_2, \ldots g_n]$. are used to compute the MRF energy equation [20] defined as

$$E(g, h) = \sum_{i \in Q} F_i^h(g_i) + \lambda \sum_{(i,j) \in O} R_{i,j}(g_i, g_j), \qquad (23)$$

where $Q = \{q_1, \ldots, q_n\}$ is a collection of n label superpixels in the video sequence, O contains four spatially adjacent label superpixels in the same video frame and two temporally adjacent label superpixels in adjacent video frames, is a balance parameter, and i and j are superpixels indices. Each superpixel is set to 0 or 1, corresponding to the background or foreground, respectively. The temporal neighbors of the superpixels in the next video frame are assigned by optical flow vector displacement between two consecutive video frames. The relevant spatiotemporal map is thus defined [11].

To compute the unary cost of labeling superpixels by GMM, the RGB color and the position information of the foreground or background are used to generate the unary potential F_i^h defined as

$$F_i^h(g_i) = -log\left(\alpha U_i^c(g_i, h) + (1 - \alpha)U_i^m(g_i, h)\right), \qquad (24)$$

where $U_i^c(\cdot)$ and $U_i^m(\cdot)$ denote the color-induced cost and local shape match-induced cost, respectively. The similarity between two superpixels can supply useful label information. The standard contrast correlation function [21] is employed, which assigns the same label to adjacent superpixels with similar color(s). The RGB color features are extracted and the backward optical flow vectors are considered as motion features. A high pairwise cost is obtained if adjacent superpixels with similar features are assigned different labels.

Note that the optimal solution of the MRF energy function is obtained based on the graph-cut minimization algorithm [20], and the 3×3 median filter is used to filter out unwanted noise.

3   Experimental Results

In this study, the proposed approach is implemented by Matlab 9.6 (R2019a) on Intel Core i7-6700 K CPU 4.0 GHz-Microsoft Windows 10 platform with 32 GB main memory. To evaluate the proposed video object segmentation approach, densely annotated video segmentation (DAVIS) dataset [22] was used. DAVIS dataset consists of 50 high-quality, full-HD video sequence sets (3455 annotated video frames) containing appearance changes, motion blur, occlusion, etc.

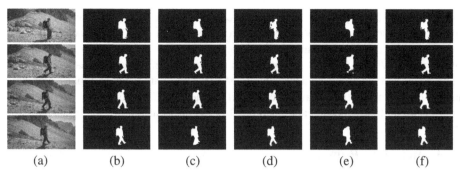

Fig. 2. Video object segmentation results of video frames 15, 35, 55, 75 in video sequence "DAVIS hike": (a) the original frames; (b) ground truth; (c)–(f) video object segmentation results by Taylor et al.'s approach [10], Jang et al.'s approach [12], Wang et al.'s approach [14], and the proposed approach.

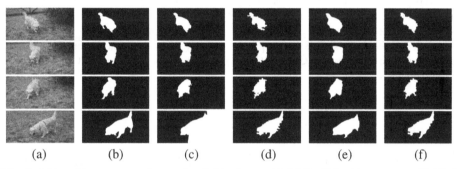

Fig. 3. Video object segmentation results of video frames 10, 25, 30, 50 in video sequence "DAVIS dog": (a) the original frames; (b) ground truth; (c)–(f) video object segmentation results by Taylor et al.'s approach [10], Jang et al.'s approach [12], Wang et al.'s approach [14], and the proposed approach.

Table 1. In terms of F, J, AP, and MAE, performance comparisons between three comparison approaches and the proposed approach on DAVIS dataset.

Approaches	F	J	AP	MAE
Taylor et al. [10]	0.567	0.514	0.488	0.076
Jang et al. [12]	0.592	0.522	0.506	0.143
Wang et al. [14]	0.697	0.579	0.556	0.044
Proposed	**0.707**	**0.590**	**0.572**	**0.044**

To evaluate the quality of video object segmentation results, both objective and subjective quality measures are employed. Four objective evaluation metrics, namely, F-score (F), Jaccard index (J), average precision (AP), mean absolute error (MAE), are employed [22–24]. To evaluate the performance of the proposed video object seg-mentation approach, three comparison approaches, Taylor et al.'s approach [10], Jang et al.'s approach [12], and Wang et al.'s approach [14], are employed. In terms of four object metrics F, J, AP, and MAE, performance comparisons between three comparison approaches and the proposed approach on DAVIS dataset are listed in Table 1. For sub-jective quality evaluation, some video object segmentation results of three comparison approaches and the proposed approach on DAVIS dataset are shown in Figs. 2 and 3.

4 Concluding Remarks

In this study, a video object segmentation approach using convex optimization of fore-ground and background distributions is proposed. Optical flow computation, superpixel segmentation, convex optimization with a mixed energy function, and maximum a pos-teriori (MAP) estimation are employed in the proposed approach. Based on the experi-mental results obtained in this study, the performance of the proposed approach is better than those of three comparison approaches.

Acknowledgements. This work was supported in part by Ministry of Science and Technology, Taiwan, Republic of China under Grants MOST 106-2221-E-194-057-MY2 and MOST 108-2221-E-194-049.

References

1. Bai, X., Wang, J., Simons, D., Sapiro, G.: Video SnapCut: robust video object cutout using localized classifiers. ACM Trans. Graph. **28**(3), 70.1–70.11 (2009)
2. Tsai, D., Flagg, M., Nakazawa, A., Rehg, J.M.: Motion coherent tracking using multi-label MRF optimization. Int. J. Comput. Vis. **100**(2), 190–202 (2010). https://doi.org/10.1007/s11263-011-0512-5
3. Wen, L., et al.: JOTS: joint online tracking and segmentation. In: Proceedings of 2015 IEEE International Conference on Computer Vision and Pattern Recognition (CVPR), pp. 2226–2234 (2015)
4. Tsai, Y., Yang, M., Black, M.J.: Video segmentation via object flow. In: Proceedings of 2016 IEEE International Conference on Computer Vision and Pattern Recognition (CVPR), pp. 3899–3908 (2016)
5. Grundmann, M., et al.: Efficient hierarchical graph-based video segmentation. In: Proceedings of 2010 IEEE International Conference on Computer Vision and Pattern Recognition (CVPR), pp. 2141–2148 (2010)
6. Perazzi, F., et al.: Fully connected object proposals for video segmentation. In: Proceedings of 2015 IEEE International Conference on Computer Vision, pp. 3227–3234 (2015)
7. Jang, W., Kim, C.: Online video object segmentation via convolutional trident network. In: Proceedings of 2017 IEEE International Conference on Computer Vision and Pattern Recognition (CVPR), pp. 7474–7483 (2017)
8. Caelles, S., et al.: One-shot video object segmentation. In: Proceedings of 2017 IEEE International Conference on Computer Vision and Pattern Recognition (CVPR), pp. 5320–5329 (2017)

9. Zhang, D., Javed, O., Shah, M.: Video object segmentation through spatially accurate and temporally dense extraction of primary object regions. In: Proceedings of 2013 IEEE International Conference on Computer Vision and Pattern Recognition (CVPR), pp. 628–635 (2013)

10. Taylor, B., Karasev, V., Soatto, S.: Causal video object segmentation from persistence of occlusions. In: Proceedings of 2015 IEEE International Conference on Computer Vision and Pattern Recognition (CVPR), pp. 4268–4276 (2015)

11. Luo, B., et al.: An unsupervised method to extract video object via complexity awareness and object local part. IEEE Trans. Circ. Syst. Video Technol. **28**(7), 1580–1594 (2018)

12. Jang, W., Lee, C., Kim, C.: Primary object segmentation in videos via alternate convex optimization of foreground and background distributions. In: Proceedings of 2016 IEEE International Conference on Computer Vision and Pattern Recognition (CVPR), pp. 696–704 (2016)

13. Wang, W., et al.: Saliency-aware video object segmentation. IEEE Trans. Pattern Anal. Mach. Intell. **40**(1), 20–33 (2018)

14. Wang, W., Shen, J., Shao, L.: Video salient object detection via fully convolutional networks. IEEE Trans. Image Process. **27**(1), 38–49 (2018)

15. Liu, C.: Beyond pixels: exploring new representations and applications for motion analysis. Electrical Engineering and Computer Science at the Massachusetts Institute of Technology (2009)

16. Achanta, R., et al.: SLIC superpixels compared to state-of-the-art superpixel methods. IEEE Trans. Pattern Anal. Mach. Intell. **34**(11), 2274–2282 (2012)

17. Zhou, D., et al.: Ranking on data manifolds. In: Advances in Neural Information Processing Systems, pp. 169–176 (2004)

18. Boyd, S., Vandenberghe, L.: Convex Optimization. Cambridge University Press, Cambridge (2004)

19. Lee, C., et al.: Multiple random walkers and their application to image cosegmentation. In: Proceedings of 2015 IEEE International Conference on Computer Vision and Pattern Recognition (CVPR), pp. 3837–3845 (2015)

20. Fulkerson, B., Vedaldi, A., Soatto, S.: Class segmentation and object localization with superpixel neighborhoods. In: Proceedings of 2009 IEEE 12th International Conference on Computer Vision, pp. 670–677 (2009)

21. Lee, Y.J., Kim, J., Grauman, K.: Key-segments for video object segmentation. In: Proceedings of 2011 International Conference on Computer Vision, pp. 1995–2002 (2011)

22. Perazzi, F., et al.: A benchmark dataset and evaluation methodology for video object segmentation. In: Proceedings of 2016 IEEE International Conference on Computer Vision and Pattern Recognition (CVPR), pp. 724–732 (2016)

23. Lou, J., Xu, F., Xia, Q., Yang, W., Ren, M.: Hierarchical co-salient object detection via color names. In: Proceedings of 2017 Asian Conference on Pattern Recognition, pp. 1–7 (2017)

24. Perazzi, F., et al.: Saliency filters: contrast based filtering for salient region detection. In: Proceedings of 2012 IEEE International Conference on Computer Vision and Pattern Recognition (CVPR), pp. 733–740 (2012)

Computer Vision

Deep Learning for Partial Fingerprint Inpainting and Recognition

Marc-André Blais⊕, Andy Couturier⊕, and Moulay A. Akhloufi$^{(\boxtimes)}$⊕

Perception, Robotics, and Intelligent Machines Research Group (PRIME),
Department of Computer Science, Université de Moncton,
Moncton, NB E1A 3E9, Canada
{emb9357,eac6996,moulay.akhloufi}@umoncton.ca

Abstract. Image completion and inpainting has been widely studied by the computer vision research community. With the recent growth and availability of computation power, we are now able to perform more complex inpainting than ever before. Techniques based on both learning and non-learning methods have been proposed for image inpainting. Some of these approaches have been used for fingerprint image enhancement. However, we lack techniques for fingerprint completion using deep learning. This is especially the case for techniques with the goal of augmenting the number of correct minutiae matchpoints for fingerprint recognition. This paper proposes new deep architectures to improve the accuracy of prints matching in live scan images. The proposed techniques have been tested using a professional software for fingerprint matching to evaluate the performance of deep learning in that aspect. The obtained results are promising and show an increase of 36.94% in minutiae match points identification.

Keywords: Fingerprint recognition · Biometrics · Convolutional neural networks · Inpainting · Minutiae

1 Introduction

Fingerprint analysis which consists of using ridges in a fingerprint to identify a person is a common method of forensics analysis that exists since the 19th century [25]. Like DNA, fingerprints are nearly unique to each individual which results in them being an excellent identifier [11]. In 2014, in the USA alone, almost 300 000 requests were made to publicly funded forensic crime labs for prints detection and analysis [9]. In a typical scenario, once the fingerprint is found and collected (e.g., at a crime scene), it is matched against an existing database of live scan of ink-based images of fingerprints. When analyzing prints, three common patterns can be found in most fingerprints [15]. The loop, whorl and arch patterns are the three types of ridges that are commonly found in prints (see Fig. 1).

This work was supported in part by the Natural Sciences and Engineering Research Council of Canada (NSERC), [funding reference number RGPIN-2018-06233].

© Springer Nature Switzerland AG 2020
A. Campilho et al. (Eds.): ICIAR 2020, LNCS 12131, pp. 223–232, 2020.
https://doi.org/10.1007/978-3-030-50347-5_20

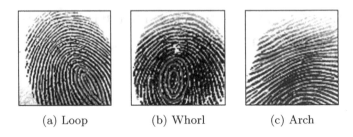

(a) Loop   (b) Whorl   (c) Arch

Fig. 1. Types of fingerprint patterns

A number of smaller points called minutiae are also found in any prints. An analyst compares fingerprints using the identifiers such as the patterns and minutiae points to declare a match between two prints. When comparing the prints, an analyst may require several hours to identify matching characteristics. However, for our analysis we will use specialized software to find patterns and minutiae and compare them automatically. The software will provide the number of matches that will be used as a metric to evaluate our models. Matching fingerprints can be difficult as it often requires a minimum number of matching pairs of points to declare that two fingerprints are from the same person. In 2011, a survey of 73 countries performed by INTERPOL identified 44 countries that are using a "point standard" [10,26]. Indeed, 24 of these countries legally require at least 12 minutiae matches. Some countries such as Italy even have higher standards and require 16 to 17 points [7]. In these conditions, fingerprint matching with incomplete live scan prints may be difficult. Moreover, latent fingerprints typically contain only 20 to 30 minutiae points which require the live scan images to be fully completed [27]. Therefore, in some situations even if only a small portion of the fingerprint is missing, identification by matching points may be impossible.

Furthermore, with the recent advancements in biometric technologies aimed at the consumer market (e.g., smartphones fingerprint scanners), there is an increased demand for these technologies. Such applications are even more challenging due to the fact that consumer devices have lower quality fingerprint scanners, have limited computation resources and must analyze the fingerprints in real-time. This motivates the need for robust and efficient partial fingerprint matching techniques. The most common approach when dealing with partial fingerprints is a direct matching with full or other partial fingerprints. This paper proposes a completely different approach to the problem by first enhancing the fingerprint before matching. The proposed approach completes the fingerprint by inferring the missing parts through deep inpainting. The results show that, following this prepossessing of the fingerprint, a greater number of matching minutiae points can be obtained thus improving fingerprint recognition.

2   Related Work

To our knowledge, research on fingerprint completion with the goal of restoring patterns and minutiae with deep learning is non-existent. However, research on image inpainting has been ongoing for two decades now. Bertalmio *et al.* published one of the earliest and most cited works on image inpainting [4]. At the time, multiple algorithms already existed for denoising and inpainting but required multiple images and human involvement by opposition to Bertalmio *et al.* approach. Nowadays, the state of the art in this area is using deep convolutional neural networks (CNN) [17]. The only work we've been able to find on the subject of fingerprint inpainting has been performed as part of the 2018 Chalearn LAP Inpainting Competition [6]. The data for the competition was generated using a synthetic fingerprint generator called Anguli [12]. Noise, occlusion and multiple types of degradation were added to the generated ground truth images to build a dataset for the competition. An unpublished paper from Mansar describing the winning approach has been made available on arXiv [19]. Mansar's architecture was inspired by [20]. The architecture is similar to a U-Net [21] but is using skip connections similar to ResNet [13] instead of channel concatenations. The network was trained using the Adam optimizer [14] and a l_1 loss. Results indicated a PSNR of 17.7 and a SSIM of 0.84. Despite initially looking like a similar problem, we cannot confidently compare our results to this work. As mentioned, not only was our dataset different, but the core of our problem slightly differs. This competition goal was to denoise, inpaint small sections and remove the background of the images, while our goal was to inpaint large missing portions of fingerprints. Furthermore, we also focused on the increase of matching minutiae point rather than the PSNR as our evaluating metric. This permits to evaluate the performance of our approach for real world applications such as fingerprint recognition.

Methods have also been proposed specifically for partial fingerprint matching. One possible approach is to develop new hand-crafted features more robust to occlusion instead of using only traditional minutiae features. In this area, Lee *et al.* proposed new ridge shape features (RSFs) in addition to traditional minutiae features [16]. More recently and similarly, Castillo-Rosado and Hernández-Palancar proposed new Distinctive Ridge Point (DRP) features and an improved triangle-based representation which is also applied to traditional minutiae features [5]. Aravindan and Anzar undertaken a slightly different approach and proposed using standard SIFT features [18] extracted from wavelet decomposed images of the fingerprints [3]. For these approaches to be implemented in forensics and fingerprint comparison systems, a complete system redesign would be necessary as they change the very nature of how the fingerprints are matched. In comparison, our approach would not involve this type of modification as it can be applied as a preprocessing step before the fingerprint is passed to existing systems. Another class of approaches has also been developed more specifically for the fingerprint scanners used in mobile devices. This type of scanners are made to have a reduced footprint and therefore produce partial fingerprints, but at a very high-resolution. For this scenario, deep features extracted with CNNs have been very successful. Zhang and Feng [28] proposed such an approach using deep joint KNN-triplet embeddings. Training samples were carefully crafted using a K-Nearest-Neighbor (KNN) policy based on the location of the partial print on the finger. Triplet loss [22] was used to map the features in an Euclidean space and was combined with a weighted softmax loss to accelerate convergence. Recently, Anand and Kanhangad [2] proposed a similar approach but by first extracting the pores present in the partial fingerprints with a DeepResPore network [1] and then applying a triplet loss trained CNN to generate embeddings. The main drawback of these approaches is the difficulty in explaining why two fingerprints are matching or not matching. This makes these approaches better suited for consumer biometrics and unsuited for forensics and latent fingerprints recognition.

3   Proposed Approach

As previously stated, our proposed approach is based on image inpainting. Using inpainting we restore missing parts of a fingerprint in order to reconstruct a complete fingerprint. Once the fingerprint is reconstructed, we apply professional software based on traditional minutiae matching. The goal is to obtain more valid minutiae matches with the reconstructed fingerprint than with the partial fingerprint.

3.1   Architectures

We propose and compare 3 different CNN architectures for fingerprint inpainting. These architectures are built from partial convolutions, a concept that was proposed by Liu et al. from Nvidia for irregular holes inpainting [17]. Partial convolutional layers are made of a masked and re-normalized convolution operation followed by a mask-update step. The mask is updated at each partial convolutional layer to remove the portion of the mask corresponding to the portion of the image that has been filled. Therefore, the mask is propagated through the network with the image. This allows for the CNN to only consider non-hole regions of the image while reconstructing the missing parts. While going through the network, the holes are progressively filled until the inpainting is completed.

Our first architecture is similar to the one proposed in [17]. It takes the form of a U-Net-like architecture [21] where the convolutions were replaced by partial convolutions. The decoder is using nearest neighbor up-sampling and the input to each of its layers is concatenated with the output feature map and the mask from the corresponding layers in the encoder. We use this model as a benchmark for our other models since it has proved to be capable in the domaine of inpainting [17]. This architecture is illustrated in Fig. 2.

Our second and third models are modified versions of the previous U-Net-like architecture. Both architectures have the same encoding phase as previously. However, following the initial encoding, we add partial decodings and encodings phases before the final decoding phase. These partial encoders and decoders have half of the size of the initial encoder and the final decoder, respectively. This approach reproject the features from a lower feature space to a higher feature space repeatedly in an Up-Down fashion. The goal is to allow the network to self correct the lacks in the initial encoding phase and better prepare the final decoding phase. Our second architecture, called W-Net, is W-shaped with a single partial phase and is illustrated in Fig. 3. The third architecture, called DW-Net, has 3 partial phases and is illustrated in Fig. 4. The role of the latter is to push further the Up-Down concept and compare the results with the former W-Net and the traditional U-Net architectures.

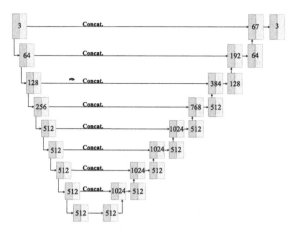

Fig. 2. U-Net architecture similar to [17].

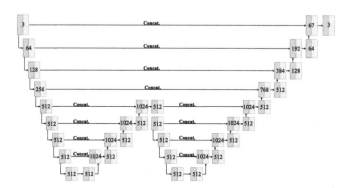

Fig. 3. W-Net architecture.

3.2   Loss and Hyperparameters

The three networks were trained for 400 epochs with a mini-batch size of 16 using the Adam optimizer [14] with a learning rate of 0.0002. The loss function we minimized is the total loss (L_{total}) presented in [17]. It is a linear combination

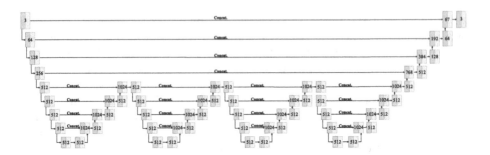

Fig. 4. DW-Net network architecture.

of 5 terms: an l_1 loss on the hole part of the output image (L_{hole}), an l_1 loss on the non-hole part of the output image (L_{valid}), a perceptual loss ($L_{perceptual}$) based on the features of a ImageNet-trained VGG16 [24], a style-loss term ($L_{style_{out}} + L_{style_{comp}}$), and a total variation loss (L_{tv}). The total loss is given by Eq. 1.

$$L_{total} = L_{valid} + 6L_{hole} + 0.05L_{perceptual}$$
$$+ 120(L_{style_{out}} + L_{style_{comp}}) + 0.1L_{tv} \qquad (1)$$

4   Experimental Results

4.1   Dataset

The dataset we employed was composed of a series of 6000 fingerprints from the SOCOFing data set [23]. Another popular dataset from a Chalearn competition was also considered at first since it contained more images. However, as mentioned in a previous section, this dataset consisted of computer generated (synthetic) fingerprints. We opted for testing and reporting the results on SOCOFing dataset since it contains real images. Nonetheless, using both datasets in the future and having the ability to compare the results to previous work could be interesting. Combining the datasets could also help in obtaining a better level of generalization and better results. The only modification performed on the dataset was to resize the images to 256×256 pixels. The resulting dataset was split into 75%, 15% and 10% for training, validation and testing, respectively. No data augmentation was used as the dataset had plenty of images and altering the fingerprints may affect the accuracy of the models. For example, altering the fingerprints could have caused distortion in the minutiae patterns, rendering them unusable for recognition. The segmentation masks were randomized at every iteration to achieve the desired generalization.

4.2   Models Performance

The three models are compared using the loss and the peak signal-to-noise ratio (PSNR) obtained on the test set. However, comparing the architectures with only these may lead to the wrong conclusions. While these metrics are important to evaluate the quality of the reconstruction, they cannot convey by themselves alone how much of the recognition capability has been restored by the proposed approach. Therefore, we analyze the increase in the number of valid minutiae match points using 35 images selected randomly in the test set. For this part of the solution validation, we used CSIpix Matcher 5 [8] to manually compare the fingerprints. We first compared the partial fingerprints with the original fingerprints to get the number of valid matches (Avg./w partial) and then, we have done the same for the restored fingerprints and the original fingerprints (Avg./w predicted). These quantitative results are presented in Table 1.

Table 1. Quantitative results.

	U–Net	W–Net	DW–Net
Loss	0.06	0.07	**0.04**
PSNR (dB)	26.80	24.59	**27.85**
Avg./w partial	13.13	13.13	13.13
Avg./w predicted	17.86	17.61	**17.94**
Increase in avg.	4.76 (36.25%)	4.50 (34.27%)	**4.85 (36.94%)**

As seen in Table 1, the DW-Net architecture achieved the best PSNR with 27.85 dB and the best increase in average of valid minutia matches with 36.94%. Before inpainting, we had 13.13 valid minutia matches in average and after inpainting with DW-Net we obtained 17.94 valid matches. As previously stated, some countries such as Italy require 16 to 17 minutia matches to consider that two fingerprints are from the same person for legal purposes. Therefore, in this scenario, with our approach, we could have identified the owner of a fingerprint, which would not have been possible with a minutiae-based approach alone. Furthermore, the worst increase in valid minutia matches we obtained was with W-Net that scored 34.27 % which is still very significant. This observation shows the strong ability of deep inpainting for the restoration of characteristics to increase the performance of minutiae-based fingerprint recognition.

In Fig. 5, we present some qualitative results obtained with the same fingerprint and mask for the three networks. As we can see, U-Net and W-Net are similar while DW-Net seems to lead to better fingerprint completion with less blur.

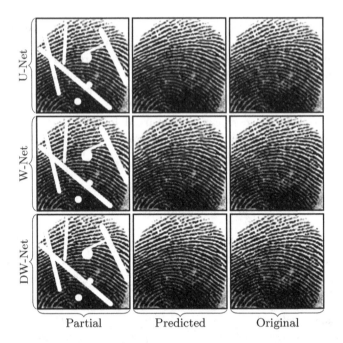

Fig. 5. Example of obtained results

5 Conclusion

The purpose of this work is to show the potential of deep inpainting for the restoration of live scan fingerprints for fingerprint recognition in forensic applications. Three architectures were proposed for this task. With a training dataset limited to 4500 fingerprints and with only 400 epoch of training, we were able to obtain an improvement of 36.94% in fingerprint recognition performance. This clearly demonstrates the value of the proposed approach for the increase in performance of minutiae-based finger recognition. Furthermore, the results demonstrated the superiority of the DW-Net architecture and the use of multiple partial decoding and encoding phases over the traditional U-Net architecture. Possible future works include the tuning of our current architectures, the evaluation of the effect of an adversarial loss, and the development of new recognition-aware approaches for inpainting.

References

1. Anand, V., Kanhangad, V.: Pore detection in high-resolution fingerprint images using deep residual network. J. Electron. Imaging **28**(2), 020502 (2019)
2. Anand, V., Kanhangad, V.: PoreNet: CNN-based pore descriptor for high-resolution fingerprint recognition. arXiv:1905.06981 [cs], May 2019

3. Aravindan, A., Anzar, S.M.: Robust partial fingerprint recognition using wavelet SIFT descriptors. Pattern Anal. Appl. **20**(4), 963–979 (2017). https://doi.org/10.1007/s10044-017-0615-x

4. Bertalmio, M., Sapiro, G., Caselles, V., Ballester, C.: Image inpainting. In: Proceedings of the 27th Annual Conference on Computer Graphics and Interactive Techniques, SIGGRAPH 2000, pp. 417–424. ACM Press/Addison-Wesley Publishing Co., New York (2000)

5. Castillo-Rosado, K., Hernández-Palancar, J.: Latent fingerprint matching using distinctive ridge points. Informatica **30**(3), 431–454 (2019)

6. Chalearn LAP Inpainting Competition: Track 3. Denoising and inpainting for fingerprint verification. https://competitions.codalab.org/competitions/18426#learn_the_details. Accessed Jan 2020

7. Champod, C., Chamberlain, P.: Fingerprints, Chap. 3. Routledge (2009)

8. CSIpix: CSIpix matcher (2019). https://www.csipix.com/. Accessed Jan 2020

9. Durose, M.R., Burch, A.M., Walsh, K., Tiry, E., Bureau of Justice Statistics (BJS), US Dept of Justice, Office of Justice Programs, United States of America: Publicly funded forensic crime laboratories: resources and services, 2014. Impressions **50**(44), 40 (2016)

10. Farelo, A.: Fingerprints survey 2011. In: 7th International Symposium on Fingerprints (2011)

11. Galton, F., Galton, S.F.: Finger Prints. Macmillan and Company, London (1892)

12. Haritsa, J., Ansar, A.H., Wadhwani, K., Jadhav, S.: Anguli: synthetic fingerprint generator. https://dsl.cds.iisc.ac.in/projects/Anguli/. Accessed Jan 2020

13. He, K., Zhang, X., Ren, S., Sun, J.: Deep residual learning for image recognition. In: The IEEE Conference on Computer Vision and Pattern Recognition (CVPR), June 2016

14. Kingma, D.P., Ba, J.: Adam: a method for stochastic optimization. In: Conference Track Proceedings of 3rd International Conference on Learning Representations, ICLR 2015, San Diego, CA, USA, 7–9 May 2015 (2015)

15. Kücken, M., Newell, A.C.: Fingerprint formation. J. Theor. Biol. **235**(1), 71–83 (2005)

16. Lee, W., Cho, S., Choi, H., Kim, J.: Partial fingerprint matching using minutiae and ridge shape features for small fingerprint scanners. Expert Syst. Appl. **87**, 183–198 (2017)

17. Liu, G., Reda, F.A., Shih, K.J., Wang, T.C., Tao, A., Catanzaro, B.: Image inpainting for irregular holes using partial convolutions. In: The European Conference on Computer Vision (ECCV), September 2018

18. Lowe, D.G.: Distinctive image features from scale-invariant keypoints. Int. J. Comput. Vis. **60**(2), 91–110 (2004)

19. Mansar, Y.: Deep end-to-end fingerprint denoising and inpainting. arXiv:1807.11888 [cs], July 2018

20. Mao, X.J., Shen, C., Yang, Y.B.: Image restoration using convolutional autoencoders with symmetric skip connections. arXiv:1606.08921 [cs], June 2016

21. Ronneberger, O., Fischer, P., Brox, T.: U-Net: convolutional networks for biomedical image segmentation. In: Navab, N., Hornegger, J., Wells, W.M., Frangi, A.F. (eds.) MICCAI 2015. LNCS, vol. 9351, pp. 234–241. Springer, Cham (2015). https://doi.org/10.1007/978-3-319-24574-4_28

22. Schroff, F., Kalenichenko, D., Philbin, J.: FaceNet: a unified embedding for face recognition and clustering. In: The IEEE Conference on Computer Vision and Pattern Recognition (CVPR), June 2015

23. Shehu, Y.I., Ruiz-Garcia, A., Palade, V., James, A.: Sokoto coventry fingerprint dataset. arXiv:1807.10609 [cs], July 2018
24. Simonyan, K., Zisserman, A.: Very deep convolutional networks for large-scale image recognition. arXiv:1409.1556 [cs], September 2014
25. Tewari, R.K., Ravikumar, K.V.: History and development of forensic science in India. J. Postgrad. Med. **46**(4), 303 (2000)
26. Ulery, B.T., Hicklin, R.A., Roberts, M.A., Buscaglia, J.: Measuring what latent fingerprint examiners consider sufficient information for individualization determinations. PLoS One **9**(11), p1–16, 16 p. (2014)
27. Wieclaw, L.: A minutiae-based matching algorithms in fingerprint recognition systems. J. Med. Inform. Technol. **13**, 65–71 (2009)
28. Zhang, F., Feng, J.: High-resolution mobile fingerprint matching via deep joint KNN-triplet embedding. In: Thirty-First AAAI Conference on Artificial Intelligence (2017)

A Visual Perception Framework to Analyse Neonatal Pain in Face Images

Lucas Pereira Carlini[1]([✉])[iD], Juliana C. A. Soares[2][iD], Giselle V. T. Silva[2][iD],
Tatiany M. Heideirich[2][iD], Rita C. X. Balda[2][iD], Marina C. M. Barros[2][iD],
Ruth Guinsburg[2][iD], and Carlos Eduardo Thomaz[1][iD]

[1] University Center of FEI, São Bernardo do Campo, SP, Brazil
lucaspcarlini10@gmail.com, cet@fei.edu.br
[2] Federal University of São Paulo, São Paulo, SP, Brazil
ruth.guinsburg@gmail.com

Abstract. Neonatal pain assessment by facial expressions are currently among the most used methods in the clinical practice, due to the fact that the human being, at an early stage of life, is not able to verbally communicate pain. Therefore, the pain assessment and its subsequently treatment are carried out by an indirect and non-objective analysis of reactions of the neonate when facing a painful procedure. This work proposes a computational framework to investigate the visual perception patterns of adults when assessing pain in order to better understand the relevance of neonate facial features commonly used by health professionals when evaluating pain in newborn babies. The results showed that there is no statistical difference of visual fixation among all groups of volunteers, whether they are health professionals or not.

Keywords: Newborn face images · Eye-tracking · Pain

1 Introduction

Neonatal pain assessment by facial expressions are currently among the most used methods in the clinical practice, due to the fact that the human being, at an early stage of life, is not able to verbally communicate pain. Therefore, the pain assessment and its subsequently treatment are carried out by an indirect and non-objective analysis of reactions of the neonate when facing a painful procedure.

In recent years, some studies have been done in order to develop automatic computational frameworks to evaluate pain in newborn babies [6,14,17,19,22, 23]. These studies have mainly focused on only behavioural indicators of pain such as facial expressions and infant reactions. More specifically, the methodology proposed by Heiderich [14] was successful to automatically evaluate neonatal pain by capturing the newborn facial image, decoding it and, lastly, classifying

---

Supported by FEI and FAPESP.

A. Campilho et al. (Eds.): ICIAR 2020, LNCS 12131, pp. 233–243, 2020.
https://doi.org/10.1007/978-3-030-50347-5_21

it as present or absent pain in an almost instantaneous time interval. The study done by Teruel [19] proposed a sequence of computational procedures in order to detect, interpret and classify patterns in frontal face images for automatic recognition of pain in neonates. The method used data transformation and extraction of statistical features from a neonate image database, allowing the interpretation and modelling of the subjectivity of trained health professionals enabling automatic identification. More recently, Brahnam [6] developed an open database of neonatal pain videos containing video segments of neonates experiencing an acute pain stimulus and/or in periods of rest. Using this database, Brahnam developed a machine learning approach based on Support Vector Machine that outperforms the human judgement [5,6].

Although these studies present feasible applications in the clinical practice, none of them gives information regarding the relevance of the facial features that defines pain used by health professionals when coding and evaluating neonatal pain, only identifying the presence of pain through specific facial actions expressed by the neonate.

Differently from others, this work proposes the idea of analysing the visual perception of health professionals and non-health professionals adults when facing the task of pain evaluation in neonates. We approach this problem through the acquisition of human eye movements, using an eye-tracking device, to analyse frontal images of newborns experiencing painful procedures or periods of rest. Subsequently, in order to understand the relationship between neonatal facial features to procedural pain, we investigate the differences among the distinct sample groups through a pattern recognition framework.

2   Fundamental Concepts

2.1   Neonatal Pain

Until the mid-1980s, it was assumed that the central nervous system of newborn babies was not fully developed, consequently, not being able to sense and suffer from pain [14]. However, research done in the latter years of 1980 showed that the central nervous and nociceptive systems are sufficiently developed in the sixth month of gestation [1,8,10]. Studies also observed that the inhibitory pathways of painful stimulus are not fully developed, leading to an increased sensitivity of pain [1,2].

The non-treated pain felt by neonates is associated with changes in their respiratory, cardiovascular and metabolic stability, increasing mortality in neonatal intensive care units. In the short-term, neonates may suffer, as a consequence of pain, irritability, inattention, change in rest pattern, dietary denial and interference in the mother-child relationship [14]. However, in the long-term, pain may cause degrading effects on the neurological and behavioural development such as cognitive problems, alterations in the brain development leading to learning disabilities and hypersensitivity to painful and non-painful stimuli [4,12]. Therefore, new studies regarding neonatal pain assessment have been developed ever since.

The most common observations reported by health professionals when treating neonatal pain are crying, irritability, sudden movements, and change in their facial expression and behaviour [16].

Due to the range of sounds, most people believe that crying is the best metric to estimate the presence and, if necessary, intensity of pain or discomfort in their newborn babies. However, it was reported that almost half of newborn babies does not cry in painful interventions, meanwhile, stressful stimulus may lead to crying as well. Therefore, although useful, crying alone is not reliable to verify the presence of pain [11]. Another useful method to verify the presence of neonatal pain is the analysis of their movements. This can be justified by the fact that newborn babies have a standardised movement. Consequently, changes in that pattern, such as sudden and disorderly movements, may indicate the presence of pain.

Lastly, pain presence may be verified through the analysis of the facial expression of the neonate. Although this analysis may be subjective, it is a noninvasive method that has been widely used in clinical practice. Due to the facial expressiveness, face is a reliable source to verify the emotional condition and pain sensitivity in neonates [14].

2.2   Neonatal Facial Coding System

One of the most known and used methods by health professionals to evaluate pain through facial expression is the Neonatal Facial Coding System (NFCS) developed by Grunau and Craig [10,11]. As observed by Grunau, the analysis of neonatal facial expression delivers valid information regarding the nature and intensity of the pain allowing better communication between the neonate and his/her caregiver. It should be noted that, as confirmed by subsequent studies [11,13,18], this set of facial actions appears just in neonates submitted to pain but does not appear in stressful but non-painful procedures.

In short, the 10 facial actions of the NFCS can be described as follows: brow lowering, eyes squeezed shut, deepening of the naso-labial furrow, open lips, vertical mouth stretch, horizontal mouth stretch, taut tongue, chin quiver, lip purse, and one which has been found to be counterindicative of pain in term infants: tongue protrusion. It was latter reported by Grunau that there is an emphasis on superior facial actions such as contraction of the forehead with lowering of the eyebrows, narrowing of the eyelids and/or closing of the eyes and frown and/or raised cheeks [9].

Grunau [11] observed that 90% of these facial actions are featured by neonates in pain, and 98% of term infants featured, at least, three of these facial actions. Therefore, when the neonate features three or more of the facial actions commented above, it is considered that the newborn is suffering from pain and is in need of treatment.

3   Materials and Methods

3.1   Volunteers

All data were collected at the São Paulo Hospital, a university-affiliated hospital of the Federal University of São Paulo, São Paulo, Brazil.

The experiments were conducted with the participation of 143 volunteers divided into four groups of study:

- 44 physicians: 4 paediatricians and 40 neonatologists;
- 40 health professionals: 17 nursing assistants, 10 nurses, 5 physiotherapists and 8 speech therapists;
- 29 parents of newborn;
- 30 others (non-physicians, non-health professionals, and non-parents of newborn).

Some of the demographic characteristics of the participants are:

- age of 34,2 (mean) $\pm$ 10,2 (SD) years;
- 78 women in the health group and 38 women in the non-health group;
- 22 volunteers of the health group and 50 of the non-health group has, at least, one children;
- 94 of the total population are graduated.

3.2   Hardware

The experiments were conducted inside a closed room with artificially controlled lighting within specifications between 300 and 1000 lx and positioned outside the visual field of the participant.

Data were collected by the eye-tracking device Tobii TX300, shown in Fig. 1. This device is able to capture data in a frequency of 300 Hz and consists of a 23-in. TFT monitor with an infrared lighting system and two video cameras located at the bottom of the equipment.

In addition to the eye-tracking device, a laptop computer was used with the Tobii Studio software in order to calibrate the equipment and to store the collected data. This computer has a Intel Core I7, 16 GB of RAM memory and Microsoft Windows 7 operating system.

3.3   Framework

The proposed framework is a computational experiment in which volunteers performed pain assessment on several face images of neonates evaluating each one using a numerical scale ranging from 0 (no pain) to 10 (extreme pain). In each session of the procedure, information regarding the ocular evaluation strategy of each volunteer was recorded by the eye-tracking equipment. Exclusion criteria was applied to volunteers with diagnoses of epilepsy (seizure) and/or severe ocular problems.

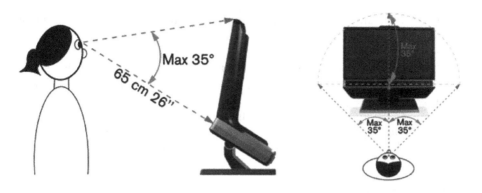

Fig. 1. Recommended positioning.

The image data set used to design the proposed framework was developed by health professionals and researchers and was approved by the Ethics Committee for Research of the Federal University of São Paulo (1299/09, 3.116.151 and 3.116.146). Twenty images of ten different neonates were selected. Each pair of images consists of one image of the neonate at rest and another image after a painful procedure.

The experimental procedure, illustrated in Fig. 2, is composed by 3 steps: (1) An instruction screen is shown to the subject; (2) Two evaluation trials are presented, so that the subjects learn and comprehend the experiment; (3) The experimental procedure begins. Each neonate image to be evaluated is shown randomly to the volunteer for seven seconds.

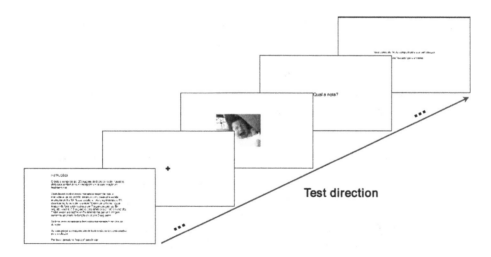

Fig. 2. Proposed framework.

The neonates images were separated in the experiment by a screen containing a cross as the central fixation point. As proposed, this cross was shown for two seconds [15] so that the ocular movement of all volunteers start at the same area on screen. However, due to the ocular inertia caused by the cross, all ocular movement performed by the participants in the initial 300 ms of the stimulus were discarded.

For each neonate image, the participant had 3 s to assign a score for the displayed image. The total time to perform the experiment was approximately 5 min for each volunteer.

4   Results and Discussion

This section is divided into three parts: (1) Analysis of the results obtained through the evaluation of pain by the numerical scale; (2) Discussion of the results shown in heat maps acquired by the ocular movement from each sample group; (3) A pattern recognition framework is used to investigate the differences among the groups of volunteers.

4.1   Numerical Scale

From 143 volunteers, we obtained 2860 numeric evaluations, half of them referring to images of newborns in painful procedure and the other half referring to images of newborns at rest. A summary is shown in Tables 1 and 2, where the Health Professionals group refers to physicians and other health professionals (i.e. nurses), and the Non-health professionals include parents and others.

Table 1. Numerical evaluations of neonates experiencing painful procedure.

Volunteer group	Mean $\pm$ SD	Median	25–75%	Min–Max
General	6,9 $\pm$ 1,7	7,3	6,0–8,1	2,1–9,7
Health professionals	7,0 $\pm$ 1,6	7,4	6,0–8,1	2,1–9,4
Non-health professionals	6,8 $\pm$ 1,8	7,1	5,8–8,1	2,7–9,7

Table 2. Numerical evaluations of neonates experiencing periods of rest.

Volunteer group	Mean $\pm$ SD	Median	25–75%	Min–Max
General	1,0 $\pm$ 1,2	0,6	0,2–1,4	0,0–6,5
Health professionals	0,8 $\pm$ 0,8	0,8	0,2–1,1	0,0–4,2
Non-health professionals	1,3 $\pm$ 1,6	0,7	0,2–1,6	0,0–6,5

There were similar results when analysing evaluations of neonates during painful procedure, as shown by similar means and standard deviations presenting no statistical differences ($p = 0.551$). However, when evaluating neonates at rest, a better agreement was shown by the health professionals with inferior standard deviation. It was observed a statistical difference between the groups ($p = 0.022$).

A threshold has been defined in order to categorise the proposed numerical scale, leading to a binary classification (with or without pain). Therefore, evaluations below and equal three were defined as neonate without pain, and evaluations greater than three were defined as neonate with pain. The results are shown in Table 3.

Table 3. Accuracy to evaluate the presence of pain (Mean ± SD).

Volunteer group	With & without pain	With pain	Without pain
General	$88,9 \pm 12,2\%$	$88,5 \pm 17,7\%$	$89,4 \pm 20,8\%$
Health professionals	$91,6 \pm 10,0\%$	$89,5 \pm 16,6\%$	$93,6 \pm 13,0\%$
Non-health professionals	$85,2 \pm 14,2\%$	$87,0 \pm 19,1\%$	$83,4 \pm 27,5\%$

When analysing the correct responses to neonates with pain, no statistical difference was found ($p = 0.405$). However, a statistical difference was observed when analysing images of neonates without pain ($p = 0.010$), leading to a statistical difference of all correct responses between the two groups ($p = 0.004$).

These results show that health professionals are better to identify the absence of pain and are slightly better to identify its presence. These findings differ from those observed by Balda [3], where a higher percentage of correct responses to identify the presence of pain was presented by the non-health professionals group. However, in accordance to Balda's findings [3], the health professional group presented higher accuracy to identify the absence of pain. This may be related to practical experience of the group to neonates in intensive care units [3].

4.2 Heat Maps

Figures 3 and 4 show examples of results found by our eye-tracking experiment. These heat maps show how spatial fixation is distributed over the stimulus, therefore, revealing the focus of visual attention of the participants.

These results show a common visual pattern for all groups. There is a general interest divided between the eyes, nose and mouth of the neonate, shown in tones of red and yellow. No distinct visual pattern was found to a specific sample group.

Finally, the areas visualised by the volunteers are the same areas proposed to be analysed by the Neonatal Facial Coding System [10], indicating that the facial features that defines pain are among the ones of the NFCS. However, it is noteworthy that health professionals did not present clear differences in their visual strategies compared to the group of non health care participants. These

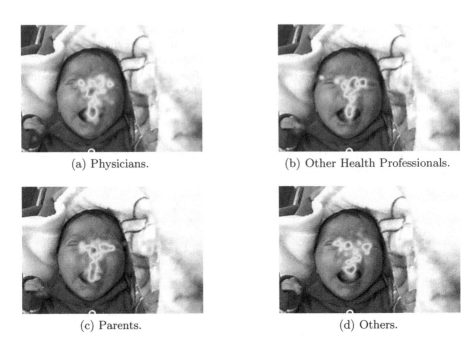

(a) Physicians.   (b) Other Health Professionals.

(c) Parents.   (d) Others.

Fig. 3. Heat maps of neonate during painful procedure by sample group.

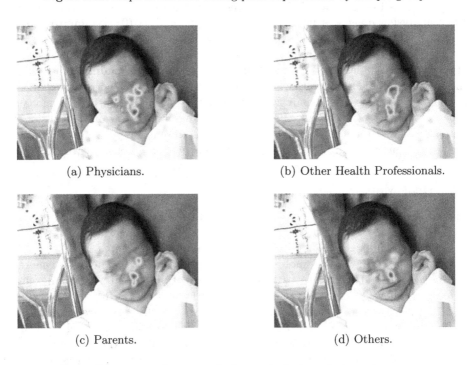

(a) Physicians.   (b) Other Health Professionals.

(c) Parents.   (d) Others.

Fig. 4. Heat maps of neonate during period of rest by sample group.

results raise issues about the implicit knowledge we humans have when faced with the task of assessing pain in newborns through facial perception.

4.3 Statistical Analysis

In order to investigate the differences among the distinct sample groups, we used a pattern recognition framework as proposed by Thomaz [20]. The Maximum Uncertainty Linear Discriminant Analysis (MLDA) is a LDA-based [7] approach based on a straightforward covariance selection method [21] for the within scatter matrix overcoming both the singularity and instability problems of the original method.

To do so, areas of interest (AOI) were manually selected in each neonate face image based on areas of analysis of the NFCS: (1) forehead, (2) left eyelid, (3) right eyelid, (4) left naso-labial furrow, (5) right naso-labial furrow, (6) mouth and (7) "not an AOI". For all volunteers, data time of these areas were collected and preprocessed using the Tobii Studio software.

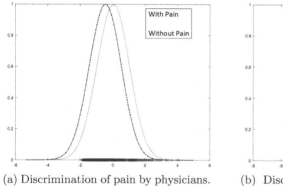 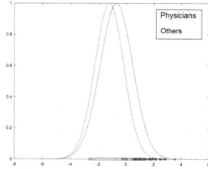

(a) Discrimination of pain by physicians.   (b) Discrimination between physicians and others for neonate in pain.

Fig. 5. Example of MLDA results.

Figure 5a shows the discrimination of the visual fixations of physicians to images of neonate during painful procedure and during periods of rest (without pain). The presented result shows that there is no difference in the physicians visual perception towards pain. In other words, physicians visual analysis is the same regardless of the presence/absence of pain. Similar results were found analysing other groups of volunteers of this work.

Figure 5b shows the attempt to discriminate the visual perception of physicians to other towards pain. This figure shows that there is no discrimination, or difference, between both groups. Similar results were found for all comparisons between groups. Although the results presented that all groups of volunteers look at AOIs as proposed by NFCS, there is no discrimination among groups on how they look at neonate faces, since all of them look, essentially, at the same regions.

5   Conclusions

The proposed framework described novel results to better understand visual perception regarding the pain phenomenon by adults belonging to various study groups, whether they are health professionals or not.

As expected, the overall results of the numerical scale analysis showed a better evaluation of pain by health professionals. Interestingly, however, there is no statistical difference of visual fixations among all groups of volunteers when facing the task of pain assessment using neonate faces. Even having specific knowledge in the area, the sample group of health professionals present an holistic visual perception based, essentially, on the same areas of visual fixations of untrained adults.

As future work, we intend to perform an analysis of the pupillary response in order to investigate the time of visual analysis of each group of volunteer. These data have already been acquired by the Tobii device. We also intend to perform a deeper discriminant analysis using different approaches of data mining and pattern recognition.

References

1. Anand, K.J., Carr, D.B.: The neuroanatomy, neurophysiology, and neurochemistry of pain, stress, and analgesia in newborns and children. Pediatr. Clin. North Am. **36**(4), 795–822 (1989)
2. Anand, K.J., Hickey, P.R., et al.: Pain and its effects in the human neonate and fetus. N. Engl. J. Med. **317**(21), 1321–1329 (1987)
3. Balda, R.C., Guinsburg, R., de Almeida, M.F.B., de Araújo Peres, C., Miyoshi, M.H., Kopelman, B.I.: The recognition of facial expression of pain in full-term newborns by parents and health professionals. Arch. Pediatr. Adolesc. Med. **154**(10), 1009–1016 (2000)
4. Balda, R.C., Guinsburg, R.: Avaliação da dor no período neonatal. Diagnóstico e tratamento em neonatologia, pp. 577–585. Atheneu, São Paulo (2004)
5. Brahnam, S., Chuang, C.-F., Shih, F.Y., Slack, M.R.: SVM classification of neonatal facial images of pain. In: Bloch, I., Petrosino, A., Tettamanzi, A.G.B. (eds.) WILF 2005. LNCS (LNAI), vol. 3849, pp. 121–128. Springer, Heidelberg (2006). https://doi.org/10.1007/11676935_15
6. Brahnam, S., Nanni, L., McMurtrey, S., Lumini, A., Brattin, R., Slack, M., Barrier, T.: Neonatal pain detection in videos using the iCOPEvid dataset and an ensemble of descriptors extracted from Gaussian of local descriptors. Appl. Comput. Inform. (2019). https://www.sciencedirect.com/science/article/pii/S2210832718303831?via%3Dihub
7. Fisher, R.A.: The use of multiple measurements in taxonomic problems. Ann. Eugen. **7**(2), 179–188 (1936)
8. Golianu, B., Krane, E.J., Galloway, K.S., Yaster, M.: Pediatric acute pain management. Pediatr. Clin. North Am. **47**(3), 559–587 (2000)
9. Grunau, R.E., Oberlander, T., Holsti, L., Whitfield, M.F.: Bedside application of the neonatal facial coding system in pain assessment of premature infants. Pain **76**(3), 277–286 (1998)
10. Grunau, R.V., Craig, K.D.: Pain expression in neonates: facial action and cry. Pain **28**(3), 395–410 (1987)

11. Grunau, R.V., Johnston, C.C., Craig, K.D.: Neonatal facial and cry responses to invasive and non-invasive procedures. Pain **42**(3), 295–305 (1990)
12. Guinsburg, R.: Avaliação e tratamento da dor no recém-nascido. J. Pediatr (Rio J.) **75**(3), 149–60 (1999)
13. Guinsburg, R., et al.: Are behavioral scales suitable for preterm and term neonatal pain assessment? In: Proceedings of the 8th World Congress on Pain. International Association of Study Pain (IASP) Press (1997)
14. Heiderich, T.M., Leslie, A.T.F.S., Guinsburg, R.: Neonatal procedural pain can be assessed by computer software that has good sensitivity and specificity to detect facial movements. Acta Paediatr. **104**(2), e63–e69 (2015)
15. Holmqvist, K., Nyström, M., Andersson, R., Dewhurst, R., Jarodzka, H., Van de Weijer, J.: Eye Tracking: A Comprehensive Guide to Methods and Measures. OUP, Oxford (2011)
16. Neves, F.A.M., Corrêa, D.A.M.: Dor em recém-nascidos: a percepção da equipe de saúde. Ciência, Cuidado e Saúde **7**(4), 461–467 (2008)
17. Pal, P., Iyer, A.N., Yantorno, R.E.: Emotion detection from infant facial expressions and cries. In: 2006 IEEE International Conference on Acoustics Speech and Signal Processing Proceedings, vol. 2, pp. II–II. IEEE (2006)
18. Pereira, A.L.S.T., Guinsburg, R., de Almeida, M.F.B., Monteiro, A.C., dos Santos, A.M.N., Kopelman, B.I.: Validity of behavioral and physiologic parameters for acute pain assessment of term newborn infants. São Paulo Med. J. **117**(2), 72–80 (1999)
19. Teruel, G.F., Heiderich, T.M., Guinsburg, R., Thomaz, C.E.: Analysis and recognition of pain in 2D face images of full term and healthy newborns. In: Proceedings of the XV Encontro Nacional de Inteligencia Artificial, ENIAC 2018, pp. 228–239 (2018)
20. Thomaz, C.E., et al.: A multivariate statistical analysis of the developing human brain in preterm infants. Image Vis. Comput. **25**(6), 981–994 (2007)
21. Thomaz, C.E., Gillies, D.F., Feitosa, R.Q.: A new covariance estimate for bayesian classifiers in biometric recognition. IEEE Trans. Circ. Syst. Video Technol. **14**(2), 214–223 (2004)
22. Vempada, R.R., Kumar, B.S.A., Rao, K.S.: Characterization of infant cries using spectral and prosodic features. In: 2012 National Conference on Communications (NCC), pp. 1–5. IEEE (2012)
23. Zamzmi, G., Kasturi, R., Goldgof, D., Zhi, R., Ashmeade, T., Sun, Y.: A review of automated pain assessment in infants: features, classification tasks, and databases. IEEE Rev. Biomed. Eng. **11**, 77–96 (2017)

Combining Asynchronous Events and Traditional Frames for Steering Angle Prediction

Abdoulaye O. Ly and Moulay A. Akhloufi$^{(\boxtimes)}$

Perception, Robotics, and Intelligent Machines Research Group (PRIME),
Department of Computer Science, Université de Moncton, Moncton, NB, Canada
{eal4944,moulay.akhloufi}@umoncton.ca

Abstract. Advances in deep learning over the last decade enabled by
the availability of more computing resources have revived interest in
end-to-end neural network methods for command prediction in vehicle
control. Most of the existing frameworks in the literature make use of
visual data from conventional video cameras to infer low level (steering
wheel, speed, etc.) or high level (curvature, driving path and more) commands for actuation. In this paper, we propose an efficient convolutional
neural network model that takes both perceptual data in the form of signals (events) from an event-based sensor and traditional frames from the
same camera to generate steering wheel angle. We show that our model
outperforms many state-of-the-art deep learning approaches using just
one type of input among regular frames or events while being much more
efficient.

Keywords: Steering angle prediction · Event-based vision · Deep
neural networks · ConvNets · Autonomous driving

1 Introduction

A traditional video sequence consists of successive 2D images appearing in a
synchronous mode. Each captured image from a standard camera has no relationship with the previous one leading to a loss of information between two
consecutive frames. With such sensor, the illusion of motion and continuity is
simulated by the amount of frames captured per time unit. For instance, for
movies a frame rate of 24 frames per second (fps) is believed to be the minimum
standard to create the effect of animation for the human eye. Below that threshold, the interruption between frames becomes more apparent and the optical
sensation of continuous movement disappears.

However, the way traditional video cameras capture images does not symbol-
ize the operating mode of the human eye. Instead, this latter has independent

Thanks to the Natural Sciences and Engineering Research Council of Canada (NSERC),
[funding reference number RGPIN-2018-06233].

A. Campilho et al. (Eds.): ICIAR 2020, LNCS 12131, pp. 244–252, 2020.
https://doi.org/10.1007/978-3-030-50347-5_22

receptors that are sensitive to illumination. Since the receptive fields are independent, each of them is refreshed only when a change of illumination is observed in an asynchronous manner. That is where comes into play the event-vision based cameras. Such kind of sensors approximately simulate our vision by providing independent pixels. Hence, instead of having a full new frame at every step, each individual pixel send a signal formerly called event $e = (x, y, i, p, t)$ where x and y represent the pixel coordinates, i the change in intensity, p the sign of the polarity and t the time of occurrence. The signals are generated asynchronously, in other words only when the previous value and the current value of a pixel are different.

In this paper we take advantage of the information provided by both an event-based camera and a conventional camera (see Fig. 1) to solve the challenging task of steering angle prediction for autonomous vehicle control. Most of the proposed methods in the literature make use of conventional images captured as inputs. However, with the proposed approach:

- We will demonstrate quantitatively that using asynchronous events with normal frames, performance can be improved in the task of steering angle prediction in real world environments.
- We use more efficient networks which is necessary and crucial in the context of autonomous vehicle control in general.

Fig. 1. On the left, standard grayscale images with ground thruth (in green) and predicted angle (in blue). On the right, event frames generated from 50 ms of accumulated signals from an event camera. (Color figure online)

2   Related Work

Using a neural network to predict control command for autonomous vehicles has been first achieved by Pomerleau [17] around three decades ago with the project ALVINN. In recent years many end-to-end deep learning based methods inspired from Pomerleau's work has been proposed with the rise of deep learning and the availability of more computing ressources. Bojarski *et al.* [2] proposed an end-to-end deep learning method to steer a car solely from raw images taken with a front facing camera. Codevilla *et al.* [3] proposed an end-to-end approach via conditional imitation learning. The authors suggested the use of driver's intention as an auxiliary input during the training of an imitative agent instead of inferring the actions solely from the visual input. This helps deal with ambiguities introduced upon reaching crosswalks or intersections. Toromanoff *et al.* [22] make use of visual data from a fisheye camera as input to their Convolutional Neural Network (CNN) [12] based models to output a steering angle. Hubschneider *et al.* [11] published DriveNet, an CNN model fed with 3 images separated by 10 m of driving each to capture a wider angle of the environment from a single front-facing camera and increase the ability of their model to make sharp turns. Different from prior work, Li *et al.* [14] proposed InfoGAIL an imitative learning algorithm based on Generative Adversarial Imitative Learning (GAIL) [9] developed to mimic expert behavior in a complex multidimensional environments from few visual demonstrations using Generative Adversarial Networks (GANs) [6]. Eraqi *et al.* [5] developed a model with Long Short Term Memory (LSTM) [10] to estimate steering angle with Comma.ai driving dataset [19]. Xu *et al.* [23] make use of dilated convolutions [24] and LSTM units to generate high level control commands from a video sequence. Maqueda *et al.* [15] recently published a novel approach that takes raw data from an event-camera as input to achieve better performance than some conventional frames based methods.

3   Proposed Approach

Using Maqueda *et al.* [15] work as our baseline and inspired by Li *et al.* [13] who combined both events and standard frames to achieve state of the art result in object detection in the context of autonomous vehicles, we stack both event frames and conventional frames to use them as input of our deep network model based on EfficientNets [21]. Our approach is summarized in Fig. 2.

3.1   From Events to Frames and Data Preprocessing

ConvNets are designed to take conventional images as input, not a sequence of asynchronous events. To mitigate this issue, the events are processed and converted into the same format as normal frames. First, we group the events into non-overlapping arrays corresponding to 50 ms of driving time. Then, from every array we construct two 2D histograms with each having a number of bins equal to the number of individual pixels. In the first histogram, we accumulate

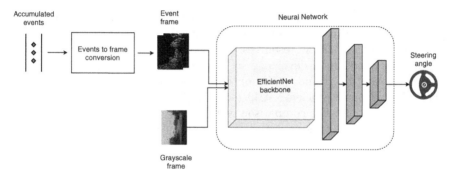

Fig. 2. Summary of our approach. We accumulate and convert signals from the event camera into a frame (event frame). The event frame is then stacked together with the corresponding standard image giving the final input for our EfficientNet [21] based model which outputs a steering angle.

signals with positive variation in intensity and in the second we compile events with negative polarity. Following that, we substract the negative histogram from the positive histogram to get a 16-bit image. To obtain our final input, the event frame is casted to a 8-bit format and stacked together with the corresponding grayscale frame captured from the same camera to form one single frame with two channels.

Before feeding the data to the network, the inputs are resized into frames of size 60 × 80 and normalized in the range $[0, 1]$ with respect to ImageNet [4] means and standard deviations. Finally, the steering wheel angles are squished into the range $[-1, 1]$ with -1 and 1 reprensenting -180 and 180°, respectively.

3.2 EfficientNets

In general, a CNN is scaled either by increasing its number of layers (depth dimension) or number of kernels (width dimension). Increasing the input size (resolution dimension) is also an interesting way to scale CNNs. Indeed, those methods help capture more features and hence increase performance, but only until a certain threshold. For instance, Resnet1000 does not achieve greater performance than Resnet with just 100 layers [8]. Recently, Tan and Le [21] came up with an interesting solution that consists of scaling all three dimensions at the same time. A method they named compound scaling. However, manually tweaking those parameters to find the optimal values can be tedious and slow. To mitigate that issue, the authors proposed a scaling approach with a compound coefficient ϕ to uniformly scale the three dimensions in the following way:

$$depth = \alpha^\phi, width = \beta^\phi, resolution = \gamma^\phi$$
$$s.t. \alpha\beta^2\gamma^2 \approx 2 \tag{1}$$
$$\alpha \geq 1, \beta \geq 1, \gamma \geq 1$$

where α, β and γ are constants that represent how computing resources are attributed to each dimension and ϕ is a parameter that can be adjusted manually according to available resources. Utilizing the compound scaling method, a baseline architecture is developed by setting ϕ to 1 and using a grid search algorithm to find α, β and γ. An optimal baseline utilizing Inverse Residual Blocks (IRB) named EfficientNetB0 (see Fig. 3) is constructed with $\alpha = 1.2$, $\beta = 1.1$ and $\gamma = 1.15$. For comparison, with similar performances on ImageNet, EfficentNetB0 has 4.9 times fewer parameters than Resnet50. Other variants of EfficientNets are computed by fixing α, β and γ and tweaking ϕ.

Fig. 3. EfficientNetB0 base architecture with Inverse Residual Blocks (simulator to those found in MobileNetV2 [18]).

3.3   Network Architecture

We considered 5 EfficientNets (B0 to B5) as extractors of meaningful features. The generated feature maps are then flattened with a global average pooling layer and fed to two consecutive fully connected layers. The first fully connected have 1024 neurons and is activated with ReLU non-linearity function [16], known to be effective for avoiding a vanishing or an exploding gradient. The last layer consists of just one neuron to output the steering angle in the range $[-1, 1]$ using tanh as activation function. Our Fully connected layers were initialized with He variance scaling method [7] which generally works well with ReLU activation.

4   Experimental Results

4.1   Dataset

We trained and validated our model using DAVIS Driving Dataset (DDD17) [1] known as the first public dataset bringing together event-based vision and traditional frames for end-to-end autonomous driving. Both event signals and grayscale frames were captured with the same DAVIS 346B prototype camera at a resolution of 346×260 pixels. The recording time totals over 12 h or around 436 GB in size. Perceptual data are recorded along with data from several other sensors such as GPS, INS, etc. The GPS gives latitude and longitude coordinates while the INS helps collect the vehicle speed and orientation. Additionally, the steering angle ranging from −600 and +600°, the position of the accelerator pedal, the position of the transmission gear, the status of the brake pedal and more are provided within the dataset. DDD17 covers city and highway driving in various scenarios including daytime, evening and night. It also contains driving sequences for both wet and dry weather conditions.

To develop and test our model, we removed calibration data (which mostly consisted of steering the vehicle at a standstill) and split the rest of the dataset into consecutive short sequences of 40 and 20 s respectively for training, validation and test. This resulted finally in over 880k frames for training and validation, and around 294k frames for testing.

4.2   Training Settings and Evaluation Metrics

To train our model, we opted for SGD optimizer with a learning rate of 0.001 and a momentum of 0.99. The choice of SGD is motivated by its good generalization capability despite needing usually more time before reaching convergence [20].

To evaluate our model, we use the Root Mean Squared Error (RMSE). This metric is more interesting for comparing between different methods as it penalizes more severely large errors which are undesirable for a task like steering angle prediction. For that reason, we used it as our loss function during training. RMSE is given by Eq. (2).

$$RMSE = \sqrt{\frac{1}{n} \sum_{i=1}^{n} (y_i - \hat{y}_i)^2} \tag{2}$$

4.3   Comparison of EfficientNets Variants

In order to determine the best performing visual encoder, we trained our model with each of the 5 variants of EfficientNets as feature extractor. We considered testing the baseline EfficientNetB0 to the bigger network EfficientNetB5. The results (Fig. 4) show that version 5 performs the best on DDD17 dataset and the performance of the model doesn't always improve with a larger backbone size. For example, the variant 3 gives the worst performance and EfficientNetB0 which has far less parameters than the other variants generalizes better than B1 to B4.

4.4   Performance on Different Subsets of the Dataset

To gauge the performance regarding different illumination conditions, we grouped the data into several subsets with respect to time (day, night and evening). Hence, we evaluated our best performing model on each portion of the dataset. Table 1 shows that the EfficientNetB5 based model performs better on evening and struggles more with night data. Arguably the reason is, on the one hand meaningful features are difficult to extract from the dark and on the other hand frames are too noisy (due to sun reflections for instance) when the camera is exposed to extreme lighting conditions.

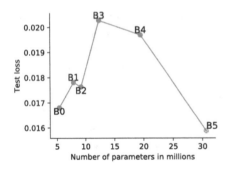

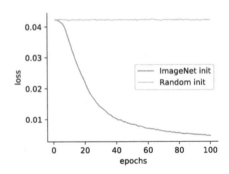

Fig. 4. Performance with different variant of EfficientNets as backbone (B0 to B5).

Fig. 5. Learning performance with and without transfer learning.

Table 1. Comparing the performance of our EfficientNetB5 based model on different illumination conditions.

Time	RMSE in degree
Day	2.73
Evening	**2.45**
Night	3.64

4.5 Transfer Learning

Transfer learning is a popular method for training deep learning models. It consists of starting the training with weights obtained from a previous training on a different dataset instead of initializing the parameters of the network with random values. This process generally helps during training by allowing a faster convergence. Our model is not an exception to that rule and Fig. 5 shows that transfer learning with ImageNet weights has considerably benefited our network during training. Indeed, our B5 network does not seem to learn anything relevant when initialized with random values even after 100 epochs.

4.6 Advantage of Combining Images and Events and Performance Comparison with Existing Models

We evaluated our model against two state-of-the-art methods proposed in the literature using RMSE and floating-point operations per second (FLOPs). The comparison (Table 2) shows that our model outperforms both of them with a considerable margin. Additionally, our model with EfficientNetB0 as backbone achieves greater performance on DDD17 than Nvidia Pilotnet [2] and Maqueda *et al.* [15] model while being 17X and 21X more efficient, respectively.

Finally, we demonstrated the added benefits of using both traditional images and event frames. Indeed, the performance is doubled compared to using only standard images as network input, while a significant improvement is achieved compared to using event frames alone.

Table 2. Our model vs existing state-of-the-art deep models and added benefits of combining standard images and dvs frames in steering angle prediction on DDD17 dataset.

Model	Data type	FLOPs in millions	RMSE in degree
Pilotnet [2]	Image	545.3	6.48
Maqueda *et al.* [15]	Events	699.2	3.61
Ours (EB0)	Image	32.0	6.55
Ours (EB0)	Events	32.0	3.42
Ours (EB0)	Both	**32.0**	**3.02**
Ours (EB5)	Both	508.0	**2.86**

5 Conclusion

Our work demonstrated that greater performance can be achieved by using deep efficient networks and combining signals from an event-based camera and traditional frames compared to just using one type of data as a network input. Indeed much more information can be captured by using both events and normal frames since the former can give detailed cues about changes that occurred over the previous several milliseconds, while the latter captures the whole scene at a specific point in time. Furthermore, our model is based on the recently proposed EfficientNet architectures which are known for their proven efficiency. Future work includes testing with deeper EfficientNet variants, exploring other fusion methods, testing with more datasets, and developing a multimodal framework capable of combining multiple type of inputs in autonomous driving applications.

References

1. Binas, J., Neil, D., Liu, S.C., Delbruck, T.: DDD17: end-to-end DAVIS driving dataset. In: ICML Workshop on Machine Learning for Autonomous Vehicles, November 2017
2. Bojarski, M., et al.: End to end learning for self-driving cars. CoRR, April 2016
3. Codevilla, F., Miiller, M., López, A., Koltun, V., Dosovitskiy, A.: End-to-end driving via conditional imitation learning. In: ICRA, pp. 4693–4700, May 2018
4. Deng, J., Dong, W., Socher, R., Li, L.J., Li, K., Fei-Fei, L.: ImageNet: a large-scale hierarchical image database. In: CVPR, pp. 248–255, June 2009
5. Eraqi, H.M., Moustafa, M.N., Honer, J.: End-to-end deep learning for steering autonomous vehicles considering temporal dependencies. In: Machine Learning for Intelligent Transportation Systems Workshop, October 2017

6. Goodfellow, I.J., et al.: Generative adversarial nets. In: NIPS (2014)
7. He, K., Zhang, X., Ren, S., Sun, J.: Delving deep into rectifiers: surpassing human-level performance on ImageNet classification. In: Proceedings of ICCV 2015, pp. 1026–1034. IEEE Computer Society (2015)
8. He, K., Zhang, X., Ren, S., Sun, J.: Deep residual learning for image recognition. In: CVPR, pp. 770–778, June 2016
9. Ho, J., Ermon, S.: Generative adversarial imitation learning. In: Lee, D.D., Sugiyama, M., Luxburg, U.V., Guyon, I., Garnett, R. (eds.) NIPS, pp. 4565–4573 (2016)
10. Hochreiter, S., Schmidhuber, J.: Long short-term memory. Neural Comput. 9(8), 1735–1780 (1997)
11. Hubschneider, C., Bauer, A., Weber, M., Zöllner, J.M.: Adding navigation to the equation: turning decisions for end-to-end vehicle control. In: ITSC, pp. 1–8 (2017)
12. LeCun, Y., Haffner, P., Bottou, L., Bengio, Y.: Object recognition with gradient-based learning. Shape, Contour and Grouping in Computer Vision. LNCS, vol. 1681, pp. 319–345. Springer, Heidelberg (1999). https://doi.org/10.1007/3-540-46805-6_19
13. Li, J., Dong, S., Yu, Z., Tian, Y., Huang, T.: Event-based vision enhanced: a joint detection framework in autonomous driving. In: ICME, pp. 1396–1401. IEEE, Shanghai, July 2019
14. Li, Y., Song, J., Ermon, S.: InfoGAIL: interpretable imitation learning from visual demonstrations. In: NIPS, March 2017
15. Maqueda, A.I., Loquercio, A., Gallego, G., Garcia, N., Scaramuzza, D.: Event-based vision meets deep learning on steering prediction for self-driving cars. In: CVPR, pp. 5419–5427, June 2018
16. Nair, V., Hinton, G.E.: Rectified linear units improve restricted Boltzmann machines. In: Proceedings of the 27th International Conference on International Conference on Machine Learning, ICML2010, Madison, WI, USA, pp. 807–814 (2010)
17. Pomerleau, D.: ALVINN: an autonomous land vehicle in a neural network. In: NIPS (1988)
18. Sandler, M., Howard, A.G., Zhu, M., Zhmoginov, A., Chen, L.C.: MobileNetV2: inverted residuals and linear bottlenecks. In: CVPR, pp. 4510–4520 (2018)
19. Santana, E., Hotz, G.: Learning a driving simulator. CoRR, August 2016
20. Schaul, T., Antonoglou, I., Silver, D.: Unit tests for stochastic optimization. In: ICLR, December 2013
21. Tan, M., Le, Q.V.: EfficientNet: rethinking model scaling for convolutional neural networks. In: ICML (2019)
22. Toromanoff, M., Wirbel, E., Wilhelm, F., Vejarano, C., Perrotton, X., Moutarde, F.: End to end vehicle lateral control using a single fisheye camera. In: IROS, August 2018
23. Xu, H., Gao, Y., Yu, F., Darrell, T.: End-to-end learning of driving models from large-scale video datasets. In: CVPR, pp. 3530–3538, July 2017
24. Yu, F., Koltun, V.: Multi-scale context aggregation by dilated convolutions. CoRR (2015)

Survey of Preprocessing Techniques and Classification Approaches in Online Signature Verification

Mohammad Saleem$^{(\boxtimes)}$ ⓘ and Bence Kovari ⓘ

Budapest University of Technology and Economics, Muegyetem rkp. 3, Budapest 1111, Hungary
{msaleem,kovari}@aut.bme.hu

Abstract. This paper reviews the latest results in the field of online signature verification and summarizes the previously published major surveys and also over 30 papers from the last decade. We examine the steps of the verification process and show the most popular approaches used. Our results show that alignment and scaling are the most common methods used in preprocessing. Position, velocity, and pressure are the most commonly used measures for feature extraction while dynamic time warping is the most commonly used approach for verification. A comparison between these methods using different databases concludes this work. The error rate varies between 0.77% to 7.13%, with an average of 2.94%. The results and comparisons published in this paper may help researchers choose the most promising approaches for their systems.

Keywords: Pattern recognition · Online signature verification · DTW · Preprocessing

1 Introduction

Although other approaches like finger or face print analysis are more accurate, for historical reasons signatures are still widely used and deeply embedded in many fields in our life. In computer-aided signature verification, we distinguish two type of signatures. In case of offline signatures, the signature data refers to an image of the signature on a paper such as bank check or any other document. In the case of an online signature, the whole process of signing is captured using some kind of device, e.g. a tablet or digital pens. These devices capture many features of the signatures, like position, pressure, velocity etc. as a function of time, thereby adding valuable extra information for the verification process.

Several thousands of papers have been published about automatic signature verification. Previous surveys have summarized these earlier papers on the field. In this work, we study the latest papers from the last two decades while focusing on the researches from the past few years. We examine the different steps of the signature verification process and analyze the most popular approaches. We conclude our work in tables which show the most promising approaches by comparing their results using different databases.

© Springer Nature Switzerland AG 2020
A. Campilho et al. (Eds.): ICIAR 2020, LNCS 12131, pp. 253–266, 2020.
https://doi.org/10.1007/978-3-030-50347-5_23

Online signature verification can be divided into four main steps: data acquisition, preprocessing, feature extraction, and verification. Data acquisition can be performed by different electronic devices. After data acquisition, preprocessing methods are applied to the signature data to reduce the noise and certain differences between the signatures. These differences between the signatures of the same signer occur because the signer cannot draw an exact signature every time, the scale, alignment or rotation can be different. Thus, preprocessing is an important step to enhance the verification results. The next step is feature extraction. Online signatures contain a variety of features such as position, velocity, pressure, acceleration, pen-up durations etc. (see Table 2) that can be utilized during this process. The last step is the actual verification where similarity measurement methods and classification methods are applied to differentiate between original and forged signatures. Distance-based methods such as DTW are common in this field, but there are also several papers which have reported about neural network-based approaches.

The evaluation of signature verification systems is done by calculating their error rates. There are two type of errors: false acceptance rate (FAR), where the forged signature is verified as genuine, and the false rejection rate, where the genuine signature is verified as being forged. Equal error rate (EER) or average error rate (AER) is used to compare the verification systems' accuracy.

All the previously mentioned steps are discussed in the following sections. Section 2 discusses the methodology of signature verification. The last section evaluates the systems and provides comparisons between the systems that have been published in the last two decades. The survey ends with a brief conclusion of the work.

2   Methodology

Online signature verification systems consist of four main stages which are data acquisition, pre-processing, features extraction and verification. In this section, the four stages are discussed in details and the best results of each stage are shown.

2.1   Databases and Data Acquisition

The acquisition of signatures is done using special input devices. This can be performed by different electronic devices such as the pen tablets, touch screens or PDAs [1]. The pens can detect different features such as position, velocity, pressure etc. The pen horizontal and vertical movement describes the position of a signature point in order to retrieve online data such as the pressure applied while using a sensitive tablet. There are also other approaches, such as one that involves a stylus containing a small CCD camera [2] and a wired-glove device [3].

An online signature that was acquired using a pressure-sensitive tablet as a time function.

$$S(n) = \left[x(n)y(n)p(n)t(n)\right]^{T} \tag{1}$$

$n = 1$ to N, where N is the number of the points recorded, the position of the signature is represented by x(n) and y(n), and p(n) and t(n) represents the pressure and time stamp, respectively [4].

There are several signatures databases available for research purposes. In this section, we are going to enumerate some of the most widely used ones. The SVC2004 (Signature verification competition 2004) [5, 6] database contains two different databases with the same signatures, but one of them contains X and Y coordinates, timestamp, and pen status, and additional features are available in the other one, such as azimuth, altitude, and pressure [7]. Each database contains signatures from 40 signers. Each signer has 20 genuine signatures and 20 skilled forgeries.

The SUSIG (Sabanci University Signature database) database is also widely used in this regard. It consists of two parts: visual sub-corpus, which was collected using Interlink ePad-ink tablet, and the blind sub-corpus, which was collected using Wacom Graphire 2 tablet. In the first part, each signer has 20 genuine and 10 forged signatures. The second part consists of 10 genuine and 10 forged samples by each signer [7]. The Interlink tablet has an LCD screen dimensions of 3 × 2.20 inches, a resolution of 300 dpi, and its sampling rate is 100 Hz. The Wacom tablet's dimensions are 5.02 × 3.65 inches with a 100 Hz sampling rate [8, 9].

The MCYT (Ministerio de Ciencia y Tecnologı´a, Spanish Ministry of Science and Technology) database contains signatures from 330 individuals; each signer has 25 genuine signatures and 25 forged signatures collected for him/her [4]. The skilled forgeries are collected by five forgers. The signatures features consist of position, pressure, azimuth, and altitude. The tablet used here has a sampling rate of 100 Hz [10].

BioSecure Multimodal Database was captured using WACOM Intuos 3 pen tablet with a sampling rate of 100 Hz. The database was captured in two sessions and the duration between the first and second session was two months. For each of the 120 signers, 30 genuine and 20 forgeries were collected. The features captured in this database are X and Y coordinates, azimuth angle, altitude angle, time stamp, and pressure [11] (Table 1).

Table 1. Some databases used in the last two decades

Database	Signers	Genuine	Skilled	dpi	Frequency	References
SVC2004	40	800	800		100 Hz	[7, 20–32]
MCYT	330	6600	8250	5080	100 Hz	[4, 19, 21, 23–25, 27, 33–38]
BioSecure	120	3600	2400		100 Hz	[11, 39]
SigWiComp'13	31	1302	1116	50	200 Hz	[13]
SUSIG	94	1880	940	300	100 Hz	[4, 7, 8, 20, 31–33, 38, 40, 41]
SIGMA	200	2000	1000	5080	200 Hz	[16]
ATVS	350	8750				[31]

A Japanese signature dataset was used in SigWiComp2013 [12]. It has been captured with an HP EliteBook 2730p tablet and used for the abovementioned database, with a sampling rate of 200 Hz and 50 dpi. The number of the users was 31; for each user, 42 genuine signatures and 36 forged signatures were collected [13, 14].

SIGMA is a Malaysian signature database. It consists of over 6,390 genuine signatures and 2,130 forged signatures for Malaysian nationals [15]. All the forged signatures in SIGMA database are skilled forgeries. The resolution of the tablet is 5080 dpi, and it has a sampling frequency of 200 Hz and 1024 pressure levels. This database was used in [16] to test the signature verification system.

The common databases such as MCYT, SVC2004, and SUSIG are very important because they are human-made signatures, but at the same time they contain limited amount of data and also store private data. In order to avoid these restrictions, synthetic databases such as ATVS [17] were produced using a generative model based on information that was obtained after analyzing real signatures [18].

Some researchers have used their own databases in their work. Ibrahim et al. (Ibrahim 2010) used their own database, which consisted of signatures from 25 signers; the total number of signatures was 21,250 (15,000 genuine and 6,250 forgeries).

2.2 Feature Extraction

Feature extraction is one of the main steps of signature verification. There are two types of features: functions and parameters features. In the case of function features, the values are described as a function of time, while in the parameters the features are considered as a vector of elements. Usually, function feature consumes more time for processing than the parameter features [42], but they give better results.

Table 2. Some features used in the last two decades

Feature	References
Position	[13, 19, 20, 22, 24, 25, 27, 29, 33, 35, 41, 45–47]
Velocity	[13, 19, 24, 25, 33, 35, 41, 45, 47, 48]
Pressure	[19, 20, 22, 24, 25, 33, 35, 41, 47, 49]
Acceleration	[25, 33, 35, 41]
Wavelet-based features	[30]
Azimuth	[20]
Timestamp	[20, 24, 49]
Normalized Fourier Descriptor	[48]
Normalized central moments	[48]
Angle based features	[22, 24, 35]
Log curvature radius	[13]
Total acceleration magnitude	[13]
DCT coefficients	[7]

The parameter features are divided into two types, local and global. Global features describe the whole signature, such as pen lifts and time duration, while the local features are extracted from specific parts of signatures.

The most widely used features are position, velocity, and acceleration. Position can be acquired directly from the input device or pen movement, while there are other features which can be derived numerically from other features. However, recently specific devices have been developed to provide these features directly during the signing process [43, 44].

The other type of features is the parameter features: total signature duration, number of pen lifts while signing, and pen-up/pen-down time ratio. Other parameters like average, root mean square, max. and min. of position, speed, acceleration, etc. can be derived from the analysis of direction or other features. Fourier transform and wavelet transform can derive the coefficient used in signature verification. Table 2 shows some of the feature used in the verification system.

2.3 Preprocessing

The aim of preprocessing is to enhance the captured signatures in order to obtain the same type of feature information, like position or velocity, and thereby improve the accuracy of the system. In this section, we discuss the most common preprocessing methods.

The most common preprocessing step is normalization, where we can differentiate between several of its kinds: normalization of the horizontal position and vertical position (alignment), minimum and maximum normalization [32], length normalization (scaling) [48], time normalization [35] and z-normalization [40]. Also, up-sampling normalization and down-sampling normalization may be applied [16]. [48] Normalized moments and normalized Fourier descriptors were used to make the signature features scale, rotation, and displacement invariant. Signature alignment is widely used for preprocessing. It is done by subtracting a value from each point of the signature to re-align it so that it starts or ends in a specific point, which improve the results of the similarity matching of the signatures. Some articles refer to alignment as position normalization, location normalization, or translation. Xia et al. [25] align the signature based on Gaussian Mixture Model to obtain the best matching results. We may also find other variants for alignment [19, 29].

Signature scaling (or length normalization) is also used to reduce the error in similarity measurement by scaling the signature by a specific ratio. Scaling can be applied horizontally, vertically, or in both directions. Similar to alignment, this is a common approach in signature verification systems [30, 50]. A signer may sign his/her signature with differences in the rotation angle. In order to obtain better results, rotation preprocessing may be applied [25, 51]. Rotation based on orthogonal regression was used in [52] and the rotation angle was removed using DTW in [28].

Pen-up duration refers to the time when the pen is not touching the input device. Forgery signatures usually take a longer time in the pen-up duration compared to the original signatures. This can be used to detect the forged signatures [4]. In most cases, this feature is discarded. Yanikoglu et al. [4] filled the pen-up duration with imaginary points using different methods (as an example, one can fill up imaginary points every 30 ms while using a 100 Hz input device). In the same research, Yanikoglu et al. applied drift and mean removal to remove the baseline drift component of the signature. Linear regression with least square error was used for this purpose while the mean removal done by subtracting the mean value of the points.

Some points of the signature may have falsely become its part because of the high sensitivity of the input device. According to [19] these points have low pressure values and should be set to zero since they are not part of the signature. Thus, a threshold can be applied to remove these false captured values. Ibrahim et al. [19] used Eq. (2) to calculate this threshold:

$$t_j^i = \frac{1}{M} \sum_{m-1}^{M} z_j^i(m) - \sqrt{\frac{1}{M} \sum_{m-1}^{M} \left(z_j^i(m) - \frac{1}{M} \sum_{m-1}^{M} z_j^i(m) \right)^2} \qquad (2)$$

Table 3. Preprocessing methods used in the last two decades

Preprocessing		References
Normalization	Alignment, alignment of the center of gravity, translation, location normalization, alignment based on GMM, mean removal	[9, 11, 14, 19, 25, 29, 45, 51]
	Scaling, size normalization, horizontal scaling, vertical scaling, length normalization	[19, 28, 30, 35, 47, 50, 53]
	Rotation, rotation normalization, removing angle using DTW	[7, 19, 25, 28, 45, 47, 50–53]
	Time normalization	[35]
	Normalization based on the standard z-norm	[24, 40]
	Down-sampling normalization	[16]
	Min. normalization	[32]
	Max. normalization	[32]
Pen-up duration		[4]
Zero pressure removal		[19]
Resampling	Smoothing	[19, 45, 46, 51]
	Equal spacing	[35, 37, 46]
	Resampling using cubic spline	[19, 30, 45]
	Up-sampling normalization	[16]
	Down-sampling normalization	[16]
Drift removal		[9]
Filtering	Noise removal	[53]
	Filtering	[35]

There are some other preprocessing steps that are used to enhance the results of the signature verification. In [35], the average signals are transformed to an equally spaced 256-point using linear interpolation. Arora et al. [26] converted the signature into a coordinate system by calculating the derivatives of different parameters up to the second order. This produced a vector of the first and second parameters of the coordinates, the pressure, the speed and the angle, which were used in their verification system [see Eq. (3)].

$$V_i = \left[X^1, Y^1, P^1, \Phi^1, X^2, Y^2, P^2, \Phi^2 \right] \tag{3}$$

Nilchiyan et al. [30] used the method of resampling using cubic spline interpolation. The number of signature points is not the same for the signature and the reference signature; thus, resampling is applied to make the number of sampled points the same as the reference points. Table 3 shows a conclusion of the mentioned preprocessing methods and the articles in which they are used.

2.4 Similarity Measurements and Classification

After signature acquisition, preprocessing and feature extraction the signatures are ready to be compared with the original signatures. One of the most popular methods for the distance-based measurement is dynamic time warping (DTW).

DTW algorithm finds the best non-linear alignment of two-time series such that the overall distance between them is minimized. It has shown promising results in the signature verification field [54]. As it calculates the distance between two signatures, it is commonly used in a threshold-based classification approaches, like in [21, 33]. Yanikoglu et al. [4] presented a novel online signature verification system based on the Fast Fourier Transform (FFT); this approach enhanced the performance of the DTW by up to about 25%.

Another approach presented in [22] enhanced DTW by utilizing the code-vectors created through a Vector-Quantization (VQ) method. The combination of scoring/voting methods of DTW/VQ showed an enhanced result of the signature verification. VQ approaches were also presented in [24], which not only enhanced the verification system but also increased the speed of the process. In [25] a modified DTW with signature curve, constraint is presented that improves the efficiency of the system. Besides DTW, other different distance-based approaches are used in signature verification: Mahalanbis distance [11], Kolmogorov Smirnov distance [55], and Manhattan, Chebyshev, and Euclidean distances [19, 26].

Another verification technique using discrete cosine transform (DCT) and sparse representation was presented in [20], and it showed a competitive result as compared to functional approaches. Moreover, it is simpler and easier for the matching process.

Artificial intelligence methods, like different approaches based on neural networks (NN), haven't been widely used in signature verification systems as they require a large amount of data for training. In [48], a multi-layer perception (MLP) neural network was used for the classification with one input layer, one hidden layer, and one output layer. A novel back-propagating recurrent neural network (RNN) was presented to improve the verification performance in [27]. Length-normalized path signatures (LNPS) was also applied to the system because of its properties such as scale and rotation invariance. Support vector machines (SVM) contain the supervised model learning algorithms used in classification [56]. In this research, SVM has been used in signature verification [29, 45]. The advantages of using SVM are that they have a convex objective function with efficient training algorithms and good generalization properties [57].

Table 4. Verification techniques used in the last two decades

Method			Reference
Distance-based approaches:	DTW-based approaches	DTW/threshold	[8, 21, 28, 33, 36, 40, 41, 45, 46, 51]
		DTW/FFT	[4]
		DTW/Vector-Quantization	[22]
		DTW/curve constraint and GMM for matching	[25]
	Other distance-based approaches	Mahalanobis distance	[11]
		Manhattan distance	[26]
		Chebyshev distance	[26]
		Euclidean distance	[19, 26]
Vector-Quantization			[24]
Discrete Cosine Transform			[20]
Neural Networks:		Neural Networks (MLP)	[16, 48]
		Recurrent Neural Networks (with LNPS)	[27]
		Neural Networks	[30, 39]
SVM			[29, 38, 45]
Gaussian Mixture Model (GMM)			[25, 35, 37, 49]
Hidden Markov Model (HMM)			[49]
K-Fold Cross-Validation			[31]
Parzen window classifier			[7]
Naïve Bayesian (NB)			[38]
Nearest neighbor			[38]
Principal component analysis (PCA)			[38]
Linear discriminant analysis (LDA)			[38]

Many other approaches can be used for the verification step, such as Gaussian Mixture Model (GMM) [25, 35], Hidden Markov Model (HMM) [49], K-Fold Cross-Validation [31], Parzen Window Classifier [7], Naïve Bayesian (NB), nearest neighbor, principal component analysis, and linear discriminant analysis [38]. Table 4 summarizes these verification methods.

3 Evaluation and Comparisons

In the evaluation phase, the signature verification system is supposed to produce results with the least error rate possible. The system should classify the tested signature as either genuine or forged. If the system classifies a genuine signature as forged or a forged signature as genuine, the result will be wrong and the error rate will increase. Two types of errors should be calculated to evaluate the system correctly.

The first type is the false rejected rate (FRR) and the second is the false acceptance rate (FAR). The average of these error rates (AER) is used to compare the verification systems. Many previous signature verification competitions have been organized to evaluate the proposed verification methods, such as SVC2004 [6], BSEC2009 [58], ESRA'2011 [59], SigComp2011 [60], SigWiComp2013 [12], and SigWiComp2015 [54].

Table 5. A comparison between different methods using SVC2004 database

Reference	Year	EER/AER
[52]	2015	0.83%
[7]	2012	2.04%
[27]	2017	2.37%
[32]	2013	2.56%
[25]	2017	2.63%
[22]	2016	2.73%
[62]	2020	2.62%

Table 6. A comparison between different methods using MCYT database

Reference	Year	EER/AER
[19]	2010	1.09%
[38]	2016	1.10%
[22]	2016	1.55%
[25]	2017	2.15%
[21]	2017	2.33%
[33]	2015	2.74%
[61]	2019	3.09%

In this survey, we focused on the articles from the last decade. The next section provides a brief comparison between different methods using different databases. Table 5 shows a comparison between the various methods used on the SVC2004 database, Table 6 shows the same for MCYT database, and Table 7 shows the same for SUSIG database. These are the most widely used databases. For the other databases, Table 8 provides a comparison between the different methods that have been presented in the last few years. Each method shows the database, the preprocessing method, the features and verification methods that are used.

Table 7. A comparison between different methods using SUSIG database

Reference	Year	EER/AER
[52]	2015	0.77%
[32]	2013	1.30%
[7]	2012	1.49%
[38]	2016	1.92%
[41]	2015	2.13%
[21]	2017	2.89%
[33]	2015	3.09%
[40]	2015	3.61%

Table 8. A Comparison between methods presented in the last few years

Ref	Year	Preprocessing	Verification	Database	EER
[62]	2020	–	Different methods	SVC2004	2.62%
[61]	2019	–	SM-DTW	MCYT	3.09
[39]	2018	–	RNN	BiosecurID	4.75%
[25]	2017	Alignment, Scaling, Rotation	DTW/GMM	MCYT	2.15%
				SVC2004	2.63%
[27]	2017	–	RNN/LNPS	MCYT	2.37%
[34]	2017	–	Threshold	MCYT	4.60%
[38]	2016	–	Different methods	MCYT	1.10%
				SUSIG	1.92%
[22]	2016	Normalization		MCYT	1.55%
				SVC2004	2.73%
[52]	2015	Scaling, Data normalization	K-Fold Cross-Validation	SVC2004	0.83%
				SUSIG	0.77%
[41]	2015	Value and length normalization	DTW/Threshold	SUSIG	2.125%
[37]	2015	Filtering, Equal spacing, Location, time and size normalization	DTW/GMM	MCYT	2.74%
[33]	2015	–	DTW/Threshold	MCYT	2.74%
				SUSIG	3.09%
[20]	2015	Translation, size and rotation normalizations	Discrete cosine transforms DCT	SVC2004	5.61%
				SUSIG	2.98%
[30]	2015	Resampling using cubic spline, Scaling	ANN	SVC2004	2.75%
[36]	2015	–	DTW	MCYT	4.10%
[49]	2015	–	HMM/GMM		1.40%

4 Conclusion

Previous surveys have summarized the previously published articles about online signature verification. In this survey, we have summarized the recent articles in the field. We have also identified and compared the most widely used and the most promising approaches in each step of the verification.

The results showed that the most-used databases are SVC2004, SUSIG, and MCYT. Alignment and scaling are commonly used in the preprocessing steps and position, velocity, and pressure are used for the features. Our research showed that dynamic time warping is still among the most popular and shows the most promising results in the verification phase.

These results are compared in different tables that show the error rates of applying the studied techniques, which may help researchers choose the most significant and useful approaches for each step of their work in the field. Applying the same approach on different databases will result in different error rates, therefore, a comparison the between approaches that are applied for the same database are presented in this paper in order to give an accurate and meaningful results. Around 30 papers from the last decade are compared in detail, which provide the approaches used in each step in Table 8. The error rate varies between 0.77% to 7.13%, with an average of 2.94%.

The future aim in online signature verification is to present a system with the least possible error rate. These results and summarization will hopefully help researchers in this purpose.

Acknowledgment. Project no. FIEK_16-1-2016-0007 has been implemented with the support provided from the National Research, Development and Innovation Fund of Hungary, financed under the Centre for Higher Education and Industrial Cooperation - Research infrastructure development (FIEK_16) funding scheme.

References

1. Guru, D.S., Prakash, H.N.: Online signature verification and recognition: An approach based on symbolic representation. IEEE Trans. Pattern Anal. Mach. Intell. **31**(6), 1059–1073 (2009)
2. Muramatsu, D., Matsumoto, T.: An HMM on-line signature verification algorithm. In: Kittler, J., Nixon, M.S. (eds.) AVBPA 2003. LNCS, vol. 2688, pp. 233–241. Springer, Heidelberg (2003). https://doi.org/10.1007/3-540-44887-X_28
3. Kamel, N.S., Sayeed, S., Ellis, G.A.: Glove-based approach to on-line signature. IEEE T-PAMI **30**, 1109–1113 (2006)
4. Yanikoglu, B., Kholmatov, A.: Online signature verification using Fourier descriptors. EURASIP J. Adv. Sig. Process. (2009). https://doi.org/10.1155/2009/260516
5. SVC: The first international signature verification competition. http://www.cs.ust.hk/svc2004
6. Yeung, D.-Y., et al.: SVC2004: first international signature verification competition. In: Zhang, D., Jain, A.K. (eds.) ICBA 2004. LNCS, vol. 3072, pp. 16–22. Springer, Heidelberg (2004). https://doi.org/10.1007/978-3-540-25948-0_3
7. Rashidi, S., Fallah, A., Towhidkhah, F.: Feature extraction based DCT on dynamic signature verification. Sci. Iranica **19**(6), 1810–1819 (2012)
8. Khalil, M.I., Moustafa, M., Abbas, H.M.: Enhanced DTW based on-line signature verification. In: IEEE International Conference on Image Processing (ICIP), vol. 16, pp. 2713–2716 (2009)

9. Yanıkoğlu, B.: SUSIG: an on-line handwritten signature database, associated protocols and benchmark results. Pattern Anal. Appl. (2008)

10. Ortega-Garcia, J., et al.: MCYT baseline corpus: a bimodal biometric database. IEE Proc. Vis. Image Sig. Process. **150**(6), 395–401 (2003)

11. Tolosana, R., Vera-Rodriguez, R., Fierrez, J., Ortega-Garcia, J.: Feature-based dynamic signature verification under forensic scenarios. In: 2015 International Workshop on Biometrics and Forensics (IWBF). IEEE (2015)

12. Malik, M.I., Liwicki, M., Alewijnse, L., Ohyama, W., Blumenstein, M., Found, B.: ICDAR 2013 competitions on signature verification and writer identification for on-and offline skilled forgeries (SigWiComp 2013). In: 2013 12th International Conference on Document Analysis and Recognition, pp. 1477–1483. IEEE, August 2013

13. Zeinali, H., BabaAli, B.: On the usage of i-vector representation for online handwritten signature verification. In: IAPR International Conference on Document Analysis and Recognition (ICDAR), vol. 14, pp. 1243–1248 (2017)

14. Ahrabian, K., BabaAli, B.: On usage of autoencoders and siamese networks for online handwritten signature verification. arXiv preprint arXiv (2017)

15. Ahmad, S.M.S., Shakil, A., Ahmad, A.R., Agil, M., Balbed, M., Anwar, R.M.: SIGMA-A Malaysian signatures' database. In: 2008 AICCSA. IEEE/ACS International Conference on Computer Systems and Applications, pp. 919–920 (2008)

16. Malallah, F.L., Ahmad, S.M.S., Adnan, W.A.W., Arigbabu, O.A., Iranmanesh, V., Yussof, S.: Online handwritten signature recognition by length normalization using up-sampling and down-sampling. Int. J. Cyber-Secur. Digit. Forensics (IJCSDF) **4**, 302–313 (2015)

17. http://atvs.ii.uam.es/atvs/databases.jsp

18. Galbally, J., Plamondon, R., Fierrez, J., Ortega-Garcia, J.: Synthetic on-line signature generation Part I: methodology and algorithms. Pattern Recogn. **45**(7), 2610–2621 (2012)

19. Ibrahim, M.T., Khan, M.A., Alimgeer, K.S., Khan, M.K., Taj, I.A., Guan, L.: Velocity and pressure based partitions of horizontal and vertical trajectories for on-line signature verification. Pattern Recogn. **43**(8), 2817–2832 (2010)

20. Liu, Y., Yang, Z., Yang, L.: Online signature verification based on DCT and sparse representation. IEEE Trans. Cybern. **45**(11), 2498–2511 (2015)

21. Song, X., Xia, X., Luan, F.: Online signature verification based on stable features extracted dynamically. IEEE Trans. Syst. Man Cybern. Syst. **47**(10), 2663–2676 (2017)

22. Sharma, A., Sundaram, S.: An enhanced contextual DTW based system for online signature verification using vector quantization. Pattern Recogn. Lett. **84**, 22–28 (2016)

23. Doroz, R., Porwik, P., Orczyk, T.: Dynamic signature verification method based on association of features with similarity measures. Neurocomputing **171**, 921–931 (2016)

24. Pascual-Gaspar, J.M., Faundez-Zanuy, M., Vivaracho, C.: Fast on-line signature recognition based on VQ with time modeling. Eng. Appl. Artif. Intell. **24**(2), 368–377 (2011)

25. Xia, X., Chen, Z., Luan, F., Song, X.: Signature alignment based on GMM for on-line signature verification. Pattern Recogn. **65**, 188–196 (2017)

26. Arora, M., Singh, H., Kaur, A.: Distance based verification techniques for online signature verification system. In: Recent Advances in Engineering & Computational Sciences (RAECS), pp. 1–5 (2015)

27. Lai, S., Jin, L., Yang, W.: Online signature verification using recurrent neural network and length-normalized path signature descriptor. In: Document Analysis and Recognition (ICDAR), pp. 400–405 (2017)

28. Mohammadi, M.H., Faez, K.: Matching between important points using dynamic time warping for online signature verification. J. Sel. Areas Bioinf. (JBIO) (2012)

29. Kholmatov, A., Yanikoglu, B.: Identity authentication using improved online signature verification method. Pattern Recogn. Lett. **26**(15), 2400–2408 (2005)

30. Nilchiyan, M.R., Yusof, R.B., Alavi, S.E.: Statistical on-line signature verification using rotation-invariant dynamic descriptors. In: Control Conference (ASCC), pp. 1–6 (2015)
31. Fayyaz, M., Hajizadeh_Saffar, M., Sabokrou, M., Fathy, M.: Feature representation for online signature verification. arXiv preprint arXiv:1505.08153 (2015)
32. Ansari, A.Q., Hanmandlu, M., Kour, J., Singh, A.K.: Online signature verification using segment-level fuzzy modelling. IET Biometrics 3(3), 113–127 (2013)
33. Fischer, A., Diaz, M., Plamondon, R., Ferrer, M.A.: Robust score normalization for DTW-based on-line signature verification. In: 2015 13th International Conference on Document Analysis and Recognition (ICDAR), pp. 241–245. IEEE (2015)
34. Guru, D.S., Manjunatha, K.S., Manjunath, S., Somashekara, M.T.: Interval valued symbolic representation of writer dependent features for online signature verification. Expert Syst. Appl. **80**, 232–243 (2017)
35. López-García, M., Ramos-Lara, R., Miguel-Hurtado, O., Cantó-Navarro, E.: Embedded system for biometric online signature verification. IEEE Trans. Ind. Inform. **10**, 491–501 (2014)
36. Tolosana, R., Vera-Rodriguez, R., Ortega-Garcia, J., Fierrez, J.: Preprocessing and feature selection for improved sensor interoperability in online biometric signature verification. IEEE Access **3**, 478–489 (2015)
37. Francis, F., Aparna, M.S., Vincent, A.: Biometric online signature verification. IOSR J. Electron. Commun. Eng. 82–89 (2015)
38. Manjunatha, K.S., Manjunath, S., Guru, D.S., Somashekara, M.T.: Online signature verification based on writer dependent features and classifiers. Pattern Recogn. Lett. **80**, 129–136 (2016)
39. Tolosana, R., Vera-Rodriguez, R., Fierrez, J., Ortega-Garcia, J.: Exploring recurrent neural networks for on-line handwritten signature biometrics'. IEEE Access **6**, 5128–5138 (2018)
40. Diaz, M., Fischer, A., Plamondon, R., Ferrer, M.A.: Towards an automatic on-line signature verifier using only one reference per signer. In: Document Analysis and Recognition (ICDAR), pp. 631–635 (2015)
41. Pirlo, G., Cuccovillo, V., Diaz-Cabrera, M., Impedovo, D., Mignone, P.: Multidomain verification of dynamic signatures using local stability analysis. IEEE Trans. Hum.-Mach. Syst. **45**, 805–810 (2015)
42. Plamondon, R., Lorette, G.: Automatic signature verification and writer identification—the state of the art. Pattern Recogn. **22**, 107–131 (1989)
43. Ohishi, T., Komiya, Y., Morita, H., Matsumoto, T.: Pen-input online signature verification with position, pressure, inclination trajectories. In: Parallel and Distributed Processing Symposium (IPDPS-2001) (2001)
44. Omata, S.: Development of the new digital sign pen system using tactile sensor for handwritten recognition. In: Proceedings of the Technical Digest 18th Sensor Symposium, pp. 131–136 (2001)
45. Radhika, K.S., Gopika, S.: Online and offline signature verification: a combined approach. Proc. Comput. Sci. **46**, 1593–1600 (2015)
46. Jain, A.K., Griess, F.D., Connell, S.D.: On-line signature verification. Pattern Recogn. **35**, 2963–2972 (2002)
47. Khan, M.K., Khan, M.A., Khan, M.A., Ahmad, I.: On-line signature verification by exploiting inter feature dependencies. In: Pattern Recognition, vol. 2, pp. 796–799 (2006)
48. Al-Shoshan, A.: Handwritten signature verification using image invariants and dynamic features. In: 2006 International Conference on Computer Graphics, Imaging and Visualization, pp. 173–176. IEEE (2006)
49. Tolosana Moranchel, R., Vera-Rodriguez, R., Ortega-Garcia, J., Fierrez, J.: Update strategies for HMM-based dynamic signature biometric systems (2015)

50. Chadha, A., Jyoti, D., Roja, M.M.: Rotation, scaling and translation analysis of biometric signature templates. arXiv preprint arXiv, vol. 2, pp. 1419–1425 (2011)
51. Wirotius, M., Ramel, J.Y., Vincent, N.: Selection of points for on-line signature comparison. In: Frontiers in Handwriting Recognition (2004)
52. Fayyaz, M., Saffar, M.H., Sabokrou, M., Hoseini, M., Fathy, M.: Online signature verification based on feature representation. In: Artificial Intelligence and Signal Processing (AISP), pp. 211–216 (2015)
53. Jindal, U., Dalal, S., Dahiya, N.: A combine approach of preprocessing in integrated signature verification (ISV). Int. J. Eng. Technol. 7, 155–159 (2018)
54. Malik, M.I., et al.: ICDAR2015 competition on signature verification and writer identification for on-and offline skilled forgeries (SigWIcomp2015). In: 13th International Conference on Document Analysis and Recognition (ICDAR), pp. 1186–1190. IEEE (2015)
55. Griechisch, E., Malik, M.I., Liwicki, M.: Online signature verification based on kolmogorov-smirnov distribution distance. In: Frontiers in Handwriting Recognition, pp. 738–742 (2014)
56. Cortes, C., Vapnik, V.: Support-vector networks. Mach. Learn. 20, 273–297 (1995). https://doi.org/10.1007/BF00994018
57. El-Henawy, I., Rashad, M., Nomir, O., Ahmed, K.: Online signature verification: state of the art. Int. J. Comput. Technol. 4, 664–678 (2013)
58. Houmani, N., et al.: BioSecure signature evaluation campaign (BSEC'2009): evaluating online signature algorithms depending on the quality of signatures. Pattern Recogn. 45(3), 993–1003 (2012)
59. Houmani, N., et al.: BioSecure signature evaluation campaign (ESRA'2011): evaluating systems on quality-based categories of skilled forgeries. In: 2011 International Joint Conference on Biometrics (IJCB). IEEE (2011)
60. Liwicki, M., et al.: Signature verification competition for online and offline skilled forgeries (sigcomp2011). In: 2011 International Conference on Document Analysis and Recognition (ICDAR). IEEE (2011)
61. Parziale, A., Diaz, M., Ferrer, M.A., Marcelli, A.: SM-DTW: stability modulated dynamic time warping for signature verification. Pattern Recogn. Lett. 121, 113–122 (2019)
62. Chandra, S.: Verification of dynamic signature using machine learning approach. Neural Comput. Appl. 1–21 (2020). https://doi.org/10.1007/s00521-019-04669-w

SSIM Based Signature of Facial Micro-Expressions

Vittoria Bruni[1,2(✉)] ⓘ and Domenico Vitulano[1,2] ⓘ

[1] Department of Basic and Applied Science for Engineering,
University of Rome La Sapienza, Via A. Scarpa 16, 00161 Rome, Italy
[2] Institute for Calculus Applications, CNR, Rome, Italy
{vittoria.bruni,domenico.vitulano}@uniroma1.it

Abstract. Facial microexpressions (MEs) play a crucial role in the non verbal communication. Their automatic detection and recognition on a real video is a topic of great interest in different fields. However, the main difficulty in automatically capturing this kind of feature consists in its rapid temporal evolution, i.e. MEs occur in very few frames of video acquired by a conventional camera. In this paper a first study concerning the perceptual characteristics of ME is performed. The study is based on the observation that MEs are visible by a human observer, even though they are very rapid, and almost independently of the context. The Structural SIMilarity index (SSIM), which is a common perception-based metric, has been then used to detect a sort of fingerprint of MEs, that will be indicated as PES (Perceptual Expression Signature). The latter is able to efficiently guide the preprocessing step for MEs recognition procedure, as it allows for a fast video segmentation by providing only those frames where a ME occurs with high probability. Preliminary empirical studies on MEs in the wild have confirmed the feasibility of such an approach.

Keywords: Facial Microexpression · Perceptual fingerprint · SSIM

1 Introduction

The increasing use of social media has opened up new ways of facing problems that appeared resolvable just by humans. One of the most interesting and attractive topics for the Scientific Community is the automatic detection of the emotional state of a subject in a video sequence [11]. A pioneering study of this kind of non verbal communication was firstly carried on by Haggard and Isaacs in 1966 [6] and it has been successively developed by Ekman and Friesen—from 1969 on [3]. Facial micro expressions (MEs) play a key role in a non verbal communication. They are defined as "very brief, subtle, and involuntary facial expressions which normally occur when a person either deliberately or unconsciously conceals his or her genuine emotions" [4,19]. MEs are characterized by a very short duration: ranging from 1/25 to 1/5 of a second (recently relaxed to a maximum duration of 1/2 s) [19]. Unfortunately, MEs are very difficult to be

© Springer Nature Switzerland AG 2020
A. Campilho et al. (Eds.): ICIAR 2020, LNCS 12131, pp. 267–279, 2020.
https://doi.org/10.1007/978-3-030-50347-5_24

detected by a human being [13] since a short duration usually is combined with a very low intensity as well as just a partial face motion. In this case, an effective computational framework is not only an help but a strong necessity to catch the emotional state of the subject under study. MEs convey a lot of information that a subject tries to hide. That's why MEs are currently under study in very different fields like business, medicine, forensic and security [5,18].

ME automatic detection usually involves two steps: *i)* spotting and *ii)* recognition. Spotting consists of finding out frames containing a ME while recognition is oriented to classify ME type—i.e., the subject emotional state. This paper will focus on ME spotting. Existing approaches addressing the spotting problem generally consist of various phases that involve different delicate operations on video sequences—see next section for a very short review. Coarsely speaking, facial points registration and tracking, salient face regions detection under noisy conditions (i.e., all movements but MEs), ME feature description and recognition are required—see Fig. 1 for a block scheme of salient required actions in spotting. However, a framework composed of a very sophisticated chain may result too much expensive in real-time investigations, especially if one considers that a 'real world' video is usually long and may contain various MEs along with additional unavoidable face movements. This paper presents a first attempt to develop a framework that is able to detect subsequences containing MEs with high probability, by means of simple operations. Such an approach is motivated by two main reasons. The first one is to build a fast preprocessing step where just a small subset of short subsequences from a long video are detected with the least computational time. The second reason is more challenging: to try to catch the 'sixth sense' of an observer that detects a ME of his interlocutor; he captures something strange even though he is not able to clearly specify details. The proposed approach shows that it is possible to find a perceptive emotional signature (PES) that characterizes MEs. To this aim, the well known Structural SIMilarity index (SSIM) [16] evaluated on pairs of subsequent frames is adopted due to its high correlation with human visual system as well as its explicit dependency on a structural term that straightforwardly captures temporal motion. This operation produces an asymmetric probability distribution for the metric, due to the fact that before ME's apex (maximum expression of ME) there's at least one frame containing no (or minimal) motion—due to the interlocutor

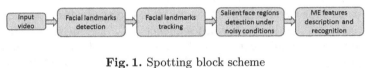

Fig. 1. Spotting block scheme

Fig. 2. Sequence 15.1 from ME-view database [9]. From left to right: neutral, onset, apex, offset and neutral state of a spontaneous ME (surprise).

need of hiding his own emotional state. The presence of ME motion is then, very often, an outlier of a very concentrated distribution. The advantage of such an approach is then twofold. First, it allows to drastically reduce the computational effort in finding ME subsequences on which successively performing available and more sophisticated approaches. This hierarchical procedure can help to build real time frameworks. Second, to the best of the authors' knowledge, this is the first attempt to better understand the perceptual contribution of this kind of non verbal communication.

The remainder of the paper is organized as follows. Next section contains a very short review of the related state of the art. Section 3 contains preliminary studies and observations that support the proposed model, while Sect. 4 presents some experimental results. The last section draws the conclusions.

2 State of the Art

MEs spotting is not limited to a rough partition of a video sequence in binary subsequences: the ones containing MEs (1st type) and the ones that didn't (2nd type). As matter of fact, it is very complicated as it consists of preprocessing, feature description and ME detection [11]. Preprocessing, in turn, involves different and distinct operations, such as landmark detection, landmark tracking, registration, masking and region retrieval. A good and relatively recent review can be found in [11]. However, without many details it can be argued that all the aforementioned phases are very delicate. Their cascade requires a very high precision in each phase in order to avoid an error spreading that may definitely inficiate the final result. Existing literature concerning ME spotting can be classified into two groups: classifier-based methods and rule-based methods. The first class includes frame-by-frame methods [12], that are not too much robust to spontaneous MEs, and temporal methods [14], that take into account frame relations by defining strain temporal maps, resulting more suitable for spontaneous MEs detection. Features difference analysis is used in [10,17], where facial motion variations are taken into account. However, they suffer from the dependence on the predefined temporal window that limits they adaptivity to videos having different rates. As eye blinking can represent a false alarm, in [2] an attempt to distinguish between MEs and eye movements has been presented by analyzing the phase variations between frames based on the Riesz Pyramid. A different class of methods focuses on apex frame detection [8,20] by using geometric and/or appearance features of specific face components.

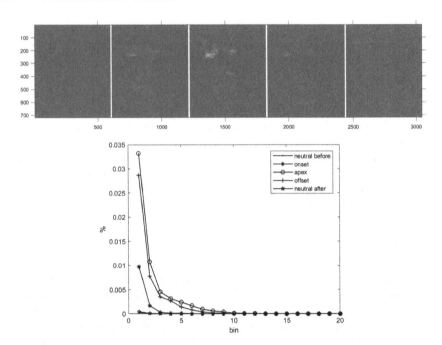

Fig. 3. *Top*) S map of two consecutive frames of the sequence in Fig. 2. *Bottom*) S distribution corresponding to the different phases characterizing ME temporal evolution. As it can be observed, S map is almost 'dark' (low S values are locally measured in the image) as the frames are considered almost 'visually' similar except for the region where the ME occurs. This is measured by a change in S distribution which occurs far from the mean value (white pixels in S maps).

In this paper we aim at investigating some particular temporal ME features; specifically, those related to the visual perception of micro-movements. The final goal is to define a specific perceptual fingerprint that could fasten or automatize some of the existing procedures.

3   The Proposed Model

MEs represent transients in the temporal motion sequence. They are mainly composed of onset, apex, offset, and neutral phases (see Fig. 2) [15]. The main problem in MEs analysis is that the phases described above occur in very few frames and are mostly local. However, an empirical study revealed that while the first two phases are common to all MEs, the last two are not. Offset and neutral can be rapid in case of a spontaneous reaction, or they may be quite slow whenever the expression is partially controlled—as, for example, whenever the subject remains in the new pose for (further) masking purposes. This is the reason why in this paper we investigate the possibility of revealing and checking just onset and apex through the use of a global visual perception-based measure.

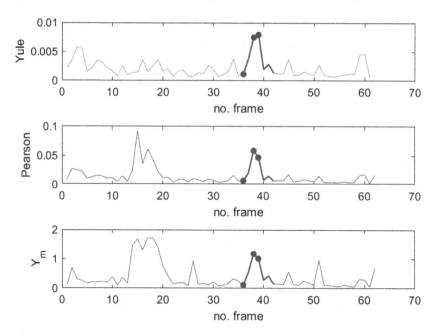

Fig. 4. Pearson, Yule and modified Yule (Y_m) absolute indexes, as defined in the text, for the sequence in Fig. 2. All of them show a typical behaviour in correspondence to the ME (bold lines) which is consistent with the temporal phases of an ideal (fully spontaneous) ME. Dot markers are in correspondence to onset, apex and starting point of the offset and they represent the perceptual fingerprint (PES) of any ME.

In fact, since human eye is, in some sense, able to perceive ME at a certain speed, in correspondence to the frames involving a ME we expect a certain contribution to a standard image quality assessment measure which is able to replicate vision mechanisms. In particular, it will be shown that MEs are characterized by a fingerprint in a specific perceptual measure, namely the *Structural SIMilarity* index (SSIM) [16]. The latter is a full-reference image quality assessment measure that correlates well with human perception. It evaluates the visual difference between two corresponding blocks (I and J) of two images as follows

$$SSIM(I,J) = \underbrace{\frac{2\mu_I\mu_J + C_1}{\mu_I^2 + \mu_J^2 + C_1}}_{luminance\ adaptation} \underbrace{\frac{2\sigma_I\sigma_J + C_2}{\sigma_I^2 + \sigma_J^2 + C_2}}_{contrast\ masking} \underbrace{\frac{\sigma_{IJ} + C_3}{\sigma_I\sigma_J + C_3}}_{spatial\ correlation}, \qquad (1)$$

where μ_I, μ_J, σ_I and σ_J respectively are the sample means and standard deviations of I and J, σ_{IJ} their covariance, while C_1, C_2 and C_3 are numerical stabilizing constants. Despite its simplicity, this measure is able to properly merge three main features to which human eye is mostly sensitive, i.e. luminance, contrast and structure, and the corresponding mechanisms, i.e. luminance adaptation, contrast masking, contrast and structures sensitivity. In particular, luminance and contrast gain control allows to maintain perceptual sensitivity under different lighting conditions, while contrast masking mainly measures to what extent an object having specific frequencies is visible whenever embedded in a background having similar frequencies. SSIM values belong to the range $[-1, 1]$: the greater this value, the better the quality. As a matter of fact, in the sequel

$$S(I, J) = 1 - SSIM(I, J) \qquad (2)$$

will be considered as it is consistent with the concept of distance, i.e. $S(I, J) \geq 0$, $S(I, J) = 0$ if and only if $I = J$, while the more $S(I, J)$ far from zero, the larger the difference between I and J. S can be computed locally (in a neighborhood of each image pixel) and it can be rewritten in the following form

$$S(I, J) = 1 - \underbrace{\frac{2\mu_I\mu_J + C_1}{\mu_I^2 + \mu_J^2 + C_1}}_{S_1(I,J)} \underbrace{\frac{2\sigma_{IJ} + C_2}{\sigma_I^2 + \sigma_J^2 + C_2}}_{S_2(I,J)}, \qquad (3)$$

where S_1 corresponds to luminance adaptation, while S_2 is related to contrast masking and structure sensitivity. This form allows to straightforward have an interesting mathematical interpretation for SSIM [1] as $\sqrt{1 - S_1}$ and $\sqrt{1 - S_2}$ are two normalized metrics in $\mathbf{R}^n$. S is a good candidate for revealing facial movements between subsequent frames since the latter actually represent a structural distortion between two consecutive frames. In particular, ME represents a local structural distortion in the face region which contributes to a change of S temporal distribution; in particular, we expect that S values distribution has a considerable change toward its tails, as shown in Fig. 3. The more perceptually significant ME, the more significant S distribution modification.

In order to identify and characterize such expected perceptual change, the distribution of S map has been considered and some of its classical statistical features have been evaluated. In particular, its asymmetry has been analysed. S values computed just in correspondence to face region actually provide a quite asymmetric and unimodal distribution whose mode is in correspondence to the minimum value of S, i.e. close to 0 (see Fig. 3 bottom). In fact, the skin does not locally provide significant contribution to S due to its visual homogeneity. Unfortunately, robust statistical tools for asymmetric data are not so numerous as the mean value does not represent a consistent estimate of the central value for asymmetric data. As a consequence, the Fisher definition of skewness [7] (the one depending on the third moment) is not the best choice. For similar reasons, the standard deviation could provide ambiguous values in the standardization of the measure. On the basis of these observations, absolute asymmetry indexes have been analysed in the sequel. In particular, measures based on median value and quantile/range values have been taken into account, as they are less sensitive to the extreme values, without completely discarding the same extreme values. The following absolute indexes have been then selected.

The second *Pearson's coefficient* of skewness compares mean value and median; even though it still depends on the mean, the comparison of mean and median is sensitive to the observed change in S distribution in the presence of a ME. Its absolute version is defined as $P = (E - Q_2)$, where E is the mean and Q_2 is the median value of the analysed data. Similarly, the *Yule's coefficient* is defined as $Y = Q_3 - 2Q_2 + Q_1$, where Q_i is the i-th quartile. Even in this case the normalization factor has been omitted. Finally, a modification of the Yule's coefficient has been considered, i.e.

$$Y_m = M - 2Q_2 + m, \tag{4}$$

where $M - m$ is the range of the S values. Figure 4 shows the plot of the three indexes for the sequence in Fig. 2. It is interesting to observe that, in correspondence to the ME, the three coefficients show a similar and specific profile which replicates the temporal phases of ME: neutral, onset, apex, offset, neutral. This behaviour represents the ideal fingerprint of the ideal ME in the distribution of the perceptual measure in correspondence to the face. As it can be observed, a rapid and significant change of the index occurs between onset and apex, as opposite to the one between apex and the starting point of the offset phase. This kind of profile represents the actual perceptual fingerprint of a ME and it will be denoted by PES in the sequel. In particular, with regard to Y_m, by denoting with t_{on}, t_{ap}, t_{off} respectively the temporal instants corresponding to the onset, apex and offset, we have

$$R = \frac{Y_m(t_{ap}) - Y_m(t_{on})}{|Y_m(t_{ap}) - Y_m(t_{off})|} >> 1. \tag{5}$$

On the contrary, the temporal perceptual index behaviour from the offset to the neutral state is less predictable due to the induced (intentional) masking. The next section will be devoted to empirically support this statement.

4   Experimental Results and Conclusions

In this section some sequences (in the wild) from the publicly available dataset ME-view (Micro Expression VIdEo in the Wild) [9] have been analysed according to the considerations made in the previous section. The aim has been to evaluate if it is possible to recognize the fingerprint (PES) described above even when the latter does not represent the main content of the analysed group of frames. The perceptual quantity S, as defined in Eq. (2), has been then evaluated between consecutive frames using the default settings for SSIM and the three asymmetry absolute indexes (Pearson, Yule and modified Yule) have been computed. In order to have more precise values, an automatic face detection algorithm has been applied to each video frame and S distribution has been computed by considering only pixels belonging to the face of the video main subject. The Matlab function vision.CascadeObjectDetector has been adopted with default settings; that is why the selected rectangular-shape regions may also contain a small part of background pixels.

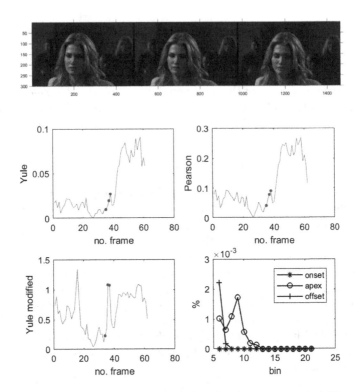

Fig. 5. Sequence 14.1 of ME-view dataset: example of contempt. *Top)* Three representative frames of the sequence: onset, apex and offset. *Bottom)* Behaviour of the three asymmetry index where PES is marked, and a detail of S histograms related to the three corresponding significant frames.

Presented tests concern two MEs different from surprise (shown in the previous section), i.e., contempt in a noiseless context and happiness in a noisy context, as well as other MEs in the wild context. The tests are oriented to: *i)* evaluate the most informative and robust asymmetry index; *ii)* validate the hypotheses made in the previous section. As it can be observed in Figs. 5 and 6, both contempt and happiness show a behaviour which is comparable and consistent with the ideal PES shown in Fig. 4, and it is especially evident for the modified Yule index and in the noisy scenario. What it is important to notice is that a significant transient occurs in correspondence to the lapse time between onset and apex; on the contrary, the offset behaviour strongly depends on the degree of ME spontaneousness: whenever it seems to be controlled, the contribution of ME in its offset phase is masked by the other simulated and measurable changes in the sequence—see Fig. 6. However, PES still is recognizable in correspondence to the frames capturing ME. In particular, we have $R = 129.73$ and $R = 3.47$, respectively for ME in Fig. 5 and Fig. 6. The same figures also show S histograms in correspondence to onset, apex and offset. As it can be observed,

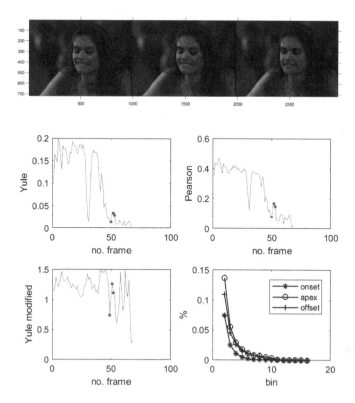

Fig. 6. Sequence 11.3 of ME-view dataset: example of noisy happiness. *Top)* Three representative frames of the sequence: onset, apex and offset. In this case the pose of the subject is not static before ME; in addition, ME is simultaneous to an eye blink. *Bottom)* Behaviour of the three asymmetry index where PES is marked, and a detail of S histograms related to the three corresponding significant frames.

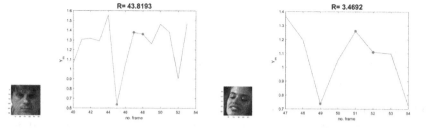

Fig. 7. Two MEs from ME-view dataset. For each sequence, the extracted face region on the first frame of ME sequence and corresponding Y_m index of S distribution are shown. Dots mark PES profile. Even though evident voluntary masking actions have been performed by the subject, the ratio R still is consistent with MEs in Fig. 8 (>3).

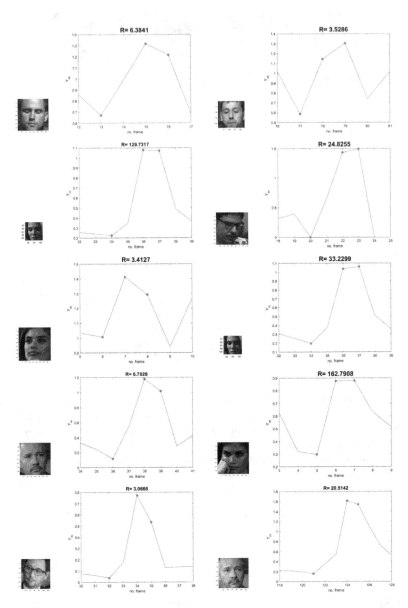

Fig. 8. Ten MEs from ME-view dataset. For each sequence, the extracted face region on the first frame of ME sequence and corresponding Y_m index of S distribution are shown. Dots mark PES profile that can be recognized, independently of both the context ('in the wild') and ME type. Each plot also contains the value of the ratio R, as defined in Eq. (5).

apex provides a distribution that is very different from the ME onset, while it is more or less similar to the offset, according to ME spontaneousness. These observations are further supported by the results shown in Fig. 8. The latter refers to the modified Yule index Y_m on ten MEs from ME-view dataset. The typical perceptual signature (PES) is almost evident even in 'wild conditions', as also confirmed by the value of the ratio R, defined as in Eq. (5)—from experimental results, we observed that $R > 3$ for all MEs. To further emphasize the typical behaviour (PES) of ME in the first part of its temporal evolution and the lack of specific feature for the decreasing one, Fig. 7 shows some results concerning MEs that are masked by more or less involuntary masking movements. As it can be observed, PES, even though less marked, still is recognizable and the ratio R still is significant. It is also worth observing that, PES profiles characterize other involuntary face expressions that have not been indexed in the dataset, including eye blinks—see for examples, frames 13–15 in Fig. 4. However, this is consistent with the feasibility study conducted in this paper that aims at representing a very preliminary attempt to characterize spontaneous and rapid MEs, as also blinks are, in an objective manner.

5 Conclusions

The paper has presented a preliminary study concerning the definition of a perceptual fingerprint for fast and spontaneous microexpressions (MEs) in video sequences, namely perceptual expression signature (PES). By characterizing MEs as a sort of a local and temporal discontinuity in the vision process of a video sequence, PES has been defined as the modification provided by ME in the distribution of the well known image quality assessment measure, the Structural SIMilarity index (SSIM), whenever computed between two successive frames. Preliminary analyses on MEs in the wild showed that PES seems to be a good candidate for MEs spotting preprocessing and its characterization may allow to select GOFs containing MEs by means of very few and simple operations. Even though such a procedure unavoidably provides false alarms, it represents a computationally advantageous preprocessing procedure as it limits the use of expensive operations, like pixel-based motion estimation, registration, masking and so on, only to a reduced number of video frames. Future research will investigate more in depth this point. In particular, the advantage in using the proposed method as a preprocessing step to the existing detection and classification methods will be evaluated quantitatively and the role of the selected image quality assessment measure will be studied. Anyway, PES can be seen as a first contribution to a new perceptual description of MEs and then can represent a possible basis for the definition of a future perception-based framework for MEs spotting.

References

1. Brunet, D., Vrscay, E.R., Wang, Z.: On the mathematical properties of the structural similarity index. IEEE Trans. Image Process. **21**(4), 1488–1499 (2012)
2. Duque, C., Alata, O., Emonet, R., Legrand, A.-C., Konik, H.: Micro-expression spotting using the Riesz pyramid. In: WACV Proceedings, Lake Tahoe (2018)
3. Ekman, P., Friesen, W.V.: Nonverbal leakage and clues to deception. Psychiatry **32**, 88–106 (1969)
4. Ekman, P.: Telling Lies: Clues to Deceit in the Marketplace, Politics, and Marriage (Revised Edition). WW Norton & Company, New York (2009)
5. Ekman, P.: Lie catching and microexpressions. In: Martin, C. (ed.) The Philosophy of Deception, pp. 118–133. Oxford University Press (2009)
6. Haggard, E.A., Isaacs, K.S.: Micromomentary facial expressions as indicators of ego mechanisms in psychotherapy. In: GottschalkArthur, L.A., Auerbach, H.A. (eds.) Methods of Research in Psychotherapy. TCPS, pp. 154–165. Springer, Boston (1966). https://doi.org/10.1007/978-1-4684-6045-2_14
7. Kendall, M., Stuart, A.: The Advanced Theory of Statistics. Chareles Griffinn & Company Limited, London (1976)
8. Ma, H., An, G., Wu, S., Yang, F.: A region histogram of oriented optical flow (RHOOF) feature for apex frame spotting in micro-expression. In: Proceedings of the International Symposium on Intelligent Signal Processing and Communication Systems (ISPACS), Xiamen, pp. 281–286 (2017)
9. MEVIEW homepage. http://cmp.felk.cvut.cz/~cechj/ME/
10. Moilanen, A., Zhao, G., Pietikainen, M.: Spotting rapid facial movements from videos using appearance-based feature difference analysis. In: Proceedings of the 22nd International Conference on Pattern Recognition (ICPR), Stockholm, pp. 1722–1727 (2014)
11. Oh, Y.-H., See, J., Le Ngo, A.C., Phan, R.C.-W., Baskaran, V.M.: A survey of automatic facial micro-expression analysis: databases, methods, and challenges. Front. Psychol. **9**, article no. 1128 (2018)
12. Polikovsky, S., Kameda, Y.: Facial micro-expression detection in hi-speed video based on facial action coding system (FACS). IEICE Trans. Inf. Syst. **96**, 81–92 (2013)
13. Porter, S., Ten Brinke, L.: Reading between the lies identifying concealed and falsified emotions in universal facial expressions. Psychol. Sci. **19**, 508–514 (2008)
14. Shreve, M., Godavarthy, S., Goldgof, D., Sarkar, S.: Macro-and micro-expression spotting in long videos using spatio-temporal strain. In: Proceedings of the 2011 IEEE International Conference on Automatic Face & Gesture Recognition and Workshops (FG 2011), Santa Barbara, pp. 51–56 (2011)
15. Valstar, M.F., Pantic, M.: Fully automatic recognition of the temporal phases of facial actions. IEEE Trans. Syst. Man Cybern. Part B **42**, 28–43 (2012)
16. Wang, Z., Bovik, A.C., Sheikh, H.R., Simoncelli, E.P.: Image quality assessment: from error visibility to structural similarity. IEEE Trans. Image Process. **13**, 600–612 (2004)
17. Wang, S.-J., Wu, S., Qian, X., Li, J., Fu, X.: A main directional maximal difference analysis for spotting facial movements from long-term videos. Neurocomputing **230**, 382–389 (2016)
18. Weinberger, S.: Airport security: intent to deceive? Nature **465**, 412–415 (2010)

19. Yan, W.-J., Wu, Q., Liang, J., Chen, Y.-H., Fu, X.: How fast are the leaked facial expressions: the duration of micro-expressions. J. Nonverbal Behav. **37**, 217–230 (2013). https://doi.org/10.1007/s10919-013-0159-8
20. Yan, W.J., Chen, Y.H.: Measuring dynamic micro-expressions via feature extraction methods. J. Comput. Sci. **25**, 318–326 (2017)

Learning to Search for Objects in Images from Human Gaze Sequences

Afonso Nunes, Rui Figueiredo, and Plinio Moreno[✉]

Institute for Systems and Robotics, Instituto Superior Técnico,
Universidade de Lisboa, Lisbon, Portugal
afonsofrnunes@tecnico.ulisboa.pt,
{ruifigueiredo,plinio}@isr.tecnico.ulisboa.pt

Abstract. Human vision relies on saccades to extract high quality information on small areas of the field of view, pointing the high resolution region of the retina (i.e. fovea) to the regions of interest. The eye motions are guided by top-down information provided by the task, which in our case is the search for a given object. In this work we propose a Recurrent Neural Network (RNN) model that learns from human demonstrations how to explore an image. The exploration samples are obtained from eye tracking data acquired while subjects inspect images. The proposed model extracts visual features from Convolutional Neural Networks (CNNs), which correspond to the input of the RNN. The contribution of this work is to consider the visual features along with the object label in a new model that is able to search for a given object in an image. We make a comparative study on the importance of context during object search tasks, showing that foveated images perform better than uniform image region crops.

Keywords: Active perception · Visual search · Eye tracking · Selective visual attention · Deep network architecture

1 Introduction

In this work we propose an architecture based on Recurrent Neural Networks (RNNs), which predicts the forthcoming fixation points for the task of visual search of objects. The RNN receives as input features from the final layers of a Convolutional Neural Network (CNN) that were obtained in object classification tasks. To mimic the behavior of human gaze sequences, the CNN features are localized in the neighborhood of the human gaze fixations. Experiments on visual search for a given object category demonstrate the prediction capabilities of the architecture. Finally, we compare the trade-off between using biologically inspired artificial foveal vision mechanisms against standard uniform Cartesian crops. The remainder of the article is structured as follows: In Sect. 2, we overview the state-of-the-art in saliency and eye fixation predictive modeling. In Sect. 3, we describe in detail the proposed methodologies. Finally, in Sect. 4 we experimentally validate our method and in Sect. 5 we wrap up with conclusions and draw ideas for future work.

© Springer Nature Switzerland AG 2020
A. Campilho et al. (Eds.): ICIAR 2020, LNCS 12131, pp. 280–292, 2020.
https://doi.org/10.1007/978-3-030-50347-5_25

2   Related Work

We briefly overview the state-of-the-art in artificial foveal vision and gaze prediction models which deal with the problem of extracting important image subregions and predicting where eye fixations should occur.

(a) EASY image   (b) HARD image

Fig. 1. Example scan-paths that emerge with our method during task-dependent visual search. The training set of this model is the mixed dataset.

2.1   Space-Variant Foveal Vision

Unlike uniform vision provided by conventional imaging sensors, human vision is space-variant, due to the uneven organization of the photo-receptors in the retina. Visual acuity, provided by the cones, is highest at the fovea, located in the center of the retina, and declines monotonically towards the periphery, with increasing eccentricity. This is a natural way of reducing the amount of information streamed to the brain, in order to cope with power, neuronal transmission bandwidth limitations, and the brain machinery processing capacity. In order to efficiently explore and understand the surrounding environment [1], humans have developed a set of attention and oculo-motor mechanisms, namely saccades, that allow them to actively and sequentially direct their eyes towards different regions of interest in the surrounding environment, and thus, to cleverly compensate for the aforementioned limitations.

In the work of [2] the authors proposed a foveation mechanism for digital image streaming in low-bandwidth communication channels, that allows the user to point the high spatial resolution focus to regions of interest, with pointing devices (e.g. eye tracker), being suitable for studies involving eye movements. The method starts by building a Laplacian pyramid, then, each level is multiplied by an exponential kernel, centered at the foveation point, up-sampled and summed with the previous levels, to obtain an image that matches the psychophysical space-variant contrast sensitivity of the human visual system (HVS). Matching the falloff resolution of the HVS, makes optimal use of compression resources, by discarding only the details that cannot be resolved by the human eye, via manipulation of the exponential kernel standard deviation. Inspired by the previous approach we use the real-time foveation method of [3] to study foveal vision impact on gaze sequence modeling (see Sect. 3.1).

2.2   Gaze Sequence Modelling

The Bayesian framework for saliency learning in [4] proposes extract natural statistics for saliency (SUN). The approach relies on features learned from a set of natural images, which correspond to bottom-up saliency and provide the prior distribution of the data samples. The prior is compared to the target features in the images through mutual information, and the features with largest mutual information correspond to salient regions in the image. This procedure was done during object search for a given object.

Most of the scan path prediction models rely on visual appearance characteristics, ignoring the previous fixation points and their visual features. More recent works have incorporated the previous samples to predict the eye fixations. The visual scanpath prediction method proposed in [5] combines low-level features provided by hand-crafted filters with high-level object semantics, in a reinforcement learning framework. The policy aims to mimic the human gaze fixation and it is obtained by a least-squares iterative algorithm. The attention model proposed in [6] uses a recurrent neural network to control the fixation point of a low-dimensional, space-variant resolution retina-like image representation. The authors formulate the gaze control problem as a Partially Observable Markov Decision Process (POMDP) and employ reinforcement learning techniques to learn policies that maximize task-related rewards. The main limitation of these models is the action space size, which constraint the application to very small images.

We follow the biologically plausible idea of mimicking humans while searching for objects, using eye fixation data [5,7] acquired with gaze tracking devices. These models aim to imitate the gaze scan-path of humans in a supervised learning approach, which infer eye fixation sequences for the task. In [7], a prediction method that uses CNNs for feature extraction and Long Short Term Memory (LSTMs) networks for gaze sequence modeling in the case of free-viewing (i.e. bottom-up saliency). In this work, we extend the architecture of [7] to perform not only free viewing [8], but also cued object search tasks.

3   Methodologies

We define visual search as a sequence of points in 2D image coordinates. We assume that the points of a sequence are not independent, in the sense that previous information affects future decisions of where to look next. In the remainder of this section we describe in detail the modules behind the proposed visual search approaches, including the artificial foveation model and the neural network architectures for sequential gaze prediction.

3.1   Artificial Foveation System

Our real-time foveation system is based on the method proposed in [9] for image compression. The approach comprises four steps: 1) Building a Gaussian pyramid, 2) compute the Laplacian pyramid and 3) apply exponential weighting kernels. These kernels are centered at a given fixation point (u_0, v_0) which defines the focus of attention. Figure 2 depicts examples of resulting foveated images.

(a) $f_0 = 50$ (b) $f_0 = 100$ (c) $f_0 = 150$

Fig. 2. Example images obtained with our foveation system where f_0 (in px) defines the size of the region with highest acuity (the fovea), from a 405×405 px image uniform resolution image.

3.2   Feature Extraction with Convolutional Neural Networks

We use a CNN to reduce the dimension of the input by extracting low-dimensional features of the images. We rely on the VGG16 model [10], pre-trained on the ImageNet dataset [11] for image classification. We drop the 3 last fully-connected layers, since we are only interested in feature map extraction. The feature maps consist of $16 \times 16 \times 512$ tensors that preserve the main characteristics of the original image. They correspond to a lower-dimensional spatial quantization of the original image into a 16×16 grid, in which each of the 256 regions are represented by a 512-long feature vector.

Formally, let $\mathcal{K} = (1, ..., 16; 1, ..., 16)$ represent the set of possible fixation points and let $\mathcal{X} = \{\mathbf{x}^k : k \subset \mathcal{K}\}$, designate the feature map set with $\mathbf{x}_t^k$ represent the feature vector extracted from the image region k.

3.3   Gaze Sequence Modeling with RNNs

In this work we utilize RNNs for gaze scan-path prediction, a subclass of Artificial Neural Networks (ANNs) that, unlike standard *feed-forward* ANNs, that

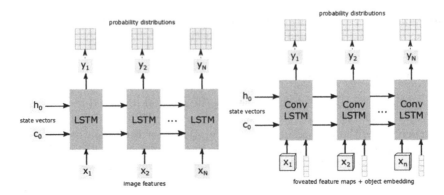

Fig. 3. Schematic drawing of our RNN models. Left: context-free architecture. Right: foveated context architecture

keeps an internal state as it processes sequential data. The internal state of the network is updated at each time step and affects subsequent predictions, allowing temporal dynamic behavior. Our model can be trained and tested with variable length fixation scan paths, and works in a modular, self-recurrent way.

Context-Free Architecture. The neural network we use to model context-free sequential vision is depicted in Fig. 3 and is based on the *Keras's* implementation of LSTMs [12]. For each input vector $\mathbf{x}_t^k \in \mathcal{X}$ at time t, the network outputs an array $\mathbf{y}_t \in \mathcal{Y}$ where $\mathcal{Y} = \{y^k : k \in \mathcal{K}\}$ represents the probability distribution map over the fixation point grid. The h_0 and c_0 are initial state vectors representing prior knowledge our model has, before analyzing any input. To estimate these values we introduced a simple fully connected layer between a low-resolution version of the input maps $\mathbf{x} \in \mathcal{X}$ and the initial state vectors. To train our RNN model we attempt to find the best set of network parameters θ for a given image I, by minimizing the following log-likelihood formula for $S = \{\mathbf{x}_0^{k_0}, ..., \mathbf{x}_T^{k_T}\}$

$$L(S|I, \theta) = \sum_{t=1}^{T} \log P(\mathbf{y}_{t+1}|\mathbf{x}_t^{k_t}, \mathbf{c}_{t-1}, \mathbf{h}_{t-1}) \tag{1}$$

where $\mathbf{h}_t$ represents sequential time step state vectors. Thus, in the training phase, the network is given by a sequence $\mathbf{x}_t$ and $\mathbf{y}_t$ $(t = 1, ..., T)$ and the best parameters are estimated using standard back-propagation.

In the testing phase, at each time-step the network yields a probability map $\mathbf{y}$ of the next location to look at. However, maximizing the likelihood of the whole sequence in all its steps is computationally intractable, since 256^N hypotheses need to be evaluated. We use a beam-search algorithm to compute the $n = 20$ most promising paths at each time step.

Foveated Context Architecture. The network used to model foveal vision is depicted in Fig. 3. It is based on the *Keras*'s implementation of ConvL-STM2D [13]. At each time step, this network receives as input complete feature maps $\mathbf{x}_t = \mathcal{X}$, rather than single feature vectors. In addition, the feature maps received in this case are not extracted from regular images, but from foveated images centered at the fixation point $k \in \mathcal{K}$. Additionally, we designed this architecture to incorporate one extra linear input vector, that encodes multiple objects. This vector is combined with the input feature maps using the method proposed in [14]. First we pass the vector through a 512-unit *fully-connected* layer with *tanh* activation. This yields a vector of values in the $[-1, 1]$ interval where the length matches the depth of the feature map tensor. Then, we make the combination in such a way that each value in the *tanh*-vector will scale up the values in each of the feature map planes.

3.4 Object Search Task and Task Encoding

We consider two alternatives to encode the task information: 1) One-hot encoding and 2) Visual embedding. One-hot encoding is a binary-valued vector that has a dimension equal to the number of object classes. This vector has one component set to 1 (corresponding to the target object class) while the remaining are set to 0. This ensures all objects are represented by equidistant vectors, but disregards visual appearance similarities between object classes.

On the other hand, the visual embedding representation builds a vector that estimates the visual similarity between objects of the categories in the dataset, using an unsupervised online search approach. One image per class is searched on Google Images search engine and the pre-trained ResNet50 [15] neural network in a manner similar to the one proposed in [16].

4 Experiments and Results

We consider two eye tracking datasets to assess our visual search approaches. In the first one, participants were asked to localize people in images[1], a single-object task introduced in [17] and originally comprises 912 images. In our experiments we used only a subset containing 456 images of people. The images with people are further divided according to the relative difficulty a human would have to find them, where 95 are labeled as EASY and 361 as HARD. In the second dataset [18], the participants were asked to search for various objects in several images[2], a multiple object search task. While in the first dataset people tend to fixate the object, in the second dataset people tend to pass by the object. In all experiments described below, the model is trained using back-propagation with the *adam* optimizer and with *categorical cross-entropy* loss [19].

---

[1] Subjects were asked to fixate the target object when the object was found.

[2] For each experiment, subjects were asked to search for a particular object for two seconds and indicate if they believed the object was present or not.

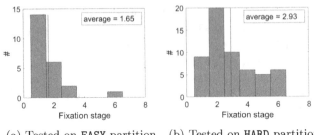

(a) Tested on EASY partition   (b) Tested on HARD partition

Fig. 4. Histograms of fixations for the model trained on EASY + HARD. On Fig. 4a shows the EASY test set whereas the ones on Fig. 4b were tested in a HARD partition.

Evaluation Metrics. We use two performance metrics for our gaze prediction model: 1) object search *accuracy* and 2) number of fixations to reach the target. We consider the model to have found the target if its scan-path includes a location less than 2 cells apart from the known one. We compute the histogram with the number of fixations it took to fixate the target in the testing images.

Table 1. Object search accuracy with several fovea sizes f_0 tested on both EASY and HARD partitions. Results are averages of 3 experiments on random train/test partition splits. The rightmost column shows the accuracy of the context-free model

Test set	Context-based architecture (%)			Context-free (%)
	$f_0 = 50\text{px}$	$f_0 = 75\text{px}$	$f_0 = 100\text{px}$	
EASY	56.14 ± 3.04	73.68 ± 5.27	68.42 ± 9.12	$67.77 \pm 11.03\%$
HARD	52.31 ± 4.01	49.54 ± 4.47	49.08 ± 6.99	$50.35 \pm 9.51\%$

Context-Free Architecture for Single Object Search. According to the difficulty labels provided by the data-set, we use these partitions to check if our model is sensible to human-assessed difficulty.

The relative size of the training and testing subsets to 90% and 10% of the entire data-set, respectively, and using 10% of the training set as validation set. Figure 1 shows examples with the scan-path generated by our model. We generate fixation sequences of length 6 for each image in the testing set, since we concluded from the data that on average, search tasks can be accomplished within this limit. In Fig. 1a we observe that our model successfully finds pedestrians in less than 4 fixation steps. After fixation 4, it remains in the same patch, although not specifically programmed to do this. In Fig. 1b illustrates that rather than searching randomly through the image, our model makes informed decisions and avoids unlikely locations such as the sky or the treetops. Table 1 shows the accuracy of the model trained in the mixed data-set. The best accuracy is around 74%, which is significantly better than random selection (50%).

(a) $f = 75px$, HARD   (b) $f = 100px$, HARD

Fig. 5. Example fixation sequences generated by our model on HARD partitions.

We also analyze the number of fixation points to reach the goal as the second performance criterion. In the case of EASY images the architecture reached the goal in less number of fixations than the HARD images model. Figure 4 shows that the average number of fixations is similar to the human ground-truth data.

Foveated Context Architecture for Single Object Search. The architecture of Fig. 3 does not include the object encoding vector, however receives the feature map $\mathbf{x}$. Since we concluded that the best results are achieved when the model is trained on the mixed data-set, we focus on this partition for training, but keep testing on the EASY and HARD partitions separately (Fig. 5).

From Table 1 and Fig. 6, we notice a significant increase in performance when the $f_0 = 75px$ followed by a performance drop at $f_0 = 100px$. This unexpected result, may be related to the fact that larger foveas activate a larger number of weights in the Convolutional layer. Further experiments, such as reducing the network's number of free weights and add more samples, may be attempted in this regard. Nevertheless, the results obtained with $f_0 = 75px$ show an important performance upgrade when compared with results from the context-free architecture. We justify this improvement by the fact that this architecture has access to peripheral context. As opposed to the previous experiment, in this one the network doesn't seem to have learned to keep at the same fixation once found the target. This task is more difficult to handle when the network is dealing with context, and the data was not enough for it to mimic this trait.

Cued Multiple Object Search Task. As expected the results in the previous section have shown that using artificial foveal vision while performing people search tasks is beneficial when compared to a context-free approach. We notice an important limitation in the models developed: they can only perform one task

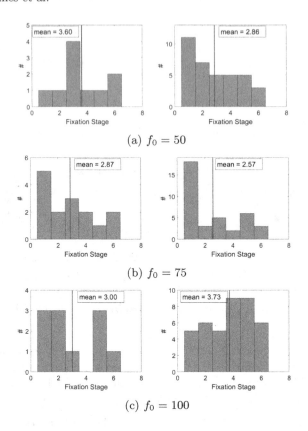

(a) $f_0 = 50$

(b) $f_0 = 75$

(c) $f_0 = 100$

Fig. 6. Histograms of the number of fixations it took for the model to find the person in the image. The histograms on the left relate to EASY images while the ones on the right relate to HARD images. Fovea size is measured in px.

per training process. For instance, if we choose to start looking for a different object, we must re-train the neural network with an appropriate data-set, and all previous knowledge is lost. To overcome this situation, we introduced the target object class as an additional vector (see Sect. 3.4). We train the foveated context architecture on the multi-task dataset.

Foveated Context Architecture. We use 80% of the multi-task dataset for training and the remaining 20% for testing. From the training set we also set apart 10% to be used as the validation set, using 15 object classes. In the testing phase we generate sequences of 8 fixations. We studied 3 variables: 1) the size of the fovea, 2) the number of known objects 3) the type of used encodings.

Figure 7 shows two examples of successful target discovery in the first 8 fixations analyzed by our model. The accuracy of the multiple-class model (around 73%) is very similar to the single model in Table 1 (around 74%). This result shows that the object encoding provides very useful information and the multiple model attains similar performance to the single model. Table 2 and Fig. 8

Table 2. Object search accuracy with several fovea sizes f_0 and types of objects encodings. Results are averages of 3 experiments on random train/test partitions.

	Context-based architecture (%)			Context-free (%)
Test set	$f_0 = 50$px	$f_0 = 75$px	$f_0 = 100$px	
One hot encoding	$63.29 \pm 8.51\%$	$72.93 \pm 4.06\%$	$66.66 \pm 8.88\%$	$60.26 \pm 11.75\%$
Visual embedding	$57.55 \pm 6.91\%$	$66.08 \pm 2.86\%$	52.42 ± 13.49 %	$55.13 \pm 4.44\%$

(a) *boat*, $f = 100px$ (b) *plant*, $f = 50px$
one-hot encoding   google encoding

Fig. 7. Example fixation sequences generated by our model, trained to search 15 different objects.

shows that *one-hot encoding* task representation achieved better results than *visual embedding*. This suggests that, at least for the set of objects known by the network in our experiments, the simplicity of *one-hot encoding* was more favorable than using *visual embeddings*. Further experiments with a larger number of object classes may show the advantages of the *visual embeddings*. Additionally, the results for $f_0 = 75$ is once again the best in the experiment, both in accuracy and in the mean number of fixation steps required to find the target object.

5   Conclusions and Future Work

In this work we propose a gaze sequence predictive model that uses context information for visual search tasks based on RNNs. The foveated architecture that considers contextual information is successful at mimicking human gaze behaviors when visually inspecting images, and when searching for particular targets. The importance of context in such tasks was studied and foveal context was demonstrated to be favorable when learning from human demonstrations.

We also developed a multi-task capable neural network architecture which has shown a promising performance at object search tasks for up to 15 different

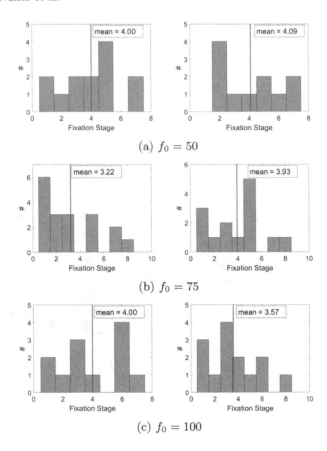

Fig. 8. Histograms of the number of fixations it took for the model to find the designated object. The histograms on the left relate to *one-hot encoding* while the ones on the right relate to *visual embedding*. Fovea size is measured in px.

known object classes. We expect to improve and continue experiments, specifically for multiple-object search, where we aim to study the effect of adding more to the list of known objects, and check which of the proposed encodings are more suitable in these cases. Also, the study of more complex foveated context architecture networks is expected to lead to networks that can handle larger foveas, and therefore increasingly approximate to human performance. We also expect to improve the networks' capability of recognizing when the target object is found and stop at that point. This may be achieved by providing additional training data. The main limitation of our current implementation is that it only allows searching for a single known object class, which needs to be present in the training dataset. In the future, we intend to improve our model with the ability of searching for multiple known objects, by extending the input feature vector with the task, using for instance a "one hot encoding" of the class of interest.

Acknowledgements. To the grant program "New Talents in Artificial Intelligence" from Fundação Calouste Gulbenkian, the Portuguese Science Foundation (FCT) funding [UID/EEA/50009/2019] and LARSyS - FCT Plurianual funding 2020–2023.

References

1. Posner, M.: Cognitive Neuroscience of Attention. Guilford Press (2012). http://books.google.pt/books?id=8yjEjoS7EQsC
2. Geisler, W.S., Perry, J.S.: Real-time foveated multiresolution system for low-bandwidth video communication. In: Photonics West 1998 Electronic Imaging, pp. 294–305. International Society for Optics and Photonics (1998)
3. Almeida, A.F., Figueiredo, R., Bernardino, A., Santos-Victor, J.: Deep networks for human visual attention: a hybrid model using foveal vision. In: Ollero, A., Sanfeliu, A., Montano, L., Lau, N., Cardeira, C. (eds.) ROBOT 2017. AISC, vol. 694, pp. 117–128. Springer, Cham (2018). https://doi.org/10.1007/978-3-319-70836-2_10
4. Zhang, L., Tong, M.H., Marks, T.K., Shan, H., Cottrell, G.W.: Sun: a Bayesian framework for saliency using natural statistics. J. Vis. **8**(7), 32–32 (2008)
5. Jiang, M., Boix, X., Roig, G., Xu, J., Van Gool, L., Zhao, Q.: Learning to predict sequences of human visual fixations. IEEE Trans. Neural Netw. Learn. Syst. **27**(6), 1241–1252 (2016)
6. Mnih, V., Heess, N., Graves, A., et al.: Recurrent models of visual attention. In: Advances in Neural Information Processing Systems, pp. 2204–2212 (2014)
7. Ngo, T., Manjunath, B.: Saccade gaze prediction using a recurrent neural network. In: 2017 IEEE International Conference on Image Processing (ICIP), pp. 3435–3439. IEEE (2017)
8. Nunes, A., Figueiredo, R., Moreno, P.: Learning to perform visual tasks from human demonstrations. In: Morales, A., Fierrez, J., Sánchez, J.S., Ribeiro, B. (eds.) Pattern Recognition and Image Analysis, pp. 346–358. Springer, Cham (2019). https://doi.org/10.1007/978-3-030-31321-0_30
9. Burt, P.J., Adelson, E.H.: The Laplacian pyramid as a compact image code. IEEE Trans. Commun. **31**, 532–540 (1983)
10. Simonyan, K., Zisserman, A.: Very deep convolutional networks for large-scale image recognition. In: International Conference on Learning Representations (2015)
11. Russakovsky, O., et al.: ImageNet large scale visual recognition challenge. Int. J. Comput. Vis. **115**(3), 211–252 (2015). https://doi.org/10.1007/s11263-015-0816-y
12. Hochreiter, S., Schmidhuber, J.: Long short-term memory. Neural Comput. **9**, 1725–1780 (1997)
13. Shi, X., Chen, Z.: Convolutional LSTM network: a machine learning approach for precipitation nowcasting (2015)
14. Levine, S., Pastor, P., Krizhevsky, A., Ibarz, J., Quillen, D.: Learning hand-eye coordination for robotic grasping with deep learning and large-scale data collection. Int. J. Robot. Res. **37**(4–5), 421–436 (2018)
15. He, K., Zhang, X.: Deep residual learning for image recognition (2015)
16. Shulga, D.: Word embeddings using deep neural network image classifier (2018). https://towardsdatascience.com/creating-words-embedding-using-deep-neural-network-image-classifier-ae2594d3862d
17. Ehinger, K.A., Hidalgo-Sotelo, B., Torralba, A., Oliva, A.: Modelling search for people in 900 scenes: a combined source model of eye guidance. Vis. Cogn. **17**(6–7), 945–978 (2009)

18. Koehler, K., Guo, F., Zhang, S., Eckstein, M.P.: What do saliency models predict. J. Vis. **14**, 14 (2014)
19. Buja, A., Stuetzle, W., Shen, Y.: Loss functions for binary class probability estimation and classification: Structure and applications (2005)

Detecting Defects in Materials Using Deep Convolutional Neural Networks

Quentin Boyadjian$^{(\boxtimes)}$ ⓘ, Nicolas Vanderesse ⓘ, Matthew Toews ⓘ,
and Philippe Bocher ⓘ

École de Technologie Supérieure,
1100, rue Notre-Dame Ouest, Montreal, QC H3C 1K3, Canada
quentin.boyadjian.1@ens.etsmtl.ca

Abstract. This paper proposes representing and detecting manufacturing defects at the micrometre scale using deep convolutional neural networks. The information theoretic notion of entropy is used to quantify the information gain or mutual information of filters throughout the network, where the deepest network layers are generally shown to exhibit the highest mutual information between filter responses and defects, and thus serve as the most discriminative features. Quantitative detection experiments based on the AlexNet architecture investigate a variety of design parameters pertaining to data preprocessing and network architecture, where the optimal architectures achieve an average accuracy of 98.54%. CNNs are relatively easy to perform and give impressive achievements in classification tasks. However, the informational complexity coming from the depth of networks represents a limit to improve their capabilities.

Keywords: Convolutional neural network · AlexNet · Ti-6Al-4V · Texture classification

1 Introduction

The spatial organization of materials at the microscopic scale is currently referred to as *microstructure*. The control of microstructure is of utmost importance for a wide array of engineering applications where materials play a structural or a functional role. Indeed, macroscopic mechanical, thermal, or electrical properties of a material depend on many microstructural characteristics at scales ranging from the nanometer to the millimeter.

In the field of metallic materials, the easiest technique for characterizing the surface of a specimen is optical microscopy, referred to as metallography. It can convey a large amount of information about the material, its history, and its expected in-service behavior. It is no surprise, then, that metallography has been holding a close relationship with image analysis over the last decades. Most of the quantitative studies in this field are oriented toward the segmentation and statistical quantification of features of interest, especially the grains (i.e., elementary crystalline units of the material) and second-phase particles, inclusions

© Springer Nature Switzerland AG 2020
A. Campilho et al. (Eds.): ICIAR 2020, LNCS 12131, pp. 293–306, 2020.
https://doi.org/10.1007/978-3-030-50347-5_26

or defects [1–7]. The analysis of the textures found in these images been a matter of interest for some applications, yet to a lesser degree[1]. Most efforts in that direction are focused on texture quantification by statistical, structural and transform-based methods [8–12]. The application of convolutional neural networks appears limited, with a few recent exceptions [13–16]. One major limitation to the penetration of modern image analysis techniques in materials science, as discussed in [17], may be the financial and time cost for the production of microstructural images (micrographs), as it requires careful specimen preparation, expertise, and expensive equipment [18]. Analysis procedures must then be adapted to size-limited datasets.

Among metallic materials of industrial importance, Titanium alloys, especially the most common Ti-6Al-4V (Titanium alloyed with 6% Aluminum and 4% Vanadium), are used in aerospace, chemistry, and biomedical applications [19]. Their microstructures are usually complex and vary in many aspects, depending on the parameters of the manufacturing process. This has motivated several studies aimed at assessing them by image analysis [9, 20–24]. Ti-6Al-4V at room temperature presents two phases with different characteristics named α and β [19, 25, 26]. A critical requirement for many Ti-6Al-4V industrial parts is that they should present a bimodal microstructure constituted by globular α grains surrounded by a fine mixture of β and α grains. This is illustrated in Fig. 1, where the surface of a specimen is imaged in optical microscopy. The α grains appear with bright shades and the mixture of fine α - β grains with dark shades. The goal of the manufacturing process is to ensure that the α grains are roughly spheroidal (i.e., circular when observed in 2D), homogeneously distributed throughout the volume, and surrounded by a fine layer of α - β mixture.

Difficulties arise when some α grains are not correctly spheroidized by the process. An example is presented in Fig. 1(a): an elongated feature extending over ca. $100\,\mu m$ can be observed at the center of the image. It corresponds to an insufficiently fragmented α grain. Such defects are referred to as α_{GB} (Grain Boundary). They must be detected as they can compromise the mechanical performance of the finished product. In the industrial context, the detection of these features is expert-based, with trained technicians visually evaluating a series of digital images and measuring the amount of defect within each, if any. As this is a tedious and time-consuming task, a need exists for automatizing it. This difficulty motivated the search for a more robust approach, based on the representation of the texture in each image and its classification.

The field of texture analysis has seen significant advances in the last 20 years, with the elaboration of the Bag-of-Words paradigm derived from linguistics for texture representation, and the onset of CNNs, made up of several layers of nonlinear feature extractors [27, 28]. The latter demonstrated high performance in

---

[1] It should be noted that the term *texture* in the context of materials science, almost always refers to crystallographic texture, i.e., the dominant crystallographic orientation of a set of grains, and in some cases to the morphological texture. Consequently, this confusion may not help the diffusion of texture analysis in the materials science and engineering community.

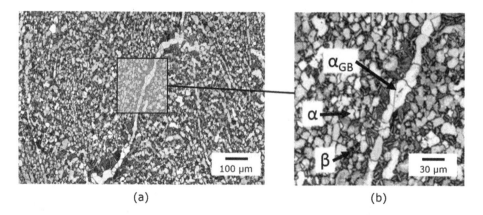

Fig. 1. (a): Micrograph of a Ti-6Al-4V with α_{GB} defect; (b): Close-up on α_{GB}.

building top quality features learned from large datasets, by contrast with hand-crafted approaches based on predefined filter banks. CNNs are usually trained and applied to sets of several hundreds of images (Table 3 in [28], Table 3 in [29]). By contrast, microstructural pictures of a given material are generally in a much lower number, which possibly puts some limitation on the accuracy of CNNs in this area. However, a recent study in the medical field showed efficient results of AlexNet [30] for a binary classification problem with a dataset consisting of less than 300 images [31]. This result has motivated the choice of AlexNet in this work for the detection of microstructural defects in Ti-6Al-4V specimens with a reduced dataset. As a first approach, the CNN was trained and tested with different hyper-parameters and datasets.

Information theory [32] is a powerful tool for quantifying the statistical link between discriminative network filter responses and classes of interest, i.e., the information bottleneck method studies the mutual information between filter responses [33]. Special attention was paid to the evaluation of the information flow [34] across the layers, so as to gain insights into their role in characterizing defects.

2 Method

2.1 Design of Experiments

To the best of the authors' knowledge, the study of defects in optical microscopy images as proposed in this work is relatively novel in the field of texture analysis. This motivated an approach in which several image parameters and CNN hyper-parameters were allowed to take several values, to define the optimal combination for detecting potential defects in the images. This work proposes a Design of Experiments (DoE) to evaluate the factors suspected to limit the final accuracy of CNN for the classification. The DoE focuses on three parameters referring to the dataset preparation, on the one hand, and three hyper-parameters related

Table 1. Design of experiments.

Parameters types	Parameters	Levels	Units
Dataset	Field of view	[293x293–586x586]	μm^2
	Overlap	[1–50]	%
	Minimal defect area	[500–1500]	μm^2
CNN architecture	Kernel size of first layer	[7 × 7–15 × 15]	pixels
	Dropout	[10–50]	%
	Validation split	[10–30]	%

to the CNN architecture, on the other hand. They are summed up in Table 1 and exposed in the next sections.

The use of a fractional factorial design of type 2^{6-2} reduced the required number of experiments from 64 to 16 and to keep a resolution of IV. A center point is added to take into account a potential non-linearity in the modelling. For each experiment with a given dataset and a set of hyper-parameters, the validation accuracy was recorded at each iteration. The value after 50 iterations was considered as the final accuracy of the model, evaluating its overall performance for classifying the images and providing a metric for comparison to the other models.

2.2 Dataset Generation

A set of 380 optical micrographs of Ti-6Al-4V specimens was acquired in industrial conditions using different magnifications and cameras. The field of view could vary between $900 \times 630\,\mu m^2$ and $1775 \times 1330\,\mu m^2$. 216 images of this dataset contain a visible defect. Since the field of view, illumination, and numerical resolution could vary between the images, they were preprocessed to produce as a "clean" dataset as possible. The open-source program Fiji was used for that purpose [35,36]. The images were first resampled to the same resolution, $1.29\,\mu m$/pixel, and corrected for uneven illumination with a pseudo-flatfield algorithm. Their intensity histogram was also normalized. By contrast with the original AlexNet architecture [30], which processes RGB images, the images in this work were 8-bit.

The preprocessed images were subdivided into smaller images (tiles) to produce different datasets with various overlap, field of view, and minimal amount of defect present in the image. The overlap ranged from 0 to 50% ("Overlap" in Table 1), allowing for the possibility to increase the data with repeated portions of images. Since the defects can vary in size and shape, the field of view covered by each tile could vary from 293 to $586\,\mu m^2$ ("Field of view" in Table 1). For supervised learning, the tiles needed to be dispatched in two classes, i.e., "containing a defect" or not. This task was accomplished by segmenting the initial grayscale images and manually measuring the amount of defects in each tile.

The minimum defect area necessary to consider the tile as containing a defect or not could take values 500 and $1500 \, \mu m^2$ ("Minimal defect area" in Table 1).

After cropping, all the tiles had numerical dimensions 227×227 pixels to fit with the AlexNet-CNN recommendations. Some non-defect images were randomly removed to generate a balanced dataset with the same amount of pictures, ca. 400, in both classes. The dataset was augmented by applying horizontal and vertical mirror transformations, as well as $90°$ rotations.

Figure 2 presents some pictures from a dataset with a field of view of $293 \times 293 \, \mu m^2$ and a minimum defect area of $1500 \, \mu m^2$. Informally described, the images without defects present similar textures characterized by some degree of granularity, due to the aforementioned process of α phase fragmentation. The overall contrast is constant among the images, as the initial images have been normalized, but the coarseness can vary depending on the amount of α/β phase mixture (dark areas). By contrast, the images with defects present a discontinuity in texture, materialized by a more or less thin and tortuous shape. Closer inspection reveals that several textures, mostly differing in isotropy, can coexist in the same image (e.g., in the second image without defect starting from the upper left-hand corner). Therefore, an efficient model has to consider the variety of morphology as a unique class.

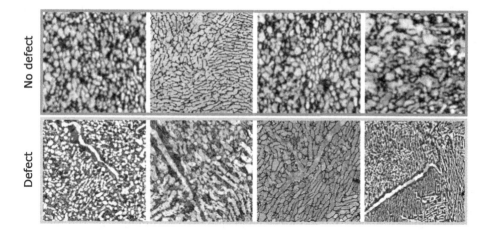

Fig. 2. Typical dataset images extracted from the initial micrographs (227×227 pixels).

2.3   CNN Architecture

The method presented here is based on the AlexNet architecture [30]. The programming language is Python 3.5 extended with the TensorFlow 2.0 machine learning platform [37]. Keras library is also used to define the layer hyperparameters [38]. The parameters used in this study are very close to the general AlexNet settings. The activation function for the five convolutional layers is the

Rectification Linear Unit (ReLU). The last three fully connected layers (6, 7, 8) are regularized with a dropout whose value depending on the experiment (Table 1), and the last layer is a softmax binary classifier.

Three hyper-parameters of the CNN were allowed to vary. The kernel size of the first layer could take values 7×7 or 15×15 pixels in order to evaluate how this characteristic was related to the dimensions of the defects. The dropout value in the fully connected layers was comprised between 0.1 and 0.5. The ratio of initial images used for fitting was automatically chosen for statistical purposes and varied between 0.1 to 0.3.

2.4   Performance Evolution

After performing the seventeen experiments from the DoE, the model with the higher accuracy was selected for a further investigation aimed at measuring the contribution of each layer to the final binary classification. Previous authors derived various metrics from information theory and Shannon entropy for evaluating the performance of a classifier, e.g., Confusion Entropy (CEN) [39], Modified CEN [40] or mutual information score. In this work, the concept of mutual information was considered. Indeed, as discussed in [34], it provides a mathematically grounded metric for quantifying the information flow through the CNN layers. Given two discrete random variables F and C (e.g., feature and class of an object), the mutual information can be expressed by the difference between the marginal entropies of F and C, and their joint entropy:

$$I(F, C) = H(F) + H(C) - H(F, C) \tag{1}$$

where $I(F, C)$ is the quantity of information obtained on one variable by the observation of the other. $H(F)$ and $H(C)$ are the marginal entropies, and $H(F, C)$ is the joint entropy. A perfect classifier is characterized by mutual information of 1, while the worst one, in the case of two classes and two labels, is 0.

For each layer of the model, the performance of each filter as a classifier was measured by calculating its mutual information score. Figure 3 sums up the principle of the mutual information analysis for the best model.

The calculation was based on the confusion matrix summing up the relative amounts of true positives (defect correctly detected), true negatives (absence of defect correctly identified), and false positives and false negatives (presence/absence of defect wrongfully detected).

A set of randomly chosen 200 images, 100 with defects, 100 without, were analyzed by the trained CNN. For each filter, the maximum values of the feature maps are recorded and reported in two histograms, one for each class with/without defect. Depending on the capacity of the classifier, the histograms can be more or less distinct. The mutual information is calculated for discrimination threshold values spanning the whole range of the histograms, in the same manner as for the derivation of a Receiver operating characteristic (ROC) curve. The performance of the filter for separating both classes is then considered as the

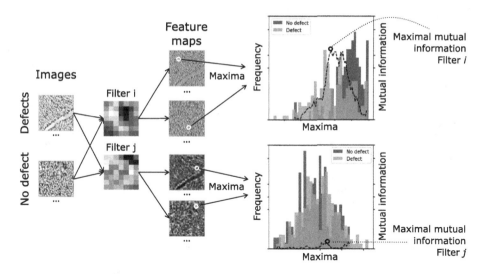

Fig. 3. Principle of the CNN mutual information analysis for two filters i and j. The output maximal mutual information, depicted on the right, shows that filter i has a higher discriminating power.

maximal mutual information value found, corresponding to the optimal threshold value. This operation is repeated for all the filters of each layer. The maximal mutual information values are then recorded and reported in a series of 5 histograms, one for each convolutional layer, summing up the abilities of its filters to correctly label the images.

3   Results

The learning progression of a model is represented by the evolution of the accuracy at each iteration. The Fig. 4 presents the learning curves of the 16 experiments.

Even though there are six varying parameters, the behavior of learning curves diverges into two different ways. The two groups revealed in the Fig. 4b are differentiated by the validation split ratio. In the case of a validation split of 30%, the mean accuracy of the model after 50 iterations reaches 95.67%. In the case of a validation split of 10%, this value of mean accuracy increase to 98.54%. It appears that all models are stabilized at the end of the experiment, i.e., after 50 iterations.

To evaluate the classification ability of the model layer by layer, the mutual information is assessed for each filter, as mentioned earlier (Fig. 3). It is then possible to observe the successive convolution of two images of defect and no-defect by the best filters of each layer through the network. The intensity distribution of each feature map is reported in histograms in Fig. 5.

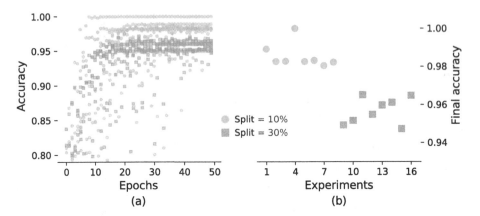

Fig. 4. (a): Bundle of learning curves obtained from the DoE; (b): Final accuracy values showing two distinct groups according to the validation split value 0.1 or 0.3.

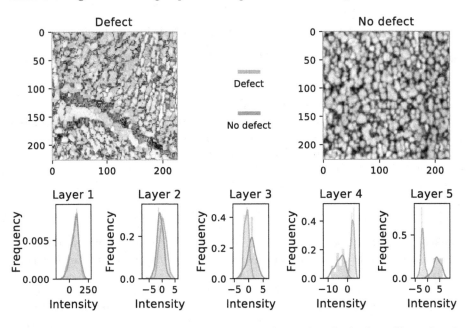

Fig. 5. Intensity histogram of the feature maps obtained with the best filter of each layer. Successful classification after the third layer.

While both histograms are overlaid in the two first layers, they start to separate at the third layer. The fourth and fifth layers exhibit two distinct distributions of intensity that reveal the successful classification of the initial images.

To evaluate the effect of the sixth factors studied in DoE, a diagram of the main effects is presented in Fig. 6.

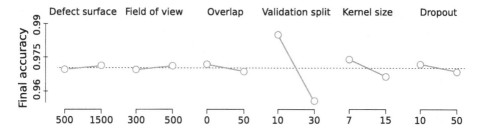

Fig. 6. Results of design of experiments. Main effects diagram.

As mentioned in Fig. 4, the validation split is of first importance in the final accuracy of the model. By comparison, the other parameters are of minor impact. The kernel size of the first convolution layer has a slight influence on the ultimate accuracy and has to be set to 7×7 pixels to increase the model performance. The overlap between successive images, which can induce redundant information, does not seem to affect the response of the models.

The mutual information histograms of all filters in each convolutional layer (model 6 in Fig. 4) are plotted in Fig. 7a. The histogram for the first convolutional layer is bimodal, showing that a significant amount of high-level filters induce different responses from both classes of images. The overall distribution for layer 2 is gathered towards low values. The distributions for layers 3, 4, and 5 appear similar, yet with increasing extreme values. This suggests that some low-level/long-range filters perform better and better with the CNN depth. This behavior is estimated in Fig. 7b, where the mutual information value separating each histogram in a 90 vs. 10% frequency ratio (highest decile) is plotted against the layer number.

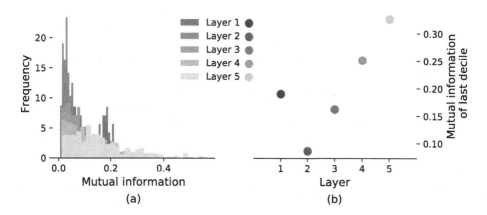

Fig. 7. (a): Distribution of mutual information in successive layers of model 6; (b): Highest decile values of histograms shown in (a).

The last decile of the mutual information first decreases between the first and second layers, then linearly increases up to the fifth layer. This expresses the cumulative information gain brought by each deep layer and suggests that these are necessary to capture the low-level features that distinguish the images with and without defects.

4   Discussion

The results presented in Fig. 4 indicate that all the models quickly reach an excellent accuracy, higher than 95%. As a matter of fact, one of the models achieves a theoretical accuracy of 100% (experiment 4 in Fig. 4b). However, the accuracy metric is highly correlated to the number of pictures randomly selected to validate the model at each iteration. For that reason, the final accuracy can take values exceptionally high and must be put into perspective.

The mutual information brings some additional knowledge about the network operation. The analysis of the mutual information through the network shows that the classification efficiency is non-linear. First of all, the bi-modality of the mutual information distribution observed in the first layer can be attributed to the heterogeneity of the textures at a small scale (as evidenced by Fig. 2). Indeed, a recent study on Texture-CNN (T-CNN) [41] showed that the three first layers of AlexNet are efficient in textures recognition, whereas the fourth and fifth layers are more suitable to describe shapes. In the present work, the classification efficiency increases from the third layer and becomes significant starting from the fourth layer. In the two last layers, the mutual information is high enough to separate the α_{GB} defects from the background texture. Based on this observation, a typical α_{GB} defect seems to more recognizable by the texture discontinuity that it causes than by its texture itself.

The consideration of 227×227 pixels tiles instead of large initial images has been made in the first instance to increase the dataset size and so to improve the final model accuracy. Additionally, this method can be reversed to return the localization of the defects in the initial images. For example, Fig. 8 shows a map in which the colors correspond to the average occurrence probability of a defect. It was obtained by dividing the initial image in 227×227 pixels tiles separated by 5 pixels, which were processed by the trained model. The final classification score of each tile was then summed and averaged at each pixel to produce the colormap overlaid on the initial image. The central defect is clearly detected (values close to 1). The upper left zone of the image appears with slightly lower values, which may be caused by the directional texture observed at this location, different from the rest of the image.

Further work shall concentrate on identifying the images that respond well to the classification, especially in the first layer. Conversely, visualizing the best performing filters of this layer will bring insights into the most significant features that make up the texture representation of the material.

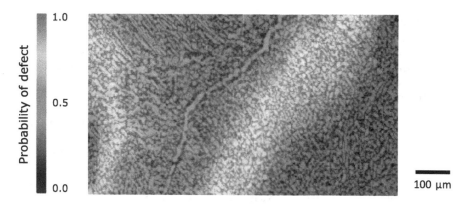

Fig. 8. Prediction map with overlaid tones corresponding to the detection probability of a defect.

5   Conclusion

In this paper, the use of AlexNet architecture was found to be a promising solution for the detection of specific geometric features in materials images (α_{GB} in Ti-6Al-4V micrographs). In a first approach, a design of experiments including six factors with two levels, related to the dataset and to the CNN, revealed an optimal model with an ultimate classification accuracy of 98.54%. Among these six parameters, the validation split ratio in the training step is of significant importance. The ultimate accuracy increases when the validation split ratio decreases in the range of 30% to 10%.

In addition to the statistical analysis of the main effects, the mutual information provided by the entropy theory has been used. This approach provides a powerful tool to understand the evolution of the information gain through the network. More precisely, it allows to evaluate the benefits of each filter in each layer. In the general context of texture classification, the convolution Neural Networks based on AlexNet are efficient in the first layers. But in the specific case of α_{GB} detection, the use of mutual information theory pointed out the benefits brought by deep layers. In this way, and contrary to the initial approach, it has been stated that the real challenge in the α_{GB} detection analysis lies in the microstructure discontinuity characterization rather than in texture recognition. In addition to that statement, there is strong evidence that adding deeper layers to the AlexNet architecture could increase the efficiency of the classification. Further efforts will focus on this opportunity to improve the efficiency of AlexNet in this context.

References

1. Gauthier, G., Coster, M., Chermant, L., Chermant, J.-L.: Morphological segmentation of cutting tools. Microsc. Microanal. Microstruct. **7**(5–6), 339–344 (1996)
2. Wejrzanowski, T., Spychalski, W., Różniatowski, K., Kurzydłowski, K.: Image based analysis of complex microstructures of engineering materials. Int. J. Appl. Math. Comput. Sci. **18**(1), 33–39 (2008)
3. Lee, S.G., Mao, Y., Gokhale, A.M., Harris, J., Horstemeyer, M.F.: Application of digital image processing for automatic detection and characterization of cracked constituent particles/inclusions in wrought aluminum alloys. Mater. Charact. **60**(9), 964–970 (2009)
4. Banerjee, S., Ghosh, S.K., Datta, S., Saha, S.K.: Segmentation of dual phase steel micrograph: an automated approach. Measurement **46**(8), 2435–2440 (2013)
5. Vanderesse, N., Anderson, M., Bridier, F., Bocher, P.: Inter- and intragranular delta phase quantitative characterization in inconel 718 by means of image analysis. J. Microsc. **261**(1), 79–87 (2016)
6. Meimandi, S., Vanderesse, N., Thibault, D., Bocher, P., Viens, M.: Macro-defects characterization in cast CA-6NM martensitic stainless steel. Mater. Charact. **124**, 31–39 (2017)
7. Dutta, T., Das, D., Banerjee, S., Saha, S.K., Datta, S.: An automated morphological classification of ferrite-martensite dual-phase microstructures. Measurement **137**, 595–603 (2019)
8. Cord, A., Bach, F., Jeulin, D.: Texture classification by statistical learning from morphological image processing: application to metallic surfaces. J. Microsc. **239**, 159–166 (2010)
9. Ducato, A., Fratini, L., La Cascia, M., Mazzola, G.: An automated visual inspection system for the classification of the phases of Ti-6Al-4V titanium alloy. In: Wilson, R., Hancock, E., Bors, A., Smith, W. (eds.) CAIP 2013. LNCS, vol. 8048, pp. 362–369. Springer, Heidelberg (2013). https://doi.org/10.1007/978-3-642-40246-3_45
10. DeCost, B.L., Holm, E.A.: A computer vision approach for automated analysis and classification of microstructural image data. Comput. Mater. Sci. **110**, 126–133 (2015)
11. Jeulin, D.: Morphological probabilistic hierarchies for texture segmentation. Math. Morphol. - Theory Appl. **1**(1) (2016)
12. Gupta, S., Sarkar, J., Kundu, M., Bandyopadhyay, N.R., Ganguly, S.: Automatic recognition of SEM microstructure and phases of steel using LBP and random decision forest operator. Measurement **151**, 107224 (2020)
13. Chowdhury, A., Kautz, E., Yener, B., Lewis, D.: Image driven machine learning methods for microstructure recognition. Comput. Mater. Sci. **123**, 176–187 (2016)
14. DeCost, B.L., Francis, T., Holm, E.A.: Exploring the microstructure manifold: Image texture representations applied to ultrahigh carbon steel microstructures. Acta Materialia **133**, 30–40 (2017)
15. Lin, J., Ma, L., Yao, Y.: Segmentation of casting defect regions for the extraction of microstructural properties. Eng. Appl. Artif. Intell. **85**, 150–163 (2019)
16. Stan, T., Thompson, Z.T., Voorhees, P.W.: Optimizing convolutional neural networks to perform semantic segmentation on large materials imaging datasets: X-ray tomography and serial sectioning. Mater. Charact. **160**, 110119 (2020)
17. Dimiduk, D.M., Holm, E.A., Niezgoda, S.R.: Perspectives on the impact of machine learning, deep learning, and artificial intelligence on materials, processes, and structures engineering. Integr. Mater. Manuf. Innov. **7**(3), 157–172 (2018)

18. Vander Voort, G.F.: ASM Handbook, Volume 9: Metallography And Microstructures (ASM Handbook). ASM International (2004)
19. Lütjering, G., Williams, J.C.: Titanium. Springer, New York (2007). https://doi.org/10.1007/978-3-540-73036-1
20. Chrapoński, J., Szkliniarz, W.: Quantitative metallography of two-phase titanium alloys. Mater. Charact. **46**(2–3), 149–154 (2001)
21. Tiley, J., et al.: Quantification of microstructural features in $\alpha\beta$ titanium alloys. Mater. Sci. Eng.: A **372**(1–2), 191–198 (2004)
22. Vanderesse, N., Maire, E., Darrieulat, M., Montheillet, F., Moreaud, M., Jeulin, D.: Three-dimensional microtomographic study of widmanstätten microstructures in an alpha/beta titanium alloy. Scripta Materialia **58**(6), 512–515 (2008)
23. Li, H., Ji, Z., Yang, H.: Quantitative characterization of lamellar and equiaxed alpha phases of $(\alpha + \beta)$ titanium alloy using a robust approach for touching features splitting. Mater. Charact. **76**, 6–20 (2013)
24. Zhao, H., Ho, A., Davis, A., Antonysamy, A., Prangnell, P.: Automated image mapping and quantification of microstructure heterogeneity in additive manufactured TI6AL4V. Mater. Charact. **147**, 131–145 (2019)
25. Sharma, H., van Bohemen, S.M.C., Petrov, R.H., Sietsma, J.: Three-dimensional analysis of microstructures in titanium. Acta Materialia **58**(7), 2399–2407 (2010)
26. Foltz, J.W., Welk, B., Collins, P.C., Fraser, H.L., Williams, J.C.: Formation of grain boundary α in β Ti alloys: its role in deformation and fracture behavior of these alloys. Metall. Mater. Trans. A: Phys. Metall. Mater. Sci. **42**, 645–650 (2011)
27. Chatfield, K., Simonyan, K., Vedaldi, A., Zisserman, A.: Return of the devil in the details: delving deep into convolutional nets (2014)
28. Liu, L., Chen, J., Fieguth, P., Zhao, G., Chellappa, R., Pietikäinen, M.: From BoW to CNN: two decades of texture representation for texture classification. Int. J. Comput. Vis. **127**(1), 74–109 (2018)
29. Liu, L., et al.: Deep learning for generic object detection: A survey. CoRR, abs/1809.02165 (2018)
30. Krizhevsky, A., Sutskever, I., Hinton, G.E.: Imagenet classification with deep convolutional neural networks. In: Pereira, F., Burges, C.J.C., Bottou, L., Weinberger, K.Q. (eds.) Advances in Neural Information Processing Systems 25, pp. 1097–1105. Curran Associates Inc. (2012)
31. Wang, S.H., Lv, Y.D., Sui, Y., Liu, S., Wang, S.J., Zhang, Y.D.: Alcoholism detection by data augmentation and convolutional neural network with stochastic pooling. J. Med. Syst. **42**(1), 2 (2018)
32. Cover, T.M., Thomas, J.A.: Elements of Information Theory. Wiley, Hoboken (2012)
33. Tishby, N., Zaslavsky, N.: Deep learning and the information bottleneck principle. In: 2015 IEEE Information Theory Workshop (ITW), pp. 1–5. IEEE (2015)
34. Chaddad, A., Naisiri, B., Pedersoli, M., Granger, E., Desrosiers, C., Toews, M.: Modeling Information Flow Through Deep Neural Networks. arXiv e-prints, page arXiv:1712.00003, November 2017
35. Schneider, C.A., Rasband, W.S., Eliceiri, K.W.: NIH image to ImageJ: 25 years of image analysis. Nat. Methods **9**(7), 671–675 (2012)
36. Schindelin, J., et al.: Fiji: an open-source platform for biological-image analysis. Nat. Methods **9**(7), 676–682 (2012)
37. Abadi, M., et al.: TensorFlow: large-scale machine learning on heterogeneous systems (2015). Software available from tensorflow.org
38. Chollet, F., et al.: Keras (2015). https://keras.io

39. Wei, J.-M., Yuan, X.-J., Qing-Hua, H., Wang, S.-Q.: A novel measure for evaluating classifiers. Expert Syst. Appl. **37**(5), 3799–3809 (2010)
40. Delgado, R., Núñez-González, J.D.: Enhancing confusion entropy as measure for evaluating classifiers. In: Graña, M., et al. (eds.) SOCO'18-CISIS'18-ICEUTE'18. AISC, vol. 771, pp. 79–89. Springer, Cham (2019). https://doi.org/10.1007/978-3-319-94120-2_8
41. Andrearczyk, V., Whelan, P.F.: Using filter banks in convolutional neural networks for texture classification. Pattern Recogn. Lett. **84**, 63–69 (2016)

Visual Perception Ranking
of Chess Players

Laercio R. Silva Junior$^{(\boxtimes)}$ and Carlos E. Thomaz

Centro Universitario FEI, Sao Paulo, Brazil
{laercio.silva,cet}@fei.edu.br

Abstract. In this work, we have carried out a performance analysis of chess players comparing a standard ranking measure with a novel one proposed here. Using the idea of treating participants eye movements, when answering several on-screen valid chess questions of distinguished complexities, as high-dimensional spatial attention patterns we have shown that expertise is consistently associated with the ability to process visual information holistically using fewer fixations rather than locally focusing on individual pieces. These findings might disclose new insights for predicting chess skills.

Keywords: Visual perception · Eye-tracking · Chess

1 Introduction

Chess has provided an inspiring, scientific, and multidisciplinary domain to understand the human cognitive system in problem-solving activities [1–4,8–11].

In the last years, biosignals like positron emission tomography [12], electroencephalography [13,14], functional magnetic resonance imaging [5–7] and eye movements [15–17] have been used not only to verify what brain areas are activated or where a chess player looks at the board, but also to describe and explain differences between chess experts and novices depending on their responses to chessboard configurations presented on a computer screen.

Following these earlier investigations, we have moved one step further and explored in this work the potential role of such biosignals' measurements as ranking metrics *de facto* to analyze the performance of chess players. More specifically, we have implemented a novel chess ranking measure based on eye movements and compared its results with the traditional metric based on high accuracy and short reaction time. In all experiments carried out, the visual perception measure has ensured the best classification of the participants' expertise on a question-by-question basis.

The remaining sections of this paper can be summarized as follows. We provide in Sect. 2 a brief description of the eye-tracking apparatus and all participants involved in this study. In Sect. 3, we explain the experimental design and

Supported by the Brazilian agencies FAPESP, CNPq and CAPES.

A. Campilho et al. (Eds.): ICIAR 2020, LNCS 12131, pp. 307–315, 2020.
https://doi.org/10.1007/978-3-030-50347-5_27

the eye movements used for data processing. The standard and novel ranking measures are described in Sect. 4 and the main results presented in Sect. 5. Conclusions highlighting the main contribution of this paper can be found in Sect. 6.

2   Apparatus and Participants

Eye movements were recorded with a Tobii TX300 equipment that comprises an eye tracker unit integrated to the lower part of a 23in TFT monitor. The eye tracker performs binocular tracking at the data sampling rate of 300 Hz, and has minimum fixation duration of 60 ms and maximum dispersion threshold of 0.5°. These are the eye tracker defaults for cognitive research. Data collection were performed with the use of the Tobii Studio programming package running on an attached notebook (Core i7, 16Gb RAM and Windows 7).

A total number of 32 participants, aged from 6 to 54 years, were involved in this study, with different qualifications: 4 professional chess players with ELO rating [18], 4 chess teachers, 4 school children who commonly compete in national chess championships, and 20 participants who know chess but not practise it regularly. All subjects participated on a voluntary basis and written informed consent was obtained from all participants.

3   Experimental Design and Data Processing

The experimental design consists of 50 on-screen questions related to full size (8×8) and valid chessboard configurations divided into 5 categories of distinguished complexities [12–14]: Object recognition (C1), where participants had to simply respond whether or not, for example, a specified chess piece was on the board; Check detection (C2), where participants should respond whether or not a specified king was in check; Checkmate judgment (C3), where participants should determine whether or not a specified king was checkmate; Checkmate in one move (C4), in which the decision was whether or not exists a piece on the board that could checkmate a specified king in the next move; Rule retrieval (C5), in which participants analyzed whether or not a simple, single move of a specific piece is valid. Each category is composed of 10 questions equally distributed among positive and negative answers.

The experiments began with a calibration procedure as implemented in the Tobii apparatus. Participants were seated in front of the eye tracker and instructed to respond the on-screen questions by pressing corresponding keys labeled yes or no [14]. On each trial, the question to be solved was shown only once before its chessboard diagram, presented afterwards on a new screen. All the stimuli were presented centralized on a black background using the 23in TFT monitor with a screen resolution of 1280×1024 pixels. All chessboard configurations were visualized on the TFT monitor with 800 pixels wide and 800 pixels high. Each question followed by its corresponding chess diagram preceded the next pair of question and chess diagram stimuli until all the 50 trials were presented. Figure 1 shows a trial example of the experimental design. The time of presentation of each stimulus was controlled by the participants themselves, but they were instructed to produce their responses as correctly and quickly as possible.

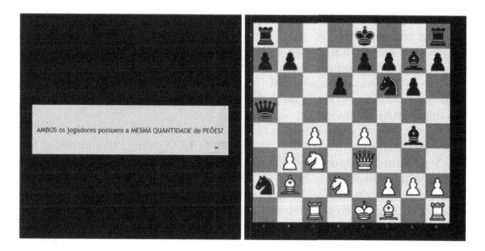

Fig. 1. A trial example of the experimental design.

During each experiment the participant's response, reaction time and eye movements were registered. We considered only chessboard data from participants for whom 40% or more of their gaze samples were collected by the eye tracker. Missing signal detection with 60ms (interval time of an eye blink) or less were interpolated. All data signals were then filtered using a weighted moving average method to remove noise generated by the equipment, and micro and macro movements from the eyes and head, respectively.

The relative duration heat maps were used to describe the accumulated fixation duration on different locations in the chessboard diagrams at the resolution of 800 × 800 pixels from all participants and from all chessboard stimuli. These relative duration heat maps have been encoded in gray-scale spatial attention maps using 8-bits per pixel.

4   Ranking Measures

To quantify a traditional discriminant measure, we have used the general Volke's strategy of high accuracy and short reaction time calculated as [13]:

$$V_j = \left(K_j - \frac{K}{2} \right) \cdot \frac{RT}{RT_j}, \tag{1}$$

where V_j is the performance value of participant j, K_j the participant's number of correct responses, K the total number of pre-defined trials, RT the mean reaction time across all participants and pre-defined trials, and RT_j the participant's mean reaction time across all pre-defined trials. These performance values served as a discriminant measure of the participants' chess skills on a question-by-question basis, considering only the subjects classified here as belonging to the sample group of novices or experts.

The general performance rule to label mastership of chess players is the ELO rating [18]. Since here not all the subjects have ELO rating, we have used the Volke's performance values the participants reached in all questions of all categories as a measure of their expertise. We have considered novices and experts all the subjects whose overall Volke's performance values arranged from smallest to largest correspond to the first and fourth statistical quartiles respectively.

To quantify a visual perception discriminant measure between these novices and experts sample groups, we propose the idea of treating each participant's spatial attention map as a pattern in an n-dimensional space by concatenating the rows of its corresponding data matrix. Let an $N \times n$ matrix $\mathbf{X}$ be composed of N visual patterns with n values, that is, $\mathbf{X} = (\mathbf{x}_1, \mathbf{x}_2, \dots, \mathbf{x}_N)^T$. A straightforward multivariate linear method to calculate the discriminant score of the participants is via the well-known computation of the $\mathbf{q}$ leading eigenvector of $\mathbf{S}_w^{-1}\mathbf{S}_b$ (Fisher's criterion), where

$$\mathbf{S}_b = \sum_{i=1}^{g} N_i (\bar{\mathbf{x}}_i - \bar{\mathbf{x}})(\bar{\mathbf{x}}_i - \bar{\mathbf{x}})^T, \tag{2}$$

$$\mathbf{S}_w = \sum_{i=1}^{g} \sum_{j=1}^{N_i} (\mathbf{x}_{ij} - \bar{\mathbf{x}}_i)(\mathbf{x}_{ij} - \bar{\mathbf{x}}_i)^T, \tag{3}$$

$\mathbf{x}_{ij}$ is the n-dimensional visual pattern of participant j from group i, N_i the number of visual patterns from group i, $\bar{\mathbf{x}}_i$ the unbiased sample mean of group i, $\bar{\mathbf{x}}$ the grand mean vector of $\mathbf{X}$, and g the total number of groups, that is, $g = 2$ here.

To avoid the computational and mathematical difficulties in handling such large, singular $\mathbf{S}_w$ matrix in the current small sample size problem ($N \ll n$), we have firstly projected all spatial attention maps on their principal components $\mathbf{P}$ with non-zero eigenvalues [19] and used a regularized version of $\mathbf{S}_w$ [20] to compute $\mathbf{q}$. Thus, we arranged the data matrix $\mathbf{X}$ to be exclusively composed of novices and experts visual patterns in each chessboard diagram, calculated $\mathbf{P}$ and $\mathbf{q}$ for these two sample groups, and considered the classification score

$$H_j = \mathbf{x}_{ij}^T \mathbf{P} \mathbf{q} \tag{4}$$

as the visual perception discriminant measure of participant j from sample group i in each question.

To assess the degree of monotonicity between both discriminant measures, we calculated the standard Spearman's correlation [21] given by

$$\rho = \frac{\sum_{j=1}^{N}(R_j - \bar{R})(Q_j - \bar{Q})}{\sqrt{\sum_{j=1}^{N}(R_j - \bar{R})^2 \sum_{j=1}^{N}(Q_j - \bar{Q})^2}}, \tag{5}$$

where R_j and Q_j represent, to a given on-screen question and chessboard diagram, the rankings of the same set of N paired participants determined respectively by their V_j and H_j discriminant measures described in Eqs. (1) and (4).

5   Results

We adopted a leave-one-out validation method to estimate the classification accuracy of the visual perception discriminant measure. The standard sample group mean of each class has been calculated from the corresponding discriminant scores and the minimum Euclidean distance from each class mean has been used to assign a test sample to either the novices or experts classes.

Table 1 shows the average values of visual perception accuracy and Spearman correlation of each category.

Table 1. Average values of each category.

Category	Visual perception accuracy	Spearman correlation
C1	0.988	0.029
C2	0.987	−0.461
C3	0.994	−0.220
C4	0.989	−0.094
C5	0.985	0.039

According to Table 1, the visual information that the novices and experts have used when making their on-screen decisions are highly discriminant (greater than 98%) in all categories. Interestingly, there is no similarity (zero correlation) or even disagreement (negative correlation) between the series of paired participants ranked by the Volke's and visual perception discriminant measures, suggesting that the traditional performance measure might be imperfect or incomplete.

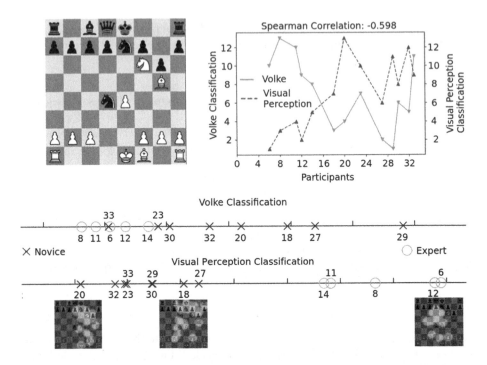

Fig. 2. (Top left) Chessboard diagram of the C5 (one of the easiest categories) on-screen question "May the WHITE KNIGHT be captured by a BLACK PAWN?". The correct answer is no; (Top right) Spearman's correlation of the degree of monotonicity between the series of paired participants ranked by the Volke and Visual Perception classifications shown as one-dimensional discriminant axes (in the middle); (Bottom) From left to right, corresponding spatial attention maps of the participants 20 (novice), 18 (novice), and 6 (expert).

Figures 2 and 3 depict the questions with the lowest and highest number of correct responses, respectively, as examples. As can be seen, although overall we might expect that experts had fewer errors and shorter reaction times than novices when considering all questions, on a question-by-question basis expertise is consistently associated with the participants ability to process visual information holistically using fewer fixations rather than locally focusing on individual pieces. This outcome highlights that treating each participant's spatial attention map as a high-dimensional pattern might disclose new explanations of the highest level of skilled performance in chess.

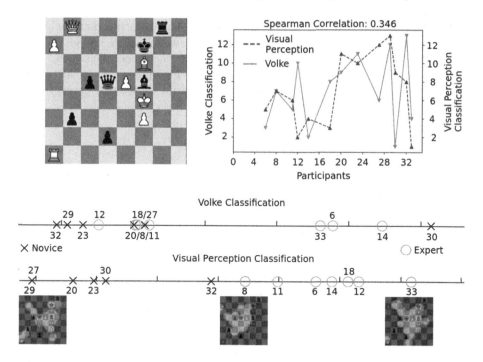

Fig. 3. (Top left) Chessboard diagram of the C4 (most difficult category) on-screen question "May the BLACK QUEEN achieve checkmate in ONE move?". The correct answer is no; (Top right) Spearman's correlation of the degree of monotonicity between the series of paired participants ranked by the Volke and Visual Perception classifications shown as one-dimensional discriminant axes (in the middle); (Bottom) From left to right, corresponding spatial attention maps of the participants 29 (novice), 8 (expert), and 33 (expert).

6   Conclusion

This work proposed and implemented a visual perception ranking measure based on eye movements to assess the performance of chess players. Using several on-screen questions of distinguished complexities, our findings revealed that the visual information that the participants used on a question-by-question basis when making their decisions are discriminant and consistent regarding their overall performance when compared with the traditional measure of high accuracy and short reaction time. These findings provide additional empirical evidence to emphasize the supplementary role of eye movement measurement on predicting chess skills.

Future work will explore perceptual expertise based on international ELO rating (which classifies chess players all over the world) with the visual perception ranking proposed here aiming to uncover domain-general characteristics of knowledge in chess. We believe that the method proposed may help to predict expertise not only in chess, but any other domain that visual perception is important to achieve such outperformance.

References

1. Groot, A.: Het denken van den schaker: een experimenteel-psychologische studie, p. 315. Noord-Hollandsche Uitgevers Maatschappij, Amsterdam (1946)
2. Chase, W., Simon, H.: Perception in chess. Cogn. Psychol. **4**(1), 55–81 (1973)
3. Chase, W., Simon, H.: The mind's eye in chess. Vis. Inf. Process. 215–281 (1973)
4. Campitelli, G., Gobet, F.: The mind's eye in blindfold chess. Eur. J. Cogn. Psychol. **17**(1), 23–45 (2005)
5. Duan, X., et al.: Functional organization of intrinsic connectivity networks in Chinese-chess experts. Brain Res. **1558**, 33–43 (2014)
6. Krawczyk, D., Boggan, A., McClelland, M., Bartlett, J.: The neural organization of perception in chess experts. Neurosci. Lett. **499**(2), 64–69 (2011)
7. Bilalić, M., Langner, R., Ulrich, R., Grodd, W.: Many faces of expertise: fusiform face area in chess experts and novices. J. Neurosci. **31**(28), 10206–10214 (2011)
8. Hambrick, D., Campitelli, G., Macnamara, B.: Cognitive Processes in Chess, The Science of Expertise: Behavioral, Neural, and Genetic Approaches to Complex Skill. Routledge, Abingdon (2017)
9. Ericsson, K., Hoffman, R., Kozbelt, A.: The Cambridge Handbook of Expertise and Expert Performance. Cambridge University Press, Cambridge (2018)
10. Bilalić, M.: The double take of expertise: neural expansion in associated with outstanding performance. Curr. Dir. Psychol. Sci. **27**(6), 462–469 (2018)
11. Gobet, F.: The future of expertise: the need for a multidisciplinary approach. J. Expertise **1**(2), 1–7 (2018)
12. Nichelli, P., Grafman, J., Pietrini, P., Alway, D., Carton, J., Miletich, R.: Brain activity in chess playing. Nature **369**, 191 (1994)
13. Volke, H.-J., Dettmar, P., Richter, P., Rudolf, M., Buhss, U.: On-coupling and off-coupling of neocortical areas in chess experts and novices. J. Psychophysiol. **16**, 23–36 (2002)
14. Silva-Junior, L., Thomaz, C.: A multivariate correlation assessment of chess proficiency using brain signals. In: Proceedings of the XV Workshop de Visao Computacional (WVC), pp. 10–15. IEEE, Brazil (2019)
15. Reingold, E., Sheridan, H.: Eye movements and visual expertise in chess and medicine. In: Oxford Handbook on Eye Movements, USA (2011)
16. Sheridan, H., Reingold, E.: Expert vs. novice differences in the detection of relevant information during a chess game: evidence from eye movements. Front. Psychol. **5**, 941 (2014)
17. Sheridan, H., Reingold, E.: Chess players' eye movements reveal rapid recognition of complex visual patterns: evidence from a chess-related visual search task. J. Vis. **17**(3), 4 (2017)
18. Elo, A.: The Rating of Chess Players. Arco Pub, Nagoya (1978)
19. Johnson, R., Wichern, D.: Applied Multivariate Statistical Analysis. Prentice Hall, New Jersey (1998)

20. Thomaz, C., Kitani, E., Gillies, D.: A maximum uncertainty LDA-based approach for limited sample size problems - with application to face recognition. J. Braz. Comput. Soc. **25**, 7–18 (2006)
21. Costa, J., Soares, C.: A weighted rank measure of correlation. Aust. New Zealand J. Stat. **47**(4), 515–529 (2005)

Video Tampering Detection
for Decentralized Video Transcoding
Networks

Rabindranath Andujar[1]($\boxtimes$), Ignacio Peletier[1], Jesus Oliva[1],
Marc Cymontkowski[1], Yondon Fu[2], Eric Tang[2], and Josh Allman[2]

[1] Haivision, 2600 Blvd. Alfred-Nobel, 5th Floor, Montreal, QC H4S 0A9, Canada
randujar@haivision.com, info@haivision.com
[2] Livepeer, 16 Vestry St, Floor 4, New York, NY 10013, USA
contact@livepeer.org
http://www.haivision.com
http://www.livepeer.org

Abstract. This paper introduces a complete methodology based on
Machine Learning and Computer Vision techniques for the verification of
video transcoding computations in decentralized networks, particularly
the Open Source project Livepeer. A base video dataset is presented,
with over 180k samples transcoded using the x264 codec. As a novelty,
we propose a set of four features computed as a full reference comparison
between the source and the rendered videos. Using these features, a One
Class Support Vector Machine is trained to identify good encodings with
a high accuracy. Experimental results are presented and the particular
constraints of this use case are explained.

Keywords: Decentralized networks · Novelty detection · Computer
vision feature extraction

1 Introduction

Video transcoding is a compute-heavy process that has traditionally carried a
high technical and monetary cost. It is the process of digitally obtaining copies of
a multimedia file resulting in smaller, more storage - and network - efficient clones
of the original, or simply device compatible ones. File size reduction has obvious
advantages for the purpose of video transport, as the sources are generally large
and consume a large amount of bandwidth. Format encoding is often needed
to provide compatibility between different target receivers. Recently, a number of initiatives based on peer-to-peer (P2P) transcodifications have appeared
seeking to reduce those costs by means of open collaborative networks where
the participants are rewarded by means of cryptocurrencies or "tokens". The
combination of open, permissionless networks and immutability associated with

---

Supported by Livepeer and Haivision.

A. Campilho et al. (Eds.): ICIAR 2020, LNCS 12131, pp. 316–327, 2020.
https://doi.org/10.1007/978-3-030-50347-5_28

cryptocurrency ledgers attracts byzantine (adversarial) behaviors: any participant can attempt to "break the protocol" without immediate consequences from within the network. This imposes the need for a verification mechanism to decide whether transcoding work was done correctly. In this article, we will be presenting a combination of Computer Vision and Machine Learning techniques that have been assembled in a tool that enables broadcaster nodes in one such P2P network to verify whether a job has been executed properly with a given degree of confidence.

2   Related Work

Sophisticated digital image and video editing tools have become increasingly powerful and available to the public. As a result, video forgery and tamper detection have become fields of very active research over the years to keep pace with the myriad of malicious attacks seeking to misinform, cheat or simply entertain an ever increasing digital multimedia audience. Excellent surveys on the topic of digital forensics where techniques for exploiting the statistics of digital images and, ultimately, video frames, can be found elsewhere [1,6,9,10]. On the other hand, decentralized platforms where computation is outsourced to trustless providers have flourished in the recent past. In all of them, the evaluation of the work performed by the providers needs to be checked prior to accepting payment. TrueBit, BOINC, iExec and Golem are but a few good examples of how these networks perform such evaluation [7,17]. The approach of TrueBit (and by extension that of iExec) to validate the proof of work, however universal, is computationally expensive. A reputation based system like the one used in the BOINC network avoids at once the problem of verification, but may become too centralized and lead to unbalanced monopolistic behaviors undesirable in the long run. Finally, the Golem network takes a more problem-specific path where verification is made over 3D render job tasks. Obviously, their solution was of no use to our purposes although similar tools were used. Our specific application is the Livepeer network [12]. Its protocol establishes the common ground for a video transcoding community based on P2P, trustless nodes. The aim of our research is to introduce economic disincentive for cheating in the network. Due to the non-deterministic nature of the transcoding operation, when multithreaded floating point calculation is used, one cannot simply re-transcode and compare the resulting hashes. However, one can exploit the fact that verification can be done on probabilistic grounds and avoid the need for computing the whole video sequence. Unlike in forgery detection, evaluation of the work must focus on the actual process of obtaining the media, not in the produced media itself. In this document we present a use case illustrative of the application of a novel set of tamper detection techniques for the verification of video transcoding work.

3   Peer-to-peer Networks, Byzantine Attacks and Beyond

Peer-to-peer collaboration is a well-covered area of research with intense activity due to the recent emergence of decentralized, permissionless systems. Such systems are resourced by nodes highly unlike each other from a technical perspective. Hence, they can not be designed based on any assumptions regarding reliability, bandwidth, or computational power. Instead, they must be made globally fault tolerant and massively scalable [4]. In these networks, any form of violation of the policies established in the system can be considered as an attack. The form of such attacks has been widely investigated. There are several models for the behavior of nodes in cooperative services, of which the Byzantine-Altruistic-Rational (BAR) is one of the most complete to date [2,11]. In the BAR model, not only are Byzantine node failures considered -arbitrary deviations from the established protocol- but also rational types of failures caused by selfish, targeted departures from the program with the aim of increasing a failing node's net benefit in detriment of the network. We have taken such node behavior into account and designed frame features that when fed to a one-class classifier [15] provide a high degree of accuracy while remaining resilient to attacks of any kind.

4   A Large Video Dataset for Training Machine Learning Estimators

Video codec (COdifier - DECodifier) protocols establish the rules that video compression algorithms need to implement. As of the writing of this article, H.264/MPEG-4 AVC, H.265/HEVC and VP9 form the vast majority of codecs in use [18]. The downside of video transcodification is that, in general, it involves lossy compression of the multimedia information. This loss of information, while improving the efficiency of the transmission, affects the final quality of the spectator's experience (QoE) by introducing undesired artifacts at the time of decoding. As a result, the task of adjusting video compression parameters comes down to a trade off between generating the least visually perceptible artifacts (blockiness, banding, blurring,...) while minimizing transmission artifacts (rebuffering, packet loss,...). Research into and development of different QoE metrics that allow for quantifying the impact of both sorts of artifacts have been going on for years. With the purpose of enabling common grounds for benchmarking these metrics, several video datasets have been made publicly available by different sources [5,13,20]. However, the extension of these datasets is limited in number of samples or diversity of topics, as they offer only a few tens of source raw videos. This makes them unsuitable for the purpose of training Machine Learning models, where large datasets are preferred. More recently, the UGC Dataset (containing a substantially larger amount of source videos) has been released by the YouTube Media Algorithms team [21]. Nevertheless, this dataset puts its emphasis on User Generated Content (UGC), lacking generality for our purposes. Due to the limitations mentioned above, we determined it would be necessary to generate our own dataset. For the sake of simplicity we limited ourselves to the creation of H.264 encodings, and sample lengths of 10 s. Once the source videos were collected, we proceeded to generate a number of renditions with two characteristics: those transcoded with standard H.264 parameters and those where the set of parameters involved some form of tampering.

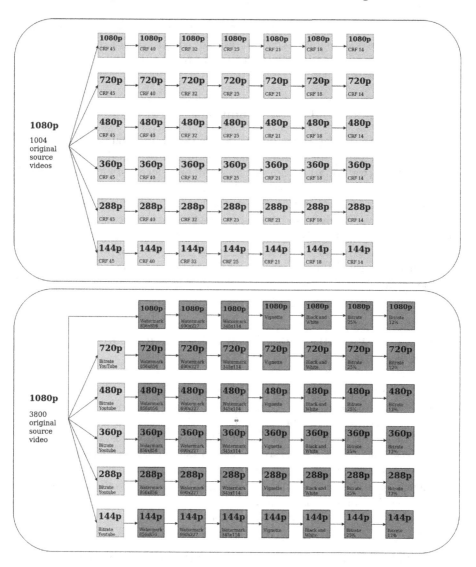

Fig. 1. Diagram representing the different kind of renditions generated for both quality targeted sources (above) and bitrate targeted sources (below). Boxes in red are labeled as attacks, whereas green boxes correspond to untampered videos. (Color figure online)

4.1 The Untampered Subset of Renditions

From a first set of 3800 source videos, we shaped a subset of untampered copies at vertical resolutions of 720, 480, 360, 288 and 144 pixels. The encodings for each resolution were obtained by fixing a target bitrate in the encoder for each of them using YouTube's indications [8]. This gave us about 19000 not tampered samples. Another set of 1004 source videos was used to further generate quality-targeted copies. These were obtained by applying different constant rate factors (CRF) in the encoder parameters (45, 40, 32, 25, 21, 18, 14, respectively) at each of the previously mentioned resolutions. In total, this amounted to another 35140 untampered samples.

4.2 The Tampered Subset of Renditions

For the generation of renditions labeled as tampered, we assumed two possible scenarios: one in which an attacking node manipulates the video by inserting undesired filters (watermarks, vignetting...) and another where it delivers renditions that require lower computational effort. The former is meant to account for byzantine attacks of irrational origin, in which nodes do not necessarily obtain an immediate benefit. Because the extent of these attacks can never be made fully comprehensive (there is an infinite number of possibilities in both scenarios), this problem is better addressed under the perspective of novelty detection, as we will see in the following section. These renditions were derived directly from the bitrate-targeted sources previously described, as can be seen in Fig. 1 above.

5 A Set of Features for Attack Detection Based on Computer Vision

As a first intuition about solving the problem, one would be tempted to use well established objective full-reference video quality metrics to validate the degree of correctness. A number of them are available, such as PSNR, SSIM, MS-SSIM or even the more sophisticated VMAF or SSIMPlus, where temporal characteristics of the video are also considered [3]. This approach, however, not only proved itself too computationally expensive but also was not able to deliver a sufficiently accurate model. Table 1 presents the accuracy values of these two different classification models, using QoE metrics as the underlying differentiator (SSIM and PSNR) and our proposed method.

5.1 Inexpensive Spatial and Spatio-Temporal Features for Attack Detection

To overcome both hurdles (expensive computation together with lack of accuracy) we resorted to our own set of features based on the same principles as those of the aforementioned full-reference objective quality metrics. We researched and tested a number of approaches where inter-frame differences between an original and its renditions are characterized, on a frame-by-frame basis, focusing on different aspects of the possible distortions. Those contributing most significantly to accurate results after training were selected using a random forest model for feature importance characterization. The approach that we have developed to compare frame sequences can be described as follows. Given two sets of N frames in a sequence, pairwise comparisons can be made between the frames of the source sequence $S_n(i,j)$ and those of the rendition $R_n(i,j)$. Prior to the comparison, we have optimized the computational effort by applying two preprocessing steps in both $S_n(i,j)$ and $R_n(i,j)$:

- Resize frames to a 480×270 resolution
- Change the color space from RGB to HSV, making operations only in the V channel, which captures the changes due to illumination [16].

Different experiments were conducted to adjust the values of the resizing resolution without compromising the classification accuracy. Also, we verified that no information was lost with the elimination of the chroma channels by training models with and without them. Furthermore, specific transformations were made over the frames prior to the computation of our metrics. We have resorted to two very common computer vision techniques: Discrete Cosine Transform (Y) and Gaussian filter (G) [14,19]. In total, a set of four features was found and selected as most significant, three in the space domain and one in the time domain.

Inter-Frame Discrete Cosine Transform Difference. The pairwise difference in DCT between a source frame $S_n(i,j)$ and its rendition $R_n(i,j)$ can be computed as:

$$IFDCTD_n = \max\left(Y_{Sn} - Y_{Rn}\right) \tag{1}$$

telling the verifier how far in the energy domain rendition frames are from the source.

Inter-Frame Gaussian Mean Squared Error (IFGMSE). In the case of the gaussian filter, a straightforward subtraction of the two transformations did not render a single scalar, but a matrix. The resulting metric is then defined as the mean squared error between the gaussian transform of both frames as:

$$IFGMSE_n = \frac{1}{A \cdot B}\left\lVert G_{Sn} - G_{Rn}\right\rVert_2^2 \tag{2}$$

containing the information as to what extent the transcodification has introduced significant distortions (on average) between the source and the rendition.

Inter-Frame Gaussian Difference (IFGD). Another form of measuring such degree of distortion in absolute terms is to account for all the differences in a pixel-wise fashion, as a sum:

$$IFGD_n = \Sigma\left\lvert G_{Sn} - G_{Rn}\right\rvert \tag{3}$$

This metric serves as a complement of the previous one in defining to what extent the distortions affect the quality of the rendition.

Inter-Frame Gaussian Difference Thresholded (IFGDT). The spatio-temporal relationships between subsequent frames plays a very important role in video compression. High levels of motion between frames also represent higher amounts of information to be passed from key frames to predictive frames at encoding time. Often, this information can be dismissed, as the human visual system is known to remain oblivious to very fast changes, and this is exploited by video codecs to optimize bitrate reductions. This metric can be considered as a two-step process. In the first place, a mask (or threshold) is prepared by subtracting the next rendition frame R_{n+1} from the source frame S_n. This establishes the amount of temporal difference T_n for the given frame:

$$T_n = \left\lVert S_{n+1} - R_n \right\rVert_1 \tag{4}$$

Then, the instant difference is computed over the gaussian filtered frames as:

$$\delta_n = \left\lVert G_{Sn} - G_{Rn} \right\rVert_1 \tag{5}$$

Once the difference and the mask are available, it is possible to obtain the thresholded gaussian difference as:

$$IFGDT_n = \Sigma M\left(T_n, \delta_n\right) \tag{6}$$

where the mask function is:

$$M(x,y) = \begin{cases} 1, & \text{if } y > x \\ 0, & \text{otherwise} \end{cases} \tag{7}$$

Defining a feature where the difference between a frame and its subsequent frame is taken into account. This is expected to help discriminate high motion sequences from those with fewer changes in the time domain.

5.2   Statistical Time Aggregators

Finally each metric was aggregated in the time domain, obtaining a unique value for the whole sequence. Notwithstanding its simplicity, the best results in terms of accuracy were obtained by averaging the values over the sequence. More sophisticated aggregators such as Euclidean or Manhattan distances or statistical measures such as standard deviation or cross-correlation were tested with worse classification results.

6   One-Class Support Vector Machine for Classification

With the previously introduced set of features, one can tackle the problem of verifying the good faith computational effort from the perspective of an novelty detection problem [15]. This comes from the fact that the space of possible attacks is too large for making any attempt at creating fully comprehensive labeled datasets. However, the generation of well transcoded renditions is very straightforward, leaving the problem as that of one-class classification. The best performer among the techniques we tested was the One Class Support Vector Machine (OC-SVM). These estimators basically compute a decision function minimizing the 'volume' around selected features measured over a set of target samples. These samples being the well transcoded assets described before as non-tampered. What we obtain from this model is a one-dimensional continuous value telling us how far in the n-feature-dimensional space a given asset is from a boundary. The n-feature space in our case is conformed by the metrics extracted from the comparisons between original and renditions. Those renditions that are "within" the boundaries have positive values. Negative values correspond to outliers. Zero is the boundary itself. This boundary is computed on the basis of what a "good transcoding" is. Figure 2 displays our dataset split into attacks, training and test subsets after being presented to the OC-SVM and having their distances to the decision function computed. The set of attacks was created synthetically and comprises renditions with watermarks, unacceptably low bitrates, rotated, symmetrically flipped, or vignetted. An important constraint for this particular use case resides in the consequences of classification errors. When transcodification jobs are identified as attempts to cheat, the protocol establishes that actual capital presented as proof of stack is destroyed. For this reason, the occurrence of false negatives had to be kept at a minimum. The ν parameter of the OC-SVM was set to 0.01 to fix a True Positive Rate (TPR) of 1 - ν. This comes with a trade off in the True Negative Rate (TNR) falling off to 88.7%. Further exploration of the nature of the misclassified attacks revealed a high number of low bitrate and small watermarks among them, whose detection was difficult even to the human eye. Further research is proposed in this line using supervised learning to further increase the TNR. This however was not a top priority for the research due to the fact that the network counts on other specific mechanisms to counter effect the impact of such a small number of false positives.

6.1   The Choice of the Accuracy Metric

We have chosen an accuracy metric such as f beta, with beta = 20, just to emphasize the weight of true positives in detriment of true negatives (i.e. to give more weight to the recall). This is due to an important constraint for this particular use case: the consequences of classification errors. When transcodification jobs are identified as attempts to cheat, the protocol establishes that actual capital presented as proof of stack is destroyed. For this reason, the occurrence of false negatives had to be kept at a minimum.

7   Results

We trained an OC-SVM estimator with a full sequence of frames of each sample (up to 60 when available in the source videos) using a subset of well encoded assets (circa 15k) from our dataset. The same procedure was followed for the creation of the model used in the production API (same features, same number

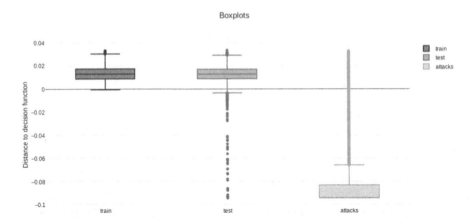

Fig. 2. Boxplot diagram of our dataset and the behavior of the assets as interpreted by our OC-SVM. The attacks subset (green) has a very large portion of its specimens very far from the decision function. The well transcoded specimens are used for training (in blue). The test set is comprised only of untampered encodings. (Color figure online)

of training specimens). In order to test its validity, we measured its accuracy in terms of True Positive Rate (TPR), True Negative Rate (TNR) and F-20 score. The size of the set of tampered videos amounts to circa 180k, and the remaining circa 4k were legitimate assets used for testing. Results are shown in Table 1. SSIM and PSNR based models are also included for comparison. For these, we took the 0.01 percentile metric values of the untampered subset and used it to prescribe a threshold below which everything was considered an attack. Moreover, to account for the effect of the resolution, we prescribed specific thresholds for each of them (720p, 480p, 360p, 288p and 144p). As can be seen, despite of the high TPR obtained by these models, the number of true negatives is unacceptably low.

Table 1. Accuracy metrics for OC-SVM trained on the dataset presented.

Frames	F-20	TNR	TPR
OC-SVM	0.9678	0.8867	0.9808
SSIM	0.9281	0.3034	0.9920
PSNR	0.9375	0.3930	0.9937

A further effort to reduce the computational cost of our method when obtaining the aggregators mentioned above, a series of experiments was carried away. Their aim was to determine to what extent the choice of a number of samples affected accuracy. Using this trained model, we iteratively repeated the prediction passing to it the average of the values of frames at random positions for each and every asset. We chose a repetition number of 500 to have a large enough sample size. The number of sampled frames was increased in steps of 5, between 5 and 55. With these results, we elaborated Table 2 aggregating the mean values after all experiments, their respective width of the 99% confidence interval and the degradation of the metrics due to reducing the sampled frames.

Table 2. Mean accuracy values (Acc.), 99% confidence intervals length (Conf.), and average metric degradation (Deg.) of the metrics after 500 experiments for each number of sampled frames.

	F20			TNR			TPR		
	Acc.	Conf.	Deg.	Acc.	Conf.	Deg.	Acc.	Conf.	Deg.
5	0.9541	0.0003	1.41	0.8915	0.0002	−0.54	0.9663	0.0003	1.48
10	0.9616	0.0002	0.64	0.8899	0.0001	−0.36	0.9741	0.0002	0.68
15	0.9639	0.0002	0.40	0.8889	0.0001	−0.25	0.9765	0.0002	0.44
20	0.9653	0.0002	0.26	0.8883	0.0001	−0.18	0.9780	0.0002	0.29
25	0.9660	0.0001	0.19	0.8879	0.0001	−0.14	0.9788	0.0001	0.20
30	0.9665	0.0001	0.13	0.8877	0.0001	−0.11	0.9793	0.0001	0.15
35	0.9668	0.0001	0.10	0.8874	0.0001	−0.08	0.9796	0.0001	0.12
40	0.9670	0.0001	0.08	0.8873	0.0001	−0.07	0.9799	0.0001	0.09
45	0.9673	0.0001	0.05	0.8872	0.0001	−0.06	0.9802	0.0001	0.06
50	0.9674	0.0001	0.04	0.8871	0.0001	−0.05	0.9804	0.0001	0.04
55	0.9676	0.0001	0.02	0.8870	0.0001	−0.03	0.9805	0.0001	0.03

In summary, we can see from the accuracy column that our model is fairly robust even when a small number of frames is sampled. The 99% confidence thresholds remain remarkably narrow for all cases. Besides, the average metric degradation column shows that by using less frames to compare, the accuracy degradation is also almost negligible. The first entry of the degradation column manifests this clearly: in the worst case of sampling just 5 frames we only lose 1.41% of F-20 with respect to computing the metrics over all 60 frames.

8   Conclusions and Further Work

A complete framework for verification of video transcoding has been presented in this article. The main innovation introduced is a set of full reference features that allow for high accuracy in the classification of well encoded videos as such. We have also introduced a large dataset of video samples with tampered and well transcoded renditions that can further be exploited to study video quality metrics. Nevertheless, the performance in the classification of poorly transcoded videos still has some room for improvements, with more than 10% of the bad transcoded samples being misclassified as good. As a future work, the undergoing research contemplates improving the classification by means of extracting visual QoE metrics using the presented set of features. These QoE metrics, such as SSIM or PSNR, can be predicted and fed to a supervised learning classifier enhancing the ability to evaluate the final transcoded result and benchmark contributors to the P2P network.

References

1. Aggarwal, R.D.S.N.: Video content authentication techniques: a comprehensive survey. Multimedia Syst. **24**(2), 211–240 (2017). https://doi.org/10.1007/s00530-017-0538-9
2. Aiyer, A.S., Alvisi, L., Clement, A., Dahlin, M., Martin, J.P., Porth, C.: BAR fault tolerance for cooperative services. ACM SIGOPS Oper. Syst. Rev. **39**(5), 45 (2005). https://doi.org/10.1145/1095809.1095816
3. Bampis, C.G., Bovik, A.C.: Feature-based prediction of streaming video QoE: distortions stalling and memory. Sig. Process.: Image Commun. **68**, 218–228 (2018). https://doi.org/10.1016/j.image.2018.05.017
4. Crowcroft, J., Moreton, T.D., Pratt, I., Twigg, A.: Peer-to-peer systems and the grid. In: The Grid 2e: Blueprint for a New Computing Infrastructure. University of Cambridge Computer Laboratory (2003)
5. Duanmu, Z., Rehman, A., Wang, Z.: A quality-of-experience database for adaptive video streaming. IEEE Trans. Broadcast. **64**(2), 474–487 (2018). https://doi.org/10.1109/tbc.2018.2822870
6. Farid, H.: Image forgery detection [a survey]. IEEE Sig. Process. Mag. **26**, 2 (2009). https://farid.berkeley.edu/downloads/publications/spm09.pdf. Accessed 27 Dec 2019
7. Fedak, G., He, H., Moca, M., Bendella, W., Alves, E.: Blockchain-based decentralized cloud computing. Technical report, iExec (2018). https://iex.ec/wp-content/uploads/pdf/iExec-WPv3.0-English.pdf. Accessed 27 Dec 2019
8. Google: Choose live encoder settings, bitrates, and resolutions (2020). https://support.google.com/youtube/answer/2853702?hl=en
9. Hammad, R.A.M.: Image quality and forgery detection copula-based algorithms. Ph.D. thesis, Cairo University (2008). https://doi.org/10.24124/2016/bpgub1124
10. Milani, S., et al.: An overview on video forensics. APSIPA Trans. Sig. Inf. Process. **1**, e2 (2012). https://doi.org/10.1017/ATSIP.2012.2
11. Nielson, S.J., Crosby, S.A., Wallach, D.S.: A taxonomy of rational attacks. In: Castro, M., van Renesse, R. (eds.) IPTPS 2005. LNCS, vol. 3640, pp. 36–46. Springer, Heidelberg (2005). https://doi.org/10.1007/11558989_4
12. Petkanics, D., Tang, E.: Livepeer white paper. Technical report, Livepeer (2018). https://github.com/livepeer/wiki. Accessed 27 Dec 2019
13. Pinson, M.H.: The consumer digital video library [best of the web]. IEEE Sig. Process. Mag. **30**(4), 172–174 (2013). https://doi.org/10.1109/msp.2013.2258265
14. Rao, K., Yip, P.: Chapter 1 - discrete cosine transform. In: Rao, K., Yip, P. (eds.) Discrete Cosine Transform, pp. 1–6. Academic Press, San Diego (1990). https://doi.org/10.1016/B978-0-08-092534-9.50007-2
15. Schölkopf, B., Williamson, R., Smola, A., Shawe-Taylor, J., Platt, J.: Support vector method for novelty detection. In: Proceedings of the 12th International Conference on Neural Information Processing, NIPS 1999, vol. 12, pp. 582–588 (1999)

16. Smith, A.R.: Color gamut transform pairs. ACM SIGGRAPH Comput. Graph. **12**(3), 12–19 (1978). https://doi.org/10.1145/965139.807361
17. Teutsch, J., Reitwießner, C.: A scalable verification solution for blockchains. ArXiv abs/1908.04756 (2019)
18. Timmerer, C., Smole, M., Mueller, C.: Efficient multi-codec support for OTT services: HEVC/h.265 and/or AV1? In: 2018 NAB BEIT Proceedings, p. 5. National Association of Broadcasters (NAB), Washington DC, USA, April 2018
19. Van der Walt, S., et al.: scikit-image: image processing in python. PeerJ **2**, e453 (2014)
20. Wang, H., et al.: Videoset: a large-scale compressed video quality dataset based on JND measurement. J. Vis. Commun. Image Represent. **46**, 292–302 (2017). https://doi.org/10.1016/j.jvcir.2017.04.009, http://www.sciencedirect.com/science/article/pii/S1047320317300950
21. Wang, Y., Inguva, S., Adsumilli, B.: YouTube UGC dataset for video compression research. In: 2019 IEEE 21st International Workshop on Multimedia Signal Processing (MMSP). IEEE, September 2019. https://doi.org/10.1109/mmsp.2019.8901772

Generalized Subspace Learning by Roweis Discriminant Analysis

Benyamin Ghojogh$^{(\boxtimes)}$ (ID), Fakhri Karray (ID), and Mark Crowley (ID)

Department of Electrical and Computer Engineering, University of Waterloo,
Waterloo, ON, Canada
{bghojogh,karray,mcrowley}@uwaterloo.ca

Abstract. We present a new method which generalizes subspace learning based on eigenvalue and generalized eigenvalue problems. This method, Roweis Discriminant Analysis (RDA) named after Sam Roweis, is a family of infinite number of algorithms where Principal Component Analysis (PCA), Supervised PCA (SPCA), and Fisher Discriminant Analysis (FDA) are special cases. One of the extreme special cases, named Double Supervised Discriminant Analysis (DSDA), uses the labels twice and it is novel. We propose a dual for RDA for some special cases. We also propose kernel RDA, generalizing kernel PCA, kernel SPCA, and kernel FDA, using both dual RDA and representation theory. Our theoretical analysis explains previously known facts such as why SPCA can use regression but FDA cannot, why PCA and SPCA have duals but FDA does not, why kernel PCA and kernel SPCA use kernel trick but kernel FDA does not, and why PCA is the best linear method for reconstruction. Roweisfaces and kernel Roweisfaces are also proposed generalizing eigenfaces, Fisherfaces, supervised eigenfaces, and their kernel variants. We also report experiments showing the effectiveness of RDA and kernel RDA on some benchmark datasets.

Keywords: Roweis discriminant analysis · Subspace learning · Principal component analysis · Fisher discriminant analysis · Supervised PCA

1 Introduction

Subspace and manifold learning are very useful in machine learning and pattern analysis for feature extraction, data visualization, and dimensionality reduction [1]. The submanifold of data can be either linear or nonlinear. Principal Component Analysis (PCA) [2] is one of the first methods in linear subspace learning. Fisher Discriminant Analysis (FDA) [3] is one of the first linear supervised subspace learning methods. Kernel PCA [2,4,5] uses the dual of PCA and the kernel trick [6] to handle nonlinearity. Kernel FDA [3,7] handles nonlinearity in a supervised manner. Supervised PCA (SPCA) [8] makes use of the empirical estimation of the Hilbert-Schmidt Independence Criterion (HSIC) [9]. It tries to

© Springer Nature Switzerland AG 2020
A. Campilho et al. (Eds.): ICIAR 2020, LNCS 12131, pp. 328–342, 2020.
https://doi.org/10.1007/978-3-030-50347-5_29

maximize the dependence of projected data and the labels in order to use the information of labels for better embedding.

In this paper, we propose a generalized subspace learning method, Roweis Discriminant Analysis (RDA), named after Sam Roweis (1972–2010) who contributed significantly to subspace and manifold learning. The proposed RDA is a family of infinite number of subspace learning methods including PCA, FDA, and SPCA as its special cases. The main contributions of our paper are as follows: (1) proposing RDA as a generalized subspace learning method based on eigenvalue and generalized eigenvalue problems, (2) proposing Double Supervised Discriminant Analysis (DSDA), a novel method, as one of the extreme cases in RDA, (3) proposing kernel RDA generalizing kernel PCA, kernel SPCA, and kernel FDA, (4) proposing Roweisfaces and kernel Roweisfaces for demonstrating the generalizability of the RDA approach for the eigenfaces [10], kernel eigenfaces [11], Fisherfaces [12], kernel Fisherfaces [13] and supervised eigenfaces [2], and (5) explaining the reasons behind some of the characteristics of PCA, SPCA, and FDA such as (I) why SPCA can be used for both classification and regression but FDA is only for classification, (II) why PCA and SPCA have their dual methods but FDA does not have a dual, (III) why kernel PCA and kernel SPCA can use kernel trick but kernel FDA uses representation theory rather than kernel trick, and (IV) why PCA is the best linear method for reconstruction.

Background on Subspace and Projection: Let $\boldsymbol{X} = [\boldsymbol{x}_1, \ldots, \boldsymbol{x}_n] \in \mathbb{R}^{d \times n}$ and $\boldsymbol{X}_t = [\boldsymbol{x}_{t,1}, \ldots, \boldsymbol{x}_{t,n_t}] \in \mathbb{R}^{d \times n_t}$ be the training and test data, respectively, where n, n_t, and d are the training size, test size, and the dimensionality, respectively. The projection of data $\boldsymbol{X}$ into the p-dimensional subspace $(p \leq d)$ and its reconstruction after the projection are $\mathbb{R}^{p \times n} \ni \widetilde{\boldsymbol{X}} := \boldsymbol{U}^\top \boldsymbol{X}$ and $\mathbb{R}^{d \times n} \ni \widehat{\boldsymbol{X}} := \boldsymbol{U}\boldsymbol{U}^\top \boldsymbol{X} = \boldsymbol{U}\widetilde{\boldsymbol{X}}$, respectively [14], where $\boldsymbol{U} \in \mathbb{R}^{d \times p}$ is the projection matrix. Likewise, the projection and reconstruction of the out-of-sample data are $\mathbb{R}^{p \times n_t} \ni \widetilde{\boldsymbol{X}}_t := \boldsymbol{U}^\top \boldsymbol{X}_t$ and $\mathbb{R}^{d \times n} \ni \widehat{\boldsymbol{X}}_t := \boldsymbol{U}\widetilde{\boldsymbol{X}}_t$, respectively.

The covariance matrix, or the total scatter, is defined as:

$$\mathbb{R}^{n \times n} \ni \boldsymbol{S}_T := \breve{\boldsymbol{X}}\breve{\boldsymbol{X}}^\top = \boldsymbol{X}\boldsymbol{H}\boldsymbol{H}\boldsymbol{X}^\top = \boldsymbol{X}\boldsymbol{H}\boldsymbol{X}^\top, \tag{1}$$

where $\mathbb{R}^{n \times n} \ni \boldsymbol{H} := \boldsymbol{I} - (1/n)\boldsymbol{1}\boldsymbol{1}^\top$ is the idempotent centering matrix and $\breve{\boldsymbol{X}} := \boldsymbol{X}\boldsymbol{H}$.

Consider a scatter $\boldsymbol{S}$. The term $\mathbf{tr}(\boldsymbol{U}^\top \boldsymbol{S} \boldsymbol{U})$, where $\mathbf{tr}(.)$ is trace of matrix, can be interpreted as the variance of the projected data. Maximizing this variance with orthogonal bases is:

$$\underset{\boldsymbol{U}}{\text{maximize}} \quad \mathbf{tr}(\boldsymbol{U}^\top \boldsymbol{S} \boldsymbol{U}), \qquad \text{subject to} \quad \boldsymbol{U}^\top \boldsymbol{U} = \boldsymbol{I}, \tag{2}$$

whose solution is $\boldsymbol{S}\boldsymbol{U} = \boldsymbol{U}\boldsymbol{\Lambda}$ which is the eigenvalue problem for $\boldsymbol{S}$ [15]. The eigenvectors and eigenvalues are sorted from the leading (largest eigenvalue) to the trailing (smallest eigenvalue) because we are maximizing in the optimization problem (the reason lies in the second order condition).

Now consider two types of scatters, e.g., $S_1 \in \mathbb{R}^{n \times n}$ and $S_2 \in \mathbb{R}^{n \times n}$. Maximizing the variance while the manipulated bases by S_2 are orthogonal is:

$$\underset{U}{\text{maximize}} \quad \mathbf{tr}(U^\top S_1 U), \qquad \text{subject to} \quad U^\top S_2 U = I, \tag{3}$$

whose solution is the generalized eigenvalue problem (S_1, S_2) [15]. Many of the subspace learning methods have the optimization form of Eq. (2) or Eq. (3).

Background on PCA, FDA, and SPCA: The optimization problem in PCA is expressed as [2]:

$$\underset{U}{\text{maximize}} \quad \mathbf{tr}(U^\top S_T U), \qquad \text{subject to} \quad U^\top U = I, \tag{4}$$

where $S_T \in \mathbb{R}^{n \times n}$ is the total scatter defined in Eq. (1). On the other hand, FDA maximizes the Fisher criterion which is a generalized Rayleigh-Ritz quotient [16]. The optimization in FDA is [3]: maximize $\mathbf{tr}(U^\top S_B U)$, subject to $U^\top S_W U = I$, where S_B and S_W are the between and within scatters, respectively. The total scatter can be considered as the summation of the between and within scatters [17]: $S_T = S_B + S_W \implies S_B = S_T - S_W$. Therefore, the optimization in FDA can be:

$$\underset{U}{\text{maximize}} \quad \mathbf{tr}(U^\top S_T U), \qquad \text{subject to} \quad U^\top S_W U = I. \tag{5}$$

Comparing the Eqs. (4) and (5) gives a hint for the connection between PCA and FDA.

SPCA [8] uses the empirical estimation of the HSIC [9]. It uses HSIC for the projected data $U^\top X$ and the labels Y and maximizes the dependence of them. Its optimization is [2]:

$$\underset{U}{\text{maximize}} \quad \mathbf{tr}(U^\top X H K_y H X^\top U), \qquad \text{subject to} \quad U^\top U = I, \tag{6}$$

where K_y is the kernel matrix over the labels. Hence, the SPCA directions are the eigenvectors of $X H K_y H X^\top$. This term, restricted to a linear kernel for K_y, is used as the between scatter in [18] hinting for a connection between SPCA and FDA. Overall, comparing Eqs. (4), (5), and (6) and considering the general forms in Eqs. (2) and (3) show that these methods belong to a family of methods based on eigenvalue and generalized eigenvalue problems. This gave us a motivation to propose RDA.

2   Roweis Discriminant Analysis

2.1   Methodology

RDA aims at maximizing the $\mathbf{tr}(U^\top R_1 U)$ interpreted as the scatter of projection, while requiring the manipulated projection directions to be orthonormal. Therefore, the optimization of RDA is formulated as:

$$\underset{U}{\text{maximize}} \quad \mathbf{tr}(U^\top R_1 U), \qquad \text{subject to} \quad U^\top R_2 U = I, \tag{7}$$

where R_1 and R_2 are the first and second *Roweis matrices* defined as:

$$\mathbb{R}^{d \times d} \ni R_1 := XHPHX^\top, \tag{8}$$

$$\mathbb{R}^{d \times d} \ni R_2 := r_2 S_W + (1 - r_2) I, \tag{9}$$

respectively, where:

$$\mathbb{R}^{n \times n} \ni P := r_1 K_y + (1 - r_1) I. \tag{10}$$

The $r_1 \in [0, 1]$ and $r_2 \in [0, 1]$ are the first and second *Roweis factors*. Note that HPH in Eq. (8) is double-centered P. The solution to Eq. (7) is the generalized eigenvalue problem (R_1, R_2) [15]. We define the *Roweis criterion* which is maximized in RDA as $\mathbf{tr}(U^\top R_1 U)/\mathbf{tr}(U^\top R_2 U)$. This criterion is a generalized Rayleigh-Ritz quotient [16].

2.2   The Special Cases of RDA and the Roweis Map

Consider the Eqs. (8), (9), and (10). If we consider the extreme cases of r_1 and r_2, we find an interesting relationship:

$$r_1 = 0, \, r_2 = 0 \implies \text{RDA} \equiv \text{PCA}, \tag{11}$$

$$r_1 = 0, \, r_2 = 1 \implies \text{RDA} \equiv \text{FDA}, \tag{12}$$

$$r_1 = 1, \, r_2 = 0 \implies \text{RDA} \equiv \text{SPCA}, \tag{13}$$

by comparing Eq. (7) with Eqs. (4), (5), and (6) and noticing the Eq. (1). We see that PCA, FDA, and SPCA are all special cases of RDA.

In fact, RDA is a family of infinite number of algorithms for subspace learning with different values of r_1 and r_2. We define a map, named *Roweis map*, which includes the infinite number of special cases of RDA where three of its corners are PCA, FDA, and SPCA. The rows and columns of the Roweis map are the values of r_1 and r_2, respectively. Figure 1-a shows this map.

The case $r_1 = r_2 = 1$ is not yet proposed in the literature, where Eq. (7) is:

$$\underset{U}{\text{maximize}} \quad \mathbf{tr}(U^\top XHK_yHX^\top U), \qquad \text{subject to} \quad U^\top S_W U = I, \tag{14}$$

whose solution is the generalized eigenvalue problem $(XHK_yHX^\top, S_W)$ [15]. This optimization uses the labels twice, once in the kernel over the labels and once in the within scatter; hence, we name it *Double Supervised Discriminant Analysis (DSDA)*.

2.3   Properties of the RDA

Properties of the Roweis Factors: According to Eqs. (9) and (10), we have:

$$P = \begin{cases} K_y & \text{if } r_1 = 1, \\ I & \text{if } r_1 = 0. \end{cases} \qquad R_2 = \begin{cases} S_W & \text{if } r_2 = 1, \\ I & \text{if } r_2 = 0. \end{cases} \tag{15}$$

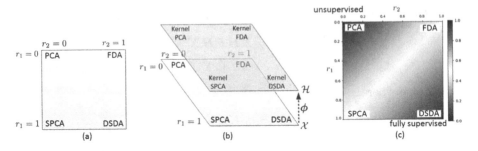

Fig. 1. (a) The Roweis map including infinite number of subspace learning methods and its special cases, (b) the map in its input and feature spaces where the map in the feature space is pulled from the map in the input space, and (c) the supervision level shown on the Roweis map.

Therefore, we can conclude that if the Roweis factor is zero and one, we do not use the labels and we fully use the labels, respectively. Therefore, the Roweis factor is a measure of using labels or being supervised. As we have two Roweis factors, we define $[0, 1] \ni s := (r_1 + r_2)/2$ as the *supervision level* which is a planar function depicted in Fig. 1-c. Note that the extremes $s = 0$ and $s = 1$ refer to the unsupervised and fully (double) supervised subspace learning, respectively, while $s = 0.5$ uses the labels once as in both FDA and SPCA.

The K_y is a soft measure of similarity between the labels while the S_W uses the labels strictly for knowing which data instance belongs to which class. It shows that if we use S_W ($r_2 \neq 0$), the labels must be for classes in classification; however, if using solely K_y ($r_2 = 0$), the labels can be either for classification or regression. This sheds light to why SPCA (with $r_2 = 0$) can be used for both classification and regression tasks [8] but FDA (with $r_2 = 1$) is only for classification.

Properties of the Roweis Matrices: The within scatter S_W, the kernel matrix K_y, and the identity matrix are positive semi-definite and symmetric and $r_1, r_2 \in [0, 1]$, so $P \succeq 0, R_1 \succeq 0, R_2 \succeq 0, R_1 = R_1^\top, R_2 = R_2^\top, P = P^\top$. We also have $\mathbb{R}^{n \times n} \ni K_y := \Phi(Y)^\top \Phi(Y)$ where $\Phi(Y) \in \mathbb{R}^t$ is the pulled Y to the feature space [6], where usually $t \gg \ell$. Hence, $\mathbf{rank}(K_y) \leq \min(n, t)$. According to Eq. (10) and the subadditivity property of the rank, we have $\mathbf{rank}(P) \leq \mathbf{rank}(K_y) + \mathbf{rank}(I_n) \leq \min(n, t) + n$. In the extreme cases $r_1 = 0$ and $r_1 = 1$, the rank of P is n and $\leq \min(n, t)$, respectively. According to Eq. (8), we have $\mathbf{rank}(R_1) \leq \min(\mathbf{rank}(X) + \mathbf{rank}(H) + \mathbf{rank}(P)) \leq \min(d, n - 1, t) = \min(d, n - 1)$, where the -1 is because of subtracting the mean in centering the matrix. Also we have $\mathbf{rank}(S_W) \leq \min(d, n - 1)$. According to Eq. (9) and the subadditivity property of the rank, we have $\mathbf{rank}(R_2) \leq \mathbf{rank}(S_W) + \mathbf{rank}(I_d) \leq \min(d, n - 1) + d$. In the extreme cases $r_2 = 0$ and $r_2 = 1$, the rank of R_2 is d and $\leq \min(d, n - 1)$, respectively.

Dimensionality of the RDA Subspace: We can solve the generalized eigenvalue problem (R_1, R_2) as $U = \mathbf{eig}(R_2^{-1} R_1)$ [15], where $\mathbf{eig}(.)$ stacks the eigenvectors column-wise. If R_2 is singular, we strengthen its diagonal as $U = \text{eig}((R_2 + \varepsilon I)^{-1} R_1)$, where ε is a very small positive number, large enough to make R_2 full rank [7]. We have $\text{rank}(R_2^{-1} R_1) \le \min\left(\text{rank}(R_2^{-1}), \text{rank}(R_1)\right) \le \min(d, n-1)$. Therefore, $p \le \min(d, n-1)$ which is a bound on the dimensionality of RDA subspace.

2.4 Dual RDA for $r_2 = 0$

As R_1 is symmetric and positive semi-definite, we can decompose it: $R_1 \overset{(a)}{=} \Psi_R \Omega_R \Psi_R^\top = \Psi_R \Omega_R^{(1/2)} \Omega_R^{(1/2)} \Psi_R^\top \overset{(b)}{=} W W^\top$, where (a) is because of SVD ($\Psi_R \in \mathbb{R}^{d \times k}$, $\Omega_R \in \mathbb{R}^{k \times k}$, $k := \min(d, n)$) and (b) is for $\mathbb{R}^{d \times k} \ni W := \Psi_R \Omega_R^{(1/2)}$. If $r_2 = 0$, we have $R_2 = I$ according to Eq. (9). In this case, the Eq. (7) becomes similar to Eq. (2) and thus the solution which is the generalized eigenvalue problem (R_1, R_2) gets reduced to the eigenvalue problem for R_1. Consider the incomplete SVD, $W = U \Sigma V^\top$, where $U \in \mathbb{R}^{d \times k}$, $V \in \mathbb{R}^{d \times k}$, and $\Sigma \in \mathbb{R}^{k \times k}$ are the left and right singular vectors and the singular values, respectively. The dual RDA exists only for $r_2 = 0$ because in SVD of W, the U is an orthogonal matrix so $U^\top U = I$. This implies that the constraint in Eq. (7) should be $U^\top U = I$ which means $R_2 = I$ so $r_2 = 0$. This clarifies why PCA and SPCA (with $r_2 = 0$) have their dual methods but FDA (with $r_2 = 1$) does not have a dual.

Note that the projection and reconstruction of the training data are $\widetilde{X} = \Sigma^{-1} V^\top \Omega_R^{(1/2)\top} \Psi_R^\top X$ and $\widehat{X} = \Psi_R \Omega_R^{(1/2)} V \Sigma^{-2} V^\top \Omega_R^{(1/2)\top} \Psi_R^\top X$, respectively, and the projection and reconstruction of the out-of-sample data are $\widetilde{X}_t = \Sigma^{-1} V^\top \Omega_R^{(1/2)\top} \Psi_R^\top X_t$ and $\widehat{X}_t = \Psi_R \Omega_R^{(1/2)} V \Sigma^{-2} V^\top \Omega_R^{(1/2)\top} \Psi_R^\top X_t$, respectively [2]. The dual RDA is very useful especially if the dimensionality of data is much greater than the sample size of data, i.e., $d \gg n$ because V is used rather than U.

3 Kernel RDA

Let $\phi : \mathcal{X} \to \mathcal{H}$ be the pulling function mapping the data $x \in \mathcal{X}$ to the feature space $\mathcal{H}$. In other words, $x \mapsto \phi(x) \in \mathbb{R}^t$ where $t \gg d$. The kernel over two vectors x_1 and x_2 is $k(x_1, x_2) := \phi(x_1)^\top \phi(x_2)$ [6]. We can have two types of kernel RDA, i.e., the dual RDA (or kernel trick) and representation theory [19]. The former holds for only two special cases but the latter works for the entire range of the Roweis map.

3.1 Kernel RDA Using Dual RDA for Special Cases

If $r_2 = 0$, we have the dual RDA and can use it for kernel RDA using the kernel trick. However, the dual RDA is useful for the kernel trick in the two cases of $r_1 = 0$ and $r_1 = 1$ because in these cases, the inner product of data points appear useful for the kernel trick. So, kernel RDA using kernel trick is valid for

$r_1 = r_2 = 0$ (i.e., PCA) and $r_1 = 0, r_2 = 1$ (i.e., SPCA). This explains why, in the literature, PCA and SPCA (with $r_2 = 0$) have their kernel methods using kernel trick (or their dual) but kernel FDA (with $r_1 = 0, r_2 = 1$) uses representation theory and not the kernel trick. Here, we do not detail the kernel RDA using the kernel trick as it is reduced to kernel PCA [4,5] and kernel SPCA [8]. For more details, refer to [2] and [20].

3.2   Direct Kernel RDA

Methodology: According to the representation theory [19], any pulled solution (direction) $\phi(u) \in \mathcal{H}$ must lie in the span of all the training vectors pulled to $\mathcal{H}$, i.e., $\boldsymbol{\Phi}(\boldsymbol{X}) = [\phi(\boldsymbol{x}_1), \ldots, \phi(\boldsymbol{x}_n)] \in \mathbb{R}^{t \times n}$. Hence $\mathbb{R}^t \ni \phi(\boldsymbol{u}) = \sum_{i=1}^{n} \theta_i \, \phi(\boldsymbol{x}_i) = \boldsymbol{\Phi}(\boldsymbol{X}) \, \boldsymbol{\theta}$, where $\mathbb{R}^n \ni \boldsymbol{\theta} = [\theta_1, \ldots, \theta_n]^\top$ is the unknown vector of coefficients, and $\phi(\boldsymbol{u}) \in \mathbb{R}^t$ is the pulled RDA direction to the feature space. The pulled directions can be put together in $\mathbb{R}^{t \times p} \ni \boldsymbol{\Phi}(\boldsymbol{U}) = [\phi(\boldsymbol{u}_1), \ldots, \phi(\boldsymbol{u}_p)]$ to have $\mathbb{R}^{t \times p} \ni \boldsymbol{\Phi}(\boldsymbol{U}) = \boldsymbol{\Phi}(\boldsymbol{X}) \, \boldsymbol{\Theta}$. where $\mathbb{R}^{n \times p} \ni \boldsymbol{\Theta} = [\boldsymbol{\theta}_1, \ldots, \boldsymbol{\theta}_p]$.

In order to have RDA in the feature space, we first kernelize the objective function of the Eq. (7):

$$\mathbf{tr}\big(\boldsymbol{\Phi}(\boldsymbol{U})^\top \boldsymbol{\Phi}(\boldsymbol{R}_1) \, \boldsymbol{\Phi}(\boldsymbol{U})\big) \overset{(8)}{=} \mathbf{tr}\big(\boldsymbol{\Phi}(\boldsymbol{U})^\top \boldsymbol{\Phi}(\boldsymbol{X}) \boldsymbol{H} \boldsymbol{P} \boldsymbol{H} \boldsymbol{\Phi}(\boldsymbol{X})^\top \boldsymbol{\Phi}(\boldsymbol{U})\big) = \mathbf{tr}\big[\boldsymbol{\Theta}^\top$$
$$\boldsymbol{\Phi}(\boldsymbol{X})^\top \boldsymbol{\Phi}(\boldsymbol{X}) \boldsymbol{H} \boldsymbol{P} \boldsymbol{H} \boldsymbol{\Phi}(\boldsymbol{X})^\top \boldsymbol{\Phi}(\boldsymbol{X}) \, \boldsymbol{\Theta}\big] = \mathbf{tr}\big(\boldsymbol{\Theta}^\top \boldsymbol{K}_x \, \boldsymbol{H} \boldsymbol{P} \boldsymbol{H} \boldsymbol{K}_x \, \boldsymbol{\Theta}\big) = \mathbf{tr}\big(\boldsymbol{\Theta}^\top \boldsymbol{M} \, \boldsymbol{\Theta}\big),$$

where $\mathbb{R}^{n \times n} \ni \boldsymbol{K}_x := \boldsymbol{\Phi}(\boldsymbol{X})^\top \boldsymbol{\Phi}(\boldsymbol{X})$ and:

$$\mathbb{R}^{n \times n} \ni \boldsymbol{M} := \boldsymbol{K}_x \, \boldsymbol{H} \boldsymbol{P} \boldsymbol{H} \boldsymbol{K}_x. \tag{16}$$

In order to kernelize the constraint in the Eq. (7), it is easier to first consider a one-dimensional subspace and then extend it to multi-dimensional subspace. We can prove (see [20]) that $\phi(\boldsymbol{u})^\top \boldsymbol{\Phi}(\boldsymbol{S}_W) \, \phi(\boldsymbol{u}) = \boldsymbol{\theta}^\top \big(\sum_{j=1}^{c} \boldsymbol{K}_j \boldsymbol{H}_j \boldsymbol{K}_j^\top \big) \boldsymbol{\theta} = \boldsymbol{\theta}^\top \boldsymbol{N} \, \boldsymbol{\theta}$, where c is the number of classes, n_j is the sample size of the j-th class, $\mathbb{R}^{n_j \times n_j} \ni \boldsymbol{H}_j := \boldsymbol{I} - (1/n_j) \mathbf{1} \mathbf{1}^\top$, $\mathbb{R}^{n \times n_j} \ni \boldsymbol{K}_j := \boldsymbol{\Phi}(\boldsymbol{X})^\top \boldsymbol{\Phi}(\boldsymbol{X}_j)$, and:

$$\mathbb{R}^{n \times n} \ni \boldsymbol{N} := \sum_{j=1}^{c} \boldsymbol{K}_j \boldsymbol{H}_j \boldsymbol{K}_j^\top. \tag{17}$$

If the subspace is one-dimensional, the constraint in the Eq. (7) is kernelized as $\phi(\boldsymbol{u})^\top \boldsymbol{\Phi}(\boldsymbol{R}_2) \, \phi(\boldsymbol{u}) \overset{(9)}{=} r_2 \, \phi(\boldsymbol{u})^\top \boldsymbol{\Phi}(\boldsymbol{S}_W) \, \phi(\boldsymbol{u}) + (1 - r_2) \, \phi(\boldsymbol{u})^\top \phi(\boldsymbol{u}) = r_2 \, \boldsymbol{\theta}^\top \boldsymbol{N} \boldsymbol{\theta} + (1 - r_2) \, \boldsymbol{\theta}^\top \boldsymbol{K}_x \, \boldsymbol{\theta} = \boldsymbol{\theta}^\top \big(r_2 \, \boldsymbol{N} + (1 - r_2) \, \boldsymbol{K}_x\big) \, \boldsymbol{\theta} = \boldsymbol{\theta}^\top \boldsymbol{L} \, \boldsymbol{\theta}$, where:

$$\mathbb{R}^{n \times n} \ni \boldsymbol{L} := r_2 \, \boldsymbol{N} + (1 - r_2) \, \boldsymbol{K}_x. \tag{18}$$

Similarly, we can extend to multi-dimensional subspace: $\mathbf{tr}\big(\phi(\boldsymbol{U})^\top \boldsymbol{\Phi}(\boldsymbol{R}_2) \, \phi(\boldsymbol{U})\big) = \mathbf{tr}\big(\boldsymbol{\Theta}^\top \boldsymbol{L} \boldsymbol{\Theta}\big)$. Hence, the Roweis criterion is $\mathbf{tr}\big(\boldsymbol{\Theta}^\top \boldsymbol{M} \, \boldsymbol{\Theta}\big) / \mathbf{tr}\big(\boldsymbol{\Theta}^\top \boldsymbol{L} \, \boldsymbol{\Theta}\big)$ in the feature space; it is a generalized Rayleigh-Ritz quotient [16]. The optimization in kernel RDA is:

$$\underset{\boldsymbol{\Theta}}{\text{maximize}} \quad \mathbf{tr}\big(\boldsymbol{\Theta}^\top \boldsymbol{M} \, \boldsymbol{\Theta}\big), \quad \text{subject to} \quad \boldsymbol{\Theta}^\top \boldsymbol{L} \boldsymbol{\Theta} = \boldsymbol{I}, \tag{19}$$

whose solution is the generalized eigenvalue problem (M, L). In kernel RDA, the directions are n-dimensional while in RDA, we had d-dimensional directions.

In kernel RDA, the projection and reconstruction of the training and out-of-sample data are $\widetilde{X} = \Phi(U)^\top \Phi(X) = \Theta^\top K_x$, $\widehat{X} = \Phi(U)\Phi(U)^\top \Phi(X) = \Phi(X)\Theta\Theta^\top K_x$, $\widetilde{X}_t = \Theta^\top K_t$, and $\widehat{X}_t = \Phi(X)\Theta\Theta^\top K_t$, where $\Phi(X)$ existing in the reconstructions are not necessarily available so we do not have reconstruction in kernel RDA.

Properties of M, N, and L: We have:

$$M = \begin{cases} K_x H K_y H K_x & \text{if } r_1 = 1, \\ K_x H K_x & \text{if } r_1 = 0, \end{cases} \qquad L = \begin{cases} N \overset{(17)}{=} \sum_{j=1}^{c} K_j H_j K_j^\top & \text{if } r_2 = 1, \\ K_x & \text{if } r_2 = 0. \end{cases}$$

We see that if $r_1 = 1$ and $r_2 = 1$, the labels are used in calculation of M and N, respectively. Thus, the Roweis factors are measures of using labels also in kernel RDA so the level of supervision is still valid.

The matrices M, N, and L are symmetric. About the ranks of these matrices, we have $\mathbf{rank}(P) \leq \min(n, t) + n$ and $\mathbf{rank}(K_x) \leq \min(n, t)$. Hence, $\mathbf{rank}(M) \leq \min\big(\mathbf{rank}(K_x) + \mathbf{rank}(H) + \mathbf{rank}(P)\big) \leq \min(n, n-1, t) = n-1$. In both the extreme cases $r_1 = 0$ and $r_1 = 1$, the rank of M is again at most $n - 1$. According to Eq. (17), we have $\mathbf{rank}(N) \leq \min(n, c - 1)$. According to Eq. (18) and the subadditivity property of rank, we have $\mathbf{rank}(L) \leq \mathbf{rank}(N) + \mathbf{rank}(K_x) \leq \min(n, c) - 1$. In the extreme cases $r_2 = 0$ and $r_2 = 1$, the rank of L is at most $\min(n, t) = n$ and $\min(n, c - 1)$, respectively.

Dimensionality of the Direct Kernel RDA Subspace: We can solve Eq. (19) as $\Theta = \mathbf{eig}(L^{-1}M)$. We have $\mathbf{rank}(L^{-1}M) \leq \min\big(\mathbf{rank}(L^{-1}), \mathbf{rank}(M)\big) \leq \min(n, c) - 1$. Therefore, the dimensionality of the kernel RDA subspace is $p \leq \min(n, c) - 1$, restricted by rank of L.

Special Cases of Kernel RDA: The Roweis map can have two layers, one for the input space and another for the feature space. The top layer is the bottom layer pulled to the feature space (see Fig. 1-b). Therefore, the four corners of Roweis map on the feature space can be considered as kernel PCA [4,5], kernel FDA [7,21], kernel SPCA [8], and kernel DSDA. The whole map includes the kernel methods of an infinite number of subspace learning algorithms.

Recall that PCA and SPCA (with $r_2 = 0$) have two kinds of kernelization which are using kernel trick (or dual of each method) and representation theory. This explains why there exist two types of kernel SPCA [8]. The kernel PCA using the kernel trick is already proposed [4,5] while the kernel PCA using representation theory is novel and proposed here.

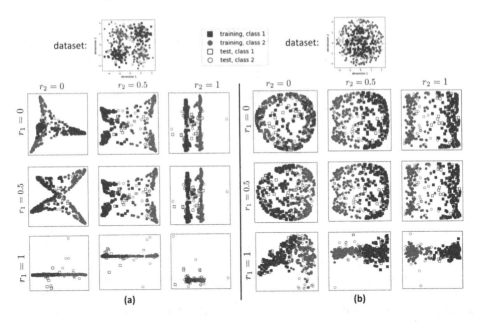

Fig. 2. The first two dimensions of the projected data in kernel RDA for (a) binary XOR dataset and (b) concentric rings dataset.

4   Experiments

4.1   Visualization: Synthetic Nonlinear Datasets

We created two synthetic nonlinear two-dimensional datasets which are binary XOR and concentric rings, shown in Fig. 2. The sample size in every dataset is 400 where 70% and 30% of the data are used for training and test, respectively. As these datasets are highly nonlinear, RDA does not separate the classes as well as kernel RDA. Therefore, the first two dimensions of the embedding in nine special cases of kernel RDA (with Radial Basis Function (RBF) kernel for K_x) are illustrated in Fig. 2. Note that in all the classification experiments in this paper, we used the Kronecker delta kernel for K_y [8]. Overall, the larger the Roweis factors get, the better the two classes are separated which is expected because the supervision level is increased. By sweeping $r_2 = 0 \rightarrow 1$, the two classes are almost collapsed into two one dimensional lines because the rank of kernel RDA is restricted by $c - 1 = 1$ when $r_2 = 1$ but this restriction does not exist for $r_2 = 0$. Another interpretation is because of taking the within scatter into account when r_2 is closer to one so the classes are collapsed.

4.2   Rowiesfaces: The Ghost Faces in RDA

For the next experiment, we used the ORL face dataset including 40 subjects each having 10 images with different expressions and poses. The data were

$r_2 = 0$ $r_2 = 0.5$ $r_2 = 1$

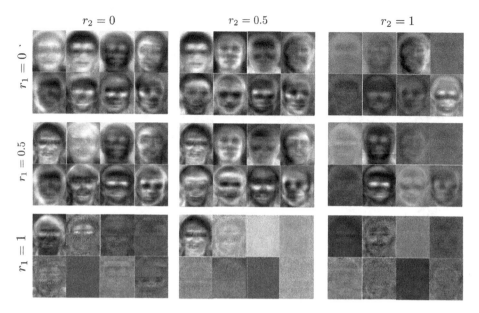

Fig. 3. The Roweisfaces: the eight leading eigenvectors for the special cases in the Roweis map where the first, fifth, and eighth eigenvectors of every case are at the top-left, bottom-left, and bottom-right, respectively.

standardized to have zero mean and unit variance. We divided the dataset into two classes of images having and not having eye glasses.

The Facial Eigenvectors: We trained nine special cases, $r_1, r_2 \in \{0, 0.5, 1\}$, of RDA and kernel RDA using the facial dataset. We name the facial eigenvectors, or ghost faces, in RDA as *Roweisfaces*. The existing special cases of Roweisfaces in the literature are eigenfaces ($r_1 = r_2 = 0$) [10,22], Fisherfaces ($r_1 = 0, r_2 = 1$) [12], and supervised eigenfaces ($r_1 = 1, r_2 = 0$) [2,8]. For $r_1 = r_2 = 1$ in Roweisfaces, we use the name *double supervised eigenfaces*. We name facial embedding using kernel RDA as *kernel Roweisfaces* whose existing special cases are kernel eigenfaces ($r_1 = r_2 = 0$) [11], kernel Fisherfaces ($r_1 = 0, r_2 = 1$) [13], kernel supervised eigenfaces ($r_1 = 1, r_2 = 0$) [2,8]. For $r_1 = r_2 = 1$ in kernel Roweisfaces, we use the name *kernel double supervised eigenfaces*.

The eigenvectors in kernel RDA are n-dimensional and not d-dimensional so we can show the ghost faces only in Roweisfaces and not kernel Roweisfaces. The trained Roweisfaces are shown in Fig. 3 for the special cases. The PCA case has captured different features such as eyes, hair, lips, nose, and face border. However, the more we consider the labels by increasing r_1 and r_2, the more features related to eyes and cheeks are extracted because of the more discrimination of having or not having glasses. Increasing r_1 tends to extract more features like Haar wavelet features [23] which are useful for face feature detection (see Viola-Jones face detector [24]). Increasing r_2, however, fades out the irrelevant features leaving merely the eyes which are important.

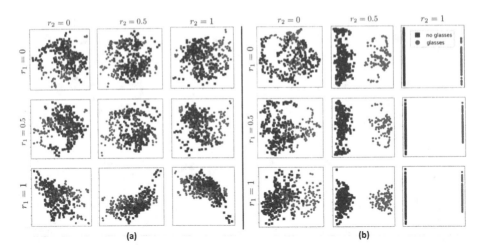

Fig. 4. The first two dimensions of the projected data in (a) Roweisfaces and (b) kernel Roweisfaces.

The Projections: The top two dimensions of projection of the facial images into the RDA and kernel RDA subspaces are shown in Fig. 4. As expected, kernel RDA separates the classes better than RDA. Also, the larger the supervision level, the better the separation. Again, for the rank-related reasons, the two classes are collapsed into one-dimensional lines for $r_2 = 1$ in kernel RDA.

The Reconstructions: Data cannot be reconstructed in kernel RDA but it can be done in RDA. Some reconstructed images for the facial dataset in Roweisfaces are shown in Fig. 5. The quality of reconstruction falls down as r_2 is increased. We explain the reason in the following. Minimizing the reconstruction error of $\boldsymbol{XA}$ (where $\boldsymbol{A}$ is symmetric) with orthonormal bases is minimize $\|\boldsymbol{XA} - \boldsymbol{UU}^\top \boldsymbol{XA}\|_F^2$, subject to $\boldsymbol{U}^\top \boldsymbol{U} = \boldsymbol{I}$, whose solution is the eigenvalue problem for $\boldsymbol{XA}^2 \boldsymbol{X}^\top$ [15]. Comparing this to the solution of Eq. (7) and noticing Eq. (8) shows we can have $\boldsymbol{A}^2 = \boldsymbol{HPH}$, $r_2 = 0$, and $\boldsymbol{R}_2 = \boldsymbol{I}$ for minimization of reconstruction error. Hence, the best setting for reconstruction is to have $r_2 = 0$. In addition, if $r_1 = 0$, the objective in this optimization becomes the error between $\boldsymbol{\breve{X}}$ and $\boldsymbol{\widehat{X}} = \boldsymbol{UU}^\top \boldsymbol{\breve{X}}$ which is the reconstruction error of centered data. This explains why PCA (with $r_2 = 0$) is the best linear method (with orthonormal bases) for reconstruction.

4.3   RDA for Classification and Regression:

Classification: To experiment on a classification task, we used a subset of the MNIST handwritten digit dataset with 5000 training and 1000 test images. The data were standardized. We used 1-Nearest Neighbor (1-NN) classifier for the projected data instances because it shows the structure of embedded data. The error rates of the classification for some special cases of RDA and kernel RDA

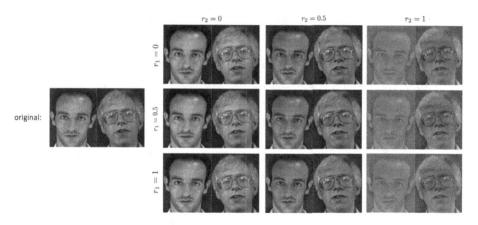

Fig. 5. The reconstructed images after projection into the RDA subspaces.

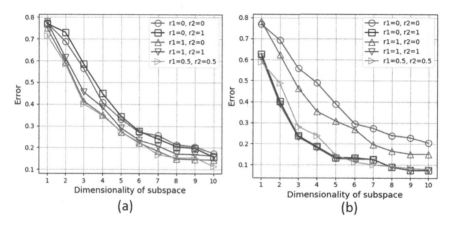

Fig. 6. The error rates for the 1-NN classification of the subset of MNIST dataset: (a) some cases in RDA, (b) some cases in kernel RDA.

are shown in Fig. 6. As expected, in most cases, the kernel RDA performed better than RDA. For RDA, the DSDA and the case $r_1 = r_2 = 0.5$ were better than PCA and FDA which makes sense because DSDA has full supervision level. Also, kernel DSDA and the kernel method for $r_1 = r_2 = 0.5$ performed much better than kernel PCA and kernel SPCA.

Regression: We used three synthetic benchmarks [25] which are for evaluating regression tasks in subspace learning. Let $X_{:i}$ and $X_{j:}$ denote the i-th column (instance) and j-th row (feature) of X, respectively. In the benchmark 1, $X \in \mathbb{R}^{4 \times n}$ and the vector of labels is $y = X_{1:}/(0.5 + (X_{2:} + 1.5)^2) + (1 + X_{2:})^2 + 0.5\varepsilon$ where $\varepsilon \sim \mathcal{N}(0,1)$ is the Gaussian additive noise and $X_{:i} \sim \mathcal{N}(0, I)$. In benchmark 2, $X \in \mathbb{R}^{4 \times n}$ and $y = \sin^2(\pi X_{2:} + 1) + 0.5\varepsilon$ where $X_{:i}$ is uniformly distributed on the set $[0,1]^4 \setminus \{x \in \mathbb{R}^4 | x_{j:} \leq 0.7, \forall j \in \{1, 2, 3, 4\}\}$.

Table 1. The average root mean squared error for regression experiments of RDA and Kernel RDA (KRDA) on the benchmark datasets.

		Benchmark 1	Benchmark 2	Benchmark 3
RDA	$r_1 = 0, r_2 = 0$	2.004 ± 0.673	0.155 ± 0.039	0.526 ± 0.413
	$r_1 = 0.5, r_2 = 0$	1.556 ± 0.446	0.055 ± 0.021	0.558 ± 0.443
	$r_1 = 1, r_2 = 0$	1.538 ± 0.441	0.048 ± 0.014	0.567 ± 0.452
KRDA	$r_1 = 0, r_2 = 0$	2.061 ± 0.701	0.155 ± 0.039	0.521 ± 0.413
	$r_1 = 0.5, r_2 = 0$	1.630 ± 0.632	0.054 ± 0.021	0.503 ± 0.394
	$r_1 = 1, r_2 = 0$	1.615 ± 0.632	0.048 ± 0.014	0.493 ± 0.390

The distribution of this benchmark is not elliptical. In benchmark 3, $\boldsymbol{X} \in \mathbb{R}^{10 \times n}$ and $\boldsymbol{y} = 0.5(\boldsymbol{X}_{1:})^2 \varepsilon$ where the noise is multiplicative here and $\boldsymbol{X}_{:i} \sim \mathcal{N}(\boldsymbol{0}, \boldsymbol{I})$. Inspired by [8], we drew 50 samples of size 100 from these benchmark distributions from each of which we took 70% and 30% of data for training and test, respectively. We used linear regression and the top two features of the projected data. We used RBF kernel for both $\boldsymbol{K}_x$ and $\boldsymbol{K}_y$. The average root mean squared errors of regression over the 50 created datasets are reported in Table 1 where only the cases with $r_2 = 0$ are used in RDA and kernel RDA because regression only applies to $r_1 = 0$ in the Roweis map. Often, the greater r_1 had better performance for the sake of larger supervision level. In most cases, kernel RDA performs better than or similar to RDA.

5   Conclusion

In this paper, we proposed RDA which generalized subspace learning including PCA, SPCA, and FDA. One of the extreme special cases is DSDA which is novel. Dual RDA for some special cases was proposed. Kernel RDA was also proposed using two methods of kernel trick and representation theory. Applying RDA and kernel RDA on facial dataset gave us Roweisfaces and kernel Roweisfaces generalizing eigenfaces, Fisherfaces, kernel eigenfaces, kernel Fisherfaces, and supervised eigenfaces. We also demonstrated some cases where DSDA, the novel method derived from the bottom-right corner of the Roweis map, provides superior preliminary results. Moreover, our analysis of the theory of RDA clarified some facts about some of the existing subspace learning methods.

References

1. Ghojogh, B., et al.: Feature selection and feature extraction in pattern analysis: a literature review. arXiv preprint arXiv:1905.02845 (2019)
2. Ghojogh, B., Crowley, M.: Unsupervised and supervised principal component analysis: Tutorial. arXiv preprint arXiv:1906.03148 (2019)
3. Ghojogh, B., Karray, F., Crowley, M.: Fisher and kernel Fisher discriminant analysis: Tutorial. arXiv preprint arXiv:1906.09436 (2019)

4. Schölkopf, B., Smola, A., Müller, K.-R.: Kernel principal component analysis. In: Gerstner, W., Germond, A., Hasler, M., Nicoud, J.-D. (eds.) ICANN 1997. LNCS, vol. 1327, pp. 583–588. Springer, Heidelberg (1997). https://doi.org/10.1007/BFb0020217
5. Schölkopf, B., Smola, A., Müller, K.R.: Nonlinear component analysis as a kernel eigenvalue problem. Neural Comput. **10**(5), 1299–1319 (1998)
6. Hofmann, T., Schölkopf, B., Smola, A.J.: Kernel methods in machine learning. Ann. Stat. 1171–1220 (2008)
7. Mika, S., Rätsch, G., Weston, J., Schölkopf, B., Müller, K.R.: Fisher discriminant analysis with kernels. In: Proceedings of the 1999 IEEE Signal Processing Society Workshop on Neural Networks for Signal Processing IX, pp. 41–48. IEEE (1999)
8. Barshan, E., Ghodsi, A., Azimifar, Z., Jahromi, M.Z.: Supervised principal component analysis: visualization, classification and regression on subspaces and submanifolds. Pattern Recogn. **44**(7), 1357–1371 (2011)
9. Gretton, A., Bousquet, O., Smola, A., Schölkopf, B.: Measuring statistical dependence with Hilbert-Schmidt norms. In: Jain, S., Simon, H.U., Tomita, E. (eds.) ALT 2005. LNCS (LNAI), vol. 3734, pp. 63–77. Springer, Heidelberg (2005). https://doi.org/10.1007/11564089_7
10. Turk, M.A., Pentland, A.P.: Face recognition using eigenfaces. In: IEEE Computer Society Conference on Computer Vision and Pattern Recognition, CVPR 1991, pp. 586–591. IEEE (1991)
11. Yang, M.H., Ahuja, N., Kriegman, D.: Face recognition using kernel eigenfaces. In: Proceedings of 2000 International Conference on Image Processing, vol. 1, pp. 37–40. IEEE (2000)
12. Belhumeur, P.N., Hespanha, J.P., Kriegman, D.J.: Eigenfaces vs. Fisherfaces: recognition using class specific linear projection. IEEE Trans. Pattern Anal. Mach. Intell. **19**(7), 711–720 (1997)
13. Yang, M.H.: Kernel eigenfaces vs. kernel Fisherfaces: face recognition using kernel methods. In: Proceedings of the Fifth IEEE International Conference on Automatic Face and Gesture Recognition, pp. 215–220 (2002)
14. Wang, J.: Geometric Structure of High-Dimensional Data and Dimensionality Reduction. Springer, Heidelberg (2012). https://doi.org/10.1007/978-3-642-27497-8
15. Ghojogh, B., Karray, F., Crowley, M.: Eigenvalue and generalized eigenvalue problems: tutorial. arXiv preprint arXiv:1903.11240 (2019)
16. Parlett, B.N.: The symmetric eigenvalue problem. Classics Appl. Math. **20** (1998)
17. Ye, J.: Least squares linear discriminant analysis. In: Proceedings of the 24th International Conference on Machine Learning, pp. 1087–1093. ACM (2007)
18. Zhang, Z., Dai, G., Xu, C., Jordan, M.I.: Regularized discriminant analysis, ridge regression and beyond. J. Mach. Learn. Res. **11**(Aug), 2199–2228 (2010)
19. Alperin, J.L.: Local Representation Theory: Modular Representations as an Introduction to the Local Representation Theory of Finite Groups, vol. 11. Cambridge University Press, Cambridge (1993)
20. Ghojogh, B., Karray, F., Crowley, M.: Roweis discriminant analysis: a generalized subspace learning method. arXiv preprint arXiv:1910.05437 (2019)
21. Mika, S., Rätsch, G., Weston, J., Schölkopf, B., Smola, A.J., Müller, K.R.: Invariant feature extraction and classification in kernel spaces. In: Advances in Neural Information Processing Systems, pp. 526–532 (2000)
22. Turk, M., Pentland, A.: Eigenfaces for recognition. J. Cogn. Neurosci. **3**(1), 71–86 (1991)

23. Stanković, R.S., Falkowski, B.J.: The Haar wavelet transform: its status and achievements. Comput. Electr. Eng. **29**(1), 25–44 (2003)
24. Wang, Y.Q.: An analysis of the Viola-Jones face detection algorithm. Image Process. On Line **4**, 128–148 (2014)
25. Li, B., Zha, H., Chiaromonte, F.: Contour regression: a general approach to dimension reduction. Ann. Stat. **33**(4), 1580–1616 (2005)

Understanding Public Speakers' Performance: First Contributions to Support a Computational Approach

Fábio Barros[1]([⊠]), Ângelo Conde[2,4], Sandra C. Soares[2,3], António J. R. Neves[1], and Samuel Silva[1]

[1] Institute of Electronics and Informatics Engineering of Aveiro,
Department of Electronics, Telecomunications and Informatics,
University of Aveiro, Aveiro, Portugal
{fabiodaniel,an,sss}@ua.pt
[2] Department of Education and Psychology,
University of Aveiro, Aveiro, Portugal
{aconde,sandra.soares}@ua.pt
[3] William James Center for Research,
University of Aveiro, Aveiro, Portugal
[4] CIDTFF—Research Center in Didactics and Technology in Training of Trainers,
University of Aveiro, Aveiro, Portugal

Abstract. Communication is part of our everyday life and our ability to communicate can have a significant role in a variety of contexts in our personal, academic, and professional lives. For long, the characterization of what is a good communicator has been subject to research and debate by several areas, particularly in Education, with a focus on improving the performance of teachers. In this context, the literature suggests that the ability to communicate is not only defined by the verbal component, but also by a plethora of non-verbal contributions providing redundant or complementary information, and, sometimes, being the message itself. However, even though we can recognize a good or bad communicator, objectively, little is known about what aspects – and to what extent— define the quality of a presentation. The goal of this work is to create the grounds to support the study of the defining characteristics of a good communicator in a more systematic and objective form. To this end, we conceptualize and provide a first prototype for a computational approach to characterize the different elements that are involved in communication, from audiovisual data, illustrating the outcomes and applicability of the proposed methods on a video database of public speakers.

Keywords: Verbal and non-verbal communication · Computational methods · Posture · Facial expressions · Voice

© Springer Nature Switzerland AG 2020
A. Campilho et al. (Eds.): ICIAR 2020, LNCS 12131, pp. 343–355, 2020.
https://doi.org/10.1007/978-3-030-50347-5_30

1 Introduction

Communication is inherent to human life, only through communication humans can interact with each other and exchange ideas and experiences. Nowadays, the capability to communicate well in public is a very important competence at the professional, academic, and personal levels.

Literature suggests that the ability to communicate is not only defined by the verbal component, but also by a set of non-verbal components since many non-verbal aspects provide redundant and/or complementary information. The literature also suggests that through the body, gestures, facial expressions and voice variations, the audience can identify several social characteristics such as competence, dominance, confidence, and others [13].

The subject of communication skills, such as in public speaking contexts, has been a topic widely studied in various areas, notably, in Education, for its relevance as a core element for the dissemination of information and knowledge. However, the advances made, through the years, about what explains good or bad communication skills has yet to reach a wider audience that could profit from it, mostly due to a arduous translation from theory to practise. One of the reasons is that researchers are often faced with a difficulty in objectively testing their hypotheses regarding the driving factors for good or bad communication due to a lack of a more quantitative setting for their research. This is where computational approaches may help. To achieve this, and as part of a long-term effort to advance the research on communication skills, the main goal of the work presented here is to bring forward a framework supporting increased objectivity in the study of communication in public, specifically by:

- Selecting, based on the literature, which aspects (channels) are most relevant in human-human communication, particularly those that have been described as having a notable impact on public communication;
- Proposing a set of computational methods describing the actions and contents present in the different communication channels identified.
- Complementing and annotating, through the proposed methods, an existing audiovisual database focusing on the study of speakers' performance.

The remainder of this paper is organized as follows: Sect. 2 presents a brief overview of research focusing public communication, and summarizes a wealth of notable datasets and libraries deemed relevant for the study and extraction of features from different communication channels. In Sect. 3 the methods proposed for the computation of different features from the selected channels are described along with a summary of the resulting data and information. Then, in Sect. 4, the methods are illustrated by applying them to an existing dataset of public speaker videos, a context for which communication skills assume a paramount role. In Sect. 5, we present a conclusion regarding the work developed and a discussion about the possible paths to advance and take advantage of the proposed approach.

2 Related Work

Human-human communication is not just about words. Although verbal communication is the main form of communication between humans, nonverbal behaviour (e.g., facial expressions, gestures, and body posture) has a very important role in communication. The information conveyed through these different channels may serve a wide variety of purposes, whether to explicitly reinforce or complement the message, as the message itself, or, inadvertently, as a barrier to its correct perception.

According to the literature, human beings seem to use expansive and open postures (becoming bigger and taking up more space) to project signs of power, confidence and assertiveness [10,12]. On the other hand, counteractive and closed postures (minimizing occupied space and shrinking body) project signs of powerlessness and low confidence. The literature also states that during communication, humans use broad gestures and expansive body postures to project dominance.

Also, human beings usually produce gestures while talking. According to the literature (e.g., [15]), such gestures are actions that are directly related to the lexical and semantic content and are particularly suited to reinforce or complement the message being conveyed. The literature also states that gestures are a crucial element for speakers, as they help to expose ideas and retrieve content that is difficult to memorize [30].

On the other hand, facial expressions can transmit countless emotions without saying a single word, and unlike some forms of nonverbal communication, they are universal. Thus, facial expressions are one of the most important aspects in human communication since they can convey the speaker's emotional state, but also intentions, through facial muscle movements, such as wrinkling eyebrows or lifting lip corners. However, facial expressions are not the only ones with an important role in nonverbal facial communication. The posture of the head and the direction of the gaze are equally important indicators of communicative intention, since they influence the level of perceived naturalness and competence [14,24].

In the contrast between verbal and non-verbal communication, literature pertaining to the verbal side states that the human being not only infers the meaning conveyed but also the way in which this is done (e.g. [19]). In this sense, prosodic clues are an integral part of human communication. Also, the literature states that there are a number of features present in audio resources that have been widely considered to understand how voices are heard and interpreted. These characteristics include, for example, volume and its variations, duration of speech, duration of pauses, consideration of a restricted lexical field (use of a group of restricted words), among others [11].

Attention to public speaking has risen, in recent years, as a valued personal communication skill and computational technology has echoed such attraction. The research community has been creating several datasets to provide the grounds to support a more systematic study of public speaking performance such as, for example, [5,7,10,26]. The present work is supported on a new dataset of

36 (18F+18M) public speaker videos. This dataset aims to establish the best social inference predictors of communicative performance. The dataset is based on thin-slice videos (30s to 50 seconds) of Portuguese TEDx orators, which were viewed by 97 participants asked to evaluate, for each video, using a visual analog scale, the emotion elicited by the presentations, first impressions (e.g., competence, warmness, confidence), and the perceived importance of several nonverbal features (e.g., gestures) on such judgments.

Considering the available datasets, one of the challenges pertains how to take the most out of the resources they provide, particularly in a way that does not loose complete sight of the theory gathered through the years to enable establishing parallels and test hypotheses. One of the most challenging aspects motivating this work is precisely the lack of a more objective knowledge about which aspects of the speaker's performance are influencing how the message is perceived and grasped. The assessments about who is a good or bad communicator are often based on the expertise of communication specialists and the subjective nature of their feedback, due to a lack of a more quantitative framework to support them, makes it difficult to understand what aspects – and their level of importance – influence the audience. Although there are several characteristics in both verbal and non-verbal communication that have been pointed out as relevant, a more systematic and quantitative approach is necessary in the improvement of studying the communication process.

In this regard, it is also important to note that the consideration of machine learning methods to build a system capable of discriminating between a good and a bad communicator is a natural goal, in the long-run, for this research. However, at this stage, we are mostly interested in adopting a framework that enables an exploratory analysis of how well we can compute features to express concepts as expansiveness, in tight collaboration with communication experts. By doing this, we hope to first create the basis for a greater multidisciplinary insight over the communication process and build a set of meaningful features that will contribute to the explicability of future machine learning approaches.

Considering the different channels that can be used to communicate, verbal and non-verbal, it is necessary to gather features allowing a computational description of their contents supporting further computational approaches to focus on the study of communication. In this regard, several technologies and software libraries can be considered.

Observations performed during the communication process allow the extraction of the necessary data for the analysis of body posture, movements and gestures, via some alternatives such as Kinect Skeletal Tracking [29], ArtTrack [16] and DeeperCut [17]. However, the OpenPose [3] library was presented in April 2017, which revolutionized the field of visual computing. Taking video frames as *input* it allows the detection and collection of values at two dimensions of the main parts of the human body in a total of 130 *keypoints*, 15 or 18 for the body, 21 for each hand, and 70 for the face.

For the extraction of facial data a few libraries have been considered, such as Menpo [21], LEAR [20], and OpenFace 2.0 [1]. From these, OpenFace 2.0, an open source library, provides the wider range of features. It detects face landmarks, head position, gaze direction, and enables recognizing the activation and intensity of several key elements of the face (Action Units) enabling a more detailed study of facial activity.

The tools OpenEAR [8], SPAC [22], and Praat [2] are some examples of what can be considered for processing and analysis of the audible component of communication. As an alternative to these, OpenSMILE (The Munich open-Source Media Interpretation by Large feature-space Extraction) [9] is strongly used by the community of researchers in the areas of voice and emotion recognition, and MIR (Music Information Retrieval). It is a flexible and modular library for signal processing and machine learning applications. Regarding voice related resources, OpenSMILE, allows the extraction of Mel Frequency Cepstral Coefficients MFCCs, Pitch, Jitter, Energy, Intensity, Zero crossing rate and others.

3   Computation Approach to Study Communication Skills

In order to better understand the phenomenon of communication at the different levels of the communication channels, a set of methods was developed that allow a computationally-based description of what happens in each of these channels (see Fig. 1. In this regard, the literature on the assessment and discussion of comunnication skills provided clues regarding which aspects could be considered. Two processing stages were considered: the first, focused on obtaining low-level characteristics e.g., wrist position, over time, describing what happens in each of the channels; the second carried out the transformation of these characteristics into high-level annotations (e.g., from hand movement coordinates into "rising hand") with the aim of allowing greater readability and better identification of relevant activities, so that they may encompass the different levels of study and the multidisciplinary nature of the research team.

3.1   Features per Communication Channel

According to Koppensteiner et al. [18], horizontal and vertical body movements affect the formation of impressions in a different way. Similarly, and according to Carney et al. [4], expansive and open postures project signs of power, dominance, confidence and assertiveness, and on the other hand, counteractive and closed postures project signs of impotence and low self-esteem. In this way and, using OpenPose, the key points of the skeleton were extracted. These were then used to compute several features characterizing communicator performance.

Human's face is another indicator of communicative intention. Facial muscle movements (Action Units), such as wrinkling eyebrows or lifting lip corners and head postures, are very important aspects in communication, since they influence the level of perceived naturalness and competence. In order to that, we extracted values related to head posture (pitch and yaw), and the activation and intensity of Action Units using Openface.

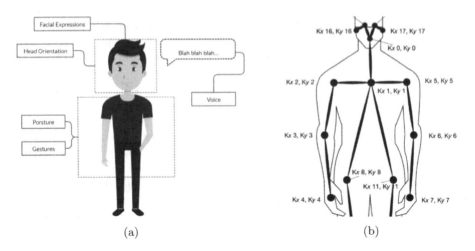

(a)   (b)

Fig. 1. On the left, identification of the different sources of communicative content (channels) considered for this work. On the right, identification of the skeleton key points considered to infer different measures describing posture, gestures, and head orientation.

Last but not least, variation of intensity, duration of speech, duration of pauses and pitch have been investigated in order to assess the voice. However, prosodic characteristics also become one of the pillars of the recognition of para-linguistic traits [6]. In this sense, with the use of Opensmile a set of features deemed relevant, based on the literature, e.g., [25], such as speech intensity, energy, pitch, jitter, loudness, and MFCCs and voice activity detection (VAD) [23], were extracted.

3.2   High Level Features and Annotations

Once the low-level descriptors associated with each of the identified communication channels were extracted, we transform these data into high-level annotations in order to give them better readability and an easier identification of relevant activities. In this sense, the high level annotations that we provide concern: posture, head movements, emotion (as expressed by the face), horizontal and vertical gestures of the harms and hands, and, also, related to the voice, moments of silence/voicing and variation of the audio intensity.

Hand gestures and head position—we use the same approach based on assessing the variation of the relevant keypoints in each sequence of ten frames. Table 1 summarize all the annotations considered and indicates which values are used to set each annotation.

Horizontal and vertical expansiveness—The amplitude of the horizontal movements is obtained by adding the distance between the neck (k_x1) and the left wrist (k_x7) and right k_x4. $H(x) = |k_x1 - k_x4| + |k_x1 - k_x7|$ (1).

The amplitude of the vertical movements is obtained by adding the distance between the neck (k_y1) and the left wrist (k_y7) and right k_y4. $H(y) = (k_x4| - k_y1) + (k_x7 - k_x1)$ (2).

Occupied area—To calculate the area occupied in each frame the values of K_xmax, K_xmin, K_ymax and K_ymin from the human body are obtained. For these values, we check which key points represent the minimum and maximum values for axes (X) and (Y) in each frame. $A = |K_xmax - K_xmin| \times |K_ymax - K_ymin|$ (3)

Table 1. On the left, criteria used to perform high level annotation of gestures and head position; on the right, the action units considered to infer the emotion expressed by the speaker.

Annotation	Criteria (10 frames)
Head Moving Right	ΔYaw > 0
Head Moving Left	ΔYaw < 0
Head Moving Up	ΔPitch < 0
Head Moving Down	ΔPitch > 0
Approach Hands	ΔWrists < 0
Separate Hands	ΔWrists > 0
Arm Going Down	$\Delta Y_{wrist} > 0$
Arm Going Up	$\Delta Y_{wrist} < 0$

Emotion	Action Units Weight		
	50%	25%	12.5%
Fear	AU 1	AU 5	AU 25
Happy	AU 12	AU 6	AU 25
Sad	AU 1	AU 4	AU 17
Angry	AU 25	AU 4	AU 9
Surprised	AU 26	AU 17	AU 2
Disgust	AU 9	AU 7	AU 4

Figure 2 illustrates the annotation of "Head Moving Right" in a sequence of frames, since the head's yaw increases over the interval.

Emotion from facial expression—in each moment of presentation we used a simple approach based on action units intensities. Firstly, based on [27,28], we selected the three most frequent action units present in each emotion: fear, happy, sad, angry, surprise and disgust, as depicted to the right of Table 1, ordered from left to right according to their predominance.

Then, for each emotion is attributed a numerical value based on the intensity of the action unit and weight of predominance. Finally, we select the emotion with the highest value, but, if the value is lower than a threshold devised empirically, during development, we attribute the neutral emotion. Figure 3 illustrates how the emotional state of "Happy" is attributed to a speaker.

Voice activity and intensity—Based on the VAD probability values, we annotate moments of silence and speech (VAD > 0). Additionally, we also annotate

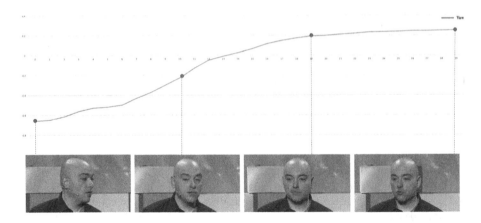

Fig. 2. Characterization of head movement: illustration of yaw variation and key video frames associated with head movement from left to right.

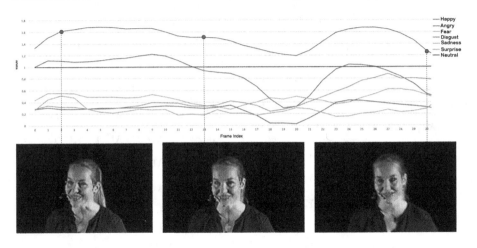

Fig. 3. Determination of emotion from facial expressions: the intensity for each emotion is determined, over time, based on AU activation, and the most intense is chosen.

voice intensity variations by using both the VAD and Voice intensity values extracted. For that purpose, we calculate the average of the intensity excluding the intervals marked as silent. Then, we consider that there is an increase in voice intensity at all moments for which the intensity is above average.

All the computed low-level descriptors along with the determined annotations and activities are stored in JSON file to facilitate, e.g., exporting the data into other tools implementing the computation of different high-level features.

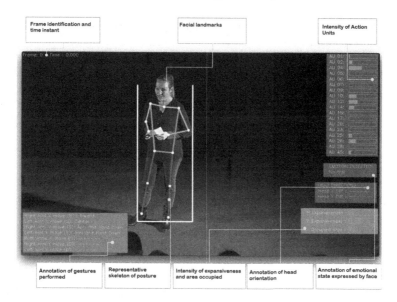

Fig. 4. Illustration of the software tool created to enable a visualization and analysis of the extracted information along the videos.

4   Results

The methods presented in this paper include a large set of data and information considered relevant for the characterisation of the different communication channels. In this sense, it was considered important to propose a visualization tool that would also support the analysis of the contributions of this work by researchers from other areas, e.g., Education and Psychology, to favour exploratory analysis of the dataset and harness expert insights in finding synergies between the computed measures and observed speaker behaviour. So, we propose a tool that performs the overlay of the computed data and information sets, on video, in real time. Figure 4 illustrates the visualization tool developed, where the computed data and annotations (e.g., intensity of the *Action Units* and gestures) are overlayed on the video stream.

This paper proposes an approach to obtain a set of data describing the activity in each communication channel, from digital audio and video, providing a first level of quantitative support for an exploratory study about understanding the communication with the adoption of computational methods.

4.1   Illustrative Application Example

To illustrate how the outcomes of the work presented in this article may support shedding some light over the study and impact of communication skills, we present an example of using the outcomes of the proposed methods to explore how the "Occupied Area" annotation might relate with the perception of good or bad communicators..

According to the literature, and as previously mentioned, more expansive and open people project signs of confidence and assertiveness. Thus, using the data computed for the occupied area, described by its (mean, standard deviation, maximum and minimum), unsupervised machine learning methods, concretely Agglomerative Clustering, were applied in order to distribute the speakers of the video dataset considered in this work. Thus, we obtained the distribution of the speakers, relative to the occupied area, during their presentation, in three groups, as illustrated in Fig. 5.

Then, the average human provided annotations for confidence and assertiveness (part of the dataset) were computed, for each of the groups, as shown in Fig. 5.

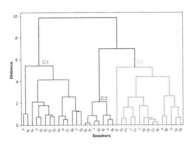

Clusters	Area	Conf.	Assert.
C1	27%	61	57
C2	30%	51	50
C3	37%	49	48

Fig. 5. Illustrative example considering the computed occupied area for clustering speakers and its relation with first impressions annotated by participants: on the left, resulting dendrogram, considering Ward's distance; on the right, average scores for computed occupied area, and corresponding annotated confidence and assertiveness.

With this basic approach and by relating the clustering with the human annotations available on data set, we have some evidence that audiences do not seem to interpret confidence and assertiveness solely based on expansive/constrained (larger/smaller occupied area) postures, hinting on the paramount importance of an understanding of the synergies among the multiple verbal and nonverbal components of communication. The work presented here is, in our opinion, a relevant first step towards that goal.

5   Conclusions

Given that public communication is an area that is still very little explored, this work has managed to make a positive contribution to its progress. Based on the literature, and since it is noticeable that communication is multimodal, i.e., a mix of the contents of several channels, it was possible to select a set of characteristics present in verbal and non-verbal communication that are deemed to have a relevant impact on human communication, in public.

Through the use of different computational tools, we successfully extract a set of elements for the characterization of multiple nonverbal features playing a role in human-human communication involving the body, face, and voice. Through these, it was also possible to implement some methods to annotate activities considered relevant that facilitate the description and interpretation of a set of actions/contents occurring during communication (e.g., raising the harms). While the proposed methods have been illustrated over a particular audiovisual dataset, they are applicable to any other videos of communicative tasks, although limited to a single speaker. In the future, our goal is to generalize our approach to encompass multiple speakers at the same time, such as in a conversation.

Interestingly, the simple application example presented, albeit preliminary, hints that some of the theoretical aspects for communication skills assessment need to be further explored, since a direct relationship between expansiveness, as represented by the occupied area, and the perception of assertive/confident speakers, as annotated by a human audience, does not stand out.

Acknowledgements. This work is partially funded by IEETA Research Unit funding (UIDB/00127/2020), by Portugal 2020 under the Competitiveness and Internationalization Operational Program, and the European Regional Development Fund through project SOCA – Smart Open Campus (CENTRO-01-0145-FEDER-000010) and project MEMNON (POCI-01-0145-FEDER-028976).

References

1. Baltrusaitis, T., Zadeh, A., Lim, Y.C., Morency, L.P.: Openface 2.0: facial behavior analysis toolkit. In: Proceedings of 13th IEEE International Conference on Automatic Face & Gesture Recognition (FG 2018), pp. 59–66. IEEE (2018)
2. Boersma, P.: Praat, a system for doing phonetics by computer. Glot. Int. **5**(9), 341–345 (2001)
3. Cao, Z., Hidalgo, G., Simon, T., Wei, S.E., Sheikh, Y.: Openpose: real-time multi-person 2D pose estimation using part affinity fields. arXiv preprint arXiv:1812.08008 (2018)
4. Carney, D.R., Cuddy, A.J., Yap, A.J.: Power posing: brief nonverbal displays affect neuroendocrine levels and risk tolerance. Psychol. Sci. **21**(10), 1363–1368 (2010)
5. Chen, L., Feng, G., Leong, C.W., Joe, J., Kitchen, C., Lee, C.M.: Designing an automated assessment of public speaking skills using multimodal cues. J. Learn. Anal. **3**(2), 261–281 (2016)
6. Cullen, A., Hines, A., Harte, N.: Perception and prediction of speaker appeal-a single speaker study. Comput. Speech Lang. **52**, 23–40 (2018)
7. Echeverría, V., Avendaño, A., Chiluiza, K., Vásquez, A., Ochoa, X.: Presentation skills estimation based on video and kinect data analysis. In: Proceedings of the 2014 ACM Workshop on Multimodal Learning Analytics Workshop and Grand Challenge, pp. 53–60 (2014)
8. Eyben, F., Wöllmer, M., Schuller, B.: OpenEAR–introducing the Munich open-source emotion and affect recognition toolkit. In: Proceedings of 3rd International Conference on Affective Computing and Intelligent Interaction and Workshops, pp. 1–6. IEEE (2009)

9. Eyben, F., Wöllmer, M., Schuller, B.: Opensmile: the Munich versatile and fast open-source audio feature extractor. In: Proceedings of 18th ACM International Conference on Multimedia, pp. 1459–1462 (2010)
10. Gan, T., Wong, Y., Mandal, B., Chandrasekhar, V., Kankanhalli, M.S.: Multi-sensor self-quantification of presentations. In: Proceedings of 23rd ACM International Conference on Multimedia, pp. 601–610 (2015)
11. Giannakopoulos, T.: pyAudioAnalysis: an open-source python library for audio signal analysis. PloS One **10**(12) (2015)
12. Gronau, Q.F., Van Erp, S., Heck, D.W., Cesario, J., Jonas, K.J., Wagenmakers, E.J.: A Bayesian model-averaged meta-analysis of the power pose effect with informed and default priors: the case of felt power. Compr. Results Soc. Psychol. **2**(1), 123–138 (2017)
13. Hall, J.A., Knapp, M.L.: Welcome to the handbook of nonverbal communication. In: Nonverbal Communication, pp. 3–10. De Gruyter Mouton, Berlin (2013)
14. Holler, J., Schubotz, L., Kelly, S., Hagoort, P., Schuetze, M., Özyürek, A.: Social eye gaze modulates processing of speech and co-speech gesture. Cognition **133**(3), 692–697 (2014)
15. Iani, F., Bucciarelli, M.: Mechanisms underlying the beneficial effect of a speaker's gestures on the listener. J. Memory Lang. **96**, 110–121 (2017)
16. Insafutdinov, E., Andriluka, M., Pishchulin, L., Tang, S., Levinkov, E., Andres, B., Schiele, B.: Arttrack: articulated multi-person tracking in the wild. In: Proceedings of the IEEE Conference on Computer Vision and Pattern Recognition, pp. 6457–6465 (2017)
17. Insafutdinov, E., Pishchulin, L., Andres, B., Andriluka, M., Schiele, B.: DeeperCut: a deeper, stronger, and faster multi-person pose estimation model. In: Leibe, B., Matas, J., Sebe, N., Welling, M. (eds.) ECCV 2016. LNCS, vol. 9910, pp. 34–50. Springer, Cham (2016). https://doi.org/10.1007/978-3-319-46466-4_3
18. Koppensteiner, M., Stephan, P., Jäschke, J.P.M.: Moving speeches: dominance, trustworthiness and competence in body motion. Pers. Individ. Differ. **94**, 101–106 (2016)
19. Kreitewolf, J., Friederici, A.D., von Kriegstein, K.: Hemispheric lateralization of linguistic prosody recognition in comparison to speech and speaker recognition. Neuroimage **102**, 332–344 (2014)
20. Martinez, B., Valstar, M.F., Binefa, X., Pantic, M.: Local evidence aggregation for regression-based facial point detection. IEEE Trans. Pattern Anal. Mach. Intell. **35**(5), 1149–1163 (2012)
21. Alabort-i Medina, J., Antonakos, E., Booth, J., Snape, P., Zafeiriou, S.: Menpo: a comprehensive platform for parametric image alignment and visual deformable models. In: Proceedings of 22nd ACM International Conference on Multimedia, pp. 679–682 (2014)
22. Özseven, T., Düğenci, M.: Speech acoustic (SPAC): a novel tool for speech feature extraction and classification. Appl. Acoust. **136**, 1–8 (2018)
23. Park, T.J., Chang, J.H.: Dempster-Shafer theory for enhanced statistical model-based voice activity detection. Comput. Speech Lang. **47**, 47–58 (2018)
24. Sadoughi, N., Liu, Y., Busso, C.: Meaningful head movements driven by emotional synthetic speech. Speech Commun. **95**, 87–99 (2017)
25. Schuller, B., et al.: The interspeech 2010 paralinguistic challenge. In: Eleventh Annual Conference of the International Speech Communication Association (2010)

26. Tanveer, M.I., Zhao, R., Chen, K., Tiet, Z., Hoque, M.E.: Automanner: an automated interface for making public speakers aware of their mannerisms. In: Proceedings of 21st International Conference on Intelligent User Interfaces, pp. 385–396 (2016)
27. Velusamy, S., Kannan, H., Anand, B., Sharma, A., Navathe, B.: A method to infer emotions from facial action units. In: Proceedings of International Conference on Acoustics, Speech and Signal Processing (ICASSP), pp. 2028–2031. IEEE (2011)
28. Vick, S.J., Waller, B.M., Parr, L.A., Pasqualini, M.C.S., Bard, K.A.: A cross-species comparison of facial morphology and movement in humans and chimpanzees using the facial action coding system (FACS). J. Nonverbal Behav. 31(1), 1–20 (2007)
29. Zhang, Z.: Microsoft kinect sensor and its effect. IEEE Multimedia 19(2), 4–10 (2012)
30. Zhen, A., Van Hedger, S., Heald, S., Goldin-Meadow, S., Tian, X.: Manual directional gestures facilitate cross-modal perceptual learning. Cognition 187, 178–187 (2019)

Open Source Multipurpose Multimedia Annotation Tool

Joed Lopes da Silva[1]([⊠]), Alan Naoto Tabata[1,2], Lucas Cardoso Broto[1,2],
Marta Pereira Cocron[1], Alessandro Zimmer[1,2], and Thomas Brandmeier[1]

[1] Research and Test Center CARISSMA, Technische Hochschule Ingolstadt,
Esplanade 10, 85049 Ingolstadt, Germany
{Joed.LopesdaSilva,Marta.PereiraCocron}@carissma.eu
{alt9707,luc2031,Alessandro.Zimmer,Thomas.Brandmeier}@thi.de
[2] Federal University of Parana, XV de Novembro, Curitiba, Parana 1299, Brazil

Abstract. Efficient tools and frameworks for image and video annotation become more necessary for pattern recognition and computer vision research as datasets for training and testing of algorithms get increasingly larger. Different software packages have been developed to deal with these tasks, but they are usually designed for specific demands, problems or are not open to the public. This paper presents an open source multipurpose tool for annotation on multimedia datasets with extended flexibility through customizable labels, option of working on a shared database for collaborative annotation and with special care given on usability and efficiency for the best user experience. The Annotation Tool is available in the following link: www.thi.de/go/thi-labeling-tool.

Keywords: Open source · Video annotation · Multipurpose · Generic annotation

1 Introduction

Annotation, according to MacMullen [13], carry multiple meanings depending on the situation. In the computer science context it is related to content and process analysis, as well as system design and functionality, with examples of functionality being image, video, text, audio and others.

Annotated datasets are fundamental for pattern recognition and computer vision systems for at least two purposes: training of the algorithm and performance evaluation. In both cases, the quality of the annotation is important for successful development of the system, since patterns are found mainly on coherent data, i.e., the concept of "garbage in, garbage out" applies.

As pattern recognition algorithms turn more complex, an increasing amount of training data becomes crucial for efficient performance. This makes the building of databases an expensive process in terms of time and human effort. The use of strategies like crowdsourcing can speed it up by separating the dataset workload among people, however, care should be taken to ensure the quality and consistency of the annotations [22].

© Springer Nature Switzerland AG 2020
A. Campilho et al. (Eds.): ICIAR 2020, LNCS 12131, pp. 356–367, 2020.
https://doi.org/10.1007/978-3-030-50347-5_31

All these factors have lead to the development of specific tools for ground truth generation and performance evaluation. Two conferences on this topic have been recently organized: the International Workshop on Visual Interfaces for Ground Truth Collection in Computer Vision Applications [18] and the International Workshop on Video and Image Ground Truth in Computer Vision Applications [19].

The remaining of the paper is organized as follows. Section 2 presents a review on annotation tools used for pattern recognition systems, while Sect. 3 shows the features and architecture of the proposed multipurpose multimedia annotation tool. Finally, Sect. 4 concludes this paper with the tool's main observations, as well as features planned for future works.

2   Related Works

Ground truth annotation tools have different functions and formats depending on their purposes. When training and testing image classification algorithms, for example, each image sample must be annotated with the real class of the represented object. On the object detection context, the position of the objects must also be set, whereas on video processing, each frame in a sequence must be described.

When working with video datasets, ViPER-GT (Video Performance Evaluation Resource) [3] is one of the most used open source tools to generate annotations. It provides a graphical user interface (GUI) and a flexible descriptor format in order to facilitate the creation and sharing of ground truth data and the representation of static and dynamic information of the videos. Besides that, the software also allows for evaluation on algorithm inference results, providing a set of configurable metrics. However, it lacks features which could improve user experience and accelerate the annotation process, such as keyboard shortcuts and semi-automatic processing.

Concerning image datasets, LabelIMG [21] is a popular annotation tool developed in Python and Qt with support for Windows, Linux and Mac operating systems. It allows either Pascal VOC or YOLO bounding box input formats and saves XML annotated metadata for each image. The downside of this tool is the lack of management properties, such as to edit images. Since its last version update, it has included shortcuts to ease the process of annotation.

Labelbox [9] provides an open source annotation interface and, for a paid enterprise version, it presents an alternate interface, that minimally define the annotation ontology and allows to work with different types of data, such as point cloud, maps and videos. Labelbox saves annotations in JavaScript Object Notation (JSON) or comma-separated values (CSV) format, with a user-friendly interface and several quality of performance control mechanisms to review the work. It is possible to quickly modify the interface in a short time using the native configurator or via a custom Javascript SDK. Besides concurrent annotation queue and flexible collaboration and management tools, the application supports bounding boxes, polygons and classifications of images and text.

As a more specific application, ODViS (Open Development for Video Surveillance) [5] is designed for video surveillance systems evaluation. It provides a framework that allows a visual analysis of error in object tracking algorithms. Although an application programming interface is offered for a more versatile use of its functions, its interface is not user friendly in a way that could speed up the annotation process.

The tools GTVT (Ground Truth Verification Tool) [1] and GTTool [6] aim to overcome these issues. By focusing on reducing user effort, both applications implement tracking algorithms in order to automate the ground truth generation for frames based on the previous instances. GTVT is limited to describing bounding-boxes data for object detection and for classification, while GTTool allows the annotation of contours for object segmentation. The latter tool also implements automatic object and contour detection algorithms and custom metadata definition.

All previous solutions, however, are more suitable for limited groups of people as they don't allow native splitting the annotation task for the same dataset. For large databases, collaboration of large groups of people can reduce time and individual efforts. Web-based platforms such as LabelMe [16] use the concept of crowdsourcing to achieve this. While its original version can be considered successful in quantitative terms of annotations, these annotation's quality are criticized [7]. It is also designed just for segmentation in still images and does not take advantage of multiple annotations of the same object to improve its description.

To overcome the limitations of LabelMe, PerLA (Performance Evaluation and Labeling Annotation) [7] is proposed, being a web-based collaborative platform for video annotation with quality control and multiple annotations combination. Like GTTool, it also implements contour detection and object tracking algorithms to automate the annotation task in a set of frames in a video sequence. Another tool with ease of work is Supervisely [20], a product which helps annotate image objects on the run via pre-built algorithms, while also allowing for continuous training according to the annotated data. Besides the provided set of features to read, change and write annotations it is also possible to develop custom plugins according to the user's requisites. Apart from other tools, Supervisely allows for project management in different layers: teams, datasets and workspaces. The annotation tool supports customizable hotkeys shortcuts; however, it lacks control mechanisms such as annotation jobs, teams, roles and activities to be performed related to the annotation task and datasets and statistics evaluation. It has a community edition for free and paid self-hosted versions.

These two previously mentioned web-based collaborative tools lack, however, in terms of flexibility as they cannot be customized for describing alternative metadata for applications in different purposes. Besides object detection, classification and segmentation in images, data annotation is useful in other contexts such as gesture recognition, behavior analysis, phonetic analysis and speech transcription. For this reason, in some cases the audio information in multimedia files is also important to be considered, which is not possible for the previous cited tools. In this sense, PRAAT [2] is a traditional tool for audio-only data annotation for linguistics and phonology research. ELAN (EUDICO Linguistic Annotator) [10] allows the use and visualization of both audiovisual information but is also designed only for textual description of the data.

Still considering the necessity of dealing with varied types of input data, VGG Image Annotation Tool (VIA) [4] is an open source, easy to use annotation software, that can be used to create ground truths for image, audio and video. It is based in HTML, CSS and Javascript thus being lightweight and standalone. As a downside, it lacks a dataset management property, but contains a good set of hotkeys shortcuts. This tool comprises a set of annotation operators such as supporting lines, dots, circles, polygons, eclipses and the option to introduce images attributes and tags. The output is a JSON file or CSV file that can be downloaded.

Besides the mentioned ones, Visual Object Tagging Tool (VoTT) [23] is an open-source annotation tool developed by Microsoft. The application works with videos and images, managing data from various local and cloud storage. It has a user-friendly interface and a deep learning feature to detect objects automatically. However, the system presents a few drawbacks, such as the necessity to host your data on Microsoft's clouding computer service and lack of a built-in API.

Finally, ANVIL [8] is proposed to be a generic video annotation tool and allows multiple annotation formats based on an user-defined coding scheme. It also offers the possibility to add descriptors referring to spatial information of the image frames rather than just temporal marks. The developers claim that the software is now being used in areas like human- computer interaction, linguistics, ethology, anthropology, psychotherapy, embodied agents, computer animation and oceanography. Its flexibility allows even to generate ground truth data for computer vision applications. As it is more specifically designed for gesture analysis, however, it does not have shortcuts that facilitate tasks for this purpose.

3   Proposal

None of the aforementioned related works are capable of simultaneously accepting data sources from a diverse set of origins, annotating either each or every data source simultaneously or are open source. With this in mind, we have developed a software capable of dealing with those details.

Our main contributions lie on two main points: the development of an annotating software which contains several customized preferences and the automated data report generation. As presented on the previous section, most tools are developed with a specific use case in mind, which in turn limits its application for that specific domain. Our tool, on the other hand, was developed with this concern and therefore accepts several different types of input data which embraces images, audio, point cloud, and general signals. As such, dealing with either indexed or sequence data is also foreseen. The output of our software is also customized. PDF reports with statistical analysis on the dataset, TXT, CSV and other annotated output formats are available. Lastly, since the core of the software works with database files, then collaborative work is also possible, since the annotation process of large data is rarely done by an individual.

3.1 Software Architecture

Different projects demands different sets of attributes for data annotation and analysis. The main goal of the proposed architecture is to provide a system with customizable features to label multiple medium types. The Fig. 1 shows the data storage architecture, which can be implemented on different storage systems such as NoSQL databases (Document Based), relational databases, or simple JSON files. The current project uses MongoDB (NoSQL) as storage system, and for the visual interface Python 3 and Qt5 (GUI Framework). To design the tool's interface, the main areas were defined and disposed in a way to allow most important sections a dedicated prominent place (in the centre or top of the screen) and less frequently used information on the bottom, or even hidden. In order to provide a user-friendly interaction, actions in the labelling tool are initiated by activating traditional buttons, dropdown lists or check boxes usually implemented in other very well-known tools. All features inside the tool are possible to be customized and grouped in different ways by the user to allow a personalised and efficient handling. Each project can have more than one file, and each file's frame can have multiple values of the custom properties created.

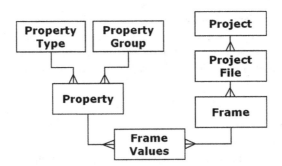

Fig. 1. Data storage architecture - each block represents an data entity

Figure 2 summarizes the recommended project workflow. First, a project is created and the files are added. Then the custom properties for the project are created and external data (from a sensor or ground truth) are imported to the database. After that the annotation process can begin. Finally, custom reports can be generated, visualized, and additional custom data can be exported.

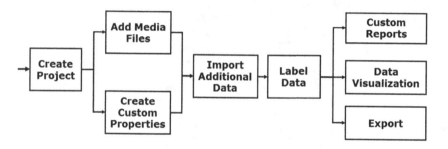

Fig. 2. Project workflow

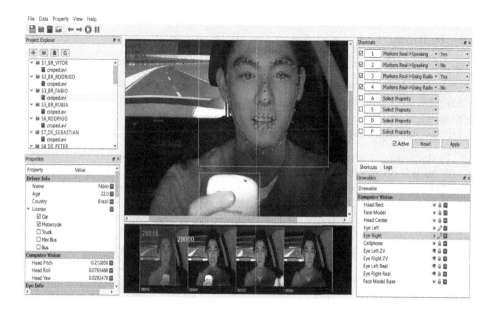

Fig. 3. Main window for video annotation

Fig. 4. Property window - example of basic information of a driver

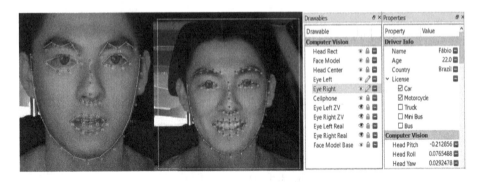

Fig. 5. Drawing window

3.2   Features

Some of the tool's key features are explained next, which include:

- Diverse input data types;
- Step-by-step x grouping labelling;
- Statistical analysis;
- Diverse labelling methods.

The proposed tool is able to accept as input and plot varied data types: image, audio, point cloud data, inertial measurement devices and vital signals. In addition to that, annotation can also be done in a frame-by-frame or in a group of frames, where on the first approach each data source is annotated individually and on the latter, every frame of the group is given the same annotation. The tool is also capable of annotating data with pre-trained algorithms which serves as a starting point for post-processing by a human expert. With the annotating process done or partially done, statistical analysis is also inferred upon the dataset, such as correlation between annotations and events, dispersion between annotations and hypothesis test.

Figure 3 shows the system's main window. When dealing with continuous time data, by using the timeline it is possible to select a range of frames to set the property values, along with user-defined key-shortcuts. This way, less time is spent on repetitive tasks, since annotation of sequential frames are usually correlated and therefore don't require individual analysis.

The property window is shown on Fig. 4, where different types of ground truth can be created. The ground truth type can be of various types: text, number, array, and even complicated array of points for polygons, such as the Deformable Face Model, Rectangles, and Ellipses, commonly used for eye iris annotation. The properties can be global data (name of the driver, age, country, and so on) or can vary each frame: face model, sensors value. Also, a filter for each property to be displayed is also available. Finally, each ground truth data type can also inherit a Reference Class, where the user can implement and define custom rules and functionalities. On Fig. 5 the property editor is shown in action alongside the drawing editor for labelling points of a face.

3.3   Statistical Analysis

Additionally to storing annotated data, commonly used statistical methods [12,14,15,24] in the automotive context are also featured on the software, with both univariate and multivariate analysis. For univariate nominal samples, the frequency and modes are given; whilst for numerical data the range (min and max), median, mean, mode, standard deviation and variance are also presented. Besides that, a module for hypothesis testing is also available with p and z-test, which then allows for ANOVA calculations. As for multivariate, focus is on dependence, with calculation of correlation (Pearson and Spearman correlations), covariance, and contingency tables for a general overview on the data distribution. Along these lines, the software also presents a UI with dispersion plotting between pairs of variables to check for possible relationships. Besides performing analysis on the created ground truth data, the software is also capable of presenting performance results to common machine learning tasks, such as mean average precision for object detection [11], precision, accuracy, recall,

Table 1. Different data type examples

Variable/Data	Type	Description
Driver personal information		
Driver's name	String	The name of the driver
Driver's age	Number	The age of the driver
Driver's license	String array	Multiple options: the driver can be able to drive small cars, motorcycles, bus and trucks
Driver's citizenship	String array	The driver can have multiple citizenship and each country has different rules for driving
Ground truth		
Head rectangle	Rectangle	The position of the driver heads in the image frame
Head pose	Number (angles)	The angles of the driver head pose (roll, pitch, yaw)
Eye position	Eye position	The position of the left and right iris in the image
Facial features	Array of points	The feature points of the driver's face: mouth and eyes
Sensors		
Inertial sensor	Number	Information about head pose (roll, pitch, yaw)
Heartbeat sensor	Number	The heartbeat frequency of the driver provided by an external sensor
Car sensors		
Car speed	Number	Speed of the car
Car brake position	Number	Brake pressing condition and amount
Steering wheel angle	Number	Steering wheel position
Computer vision		
Face tracking	Rectangle	Face points acquired by the computer vision algorithm
Speaking detection	Boolean	Result of the computer vision algorithm (true or false)
Visual focus	Number (angles)	Angles of the driver's gaze

F1-score and Receiver Operating Characteristic Curve (ROC) for classification, and mean squared error and root-mean-square deviation for regression.

3.4 Use Cases and Applications

To exemplify the proposed solution, the data collected in [17] is described, where a database of drivers in specific scenarios is built. The experiment works with different types of data and variables, as described on Table 1.

As seen on Table 1, a project can have many types of variables and data. The proposed tool is able to create all these custom properties dynamically, moreover, all the data of each frame is stored in a NoSQL database (MongoDB). It is to be noted that usage of a relational database is not convenient for such architecture, since the system would not run queries in real time; the NoSQL approach, however, can fetch the data of each frame quickly even with big datasets. The dataset described on [17] has 20 videos with 40.000 frames with each containing more than 500 data entries (numbers, strings, points). For that reason, a relational database style can not handle efficiently such amount of data, and by using MongoDB, additional operations can be performed, such as Map and Reduce to export reports and extract any needed data. The Figs. 3, 4, 5 shows the configurations used for this task.

In the Fig. 6 is presented the use case for a pupillometry study where the subject's personal information is stored, and for each frame of a video sequence the iris and the pupil positions are labeled using ellipses. In the Fig. 7 is pre-

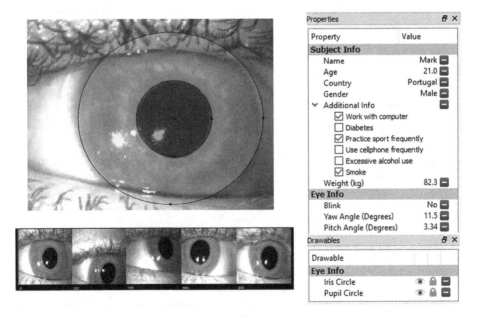

Fig. 6. Use Case - Eye Iris/Pupil study

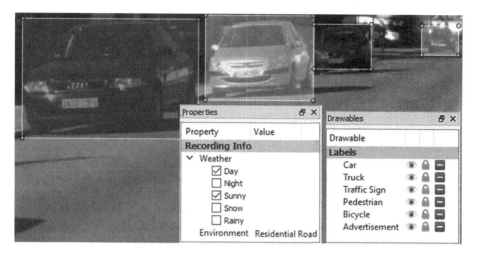

Fig. 7. Use Case - Traffic Dataset

Fig. 8. Different input data types: image and point cloud (top); and Data Synchronization window (bottom).

sented the use case for a traffic data labeling. And, in the Fig. 8, is shown the synchronized data of multiple data source files of monocular images and point cloud data.

4   Conclusion

An open source framework capable of reading data from a diverse set of sources and adapted to annotating either each type of data or data in general has been developed. It accepts mainly data sources from autonomous applications, such as image, audio, point cloud data, inertial measurement devices and vital signals.

Additionally, the developed framework is capable to handle and display large amounts of data, with the option of multiple users being able to remotely access the same database and work cooperatively. The system can be used in a variety of experiments, even projects not related to image classification. Finally, because it uses Python as the main programming language, it makes easier for third parties to integrate new plugins or to customize the application.

For future works, the authors plan on implementing additional statistical analysis, being the inter-rater reliability and intra-rater reliability tests to further aid on establishing a coherent dataset. Moreover, a usability test with potential users of the tool is also planned to improve the features, and allow users less familiar with labelling software to have a good experience.

5   To Download the Annotation Tool

The Annotation Tool developed by Technische Hochschule Ingostadt is available in the following link: www.thi.de/go/thi-labeling-tool. Please read the related terms and conditions before downloading the tool. If you use the tool in any academic work, please cite this paper.

References

1. Ambardekar, A., Nicolescu, M., Dascalu, S.: Ground truth verification tool (GTVT) for video surveillance systems. In: 2009 Second International Conferences on Advances in Computer-Human Interactions, pp. 354–359. IEEE (2009)
2. Boersma, P., et al.: The use of praat in corpus research. In: The Oxford Handbook of Corpus Phonology, pp. 342–360 (2014)
3. Doermann, D., Mihalcik, D.: Tools and techniques for video performance evaluation. In: Proceedings 15th International Conference on Pattern Recognition, ICPR-2000, vol. 4, pp. 167–170. IEEE (2000)
4. Dutta, A., Zisserman, A.: The VIA annotation software for images, audio and video. In: Proceedings of the 27th ACM International Conference on Multimedia, MM 2019. ACM, New York (2019). https://doi.org/10.1145/3343031.3350535
5. Jaynes, C., Webb, S., Steele, R., Xiong, Q.: An open development environment for evaluation of video surveillance systems. In: PETS02, pp. 32–39 (2002)
6. Kavasidis, I., Palazzo, S., Di Salvo, R., Giordano, D., Spampinato, C.: A semi-automatic tool for detection and tracking ground truth generation in videos. In: Proceedings of the 1st International Workshop on Visual Interfaces for Ground Truth Collection in Computer Vision Applications, p. 6. ACM (2012)
7. Kavasidis, I., Palazzo, S., Salvo, R.D., Giordano, D., Spampinato, C.: An innovative web-based collaborative platform for video annotation. Multimed. Tools Appl. **70**(1), 413–432 (2013). https://doi.org/10.1007/s11042-013-1419-7

8. Kipp, M.: Anvil: the video annotation research tool. In: Handbook of Corpus Phonology, pp. 420–436 (2014)
9. Labelbox (2018). https://github.com/Labelbox/Labelbox/blob/master/README.md
10. Lausberg, H., Sloetjes, H.: Coding gestural behavior with the NEUROGES-ELAN system. Behav. Res. Methods **41**(3), 841–849 (2009). https://doi.org/10.3758/BRM.41.3.841
11. Lin, T.-Y., et al.: Microsoft COCO: common objects in context. In: Fleet, D., Pajdla, T., Schiele, B., Tuytelaars, T. (eds.) ECCV 2014. LNCS, vol. 8693, pp. 740–755. Springer, Cham (2014). https://doi.org/10.1007/978-3-319-10602-1_48
12. Llaneras, R.E., Salinger, J., Green, C.A.: Human factors issues associated with limited ability autonomous driving systems: drivers' allocation of visual attention to the forward roadway (2013)
13. MacMullen, W.J.: Annotation as process, thing, and knowledge: multi-domain studies of structured data annotation. In: ASIST Annual Meeting (2005)
14. Maurer, M., Gerdes, J.C., Lenz, B., Winner, H., et al.: Autonomous Driving. Springer, Heidelberg (2016). https://doi.org/10.1007/978-3-662-48847-8
15. Muhrer, E., Reinprecht, K., Vollrath, M.: Driving with a partially autonomous forward collision warning system: how do drivers react? Hum. Factors **54**(5), 698–708 (2012)
16. Russell, B.C., Torralba, A., Murphy, K.P., Freeman, W.T.: Labelme: a database and web-based tool for image annotation. Int. J. Comput. Vis. **77**(1–3), 157–173 (2008). https://doi.org/10.1007/s11263-007-0090-8
17. da Silva, J.L., Thomas Brandmeier, A.Z.: Automatic measurement of automobile drivers attention level via computer vision. In: XXIV Congresso Brasileiro De Engenharia Biomédica (2014)
18. Spampinato, C., Boom, B., He, J.: First international workshop on visual interfaces for ground truth collection in computer vision applications. In: Proceedings of the International Working Conference on Advanced Visual Interfaces, pp. 812–814. ACM (2012)
19. Spampinato, C., Boom, B., Huet, B.: Vigta 2013: Proceedings of the International Workshop on Video and Image Ground Truth in Computer Vision Applications, pp. 812–814. ACM (2013)
20. Supervisely (2019). https://github.com/supervisely/supervisely/blob/master/README.md
21. Tzutalin: Labelimg (2015). https://github.com/tzutalin/labelImg/blob/master/README.rst
22. Vondrick, C., Patterson, D., Ramanan, D.: Efficiently scaling up crowdsourced video annotation. Int. J. Comput. Vis. **101**(1), 184–204 (2013). https://doi.org/10.1007/s11263-012-0564-1
23. VoTT: Vott (visual object tagging tool) (2019). https://github.com/microsoft/VoTT/blob/master/README.md
24. Walch, M., Lange, K., Baumann, M., Weber, M.: Autonomous driving: investigating the feasibility of car-driver handover assistance. In: Proceedings of the 7th International Conference on Automotive User Interfaces and Interactive Vehicular Applications, pp. 11–18. ACM (2015)

SLAM-Based Multistate Tracking System for Mobile Human-Robot Interaction

Thorsten Hempel$^{(\boxtimes)}$ (ID) and Ayoub Al-Hamadi$^{(\boxtimes)}$ (ID)

Neuro-Information Technology (NIT),
Otto-von-Guericke University Magdeburg,
Universitaetsplatz 2, 39106 Magdeburg, Germany
{thorsten.hempel,ayoub.al-hamadi}@ovgu.de

Abstract. The transfer from the utilization of simple robots for specifically predefined tasks to the integration of generalized autonomous systems poses a number of challenges for the collaboration between humans and robots. These include the independent orientation of robots in unknown environments and the intuitive interaction with human cooperation partners. We present a robust human-robot interaction (HRI) system that proactively searches for interaction partners and follows them in unknown real environments. For this purpose, an algorithm for simultaneous localization and mapping of the environment is integrated along with a dynamic system for determination of the partner's willingness and the tracking of the partner's localization. Interruptions of interactions are recovered by a separate recovery mode that is able to identify prior collaboration partners.

Keywords: Human-robot interaction · Slam · Interaction willingness detection

1 Introduction

The introduction of robots into industry led to significant increases of productivity and innovation due to machines' constant strength and precision. Yet, robots are mostly unable to perceive their environment and lack the ability to engage reactively with arbitrary surrounding conditions. Thus, robotic applications are used in isolated workspaces that are specifically tailored to their restricted abilities that omits useful interaction opportunities, for example, the robots assignment as carrying assistant that is autonomous following its human partner. The potential of HRI for mobile robotic applications in the industrial and healthcare environment encourages the development of new technological concepts for intuitive communications and generalized safe interactions with cooperation partners by developing awareness about their physical themselves and their environment. Several approaches have been proposed to deal with specific tasks of these objectives, whereas composing a robot system with interacting submodules involves its own challenges.

© Springer Nature Switzerland AG 2020
A. Campilho et al. (Eds.): ICIAR 2020, LNCS 12131, pp. 368–376, 2020.
https://doi.org/10.1007/978-3-030-50347-5_32

1.1   Simultaneous Localization and Mapping

Creating a map of the surrounding environment while simultaneously maintaining the robots location within is the research object of SLAM algorithms. Without access to a priori information most approaches try to solve this task as a probabilistic problem by aiming to minimize the approximation errors for the localization and environment reconstruction. Popular methods are particle filters [10], extended Kalman filters [4,14] and graph-based approaches [11] that use natural or artificial landmarks for triangulation. On the contrary, direct SLAM methods [5,8,13] operate directly on image intensities for tracking and robot localization. This enables the creation of dense maps of the environment, but requires a lot more processing power than landmark based methods. Currently SLAM systems with the highest accuracy rate rely on feature point landmarks, whereby graph-based approaches stand out due to their post-correction and optimization abilities of past landmarks and poses maintained in graph structures. The current state of the art approach from Mur-Artal et al. [12] combines these advantages with multiple graphs of different information complexities. This way the creation of large maps and trajectory graphs is viable due to the spare maintenance of rapid increasing sensor data.

1.2   Human-Robot-Interaction

Common approaches aim for the transition from a specific robot interface to reactive and adaptable actions of autonomous robots for intuitive and natural cooperation between humans and machines. One prerequisite step is the robot systems adaption to the respective human behavior and traits in order to be universally and safely applicable independently of varying human partners. This requires the analysis of potential human interaction partners to detect a persons willingness for collaboration. Recent approaches manage this complex tasks by predicting intention [9] and behavior [1], others utilize the human facial expressions [17], gesture and pose [16] to derive non-verbal feedback. However, these methods still not fulfill the requirements of robustness, versatility and generalization. In addition, evaluating interaction willingness tends to be very subjective which brings additional difficulties for assessing methods in a quantitative way.

In this paper we introduce a real-time SLAM-based robot system that determines the willingness for cooperation of potential interaction partners by estimating their head pose in relation to the robot over adapting time spans. After a successful detection the robot follows its interaction partner by utilizing detecting and tracking methods. An additional recognition module has been implemented to reactivate recent collaborations with prior interaction partners.

Section 2 gives details of the proposed systems and the used methods starting with the interaction willingness detection algorithm, followed by an examination of the tracking and identification module. Section 3 shows experimental results that are resumed and concluded in Sect. 4.

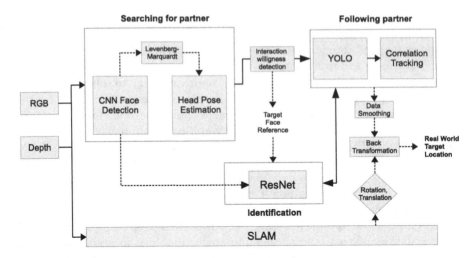

Fig. 1. Block diagram of the introduced system. The interaction modules contain three different states to process visual input. A DNN is used for face detection to search for interaction partners. The faces are further analyzed for their 3D head pose to derive the attention towards the robot. Upheld attention over multiple images is classified as interaction willingness that leads to next state: Following the partner. Visual Tracking is processed by alternating object detection and correlation tracking. The results are used to determine the world position via back transformation. A ResNet is used for interaction reactivation in the third state that matches incoming faces with prior partners' face information. After a successful match the following of the partner continues.

2   System Description

Figure 1 shows an overview of our system. For elementary orientation we chose the open source ORB-SLAM2 algorithm[1] which offers state-of-the-art realtime mapping and localization features. On top of it the HRI-System thread is dividable in three states: Searching for an interaction partner, following it, and its identification.

2.1   Interaction Willingness

We first search for faces in the incoming frames to find potential interaction partner. We use the OpenCV [3] CNN face detector and compensate its longer inference time towards other simpler face detectors by processing the network on the GPU. To derive the head pose from the detected faces, facial landmarks are extracted using dlibs landmark estimator implementation of [7]. Afterwards the head pose is estimated. We use n extracted 2D landmarks as image projections points

$$p_i = [u_i \ v_i \ 1]^T \tag{1}$$

---

[1] https://github.com/raulmur/ORB_SLAM2.

and a generalized head model with corresponding n 3D reference points

$$q_i = [x_i \ y_i \ z_i]^T. \tag{2}$$

Given this and the camera coefficients the 3D coordinates rotations and translations is recovered using the nonlinear Levenberg-Marquardt optimization by iteratively estimating rotation matrix R and translation vector t so that

$$\gamma_i \ p_i = R \ q_i + t, \tag{3}$$

where γ_i denotes the depth factor of point i.

The resulting head pose is observed over multiple frames to analyze the viewing direction. We experienced that falsely estimated head poses and affective distractions on behalf of the viewer can lead to momentary interruptions of the turning to the robot. Thus, we implemented a loading bar principle that will load faster by looking at the robot than it will unload when looking away. Persisting viewing direction towards the robot is interpreted as interaction willingness. In this case a reference face image and the face landmarks of the observed person are saved and the next state gets activated to follow the found cooperation partner.

2.2   Tracking of the Interaction Partner

Once an interaction partner is registered, the face detection gets detached by object detection to track the partners location. We search for the whole body of the person. This increases the robustness as we no longer depend on the face and following the partner also in greater distances is possible. To ensure that the right person is tracked, the detection result rectangle is initially matched with the image area of last face bounding box. As object detector we use the fast YOLOv3 model [15]. To increase the processing speed even further, the object detection is only fired every fifth frame. The tracking in intermediate frames is processed by an efficient mosse-based correlation filter [2] that offers shorter inference times and adapting of the tracking box size. Another main advantage is the reduced flickering of the bounding box in comparison to the object detection. Yet, it tends to loose track over time in scenes with increased movement. Therefore, we use object detection as a correction mechanism to rectify drifts from the tracking algorithm periodically. Visual tracking is not enough to gain knowledge about the geographical location of the interaction partner. Hence, the 2D coordinates from the interactions partner are transformed from pixel to global level,

$$P_w = [R|T] \ [M^{-1}P_h \ d|1] \tag{4}$$

where P_h denotes the homogeneous pixel coordinates and $[M]^{-1}$ the inverse camera matrix with the intrinsic and extrinsic camera parameters. Depth d is estimated by calculating the mean of an inner crop of the detection box from the depth image. Matrix $[R|T]$ provides translation and rotation information about the entire movement from the first to the current keyframe of the camera provided by the SLAM algorithm. Using these variables, we can induce the 3D world coordinates P_w that enables us to construct a position graph. The accuracy of the resulting graph depends on the performance from the SLAM process and the coordinates accuracy of the interaction partner, which are extracted from the centroid of the detection and tracking bounding boxes.

As the used object detector is trained to find the whole area of a human body, the detection rectangles can grow and shrink heavily in order to cover extending limbs from movements and gestures. These changes, as well as false detection and the natural flickering of object detectors, have a big impact on the extracted centroid, which leads to drifts and jitters in the location graph. To get rid of outliers and noise, we apply a Savitzky-Golay filter for smoothing. A median filter could also deal with it, but it would reduce local minima and maxima and thus the complete range of motion that we detect from our interaction partner. With a Savitzky-Golay moving window averaging we still incorporate extrema, but smooth the jittery bounding box movements by local polynomial regression. The result is the linear combination x_i of itself and $2 \cdot M$ nearby neighbors defined as

$$x_i = \sum_{k=-M}^{M} c_k y_{i+k} \tag{5}$$

with the data value y_{i+k} that is multiplied with the convolution coefficient c_k. For calculating the coefficients $c_{-M;M}$ we use a polynomial of higher order K defined as

$$p_i = \sum_{k=0}^{K} c_k i^k \tag{6}$$

that we calculate by minimizing the square error E,

$$E = \sum_{i=-M}^{M} (y_i - p_i)^2 \tag{7}$$

to all position data points in the moving window. This way, we preserve higher moments than using a constant. Since the calculation only depends on the polynomial order, we can prepare it beforehand to save processing time in runtime. We empirically found that a windows size $n = 2 \cdot M + 1 = 11$ and polynomial order of five work well to retain a natural movement graph after filtering.

Newly processed landmark information and a loop detection can lead to optimization and correction of the whole camera trajectory graph by the SLAM algorithm that can make the location graph inconsistent. Therefore we keep the raw data to be able to rebuild the interaction partner's location graph along with the SLAM's bundle adjustment and smooth it afterwards.

2.3   Reactivating Collaborations

If multiple object detection attempts do not detect any humans in the target area, we assume that the interaction partner has left the camera frame. This will stop any object detection and tracking and activates the state for reactivating collaboration. From now on every frame is examined for faces by a DNN face detector again. Found faces are given to a neural network for face recognition that matches them with the prior saved reference face data of the last interaction partner. We chose dlibs implemented and modified version of the ResNet-34 network [6] that provides state of the art accuracy (99,38% on LFW benchmark [18]). Once there is a successful match a new reference face image and corresponding facial landmarks are stored again and the tracking can be resumed by switching back to the previous state.

3   Experimental Results

Figure 2 shows two SLAM maps with the camera trajectory (green) and the position graph of the interaction partner (gray) in order to compare raw and filtered location graph data. We used the videos test sequence *freiburg2/desk_with_person* from the TUM dataset that shows a person sitting at a desk while the camera is moving around him. The person is barely changing its core position but simulates typical desk movements like stretching out his legs and reaching for the telephone. The movement graph in the left image strongly reflects these movements and clusters a lot of noise position graph nodes. The movement graph in the right image shows that our approach of smoothing was able to rectify a lot of oscillations that results into a more compact graph. The location graph contains even less nodes since a new node is only accepted if its distance to the previous node is more than 0.3 m.

Figure 3 illustrates a real-time experiment including all three states. The extracted frames show snapshots of the test sequence. The corresponding slam map with its tracked feature points and the movement graph of the interaction partner is shown below them. In the first image a test person enters the frame and signals interaction willingness. Thereupon, the next system state is activated leading to detecting and tracking of the whole body to build up a position graph as shown in image two to five. After that the interaction partner leaves the camera to interrupt the connection which activates the next state for rediscovering

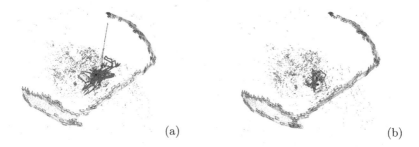

(a)   (b)

Fig. 2. Comparison between raw position data (a) and smoothed position data (b). (Color figure online)

Fig. 3. Qualitative results of an interaction through all system states. Processed image frames with corresponding feature map with position graph (view from above)

prior collaborations. The tracking stops and face identification of incoming faces begins. In the next image a second test person enters the camera frame, but is successfully ignored as it does not match the registered partner. In image seven the interaction partner enters the frame again and gets recognized. The system state is switched back and the tracking continues.

We experienced that real-time capabilities are inevitable to maintain meaningful data about the head and position estimation. This concerns especially system state transitions where information needs to be accurate and up to date to make consistent associations possible. An example is the transition from identifying a prior interaction partner to its tracking. If a known face is found, the object detector tries to find the whole body in the area of the found face. So the recognition process must be fast enough to deliver accurate corresponding face position data in case the person is moving.

We process all used models in the interactor thread on the GPU (GTX 1060). Table 1 illustrates the average processing times of our interactor thread in comparison to the SLAM tracking thread. The slowest network is YOLO that has an inference time of 45 ms. The correlation tracker takes 7 ms. In Combination with

Table 1. Processing time of the different system states compared with the SLAM's tracking thread.

Tracking thread	Interactor thread		
Tracking	Searching	Following	Identification
30 ms	8 ms	14.6 ms	15 ms

YOLO, that is only used for every fifth frame, we achieve an average thread time of 14.6 ms. The identification state needs 15 ms and is therefore in average the slowest thread state. Nevertheless we are still two times faster than the SLAM main tracking thread that takes about 30 ms on our CPU (i7 6850K).

Yet, the SLAM tracking is the backbone of our proposed system. We experienced that dynamic objects and therefore also the moving interaction partner have big impact on the accuracy and robustness of the SLAM results. We found that the estimated camera trajectory tends to shift when matched tracking features are located on the dynamic interaction partner.

4 Conclusion and Future Work

In this paper we presented a HRI system that is able to detect interaction willingness and follow the interaction partner. With a SLAM algorithm as backbone it is usable in a mobile robotic system in real unknown environments. The reactivation capabilities of prior cooperation make it flexible and robust towards interruptions of interactions. The synergy of these features with real-time capabilities enables the proposed system to be used in real world applications for service and industrial robots.

Future extensions of this work might include the creation of a dataset with typical interaction scenes and corresponding ground truths of the human partner that would enable more precise qualitative evaluations of the system's accuracy and robustness. In addition a tighter communication with the SLAM algorithm about suitable keypoint selections would be a reasonable approach for equally improving the SLAM trajectory and the accuracy of the proposed system.

Acknowledgments. This work is funded by the Federal Ministry of Education and Research (BMBF) (RoboAssist no. 03ZZ0448G-L) within 3Dsensation alliance.

References

1. Awais, M., Henrich, D.: Human-robot collaboration by intention recognition using probabilistic state machines. In: 19th International Workshop on Robotics in Alpe-Adria-Danube Region (RAAD 2010). pp. 75–80, June 2010. https://doi.org/10.1109/RAAD.2010.5524605
2. Bolme, D.S., Beveridge, J.R., Draper, B.A., Lui, Y.M.: Visual object tracking using adaptive correlation filters. In: 2010 IEEE Computer Society Conference on Computer Vision and Pattern Recognition, pp. 2544–2550 (2010)

3. Bradski, G.: The OpenCV library. Dr. Dobb's J. Softw. Tools (2000)
4. Davison, A.J., Reid, I.D., Molton, N.D., Stasse, O.: Monoslam: real-time single camera slam. IEEE Trans Pattern Anal. Mach. Intell. **29**, 1052–1067 (2007)
5. Engel, J., Koltun, V., Cremers, D.: Direct sparse odometry. CoRR abs/1607.02565 (2016). http://arxiv.org/abs/1607.02565
6. He, K., Zhang, X., Ren, S., Sun, J.: Deep residual learning for image recognition. In: 2016 IEEE Conference on Computer Vision and Pattern Recognition (CVPR), pp. 770–778 (2015)
7. Kazemi, V., Sullivan, J.: One millisecond face alignment with an ensemble of regression trees. In: 2014 IEEE Conference on Computer Vision and Pattern Recognition, pp. 1867–1874 (2014)
8. Kerl, C., Sturm, J., Cremers, D.: Dense visual slam for RGB-D cameras. In: 2013 IEEE/RSJ International Conference on Intelligent Robots and Systems, pp. 2100–2106, November 2013. https://doi.org/10.1109/IROS.2013.6696650
9. Li, S., Zhang, L., Diao, X.: Deep-learning-based human intention prediction using RGB images and optical flow. J. Intell. Robot. Syst. **97**(1), 95–107 (2019). https://doi.org/10.1007/s10846-019-01049-3
10. Montemerlo, M., Thrun, S., Koller, D., Wegbreit, B.: FastSLAM 2.0: an improved particle filtering algorithm for simultaneous localization and mapping that provably converges. In: Proceedings of the Sixteenth International Joint Conference on Artificial Intelligence (IJCAI), IJCAI, Acapulco, Mexico (2003)
11. Mur-Artal, R., Montiel, J.M.M., Tardós, J.D.: ORB-SLAM: a versatile and accurate monocular slam system. CoRR abs/1502.00956 (2015)
12. Mur-Artal, R., Tardos, J.D.: ORB-SLAM2: an open-source slam system for monocular, stereo, and RGB-D cameras. IEEE Trans. Rob. **33**(5), 1255–1262 (2017). https://doi.org/10.1109/tro.2017.2705103
13. Newcombe, R.A., Lovegrove, S., Davison, A.J.: DTAM: dense tracking and mapping in real-time. In: Metaxas, D.N., Quan, L., Sanfeliu, A., Gool, L.J.V. (eds.) ICCV, pp. 2320–2327. IEEE (2011)
14. Pire, T., Fischer, T., Castro, G., De Cristóforis, P., Civera, J., Berlles, J.: S-PTAM: stereo parallel tracking and mapping. Robot. Auton. Syst. **93**, 27–42 (2017). https://doi.org/10.1016/j.robot.2017.03.019
15. Redmon, J., Farhadi, A.: Yolov3: an incremental improvement (2018). http://arxiv.org/abs/1804.02767. cite arxiv:1804.02767Comment. Technical report
16. Svenstrup, M., Tranberg, S., Andersen, H.J., Bak, T.: Pose estimation and adaptive robot behaviour for human-robot interaction. In: 2009 IEEE International Conference on Robotics and Automation, pp. 3571–3576, May 2009. https://doi.org/10.1109/ROBOT.2009.5152690
17. Tistarelli, M., Grosso, E.: Human face analysis: from identity to emotion and intention recognition. In: Kumar, A., Zhang, D. (eds.) ICEB 2010. LNCS, vol. 6005, pp. 76–88. Springer, Heidelberg (2010). https://doi.org/10.1007/978-3-642-12595-9_11
18. Wolf, L., Hassner, T., Taigman, Y.: Effective unconstrained face recognition by combining multiple descriptors and learned background statistics. IEEE Trans. Pattern Anal. Mach. Intell. **33**(10), 1978–1990 (2011). https://doi.org/10.1109/TPAMI.2010.230

3D Computer Vision

Dense Disparity Maps from RGB and Sparse Depth Information Using Deep Regression Models

Pedro Nuno Leite[1,2]([✉]), Renato Jorge Silva[1,2], Daniel Filipe Campos[1,2], and Andry Maykol Pinto[1,2]

[1] INESC TEC, Centre for Robotics and Autonomous Systems, Porto, Portugal
pedro.nuno@inesctec.pt
[2] Faculty of Engineering of University of Porto, Porto, Portugal

Abstract. A dense and accurate disparity map is relevant for a large number of applications, ranging from autonomous driving to robotic grasping. Recent developments in machine learning techniques enable us to bypass sensor limitations, such as low resolution, by using deep regression models to complete otherwise sparse representations of the 3D space. This article proposes two main approaches that use a single RGB image and sparse depth information gathered from a variety of sensors/techniques (stereo, LiDAR and Light Stripe Ranging (LSR)): a Convolutional Neural Network (CNN) and a cascade architecture, that aims to improve the results of the first. Ablation studies were conducted to infer the impact of these depth cues on the performance of each model. The models trained with LiDAR sparse information are the most reliable, achieving an average Root Mean Squared Error (RMSE) of 11.8 cm on our own Inhouse dataset; while the LSR proved to be too sparse of an input to compute accurate predictions on its own.

Keywords: Disparity map · Sparse depth information · Convolutional neural networks

1 Introduction

A wide array of applications are highly dependent on robust depth predictions. This computer vision task is of vital importance for autonomous driving, robotic grasping, augmented reality and 3D mapping, just to name a few.

Sensor limitations can severely hinder these applications. Among the most commonly used sensors for depth estimation are stereo cameras. These make use of two different views of the same scenario to estimate the depth for each pixel, by finding correspondences in each image. Light conditions strongly affect stereo methods, as well as the lack of texture in some areas, which makes it impossible to find disparities in both frames [3]. LiDARs are another very popular choice for depth estimation, being very accurate and reliable. On the other hand, high-end models are quite expensive and, like the lower-tier ones, lack the necessary

© Springer Nature Switzerland AG 2020
A. Campilho et al. (Eds.): ICIAR 2020, LNCS 12131, pp. 379–392, 2020.
https://doi.org/10.1007/978-3-030-50347-5_33

resolution to provide dense estimations. As distance increases, this problem gets aggravated. One other less common method, and more application specific (e.g. underwater) is using Light Stripe Ranging (LSR). This method consists in projecting a set of visible stripes of light (generated by a laser diode) into the scene. The 3D information is recovered from these laser stripes by means of triangulation [12]. Although highly accurate, the depth information extracted from this method is rather sparse.

Monocular depth estimation aims at finding depth cues from a single RGB image. These features can either be global (eg. perspective, shadows and edges) or local such as focus/out-of-focus [4]. Despite the recent advancements in this field, resultant from deep-learning techniques, the use of a single monocular camera is still not accurate enough, achieving worse performances on the state-of-the-art datasets for the task (eg. KITTI and NYUDV2) [9]. An interesting way to further improve these results, is the combined use of an RGB image with a sparse depth input (RGBD-based depth prediction).

This work is then focused on predicting a robust and dense disparity estimation from a single RGB image combined with sparse depth cues. To achieve such end, two deep-learning based approaches were studied: a single Sparse-to-Dense Convolutional Neural Network (S2D CNN), and a cascade pipeline makes use of the first to compute an intermediate prediction and further refines it. The S2D CNN is a residual network proposed by Fangchang Ma *et al.* [9], re-trained to learn deep regression models for each of the aforementioned sparse inputs (stereo-based, LiDAR and LSR). Since, to the best of the authors' knowledge, there are no available datasets containing sparse depth samples obtained via the LSR technique, our own dataset was collected for this experimentation purpose. Therefore the contributions of this work are:

- An Inhouse dataset comprised of RGB images taken under different lighting conditions, as well as the corresponding sparse depth samples obtained from multiple sensors/techniques (stereo, LiDAR, LSR);
- A comparative study on how the performance of deep regression models for dense disparity estimation is affected by the intrinsic characteristics of each sparse input (e.g. accuracy, spatial distribution, sensibility to lighting conditions);
- A cascade pipeline that uses the S2D CNN as building block to generate a first intermediate prediction, later refining it with a second model.

The remainder of this article is structured as follows: Sect. 2 shortly discusses some related work; The dataset, its acquisition process and data augmentation techniques are presented in Sect. 3; Both the deep regression network as well as the cascade approach, combining multiple models, are detailed in Sect. 4; Section 5 offers a quantitative analysis of the obtained results for the different approaches; And finally, Sect. 6 summarizes the conducted work and provides a critical view of the obtained results.

2   Related Work

The usage of deep learning to overcome the many flaws and limitations of depth sensors, such as stereo cameras and LiDARs, has recently started to achieve very promising results. This section aims at discussing some of the approaches that are relevant for this work.

Depth Estimation from a Single RGB Image. Traditional methods that aim at estimating dense depth maps from RGB images alone usually rely on hand-crafted features and probabilistic models. With the recent developments in deep learning techniques, methods based on these models are able to achieve better performances. Eigen *et al.* [2] propose a two-stack CNN, the first tasked with making a prediction based on the whole image, while the second refines this prediction based on local features. Laina *et al.* [7] make use of a single, however deeper, CNN based on the ResNet architecture, for the same purpose. An unsupervised learning method is presented by Godard *et al.* [5], where depth estimation is formulated as an image reconstruction problem. This approach is based on the intuition that by learning how to reconstruct one image from the other (left-right camera setup), one is able to calculate the disparities for both cameras, using a single image. A CNN is then trained, using this insight knowledge, with a loss function that forces both disparities to be consistent with each other. Pillai *et al.* [11] use self-supervised learning for the same task. The authors propose a subpixel convolutional layer extension as well as a differentiable flip-augmentation layer (reducing the effect of occlusions), obtaining significant performance gains on the KITTI dataset benchmark.

Sensor Fusion: Depth Reconstruction from Sparse Samples. A wide range of techniques attempt to improve depth prediction by taking sparse depth inputs and fusing them with additional information from different sensors. The work proposed by Mancini *et al.* [10] uses both RGB images and optical flows as inputs for a CNN that aims to obtain fast and robust depth predictions. Uhrig *et al.* [13] propose a sparsity invariant CNN which considers the location of the missing data during the convolution process. The closest work that uses something similar to sparse depth from an LSR technique is the one presented by Liao *et al.* [8]. This study used a 2D laser mounted on a ground robot to provide a sparse depth input that would increase the accuracy of an RGB-based depth estimation model. A multi-modal auto-encoder is proposed by Cadena *et al.* [1], taking as inputs RGB images, sparse depth cues and semantic labels. The accuracy resultant from this work was comparable to using RGB alone. Fangchang Ma *et al.* [9] proposed feeding to a single encoder-decoder network the concatenation of a sparse depth sample with an RGB image. This approach serves as the base architecture of the work presented in this article.

3   Inhouse Dataset

There are a number of publicly available datasets that can be used in tasks such as depth prediction/completion (eg. KITTI, NYUDV2, Scene Flow). However, none offer the variety of sparse inputs pretended for this work, and more specifically there are no datasets with sparse depth computed from LSR techniques. To gather data from multiple sensors the authors resorted to the setup represented in Fig. 1.

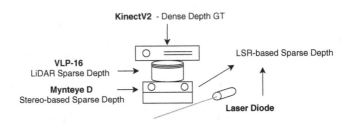

Fig. 1. Sensor setup used to collect our Inhouse Dataset.

The dense Ground Truth (GT) is given by a KinectV2 (Monocular camera + IR pattern emitter), while sparse depth samples are collected from the remaining sensors: a stereo-based method, computed from both the left and right frames of the Mynteye D camera; a pointcloud gathered from the VLP-16 LiDAR; and finally using the LSR technique (the laser stripe is segmented from the RGB frame and 3D information is extracted by means of triangulation between the laser-camera setup). All the depth samples are then projected onto a 2D plane, where pixel intensities represent depth. Since RGB-based methods are highly dependent on the lighting conditions, these were changed iteratively during every scenario to increase the variety of both the RGB and stereo-based sparse samples.

Each sample is then preprocessed online, RGB images are normalized so that each pixel $\in [0,1]$ and the pixels from the depth samples are converted to their correspondent depth in meters (according to Eq. 1). This conversion makes it more direct to compute quantitative metrics, and also to match the input representation necessary for the architecture presented in [9].

$$D(m) = D(px) \cdot \frac{(M_d - m_d)}{255} + m_d \qquad (1)$$

where D represents the Depth values; M_d and m_d correspond, respectively, to the maximum and minimum distances, in meters.

Since the amount of data is small, even more so after the train/test and train/validation splits (90–10% and 80–20% respectively), and the scenarios are somewhat limited, data augmentation is performed to improve the generalization capabilities of the models described in the following sections. Such is done both online and offline by applying random transformations to the input data:

- Random **Rotations** between $[-10, 10]$ degrees;
- Vertical and Horizontal **Flips** with a 0.5 probability;
- **Color Jitter** - brightness, saturation and contrast are scaled randomly.

The authors considered performing random crops in addition to the aforementioned transformations, however, decided against it since removing information from an already sparse input could result in a far more complex regression model. This dataset is made publicly available at[1].

4   Sparse-to-Dense CNN

The first method used to compute a dense disparity estimation from sparse samples makes use of an already existing architecture, presented by Ma *et al.* [9], and fine tunes distinct deep regression models for each of the aforementioned sparse depth inputs. A pre-trained model (provided by the Sparse-to-Dense authors[2]) on the New York University Depth dataset V2 (NYUDV2), which is composed of indoor scenarios, and the closest to our data, is used as the basis for the training.

4.1   Architecture

The Sparse-to-Dense (S2D) CNN follows the conventional Encoder-Decoder structure. The encoder, responsible for feature extraction, is composed by a ResNet followed by a convolutional layer of 1×1 kernel and batch normalization. The residual training provided by the use of a ResNet makes it easier to optimize deeper networks, since it implements identity shortcuts between layers (adding the input of said layer to its output, leading to an overall higher gradient of the block) [6]. The ResNet-18 is the chosen encoder architecture, since computational resources are indeed a constraint. However, *"...residual networks are easier to optimize, and can gain accuracy from considerably increased depth"* [6]. For this very reason we later study the impact of switching the encoder architecture to a ResNet-50. On the other hand, the decoder is comprised by four upsampling layers followed by bilinear upsampling. The module proposed by Laina *et al.* [7], UpProj, was used for the upsampling layers. It is composed of an unpooling layer followed by two distinct branches (with different number of convolutional and batch normalization layers) which are then added up and fed to a ReLU.

Figure 2 depicts the general architecture of the S2D CNN. The blocks highlighted in blue are representative of the Encoding layers, while the ones highlighted in yellow represent the layers that comprise the Decoder.

---

[1] https://tinyurl.com/inhousedataset.

[2] http://datasets.lids.mit.edu/sparse-to-dense.pytorch/results/.

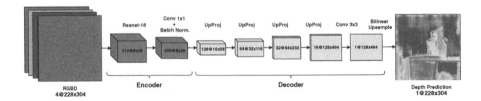

Fig. 2. The general Encoder-Decoder architecture of the Sparse-to-Dense CNN: the Encoder, highlighted in blue is composed of a ResNet followed by a convolutional layer; the Decoder, highlighted in yellow, is comprised of four UpProj modules followed by an upsampling layer. Feature maps are presented as: #features@height×width. *Adapted from* [9]. (Color figure online)

4.2   Loss Functions

In order to minimize the error (in meters) between both the depth predictions and their ground truth, the traditional l_1 and l_2 loss functions were studied as criteria. The l_2 is more sensitive to outliers, penalizing larger discrepancies (due to the squared part of the function, see Eq. 3), therefore it can lead to the appearance of artifacts in the prediction. On the other hand, the l_1 weights every error on the same scale (according to Eq. 2).

From multiple experiments we were able to conclude that the l_2 worked best across every model. Figure 3 provides a visual comparison between two predictions estimated by optimizing the l_1 and l_2 loss functions. The first lead to blurrier disparity maps, over-smoothing boundaries between objects. On the other hand, the l_2 not only computed more accurate predictions (metrically), but also captures sharper transitions, outlining edges and shapes.

$$l_1 = \frac{1}{N} \cdot \sum_{i=1}^{N} \mid y_i - \hat{y}_i \mid \tag{2}$$

$$l_2 = \frac{1}{N} \cdot \sum_{i=1}^{N} (y_i - \hat{y}_i)^2 \tag{3}$$

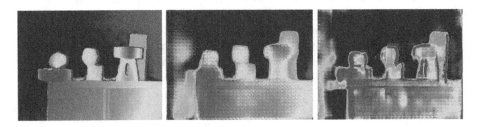

Fig. 3. A comparison between predictions obtained by optimizing the l_1 and l_2 loss functions (columns two and three, respectively). The dense ground truth is represented in the first column.

4.3 Cascade S2D CNN

A second approach, to further improve upon the results obtained from a single CNN, is based on a cascade model. Using the S2D architecture as building block, a pipeline is formed by taking its output prediction ($\hat{y}_1$), creating a new RGBD input and feeding it to another S2D model, as shown in Fig. 4. The basic concept aims to make use one of the deep regression models trained on the standalone CNN architecture to infer an intermediate prediction that would later be refined by a second model.

From the conducted experiments we found that freezing the first model (i.e. using it only for inference) leads to a more satisfying performance, easing the learning of the final model. Both CNNs are identical, the hyperparameters and optimizer were kept the same, whereas the loss function used for training the second model was changed to the l_2.

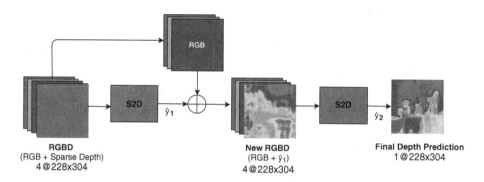

Fig. 4. Pipeline for the Cascade S2D CNN approach. An intermediate prediction is inferred by the first model, while the second one is responsible for refining it. Feature maps are presented as: #features@height×width.

5 Results

This section aims to present and offer discussion about the results obtained from the distinct approaches. Training was solely conducted on our Inhouse Dataset, since there are no other available datasets containing sparse LSR-based depth samples. The evaluation metrics used throughout this section are common for every model.

5.1 Metrics

The metrics used for evaluating how accurate each deep regression model is when compared to the dense ground truth are the following:

– **RMSE:** Root Mean Squared Error (lower is better);

- **MAE:** Mean Absolute Error (lower is better);
- **REL:** Mean Absolute Relative Error (lower is better);
- δ_1: percentage of predicted pixels whose relative error is within a threshold (see Eq. 4), a higher δ_1 indicates a better prediction [9].

$$\delta_1 = \frac{card(\{\hat{y} : max\{\frac{\hat{y}_i}{y_i}, \frac{y_i}{y_i}\}\}) < 1.25}{card(\{y_i\})} \qquad (4)$$

where y_i and $\hat{y}_i$ are the ground truth and prediction, respectively. Card represents the cardinality of a set.

Since we aim to test each model within an embedded platform (e.g. Nvidia JetsonTX2), the **average elapsed GPU time** is also considered as a metric for evaluation.

5.2 Sparse-to-Dense CNN

For the S2D CNN, training was conducted with two different setups: Nvidia 1030, for models using the ResNet-18 as the encoder; Nvidia 2080, for the models composed by a ResNet-50. On the other hand, for testing purposes, the Nvidia JetsonTX2 was used, allowing for a good perception of how these models would perform on an embedded platform and whether or not can could work in real-time applications. Choosing a fitting optimizer is rather crucial since it directly impacts the quality of the learning process. The Adadelta (with the respective learning rate equal to 1) proved the better option. The training phase is set to 150 epochs with batch size 1. For regularization sake, a small weight decay of 10^{-4} is applied across every model.

Inhouse Dataset
As stated above, all the presented experiments were performed using a JetsonTx2. Taking a look at the quantitative results presented in Table 1, one is able to conclude that all the trained models are able to run in real-time, on an embedded platform, at around 5 Hz. The regression model trained with LiDAR sparse cues clearly outperforms the two other models, achieving an average RMSE error of 11.8 cm and an average δ_1 of 97.2%. This comes as no surprise, since, even if sparse, it provides the most complete of the three inputs, providing information from the whole scenario.

One critical drawback of using stereo-based sparse inputs, is their high vulnerability to lighting conditions. Figures 5a and 5b represent the perfect example of this behavior. The model trained with sparse stereo cues has a drastic change in performance from one scenario to the other (lights on/out, respectively), leading to an average RMSE error of 14.4 cm and a REL of 11.6 cm. By observing Fig. 5b one can clearly observe the influence of the stereo depth information on the output prediction. Not being able to compute features from a poor illuminated RGB input, and taking into consideration that the color red represents lack of information, the prediction is solely guided by the very sparse cues from the depth channel. This leads to an output that lacks accuracy and detail, only

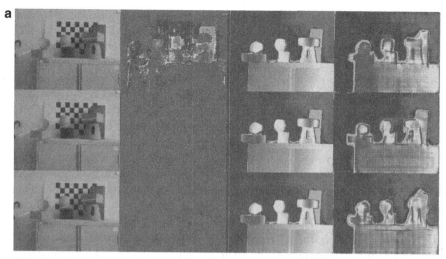

The lack of information from the LSR-based technique leads to slightly less accurate prediction when compared to the remaining models.

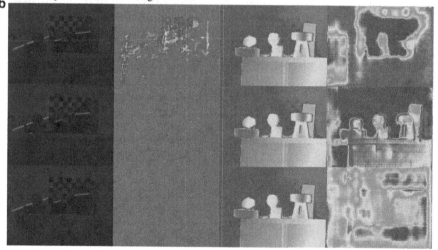

The model trained with LiDAR sparse cues maintains its performance since it is not sensible to lighting conditions. On the other hand, the remaining models drastically decrease their accuracy.

Fig. 5. Prediction obtained from each deep regression model on a scenario with distinct lighting conditions (fourth column). First and second columns represent the RGB and Sparse depth inputs, respectively, from top to bottom: stereo; LiDAR; LSR. Third column shows the common ground truth.

being able to predict the space where the stereo input provides information. The model trained with LiDAR data however, does not suffer from a dip in performance, since a radar based technology is independent from lighting conditions.

When it comes to the LSR-based model, a simple conclusion can be drawn by looking at the obtained results. The depth input it provided does not suffice by itself, being way too sparse. This can be further inferred by looking at the predictions for both the aforementioned scenarios. For a favorable lighting condition (lights on), the model uses the RGB input to make a somewhat accurate prediction, even if it misses out on some of the detail. However, when such is not possible (lights out) the model is not able to output a reasonable depth estimation. This very fact raises the question if the sparse input from the LSR is being considered at all by the model (discussed on the following section).

Overall these deep regression models are able to predict a vastly better disparity map, even if some are quite dependent of lighting conditions. The LiDAR-based model proves to be the better option since it outputs the most accurate and reliable predictions.

Ablation Study: Impact of the LSR Sparse Depth Information

This section aims to further study if the model trained with LSR-based sparse cues, is indeed using this depth information, or if the model simply makes use of the RGB images alone. For the sake of a fair comparison, an RGB only regression model was trained using the same hyperparameters as the ones used in the LSR-based model. Table 2 offers a quantitative analogy between the two models. One is able to conclude that the depth cues are actually improving the accuracy of the model. When compared to using RGB alone, the LSR sparse depth provides an average RMSE improvement of 2 cm as well as a higher percentage of correctly predicted pixels (even if sparse, the information is very accurate metrically).

Table 1. Evaluation of the distinct deep regression models on the Inhouse dataset.

	RMSE (m)	MAE (m)	REL (m)	δ_1 (%)	GPU time (s)
Stereo	0.144	0.082	0.116	94.3	0.198
LiDAR	0.118	0.058	0.105	97.2	0.199
LSR	0.159	0.101	0.135	90.8	0.192

Depending on the application such a small improvement may be crucial (e.g. close range navigation, robotic grasping), however these results serve as confirmation that the LSR technique provides too sparse of a depth input to be used on its own.

Impact of a Deeper Network

Would a deeper network (meaning, using a higher number of filters) improve the obtained results? This subsection aims to study this question by changing the encoder's architecture to a ResNet-50. For a fair comparison between models, the hyperparameters were kept the same as the ones used for the deep regression models presented above.

Table 2. Impact of the LSR sparse depth input on the deep regression model's behavior.

	RMSE (m)	MAE (m)	REL (m)	δ_1 (%)
RGB + LSR	0.159	0.101	0.135	90.8
RGB	0.181	0.119	0.154	87.1

Looking at the quantitative results shown in Table 3, one is easily able to conclude that the error metrics increased across every model. The GPU time is higher since a deeper network would obviously take longer to make calculations and compute a prediction. Still, every model is able to run at 2 Hz on the JetsonTX2. The remaining metric errors are noticeably worse, the RMSE error increases 15% on average, across every model. The model trained with LiDAR sparse depth information is the less affected by this change in enconder, likely due to the fact that the model used for the ResNet-50 had been pre-trained on depth cues very similar to the ones gathered from a LiDAR sensor.

Why would the remaining models suffer from such a decline in performance? The fact that the number of filters is increased, but the scale of the dataset used for training remains the same, is a key factor for these results. A deeper network directly implies a higher number of parameters to learn, therefore, the more data it needs. Concluding, for a bigger dataset, the ResNet would very likely perform increasingly better the higher the number of filters.

Table 3. Evaluation of the distinct deep regression models on the Inhouse dataset, using the ResNet-50 as the encoder.

	RMSE (m)	MAE (m)	REL	δ_1 (%)	GPU time (s)
Stereo	0.152	0.093	0.131	92.0	0.501
LiDAR	0.129	0.062	0.102	96.9	0.502
LSR	0.212	0.154	0.187	82.9	0.502

5.3 Cascade S2D CNN

A cascade pipeline was implemented to try and improve upon the previously obtained results. The deep regression model trained with LSR-based sparse cues was the main focus of this study, since it had the overall worse performance. Said model is then responsible for computing an intermediate prediction that will later be improved on by a second S2D CNN.

This approach proved successful, achieving an average RMSE improvement of 1.5 cm, when compared to the standalone model. Table 4 presents a quantitative analogy between both approaches. The GPU elapsed time is slightly higher since we increase the amount of necessary computations. An interesting pathway to further improve the deep regression models trained with LSR-based sparse information, would be to do additional preprocessing of this data before using it as input. The LiDAR provides the better input across all models since, even if sparse, it captures information from the whole scenario. If one is able to extend the LSR depth cue to the parts of the scenario it doesn't capture, better results are likely to be achieved.

Table 4. Comparison between the Standalone and Cascade models, trained with LSR-based sparse cues, on the Inhouse dataset.

	RMSE (m)	MAE (m)	REL (m)	δ_1 (%)	GPU time (s)
S2D	0.159	0.101	0.135	90.8	0.192
Cascade	0.146	0.086	0.128	93.1	0.351

6   Conclusions and Future Work

This paper makes use of two deep learning approaches for solving a rather crucial computer vision problem: depth completion. Having a dense and accurate representation of a scenario is of the utmost importance for applications such as autonomous driving. However, most sensors used for the purpose of depth estimation have limitations (e.g. low resolution or light sensibility) leading to incomplete and sparse disparity maps.

A single network was used as the first approach for this regression task, the Sparse-to-Dense CNN. The LiDAR sparse input leads to the better depth map prediction, averaging a RMSE error of 11.8 cm, since it is able to generalize to every scenario (it is independent from lighting conditions, unlike the stereo based cues). On the other hand, models trained with LSR-based depth performed quite poorly, indicating that this might be too sparse of an input. As a means to improve these results, we firstly studied the implications of having a deeper network (higher number of filters), however a larger amount of data would be necessary for this to be a valid solution. Finally, a cascade pipeline was implemented using the previously trained deep regression models to infer an intermediate prediction that would then be refined by a second S2D model. This final approach proved successful, showing an average improvement of around 1.5 cm.

As an immediate next step, we aim to extend the experiments conducted with the Cascade S2D CNN to the remaining sparse inputs. One other possible improvement for the LSR-based models is using the approach proposed by Liao et al. [8] as an additional preprocessing step. The thin stripe of 3D points is extended along the gravity direction and only then projected to a plane and used as the input depth map. However, by doing this one is essentially propagating misleading information throughout the image, so a possible extra step would be to use Gaussian distributions to extend the LSR information.

The influence of lighting conditions on the performance of the stereo-based models was discussed several times. The YCbCr color-space is less influenced by said conditions, since it separates luminance from chrominance. Therefore, using these channels as input, instead of the RGB ones, could increase the robustness of these models for non-favorable scenarios.

Finally, changing the current Encoder-Decoder architecture so that it allows for the late fusion of both the input image and the respective sparse depth, could be an interesting possibility to increase the weight given to the features extracted from the sparse depth information.

Acknowledgments. This work is financed by the ERDF - European Regional Development Fund through the Operational Programme for Competitiveness and Internationalisation - COMPETE 2020 Programme and by National Funds through the Portuguese funding agency, FCT - Fundação para a Ciência e a Tecnologia within project POCI-01-0145-FEDER-030010.

References

1. Cadena, C., Dick, A., Reid, I.D.: Multi-modal auto-encoders as joint estimators for robotics scene understanding. In: Robotics: Science and Systems (2016). https://doi.org/10.15607/rss.2016.xii.041
2. Eigen, D., Puhrsch, C., Fergus, R.: Depth map prediction from a single image using a multi-scale deep network. In: Advances in Neural Information Processing Systems, pp. 2366–2374 (2014)
3. Fanello, S.R., et al.: HyperDepth: learning depth from structured light without matching. In: 2016 IEEE Conference on Computer Vision and Pattern Recognition (CVPR), pp. 5441–5450 (2016). https://doi.org/10.1109/CVPR.2016.587
4. Gil, Y., Elmalem, S., Haim, H., Marom, E., Giryes, R.: MonSter: awakening the mono in stereo. In: International Conference on Computer Vision (2019). http://arxiv.org/abs/1910.13708
5. Godard, C., Mac Aodha, O., Brostow, G.J.: Unsupervised monocular depth estimation with left-right consistency. In: Proceedings - 30th IEEE Conference on Computer Vision and Pattern Recognition, CVPR 2017, pp. 6602–6611 (2017). https://doi.org/10.1109/CVPR.2017.699
6. He, K., Zhang, X., Ren, S., Sun, J.: Deep residual learning for image recognition. In: Proceedings of the IEEE Computer Society Conference on Computer Vision and Pattern Recognition, pp. 770–778 (2016). https://doi.org/10.1109/CVPR.2016.90
7. Laina, I., Rupprecht, C., Belagiannis, V., Tombari, F., Navab, N.: Deeper depth prediction with fully convolutional residual networks. In: Proceedings - 2016 4th International Conference on 3D Vision, 3DV 2016, pp. 239–248 (2016). https://doi.org/10.1109/3DV.2016.32
8. Liao, Y., Huang, L., Wang, Y., Kodagoda, S., Yu, Y., Liu, Y.: Parse geometry from a line: monocular depth estimation with partial laser observation. In: Proceedings - IEEE International Conference on Robotics and Automation, pp. 5059–5066 (2017). https://doi.org/10.1109/ICRA.2017.7989590

9. Mal, F., Karaman, S.: Sparse-to-dense: depth prediction from sparse depth samples and a single image. In: Proceedings - IEEE International Conference on Robotics and Automation, pp. 4796–4803 (2018). https://doi.org/10.1109/ICRA.2018.8460184

10. Mancini, M., Costante, G., Valigi, P., Ciarfuglia, T.A.: Fast robust monocular depth estimation for Obstacle Detection with fully convolutional networks. In: IEEE International Conference on Intelligent Robots and Systems, pp. 4296–4303 (2016). https://doi.org/10.1109/IROS.2016.7759632

11. Pillai, S., Ambruş, R., Gaidon, A.: SuperDepth: self-supervised, super-resolved monocular depth estimation. In: 2019 International Conference on Robotics and Automation (ICRA), pp. 9250–9256, May 2019. https://doi.org/10.1109/ICRA.2019.8793621

12. Pinto, A.M., Matos, A.C.: MARESye: a hybrid imaging system for underwater robotic applications. Inf. Fusion (2020). https://doi.org/10.1016/j.inffus.2019.07.014

13. Uhrig, J., Schneider, N., Schneider, L., Franke, U., Brox, T., Geiger, A.: Sparsity invariant CNNs. In: Proceedings - 2017 International Conference on 3D Vision, 3DV 2017, pp. 11–20 (2018). https://doi.org/10.1109/3DV.2017.00012

Exploitation of Dense MLS City Maps
for 3D Object Detection

Örkény Zováthi[1,2(✉)] ⓘ, Balázs Nagy[1,2] ⓘ, and Csaba Benedek[1,2] ⓘ

[1] Institute for Computer Science and Control (SZTAKI),
Kende u. 13-17, 1111 Budapest, Hungary
{zovathi.orkeny,nagy.balazs,benedek.csaba}@sztaki.hu
[2] Faculty of Information Technology and Bionics,
3in Research Group, Pázmány Péter Catholic University,
2500 Esztergom, Hungary

Abstract. In this paper we propose a novel method for the exploitation of High Density Localization (HDL) maps obtained by Mobile Laser Scanning in order to increase the performance of *state-of-the-art* real time dynamic object detection (RTDOD) methods utilizing Rotating Multi-Beam (RMB) Lidar measurements. First, we align the onboard measurements to the 3D HDL map with a multimodal point cloud registration algorithm operating in the Hough space. Next we apply a grid based probabilistic step to filter out the object regions on the RMB Lidar data which were *falsely* predicted as dynamic objects by RTDOD, although they are part of the static background scene. On the other hand, to find objects erroneously *missed* by the RTDOD predictions, we implement a Markov Random Field based point level change detection approach between the map and the current onboard measurement frame. Finally, to analyse the changed but previously unclassified segments of the RMB Lidar clouds, we apply a geometric blob separation and a Support Vector Machine based classification to distinguish the different object types. Comparative tests are provided in high traffic road sections of Budapest, Hungary, and we show an improvement of $5,96\%$ in precision, $9,21\%$ in recall and $7,93\%$ in F-score metrics against the *state-of-the-art* RTDOD algorithm.

Keywords: Lidar · City map · Registration · Change detection · Object detection

1 Introduction

Real time dynamic object detection (RTDOD) in 3D sparse point clouds is a key challenge in autonomous driving. During the past few years, several geometric [1] and deep learning [1,5,10–12,14,15] based approaches appeared in the literature, which operate on raw Rotating Multi-Beam (RMB) Lidar frames and provide output sets of oriented bounding boxes for various object categories such as vehicles, pedestrians or bicycles. As main advantage, these approaches

© Springer Nature Switzerland AG 2020
A. Campilho et al. (Eds.): ICIAR 2020, LNCS 12131, pp. 393–403, 2020.
https://doi.org/10.1007/978-3-030-50347-5_34

can simultaneously consider local shape and point density features together with global contextual information for the classification of the different point cloud segments. However, due to the low vertical density of the RMB Lidar sensor data, which quickly decreases as a function of the objects' distance from the sensor, the typical ring pattern of the point clouds, and various occlusion effects in dense urban environment, there are a number of limitations of these approaches. On one hand, *false positive* hits may be detected in point cloud regions containing static scene objects with similar appearance and context parameters to the focused dynamic scene objects. On the other hand, the point cloud blobs of several dynamic objects can be heavily merged or occluded by static street furniture elements, yielding many *false negative* detections.

Mobile Laser Scanning (MLS) technologies may be used to obtain High Density Localization (HDL) maps [6,7,9] of the cities, with providing dense and accurate point clouds from the static environment with homogeneous scanning of the surfaces and a nearly linear reduction of points as a function of the distance. Exploiting low level information from 3D city maps is a quite new research area, with a few related techniques. The HDNET [13] approach uses a prior *road map* with local *ground-height* data as reference, which helps in eliminating false object candidates detected out of the road, or above/under the ground level. However, it does not deal with the confusion of dynamic objects with static entities from the map, and therefore it cannot adjust the missing object rate. To fill this gap, we present a new approach which utilizes dense HDL maps in order to decrease in parallel both the *false negative* and *false positive* hits of RTDOD algorithms.

The key steps of the proposed algorithm are multimodal point cloud registration between the RMB Lidar measurements and the HDL maps, map based object validation, multimodal change extraction and object level change analysis. As a basis of comparison, we have chosen the *PointPillars* [5] state-of-the-art RTDOD method, which can predict object-candidates from multiple classes, together with their 3D oriented bounding boxes and class confidence values.

2 Proposed Algorithm

The workflow of the proposed approach is shown in Fig. 1. Initially, we apply a state-of-the-art RTDOD algorithm on the raw RMB Lidar frames - in the paper the *PointPillars* [5] techniques is used for this purpose - which provides us multiple vehicle and pedestrian candidates. To refine the output of RTDOD, first we need to accurately register the input RMB Lidar point cloud to the MLS based High Density Localization (HDL) map, which is achieved by a multimodal point cloud registration algorithm. After the alignment, we apply a probability map based validation step against the HDL map to remove *false positive* RTDOD predictions. Finally, for eliminating the *false negatives*, we subtract the HDL map and the already detected RTDOD objects from the actual Lidar frame, then we extract object candidate blobs in the remaining dynamic regions, and we attempt to identify the *previously undetected* dynamic objects by a Support Vector Machine (SVM) based blob-classifier.

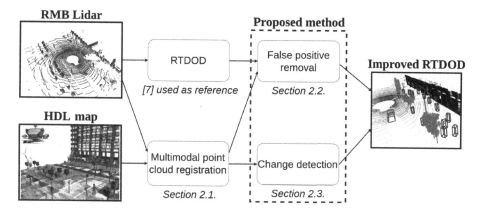

Fig. 1. Workflow of the proposed approach

2.1   Multimodal Point Cloud Registration

Let us assume that using internal navigation sensors, the current position of the vehicle is roughly known with a maximal error of 10 meters in the map's coordinate system. For accurately registering the recorded RMB Lidar frames ($\mathcal{P}_{\text{RMB}}$) to the available HDL map ($\mathcal{P}_{\text{Map}}$), we search for a rigid transform between the two point clouds in the following form:

$$\mathbf{T}_{dx,dy,dz,\alpha} = \begin{bmatrix} \cos\alpha & \sin\alpha & 0 & dx \\ -\sin\alpha & \cos\alpha & 0 & dy \\ 0 & 0 & 1 & dz \\ 0 & 0 & 0 & 1 \end{bmatrix}$$

where dx, dy, dz are the offset parameters and α is the rotation angle around the vertical axis.

To estimate the optimal transform, we apply a robust blob level voting technique in the Hough space based [8]. First, we remove the road points by a locally adaptive ground filter, and extract object-like connected blobs – called abstract objects – by region-growing in both the actual measurements and the HDL map's point cloud (see Fig. 2). Let us denote the two obtained blob sets by $\mathcal{O}_{\text{RMB}}$ and $\mathcal{O}_{\text{Map}}$, respectively. Since we can assume that the HDL map is free of dynamic objects [7], we exclude from the $\mathcal{O}_{\text{RMB}}$ set the blobs which overlap with the initial object candidate regions provided by the RTDOD. Thereafter, based on [8] we extract 8 keypoints in each abstract object candidate of $\mathcal{O}_{\text{RMB}} \cup \mathcal{O}_{\text{Map}}$. For finding the optimal parameter quartet (dx, dy, dz, α) we iterate through all possible keypoint pairs in $\mathcal{O}_{\text{RMB}} \times \mathcal{O}_{\text{Map}}$, and aggregate their votes in the Hough space.

2.2   False Positive Removal by Map Based Validation

False objects of the RTDOD algorithms often overlap with static obstacles of the background scene, thus they can be identified through analyzing their location

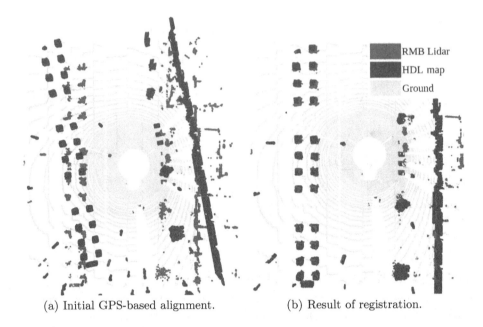

(a) Initial GPS-based alignment.   (b) Result of registration.

Fig. 2. Registration of an onboard measurement to the HDL map

in the registered HDL map. We have proposed a 2D probabilistic approach to manage this problem (see Fig. 3). First, taking a top view analysis, we project both the RMB Lidar and the registered HDL map point clouds to a discrete grid on the ground plane, with a resolution of 10 cm. Thereafter, we assign to each (i, j) cell two competing potentials describing the foreground $(P_{\text{fg}}(i, j))$ and background likelihoods $(P_{\text{bg}}(i, j))$. Foreground values are determined by the RTDOD output: for each cell covered by an object candidate, we take $P_{\text{fg}}(i, j) \in [0, 1]$ as the prediction score (i.e. confidence value) of the RTDOD network regarding the given object. The remaining cells receive $P_{\text{fg}}(i, j) = 0$. On the other hand, the background likelihoods are calculated from the projected MLS point cloud. If cell (i, j) is occluded by a static obstacle in the HDL map, we set $P_{\text{bg}}(i, j) = 1$, while for cells near to the boundaries of static objects we use a distance-based Gaussian attenuation in the P_{bg} until 1 meter in any directions (with variance parameter $\sigma = 10$). For the remaining cells, we set $P_{\text{bg}}(i, j) = 0$.

Using the constructed likelihood maps, we remove all RTDOD object candidates, which cover any cell (i, j), where $P_{\text{bg}}(i, j) \geq P_{\text{fg}}(i, j)$. Note that the adopted Gaussian soft boundary also ensures robustness of the approach against small registration errors.

2.3 Search for Missing Objects via Change Detection

Decreasing the number of missing dynamic objects of RTDOD is highly challenging, since we cannot exploit here the HDL map's object-information in a

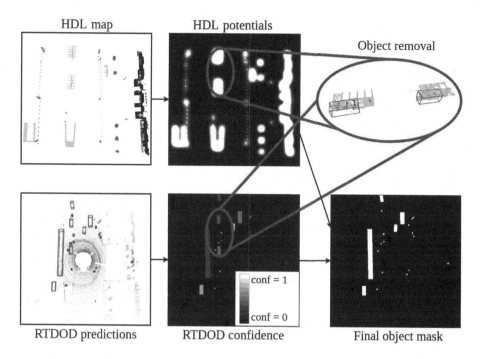

Fig. 3. False positive removal

(a) Range image representation of the RMB Lidar measurement.

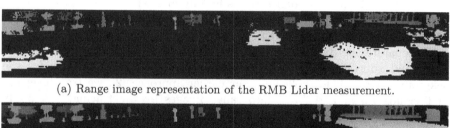

(b) Range image obtained from the HDL Map with ray tracing

(c) Markov Random Field based change mask between (a) and (b)

Fig. 4. Change detection in the range image domain

Fig. 5. Changes backprojected to the RMB Lidar frame

straightforward way, and especially for deep neural network (DNN) based detectors, the sources of mis-detections are often hard to explain intuitively. The key idea of our approach is that we separate at point level the dynamic and static regions of the input RMB Lidar cloud $\mathcal{P}_{\mathrm{RMB}}$, and search for further possible objects of interest in the dynamic segments of $\mathcal{P}_{\mathrm{RMB}}$. In this way, we expect improvement for two reason: *first* we re-locate our previously undetected objects into a different context, where a second-round detection can be successful. *Second*, if a dynamic object's point cloud is heavily merged with a static obstacle's blob, the elimination of background points can highlight the object's real shape, which step can highly facilitate the classification.

We separate the dynamic and static regions of $\mathcal{P}_{\mathrm{RMB}}$ through multimodal background subtraction, where the registered HDL map $\mathcal{P}_{\mathrm{Map}}^{*}$ provides the background point cloud. Following our earlier approach [2], we transform the point clouds $\mathcal{P}_{\mathrm{RMB}}$ and $\mathcal{P}_{\mathrm{Map}}^{*}$ into range images by ray tracing, and apply a Markov Random Field based binary change segmentation in the 2D image domain (Fig. 4). Finally, we backproject the obtained change labels from the range images to the 3D point cloud (Fig. 5).

The next step is object separation within the change regions of the $\mathcal{P}_{\mathrm{RMB}}$ cloud, which is performed by our efficient two-level grid based clustering method introduced in [1]. This process is implemented using a 2D cell map: at super cell level, a region growing algorithm is executed, where empty cells act as stopping criterion. This step may merge several nearby entities into the same object. Therefore, we apply a refinement step at the sub-cell level: a super-level object is divided into different parts, if we find a separator line composed of low density sub-cells at the fine resolution.

The above process provides as output a set of blobs, where some of them might represent further objects of interest ignored by RTDOD, while the other ones belong to a general street clutter class, which is currently out of our focus. For the final decision, we trained a Support Vector Machine with a Radial Basis Function (RBF) [4] kernel, which classifies the blobs based on the set of features listed in Table 1. After classification, the blobs labeled as vehicles or pedestrians are added to the object list of the detector.

Table 1. Feature vector used for SVM classification

No.	Description	Dim.
f_1	Number of points included in the object	1
f_2	The minimum distance to the object center	3
f_3	3D covariance matrix of the object points	6
f_4	Principial component of the object	3
f_5	3D bounding box sizes (height, width, depth)	3

3 Evaluation

We have evaluated the proposed technique on real dynamic point cloud sequences recorded by a car mounted Velodyne HDL 64-E Lidar scanner, on roads with heavy traffic in Budapest, Hungary. The High Density Localization (HDL) map was prepared in our laboratory from high resolution point clouds of a Riegl VMX-450 MLS system, provided by the city's road management company (Budapest Közút Zrt). During HDL map generation, the raw MLS data also undergo a semantic segmentation step [7] for ghost object removal and road detection. As state-of-the-art RTDOD method, we used the *PointPillars* technique [5] which was trained on a mixed dataset composed of the KITTI [3] benchmark, and additional annotated samples from our Budapest data [1].

Qualitative results are shown in Fig. 6 and 7. Figure 6 displays a large scene where the proposed model provides us a comprehensive scene interpretation, although several vehicles (both cars and trams) and pedestrians are jointly present. Figure 7 demonstrates the improvements of using our map-based approach versus the pure RTDOD technique. At the top (Fig. 7(a)(b)), we find two false vehicle predictions which are successfully removed based on the background cloud, while at the bottom (Fig. 7(c)(d)), we illustrate that even in a crowded scene with multiple pedestrians we can find new previously undetected people with our change detection based approach.

For quantitative evaluation, we have selected five heavy traffic road sections recorded in the city center of Budapest, near Deák square (Fig. 6), Múzeum boulevard, Fővám square, Károly boulevard and Kálvin square, respectively. From each location, the evaluation dataset contains 50 different frames; and in average 5 vehicles and 16 pedestrians are present in a single time frame. The numerical performance results compared to the original *PointPillars* [5] output

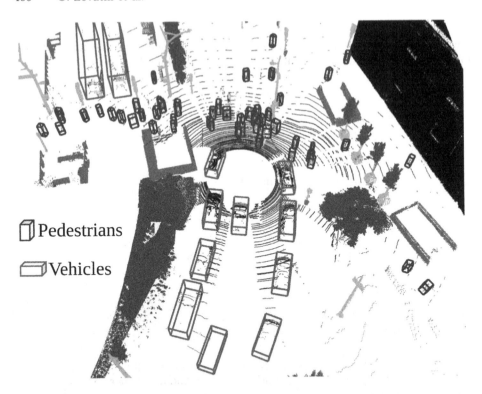

Fig. 6. Result of object detection by Deák square, Budapest

Table 2. Quantitative results versus *PointPillars* [5]

Method	Class	Precision	Recall	F-score
Only RTDOD [5]	Pedestrian	**95,62%**	67,42%	79,08%
	Vehicle	75,19%	88,19%	81,11%
	All	88,75%	72,22%	79,64%
RTDOD with the proposed method	Pedestrian	94,60%	**84,43%**	**87,52%**
	Vehicle	**95,02%**	88,19%	**91,38%**
	All	**94,71%**	**81,43%**	**87,57%**

are shown in Table 2. With the proposed false-positive removal step (Sect. 2.2), we obtained a 19,83% *precision* improvement for the vehicle class, by eliminating many false vehicle-like regions of the RMB Lidar measurements. As result of the change detection based blob classification step (Sect. 2.3), we could significantly improve the *recall* rate of pedestrians with 17.01%. In general for both classes, we observed an overall improvement of 7,93% in *F*-score, versus relying purely on the state-of-the-art RTDOD approach.

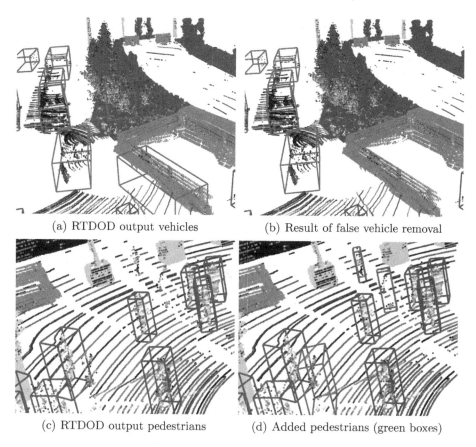

(a) RTDOD output vehicles   (b) Result of false vehicle removal

(c) RTDOD output pedestrians   (d) Added pedestrians (green boxes)

Fig. 7. Qualitative demonstration of improvements by using the proposed model (right) versus RTDOD (left) (Color figure online)

The algorithms were tested on a desktop computer with CPU implementation, where the average computation time was 100 ms per frame for the registration and 80 ms per frame for the change detection step, respectively.

4   Conclusion and Future Work

We introduced a new method to exploit High Definition Localization (HDL) maps for performance improvement of state-of-the-art Lidar based dynamic object detection algorithms. We have shown that the proposed approach can efficiently balance the precision and recall values with significant overall improvement for both vehicles and pedestrians. Most of the remaining detection errors were related to pedestrians too close to each other, and vehicles fare away where the point cloud is much sparser, which problems may be reduced by adopting object tracking in the future.

Acknowledgements. This work was supported by the National Research, Development and Innovation Fund under grant number K-120233, by the European Union and the Hungarian Government from the projects *Thematic Fundamental Research Collaborations Grounding Innovation in Informatics and Infocommunications* under grant number EFOP-3.6.2-16-2017-00013 (Örkény Zováthi and Balázs Nagy) and *Intensification of the activities of HU-MATHS-IN - Hungarian Service Network of Mathematics for Industry and Innovation* under grant number EFOP-3.6.2-16-2017-00015, and by the Michelberger Master Award of the Hungarian Academy of Engineering (Csaba Benedek).

References

1. Börcs, A., Nagy, B., Benedek, C.: Instant object detection in Lidar point clouds. IEEE Geosci. Remote Sens. Lett. **14**(7), 992–996 (2017)
2. Gálai, B., Benedek, C.: Change detection in urban streets by a real time Lidar scanner and MLS reference data. In: Karray, F., Campilho, A., Cheriet, F. (eds.) ICIAR 2017. LNCS, vol. 10317, pp. 210–220. Springer, Cham (2017). https://doi.org/10.1007/978-3-319-59876-5_24
3. Geiger, A., Lenz, P., Urtasun, R.: Are we ready for autonomous driving? The KITTI vision benchmark suite. In: Conference on Computer Vision and Pattern Recognition (CVPR) (2012)
4. Kidono, K., Miyasaka, T., Watanabe, A., Naito, T., Miura, J.: Pedestrian recognition using high-definition LIDAR. J. Robot. Soc. Japan **29**, 405–410 (2011). https://doi.org/10.1109/IVS.2011.5940433
5. Lang, A., Vora, S., Caesar, H., Zhou, L., Yang, J., Beijbom, O.: PointPillars: fast encoders for object detection from point clouds. In: IEEE Conference on Computer Vision and Pattern Recognition (CVPR) (2019)
6. Matthaei, R., Bagschik, G., Maurer, M.: Map-relative localization in lane-level maps for ADAS and autonomous driving. In: IEEE Intelligent Vehicles Symposium Proceedings, Dearborn, MI, USA, pp. 49–55, June 2014. https://doi.org/10.1109/IVS.2014.6856428
7. Nagy, B., Benedek, C.: 3D CNN-based semantic labeling approach for mobile laser scanning data. IEEE Sens. J. **19**(21), 10034–10045 (2019)
8. Nagy, B., Benedek, C.: Real-time point cloud alignment for vehicle localization in a high resolution 3D map. In: Leal-Taixé, L., Roth, S. (eds.) ECCV 2018. LNCS, vol. 11129, pp. 226–239. Springer, Cham (2019). https://doi.org/10.1007/978-3-030-11009-3_13
9. Seif, H.G., Hu, X.: Autonomous driving in the iCity-HD maps as a key challenge of the automotive industry. Engineering **2**(2), 159–162 (2016). https://doi.org/10.1016/J.ENG.2016.02.010
10. Shin, K., Kwon, Y., Tomizuka, M.: . RoarNet: a robust 3D object detection based on region approximation refinement. In: IEEE Intelligent Vehicles Symposium, pp. 2510–2515 (2018)
11. Simon, M., Milz, S., Amende, K., Groß, H.M.: Complex-YOLO: real-time 3D object detection on point clouds. arXiv abs/1803.06199 (2018)

12. Yan, Y., Mao, Y., Li, B.: SECOND: sparsely embedded convolutional detection. Sensors **18**, 3337 (2018). https://doi.org/10.3390/s18103337
13. Yang, B., Liang, M., Urtasun, R.: HDNET: exploiting HD maps for 3D object detection. In: Conference on Robot Learning. Proceedings of Machine Learning Research, 29–31 Oct 2018, vol. 87, pp. 146–155. http://proceedings.mlr.press/v87/yang18b.html
14. Yang, B., Luo, W., Urtasun, R.: PIXOR: real-time 3D object detection from point clouds. In: IEEE Conference on Computer Vision and Pattern Recognition (CVPR), pp. 7652–7660 (2018). https://doi.org/10.1109/CVPR.2018.00798
15. Zhou, Y., Tuzel, O.: VoxelNet: end-to-end learning for point cloud based 3D object detection. In: IEEE Conference on Computer Vision and Pattern Recognition (CVPR), pp. 4490–4499 (2018). https://doi.org/10.1109/CVPR.2018.00472

Automatic Stereo Disparity Search Range Detection on Parallel Computing Architectures

Ruveen Perera$^{(\boxtimes)}$ (iD) and Tobias Low (iD)

University of Southern Queensland, Toowoomba, Australia
{SirigalpatabandigeRuveen.Perera,Tobias.Low}@usq.edu.au

Abstract. From the earliest to the state-of-the-art algorithms, stereo depth estimation techniques often require a disparity search range (DSR) value to be chosen manually. However, the optimal DSR varies from one scene to another making the results depend on the operator input and operator having to optimize the configuration by using trial-and-error. In this paper we present a novel technique suitable for parallel computing architectures which detects the optimum DSR for a given scene without requiring operator input or prior knowledge of the scene. Experiments on stereo images from Middlebury, KITTI and Sceneflow bench-mark datasets indicate that our technique can automatically extract a suitable DSR value from different scenes, which leads to better consistency in matching. The technique presented here can be used with existing stereo algorithms to limit the size of the cost volume as it is being built (without requiring pre-processing or operator input). A CUDA based implementation of our method can deliver real-time performance on consumer grade GPUs at high frame rates.

Keywords: Stereo vision · Stereo vision on GPU · Automatic disparity search range · Depth estimation

1 Introduction

Advancements in the field of stereo vision have resulted in algorithms that can produce accurate results [1] in challenging environments under varying scene conditions, efficiently [18] and in real-time [19]. In most such algorithms however, some form of parameter inputs from the operators are required to produce the optimal results. Disparity Search Range (DSR) is one such parameter which is often configured at the initiation phase of a stereo algorithm. DSR is commonly seen in algorithms regardless of the stereo matching technique used; local, global or semi-global. For example, even in machine learning based state-of-the-art (SOTA) stereo algorithms; GA (Guided Aggregation) Network [1], Pyramid Stereo Matching Network [2], CSPN-Convolution Spatial Propagation Network [3]; users often have to specify the maximum DSR value, which leads to the requirement for a method that extracts a suitable DSR for a given scene efficiently without scene-specific initialization of parameters.

In this study we examine the movement of matching-cost-minima during layer-wise construction of a matching-cost-volume for a stereo image pair, in order to find

© Springer Nature Switzerland AG 2020
A. Campilho et al. (Eds.): ICIAR 2020, LNCS 12131, pp. 404–416, 2020.
https://doi.org/10.1007/978-3-030-50347-5_35

suitable criteria to limit the size of the cost volume when the maximum disparity for the scene is reached (thereby determining the maximum DSR). For simplicity, we use basic cost aggregation methods such as Absolute Difference (AD), Sum-of-Absolute-Differences (SAD) and Sum-of-Squared-Differences (SAD) with different mask sizes in our experiments. However, any matching cost-calculation, cost-aggregation and disparity-selection/regularization method can be used to aid in producing even better results. This study assumes that a calibrated pair of images is available before processing can begin.

The paper is structured as follows. First, a brief discussion of the background of stereo vision and the implications of DSR on the accuracy of the disparity estimation is presented. Next, prior studies in literature on the same topic are discussed with emphasis on their progression, merits and drawbacks. Following this, a novel metric for DSR estimation is introduced together with algorithms and experiments to identify the point at which an increase in DSR stops producing improvements in matching, making it less productive to continue searching along the horizontal scan lines. The algorithm is then evaluated with experiments using standard datasets. Finally, a summary of our CUDA based implementation and future work rounds off the paper.

2 Background

Detecting DSR in advance is not a novel concept. It has been studied for a long time and there are many methods which capture DSR automatically. However, such methods frequently use a sparse set of pixels from the scene to serve as a sample to provide the optimal disparity search range [4, 5]. For determining the candidate points as samples, various feature detectors can be used. For example, in [7] the researchers have used SURF as the feature detector to identify the key points from the scene. Although this method is a better alternative than relying on a random set of image points, it still suffers from the drawbacks associated with the sparse techniques. The whole process depends on SURF method detecting the important (especially close-range) image points and outliers can cause inaccuracies besides requiring pre-processing to determine the DSR.

In some instances [6], a stack of images has been used with multiple resolutions by converting original images into low resolution images for an initial estimate before increasing the resolution until they reach the final resolution. They have also analyzed the drawbacks of having sparse set of points for initial estimation and have pointed out how knowledge of some close-range objects can be lost in the process. Such multi-resolution layered approaches add to the computational complexity in terms of image pre-processing and require multiple iterations when progressing in coarse-to-fine estimation process. However, in [9] the researchers claim to have managed to recover the losses in performance by using the gains in performance through DSR reduction.

Some techniques combine coarse/sparse and image pyramid/coarse-to-fine approaches. For example, in a study [8], down sampled images have been used at the initial stage. However, they revert to dense approach at later stages of the algorithm to ensure that they can cater for the outliers. The drawback however is the computational complexity because of combining multiple stages together.

Disparity search range for the current image pair can be optimized using the disparity map from the previous pair of images in a stereo sequence. In [12], researchers have studied the possibility, showing that it is possible to achieve good results if the disparity estimates from the previous pair of images are reliable. However, the propagation of error estimates cannot be completely ruled out from their approach.

It is also possible to determine DSR adaptively for each pixel based on the other pixels in the neighborhood. As part of a project to develop a disparity estimation algorithm targeting driver assistance systems [10], researchers have used the disparity from the previous image rows to determine the applicable DSR for the current pixel. The same approach has been utilized in one of the recent studies [11]. Although it is apparent from the design that the computational burden is high for calculating per pixel DSR, they have claimed to have achieved a comparable level of performance. However, when compared with the latest implementations of algorithms like Semi-Global-Matching (that produces better results with only a single disparity search range value for the whole image), it is not computationally efficient to calculate DSR for every pixel.

When reviewing the past studies, it is apparent that better results have been achieved by using optimized disparity search range. However, the computational cost, complexity and inadequate coverage of the whole scene can be identified as some of the drawbacks of the existing methods.

3   Our Approach

We have proposed a novel metric named "Sum of new cost minima SNCM" (described in detail in Sect. 3.2), which can be used to determine the maximum depth of a matching-cost-volume. The proposed metric was analyzed using stereo image datasets in order to evaluate the feasibility of using the same for recovering the cut-off point in disparity search. The novel algorithm which was developed based on the findings, is able to estimate a suitable DSR value for a stereo image pair as part of the cost volume creation process itself. Our approach is different from the others because of not relying on pre-processing steps, down sampling or previous stereo results.

3.1   Context and Assumptions

The process of creating the matching-cost volume in stereo matching algorithms can be perceived as a process of stacking 2-dimentional (2D) arrays of costs (for all the pixels in the image) on top of each other up to the maximum expected disparity. Usually, users must specify the maximum expected disparity as an external input which (together with image dimensions) determines the size of the cost volume. However, in this study we assume that such a value is not available at the time of construction of the cost volume and therefore the termination criteria must be determined dynamically as part of the cost volume creation process.

3.2   Development of the Novel Metric

As new layers are being added to a stereo cost volume as shown in Fig. 1, it is possible for the cost minima associated with some pixels to move to the newest layer because of better matching.

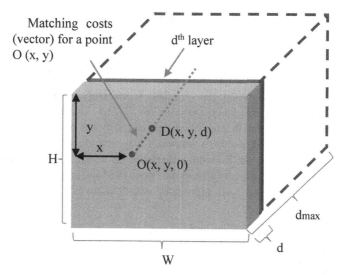

Fig. 1. A partially built matching cost volume for a stereo image pair with the dth layer being the latest (*W, H* - image width and height in pixels, d = current disparity, *dmax* - maximum disparity for the scene in pixels).

According to Fig. 1, local matching-cost-minima for a point (O) with coordinates (x, y) on the reference image, should reside on a series of values from O to D (referred to as OD hereafter). Since all disparity values along OD have equal likelihood of being minima values on OD (assuming random distribution of cost minima within OD and the best match for the point is located at a higher disparity than (d)), we can estimate the probability of the minima lying on the dth layer. Therefore, the probability (P) of having at least one minima located at the dth layer of a cost volume which is partially built up to disparity (d), can be calculated using the Eq. (1) where N denotes the number of pixels of which the cost minima have not yet stabilized by disparity (d).

$$P(At\ least\ one\ minima\ at\ d) = \begin{cases} 1 - \left(\frac{d-1}{d}\right)^{N}, & 0 < d \leq dmax \\ 0, & d > dmax \end{cases} \quad (1)$$

From Eq. (1), it can be deduced that the probability of having cost extrema located at the current layer of a partially built cost volume, remains high as long as the current disparity is lower than the maximum disparity and N is sufficiently large. In other words, when there are foreground objects which occupy N pixels in the image that have not matched correctly by disparity (d), there is a higher probability (depending on the value of N) of locating cost minima at d^{th} layer of a partially built cost volume. Based on that, a metric called **Sum of New Cost Minima** (abbreviated SNCM) was defined to represent the total number of minima that moves to the newest layer of a partially built cost volume.

SNCM Definition: SNCM is the total sum of matching cost minima that shifts to the layer at disparity (d) as soon as the dth layer is added to the cost volume. For the purpose of this study we calculate SNCM as a percentage of the total number of pixels in a stereo image (left or right).

According to the Eq. (1), the probability of locating cost minima at the newest layer (or having a non-zero SNCM value at the current disparity - by definition) is high as long as the maximum disparity has not been reached. Conversely, if the cost minima keep moving to newly added layers of a cost volume (or SNCM value for the current layer is high), then it can be concluded that the maximum disparity has not been reached and the cost volume creation process needs to continue. A typical distribution of SNCM over a disparity range larger than the maximum disparity for a scene can be found in Fig. 2 which shows the SNCM profile for the popular "cones" image pair from the Middlebury 2003 stereo dataset [13] using costs aggregated with SAD over a 3×3 window.

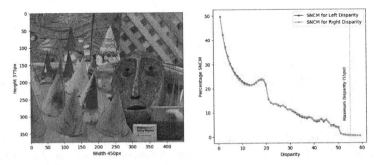

Fig. 2. Variation of SNCM for the classic stereo pair – Middlebury Cones [13]. SNCM profile for the left and right disparities have similar profiles. SNCM reaches a low value plateau around the maximum disparity for the image pair.

Due to the dependency of SNCM on the stability of minima (by definition) at a particular layer, SNCM should become negligibly small once the best matches for all pixels have been established (with the exception of high image noise, repetitive/no texture that spans the whole image and very small foreground objects). To evaluate the robustness of the metric, optical and synthetic images from 3 datasets were used (Middlebury, KITTI and Sceneflow).

According to the results (as shown in Fig. 3), it could be observed that the SNCM value stays high as expected, before the maximum disparity is reached and then reaches a low value plateau afterwards.

Effect of Image Noise. To evaluate the effect of Image noise on SNCM, varying levels of noise (normally distributed Gaussian noise with a noise factor to determine how much of noise is added to each pixel) were added to the image pairs and SNCM profiles were plotted on the same chart. Results for two images from KITTI and Middlebury images is shown in Fig. 4. From the figure, it can be seen that the image noise can cause cost minima to keep shifting layers beyond the maximum disparity. However, large deviations are observable only when the noise levels are significantly high.

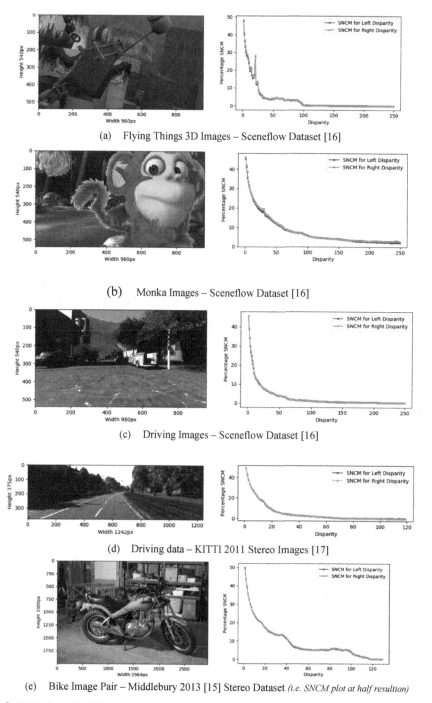

(a)   Flying Things 3D Images – Sceneflow Dataset [16]

(b)   Monka Images – Sceneflow Dataset [16]

(c)   Driving Images – Sceneflow Dataset [16]

(d)   Driving data – KITTI 2011 Stereo Images [17]

(e)   Bike Image Pair – Middlebury 2013 [15] Stereo Dataset *(i.e. SNCM plot at half resultion)*

Fig. 3. Variation of SNCM for various image pairs from Middlebury, KITTI and Sceneflow datasets.

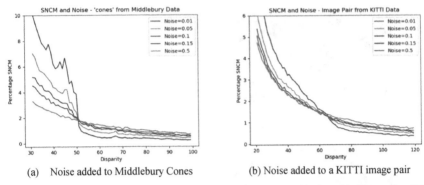

(a)   Noise added to Middlebury Cones   (b) Noise added to a KITTI image pair

Fig. 4. Variation of the SNCM profile due to varying degrees of noise. (a) Shows the SNCM profiles for "Cones" image pair from Middlebury [13] dataset. (b) Shows the same for an image pair from KITTI [17] dataset.

Effect of Cost Aggregation Method and Mask Size. As mentioned earlier, use of SAD for cost aggregation is arbitrary and any matching cost/aggregation method can be used. Figure 5(a) shows the SNCM variations for the Middlebury 2003 "Cones" image pair with 3 different cost aggregation methods (SAD, SSD and AD) whereas Fig. 5(b) shows the variation of SAD-based SNCM with different aggregation window (Mask) sizes. As per the results, SNCM value reaches a low value plateau regardless of the cost aggregation method (even in the case of Absolute Difference – AD) or the mask size used. However, robust aggregation methods and larger mask sizes tend to generate steeper descent towards the plateau due to less-ambiguous matching.

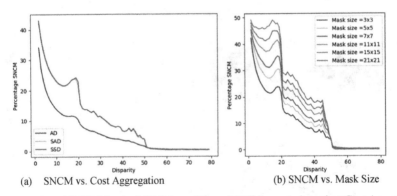

(a)   SNCM vs. Cost Aggregation   (b) SNCM vs. Mask Size

Fig. 5. Variation of SNCM for the Middlebury "Cones" [13] image pair against Cost Aggregation algorithm (a) and Mask Size (b); AD – Absolute Difference, SAD – Sum of Absolute Difference, SSD – Sum of Squared Difference

4   The Algorithm

To simulate the sequential addition of the layers to the cost volume, the left or the right image is rolled over other image horizontally, 1 pixel at a time while capturing the pixel intensity differences applicable for all the pixels at each step. Since the two images have equivalent dimensions, the non-overlapping areas of the sliding image are padded with zeros. After obtaining the difference image, all the values are converted to absolute values. If a mask is used for block wise aggregation, a 2D convolution is performed with a square kernel (with the same dimensions as the mask) which provides the matching costs for the current layer of the cost volume.

4.1   SNCM Calculation

SNCM value for the current layer (d^{th} layer in Fig. 1) of a cost volume can be computed by summing the total number of cost minima that reside in the same layer in the absence of any other layers after the dth layer (in other words only the layers from 1 to (d) are used for the calculation of SNCM value at the dth layer).

4.2   Detection of Max Disparity

The SNCM calculation is repeated continuously until the value reaches a low plateau which indicates that the maximum disparity has been reached. The plateau can be detected by using a threshold for the percentage SNCM and the gradient.

4.3   Computational Complexity

Calculating the SNCM value for each layer of the cost volume is much suited for parallel computing architectures in which case a separate thread can be allocated to each of the pixels in the image. However, calculation of SNCM at each layer is not computationally efficient on CPU environments. Therefore, we introduce two separate methods for GPU and CPU environments. We propose a back tracking algorithm for CPU based environments and a CUDA based parallel processing algorithm for GPU.

Backtracking Algorithm for CPU: While the cost volume is being constructed, this algorithm first extracts the initial layer (which could be the second layer or any following layer) and calculates the new cost minima in that particular layer and stores the value and proceeds. In the subsequent steps, a constant value can be added to the current disparity value to skip layers or the gradient of the SNCM values can be used to calculate the next step size. In the implementation used for evaluation - Fig. 6(a), the value is set proportionately to the current value of the SNCM which helps overshoot the optimal DSR and reach the SNCM plateau. SNCM plateau can be detected by comparing the percentage of SNCM against a small numeric constant or by using the gradient of the average value across multiple steps. Once the SNCM plateau is detected the algorithm back-tracks along the previously stored steps and then conduct a search between the last recorded values while halving the search range in every step. Search ends when the search range equals to 1 pixel and then the higher value of the two values at the each end of the search range is selected as the optimal DSR value.

Algorithm for GPU: To generalize the requirements for the algorithm on GPUs, we assume a fixed cost-volume-width and height for all images, inspired by the state-of-the-art stereo algorithms which convert the input images to a fixed-sized internal cost volume [1–3]. However, we do not restrict the size in terms of depth. Instead, we use thread synchronization to aggregate the movement of minima on to the newest layer as shown in Fig. 6(b). Although this introduces a small penalty in performance, a high frame rate is still achievable.

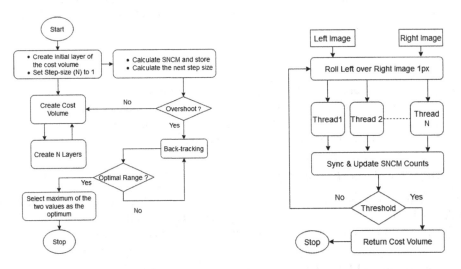

(a) Algorithm for sequential processing   (b) Algorithm for parallel processing

Fig. 6. Flowcharts of the backtracking algorithm (a) for CPU based processing and (b) for GPU based processing

5   Results and Evaluation

For evaluation, the developed algorithm was used to estimate disparity maps of various image pairs from KITTI and Middlebury stereo image datasets at different resolution levels while calculating the disparity range automatically (cost aggregation was set to SAD with a window of size 11×11 pixels). The left-right consistency was also calculated for the disparity values in the neighborhood (of the predicted value) in order to find out whether the auto-selected DSR values lead to better consistency in matching. A summary of results is shown in Table 1. It is apparent from the results that auto-detected DSR values contribute to gains in left-right consistency when compared with the results obtained by setting the DSR to a higher value manually.

Further analysis of left-right consistency was carried out using the disparity values in the neighborhood of the automatically selected DSR in order to determine the effect on left-right consistency, results of which is shown in Table 2. It can be observed from the results that the auto-selected DSR values coincide approximately with the range of DSR values which provides the highest left-right consistency.

Table 1. Left-right consistency comparison for manual and automatic DSR

Image pair	Resolution	DSR (manual)	Left-right consistency (manual)	DSR (auto)	Left-right consistency (auto)
Middlebury Cones	450×375	64	91.46	53	91.77
Middlebury Cones	225×187	32	93.3	26	93.31
Middlebury Teddy	450×375	64	89.4	45	89.48
Middlebury Teddy	225×187	32	90.47	23	90.47
Middlebury Art	695×555	128	78.68	109	78.75
Middlebury Art	347×277	64	81.4	55	81.52
Middlebury Bowling	626×555	64	88.81	30	88.91
Middlebury Bowling	313×277	32	92.88	15	92.84
KITTI(2015) Sample 1	1242×375	72	86.07	66	86.08
KITTI(2015) Sample 2	1242×375	72	85.38	66	85.4
Middlebury Bike	741×500	64	86.46	58	86.46
Middlebury Bike	1482×1000	128	81.42	117	81.44

5.1 Performance CPU vs. GPU

In order to compare the performance of CPU and GPU (CUDA-based) implementations of the algorithm, a scaled set of image pairs were used with resolutions below 512×384. An AMD CPU (1.8 GHz) was used for the CPU-based algorithm whereas a NVIDIA GTX1070 was used as the hardware platform for the GPU-based implementation. Again the stated resolution was selected based on the internal cost volume size of state-of-the-art machine-learning-based algorithms like GA-Net [1] and PSM-Net [2]. CPU-based

Table 2. Comparison of the left-right consistency associated with the automatically reported DSR value with the maximum in the neighborhood (optimum DSR range)

Image pair	DSR (Auto)	LR consistency	Optimum disparity range	Maximum LR consistency	Difference
Middlebury Cones	53	91.77	53–55	91.77	0
Middlebury Cones	26	93.31	24–29	93.32	−0.01
Middlebury Teddy	45	89.48	42–44	89.54	−0.06
Middlebury Teddy	23	90.47	19–26	90.78	−0.31
Middlebury Art	109	78.75	109–115	78.75	0
Middlebury Art	55	81.52	52–55	81.6	−0.08
Middlebury Bowling	30	88.91	26–30	89.12	−0.21
Middlebury Bowling	15	92.84	09–19	93.54	−0.7

algorithm was used without backtracking, hence increasing the computational overhead because of having to calculate SNCM at every disparity. SNCM was calculated using SAD with an aggregation window size of 3×3 and SNCM threshold was set to 0.5% in order to determine the disparity automatically. The results are shown in Table 3. According to the results, it can be seen that the CPU-based algorithm has produced depth maps in less than 1 s in spite of having to calculate SNCM at every disparity. In contrast, the performance of the GPU-based algorithm is far better than the CPU-based algorithm as evident from the speed factor (up to 19 times faster).

5.2 Computational Overhead of SNCM

On a NVIDIA GTX2080 GPU, using a thread block size of (32, 32) and grid size of (12, 16), authors were able to compute automatic cost volumes of varying depth with 512×384 image resolution (which is larger than the internal cost volume size of SOTA algorithms like GA [1] Stereo and PSM [2]) with only a 20 ms (on average) overhead per image pair.

Table 3. Comparison of computational times for GPU and CPU for various image pairs

Dataset	Image pair	Resolution	Processing time on CPU (s)	Processing time on GPU (s)	Speed factor
Middlebury 2003	Cones	450×375	0.703116	0.038334	18.34
Middlebury 2003	Teddy	450×376	0.687466	0.03809	18.05
Middlebury 2005	Art	463×370	0.687497	0.049779	13.81
Middlebury 2006	Bowling	417×370	0.656245	0.070106	9.36
Middlebury 2014	Bike	494×333	0.249978	0.031072	8.05
KITTI 2015	Scene flow	414×125	0.578125	0.029677	19.5
Scene flow	Driving	480×270	0.421845	0.07589	5.56

6 Conclusion and Future Work

In this paper, we have introduced a novel algorithm which can extract the optimal Disparity Search Range (DSR) for a given scene by using a custom developed metric called Sum-of-New-Cost-Minima (SCNM). Through experiments on stereo images from Middlebury, Sceneflow and KITTI bench-mark datasets, the proposed algorithm was shown to correctly estimate an optimal DSR value, leading to a higher left-right consistency. Furthermore, the algorithm was also able to extract optimum DSR values despite changes in resolution. Efficiency of the proposed algorithm can be increased by segregating large images in to manageable blocks and processing them in parallel. Optimization of the CUDA code of the GPU-based algorithm can yield even better performance. The technique can be incorporated in to machine-learning-based stereo vision algorithms to learn maximum disparity search range (DSR) automatically which can lead to more accurate estimates of DSR.

References

1. Zhang, F., Prisacariu, V., Yang, R., Torr, P.H.: GA-net: guided aggregation net for end-to-end stereo matching. In: Proceedings of the IEEE Conference on Computer Vision and Pattern Recognition, pp. 185–194 (2019)
2. Chang, J.R., Chen, Y.S.: Pyramid stereo matching network. In: Proceedings of the IEEE Conference on Computer Vision and Pattern Recognition, pp. 5410–5418 (2018)
3. Cheng, X., Wang, P., Yang, R.: Learning depth with convolutional spatial propagation network. In: IEEE Transactions on Pattern Analysis and Machine Intelligence (2019)
4. Geiger, A., Roser, M., Urtasun, R.: Efficient large-scale stereo matching. In: Kimmel, R., Klette, R., Sugimoto, A. (eds.) ACCV 2010. LNCS, vol. 6492, pp. 25–38. Springer, Heidelberg (2011). https://doi.org/10.1007/978-3-642-19315-6_3

5. Zhang, Z., Shan, Y.: A progressive scheme for stereo matching. In: Pollefeys, M., Van Gool, L., Zisserman, A., Fitzgibbon, A. (eds.) SMILE 2000. LNCS, vol. 2018, pp. 68–85. Springer, Heidelberg (2001). https://doi.org/10.1007/3-540-45296-6_5

6. Kostková, J., Sara, R.: Automatic disparity search range estimation for stereo pairs of unknown scenes. In: Proceedings of the Computer Vision Winter Workshop, pp. 1–10 (2004)

7. Min, D., Yea, S., Arican, Z., Vetro, A.: Disparity search range estimation: enforcing temporal consistency. In: Proceedings of the 2010 IEEE International Conference on Acoustics, Speech and Signal Processing, pp. 2366–2369. IEEE (2010)

8. Smirnov, S., Gotchev, A., Hannuksela, M.: A disparity range estimation technique for stereo-video streaming applications. In: Proceedings of 2013 IEEE International Conference on Multimedia and Expo Workshops (ICMEW), pp. 1–4. IEEE (2013)

9. Sizintsev, M., Wildes, R.P.: Coarse-to-fine stereo vision with accurate 3D boundaries. Image Vis. Comput. **28**(3), 352–366 (2010)

10. Ozgunalp, U., Ai, X., Zhang, Z., Koc, G., Dahnoun, N.: Block-matching disparity map estimation using controlled search range. In: Proceedings of 2015 7th Computer Science and Electronic Engineering Conference (CEEC), pp. 35–40. IEEE (2015)

11. Ma, H., et al.: Multiple lane detection algorithm based on optimised dense disparity map estimation. In: Proceedings of 2018 IEEE International Conference on Imaging Systems and Techniques (IST), pp. 1–5. IEEE (2018)

12. Mun, J.H., Ho, Y.S.: Guided image filtering based disparity range control in stereo vision. Electron. Imaging **2017**(5), 130–136 (2017)

13. Scharstein, D., Szeliski, R.: High-accuracy stereo depth maps using structured light. In: Proceedings of 2003 IEEE Computer Society Conference on Computer Vision and Pattern Recognition, 2003, vol. 1, pp. I–I. IEEE (2003)

14. Hirschmuller, H., Scharstein, D.: Evaluation of cost functions for stereo matching. In: Proceedings of 2007 IEEE Conference on Computer Vision and Pattern Recognition, pp. 1–8. IEEE (2007)

15. Scharstein, D., et al.: High-resolution stereo datasets with subpixel-accurate ground truth. In: Jiang, X., Hornegger, J., Koch, R. (eds.) GCPR 2014. LNCS, vol. 8753, pp. 31–42. Springer, Cham (2014). https://doi.org/10.1007/978-3-319-11752-2_3

16. Mayer, N., et al.: A large dataset to train convolutional networks for disparity, optical flow, and scene flow estimation. In: Proceedings of the IEEE Conference on Computer Vision and Pattern Recognition, pp. 4040–4048 (2016)

17. Geiger, A., Lenz, P., Stiller, C., Urtasun, R.: Vision meets robotics: the KITTI dataset. Int. J. Robot. Res. **32**(11), 1231–1237 (2013)

18. Hirschmüller, H., Buder, M., Ernst, I.: Memory efficient semi-global matching. In: ISPRS Annals of the Photogrammetry, Remote Sensing and Spatial Information Sciences, vol. 3, pp. 371–376 (2012)

19. Zha, D., Jin, X., Xiang, T.: A real-time global stereo-matching on FPGA. Microprocess. Microsyst. **47**, 419–428 (2016)

Multi-camera Motion Estimation with Affine Correspondences

Khaled Alyousefi[1]($\boxtimes$) and Jonathan Ventura[2]

[1] University of Colorado, Colorado Springs, CO 80918, USA
kalyouse@uccs.edu
[2] California Polytechnic State University, San Luis Obispo, CA 93407, USA
jventu09@calpoly.edu

Abstract. We present a study of minimal-case motion estimation with affine correspondences and introduce a new solution for multi-camera motion estimation with affine correspondences. Ego-motion estimation using one or more cameras is a well-studied topic with applications in 3D reconstruction and mobile robotics. Most feature-based motion estimation techniques use point correspondences. Recently, several researchers have developed novel epipolar constraints using affine correspondences. In this paper, we extend the epipolar constraint on affine correspondences to the multi-camera setting and develop and evaluate a novel minimal solver using this new constraint. Our solver uses six affine correspondences in the minimal case, which is a significant improvement over the point-based version that requires seventeen point correspondences. Experiments on synthetic and real data show that, in comparison to the point-based solver, our affine solver effectively reduces the number of RANSAC iterations needed for motion estimation while maintaining comparable accuracy.

Keywords: Ego-motion estimation · Generalized cameras · Epipolar constraint · Affine correspondences

1 Introduction

Motion estimation from video is an important task in computer vision, robotics, and self-driving cars. Most techniques use the standard pipeline of point feature matching and minimal-case motion estimation inside a RANSAC loop [12, 27,33]. Epipolar geometry is the foundation for minimal-case motion estimation solvers [16]. In particular, the 3×3 essential matrix relates corresponding

This material is based upon work supported by the National Science Foundation under Grant No. 43000365.

Electronic supplementary material The online version of this chapter (https:// doi.org/10.1007/978-3-030-50347-5_36) contains supplementary material, which is available to authorized users.

points in two calibrated views according to the relative pose between them [16]. Recently, authors have developed a corresponding theory of epipolar geometry for affine correspondences, i.e., correspondences consisting of affine frames instead of points [6,9,32].

A separate branch of research investigates generalized epipolar geometry, where the assumption of a single optical center is relaxed [29]. The generalized epipolar constraint relates point correspondences observed by a moving multi-camera rig, such as a collection of cameras rigidly mounted on a vehicle or robot. With enough point correspondences between the camera views, ego-motion can be estimated from the generalized essential matrix [37].

In this paper, we unite these two branches of epipolar geometry and develop a new epipolar constraint on affine correspondences observed in a moving multi-camera rig. In addition, we apply this new constraint to adapt an existing generalized relative pose solver [20] to use affine correspondences instead of point correspondences. Since an affine correspondence gives three constraints on the epipolar geometry, versus the single constraint given by a point correspondence, an affine-compatible version of the point solver requires three times fewer correspondences in a minimal sample [4,32]. Reducing the minimal sample size is useful in RANSAC-style [11] sampling where a smaller sample size corresponds to fewer iterations of sampling. For the linear solver of Li *et al.* [20], we reduce the minimal sample size from seventeen to only six, thus making the method more practically useful in a random sampling regime for robust motion estimation from correspondences corrupted by outliers.

We compare the point and affine versions of the solver in an evaluation on image sequences with ground truth poses [14] as well as with synthetic data. While affine solvers benefit from the extra epipolar constraints and so require fewer correspondences, affine correspondences themselves are known to be noisier than point correspondences [9]. However, in our experiments with synthetic and real data, we found that our solver using affine correspondences produces comparable – or even better – accuracy than the point-based solver.

Related work is surveyed in Sect. 2 and the relevant results on affine correspondences are summarized in Sect. 3. This article will also present how to develop a multi-camera epipolar constraint on affine correspondences and how to adapt an existing minimal solver to use it in Sect. 4. Our new minimal solver on synthetic and real data is evaluated in Sect. 5. Finally, the results are discussed in Sect. 6, and a summary of our results and directions for future work are presented in Sect. 7.

2   Related Work

Bentolila *et al.* showed that affine correspondences induce three linear constraints on the fundamental matrix [6]. Raposo *et al.* re-derived these constraints in a simpler form and analyzed their use for structure-from-motion tasks [32]. Eichhardt *et al.* extended the constraint to include non-pinhole cameras [9].

The constraints from affine correspondences are useful in addressing many problems, such as visual odometry and plane segmentation. Barath *et al.* proposed a method for accurately estimating local affine transformations, which are compatible with a given fundamental matrix [5]. Affine correspondences can also be used to estimate a planar homography [2,3] from one point correspondence and the related affine transformation. Additionally, affine correspondences offer clear advantages when solving many other problems, such as image rectification under radial distortion [30], surface normal estimation [10,17], and piece-wise planar reconstruction [31].

Affine region detection has been studied for decades [25,39]. Many affine detectors have been proposed, including: Maximally Stable Extremal Regions (MSER) [22], the affine-adapted Harris detector [23], and the Hessian affine detector [24]. Ouyang *et al.* proposed Affine-SIFT that is robust to illumination and rotation, but is computationally expensive [28]. Furnari *et al.* proved that affine detectors can be successfully applied to the radially distorted images using fisheye lenses [13].

While affine correspondences provide more information than point correspondences, they are more sensitive to noise. Eichhardt *et al.* discussed techniques to mitigate the noise in affine correspondences [9], and proposed a hybrid version of LO-RANSAC [18] with a new affine solver that samples and tests from two correspondences in the minimal case. They showed that, by using local optimization in the RANSAC loop, it is possible to avoid expensive photometric refinement of the affine correspondences. If the camera motion is already known, Barath *et al.* proposed a method for correcting the affine correspondences to make them more consistent with the epipolar geometry [5].

Pless introduced a generalized camera model that depicts a rigid configuration of cameras as one generalized camera [29]. Sturm proposed a different generalized camera model that achieved similar results [36]. However, neither Pless nor Sturm provide results using real-world examples. Stewénius *et al.* suggested a minimal solver for the generalized camera relative pose that produces 64 solutions, however, it is computationally expensive [35]. Li *et al.* introduced a seventeen-point linear solution for the problem that produces only one solution, but requires a large sample size [20]. Ventura *et al.* proposed a fast, real-time solver that uses a first-order approximation to relative pose [41]. Molnár *et al.* derived a generalized epipolar constraint along the epipolar curves [26].

To the best of our knowledge, this work is the first to describe a multi-camera epipolar constraint on affine correspondences and introduce a solver for multi-camera relative pose from affine correspondences.

3   The Epipolar Constraint on Affine Correspondences

This section will review the theory of epipolar geometry for perspective cameras and the extension to affine correspondences developed by Raposo *et al.* [32]. Next, we will develop a form of the multi-camera epipolar constraint that is compatible with affine correspondences.

3.1   Epipolar Constraint

The epipolar constraint relates homogeneous points $\mathbf{u}$ and $\mathbf{v}$ by

$$\mathbf{v}^T \mathsf{E} \mathbf{u} = 0 \qquad (1)$$

where $\mathbf{u}$ and $\mathbf{v}$ are the points normalized by the intrinsic camera matrices in the first and second images, respectively, and E is the 3×3 essential matrix. If the first and second cameras have pose matrices $[\mathsf{I} \mid \mathbf{0}]$ and $[\mathsf{R} \mid \mathbf{t}]$, respectively, then

$$\mathsf{E}(\mathsf{R}, \mathbf{t}) = [\mathbf{t}]_\times \mathsf{R} \qquad (2)$$

3.2   Epipolar Constraint on Affine Correspondences

An affine correspondence between points $\mathbf{p}$ and $\mathbf{q}$ is parameterized by a 2×2 matrix $\mathsf{A} = \begin{bmatrix} A_{11} & A_{12} \\ A_{21} & A_{22} \end{bmatrix}$ and 2D points $\mathbf{x} = \begin{bmatrix} x_1 \\ x_2 \end{bmatrix}$ and $\mathbf{y} = \begin{bmatrix} y_1 \\ y_2 \end{bmatrix}$, as shown in Fig. 1(a), such that

$$\mathbf{q} = \mathsf{A}\mathbf{p} + (\mathbf{y} - \mathsf{A}\mathbf{x}). \qquad (3)$$

An affine correspondence induces a family of homographies parameterized by $\mathbf{g} = \begin{bmatrix} g_3 \\ g_6 \end{bmatrix}$ [32]:

$$\mathsf{H} = \begin{bmatrix} \mathsf{A} + \mathbf{y}\mathbf{g}^T & \mathbf{y} - (\mathsf{A} + \mathbf{y}\mathbf{g}^T)\mathbf{x} \\ \mathbf{g}^T & 1 - \mathbf{g}^T \mathbf{x} \end{bmatrix}. \qquad (4)$$

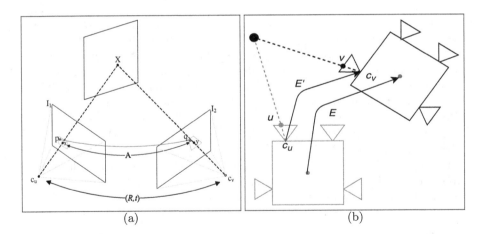

(a)   (b)

Fig. 1. (a) An affine correspondence (AC) between points $\mathbf{p}$ and $\mathbf{q}$ is parameterized by a 2×2 affine matrix A and 2×1 points $\mathbf{x}$ and $\mathbf{y}$. (b) Illustration of the generalized epipolar constraint. A multi-camera rig consists of cameras fixed at different offsets from the center of the rig. Observations $\mathbf{u}$ and $\mathbf{v}$ of a 3D point are constrained by the generalized essential matrix E', which incorporates the rotation and translation of the rig as well as the camera offsets $\mathbf{c_u}$ and $\mathbf{c_v}$.

A homography H is compatible with an essential matrix E if

$$H^T E + E^T H = 0. \tag{5}$$

Plugging Eq. 4 into Eq. 5 gives an epipolar constraint on affine correspondences. Raposo *et al.* [32] showed how to reduce this constraint to a linear system

$$M\overline{E} = 0 \tag{6}$$

where M is the following 3×9 matrix[1]:

$$M^T = \begin{bmatrix} x_1 y_1 & a_3 x_1 & y_1 + a_1 x_1 \\ x_1 y_2 & a_4 x_1 & y_2 + a_2 x_1 \\ x_1 & 0 & 1 \\ x_2 y_1 & y_1 + a_3 x_2 & a_1 x_2 \\ x_2 y_2 & y_2 + a_4 x_2 & a_2 x_2 \\ x_2 & 1 & 0 \\ y_1 & a_3 & a_1 \\ y_2 & a_4 & a_2 \\ 1 & 0 & 0 \end{bmatrix}. \tag{7}$$

Accordingly, each affine correspondence gives three linear constraints on the essential matrix. This is a significant advantage over point correspondence, which only gives one linear constraint. Raposo *et al.* [32] showed that the linear constraints on the essential matrix used by Stewénius *et al.* [34] can be replaced with the linear constraints in Eq. 6 derived from affine correspondences. The non-linear part of the solver by Stewénius *et al.* [34] stays the same. The result is a minimal solver for the essential matrix, which only requires two affine correspondences instead of five point correspondences.

4   Multi-camera Motion Solvers Using Affine Correspondences

This section reviews the epipolar geometry of generalized cameras [29] and shows how to develop a generalized epipolar constraint and minimal solvers for multi-camera relative pose using affine correspondences.

4.1   Generalized Epipolar Constraint

Consider that we have a multi-camera rig, where the first and second cameras are at an offset from the origin of the rig. The 3D offsets of the first and second camera are written as c_u and c_v, respectively (see Fig. 1(b)).

In a normal pinhole camera, the rays must all intersect at a common point, the optical center of the camera. We can imagine the multi-camera rig as a single

---

[1] The original C matrix in [32], Eq. 21, has a typo. The cell $C(2,3)$ should be written as: $-x_1(g_6 * x_2 - 1)$.

"generalized" camera, which samples rays without restriction. A ray passing through an offset camera can be represented in Plücker coordinates as

$$l_u = \begin{bmatrix} u \\ c_u \times u \end{bmatrix}. \tag{8}$$

The generalized epipolar constraint [29] relates rays in two generalized cameras by

$$\begin{bmatrix} v^T & (c_v \times v)^T \end{bmatrix} \begin{bmatrix} [t]_\times R R \\ R & 0 \end{bmatrix} \begin{bmatrix} u \\ c_u \times u \end{bmatrix} = 0. \tag{9}$$

This can be written equivalently as

$$v^T([t]_\times R)u + v^T R([c_u]_\times u) + ([c_v]_\times v)^T Ru = 0. \tag{10}$$

Re-Writing as an Essential Matrix: The generalized epipolar constraint is typically written using the 6×6 matrix given in Eq. 9. Here, we show how to re-write the constraint with a 3×3 matrix, which is analogous to the perspective essential matrix but dependent on the two camera offsets.

The generalized epipolar constraint (Eq. 10) can be re-written as

$$v^T([t]_\times R)u + v^T(R[c_u]_\times)u - v^T([c_v]_\times R)u = 0 \tag{11}$$

using the fact that $[a]_\times^T = -[a]_\times$. After grouping terms we have

$$v^T([t]_\times R + R[c_u]_\times - [c_v]_\times R)u = 0. \tag{12}$$

Now we can define an essential matrix for offset cameras as

$$E'(R, t, c_u, c_v) \equiv [t]_\times R + R[c_u]_\times - [c_v]_\times R \tag{13}$$

so that

$$v^T E'(R, t, c_u, c_v)u = 0. \tag{14}$$

Note that

$$E'(R, t, c_u, c_v) = E(R, t) + R[c_u]_\times - [c_v]_\times R. \tag{15}$$

This re-written generalized essential matrix (Eq. 15) is a 3×3 matrix relating homogeneous points in two cameras, just like the perspective essential matrix (Eq. 2). However, it depends on the camera offsets c_u and c_v in addition to the rotation R and translation t between the two cameras. When both cameras have zero offset ($c_u = c_v = [0\ 0\ 0]^T$), the generalized essential matrix is reduced to the perspective essential matrix.

4.2   Generalized Epipolar Constraint on Affine Correspondences

As we have shown in the previous section, the generalized epipolar constraint is analogous to the normal epipolar constraint, since it relates perspective projections in two cameras related by rotation and translation. The only difference is that the generalized epipolar constraint incorporates a 3D offset vector for each camera.

Given our 3×3 formulation of the generalized essential matrix E' (Eq. 13), it is simple to produce the generalized epipolar constraint on affine correspondences. We simply replace the perspective essential matrix in Eq. 6 with the generalized essential matrix (Eq. 13):

$$\mathsf{M}\overline{\mathsf{E}'} = \mathbf{0}. \tag{16}$$

4.3   Minimal Solver

Using the linear constraints on the generalized essential matrix given in Eq. 16, we can reformulate existing solutions for the generalized essential matrix to use affine correspondences instead of point correspondences. In this paper, we focus on the seventeen-point linear solution presented by Li *et al.* [20].

Because each affine correspondence gives three constraints, we can reduce the number of correspondences needed for each solver. The linear solution needs seventeen point correspondences but only six affine correspondences, making its use more practical in terms of RANSAC iterations.

4.4   Linear Solution

To produce the linear solution, following [20], we parameterize the essential matrix E and the rotation matrix R, separately, so that the problem has eighteen parameters (nine for the essential matrix and nine for the rotation matrix).

By plugging this into Eq. 16 and re-arranging it, we arrive at a new 3×18 matrix of coefficients. The first nine columns are equal to M, and the second nine columns contain coefficients involving $\mathbf{c_u}$ and $\mathbf{c_v}$[2]. From this point forward the solution procedure is essentially the same as [20]; the solution is briefly summarized here.

Stacking the equations for all six affine correspondences results in an 18×18 matrix of coefficients A such that $\mathsf{A} \begin{bmatrix} \mathsf{E} \\ \mathsf{R} \end{bmatrix} = \mathbf{0}$. We break A into two matrices $\mathsf{A}_{\mathsf{E}'}$ and A_{R} such that $\mathsf{A}_{\mathsf{E}'}\mathsf{E}' + \mathsf{A}_{\mathsf{R}}\mathsf{R} = \mathbf{0}$. A solution for E' is then found by solving

$$(\mathsf{A}_{\mathsf{R}}\mathsf{A}_{\mathsf{R}}^{+} - \mathsf{I})\mathsf{A}_{\mathsf{E}'}\overline{\mathsf{E}'} = \mathbf{0} \tag{17}$$

where $\mathsf{A}_{\mathsf{R}}^{+}$ is the pseudo-inverse of A_{R}.

The solution for the rotation is found by decomposing the essential matrix into two possible rotations [16]. A correctly scaled translation can be found by plugging the rotation solution into the generalized epipolar constraints for point correspondences (Eq. 10) and solving for $\mathbf{t}$.

---

[2] The full matrix of coefficients is written out in the supplementary material.

Table 1. Names and descriptions of solvers tested in our evaluation. N is the number of correspondences needed. The generalized methods directly estimate the rotation and then the translation.

Name	Rotation	Translation	N
Generalized Linear – Point Correspondences (GL-PC) [20]	Point	Point	17
Generalized Linear – Affine Correspondences (GL-AC) (ours)	Affine	Point	6

5 Evaluation

We evaluated the minimal solvers shown in Table 1 on synthetic and real data in terms of accuracy. All minimal solvers were implemented in C++. We compare the accuracy of our minimal solver using affine correspondences with the traditional solver that uses point correspondences.

5.1 Evaluation on Synthetic Data

The solvers were tested using synthetically generated data with varying levels of Gaussian noise added to the observations. The first camera rig in each problem is located at the origin with identity rotation; and, the second camera rig has a random rotation R and a random translation t of unit norm. The observation cameras are at offsets c_u and c_v randomly sampled from $[-1\ 1]^3$. Each point correspondence between the two synthetic views is generated by randomly sampling a 3D point x with norm between $[4\ 8]$ and then projecting this point to the first and second cameras. The observations of the point in the first and second cameras are $u = \pi(x - c_u)$ and $v = \pi(Rx + t - c_v)$, respectively, where $\pi(\cdot)$ is the pinhole projection function.

The affine correspondences between the two views are computed as follows. The point x is assumed to lie on a planar surface with normal pointing to the origin. We create four corner points of a box on the planar surface with side lengths of .02 units. These corner points are projected to the first and second cameras to produce observation points x_i and y_i, respectively, where $i = 0, 1, 2, 3$. The affine part A of the affine correspondence consists of a 2×2 matrix that relates the corner points in the first and second cameras by $y_i = A(x_i - u) + v$. We compute the 3×3 homography matrix H from the projections of the corner points, and then compute the affine matrix A [3] as follows:

$$A = s^{-1} \begin{bmatrix} H_{1,1} - H_{3,1}y_1 & H_{1,2} - H_{3,2}y_1 \\ H_{2,1} - H_{3,2}y_2 & H_{2,2} - H_{3,2}y_2 \end{bmatrix} \tag{18}$$

where $s = x_1 H_{3,1} + x_2 H_{3,2} + H_{3,3}$.

Following [9], we add Gaussian noise to the center point observations and to the 2×2 affine matrix coefficients. The standard deviations of the noise added to the points and affine coefficients are controlled independently. We generated 10,000 problems for each noise level.

For each problem, we compute the rotation and translation using the minimal number of point or affine correspondences. Because the solvers return multiple solutions, we choose the lowest error observed over all solutions for each metric.

Figure 2 plots the mean rotation and translation errors over a range of noise standard deviation settings. It shows that with low levels of noise added to the affine coefficients, our Generalized Linear solver on Affine Correspondences (GL-AC) outperforms its counterpart solver on Point Correspondences (GL-PC). However, when adding noise to the affine parameters in A, the accuracy of the GL-AC solver decreases. The GL-PC solver is clearly not affected by noise added to the affine coefficients.

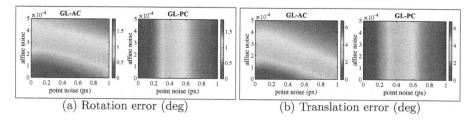

(a) Rotation error (deg)   (b) Translation error (deg)

Fig. 2. Mean rotation and translation errors of the generalized solvers on affine (GL-AC) and point (GL-PC) correspondences under different noise levels.

5.2   Evaluation on Real Data

Our GL-AC solver was evaluated using the first eleven sequences from the KITTI visual odometry dataset [14]. This dataset contains stereo image sequences captured at 10 Hz from a car driving around a small city. The sequences come with associated ground truth trajectories acquired using a high-accuracy GPS receiver and inertial navigation system. The KITTI sequences consist of rectified left-right stereo image pairs and an associated ground truth pose for each frame.

Feature Matching: To establish the affine correspondences, we first extract the affine-covariant features in each image. We use the SIFT detector [21] with affine covariant shape estimation [23], as implemented in the VLFeat library [40].

In each sequence, the affine correspondences are found by following a quad-matching procedure (inspired by Geiger *et al.* [15]), which involves the left and right images at the current timestep and the next timestep. Features are matched from the first left image to the first right image, then to the next right image, the next left image, and back to the first left image. If the matching process does not end at the same feature from which it started, the sequence of matches is discarded. We used the matching algorithm proposed by Lowe [21] that discards incorrect matches due to ambiguous features according to a distance ratio test.

For each set of four matched features across the four images, a non-linear refinement technique is applied to improve the quality of matches. At each step of the non-linear refinement, each of the four affine frames is projected to the canonical frame, using a patch size of 11 × 11. Then, we compute and add up the sum squared error between each pair of projected frames. The total error is minimized by five iterations of Levenberg-Marquardt non-linear optimization, adjusting each of the four affine frames at each iteration.

Relative Pose Estimation: We apply both the point-based (GL-PC) and affine-based (GL-AC) versions of the generalized linear solver to each consecutive pair of stereo pairs in the eleven test KITTI sequences. For better analysis, the relative pose was estimated with and without applying the nonlinear refinement (described in Sect. 5.2). Each quad-match contributes four possible correspondences to the total set of correspondences considered at each frame. We used either the center points or the affine frames, depending on the solver used.

To robustly estimate the relative pose in the presence of outliers, some version of Random Sample Consensus (RANSAC) [11] needs to be applied. We experimented with LO-RANSAC [7,9,18], but found that this greatly increased the computation time. Therefore, we applied MSAC (M-estimator SAmple and Consensus) [38] with a probability of success of 0.99, and then applied a robust optimization scheme after the MSAC process is completed.

For inlier testing with generalized solvers, we performed linear triangulation using the stereo pair at the current timestep and projected the triangulated point to the left frame of the next timestep. In both cases, we used an inlier threshold of 0.65 pixels.

To refine the MSAC result, we updated the estimated relative pose to minimize the re-projection error of the triangulated points in the next timestep. Formally, we found the relative pose parameters R and **t** that minimized the re-projection error

$$C(\mathsf{R}, \mathbf{t}) = \sum_i \rho(\|\pi(\mathsf{R}\mathbf{x_i} + \mathbf{t} - \mathbf{c_{v_i}})) - \pi(\mathbf{v_i})\|^2) \qquad (19)$$

where $\mathbf{x_i}$ is the i-th triangulated point in the world coordinate frame and $\rho(\cdot)$ is the Huber cost function, which reduces the influence of outliers. We parameterized R using the axis-angle representation and implemented the optimizer using the Ceres library [1]. The optimizer was run for a maximum of 100 iterations. In comparison to full bundle adjustment, this non-linear refinement step was efficient because we only updated the six pose parameters and kept the 3D points fixed.

Results: For each sequence, the per-frame error was calculated in rotation and translation direction, according to the provided ground truth. Table 2 shows the results for all tested KITTI sequences.

Table 2. The results on KITTI seq.00 through 10. For each measure, we report the mean value. Our proposed affine solver shows comparable rotation and translation error to the point solver. However, the affine solver is faster; and it requires fewer iterations to converge to a solution. A statistical t-test was performed to confirm this result.

Measure	Rotation err. (deg)		Translation err. (deg)		No. of iterations		Run time (ms)	
Solver	GL-PC	GL-AC	GL-PC	GL-AC	GL-PC	GL-AC	GL-PC	GL-AC
Seq. 00	0.063	0.06	1.429	1.459	1558	1469	251	209
Seq. 01	0.065	0.066	6.693	6.363	1994	1655	263	188
Seq. 02	0.045	0.045	1.058	1.075	1139	1253	212	207
Seq. 03	0.037	0.037	1.038	1.102	1594	1216	338	237
Seq. 04	0.037	0.036	0.683	0.69	1656	631	311	124
Seq. 05	0.042	0.04	3.015	3.043	1490	1274	254	194
Seq. 06	0.039	0.039	0.889	0.872	1880	1336	285	180
Seq. 07	0.056	0.062	6.623	6.808	1598	1259	287	201
Seq. 08	0.039	0.04	2.572	2.584	1556	1394	258	205
Seq. 09	0.041	0.041	0.797	0.805	1653	1468	264	207
Seq. 10	0.046	0.046	1.467	1.469	1454	1431	231	194
Average	0.046	0.047	2.388	2.388	1597	1308	269	195

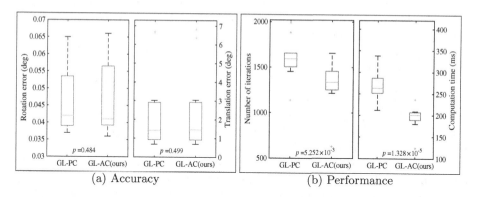

(a) Accuracy   (b) Performance

Fig. 3. Accuracy and performance of the GL-AC and GL-PC solvers on KITTI dataset [14] sequences 0 through 10 using refined correspondences. The p-values of the performed t-test are shown on each plot. Plot (a) shows that the accuracy of both solvers are almost the same. The p-values of the t-test show no significant differences between the two solvers in term of accuracy. On the other hand, the plot of performance (b) shows that the GL-AC solver is faster and takes fewer iterations to converge. The p-values of the t-test confirm the higher performance of our Affine solver.

The estimated trajectories between the two generalized solvers for all KITTI sequences were equivalently the same[3]. The trajectories were formed by integrating the relative pose at each timestep. An accumulation of drift is expected since no loop closure or bundle adjustment was applied; this allowed for an isolated comparison of the various relative pose solvers.

6   Discussion

In our tests, we reported the mean rotation and translation angle error, as well as the average number of iterations and the computation time, as shown on Table 2. We rigorously refined the affine correspondences according to a photometric error. The refinement process was not optimized for speed in the experiment; the average refinement time of an AC was about two seconds, but the refinement could be parallelized for faster performance. The results show that our affine solver (GL-AC) outperformed its point solver counterpart while maintaining similar accuracy. Our GL-AC solver converged more quickly with fewer MSAC iterations on affine correspondences.

Figure 3 presents a statistical analysis of the experimental results, which supports our conclusion that there is a significant advantage to using our generalized affine solver over point solvers. Despite the noisy affine part, our affine-based solution was able to achieve similar accuracy to the point-based solution. The reported mean rotation and translation angle errors of our novel solver using affine correspondences was about the same as the existing solver, based on point correspondences. A statistical t-test found p-values between 0.35 and 0.5. The translation scale ratio for all solvers was basically equivalent. Visually, the integrated trajectories of all solvers look similar.

Moreover, our affine solver benefits from the fact that fewer correspondences are required compared to point solvers. Compared to the state-of-the-art SLAM systems [8,19], our method does not incorporate loop closure or 3D mapping. The results show that the computation time and average number of MSAC iterations are both less when using the affine solver. The p-values of the t-tests were very small, showing a significant benefit to using our generalized linear affine solver (GL-AC). We chose a low inlier threshold because increasing the inlier threshold caused the number of iterations required by the affine solver to increase faster than that required by the point solver. This indicates that ACs are noisier than PCs.

7   Conclusion

In this work, we show how to extend the epipolar constraint on affine correspondences [32] to the generalized multi-camera setting. We used our new generalized constraint to create a generalized relative pose solver using affine correspondences. As noted, an affine correspondence gives three constraints on the epipolar

---

[3] All plots and error tables for all KITTI sequences 0 through 10 are provided in the supplementary material.

geometry, allowing for a reduced sample size in comparison to using point correspondences. Our method uses, minimally, six point correspondences instead of seventeen, as required by the corresponding point-based method. Evaluation on a large image sequence dataset validates our approach. The accuracy of the affine solver (GL-AC) was found to be comparable with that of the equivalent point-based solver. Furthermore, as a result of the fewer required correspondences, the affine solver was faster and took fewer iterations for MSAC to converge.

Future work will explore applying the approach to other multi-camera motion estimation solutions [41] and developing a fast and accurate multi-camera affine correspondence algorithm to support real-time operation of our system.

References

1. Agarwal, S., Mierle, K., et al.: Ceres solver. http://ceres-solver.org
2. Barath, D.: P-HAF: homography estimation using partial local affine frames. In: 12th International Conference on Computer Vision Theory and Applications (2017)
3. Barath, D., Hajder, L.: A theory of point-wise homography estimation. Pattern Recogn. Lett. **94**, 7–14 (2017)
4. Barath, D., Hajder, L.: Efficient recovery of essential matrix from two affine correspondences. IEEE Trans. Image Process. **27**, 5328 (2018)
5. Barath, D., Matas, J., Hajder, L.: Accurate closed-form estimation of local affine transformations consistent with the epipolar geometry. In: 27th British Machine Vision Conference (BMVC) (2016)
6. Bentolila, J., Francos, J.M.: Conic epipolar constraints from affine correspondences. Comput. Vis. Image Underst. **122**, 105–114 (2014)
7. Chum, O., Matas, J., Kittler, J.: Locally optimized RANSAC. In: Michaelis, B., Krell, G. (eds.) DAGM 2003. LNCS, vol. 2781, pp. 236–243. Springer, Heidelberg (2003). https://doi.org/10.1007/978-3-540-45243-0_31
8. Cvišić, I., Ćesić, J., Marković, I., Petrović, I.: SOFT-SLAM: computationally efficient stereo visual simultaneous localization and mapping for autonomous unmanned aerial vehicles. J. Field Robot. **35**(4), 578–595 (2018)
9. Eichhardt, I., Chetverikov, D.: Affine correspondences between central cameras for rapid relative pose estimation. In: Ferrari, V., Hebert, M., Sminchisescu, C., Weiss, Y. (eds.) ECCV 2018. LNCS, vol. 11210, pp. 488–503. Springer, Cham (2018). https://doi.org/10.1007/978-3-030-01231-1_30
10. Eichhardt, I., Hajder, L.: Computer vision meets geometric modeling: multi-view reconstruction of surface points and normals using affine correspondences. In: IEEE International Conference on Computer Vision (2017)
11. Fischler, M.A., Bolles, R.C.: Random sample consensus. Commun. ACM **24**(6), 381–395 (1981)
12. Fischler, M.A., Bolles, R.C.: Random sample consensus: a paradigm for model fitting with applications to image analysis and automated cartography. In Readings in Computer Vision, pp. 726–740. Elsevier (1987)
13. Furnari, A., Farinella, G.M., Bruna, A.R., Battiato, S.: Affine covariant features for fisheye distortion local modeling. IEEE Trans. Image Process. **26**(2), 696–710 (2017)
14. Geiger, A., Lenz, P., Urtasun, R.: Are we ready for autonomous driving? The kitti vision benchmark suite. In: Conference on Computer Vision and Pattern Recognition (CVPR), pp. 3354–3361 (2012)

15. Geiger, A., Ziegler, J., Stiller, C.: StereoScan: dense 3D reconstruction in real-time. In: IEEE Intelligent Vehicles Symposium (2011)
16. Hartley, R.I., Zisserman, A.: Multiple View Geometry in Computer Vision, 2nd edn. Cambridge University Press, Cambridge (2004). ISBN 0521540518
17. Köser, K.: Geometric estimation with local affine frames and free-form surfaces. Shaker (2009)
18. Lebeda, K., Matas, J., Chum, O.: Fixing the locally optimized RANSAC-full experimental evaluation. In: British Machine Vision Conference, pp. 1–11. Citeseer (2012)
19. Lenac, K., Ćesić, J., Marković, I., Petrović, I.: Exactly sparse delayed state filter on lie groups for long-term pose graph SLAM. Int. J. Robot. Res. **37**(6), 585–610 (2018)
20. Li, H., Hartley, R., Kim, J.: A linear approach to motion estimation using generalized camera models. In: 2008 IEEE Conference on Computer Vision and Pattern Recognition, pp. 1–8 (2008)
21. Lowe, D.G.: Distinctive image features from scale-invariant keypoints. Int. J. Comput. Vis. **60**(2), 91–110 (2004)
22. Matas, J., Chum, O., Urban, M., Pajdla, T.: Robust wide-baseline stereo from maximally stable extremal regions. Image Vis. Comput. **22**(10), 761–767 (2004)
23. Mikolajczyk, K., Schmid, C.: An affine invariant interest point detector. In: Heyden, A., Sparr, G., Nielsen, M., Johansen, P. (eds.) ECCV 2002. LNCS, vol. 2350, pp. 128–142. Springer, Heidelberg (2002). https://doi.org/10.1007/3-540-47969-4_9
24. Mikolajczyk, K., Schmid, C.: Scale & affine invariant interest point detectors. Int. J. Comput. Vis. **60**(1), 63–86 (2004)
25. Mikolajczyk, K., et al.: A comparison of affine region detectors. Int. J. Comput. Vis. **65**, 43–72 (2005)
26. Molnár, J., Csetverikov, D., Kató, Z., Baráth, D.: A theory of camera-independent correspondence. In: 10th National Conference of Image Processing and Image Recognition (2015)
27. Nistér, D.: An efficient solution to the five-point relative pose problem. IEEE Trans. Pattern Anal. Mach. Intell. **26**(6), 0756–777 (2004)
28. Ouyang, P., Yin, S., Liu, L., Zhang, Y., Zhao, W., Wei, S.: A fast and power-efficient hardware architecture for visual feature detection in affine-sift. IEEE Trans. Circ. Syst. **65**(10), 3362–3375 (2018)
29. Pless, R.: Using many cameras as one. In: Computer Vision and Pattern Recognition, vol. 2, pp. II–587. IEEE (2003)
30. Pritts, J., Kukelova, Z., Larsson, V., Chum, O.: Radially-distorted conjugate translations. In: Proceedings of the IEEE Conference on Computer Vision and Pattern Recognition, pp. 1993–2001 (2018)
31. Raposo, C., Barreto, J.P.: πMatch: monocular vSLAM and piecewise planar reconstruction using fast plane correspondences. In: Leibe, B., Matas, J., Sebe, N., Welling, M. (eds.) ECCV 2016. LNCS, vol. 9912, pp. 380–395. Springer, Cham (2016). https://doi.org/10.1007/978-3-319-46484-8_23
32. Raposo, C., Barreto, J.P.: Theory and practice of structure-from-motion using affine correspondences. In: Proceedings of the IEEE Conference on Computer Vision and Pattern Recognition, pp. 5470–5478 (2016)
33. Scaramuzza, D., Fraundorfer, F.: Visual odometry [tutorial]. IEEE Robot. Autom. Mag. **18**(4), 80–92 (2011)
34. Stewénius, H., Engels, C., Nistér, D.: Recent developments on direct relative orientation. ISPRS J. Photogramm. Remote Sens. **60**(4), 284–294 (2006)

35. Stewénius, H., Nistér, D., Oskarsson, M., Åström, K.: Solutions to minimal generalized relative pose problems. In: OMNIVIS 2005: The 6th Workshop on Omnidirectional Vision, Camera Networks and Non-Classical Cameras (2005)
36. Sturm, P.: Multi-view geometry for general camera models. In: 2005 IEEE Computer Society Conference on Computer Vision and Pattern Recognition, CVPR 2005, vol. 1, pp. 206–212. IEEE (2005)
37. Sturm, P., Ramalingam, S., Tardif, J.-P., Gasparini, S., Barreto, J.: Camera models and fundamental concepts used in geometric computer vision. Found. Trends® Comput. Graph. Vis. **6**, 1–183 (2011)
38. Torr, P.H.S., Zisserman, A.: MLESAC: a new robust estimator with application to estimating image geometry. Comput. Vis. Image Underst. **78**(1), 138–156 (2000)
39. Tuytelaars, T., Mikolajczyk, K., et al.: Local invariant feature detectors: a survey. Found. Trends Comput. Graph. Vis. **3**, 177–280 (2008)
40. Vedaldi, A., Fulkerson, B.: VLFeat: an open and portable library of computer vision algorithms (2008). http://www.vlfeat.org/
41. Ventura, J., Arth, C., Lepetit, V.: An efficient minimal solution for multi-camera motion. In: Proceedings of the IEEE International Conference on Computer Vision, pp. 747–755 (2015)

Author Index

Printed in the United States
By Bookmasters